Securing the Seas

Securing the Seas

The Soviet Naval Challenge and Western Alliance Options

Paul H. Nitze, Leonard Sullivan, Jr.,
and the Atlantic Council Working Group
on Securing the Seas

AN ATLANTIC COUNCIL POLICY STUDY

Westview Press / Boulder, Colorado

The Atlantic Council Policy Series

All rights reserved. No part of this publication may be reproduced or transmitted in any form or by any means, electronic or mechanical, including photocopy, recording, or any information storage and retrieval system, without permission in writing from the publisher.

Copyright © 1979 by the Atlantic Council of the United States

Published in 1979 in the United States of America by
  Westview Press, Inc.
  5500 Central Avenue
  Boulder, Colorado 80301
  Frederick A. Praeger, Publisher

Library of Congress Cataloging in Publication Data
Nitze, Paul H.
  Securing the seas.
  (The Atlantic Council policy series)
  Includes index.
  1. Sea power. 2. Navies. 3. North Atlantic Treaty Organization. 4. United States. Navy. 5. Russia (1923- U.S.S.R.). Voenno-Morskoĭ Flot. I. Sullivan, Leonard, 1925- joint author. II. Atlantic Council's Working Group on Securing the Seas. III. Title. IV. Series: Atlantic Council of the United States. The Atlantic Council policy series.
VA10.N57   359'.03'091821   78-10423
ISBN 0-89158-359-9
ISBN 0-89158-360-2 pbk.

Printed and bound in the United States of America

Contents

List of Tables and Figures xv
List of Photographs xix
Foreword, Kenneth Rush xxiii
Preface xxv
Working Group on Securing the Seas xxix

Summary of Policy Conclusions and Recommendations 1

1. Introduction 3
   The Role of the Seas in the World Balance of Influence 3
   Five New Factors in the Current Use of the Seas 4
      Nuclear Warfare 4
      Emergence of the Soviet Union as a Maritime Power 6
      Military Technology 8
      Resource Interdependence 8
      The Rise of New Nations 9
   The Future Importance of the Seas 9
      Strategic Balance 10
      Conventional Force Balance 11
      Conventional-Strategic Linkage 13
      Resource Extraction from the Sea 13
      Ship Vulnerability 15
      Soviet Expansionism 15
      Substitutes for Merchant Ships 17
      Stockpiling and Prepositioning 17

v

The Continued Importance of Naval Superiority 18
  Large-Scale Conventional War with the Soviet Union 18
  War at Sea 20
  U.S. Intervention in Third World States 20
  War between Rival Client-States 21
  Economic Pressure and Intimidation against the
    Western Alliance 21
  Peacetime Postures and Perceptions 23

Atlantic Council Study Objectives 24

Atlantic Council Study Limitations 26

Atlantic Council Study Outline 28

2. Soviet Naval Evolution 31

Introduction 31

From the Beginnings to 1971 32
  Before World War II 32
  World War II 35
  Stalin the Traditionalist, 1945 to 1953 36
  Khrushchev the Innovator, 1953 to 1960 38
  The Emergence of the Modern Fleet, 1961 to 1971 42

Development of the Civil Sector 48
  The Soviet Merchant Marine 48
  Soviet Shipyards 52

Toward the Future: 1971 to the Present 53

3. The Soviet Fleet Today 57

Current Status and Funding 57
  Types and Force Levels 57
  Fleets and Organizational Structure 58
  The Naval Budget 59

Constraints on Soviet Naval Operations and Growth 59
  Geographic Constraints 59
  Political Constraints 63
  Domestic Constraints 65
  Economic Constraints 66

Peacetime Influence of the Soviet Navy 66
  Nuclear Intimidation 66
  Influence in the Third World 67
  Influence in the Mediterranean 68
  Influence in the Indian Ocean 69
  Influence in Other Areas 72

Future Prospects 73
  Naval Nuclear Strategy 73
  Conventional War at Sea 74
  Possible Roles in Small Wars 76
  Domestic Economic and Political Influences 77
  Advances in Naval Technology 80

4. Allocation of Soviet Naval Forces 83

Wartime Mission Structure 83
  Strategic Nuclear Strike 84
  Destruction of Enemy Naval Forces 85
  Support for Ground Force Operations 85
  Command of Contiguous Waters 86
  Interdiction of Enemy Sea Lines of
    Communication (SLOCs) 86
  Protection of Soviet Sea Lines of Communication 88

Wartime Operational Concepts 88
  Area Defense 88
  Combined Arms 89
  Warfighting 89
  Equipment Adaptation 90
  Antiship Warfare 90
  Antisubmarine Warfare 92
  Long-Range Interdiction 93

Soviet Naval Force Levels, Composition, and
Fleet Allocations 93
  Submarine Forces 93
  Submarine Fleet Allocations 97
  Major Surface Combatants 98
  Major Surface Combatant Fleet Allocations 101
  Other Surface Combatants 101
  Other Surface Combatant Fleet Allocations 103

Allocation of Naval Ship Construction 103
Soviet Naval Aviation Forces 105
Naval Aviation Fleet Allocation 107

Wartime Mission Allocations of Soviet Naval Forces 108
   The North Atlantic 108
   The Mediterranean 111
   The Pacific 114
   The Indian Ocean 114
   Implications of Force Allocations 116

5. Western Maritime Interests 119

The Meaning of Maritime Security 119
   Sensitivity, Interdependence, and Vulnerability 119
   Determinants of Vulnerability 123

Factors Affecting Use of the Ocean 127
   Economic Conditions 127
   Technological Developments 128
   Law of the Sea 129
   Domestic Policies 131

Maritime Activities Worldwide 131
   Seaborne Commerce 132
   Fishing 134
   Seabed Resources 137

Western Uses of the Seas—By Region 139
   Atlantic Ocean 140
   Mediterranean 142
   Pacific Ocean 143
   Indian Ocean 144

Summary 146

6. Implications of Soviet Maritime Capabilities 147

Soviet Maritime Activities 147
   Shipping 148
   Fishing 151
   Offshore Resources 151

Contests at Sea 152

Contents ix

    Peacetime Competition 152
    Crisis 154
    Wartime 157
  Implications for U.S. and Allied Naval Forces 160
  Summary 164

7. Evolution of the U.S. Navy 165
  Early History 165
  The Battleship Navy 165
  The Navy after World War II 167
  Declining U.S. Navy Force Levels 170
  Quality versus Quantity in Naval Forces 171
  U.S. Naval Roles, Missions, and Versatility 172
  The Soviet Submarine and Air Threats 176
  Vulnerability of the Carriers 179
  Naval Alternatives for the Future 181

8. Allocation of U.S. and Allied Naval Forces 187
  Organization and Missions of NATO Naval Forces 187
    NATO Naval Organization 187
    NATO Naval Strategy and Missions 189
    The NATO Flanks 196
    National Missions of Naval Significance 198
    NATO Order of Battle (1978).........................200
    U.S. Atlantic Posture without NATO 203
  Organization and Missions of Allied Pacific Forces 204
    Pacific Naval Organization 204
    Pacific Naval Strategy and Missions......................205
    Indian Ocean Strategy and Missions 213
    Pacific-Indian Ocean Orders of Battle (1978) 216
  Alliance Naval Posture without the United States 218
  Alliance Naval Exercises 220

9. Comparative Force Levels, Merchant Marines, and
   Overseas Bases 221

   Soviet-Alliance Force Level Comparisons 221
      Submarines 222
      Aviation Ships 224
      Major Surface Combatants 224
      Small Combatants 224
      Amphibious Ships 224
      Naval Aviation 224
      Alliance Contributions 225
      Other Comparisons 225
      Regional Comparisons of Major Naval Elements for
         Conventional War 230

   Soviet-Alliance Merchant Marine Comparisons 231
      Static Balance 231
      Trends 234
      Composition 235
      Government Responsibilities 235
      Other Potential Applications for Merchant Ships 239
      Economy of Scale Considerations 240

   Comparisons of Soviet and Alliance Naval Bases and
   Facilities 244
      Relative Trends in Shore-Base Access 245
      Soviet Overseas Facilities 245
      U.S. Overseas Bases and Facilities 246
      Scenario-Dependence of Overseas Facilities 248

10. Comparative Alliance Naval Capabilities 251

    Introduction 251

    Comparative Surveillance Capabilities 252
       Surface Ship Surveillance 253
       Submarine Surveillance 255
       Implications of Surveillance Capabilities 258

    Comparative Ship Characteristics 259
       Aircraft Carriers 259
       Surface Combatants and Escorts 263
       Submarines 274
       Naval Weapons 277

Contents

    Mine Warfare...281

    Comparative Aircraft Characteristics 283
        Ship-Based Aircraft Systems 285
        Land-Based Aircraft 290

11. Projected Alliance Technology and Force Requirements........295

    Introduction...295

    New Naval Technology (RDT&E) 295
        Ocean Surveillance......................................295
        Antisubmarine Warfare 296
        Antiaircraft Warfare 297
        Antiship Warfare 299
        Electronics and Electronic Warfare.......................299
        Laser Warfare 300
        Mine Warfare..300
        Shore Target Attack 302
        Ship Design 302
        Aircraft Design 304
        Submarine Design 307

    Problems in Adopting New Naval Technology 307

    Characteristic Forces Required for Sealane Defense Missions....312
        Convoy Defense System Characteristics 313
        Sealane "Sanitization" System Characteristics 315
        Potential for Merchant Ship Self-Defense 316

12. Anticipated Constraints on the U.S. Navy Budget 319

    Increasing Defense's Share of Federal Spending 319

    Increasing the Navy's Share of Defense Spending 322

    Increasing the Procurement Share of the Navy's Budget 326
        Military Personnel 326
        Operations and Maintenance 327
        Procurement..327
        Research, Development, Test, and Evaluation (RDT&E) 327

    Increasing the Ship Construction Share of the Navy's
    Procurement Budget 328

    Changing the Mix within the Navy's Procurement Program 332

Reducing the Navy's Procurement Budget 334

Summary 335

13. Quantifying the Sealane Defense Problem 337

Introduction 337

Past Experience: The World War II Battle of the Atlantic 339
   U-Boat Effectiveness 339
   Countering the Submarine Threat 341

Sea Control Today 343
   Progress in Submarines and Antisubmarine Warfare 343
   The New Setting and Tactics..............................345
   An Illustrative Atlantic SLOC Campaign 349
   Simplified Analysis of the Sealane Defense Mission 351
   Exchange Ratios 358
   Conclusions from Simplified Analysis 359
   The Air Threat to Convoys 360
   ASW-Capable Merchant Vessels 361
   Advanced Mine Barriers 364
   The Use of Nuclear Weapons at Sea 364

U.S. Sea Control and Merchant Ship Force Levels 366
   The Opposing Views 366
   Uncertainties in Force Level Estimation 369

Resupply versus Prepositioning 374

Summary 380

14. Overall Assessment of Naval/Maritime Balance 383

Introduction 383

Historical Context 383
   Soviet Naval Background 383
   Current Soviet Naval Objectives 384
   U.S. Naval Background...................................385
   Current U.S. Naval Objectives............................385
   Comparative Force Level Trends 387

Strategic Context..387
   Soviet Strategic Doctrine.................................387
   U.S. Strategic Doctrine 389

Contents   xiii

    Scenario Context..390
        Nuclear Conflict Scenarios.................................390
        Conventional Warfare Scenarios 391

    Technology Context......................................392
        Detection Systems 392
        Submarine Propulsion.....................................393
        Homing Missiles..393
        Implications..395

    Assessment of Mission Capabilities 395
        General Nuclear Warfare 395
        Theater Nuclear Warfare..................................398
        Large-Scale Conventional War 399
        Intervention 403
        Client-versus-Client Wars 405
        Economic Pressure and Intimidation 406
        Military Presence 406
        Prestige 407
        Commerce...408

    Summary 408

15. Findings and Recommendations............................411

    Introduction...411

    Recommendations 412

    A. Alliance Long-Range Commitment to Naval Superiority....414
        A-1: Alliance Naval Policies and Construction Programs.....414
        A-2: The Importance of Naval Counterforce Capabilities.....416

    B. Future Alliance Naval Policies 417
        B-1: Scope of a "NATO War"..............................417
        B-2: Analysis of Soviet Interposition Capability 418
        B-3: Critical U.S. Scenarios Excluding the Alliance—and
             Vice Versa...419
        B-4: Peacetime Naval Presence 420
        B-5: Post-Nuclear Naval Force Requirements 421
        B-6: Merchant Marine Requirements.......................422

    C. Threat-Responsive Alliance Naval Capabilities.............424
        C-1: Numerically Larger Surface Navies.....................424
        C-2: Modular Design in Naval Combatants 425
        C-3: Important Technology Programs 426

D. Making Greater Use of Existing Alliance Assets 429
      D-1: Arming Merchant Ships for Escort Duty and
           Self-Defense 429
      D-2: Reducing Convoy Losses through Merchant Ship
           Design and Use 430
      D-3: Naval Partnership with Alliance 432
      D-4: NATO Role in Port Defense 433
      D-5: NATO Attention to Mine Warfare 435
      D-6: Air Force Contributions to Sealane Defense 437
   E. Decreasing Dependence on Shipping at Crucial Times 439
      E-1: Prepositioning of Military Equipment 439
      E-2: Economic Stockpiling 440
   F. Limit Soviet Naval Effectiveness 441
      F-1: Soviet Acquisition of Overseas Bases 441
      F-2: U.S. Dependence on Overseas Bases 441

16. Additional Views 443

    Julien J. LeBourgeois 443

    William Lind, Norman Polmar, Dominic A. Paolucci 445

    David B. Kassing 449

    Richard L. Garwin 451

*Appendix: Soviet Ship Characteristics, Armament, and
System Purpose* 453

Notes 459

Tables and Figures

Tables

4-1	Soviet Submarine Forces	97
4-2	Major Soviet Surface Combatants	102
4-3	Other Soviet Surface Combatants	104
4-4	Soviet Small Craft Transfers	105
4-5	Implications of Current Soviet Naval Construction	106
4-6	Soviet Naval Aviation	108
4-7	Theater Allocation by Mission—Atlantic	109
4-8	Theater Allocation by Mission—Mediterranean	113
4-9	Theater Allocation by Mission—Pacific and Indian Ocean	115
5-1	Rates of Growth of Gross National Product and Imports	121
5-2	Imports as a Share of Consumption: Mid-1970s	122
5-3	Ships Unloaded in Seaborne Trade: 1975	136
5-4	Ships Loaded in Seaborne Trade: 1975	136
5-5	Monthly Transits by Standard Ships: 1974 and 1985	136
5-6	World Fish Catch: 1975 and 1985	136
5-7	Monthly Ship Transits in the Atlantic: 1974 and 1985	145
5-8	Atlantic Ocean Fish Catch: 1975 and 1985	145

5-9	Monthly Ship Transits in the Mediterranean Sea: 1974 and 1985	145
5-10	Monthly Ship Transits in the Pacific Ocean: 1974 and 1985	145
5-11	Pacific Ocean Fish Catch: 1975 and 1985	145
5-12	Monthly Ship Transits in the Indian Ocean: 1974 and 1985	145
6-1	Illustrative Monthly Ship Transits in 1985	163
7-1	United States Naval Force Levels	171
8-1	NATO Order of Battle (1978)	201
8-2	Pacific Order of Battle (1978)	219
9-1	Comparison of Major Soviet and Alliance Naval Elements as of 1/1/78	223
9-2	Regional Comparisons of Major Naval Elements for Conventional War	232
9-3	Eleven Largest World Merchant Fleets	233
9-4	Estimated U.S. Waterborne Petroleum Imports	242
9-5	Shipping Cost of U.S. Petroleum Imports by Source and Tanker Size	242
9-6	Estimated Annual Costs of Limiting U.S. Petroleum Imports to Small Tankers In: (millions of dollars)	243
10-1	Mines Carried by Various Aircraft Types	285
12-1	Major Components of Actual Federal Spending as a Percent of Total Outlays FY 1957-FY 1977	320
12-2	Major Components of Projected Federal Spending as a Percent of Total Outlays FY 1976-FY 1982	320
12-3	Outlay Projections by Function: By Fiscal Years, in Billions of Dollars	322
12-4	Alternate Approaches to Reaching 4.5% Unemployment by FY 1982	323
12-5	Distribution of Defense Spending—Proposed FY 1978 Budget	324

12-6	Proposed Major Procurements for FY 78 (Unamended)	329
12-7	Generalized Annual Navy Procurement Requirements	329
12-8	Alternative Annual Navy Procurement Requirements	334
12-9	"Steady State" Size of U.S. Navy Fleet and Air Arm as a Function of Annual Ship/Aircraft Procurement	335
13-1	German Open Ocean Submarines—World War II	340
13-2	Allied Merchant Ship Losses from Enemy Action, By Causes: Tonnage	340
13-3	Allied Merchant Ship Losses from German U-Boat Action	341
13-4	U-Boat Campaign on the East Coast of America (January-May 1942)	342
13-5	U-Boat Campaign on the Atlantic Convoy (January-May 1943)	342
13-6	Levels of Selected U.S. Naval Forces—World War II and Exchange Ratio between Combatant Vessels and Submarines	343
13-7	Estimating Escort Requirements	371
13-8	Estimated Merchant Ship 90-Day Losses to Submarines	372

Figures

3-1	Soviet Geography	61
8-1	NATO Naval Organization	188
9-1	Changes in Naval Force Levels—U.S./U.S.S.R. (1966-1976)	226
9-2	Characteristics and Changes in General Purpose Naval Forces—U.S./U.S.S.R.	227
9-3	U.S./U.S.S.R. Combatant Ship Deliveries (1966-1976)	228
9-4	Current U.S./U.S.S.R. Maritime Balance	229
9-5	U.S./U.S.S.R. Combatant Ship-Days on Distant Deployment	230

9-6	U.S./U.S.S.R. Combatant Deployments (Average CY 66 and 76)	232
13-1	1975 Defense Department Atlantic Campaign Study Results	346
13-2	Sea Control in the Northeast Atlantic—Greenland-Iceland-United Kingdom (G.-I.-U.K. Gap) Barrier Chokepoint	350
13-3	Simplified Attrition Analysis/Varying ASW Capability	353
13-4	Simplified Attrition Analysis/Varying Submarine Pre-deployment	355
13-5	Simplified Attrition Analysis/Most Optimistic ASW Performance	356
13-6	Simplified Attrition Analysis/Worst Case Performance and/or Force Levels	357
13-7	Simplified Attrition Analysis/Impact of Arming Merchant Ships	365
13-8	Added Costs of Prepositioning versus Added Costs of Shipping Losses	378

Photographs

Chapter 1

Nuclear Warfare at Sea 5
Conventional/Strategic Linkage 14
U.S. Naval Intervention Operations 22

Chapter 2

Soviet Naval Assets of the Stalin Era 39
Naval Aircraft of the Khrushchev Era 47
Soviet Merchant Ships 51

Chapter 3

Soviet Naval Presence 71
Soviet Maritime Presence 79

Chapter 4

Soviet Amphibious and Coastal Craft 87
Modern Soviet Submarines 95

Chapter 5

U.S. Strategic Stockpiles 126
Resource Extraction from the Sea 138

Chapter 6

Soviet Cargo Ships 150
Crises Involving Naval Forces 155

Alliance Naval Forces in the Pacific 159

Chapter 7

The U.S. Battleship Navy 168
U.S. Aircraft Carrier Growth 175
New Small U.S. Aircraft Carriers 183

Chapter 8

NATO Naval Forces on the Northern Flank 191
NATO Naval Forces in the North Atlantic 193
NATO Naval Forces in the Mediterranean 197
Alliance Naval Forces in the Pacific 207
U.S. Naval Forces in the Pacific 210
U.S. Naval Capabilities in the Indian Ocean 214

Chapter 9

U.S. Military Sealift Cargo Capability 236
Economy of Scale in Tanker Design 241
Overseas Naval Bases 247

Chapter 10

Satellite Ocean Surveillance 256
Soviet Aviation-Capable Ships 262
Soviet and U.S. Cruisers 264
Soviet and U.S. Destroyers 271
Soviet and U.S. Attack Submarines 276
U.S. Tactical Standoff Antiship Missiles 282
Soviet and U.S. Land-Based Mining Aircraft 284
Soviet and U.S. Naval Strike Aircraft 287
Soviet and U.S. Carrier-Based Fighter Aircraft 289
Soviet and U.S. Land-Based ASW Patrol Aircraft 291

Chapter 11

New U.S. Naval Shipboard Air Defense Systems 298
U.S. Mine Warfare Assets 301
New U.S. Ship Designs 303
New Alliance Ship-Based Aircraft Designs 306
Problems in Adopting New Naval Technology 309

Chapter 12

New Lower-Cost U.S. Naval Designs 331

Chapter 13

U.S. World War II Convoy Experience 348
ASW-Capable Merchant Ships 363
U.S. Prepositioned Equipment 375

Chapter 14

Soviet and U.S. Forward Deployment Capability 386
U.S. Antiship Missile Capabilities 394
Soviet and U.S. Strategic Submarines 396
Naval Role in Intervention 404

Foreword

Few problems we will face in the latter part of the twentieth century are more important than control and use of the oceans of the world. This problem involves many uncertainties—uncertainties of a political, strategic, economic, and legal nature. The future of the free nations will be heavily influenced by it.

The outcome will depend primarily on the policies and behavior of the two superpowers, the United States and the Soviet Union. As the report concludes: "There is a stark contrast between the momentum of Soviet naval development and the relative indecision on the Alliance side." Certainly the persistent and unprecedented expansion of Soviet naval power in recent years has stirred speculation and concern in the Western world. What objectives do Soviet leaders have in mind? Why do they feel— as they apparently do—that they need to increase their power substantially? In view of the growing demand for consumer goods inside Russia and the other serious economic problems the Russians face, why should they continue to devote so much of their energy and resources to building up naval strength at this particular juncture? And even more significant, what does this development mean for the future of the Western Alliance and for U.S. defense efforts as we pursue our indispensable task of maintaining the freedom of the seas? This Atlantic Council study, sponsored by a grant from the Scaife Family Charitable Trusts, attempts to grapple with these and other related questions.

I want to express my very deep appreciation to Paul H. Nitze, Chairman; to Leonard Sullivan, Jr., Director and Rapporteur; and to the other members of the Working Group on Securing the Seas, who have approached their task with interest and enthusiasm and have advanced a number of constructive ideas that should prove helpful to all individuals concerned about Soviet-American relations, the balance of power, and the future of the U.S. Navy. Special thanks also go to the Scaife Family Charitable Trusts, without whose interest and support this project would not have been possible.

I should add that the views expressed in the report are those of the Working Group and not necessarily those of the Council as a whole. It should also be clear that even though the report sets forth the overall views of the Working Group, no particular member of the panel should necessarily be assumed to subscribe to all the specific views presented. In any event, the topic is a very important one, the report is a very good one, and the Council is pleased to present the findings for public discussion and debate.

Kenneth Rush
Chairman, Atlantic Council
of the United States

Preface

The past ten years have brought considerable debate over the course that should be steered by the United States Navy and most of the other fleets of the Western Alliance. During this period, the Soviet Navy has emerged into full view as a major threat to the security of the seas. In the summer of 1976, Francis Wilcox of the Atlantic Council of the United States asked me to assemble a group of knowledgeable Americans to consider the projected threats to the free use of the seas on which the West so heavily depends. A grant was obtained from the Scaife Family Charitable Trusts, the Honorable Leonard Sullivan, Jr., agreed to serve as Project Director, the Working Group was selected, and the first meeting was held on September 30, 1976.

At that time, we visualized a 250-page report in six chapters, to be completed within eighteen months, after roughly ten meetings of the Working Group. We recognized from the outset that we would not be able to consider all the likely missions for U.S. and Alliance naval forces. To keep the problem within bounds, we concentrated on issues concerning the security of the seas and the Western Alliance's essential sealanes. As so many have discovered before us, however, it is not possible to consider one aspect of the many naval missions without placing it within the context of the overall strategic balance, strategic nuclear warfare, and other naval tasks such as air and amphibious force projection.

Two years and fourteen meetings later, we have produced a 464-page, 16-chapter, report. Repeated efforts to compress the work have been unsuccessful. We feel obliged to include material on the naval history of both superpowers and on technology projections as well as to consider the broad variety of peacetime, crisis, and wartime missions in which our navies could become involved in various regions of the world. Moreover, we have set as our goal the production of a work that can be understood by lay leaders in the United States and throughout the Alliance. We have attempted to minimize the jargon and the shorthand of the "inner circle" in the hope that the debate on the future of Western navies will expand to include concerned individuals throughout the West.

This effort has involved many people with many talents. Chapters 2 and 3 are mainly the work of Donald Jameson, with liberal comments and suggestions from Norman Polmar. Michael MccGwire contributed greatly to Chapter 4. Chapters 5 and 6 are chiefly the product of David Kassing, with valuable assistance from Robert Athay, Ann Hollick, and Ellen Weis. Chapters 7 and 8 were structured by Frank Bothwell and Ira Rutberg. Chapters 10 and 11 were prepared by Reuven Leopold, with some valuable assistance from Allan Schaffer. Chapter 13 is basically the work of Charles DiBona and William O'Keefe, with important help from Ursula Guerrieri and Roland Smith. Leonard Sullivan as rapporteur contributed to the entire report and put together Chapters 1, 9, 12, 14, and 15 with help from other members of the Working Group: Gerard Mangone, Thomas Wolfe, and Seyom Brown were particularly helpful with Chapter 1, and Robert Athay with Chapter 9. The entire text has benefited greatly from the comments, wisdom, and "alternate views" of Francis Wilcox, Julien Le Bourgeois, John Foster, Richard Garwin, George McGhee, and William Lind. Julien LeBourgeois, in particular, deserves great credit for his tireless efforts to keep the focus on practical naval considerations. We were disappointed that Robert Baldwin, Eugene Fubini, and Andrew Goodpaster were compelled to withdraw from the Working Group owing to the pressure of other assignments.

Chapters 14 and 15 significantly reflect consultations during the early summer of 1978 in Japan, Germany, and England with both past and current naval experts. This final report does not constitute approval by any government—including our own. It is intended to be the work and opinions of an interested but unofficial group, dedicated to the continued security of the Western Alliance.

It should go without saying of course, that no one member of the group—including the project director and myself—can wholeheartedly agree with every word of the text that follows. Each one of us would have preferred different wording or emphasis in a few places. Those who feel most strongly have submitted "Additional Views," which are included in Chapter 16. Even these postscripts have been reviewed and debated within the Working Group. In the main, however, all the participants listed on the following pages support the work as a whole and believe it can contribute positively to the debate on this national issue.

Final editing of the manuscript was accomplished by Albert Toner.

Preface xxvii

Without his efforts it is unlikely that we would have been able to draw the entire report together.

I am indebted to the project director, the editor, and all the members of the Working Group and the Atlantic Council for their wholehearted support of this extended effort. I believe it carries an important message concerning the magnitude of the Soviet naval threat and the need for the West to direct increased attention to assuring the security of the seas.

Paul H. Nitze
Chairman,
Atlantic Council Working Group,
"Securing the Seas"

Working Group on Securing the Seas

Chairman

Paul H. Nitze, Consultant, System Planning Corporation, former delegate to SALT; former Deputy Secretary of Defense and Secretary of the Navy.

Project Director and Rapporteur

Leonard Sullivan, Jr., Defense Policy Consultant, former Assistant Secretary of Defense.

Members

Robert E. Athay, Professor of Management, Naval War College.

Frank E. Bothwell, Vice President, Tetra Tech, Inc.

Seyom Brown, Director of U.S./Soviet Relations Program, Carnegie Endowment for International Peace.

Charles J. DiBona, Executive Vice President, American Petroleum Institute.

John S. Foster, Jr., Vice President and General Manager, Energy Systems Group, TRW Defense and Space System Group; former Director of Defense Research and Engineering, Department of Defense.

Richard L. Garwin, IBM Fellow, Thomas J. Watson Research Center; former Member of Defense Science Board and President's Science Advisory Committee.

Andrew J. Goodpaster, Superintendent, U.S. Military Academy; former Supreme Allied Commander, Europe.

Ann L. Hollick, Associate Professor and Executive Director of the Ocean Policy Project, School of Advanced International Studies, Johns Hopkins University.

Donald F. B. Jameson, Secretary-Treasurer, Tetra Tech, Inc.

David B. Kassing, President, Center for Naval Analyses.

Lane Kirkland, Secretary-Treasurer, AFL-CIO.

Julien J. LeBourgeois, former President, Naval War College; former Deputy Assistant Chief of Staff of SHAPE.

Reuven Leopold, Technical Director, Ship Design Division, Naval Ship Engineering Center, U.S. Navy.

William Lind, Legislative Assistant to Senator Gary W. Hart.

George C. McGhee, former Ambassador to Germany and Turkey and Under Secretary of State.

Michael K. MccGwire, Professor of Political Science, Dalhousie University.

Gerard Mangone, Professor of International Law and Director, Center for the Study of Marine Policy, University of Delaware; Consultant to the Department of State.

William O'Keefe, Director of Management and Budget, American Petroleum Institute.

Robert E. Osgood, Dean, School of Advanced International Studies, Johns Hopkins University.

Dominic A. Paolucci, President, Santa Fe Corporation; Retired Captain, U.S. Navy.

Norman Polmar, Vice President, Santa Fe Corporation.

Chalmers M. Roberts, author and columnist; former Staff Writer for the *Washington Post*.

Ira Rutberg, Analyst, Tetra Tech, Inc.

Allan B. Schaffer, Staff Assistant to the Vice President, Ballistic Missile System Division, TRW Defense and Space System Group; former Assistant to the President, R&D Associates.

Andreas C. Schultheis, Director of Systems Research and Engineering Division, System Planning Corporation; former Project Engineer and Program Manager, Design and Development, Applied Physics Laboratory, Johns Hopkins University.

Thomas W. Wolfe, Senior Researcher, Rand Corporation; Retired Colonel, U.S. Air Force.

Ex-Officio Members

Theodore C. Achilles, Vice Chairman, Atlantic Council; former Counselor of the State Department and Ambassador to Peru.

Francis O. Wilcox, Director General, Atlantic Council; former Assistant Secretary of State; Dean, School of Advanced International Studies, Johns

Hopkins University; Chief of Staff, Senate Foreign Relations Committee.
Livingston Hartley, author.
Martha C. Finley, Assistant Director General, Atlantic Council.

Editor

Albert P. Toner, Editorial Consultant, Foreign Affairs Specialist.

Student Interns

Richard D. Sokolsky, School of Advanced International Studies, Johns Hopkins University.
Ellen J. Weis, Georgetown University.

Securing the Seas

Summary of Policy Conclusions and Recommendations

This report is the effort of a group of experts brought together by the Atlantic Council to analyze the capabilities of the Western Alliance to defend essential sea lines of communication (SLOCs) under various conditions of peace, tension, and war.

The issues are highly important; at stake are the tradition of freedom of the seas and the security interests of the entire Alliance. The Working Group finds that the Soviet Union—whose naval forces have become substantially stronger in recent years—is now capable of seriously interfering with essential shipping and challenging other Western uses of the seas.

Meanwhile, the Alliance fleets have been permitted to dwindle in numbers and, in some cases, to become obsolete. The fundamental conclusion of the study is that the West must make renewed commitments to maintaining a favorable naval balance. This will require firm long-range naval policies and construction programs to support them. Top priority should be devoted to Alliance naval counterforce capabilities. Collectively we need to build military forces large and versatile enough to neutralize or eliminate the diverse threats that the Soviets and their client-states could pose to Western security. No Alliance navy should be sized or configured solely for sealane defense operations.

Estimating military and civil losses during the early stages of confrontation at sea is a highly uncertain process; both sides would be constrained by the limits of their forces from handling all the possible assignments at once. Variations in strategies, priorities, and weapons effectiveness on both sides would greatly influence the progress of hostilities. In order to lower the losses that might be sustained by Western naval forces, merchant ships, and receiving ports, should hostilities break out, the Working Group presents a series of recommendations designed to:

- *Encourage a new Alliance commitment to the retention of a favorable naval balance by* formulating definitive Alliance naval policies and firm long-range construction programs that support them and establishing top priority for the development of Alliance naval counterforce capabilities.
- *Improve Alliance understanding of the full range of possible naval requirements, including* the increasing need for capable naval forces in the Pacific in the event of a "NATO war"; the importance of countering growing Soviet interposition capabilities; the implications of a U.S. conflict without Alliance participation and vice versa; the declining capability for continuous U.S. forward deployments of naval forces; the possible importance of the Western sealanes following the nuclear phases of a war; and Western merchant marine requirements.
- *Develop more threat-responsive Alliance naval capabilities by* creating numerically larger navies of less expensive ships; adopting "modular" design of critical weapons and sensors to facilitate conversion of merchant ships, upgrading of naval escorts, Alliance standardization and interoperability of weapons and equipment, and modernization of naval combatants; and exploiting new technology.
- *Make greater use of available Alliance assets to counter a possible Soviet anti-SLOC campaign by* converting some merchant ships to auxiliary convoy escorts and arming others for self-defense; keeping the numbers of merchant ships up, mixing economic and military cargoes within ships and within convoys, and providing self-unloading capability for those ships; improving standardization, interoperability, joint training, and command structure; giving NATO a collective responsibility for port defense and mine warfare; and applying air force assets to the naval counterforce mission.
- *Reduce Alliance dependency on shipping during the early stages of a crisis or conflict by* increasing prepositioning of military equipment near anticipated theaters of operations and intensifying national economic stockpiling throughout the Alliance.
- *Avoid increasing the projected Soviet anti-SLOC threat by* resisting the extension of Soviet overseas bases and maintaining or expanding U.S. overseas installations.

The rationale for these findings is set forth in the chapters that follow. There is a stark contrast between the momentum of Soviet naval development and the relative indecisiveness on the Alliance side. If this study succeeds in alerting Western planners to the potential problems ahead and contributes to a renewed dedication in the West to naval and maritime needs, then it will have served its purpose.

1
Introduction

The Role of the Seas in the World Balance of Influence

Two world powers emerged from the titanic struggles of World War II. The Union of Soviet Socialist Republics (U.S.S.R.), traditionally a group of land-bound peoples sprawled across Central Europe and Asia, has openly stated its intent to export its Communist doctrine around the world. The United States, facing two great oceans and traditionally dependent on the seas, has become the leader of a coalition of free democratic states in a world troubled by rising economic expectations and national revolutions. This study examines the continuing contest between these two great powers and their allies in terms of future control of the seas.

If mankind had remained incapable of traversing the oceans, we would live in a radically different world, and "Americans" would not exist. Each of the major landmasses and island chains would be a world unto itself, with unique politics, economies, and lifestyles.

Instead, man mastered the seas in his ambitious drive to expand the known world, and for the past three centuries the seas have been dominated by one nationality or another. When the British Empire ended its century of unchallenged naval supremacy after World War I, its worldwide political, economic, and military influence began to wane. By the beginning of World War II, the Axis powers of Germany, Japan, and Italy were able to present a serious threat to the free use of the seas by the opposing Allies. Allied success depended on winning the crucial sea battles of the Atlantic and the Pacific. With control of the oceans, men, war machines, and supplies then traversed the seas to the battlefields on or near the Eurasian landmass. It was primarily because of Allied success in establishing supremacy at sea that the postwar balance of power almost defied the logic of distance and geography. Continued free use of the seas for commerce has helped the United States to develop the most advanced economy the world has known.

The members of the new Western Alliance, in both the Atlantic and the Pacific Hemispheres, include the former three Axis powers of World War II and are spread over most of the continents. They hold much of the warm water coastline of both the Atlantic and the Pacific. Their major antagonist, the Soviet Union, has only limited direct access to those oceans. Present political alignments, as well as the economic strength and military balance of the West, continue to depend on the availability of the seas for the exchange of resources and finished products and, in time of war, the movement of military supplies and the projection of military force. No one ally or group of allies that share or abut the Eurasian landmass could otherwise stand alone against the military might of the Soviet Union and those less-than-voluntary allies that form her buffer states. Beyond our strategic weapons, it is the U.S. forces stationed with our allies abroad and their confidence in further reinforcements at the outset of any possible Soviet aggression that strengthen the military and political deterrent to conventional warfare.

The Western Alliance is equally dependent on seaborne commerce for the viability of its free economic system. Each nation of the Alliance derives a substantial and increasing share of its gross national product from waterborne international trade. Few countries could survive, and none could prosper, if that trade were dependent on the acquiescence of an unfriendly power. The result could well be realignment of political allegiance based primarily on geography. Permanent adverse control of the seas could very well be exploited to force the communization of the entire European, Asian, and African continents, as well as the neighboring islands such as Japan, Indonesia, Taiwan, and the United Kingdom. This development might leave Australia and North and South America as the bastions of individual and economic freedom. The full impact of such a traumatic readjustment in world political and economic alignments can hardly be imagined.

Five New Factors in the Current Use of the Seas

Five relatively recent developments—since the end of World War II— have significantly changed the importance of the seas in both the peaceful and the belligerent affairs of mankind.

Nuclear Warfare

First and foremost is the advent of nuclear weapons. Both the United States and the Soviet Union discovered that the least vulnerable of their strategic offensive forces would be those hidden beneath the surface of the seas, and they shaped their programs accordingly. As a result, a significant portion of the total strategic might of each superpower now rests within the

NUCLEAR WARFARE AT SEA

The possibility of nuclear war at sea was heralded by the atomic tests at Bikini Atoll in July of 1946 against a target fleet. (Courtesy U.S. Navy)

The first firing of a Polaris SLBM missile from a submerged submarine, the U.S.S. *George Washington* (SSBN-598), took place in July of 1960. (Courtesy U.S. Navy)

hulls of a few scores of nuclear-powered submarines, each able to launch one or more devastating nuclear warheads from each of its many ballistic rockets against targets deep in the opponent's home territory. The seas have always held an important strategic role in the political, economic, and military development of the world's nations as a medium for transportation and as the area for contests for naval supremacy. Now they provide bases for a crucial element of strategic nuclear forces as well.

The impact of nuclear weapons, however, is not limited to those deployed at sea. As long as the United States maintained a predominance in total nuclear arms, the free use of the seas could be guaranteed by the threat of nuclear retaliation. Conventional naval forces could operate under the general nuclear umbrella, regardless of the state of these forces themselves. Nuclear "parity" now removes most of that umbrella, and the conventional naval balance again becomes important in its own right.

Emergence of the Soviet Union as a Maritime Power

Second, in the last twenty years it has become increasingly apparent that the Soviet Union has decided to become a major maritime and naval power despite her limited access to the warm waters of the world's oceans. The Western Alliance must look toward serious competition from our major political and economic antagonist in the uses of the seas. This presents a severe challenge to all the functions of the sea from which the Western Alliance has benefited: as the primary means for transporting resources and goods; as a medium for the development and exploitation of resources; as a secure base for our nuclear deterrent; and as an essential right-of-way for the projection of conventional military force to other lands. The spectre of an effective, globally deployed, Soviet deepwater navy adds considerable uncertainty to the future correlation of political, economic, and military forces from which the West has in the past gained so greatly.

The Soviets' approach to military doctrine can be derived from their extensive writings and actions. They emphasize that predominant capabilities at higher levels of combat, once achieved, can open up manifold opportunities for exploitation at lower levels of engagement. In the event of major hostilities, the Soviets claim that "all factors must be strategically coordinated and exploited in terms of time and space" in order to achieve comprehensive military control of the situation as soon as possible. Such control can then be exploited to achieve the political objectives for which the war is being fought.

In conformity with these principles, the Soviets have given priority to creating the following overall military capabilities: (a) the achievement of a radically favorable shift in the strategic nuclear military relationship; (b) the ability to surround or defeat opposing ground forces—conventional and nuclear—within the various theaters of the Eurasian landmass, plus the ability to exploit those successes by investing and occupying the desired territory; and (c) the ability to destroy opposing naval forces with a view to such subsequent exploitation of command of the sea as Soviet politico-military objectives may call for in some areas.

In situations where the Soviets enjoy equal to superior military capability at the higher levels of potential combat (i.e., the strategic nuclear, theater nuclear, or theater conventional levels), they believe it proper and desirable to exploit such potential advantage in support of their stated objective of enlarging the Communist sphere of influence and control. They may do this at the sociopolitical or economic levels or by actions at the most favorable and effective lower levels of pressure and military action, preferably through client-states or movements. They are capable of coordinating the strategic use of most available assets for the accomplishment of their chosen objectives. In each case, they attempt to minimize the risks to themselves in the course selected. Examples of such pressure or military action have been seen in the past throughout the area adjacent to Soviet borders and more recently at greater distances, including the Eastern Mediterranean, the Red Sea and Persian Gulf areas, South Asia, and Africa. Such pressure can call for the use of naval forces, as in the support of Cuban forces in Angola and the current harassment of Japanese fishing vessels in the Sea of Japan.

The evolution of Soviet naval capabilities appears to have been in conformity with these general principles of Soviet military ambitions and doctrine. In the creation of its naval forces, the Soviet Union appears to have put high priority on:

1. The capability to counter U.S. sea-based strategic systems as they have evolved—initially with anticarrier systems, and later in the form of antisubmarine systems;
2. The creation and improvement of their own naval strategic warfighting capabilities, primarily ballistic and cruise missile submarines (both of longer and shorter range), and of land-based naval aircraft;
3. A submarine, air, and surface navy capable of inflicting immediate heavy damage against Alliance naval surface vessels and merchant ships, and the extensive mining of Alliance port facilities;
4. The maintenance of strong naval coastal defense and countermining capabilities as well as an expanding capability to project naval infantry within areas of friendly, land-based air cover.
5. The development of forward resupply capabilities consistent with requirements for sustained operations in distant waters—without extensive dependence on permanent shore bases abroad; and

6. The full participation of civil maritime assets in support of naval research, naval operations, and intelligence gathering.

The relative priorities and capabilities to perform these missions will be discussed in subsequent chapters.

Military Technology

The third factor, technology, has made the surface of the oceans much more vulnerable than it used to be. Until very recently, naval vessels could become "lost" to view by simply moving beyond the horizon. The advent of naval patrol aircraft during World War II began to remove some of this potential for concealment. Longer-range aircraft with vastly improved sensors and weapons are now available. The more recent advent of extensive satellite surveillance promises to make it theoretically possible to locate and track almost any ship on the high seas on an hour-by-hour basis.

The nations of the world currently operate something in excess of 26,000 commercial seagoing ships. About half of them are at sea at any one time. Of those at sea, roughly half are transporting cargo in the form of raw materials or finished products, while the other half are engaged in gathering high protein food from the sea. Of the 13,000 cargo vessels, some 5,000 are transporting that vital source of energy: oil. In comparison to the 26,000 commercially registered vessels, all the nations of the world would be hard-pressed to assemble 1,000 surface naval vessels in the open ocean.

Technology has spawned a new generation of medium- and long-range antiship missiles capable of being launched from aircraft, submarines, surface combatants, and even patrol craft. Hence, surface ships have become not only more "visible," but also easier to sink or damage. At the same time, technology has vastly improved the capabilities of both conventional and nuclear-powered submarines and their conventional and nuclear weapons. They remain difficult to detect and sink.

Thus, while the worldwide threat from land-based naval aircraft and from submarines has increased to a great extent, the worldwide threat posed by large surface combatants has probably diminished substantially, except where geography and the particular scenario make such large warships irreplaceable. In any event, the ability to detect, classify, and locate enemy surface, air, and submarine targets and to analyze, communicate, and use that information with speed has been accorded increasingly central importance by both sides as technology has quickened the pace of naval warfare. By the same token, recent Soviet writings also address the need for naval systems to provide cover, deception, and electronic warfare, and they even allude to "antisensor" warfare in future naval conflict.

Resource Interdependence

The fourth recent change in the importance of the seas derives from the increasing interdependence of the countries that harbor the world's natural resources and those that need them for their own continued growth and prosperity. Very few, if any, nations today contain all the resources required for their continued development. Those that have both food and energy may lack important minerals. The Soviets, for instance, have almost all the minerals and most of the oil they need but cannot sustain themselves reliably on internally grown food. The United States, on the other hand, is a major exporter of food but can no longer prosper on her own mineral and oil resources at present levels of consumption. Europe and Japan are not self-sufficient in any of these three basic commodity classes. The result is increasing international interdependence for the redistribution of resources required for survival. Virtually all of these essential resources must move by sea.

The Rise of New Nations

The fifth new factor of importance results from the dissolution of essentially all of the world's "empires" following World War II. In many cases, the various colonies of these empires—whether British, French, Dutch, Belgian, Spanish, or Portuguese—together provided some semblance of equilibrium in essential resources in return for a measured but inadequate development of their own societies. Now, however, the "liberation movement" is virtually complete and the number of independent and politically unaligned countries has risen drastically. Where there were once a half dozen sovereign states in Africa, for example, there are now nearly fifty. Similar fragmentation has taken place in Asia and the Middle East—and even in the Caribbean. Inexperienced, ambitious, and often resentful, these new nations of the Third World seek continued redress of both real and imagined inequities in their status. A few of these countries survive because of the rich resources they control, but they can neither use nor exploit them without outside assistance. Compared to the 1950s, the world's interdependence has risen, while its political and economic stability appears to have decreased.

Naval forces have classically been used during peacetime as a means of maintaining stability, quieting unrest, and deterring interference with the free use of the seas. The various empires of the West provided many overseas ports and facilities from which to operate these navies. Now, however, interdependence and unrest are on the upswing, and we are faced with dwindling naval resources and a diminishing number of overseas bases from which to operate them.

The Future Importance of the Seas

Based on this view of the present, what can be said about the world of the future? Will the importance of the seas continue to rise? The answer to the former must, of course, be speculative. The answer to the latter must be an unqualified affirmative. Regardless of the many unforeseen events that make predictions uncertain, some undeniable trends are worth noting. They all lead to the conclusion that the importance of the seas—to the Western Alliance, the Soviet Union, and the nations of the Third World as well—will continue to rise.

Strategic Balance

We may have to face an era in which the strategic nuclear balance tends to tilt in the direction of the Soviet Union. Although it may not be certain that the Soviet leaders are striving for strategic military supremacy, such an ambition certainly cannot be ruled out and, in fact, appears probable in view of current trends. Certainly they intend to posture themselves in such a way as to minimize the damage they would have to absorb in the unlikely— but not "unthinkable"—event of a nuclear war and to maximize their capabilities to be the ultimate winner of such a war. This is apparent from their rather impressive efforts on the civil defense front and from their recent writings on the missions of Soviet naval forces and on warfare generally.

The West seems not to understand fully the extent to which the Soviet Union subscribes to the Clausewitzian theory that war is an extension of politics. Yet Soviet military writers define four states of war: *peacetime*— during which the State pursues its Socialist-Communist objectives, including the support of "wars of national liberation"; *applying pressure*— during which military muscle may be flexed to intimidate the recalcitrant; *warfighting*—during which no available weapons are considered too terrible to use or impossible to survive; and *effecting the outcome*— during which residual forces may be displayed or used to help establish the winner. For this last role, Soviet writers identify "second echelon forces," whose purpose, in the case of the army, is to "invest" and occupy defeated lands. In the case of the navy, they often refer to U.S. carriers and nuclear-powered fleet ballistic missile submarines (SSBNs) as our "second strategic echelon" and rather clearly imply that their own new SSBNs, and whatever naval assets are required to defend them, may be withheld to act in the same role against lands they cannot hope to occupy. It is certainly not inconceivable that the Soviets would also look at Western shipping as "second echelon support" for continued military resistance *after* the initial nuclear exchanges—which they generally accept as occurring early in any full-scale war between the superpowers.

In such progressive or full-scale nuclear exchanges—if they should occur—U.S. SSBN support bases, carrier task forces, and other concentrations of Alliance naval forces would be expected to be important targets. The relatively low-value merchant ship convoys would be less likely to rate high target priority. Initially, each side would certainly target the major naval bases, port facilities, and airfields of the other targets. In the future, given enough time and warheads, it may be possible to conduct nuclear barrage attacks against SSBN bases and suspected SSBN patrol areas. Nonetheless, both sides still have reason to be confident that major elements of their sea-based nuclear strike forces would survive these initial exchanges because of the continuing difficulty of detecting and localizing at-sea submarines that are not obliged to give away their general location. The Soviets could also retain their latest SSBNs in protected coastal waters.

In view of the Western lead in antisubmarine warfare, however, it appears that the Soviets would devote a substantial portion of their naval assets to the protection of their SSBN forces. Acceptance of a "withhold" strategy, made possible by their growing nuclear forces and more capable SSBNs, might require the continued use of these defensive assets—and supporting units—after an initial nuclear exchange. Assumption of a "withhold" strategy for Western naval forces, including SSBNs and other surface elements, would also motivate the Soviets to attempt to conserve naval forces for continuing the fight in the aftermath of the initial nuclear exchanges.

In short, there is considerable indication that the still-growing Soviet strategic capabilities will have a substantial impact on the utilization of the navies of both superpowers. Naval strategic and strategic-supporting assets might be given no higher time-priority as targets in the initial exchanges of a general nuclear war than would naval nonstrategic forces. The primary function of surviving SSBN forces might be to play a crucial, if not decisive, role in determining the ultimate outcome of the war. Assuring the low vulnerability and endurance over time of these special national assets will continue to be a major driving factor in the naval developments of the two superpowers.

Conventional Force Balance

The retention of a deterrent to peacetime intimidation or conventional warfare will continue to depend in considerable measure on naval developments. The primary role of each side's nonstrategic naval forces will be to exploit—or to deny the other side's ability to exploit—the lower portions of the warfare spectrum at a distance from their homelands. The struggle for political and economic leverage by the emerging nations seems certain to involve manipulation of supply and demand and possibly of the shipping that provides a major means of equalizing the two. The behavior of these nations is also likely to generate situations that could lead to the use of force by one—or both—of the superpowers. Continuing political and economic instability may well lead to instances of military intervention. Such interventions—as well as the interposition of forces to deny them—will generally involve the exercise of naval elements.

During future periods of peacetime tension, it is not inconceivable that the Soviets might attempt to apply dramatic forms of pressure, such as: declaring certain sea areas closed to navigation; establishing a quarantine area comparable to U.S. action during the Cuban missile crisis; or the seizing, sinking, or harassing of individual ships without prior notice. Such actions would not be lightly taken, since the Soviets would be vulnerable to a variety of counteractions and would doubtless have an increasing stake in maintaining peacetime stability on the seas. Nonetheless, the West must remain capable of deterring such acts.

The Soviets no doubt realize that aircraft carriers no longer have a role in the initial nuclear strike plans of the United States. However, they still view our carriers as central to all U.S. conventional naval capabilities, and consider that, unopposed, they form the mainstay of our capabilities to intervene militarily in the affairs of other countries—such as Vietnam, Korea, and Lebanon. While the Soviets repeatedly decry direct military intervention in support of lesser states by any major power other than themselves (in what they call the "local wars of the imperialists"), they see no reason to assume that the United States will forswear such intervention in the foreseeable future. One stated purpose for the growing Soviet conventional warfare fleet (and the development of conventional weapons to go with it) is to protect Third World nations against such intervention. The U.S. carrier task force will retain the power to destroy such interposition forces in most situations, but there will be a growing uncertainty about when and where it would be wise to risk such a confrontation.

It can also be argued that the Soviets must continue to evolve a substantial conventional naval capability in order to enable them to resupply their eastern-deployed forces in a war with the People's Republic of China, owing to the vulnerability and inadequacy of their overland transportation network. (A Sino-Soviet war is considered by some to be more likely than a U.S.-Soviet conflict.) However, they are working to improve their overland routes, which will clearly be essential to the eventual development of their own vast natural resources in Central and Eastern Asia.

The Soviet Union is well on its way to becoming a major naval and merchant power, as will be demonstrated in later chapters. By comparison, the fundamental need of the Western Alliance to use the seas in peacetime or during or after a major conflict will far outstrip any claims to the economic, political, or military essentiality of the use of the seas that could reasonably be put forward by the Soviets. On this basis, it is mandatory that the Alliance maintain a naval capability sufficient to offset any Soviet attempts at sea denial. However, the achievement of prompt and total sea control in the classic sense will probably never be possible again by one nation's conventional forces.

Conventional-Strategic Linkage

There is a growing and inevitable linkage between the use of conventional force and the threat of escalation to some use of nuclear weapons—either for tactical or theater purposes or at the strategic, intercontinental level. Fifteen or twenty years ago, when the United States held uncontested nuclear supremacy or later, superiority, many people felt that Soviet attacks on the U.S. Navy could be deterred by the probability of nuclear escalation. With the advent of "nuclear parity," as we mentioned earlier, the threat of U.S. nuclear escalation may not carry the same weight it once did.

Furthermore, it can be argued that the restricted use of nuclear weapons at sea carries neither the degree of moral stigma nor the threat of further escalation that applies to their use against land targets. What would our response be if the Soviets were to destroy one U.S. carrier or ballistic missile submarine at sea with a single nuclear weapon? The answer is by no means obvious. Indeed, the uncertainty of response forms an essential ingredient of the deterrent. Nonetheless, both sides will have to design, deploy, and maneuver their ships and convoys to minimize the damage that could be done by a restricted use of nuclear weapons.

The conventional-strategic linkage in naval forces will be complicated further by the multipurpose nature of naval assets. As long as they can carry nuclear weapons, our aircraft carriers, in the pursuit of some lesser objective, can still be looked upon by the Soviets as potential platforms for launching nuclear aircraft strikes against their homeland. By the same token, ships and submarines that the Soviets may be dedicating to the neutralization of our SSBNs may appear to us as a major threat to the free passage of ships in support of conventional military objectives. Each side will continue to have difficulty in understanding the motives behind the other's multipurpose naval ship construction and deployment programs. For the past thirty years, this problem has been illustrated by the relative emphasis placed on antisubmarine warfare (ASW) by each superpower. The Soviets have feared a nuclear war more than a conventional one and have almost certainly concentrated their ASW efforts on developing a capability to counter our ballistic missile submarines and protect their own. Conversely, we have seen a conventional engagement in NATO Europe as more probable than a nuclear war and have concentrated our ASW efforts on assuring the use of the sealanes across the Atlantic.

Resource Extraction from the Sea

In the area of political and economic development, the world is going to

CONVENTIONAL/STRATEGIC LINKAGE

The attack carrier U.S.S. *Ranger* (CVA-61) is typical of the large U.S. ships that can be given either nuclear or conventional strike missions. (Courtesy U.S. Navy)

The new U.S. Navy Tomahawk cruise missile, shown here approaching the California coast after launch from the U.S.S. *Barb* (SSN-596) in a late 1977 test flight is also capable of performing either nuclear or conventional strike missions. (Courtesy U.S. Navy)

become more complicated; the use of the seas will grow more complicated as well. The increasing significance of the Third World has already been mentioned, and another new trend is certain to confuse matters even more: the increasing realization of the resource potential of the sea and its floor. A substantial and increasing share of the world's oil is drawn from offshore wells (17 percent of U.S. oil is now obtained from such sources). In addition, deep-sea mining for various minerals will soon be undertaken by the developed countries, albeit at a very slow pace. Seabed mining will take place off the shores of developing and advanced nations alike.

As the world population grows, a larger percentage of the needed nutrition may be drawn from the sea. In recognition of these trends, the world is on the verge of assigning a rather significant fraction of the total ocean areas to the countries that border them. The new 200-mile limits—as well as arrangements for the "ownership" of straits and archipelagos—will eventually cause dramatic limitations and disagreements concerning the free use of the seas. The seas will be less free than they used to be, and "ownership" is bound to generate proprietary attitudes that may restrict navigation freedom and encourage the building of naval systems capable of enforcing sovereignty. In short, many lesser nations may for the first time feel obliged to develop navies of their own—and now they can obtain a potent capability at a relatively low cost. Many of the more prosperous nations may also become more concerned about the vulnerability of their offshore assets and increase their naval and coast guard forces accordingly.

Ship Vulnerability

If modern technology had not progressed beyond the weapon development potential of World War II, the threat from various minor navies would not be very real to the superpowers. But recent developments in small, simple, relatively cheap, antiship and antiaircraft weapons can make a 70-foot shore patrol craft a serious threat to a major surface combatant at a range well beyond visual identification—even over the horizon. The real threat from Third World naval forces will not be revealed by the mere counting or weighing of capital ships. Conversely, the inherent power and destructive capacity of major ships may be seriously diminished by their susceptibility to damage (and severe embarrassment) possibly en route to some major engagement. In these new circumstances, major naval forces, because they could not be safely deployed within 250 miles of any unaligned nation's coastline—or within 50 miles of any unidentified "fishing vessels"—could find their future utility compromised.

Soviet Expansionism

There may be something to the argument that the Soviet Union, for geographic reasons, is not a "natural" seagoing power. There is also considerable evidence that the Soviets initially expanded their naval capabilities somewhat reluctantly in response to what may have seemed to them to be aggressive moves on the part of the United States and its nuclear forces. Whether or not there is merit in these assumptions is possibly of little concern for the future. Over the past twenty years, the Soviet Union has been generally preoccupied with overcoming U.S. superiority in strategic nuclear systems. The Russians have been forced to contend with the loss of the People's Republic of China as an ally with a common land border 4,500 miles long. They have had to deal with the dissatisfaction of their Eastern European "allies." The U.S.S.R. has also been faced with substantial numbers of forward-deployed Western Alliance military assets as well as with what may have appeared to it as a strong NATO military structure, and it maintained a clearly inferior naval posture.

The Soviets have done remarkably well in redressing these imbalances. Only within the past three to five years has the Soviet "superpower" really become a coequal with the United States in strategic terms. They perceive this event as a major qualitative shift in the "correlation of world forces" in their direction. The prime question now is, what will they do next? If their pursuit of "peaceful coexistence" is only a form of international conflict and struggle designed to avoid direct confrontation with the United States, then they should be able to turn more of their energies toward peaceful competition in the political and economic spheres—while supporting armed conflict only amongst the less-developed countries with "proxy force" assistance when required. For these purposes, their current naval forces appear adequate. If they intend to deny U.S. capabilities to intervene in local wars, then they will need to continue their naval buildups significantly. If, at the other extreme, they opt to increase their military forces across the board to the level required to intimidate the entire Western world and thus pressure it piecemeal into subjugation, then the West will be forced to increase the level of its energies and resources devoted to maintaining some ever-expanding military balance.

In any event, the Soviet Union appears certain to move in the direction of greater utilization of the seas for both conventional military and civil expansion. Some qualified Sovietologists infer that the Soviet leaders believe they have now reached the "third stage" in the socialist progression over imperialism, which allows them to operate worldwide without fear of being labeled adventurists or of incurring "imperialist" counteraction. In some instances, the Western Alliance has nothing to fear from these increased—and legitimate—Soviet maritime interests. In other instances, the Western way of life could be placed in jeopardy. It behooves the Alliance to enter this coming period with greater attentiveness and some apprehension until the Soviet course becomes more evident. Similarly, Western policymakers must be sensitive to the impact of their decisions and actions on Soviet intentions and developments.

Substitutes for Merchant Ships

There appear to be no plausible substitutes within the foreseeable future for commercial surface shipping and its attendant large, vulnerable port complexes. Various studies have explored the use of very large aircraft, surface effects craft, or submersibles to replace surface fleets. It is certainly practical to design aircraft that can lift more than the current limit of 100 tons and possible to design submarines or surface effect ships that can carry more than the current limit of about 1,000 tons. However, each requires a combination of hull (airframe), propulsion system, and fuel capacity that consumes a far larger share of the total vehicle weight than that required for conventional surface ships. Moreover, these alternatives would require designing vessels greater than ten times as large as current maximum practice in submarines or surface effects ships or 100 times as large as the C-5 aircraft in order to match the smallest of current seagoing cargo vessels, of which there are well over 10,000. Among these alternatives, the large, very shallow submersible appears to hold promise for the foreseeable future, but its economic feasibility is still in question.

Possibly greater reliance on cross-country and even underwater pipelines would be more practical than using aircraft, surface effect ships, or submarines for the shipment of essential petroleum products. There are already sealanes where the tanker "stream" exceeds one vessel every 50 miles, day and night. On these segments of the routes, pipelines are potentially competitive today. The problem, of course, is that these ships are not headed to the same discharge ports, and many more thousands of miles of pipeline would be required than could be generated by recycling tanker steel into pipe. Moreover, pipelines are not suited to carrying raw materials or finished products other than oil and gas. Finally, like aircraft, ships, shallow submersibles, and submarines, cross-country and underwater pipelines would be very vulnerable. Nonetheless, they may well find some additional uses as alternates to highly constrictive sea passages such as the Straits of Hormuz or the Panama Canal.

Stockpiling and Prepositioning

The world's trade seems certain to increase at least at the equivalent rate of the expected growth in real Gross National Product (GNP) and it will continue to be carried principally by surface ships, at least for the remainder of this century. Generally, continuity in shipping flow will also be required to avoid economic fluctuations. Even though the majority of this commerce is "nonessential" in the sense of national survival, there would be traumas associated with short-term interruptions of shipping flow. These can be partially offset by increased economic and strategic stockpiling by either national governments or private industry. Several recent U.S. studies, including that of a congressional commission, confirm the usefulness of some forms of stockpiling as well as the relatively minor costs involved. In large measure, economic stockpiles may be developed by the private sector. Stockpiling helps primarily with short-term interruptions in raw materials: it would be vastly more difficult to stockpile finished products at the point of sale or to stockpile raw materials for a protracted period of several years. Nonetheless, several countries already practice economic and strategic stockpiling, and others—including the United States—are expected to increase theirs.

The United States stockpiles some critical materials required for a major war and has recently decided to increase the size and scope of those accumulations. The United States also "prepositions" a portion of the basic weapons and supplies needed for a major war either in Europe or in Northeast Asia. In this case, prepositioning makes eminently good sense as long as measures are taken to limit the vulnerability of forward-based depots. Such military prepositioning will be increased in the future if Congress approves Defense Department requests. Moreover, since more Americans fly to Europe each summer as tourists than we would send as soldiers to fight the next war, there should be little problem in providing the airlift to get the troops to their prepositioned equipment—probably without suffering the heavy attrition that might be expected on the high seas. Additionally, if current attempts to increase military equipment standardization succeed within the NATO Alliance, overseas stockpiles may eventually be produced in large measure within the anticipated theater of operations by our Allies themselves.

The Continued Importance of Naval Superiority

Naval forces are probably the most versatile military elements available in the arsenals of both the East and the West. In addition to the strategic nuclear roles already discussed, they can play a crucial part in a broad variety of conventional "scenarios" that could develop in the remainder of this century. No single class of scenarios is truly representative of needed Western capabilities. Consequently, six separate but related classes of situations are presented, against which Western naval capabilities should be judged. They are arranged in the order of decreasing politico-military importance.

Large-Scale Conventional War with the Soviet Union

In the first category, there are two major subdivisions. The first set involves a large-scale theater war with the Soviet Union that has not escalated to the use of nuclear weapons and which both sides are attempting, if at all possible, to keep from escalating. The most obvious—but not necessarily the most likely one in the future—is a NATO-Warsaw Pact conventional war scenario. In the NATO arena, the possibility for nuclear escalation is widely considered by both sides. Outside that arena, there would appear to be several places where the possibility of a major superpower confrontation might also arise. Although the odds of nuclear escalation might be less, the chances for a protracted conflict might actually be higher—and demands on U.S. naval capabilities, without NATO participation, could actually be more severe. Such scenarios are not currently part of serious U.S. defense planning.

There is an unrealistic tendency to believe that such conventional wars between the United States and the Soviets would somehow be geographically limited to the area where they might start. Such assumptions seem highly inappropriate: any large-scale superpower confrontation would be more likely to spread in one form or another to any region where either superpower can exert military force or heavy political pressure.

The second set of possibilities in this class of scenarios involves a continuing large-scale war with the Soviets *after* the initial exchanges of nuclear weapons may have taken place. In this case, the objective would be to assure the survival of one's own "withheld" nuclear forces and simultaneously to rebuild the political, economic, and military infrastructure essential for preserving the Western way of life. This scenario has been given very little consideration by the Western Alliance in recent years.

Both of these scenario sets could be characterized, at least in part, as wars for the sealanes. However, the magnitude of the Western effort and the Soviet threat depends on many variables: how much prepositioning and stockpiling has been done; how long the war has gone on and is expected to continue; whether there has been time to mobilize reserve, Allied, and civil assets; how much nonessential shipping is continuing; how much prior damage has already been done to the combatants of each side; and how much effort the Soviet Navy has assigned to this mission as opposed to, say, the mining and destruction of the receiving ports. In most Soviet writings, there appears to be a preference for attacking the receiving ports, while large-scale Soviet naval maneuvers seldom appear to devote much attention to the interdiction of sea lines of communication (SLOCs). Nevertheless, it is important in this class of scenarios to focus on the capability for continued attrition of Soviet submarines and naval aircraft and the clearing of the seas of Soviet naval and other surface vessels. If there is no prospect of restoring the SLOCs—or of countering a limited diversionary Soviet thrust at them—there is little point in engaging in a protracted conventional defense, either before or after a nuclear exchange. Furthermore, an early attempt to get ships through may be necessary to induce the exposure of Soviet submarines and begin their attrition. In fact, such a situation may be inescapable if the war is preceded by a period of crisis or if mobilization and reinforcements are already en route.

War at Sea

The second class of scenarios covers potential conflicts at sea involving both Soviet and U.S. naval forces, with varying degrees of Alliance participation, but no significant ground action on the perimeter of the Soviet Union—although the threat of such ground involvement would not be ruled out. It is not clear that such scenarios are to the benefit of the Soviet Union, unless it found some compelling rationale for trying to eliminate some of our carrier task forces or wished to test or discredit our resolve. As described later, Soviet naval forces do not appear to be designed for, or deployed in, Western-style task forces, making matched-fleet battles of the World War II, Pacific type highly unlikely. The Soviets would presumably concentrate on attacks against our carriers and amphibious forces by submarines and land-based aircraft. Our efforts would presumably emphasize seeking out and sinking the enemy's individual surface ships and then working toward the attrition of his naval aircraft and submarines. The most difficult battle would be the undersea conflict in the open ocean.

U.S. Intervention in Third World States

The third class of scenarios would not involve Soviet military forces directly, but would include U.S. actions against a country receiving Soviet support in the way of equipment, training, and logistics. As in the case of Vietnam, there probably would be other client-state military intervention. Direct or indirect Allied support to the United States would be a variable. The Soviets have shown that they intend to use their maritime assets, both civil and military, to resupply their clients with both arms and "proxy" forces in support of "wars of national liberation." In Soviet doctrine, there is no inconsistency between avoiding direct superpower confrontation (through "détente" or "peaceful coexistence") and continuing the active support of armed conflict within the Third World. In this scenario, the U.S. forces would be pitted against Soviet equipment operated by client or "proxy" forces. The threat of a direct confrontation would arise if the Soviets attempted to interdict our military support to a friendly nation.

The questions raised by this scenario involve the dwindling numbers of U.S. naval assets; the reduction of their primary deterrent effect owing to their commitment to a lesser objective; their capability to go up against Soviet-supplied client-states; the risk of embarrassment over the loss of major naval elements; and the means required to discourage Soviet naval interposition. The cooperation and support of allies and normally friendly clients might be substantially reduced during such crisis periods if there were credible circumstances under which Western Alliance nations could not be assured that the United States could provide them with maritime support, or if the allies just did not wish to become involved for external or internal political or economic reasons. But the capability to provide support against such opposition is highly important. This consideration is reinforced by the significance of land-based assets bordering on the seas in a potential war at sea.

War between Rival Client-States

The fourth class of scenarios involves conflict between client-states supported by the Soviet Union and states resisting aggression, supported by the United States and various allies. It does not involve direct confrontation between U.S. and Soviet forces. In any such situation, the possibility of escalation to one of the earlier scenario stages would always be present. In fact, judgments about the relative capability and will of the two superpowers to intervene could be dominant factors in the outcome. Such scenarios might be likely among the littoral states of the Eastern Mediterranean and the Indian Ocean. Assuming a standoff in such judgments and non-intervention by the superpowers, the outcome could be heavily influenced by competitive military aid and third-party training and support. The basic factors would be the organization, will, indigenous support, and leadership of the local contestants—plus the availability of continuing military aid.

Outside intervention in the affairs of the lesser states may be constrained in the future not only by the presence and capabilities of the opposing superpowers themselves but by the existence of increasingly effective "minor" navies within the Third World. As noted earlier, these smaller nations, equipped with coastal defense, mines, and patrol craft, could become capable of heavily damaging (and embarrassing) the larger naval and maritime elements of the major powers if their ships steamed too close during periods of tension.

Economic Pressure and Intimidation against the Western Alliance

The fifth scenario class involves economic pressure and intimidation by the Soviets, their clients, or certain Third World states who might wish to threaten the economic welfare of the Western Alliance by interrupting the flow of trade in raw materials or finished goods. The Soviets—as well as some Third World countries—have the naval capability to harass and interrupt, at least partially, this vast flow of seaborne commerce if they choose to do so during a period of crisis and tension. By the same token, Soviet civil maritime assets are no less susceptible to harassment, flow interruption, internment, etc. The key questions are how critical a

U.S. NAVAL INTERVENTION OPERATIONS

Naval forces contributed greatly to intervention operations in South Korea, including this amphibious operation into Inchon in September 1950. (Courtesy U.S. Navy)

Landing craft (LCVPs) from the U.S.S. *Rockbridge* (APA-228) took units of the Sixth Marines ashore at Red Beach, Beirut, Lebanon in July 1953 to stabilize a governmental crisis in that country. (Courtesy U.S. Navy)

temporary trade interruption might be, how its impact could be lessened, and what other alternatives exist with less opportunity for reciprocal actions. In any case, it might be highly desirable in certain cases to demonstrate determination to resist trade interruption at sea by the suitable application of naval force. The possible vulnerabilities of offshore assets to disruption must also be considered.

Peacetime Postures and Perceptions

Decision makers must continually consider the relative military capabilities of the principal actors in world affairs and the conditions under which they might be used. Naval capabilities are merely one aspect of overall military balance. They have a particular bearing, however, on countries which are not physically adjacent to the U.S.S.R. or the United States, but which border on the sea and are dependent on one of these superpowers for support against the other—or against stronger neighbors. For instance, few things could be more damaging to the Western Alliance than a conviction among the European and Pacific allies that the United States would be unable to provide essential reinforcement by sea during a major confrontation with Soviet-Warsaw Pact forces. Other states could be equally discouraged by a perception that we could not or would not provide military aid during a lesser war with a neighbor.

The peacetime presence of naval forces in a given area can be significant largely as a signal of political will to use military force if necessary. The message is ineffective if the military power or the will to intervene successfully is perceived to be in doubt. If the will is real, forward deployments may be necessary to assure the timely initiative—and prior training—essential to success. Military presence, including naval elements, however, may have unfavorable political effects if long continued, depending on the specific situation involved. Long-term "fixed" forward deployments have other disadvantages: they tend to cause extraneous hardships on both crews and equipment; they reduce the inherent versatility and flexibility normally associated with naval systems; and they may lose the original connotation of their presence, becoming a crutch for, instead of a boost to, local self-confidence.

In short, judging from current trends, the remainder of this century is certain to bring significant changes in both military and civil uses of the seas—some of which we cannot foresee. The two superpowers will use the seas to base a substantial portion of their strategic and conventional military forces, and there will be an inevitable linkage between these sets of forces. The Western Alliance will become ever more dependent on the rights of free and unencumbered passage for its ships as world trade grows. No substitutes are expected to be found for the growing flow of surface shipping, although stockpiling of critical materials and prepositioning of critical weapons may decrease the possible inconvenience of short-term interruptions of the shipping stream. The Third World will gain more interest in both the use and the control of the seas and more capability to interfere with the free passage of both military and commercial vessels as technology makes all kinds of surface ships more vulnerable. At the same time, the Soviet Union, with its newfound "parity" in both conventional and nuclear forces, is certain to expand its own uses of the sea for military, political, and economic purposes. The contest for the seas will most likely increase, and the outcome of that contest in a variety of scenarios will continue to be vital to the survival and progress of the Western Alliance.

Meanwhile, naval forces will still have a long lead-time in decisionmaking, design, procurement, production, deployment, modification, and use. A new ship decided upon today may not be initially deployed for ten years; the ships may then have a service life lasting to the year 2025. The sensors, aircraft, missiles, torpedoes, or mines deployed on them, however, will continue to have a much shorter life cycle. New ships can and must have adaptability to changing roles designed and built into them. Nevertheless, the decisions made or not made today will bear upon naval capabilities for many years in the future. There will always be the pressure not to make a decision today because information leading to a better decision will be available next year. This problem can be overcome only by a steady shipbuilding program—like that of the Soviets—subject, of course, to periodic modification.

The need for types of naval developments, particularly those relating to detection, classification, localization, and command and control, would appear not to be scenario-dependent, although increasing dependence on space-based systems raises new questions for both sides. Similarly, the need for strategic nuclear offensive and defensive capabilities appears less scenario-dependent, although the Soviets' new potential for withholding their sea-based strategic systems as a determinant of the ultimate outcome of a major conflict introduces new considerations. In any event, these capabilities at higher levels of potential conflict can greatly influence scenarios at lesser levels.

The most difficult issues for the near future revolve around the amount of effort we should devote to surface-based ship platforms and their armaments as opposed to the submarine, land-based missile, and air capabilities we would need to win a future battle for control of the seas and, thus, the significant sea lines of communication.

Atlantic Council Study Objectives

Within this context, the Atlantic Council has undertaken the study that produced the results reported herein. Assuring the continued use of the sealanes under many different conditions of peace and war must remain one of the principal concerns of the Western Alliance. The problem can not be completely solved—or wished away, for that matter—by any one member of the Alliance, for it makes a common impact on the political solidarity, economic prosperity, and military security of both our Atlantic and our Pacific allies.

We have entered a period when prompt and total sea control no longer seems a realistic option. Both superpowers have substantial navies, but, as indicated earlier, many of the lesser navies of the unaligned world are now, or will shortly be, able to influence the actions of the major powers at sea—at least within 200 miles of their own national coastlines. The Western Alliance will have to settle for less than the total sea control that characterized the later stages of World War II. We will not be able to sail our ships with impunity wherever we wish. There will always be substantial risk in certain waters, but we should certainly maintain the ability to overcome attempts at sea *denial* in waters that provide essential passage.

Furthermore, we must be able to counter sea denial operations under a broad variety of circumstances. These scenarios may vary from politically motivated attempts at economic coercion to periods of crisis involving confrontations between the clients of the superpowers to an all-out confrontation between the superpowers themselves. At each level of naval contest, the means at the disposal of the adversaries and their own levels of vulnerability will be substantially different. Yet there will always be the possibility of linkage between these various levels. On the one hand, an effort by an ad hoc consortium of Third World nations to interrupt shipping could lead to involvement by the superpowers and even to the threat of nuclear escalation, if an American carrier were damaged or sunk, for instance. On the other hand, a major confrontation between the superpowers could lead to intervention by the coastal navies of the Third World. Both superpowers would presumably strive to avoid escalation—particularly as a result of unpremeditated confrontation. Nonetheless, there might well be incidents—or even accidents—in which escalation, or the threat thereof, would be brought into play.

This study, then, is devoted to the analysis of the realistic capabilities of current and projected Alliance conventional forces to prevent or offset the impact of shipping interruptions by Soviet or Third World nations during periods of: (1) protracted conventional warfare against Soviet and Warsaw Pact forces; (2) brief but intense crises or intervention involving one or both superpowers or their client-states; or (3) protracted economic warfare. In each situation, the threat of escalation is ever-present. In the case of protracted war with the Soviets, the threat of escalation to tactical or strategic nuclear weapons would be real and must be seriously considered along with its aftermath. To the extent that current Alliance forces appear inadequate in the face of potential buildups in Soviet and Third World forces, recommendations are provided for augmenting our collective capabilities within realistic budget assumptions.

Atlantic Council Study Limitations

This study does not pretend to consider the total needs of Alliance navies or their specific overall configurations. Such a comprehensive effort was not possible within the time and fiscal constraints of this Atlantic Council Working Group. Consequently, there is no authoritative treatment of the following subjects:

- The impact and extent of the new Law of the Sea negotiations are not yet fully apparent. Eventually, these arrangements, and the ability of various countries to enforce them, may further constrain Alliance naval activities on the high seas. To the extent that we have considered the near-term impact of Third World navies, however, we do provide some insight in this quarter.
- The impact of the use of chemical weapons at sea has not been studied. Soviet ships are known to be defensively equipped to survive the use of such weapons, and we know that a very substantial portion (perhaps one-third) of Soviet land force munitions contain chemical warheads. We are not certain of the offensive chemical capability of Soviet ships. To the extent that they could force whole convoys or task forces to sail through lethal clouds, they could generate substantial problems without physically damaging a single surface vessel. As of this time, the Western Alliance might well be forced to threaten retaliation with nuclear weapons against land targets if the Soviets were to violate the recent international agreements restricting the offensive use of these weapons. We cannot foresee a situation in which it would be advantageous for Alliance forces to initiate use of chemical weapons.
- We do not address the full consequences of an all-out nuclear exchange between the superpowers. However, the possible need for naval forces after such an exchange is explored because of its impact on the conservation of naval assets for that eventuality. The limited use of tactical weapons at sea is also treated, at least superficially.
- The other classic roles of naval forces and naval infantry are not addressed, even though we recognize that there are major roles to be played by fleet and marine elements beyond those required to prevent "sea denial." We have not attempted to evaluate the contribution of naval air assets in a major land war in Europe or Northeast Asia. Furthermore, we take no position on the size of U.S.

or Alliance naval forces required for unilateral or multilateral military interventions. However, we acknowledge that such forces may be more crucial to overall naval spending levels than are those required to assure continued use of the seas in contested areas. In some cases these forces may, in fact, be needed to assure continued use of the seas. For instance, the threat of physical intervention may be adequate to deter some third countries from harassing vulnerable SLOCs.

- We make no attempt to second-guess the possible impact of future progress—or lack of it—in strategic arms limitation. Considering the slow rate of current progress toward rather small changes in overall strategic postures, however, it does not appear likely that SALT will make a significant impact on the naval balance in the foreseeable future.
- For several reasons, this report also gives little consideration to the possibility of productive naval conventional arms limitation negotiations between the United States and the Soviets. First, a total naval "balance" between the Soviets and the United States does not appear to be in the best interests of the side with the substantially greater need to use the seas. Second, the Soviets already have a quantitative advantage in many areas and would surely see little reason to cut back to U.S. force levels. Third, the United States retains an advantage in individual ship size, and we see little reason to impose a limit or a reduction in our own maximum allowable ship size (by which we try to offset Soviet quantity). Fourth, it is virtually impossible to negotiate limits to qualitative improvements on either side. Fifth, naval limitations have seldom proved effective when imposed by one side on the other; it seems even less likely that voluntary, self-imposed limits would be any more successful. Sixth, the kinds of limitations that might best serve each side's purposes are rather asymmetrical. For instance, the Soviets might wish, above all, to bound our carrier-based aviation capabilities, while our chief aim might be to limit their overall new attack submarine inventory. By what measure could both sides practically agree to balance U.S. carriers off against Soviet submarines which are so different in size, cost, and capability?

Nonetheless, one primary objective of naval forces in the Alliance must be to assist in preserving the political, economic, and military cohesion provided by our extensive and growing collective use of the seas for surface shipping. The continued accomplishment of this objective is currently threatened by Soviet and certain Third World forces that appear to be growing larger and more capable with each passing year. We believe that certain measures need to be taken by the Alliance to offset these potential threats. Moreover, these matters should be of grave concern to government and lay leaders of the Western Alliance. It is our intent to present our case in such an objective and understandable manner that the attention of these groups will be focused on the areas of our concern.

Atlantic Council Study Outline

We begin our study with a brief review of the evolution of Soviet naval interests since the current regime assumed power in 1917—with the help, incidentally, of certain elements of the Russian Navy. We then assess current capabilities and limitations of the Soviets and review the manner in which their naval forces have recently been used. We make some considered projections of Soviet and Third World naval resources based on recent trends and some anticipated constraints. We estimate their overall mission capabilities (not necessarily simultaneous), and indicate some areas in which their future research and development (R&D) efforts might be more threatening. Finally, we show current force allocations among the four major Soviet fleets and estimate the most likely responsibilities of those forces for various conventional and strategic missions.

Next, the report explores Western Alliance economic sensitivity to shipping interruptions. Various means for attenuating their impact are discussed, including stockpiling. We consider the four major regions of current naval and maritime competition: the Atlantic, Mediterranean, Pacific, and Indian oceans, indicating the primary Western uses of these ocean regions and the level of peacetime shipping anticipated over the next decade. We also indicate the current and projected Soviet uses of the seas. The vulnerabilities of offshore resource facilities and the possible impacts of the Law of the Seas are treated superficially. We conclude this portion of the study with a crude estimate of the volume of economic shipping that might be kept moving during a protracted war, comparing that to the anticipated transoceanic military shipping needed and estimating the practicality of providing fleet defense for either or both.

We then trace the evolution of the U.S. Navy since before World War II and describe some of the factors implicit in the changing balance of naval power. We describe the current organization of NATO and Pacific naval forces and compare Soviet and Alliance naval and merchant fleet force levels and base structures. We also identify likely constraints on U.S. naval budgets in the foreseeable future. We describe the relative capabilities of Alliance and Soviet surveillance, ship, and aircraft weapon systems and project some developments for Western navies. We also attempt to explain some of the reasons why the reorientation of existing Western navies to new missions and technologies is a slow process. This section is concluded with a discussion of the types of forces required for Alliance sealane defense missions now and in the near future.

Next, we turn to sea control objectives and review the World War II experience of the Battle of the Atlantic. Then we look at today's naval environment and make some crude estimates of likely shipping losses and escort requirements during a war with the Soviets. We indicate the effect of possible uses of nuclear weapons at sea as well as the potential contributions from various civil assets converted during a period of mobilization. We also make some rough estimates of the value of prepositioning as an alternative to the inevitable shipping losses early in a possible conflict, before the threat is brought under control.

We end with an assessment of the current capabilities of opposing naval forces and offer conclusions and specific recommendations by which the Western Alliance can improve its capabilities to assure the availability of essential sealanes if and when they are threatened. The United States, together with its Atlantic and Pacific allies, can and must retain its access to the seas.

2
Soviet Naval Evolution

Introduction

Since the beginning of the eighteenth century, when Russia emerged as a major power in Europe, her more ambitious rulers have built fleets that other leading nations have denounced as aggressive or ridiculed for their extravagance.

Because the Soviet Union is spread over one-sixth of the land surface of the globe and its coasts lie primarily along the Arctic Ocean, it would appear to have little need for a navy for defense. Moreover, that country's seaborne exports are relatively small, no seaborne imports are essential to its survival, and it lacks a tradition of wide-ranging commercial ventures abroad. Therefore, the U.S.S.R. is unique in history for becoming a great naval power despite the absence of the conditions historically associated with the development of navies and merchant fleets.

The anomaly has not been lost on either the advocates of Soviet naval power or its critics. "Hostile propaganda tirelessly affirmed that Russia was not a maritime country, but only a continental power and therefore she needed a fleet only to decide modest tasks of defense along the shore," wrote Admiral S. G. Gorshkov, commander-in-chief of the Soviet Navy, who has dedicated much of his voluminous writing to this theme and its antithesis—that the worldwide interests of the Soviet Union demand a fleet with global reach. Gorshkov even quotes President Nixon as saying that "Soviet military requirements are different from what we need. The U.S.S.R. is a land power . . . and we are first of all a sea power and our needs therefore are different." Likening the Nixon comment to old attempts by British politicians "to prove that Russia has no need for a powerful navy," Gorshkov protests that the former President's statement is out of touch with reality and that it "contradicts the entire path of development of our navy . . . and the interests of our state. . . ."

Gorshkov explains what he means by "state interests" when he writes, "For the Soviet Union . . . sea power appears as one of the important factors of strengthening its economy, as a stimulus of scientific and technical development, as a consolidation of the economic, political, cultural and scientific ties of the Soviet people with friendly peoples and countries. . . . At the same time, sea power includes the capabilities of our armed forces to defend the nation from the threat of attack from the ocean." In summing up the thoughts expressed in his last book, *The Sea Power of the State*, the admiral notes, "Among the many factors which characterize the economic and military might of our country, an ever increasing role is assumed by its sea power, which expresses the real ability of the State to employ effectively the world ocean in the interests of the building of communism."[1]

In addition to the traditional arguments about the basis for seapower, Gorshkov touches on one additional point that has assumed grave importance only in the last two decades. The striking power of modern naval weapons, especially those equipped with nuclear warheads, has posed a problem for defensive naval forces beyond anything they had to counter in the past. Given the Soviet doctrine that assumes a real possibility of nuclear war and seeks to prepare the Soviet Union to win and survive that war if it should come, the missions to intercept carrier task forces far from shore and destroy hostile missile-carrying submarines before they have launched their weapons have had a major influence on the expansion of the Soviet Navy in the past twenty years. The other side of that coin, the development of a submarine-launched strategic strike force, has been even more important to the Soviet Navy and very likely is its greatest success. In these planning categories, the need has been clear and the response effective. But when one goes beyond them, the capabilities and particularly the intentions of the Soviet Navy become less certain. After several faltering starts, however, in the past fifteen years the U.S.S.R. has found a compelling rationale for becoming a major naval power, and this development has stimulated other maritime ambitions. The evolution of that rationale from the beginnings of the Soviet state and the goals and missions of the Soviet Navy that derive from it are the principal subjects of this chaper.

From the Beginnings to 1971
Before World War II

World War I found the Russian Navy in last place among the major navies of the world despite the excellent qualities of some of its newer ships. Subordinated to the army in both command and government interest, the navy was limited in its role during the war. Even so, it proved effective in mine warfare, combined operations, and the use of naval aviation.

With the Revolution of 1917 came the shining hour of the Russian navy in communist chronicles. On October 24, 1917, the Provisional Government ordered the cruiser *Aurora* to sea. Instead, the crew obeyed the orders of the Military Revolutionary Council, eased the warship into the Neva River, and trained guns on the Winter Palace, the last refuge of the ministers of Kerensky's Provisional Government. The gunfire of the *Aurora* (using blanks because no shells were available) was a signal for the storming of the Winter Palace and the Bolshevik ascendancy to power.

The Baltic sailors and the garrison of the Kronstadt naval fortress in Petrograd Harbor were among the most fervent revolutionaries of the time. The sailors of the Black Sea Fleet, however, balloted on their fate. As a result, nineteen destroyers were scuttled by their crews and one battleship was accidentally blown up. Another battleship, an old cruiser, and seven destroyers escaped beyond the reach of the Bolsheviks.

When the Russian revolution was over, the Baltic Fleet sailors demanded free elections by secret ballot, freedom of press and speech, the abolition of Bolshevik direction over the peasants' cultivation of their own land, and the end of absolute Bolshevik control in favor of a "true people's revolution." In February 1921, on the eve of the Tenth Communist Party Congress in Moscow, the discontent of these sailors led to riots among the workers of Petrograd. The Bolshevik government ruthlessly suppressed the counterrevolutionaries and proclaimed a state of emergency. The Bolsheviks sent troops to attack Kronstadt and executed or sent to prison camps several thousand sailors and workers who were allied with them.

The Tenth Party Congress took stringent measures to strengthen the political reliability of the navy. A strict system of political commissars was established within the navy to keep watch and, it was hoped, prevent further problems. In this political environment, the Soviet navy began life. The Baltic Fleet had only a few operational ships; the Black Sea Fleet was virtually nonexistent; and there were no major warships in the Arctic or Pacific. One dreadnought, eight destroyers, and some smaller craft constituted the operational Soviet Navy, with the remaining ships still afloat placed in reserve.

The bloody Russian civil war, followed by economic collapse, precluded for a time any serious interest in the development of a major navy. During the early 1920s, some efforts were made to recondition the existing warships. By 1928, Soviet naval strength consisted of three battleships, five cruisers, twenty-four destroyers, and eighteen submarines, plus lesser craft. While this reconstruction was in progress there was a sharp debate concerning strategy and ships. The "old school" proposed a fleet based on the offensive might of battleships and cruisers. The "young school" advocated light defensive forces—submarines, torpedo boats, naval aircraft, and possibly destroyers. Stalin, who had by then emerged as unquestioned chief of the Soviet state and the Communist party, initially appeared to decide against the "old school." The construction effort of the First Five-Year Plan (1928-1932) consisted of some five submarines.

More submarine construction followed rapidly, and the Second Five Year Plan (1933-1937) also provided for the first major surface warships constructed by the Soviets: the Leningrad class of destroyers or "leaders"; and the Kirov-class heavy cruisers (9 x 7.1-inch guns), based on Italian designs. The plan also provided for extensive modernization of the three surviving battleships, marking a turning point in Soviet naval developments. Steps were taken to include large warships in the Third Five-Year Plan that would begin in April 1937. Battleships, heavy cruisers, and other classes of surface warships were to be built, albeit at a slow pace, as well as a large number of submarines. The construction of aircraft carriers was postponed to the last year of the Five-Year Plan.

Stalin's inclination toward an oceangoing fleet may have been reinforced during the Spanish Civil War, which erupted in July 1936. Extensive Soviet logistic support for the Spanish Republicans began in October 1936 from Black Sea ports. A dozen Soviet ships reached Spanish Mediterranean ports that first month. The flow of Soviet aid soon reached such proportions that Franco was forced to plead with Mussolini for a naval blockade of the Republican ports. The Italians responded by covert attacks on Soviet merchantmen. The situation led to the establishment of an international naval patrol (essentially British and French) to hunt the "pirate" submarines and aircraft, but these halfhearted actions proved ineffective. Although the Soviet Union could supply war material, it could not protect merchant ships carrying it to Spain. The Soviet Navy had neither the warships nor the logistic capability (bases or support ships) to carry out Soviet foreign policy in the Mediterranean.

During the 1937-1939 purges of Soviet military leaders, several hundred naval officers, mostly of senior rank, were executed. On April 28, 1939, Admiral Nikolai Kuznetsov was given the task of rebuilding the decapitated Red Navy command structure and of creating an oceangoing fleet. Kuznetsov was then thirty-eight years of age and had served as commander of the Pacific Fleet for almost a year. He had also had some war experience in Spain with the Republican naval forces. Preliminary construction began during 1938-1940 on new classes of battleships, large cruisers, and light cruisers, while the already high rate of submarine construction continued. The Soviets unsuccessfully sought U.S. technical support in the design of the larger surface ships.

As Europe rushed toward war in 1939, the Soviet Union was drawn into cooperation with Nazi Germany. One result was German technical assistance to the Soviet Navy, culminating in the sale of the unfinished heavy cruiser *Lutzow* to the Soviets in 1940. That vessel was berthed at

Leningrad on June 22, 1941, the day a thousand German warplanes flew over the Soviet Union in Hitler's surprise attack. The Red Navy was still far from being a viable contemporary naval force, particularly in terms of surface ships.

World War II

The Soviet Navy was unprepared for a naval war from the viewpoint of either material or morale. The 1937–1939 purges were too recent, and the new commanders were unready for high-level commands. On the material side, by mid-1941 the Soviets could muster just 3 pre–World War I battleships and 10 cruisers, of which only 2 were of recent construction. They did, however, have 66 destroyers (half of them new) and 218 submarines. Their undersea fleet had become by far the world's largest, with roughly twice as many boats as there were in either the U.S. or the German Navy at the time.

Of the Soviet oceangoing forces, only submarines were significantly active against the Germans during World War II. Their performance was poor, and some Western authorities question whether they sank more than a hundred oceangoing ships during the entire war. In return, Soviet submarine losses are estimated at between twenty-one and thirty boats. This inferior performance is ascribed to several causes: the prevailing doctrine that the Soviet Navy's primary missions were to support land operations and coastal defense; poor tactics; lack of radar; primitive hydrophone equipment; poor training and maintenance; lack of aggressiveness (with a few notable exceptions); and poor morale. Moreover, some seventy-five to ninety of their submarines were based in the Pacific, where they did not see action until the Soviets began operations against Japanese forces in the summer of 1945.

Although the navy's contributions on the high seas were negligible, the river flotillas are considered to have made major contributions to a number of land battles and campaigns. Particularly worthy of mention was the Sea of Azov Flotilla, whose commander was Sergei Gorshkov. (As a result of earlier purges of senior officers, Gorshkov had been promoted to the rank of rear admiral in 1941 at the age of thirty-one. He was one of the youngest men to hold such rank in modern times.) During the war, Gorshkov served in cruiser-destroyer forces and in small coastal and riverine craft; he directed large and complex amphibious operations; and he commanded ground forces in combat. Perhaps most significant, he came into contact with several men who later would hold key political and military positions in the Soviet Union, among them Nikita Khrushchev and Leonid Brezhnev and Generals Malinovskiy and Grechko, both of whom were later to become marshals and ministers of defense.

The Soviet Navy made a valuable contribution to the war effort through the use of naval infantry units and ships' crews as ground troops, especially in the battles of Leningrad, Moscow, and Stalingrad. Sailors formed forty-two naval infantry brigades and several independent battalions. In all, more than 400,000 navy men were employed as ground troops during the war.

Thus, the major contribution of the navy was in joining with the real victors of the war against the Germans—the more than 11 million soldiers of the Red Army who, with almost half a million sailor comrades fighting as infantrymen and gunners, pushed back the Germans from the approaches of Moscow to the streets of Berlin. In comparison, the Soviet naval and air forces had minor roles in the final victory.

During the war, the Soviet Navy had lost several ships to enemy action, including one of the old tsarist battleships and an old cruiser (both sunk by German air attacks), and an estimated 36 destroyers. The unfinished Soviet ships at Leningrad and Nikolayev, among them battleship and cruiser hulls, had been damaged, many beyond redemption. No surface warships larger than light cruisers were completed by Soviet shipyards during the war. Some 52 submarines of prewar design were completed, enough to provide an undersea force of over 200 submarines in 1945, about the same strength as that of the Red submarine fleet when the war began four years earlier. Moreover, the nature of the war had deprived most Soviet naval commanders and seamen of big ship and deepwater experience. Combined with political and other personnel problems, this deficiency meant that the navy could not immediately become a credible force for missions other than coastal defense—even if suitable ships had been available.

At the war's end there appeared to be little prospect for immediate rejuvenation of either the personnel or the ships of the Soviet Navy. The just-concluded war had cost the U.S.S.R. the lives of some 20 million men and women (a tenth of the population); millions were crippled, and other millions, in bad or indifferent health, were returning from German labor camps. Additionally, many industrial areas had been laid waste during the war. The shipyards at Leningrad were idle and severely damaged during almost three years of German siege. Conditions were even worse along the Black Sea coast, where the Germans had captured key cities which later were retaken by the Soviets, often after savage fighting. Destruction of the yards was severe; the ports of the Black Sea, the Baltic Sea, and the Sea of Azov, as well as basins of rivers and lakes to the west of the Volga, had been reduced to ruin. The armament industry that had escaped the German invasion was employed almost entirely to make armaments for land and air warfare, neglecting the navy.

Stalin the Traditionalist, 1945 to 1953

In 1948, less than three years after the end of World War II, Stalin again undertook a major program to construct a large, modern fleet despite the many other strains on the U.S.S.R. The naval program was part of a massive rearmament effort that accompanied the return to a militantly anti-Western foreign policy and rigid ideological conformity within the Soviet Union. One clue to Stalin's concerns is found in the report by the vice president of Yugoslavia, Milovan Djilas, of a conversation with Stalin in February 1948. Stalin is quoted as saying, "What do you think, that Great Britain and . . . the United States, the most powerful state in the world—will permit you to break their line of communication in the Mediterranean Sea? Nonsense. And we have no navy. The uprising in Greece must be stopped and as quickly as possible."[2] (The context was the Communist guerrilla movement in Greece and Yugoslavia's support for it.)

As these words indicate, Stalin had observed the impact of both Allied and German naval strength on the conduct of World War II and its aftermath. His decision to develop a large surface fleet reflected a desire to expand Soviet influence between the existing boundaries and coastal seas of the "Camp of Socialism."

Rehabilitation of the war-ravaged Soviet shipbuilding industry was particularly costly because German forces had occupied most of the Baltic and Black Sea coasts of the U.S.S.R., the centers for major ship construction. By comparison, the Soviet northern, far eastern, and inland shipyards were largely unscathed, but these yards were limited to construction of relatively small surface ships and submarines. Stalin's decision to persist in the construction of a major fleet was further complicated by the lack of Soviet operational experience during the war.

Nevertheless, by the end of the 1940s the Soviet Navy had initiated several major new shipbuilding programs and resumed work on some warships started before the war. Although ambitious in scope, the tempo of construction was slow, especially on the largest classes of ships. The Stalinist approach was conventional, obviously building on the lessons of World War II as observed from the Soviet perspective and based on readily available technology. It sought, at least initially, to control the sea adjacent to the Soviet Union, to support the ground forces offensively and defensively, and, probably, to disrupt sea communications between the United States and Western Europe. During the late 1940s, the Soviets were able to lay down the keels for the first of a class of battle cruisers, twenty 19,000-ton light cruisers, and numerous destroyers. Planning was also under way for a new class of heavy cruisers and aircraft carriers, reportedly drawing from contemporary British designs.

Stalin also continued the massive submarine construction program begun in the 1930s. The wartime submarine construction program was continued at the undamaged inland yards until new designs were evolved.

Building on advanced German submarine technology, especially the Type 21 high-speed, diesel-electric craft, the first Soviet postwar submarines of the Whiskey class became operational in 1950 and eventually reached a mass production rate of almost ninety submarines during a single year. The comparatively modern Whiskey class was followed by an improved Zulu-class diesel-electric attack submarine in 1951. Still other submarine classes were started in this period. This vast Soviet undersea force was soon recognized by U.S. naval planners as the most serious threat to U.S. postwar naval supremacy.

Coupled with the surface and submarine programs, the Soviets also created a large and comparatively modern naval air arm. By the mid-1950s, the Soviet naval air arm could muster some 90,000 men and 4,000 aircraft. Almost half of the aircraft strength was in fighters to provide close support for Soviet warships operating within aircraft radius of land bases. The remainder included some bomber-type aircraft, most of which carried gravity bombs or torpedoes, and some were equipped with the first Soviet air-to-surface missiles entering service.

When Stalin died in March 1953 his plans for a large conventional oceangoing fleet were almost buried with him. In December 1954, plans for carrier and heavy cruiser construction were dropped, the just-started battle cruisers were scrapped, and the light cruiser, destroyer, and submarine programs were cut back sharply. However, three products of Stalin's efforts form important elements of the Soviet Fleet today: submarines, cruisers, and shipyard capacity. Diesel-electric submarines are still part of the fleet, with construction continuing on advanced classes to the present.

Eleven of the Sverdlov-class 19,000-ton light cruisers are still useful as flagships, gunfire support ships, training ships, and platforms to demonstrate Soviet naval presence. Most significantly, Stalin provided the postwar Soviet Union with a major shipyard capacity as well as the related heavy and light industries, research centers, and ship design bureaus. This aspect of his naval programs became the basis for subsequent Soviet naval and commercial maritime expansion and allowed the Soviets to undertake original designs based on their own technology.

Khrushchev the Innovator, 1953 to 1960

> In the mid-1950s the Central Committee of the Party laid down the path of development for the Navy... an ocean fleet capable of strategic missions of an offensive nature. The foremost position in this was taken by submarines and naval aircraft. The first foundations of a well-balanced fleet were laid—[which by virtue of] its composition and weapons characteristics is able to discharge such tasks as it is faced with, whether nuclear missile war, nonnuclear war or the support of state interests on the sea in peacetime. (Gorshkov, article in *Morskoy Sbornik* [Maritime collection], no. 2, 1967.)

Nikita Khrushchev soon assumed the leadership among Stalin's

SOVIET NAVAL ASSETS OF THE STALIN ERA

The first post–World War II Soviet attack submarine (SS) design was the Whiskey class, mass-produced at a rate of almost ninety units per year during the Stalin era. (Courtesy U.S. Navy)

Eleven Sverdlov-class cruisers are still in operation as flagships, gunfire support ships, training ships, and platforms to demonstrate Soviet naval presence. They were built during the late 1940s and early 1950s. (Courtesy U.S. Navy)

successors, and by 1955 he had fully consolidated his power. He held traditional navies in low esteem, calling naval shipbuilding programs "metal eaters," and said that the new Soviet cruisers were fit only to carry admirals on parade, although he sailed on one to England in 1955. On January 6, 1956, Admiral S. G. Gorshkov, the recent Black Sea Fleet commander, replaced N. G. Kuznetsov as naval commander-in-chief and deputy minister of defense (for navy). Kuznetsov, who had served in top navy positions from 1939 to 1947 and again from 1951 through 1955, had personified Stalin's efforts to build a large conventional big ship fleet. Khrushchev, on the other hand, proclaimed that "an important part of our military doctrine should be that we not try to compete with our adversaries in every area where they are ahead of us."

Admiral Gorshkov took command of the Soviet Navy at the beginning of a number of Krushchev-directed reductions in the armed forces, as the Soviet leader sought to replace the traditional Russian mass-of-force with high-technology weapons such as strategic missiles. Like other world leaders, Khrushchev was preoccupied with the potential impact of nuclear weapons launched from both land and sea. Such weapons made Russia more vulnerable than ever before and appeared to render existing military forces obsolete. His top priority appears to have been to redress the military imbalance caused by U.S. superiority in nuclear weapons while developing mechanisms to defend the Soviet Union against their use. In the case of the navy, this meant defense against U.S. carrier strike forces.

Scores of warships were laid up or scrapped; thousands of naval personnel were released from active duty; special pay and privileges were cut back. The naval air arm was also reduced as some 1,500 to 2,000 fighter aircraft were transferred to the unified national air defense command—to defend against U.S. nuclear-armed bombers from forward land bases and carriers. Other aircraft were transferred or discarded until the Soviet naval air arm was reduced to less than 1,000 aircraft. At the same time, the Soviet Navy also gave up two bases on foreign territory—Porkkala in Finland, at the entrance to the Gulf of Finland; and Port Arthur, near Dairen on the Liaotung Peninsula of China.

Under Gorshkov's direction, ongoing Soviet research into naval applications of guided missiles, nuclear propulsion, and other technological developments was accelerated. Two top priorities seem to have guided the development of the Soviet Fleet in this period: first, to defend against U.S. Navy carrier-based nuclear-armed aircraft, which, since 1951, had been capable of striking directly at the Soviet homeland; and, second, to develop a nuclear offensive capability for Soviet submarines. In this latter area, the Soviets were pulling ahead of the United States in the mid-1950s with their cruise missile submarines. The equivalent U.S. program had been cancelled in 1954.

Soviet Naval Evolution

A specific concept of anticarrier warfare was developed, and programs were initiated to produce large numbers of surface ships, submarines, and aircraft armed with antiship (i.e., anticarrier) missiles. In addition, many existing ships and aircraft were modified for this role. Gorshkov comments on this period in *The Sea Power of the State*, published in Moscow in 1976:

> In the second stage of the postwar development of the Navy, when in our country there was support for the establishment of a powerful submarine force, construction of surface ships, particularly oceangoing ships, was reduced. This was also brought about by the appearance of fundamentally new means of armed struggle which were presented by nuclear weapons. In the beginning, it was not clear what tasks might be handled by surface ships in the ocean and what equipment they would have to have in order to participate effectively in an armed struggle in which nuclear weapons were introduced. . . . Some specialists, hypnotized by the all-powerful atomic weapon, were persuaded that in the new circumstances, all surface vessels had lost their military value. An exception was made only for aircraft carriers. . . . Only a few of these specialists saw in the great mobility of the fleet a means not only to survive an attack by the enemy but also to preserve its capabilities to carry out wartime missions.

Gorshkov then quotes one of his colleagues, Admiral Barzho, on the effectiveness of systems to wash down ships with seawater after they have been exposed to radiation from a nuclear bomb burst.

Despite the "great debate" on the thesis that rockets would make navies obsolete and the ensuing new directives, the Soviet Navy retained most of the existing Sverdlovs as well as other smaller surface ships. Designs for new destroyer and cruiser classes specifically dedicated to intercepting enemy aircraft carriers were begun in the mid-1950s and altered to include antisubmarine and antiaircraft capabilities in the late 1950s. The conflicting target priorities between carriers and submarines, together with the realization that these ships would have to operate beyond the range of land-based fighters, led to numerous alterations in design, additions to ships under construction, and cancellation of building programs.

The Kashin-class destroyer appears to have begun as an antiaircraft escort for the Kynda-class cruiser, which is armed with 300-nautical-mile-range guided missiles designed to attack carriers.[3] The Kashin, the world's first oceangoing warship with all gas-turbine propulsion, was finally launched as an antisubmarine ship, with the apparent mission of protecting Soviet submarines as they made their way to the ocean basins in addition to more conventional tasks. The Kynda class was cut back to four ships from an initially planned twelve. Greater preoccupation with submarines and the increased vulnerability of the carrier to missile attack brought about the shift in priorities. In addition, many small combatants armed with antiship guided missiles were built, apparently to keep U.S. naval vessels away from the coastlines. Moreover, Stalin's extensive submarine building program (about twenty per year) was continued unabated into the early '60s.

In all, two new destroyer classes, three new cruiser classes, and six submarine classes were designed to counter U.S. aircraft carriers between 1955 and 1960. These included the new Echo-class nuclear submarines equipped with antiship cruise missiles. In addition, the Echo submarines, with their unlimited cruising radius, were capable of strategic attacks against the southern portions of the United States, an area that could not be reached by land-based bombers flying from the Soviet Union.

The Soviets also undertook their first ballistic missile submarine program then. Here again, existing submarines (Zulu class) were converted and then new diesel (Golf) and nuclear (Hotel) classes were built specifically to launch short-range (400 to 600 nautical miles) ballistic missiles.

Other factors of major naval significance during this period included a shift in the main naval striking forces from the Baltic, where they were vulnerable to blockade, to the Northern Fleet area, where there was more freedom of egress through the Norwegian Sea, and the start of continuous Soviet naval deployments in the Mediterranean.

Despite the large number of new designs developed during this period, the total Soviet commitment to naval warship construction was substantially smaller than during the Stalin-Khrushchev era—and has remained so ever since. Instead, Khrushchev initiated a massive merchant ship effort by converting several existing naval shipyards and building several new shipyards specifically for merchant ships. Within fifteen years this effort produced the world's numerically largest merchant fleet. Although these ships are relatively small and mainly designed for use with general cargo between relatively small ports, their total tonnage matches the Western Alliance's construction during this period.

The Emergence of the Modern Fleet, 1961 to 1971

> To challenge Capitalist naval superiority on all the seas and oceans of the world. (Gorshkov on the mission of the Soviet Navy in *Morskoy Sbornik* [Maritime collection], no. 2, 1967.)

The period of the late 1950s and early 1960s produced many rapid changes in naval capabilities as well as several important demonstrations of the increasing and overlapping roles of naval conventional and strategic weapon systems. On the conventional side of the ledger, U.S. intervention in Lebanon in 1958, following British-French intervention in Egypt over the Suez Canal in 1956, demonstrated once again the significance of conventional naval forces. The Soviets were unable to assert themselves in either confrontation. On the strategic side, the U.S. Navy sent to sea its first Polaris ballistic missile submarine, the U.S.S. *George Washington,* in 1960, thus adding to its forward-based nuclear offensive capability. In the same year, as a consequence of the emerging rift between the Soviet Union and China and China's ally, Albania, the Soviets were forced to give up their only Mediterranean base in Albania, reportedly losing a submarine tender and four Whiskey-class submarines to the Albanians in the process.

Further ominous signs of strategic inferiority were apparent to Khrushchev during these years. The United States' intercontinental strategic bomber, the B-52 had first flown in 1952 and was immediately put into production. The first U.S. land-based intercontinental missiles had been tested before 1960, and production of the first solid-propellant ICBM, the Minuteman, began in 1962. Moreover, although U.S. commitment to aircraft carriers appeared to have weakened somewhat, the first supercarrier, *Forrestal,* had entered service in 1955, and the Congress authorized the first nuclear-powered carrier, the *Enterprise,* in 1957.

In this environment, Khrushchev attempted to use his inadequate naval force to deploy his own strategic offensive capability to Cuba in 1962. His subsequent humiliation probably resulted from U.S. strategic weapon superiority and from the inability of the Soviets to project their own naval forces overseas in the face of U.S. naval strength. As a consequence, for the first time in many years their overall submarine construction program was realigned to emphasize ballistic missile boats, although significant numbers of these did not come off the ways until after Khrushchev's ouster in October 1964.

In 1967, when the U.S. Navy completed its forty-first and last Polaris submarine, the Soviet Navy launched its first Yankee-class submarine. Over the next six years, a total of thirty-four submarines of this class were completed, each of these nuclear-propelled submarines carrying sixteen SS-N-6 missiles. That class was followed on the building ways by the larger Delta series, carrying initially twelve, and then sixteen of the longer-range SS-N-8 missiles and a later version, the SS-N-18. These Delta submarines have continued in production in improved versions, with the Soviets expected to reach the SALT "limit" of sixty-two nuclear-powered ballistic missile submarines (SSBNs) in 1978.

In the late 1960s and early 1970s the role for Soviet SSBNs was not considered on a par with the intercontinental ballistic missiles (ICBMs) of the land-based Strategic Rocket Force, at least by the senior command of the Ministry of Defense. In 1968, Marshal Sokolovskiy wrote in his book *Military Strategy:*

> The main aim of fleet operations in naval theaters is to defeat the enemy's

navy and to disrupt his maritime communications. It may be necessary to deliver nuclear missile attacks on coastal targets, carry out joint operations with ground forces, provide transport and protect one's own sea communications. Nuclear submarines . . . armed with missiles will make decisive naval operations possible against a powerful maritime enemy.

Concerning the importance of the enemy's sea lines of communication (SLOCs), he added,

One of the navy's main tasks . . . will be to sever the enemy's ocean and sea transport routes. . . . Eighty to one hundred large transports would arrive daily at European ports in the event of war. . . . Operations against enemy sea lines of communications should be developed on a large scale. . . . This task might be carried out by the strategic rocket force, the long-range air force, missile submarines against naval bases, ports, channels, narrow inlets, shipyards, by destroying convoys and transports at sea, etc.

In his 1971 book, Marshal Grechko writes that the Strategic Rocket Force and the SSBNs are the main instruments for deterrence, but the SSBNs are not decisive. The Strategic Rocket Force alone is decisive. The navy is downgraded to secondary tasks. He does say, "The navy is one of the instruments of policy of the U.S.S.R. to counter threats and deter the enemy." Since that time, the statements of Gorshkov and others putting the SSBN on a par with the ICBM have not been refuted by army commentators.

The mission of protecting the Soviet Union from attack by submarine-launched missiles grew increasingly complex. The first Polaris SSBNs were armed with the 1,200-mile A-1 missile. To hit major Soviet targets with them, U.S. submarines would have to operate in restricted waters potentially vulnerable to Soviet antisubmarine systems. But the extension in range of U.S. submarine-launched ballistic missiles (SLBMs) to 2,500 miles by 1964 meant that U.S. submarines could operate along an arc from the southern coast of Greenland to Gibraltar and throughout the Mediterranean and still strike as far inland as Moscow. The advent of the Poseidon missiles introduced multiple warheads which greatly increased the damage that could be done by a single submarine. Finally, since the authorization of the Trident missile and submarine programs by the U.S. Congress in 1974, the Soviets have recognized that the U.S. SSBN threat extends over most of the oceans of the world.

Prior to the 1960s, Soviet antisubmarine warfare efforts and capabilities had been very limited—oriented primarily toward defending Soviet surface ships in coastal areas. By 1960, however, it must have been abundantly clear that a much more substantial and far-reaching antisubmarine warfare (ASW) capability would be required. The development of effective ASW capabilities is a difficult and painstaking task. It is a mission on which the U.S. Navy has worked diligently and continuously since the need was made so dramatically evident in World War II. By comparison, serious Soviet efforts in this mission area appear to have been started twenty years later and only at a time when the submarine threat graduated from an attrition-control problem against surface ships (for which the Soviets had little strategic need) to a primary nuclear threat against Soviet national survival.

The principal problems that the Soviet Navy has faced—how to deal with enemy carriers and missile submarines and how to protect their own submarines—have expanded as the ranges of aircraft and weapons have lengthened. (For a more detailed exposition of Soviet naval ship characterization, see Chapters 4 and 10.) The first all-new postwar cruiser, the Kynda, has a 250-nautical-mile guided missile for attacking carriers but needs air defense from the shore or from other ships and air support to guide the missile to its target. The Kresta I carries a helicopter for missile guidance. The Kresta II carries one helicopter and apparently better ASW gear. With this class, the primary target seems to have shifted from the aircraft carrier to the submarine. Finally, the Kara class, the most recent, adds an advanced antiaircraft missile system to the armament of the Kresta II, giving it "a formidable capability, matched by no other ship."[4] The trends that these progressive changes show are improved air defenses, improved ASW capabilities, and shorter-ranged missiles for surface targets.

Virtually every new large Soviet surface ship delivered since 1966 (aside from a small number of amphibious vessels for the Soviet marine infantry) is described by the Soviets as an antisubmarine warfare asset—and it is likely that this mission has been used within the Soviet bureaucracy as the primary justification for its construction (regardless of its ancillary capabilities). Several classes of older ships were converted for this purpose, and the four cruiser classes mentioned above and four new destroyer classes are all called big antisubmarine ships.

In a more dramatic warship development, the *Moskva* and *Leningrad* helicopter carriers appeared in 1967 and 1969, labelled as antisubmarine cruisers. Further planned construction of these ASW cruisers appears to have been stopped in favor of the 37,000-ton, Kiev-class "ASW cruisers," which have substantially greater open ocean capabilities as well as jet vertical/short take-off and landing (VSTOL) aircraft capabilities. It should be noted that these new Soviet ships borrow nothing from Western warship design.

All modern Soviet ships appear to acknowledge the fundamental Soviet belief in their own vulnerability. In addition to their primary ASW missile and helicopter armaments (which replace the earlier anticarrier missiles), they fairly bristle with torpedoes, small- and medium-caliber guns, and antiaircraft missile systems. Moreover, their high speed, relatively low endurance, limited weapon reload capability, topside weapon vulnerability, and inferior habitability (by Western standards) attest to the Soviet philosophy of a short, intense "shootout" during the opening phases of a war.

In the 1960s, the Soviet anticarrier systems already in production were quite substantial compared to the dwindling number of Western Alliance aircraft carriers. Continued updating of anticarrier capabilities appears to have been assigned primarily to the naval air force. Improved air-to-surface missiles (ASMs) were provided to the Soviet naval air arm, and several hundred Badger turbojet bombers were transferred from Soviet long-range aviation to the navy. These were later supplemented by new-production Badgers, specifically configured for missile strike, electronic jamming, and reconnaissance, as well as by some supersonic-dash Blinders. These, in turn, are now being supplemented by the new variable-wing Backfire. Soviet long-range strategic aviation has been largely displaced by Soviet ICBMs and SLBMs. In turn, long-range naval aviation assets have now displaced Soviet surface ships as a primary weapon for use against the capital ships of the West.

Finally, in addition to their new classes of SSBN submarines, the Soviets put to sea in 1967 the first of the Charlie-class nuclear-propelled cruise missile submarines, armed with eight SS-N-7 missiles. Although these weapons have a range of only 30 miles compared to several hundred miles for the original anticarrier Shaddock missiles, they can be fired while the submarine is fully submerged. These submarines, along with the older (and now obsolescent) Echo-II and Juliett cruise missile submarine and the ASM-armed land-based aircraft, are now considered the principal conventional strike forces of the Soviet Navy. Production also continues on Victor-class, nuclear-propelled torpedo attack submarines (SSNs). It is not apparent which mission capability these submarines will dominate: defense of their own SSBNs (they sometimes travel in company); attack on U.S. SSBNs; attack on U.S. carriers and other surface combatants; or attack on merchant shipping. One of the first three missions appears more likely early in a major war. It remains to be seen whether their production will increase when SSBN production limits imposed by the Strategic Arms Limitation Treaty (SALT) are reached.

In the relatively short space of fifteen years, the Soviets had redressed the strategic balance while maintaining a conventional force balance and had begun to exert economic, political, and military power well beyond their own shores. In the process, they produced a heterogeneous set of surface warships that will, in all probability, outlive their original missions (as some already have) and be available to contribute to other, more contemporary Soviet objectives. Technologically, they had made great progress. In only one area did they still lag behind the West substantially:

NAVAL AIRCRAFT OF THE KRUSHCHEV ERA

Khrushchev introduced hundreds of land-based aircraft into Soviet naval aviation, as typified by this TU-20 Bear flying over the U.S.S. *Kitty Hawk* (CVA-63), escorted by two carrier-based F-4J fighters. (Courtesy U.S. Navy)

The Soviet medium-range jet attack bomber Blinder was also introduced into Soviet naval aviation during the Khrushchev era; it is now being retired. (Courtesy U.S. Navy)

they still were forced to acknowledge the "relative invulnerability" of Western submarines despite their extensive ASW work and hydrographic research. Some of their latest ships and weapon systems appear designed around a broad area submarine detection system that still has not materialized. Despite this limitation, Gorshkov could claim in the armed forces newspaper *Red Star* in 1970:

> The age old dreams of our people have become reality. The pennants of Soviet ships now flutter in the most remote corners of the seas and oceans. Our navy is a real force and possesses the ability to resolve successfully the task of defending the state interest of the Soviet Union and the whole socialist world.

Development of the Civil Sector

The Soviet Merchant Marine

Since the mid-1950s, the Soviet Merchant Marine Fleet has been characterized by rapid, consistent growth, adding new ships produced by its own yards as well as those of Eastern and Western Europe. In recent years, it has grown by approximately one million deadweight tons annually. It is currently reported to consist of over 1,600 vessels totalling about 16 million deadweight tons, making it close to the world's largest in numbers and ranking eighth or ninth in tonnage.

Soviet production of merchant ships has continued at an almost constant rate for well over ten years. It must have been a source of some satisfaction to the Soviets to be able to use these ships in the resupply of the North Vietnamese from 1966 to 1972. By this relatively small investment they were able to sustain their surrogate's warfighting capability against the forces of "Western imperialism," eventually contributing to a victory in a war that cost the United States close to $100 billion in defense expenditures. That war also diverted this country while the Soviets successfully built up their offensive and defensive strategic forces to the extent that the Western Alliance is for the first time concerned about the possibility of "strategic inferiority" to the Soviets.

Specialized Cargo Ships. Although still smaller on the average than the vessels of other flags, the newest Soviet merchant ships have speeds comparable to those of other countries. In the last three years, the number of specialized cargo handling ships—container, barge carrier, and roll-on/roll-off vessels (ro/ro's)—has increased markedly. In 1974, the Soviets had only fifteen container ships with a deadweight tonnage of about 4 percent of U.S. flag tonnage in that category. The first Soviet ro/ro's were introduced in the same year. The first barge carriers, despite their suitability for the Soviet river transport system, were ordered only in 1975. Of the three, the ro/ro has proved most attractive. The first ships of this type were 6,000-tonners, contrasted to the 20,000-ton (and up) ro/ro's of the West. In 1975, foreign purchase and domestic production combined to expand the number and size of the ro/ro fleet substantially. The 1976–80 Five-Year Plan calls for 200,000 tons of ro/ro construction, 139,000 tons of container ships, and 80,000 tons for barge carriers; the three categories together add up to 9 percent of the total building plan.

Roll-on/roll-off ships are not as efficient as our container carriers in moving containerized cargoes between major ports. However, they offer expeditious handling of wheeled vehicles and cargo in trailers. They can operate from less well-equipped ports and are especially adaptable for the fast delivery of military vehicles, including tanks, as events in Angola have demonstrated. Consequently, these ships must be counted as part of the Soviet Navy's ability to project its forces to countries not easily reached by Soviet land forces.

Five-Year Plan Goals. The full construction program for the new Five-Year Plan calls for 5 million deadweight tons to be added to the Soviet merchant fleet by the end of 1980. Judging from past performance, actual construction will be less. The tanker building plan, 52 percent of the total, is especially likely to lag. The Soviets already have some large tankers, up to 150,000 tons, but plans for supertankers (which could not use Soviet ports because of the shallow depths) have been put off.

The dry and oil-and-dry cargo construction plan allots the largest portion to dry bulk carriers, perhaps an indication that the Soviet Union expects to need grain imports for some time to come. General-purpose freighters make up 8 percent. Timber carriers and the specialized cargo handling ships make up the rest.

General-Purpose Vessels. Despite increasing specialization, the strength of the Soviet Merchant Marine remains in relatively small, general-purpose dry cargo vessels capable of operating in small ports, which the larger and more specialized ships of the Western nations often neglect. This category still makes up over 40 percent of the total tonnage, including tankers. This pattern of construction may represent a deliberate policy on the part of the Soviet Union. In 1965, the minister of the Merchant Marine, Victor Bakayev, stated that the goal of the Soviet Merchant Marine was to enter into "free competition with the capitalist fleet . . . and to restrain the expansionist intentions of certain aggressive states and render real assistance to the newly developing countries in the growth of their economic and foreign trade."[5]

Role in Fulfilling Soviet Political and Military Goals. The Soviet

Merchant Marine directly supports the Soviet Navy by provisioning naval vessels and fueling them on the high seas and by providing such services as shipping arms into the war zone in Vietnam, supplying strategic weapons to Cuba in 1962, and transporting Cuban troops and supplies to Angola in 1976. The formidable size and centralized direction of the Soviet merchant fleet, plus its close affiliation with the Soviet Navy, place it in a special category when one is considering national power.

The commitment of the Soviet Merchant Marine to political and governmental projects may reduce its commercial potential as a competitor to Western shipping interests. On balance, however, the Soviet Merchant Marine appears certain to play a growing part in world trade between the Soviet Union and other nations, especially in cross-trading in Asia, Latin America, and Africa. If present trends continue, many of the smaller and less-developed countries of the Third World may find themselves almost entirely dependent on the Soviet Merchant Marine for their ocean transport, as some already are.

One cannot with certainty ascribe this trend to a deliberate policy aimed at the advancement of the strategic interests of the Soviet Union. For a nation with a new merchant marine, comprised primarily of relatively small general-purpose ships, the market of the Third World is certainly the easiest to penetrate. The low level of Soviet wages, the need for hard currency earnings, and the attraction of a life at sea for people whose alternative is an austere existence in the Soviet Union—all combine to make an emphasis on merchant shipping both rational and rewarding. Reliance on the merchant marine to supplement the auxiliary fleet of the Soviet Navy and to take part in the state's foreign operations, such as in Cuba, Vietnam, and Angola, might simply be a product of a practical, self-reliant system and betray no particular strategic objectives.

On the other hand, Soviet leaders have assigned explicit missions and objectives to their merchant marine. It remains entirely under the control of the central government and the navy. It is run under a system of discipline that more closely approximates naval standards than those of the merchant marine in much of the world. It has demonstrated its utility on missions of state that have little to do with commercial profitability. It is automatically disposed to respond to the directives of the government under all circumstances. Finally, if one speculates as to the motives behind Khrushchev's conversion of Stalin's plans for a large oceangoing navy into a program for a large merchant marine, one is drawn to the conclusion that Khrushchev recognized the need for warm water ports and forward bases. Perhaps he thought that the best way to cultivate such concessions from foreign countries peacefully was through the regular intercourse provided by commercial fishing and merchant fleets. Only after such installations have become available will a real worldwide oceangoing navy become

SOVIET MERCHANT SHIP

Freighters of the Soviet Merchant Marine, like this one enroute to Haiphong in the Tonkin Gulf in 1967, have proven their utility in supporting Soviet political objectives through supplying arms to client-states as well as serving as a valuable source of foreign exchange. (Courtesy U.S. Navy)

practical for the Soviets.

Soviet Shipyards

The Soviet Union maintains eighteen of the world's large shipyards plus several hundred lesser shipbuilding facilities. Four of the major Soviet yards date back to the nineteenth century. Under Stalin's prewar drive to industrialize Russia, seven major new shipyards and many smaller ones were established—including the first one each on the Arctic and Pacific coasts. During World War II, the Soviets established two more major inland yards, located along the Volga River. After the war, rehabilitation of the heavily damaged shipyards along the Baltic and Black seas was given very high priority in Soviet rebuilding efforts. Under the Khrushchev regime, the five latest major shipyards were constructed; all but one of them were intended only for commercial vessels. In addition, Khrushchev converted several existing yards totally or partially from naval to merchant construction. In fact, only one yard on each of the Soviet Union's four coastal areas, plus one yard along the Volga, are now restricted to the exclusive construction of warships and submarines.

During the past fifteen years, the Soviets have produced roughly 350 warships at these yards—over 200 of which have been submarines, both conventional- and nuclear-powered. In the same period, the United States has produced roughly 290 warships, but less than half of them have been submarines. In the main, however, U.S. ships have had almost two-and-one-half times the average Soviet tonnage, the U.S. average being heavily biased by our supercarriers. The Soviets have constructed roughly 1.5 million tons of warships, while the United States has produced approximately 2.8 million tons. Over the same period, however, the Soviets have also built over 800 merchant ships and roughly 100 oceanographic and intelligence ships. The United States has built only some 320 merchant ships. At present, neither Soviet nor U.S. shipyard capacity is fully utilized. The Soviet Navy is currently accepting about 20 surface ships and 12 submarines a year, while the U.S. Fleet is receiving roughly 10 larger surface ships and 4 submarines a year.

Today, the Soviet Union's shipbuilding industry is large, modern, and flexible. All significant shipbuilding efforts—naval and commercial—are coordinated by a centralized Ministry of Shipbuilding under a civilian minister and supported by excellent design bureaus and research facilities. In addition to sales of naval units and merchant ships to such traditional seafaring nations as Sweden, Great Britain, and Norway, the Soviets also purchase large numbers of naval and commercial ships from foreign yards. Landing ships and research-surveying ships are provided by yards in East Germany and Poland, while commercial ships are purchased from those countries as well as Japan, Denmark, Finland, and Great Britain. Often the foreign-built ships are used to import technology or to avoid starting up a specialized or difficult design.

Many Soviet yards are capable of reallocating their emphasis between commercial and naval shipbuilding in accordance with the dictates of the Kremlin. The Soviet shipbuilding industry could readily adapt to a period of mobilization or demobilization.

Toward the Future: 1971 to the Present

> During the first fifteen years after the war, the prime determinant of long-term Soviet naval policy was the threat posed by the West, although its relative significance varied in terms of national policy.... But as we move from maritime defense to maritime influence, from need-to-know to nice-to-have, then unmistakable identification of prime determinants becomes more difficult. (Michael MccGwire, in *Soviet Naval Developments* [Halifax, Nova Scotia: Dalhousie Univ., 1974] p. 178.)

The next turning point in the overall policy and mission of the Soviet Navy evidently occurred sometime in the early 1970s. It is still several years too soon to see the product of those changes, but, for the purposes of this discussion, the timing can be pegged to the Soviet Five-Year Plan begun in 1971. By that time, the Russians could welcome in a new era for themselves. They sensed a qualitative change in the "correlation of world forces" in their favor. The chronic problems of the '60s were past. Had they finally reached "Stage III" in the progression of socialism over capitalism? Could they now operate worldwide without fear of being considered adventurists? Could they begin to expand their sphere of operations without fear of "imperialist intervention?" In their ledger, the recent events on the plus side clearly outweighed the minuses. For instance:

- The United States had finally retreated from Southeast Asia, preserving no continental foothold in that part of the world.
- The United States had begun to negotiate arms control measures with the Soviets on both the strategic (SALT) and conventional Mutual and Balanced Force Reduction (MBFR) plateaus—essentially acknowledging "equivalence" in both areas.
- The Western Alliance economies were beginning to show chronic signs of stress manifested by high unemployment and persistent inflation.
- The overall effectiveness of the Western military establishment was decreasing relative to that of the Soviet Union.
- The newly emerging nations of the Third World had gained their independence from "Western imperialism" (the British, Dutch,

Belgian, French, Spanish, and Portuguese "empires" were all dismantled).
- The Warsaw Pact countries of Eastern Europe were showing relative political stability within the framework of the "Brezhnev Doctrine," and their status has subsequently been confirmed by the Helsinki Accords.
- The solidarity of the NATO countries was appearing to weaken. Difficulties between Iceland and the United Kingdom and between Greece and Turkey, plus the withdrawal of French forces from the integrated structure of the NATO fleet and the Italian, French, and Portuguese political instabilities, must all have offered encouragement to Moscow.
- The influence of communist parties and the Soviet regime was increasing in several key nations of Western Europe—especially in Italy and France.
- The Alliance's heavy dependence on Third World oil resources was changing the economic balance of power.
- During the 1973 Arab-Israeli war, the oil-exporting nations established a threefold increase in the cost of this basic commodity for virtually all oil importers.
- The Soviet Merchant Marine was opening up various foreign ports and countries to Soviet influence and exploitation as well as providing a valuable source of foreign exchange.
- The Soviet buildup of conventional forces along the Sino-Soviet borders had apparently brought a measure of stability to that area and deterred the Chinese from adventurism.
- The more recent Soviet intervention in the affairs of Angola, Somalia, and Ethiopia, using proxy forces supported by Russian merchant shipping and transport aircraft, went without effective challenge by the West. Soviet influence in the other states bordering South Africa, Rhodesia, and Southwest Africa was growing.

By comparison, the minuses on the ledger appear relatively small:

- The economy, availability of consumer goods, and standard of living of the U.S.S.R. have remained far behind those measures of advancement in the West and have even fallen further behind the situation in some of its satellite states.
- Economic stagnation has spread in Eastern Europe, especially within the key nations of Poland, East Germany, and Czechoslovakia.
- Soviet agriculture has lagged behind national demand for its

products, causing increased dependence on the West for basic food resources.
- The issue of human rights, initiated at the Belgrade Conference and highlighted by the Carter Administration, promises to be an increasing source of domestic friction and international embarrassment.
- The Soviet Union's balance of payments with the West has continued to be negative, despite increases in the price of oil.
- Fluctuations in Soviet influence in the Middle East and the Horn of Africa have remained a major frustration for Moscow. Among other factors, the new affluence of the area, combined with a reaction against Soviet heavy-handedness in Egypt and elsewhere, have reduced the role of the U.S.S.R. in Middle Eastern affairs. Long-range prospects probably are not seen by Moscow in a totally pessimistic light, however.

The Soviets must certainly believe that the next decade can be devoted to the pursuit of their own political and economic objectives at their own initiative with little to fear directly from the conventional or strategic arms of the West or the People's Republic of China. Weapons "parity" with the Western Alliance has been achieved; the benefits for them of "peaceful coexistence" have been established beyond question. For the first time in its sixty years, the Soviet Union has reason to be confident that it can probably inflict as much damage as—or more than—it would sustain in any major superpower confrontation. It is certainly a match for opposing forces on the Eurasian continent. In short, in most areas, the military initiative is theirs—if the potential gains seem worthwhile. If they do not use it, then they will be free to compete internationally for the economic and political attentions of an increasing share of the world's population.

From the narrower perspective of naval forces, the Soviets enter this new era with a mixed bag developed under three decidedly different post–World War II eras of naval development, with a good portion of these forces facing obsolescence within the next five years. A good fraction of the newer forces provide strategic offensive capability, while another significant number is currently aimed at limiting the effectiveness of our offensive nuclear forces (SSBNs and carriers)—a task which should persist well into the future. These Soviet forces, furthermore, need improved means of support when deployed on the high seas, in either the form of bases or a better service and supply fleet, as Gorshkov pointed out in August 1976 in the organ of the support elements of the Soviet armed forces, *Tyl i Snobzheniye* (Rear and supply).

In addition, they must continue to plan on the use of seaborne transport to reinforce and supply their forces deployed in the Soviet Far East, since their land transport routes are limited and vulnerable. Will this produce larger naval requirements of a new type, or will they improve their landlines of communication instead? Their merchant marine, built up at the instigation of Khrushchev, is serving them admirably in increasing their influence (and arms deliveries) among favorably disposed client-states. Will they build up a navy capable of defending this merchant marine? Both the Western economy and NATO's ability to deter Soviet expansion into Western Europe depend on the continued use of the seas in time of peace or war. Will the Soviets build up a navy to deny the use of the seas to the West or can they already perform this mission? Soviet interests in the political and economic development of the non-aligned nations are frequently incompatible with our own. Both sides may well find frequent opportunities to intervene in the affairs of these emerging nations. Will the U.S.S.R. develop a navy and support points in other countries capable of intervening on its own behalf or interposing itself in such a way as to deny U.S. intervention?

It appears to be only a matter of time before some nation of the Third World attempts to deny passage to either Soviet or U.S. shipping in an effort to exact some economic or political benefit. Will the Soviets develop a navy capable of ensuring passage of its own vessels or of denying passage to ships of the West? These uncertainties, among others, will be addressed in subsequent chapters.

3
The Soviet Fleet Today

Current Status and Funding

Types and Force Levels

The Soviet Naval Command currently has the following assets at its disposal:

- The SLBM fleet, still growing rapidly and armed with increasingly large, accurate, and sophisticated weapons. The submarines employ multiple reentry vehicles (MRVs), multiple independently targeted reentry vehicles (MIRVs), and the only operational ballistic missile guidance system using star-sighting mechanisms. The range of some currently deployed Soviet submarine-launched missiles exceeds that of planned first-generation U.S. Trident missiles.
- A major surface fleet of stable size, armed with ship-to-ship missiles and ASW weapons and capable of rapid fire and high speed, if not great staying power.
- New classes of innovative surface ships that carry aircraft—helicopters and VSTOL planes—which have, in addition to their apparent ASW capabilities, the capability to cover landings on beaches in most Third World countries.
- Probably the largest and most extensive ocean surveillance and naval intelligence gathering system in the world, including two different naval satellite systems.
- By far the largest fleet of attack submarines, with nuclear-powered units gradually replacing the older diesel-electric ones, and armed with torpedoes and surface-to-surface and underwater-to-surface missiles.
- Long-range naval aircraft—including the most modern Soviet

supersonic bomber—for patrol, antisubmarine warfare, and attack on hostile ships.
- Missile-carrying corvettes and patrol craft for coastal defense as well as a vast fleet of minelaying (and minesweeping) craft, which pose a threat to large naval vessels, no matter how well protected. These relatively inexpensive craft are also now operated by many other coastal countries friendly to the U.S.S.R. (see Chapter 4).
- A limited amphibious fleet capable of moving a modest-sized landing force anywhere on the globe and putting it ashore if aircover from other fleet elements or friendly forces is adequate.
- A rapidly expanding merchant marine that retains a preponderant number of small tramp steamers well suited to serving small ports in less-developed countries. Roll-on/roll-off and other specialized ships are also being added to the merchant marine.
- The world's largest fleet of oceanographic survey vessels and electronic intelligence collection ships, devoted to the diligent acquisition of information for the purpose of improving the capabilities and operations of the Soviet Navy.

Fleets and Organizational Structure

Soviet naval forces are divided into four principal fleets: The Northern Fleet, based in and around the Kola Peninsula to the east of Norway; the Pacific Fleet, based at Vladivostok, at Petropavlovsk on Kamchatka, and elsewhere on the Soviet Pacific Coast; the Baltic Fleet, based near Leningrad; and the Black Sea Fleet, based in the Crimea.

The Northern Fleet, which is the largest and contains the greatest number of the newer types of ships, has under its administrative command all Soviet fleet units in the Atlantic Ocean. (Presumably, some at least of the SSBNs in operational status are under the direct control of the High Command in Moscow.) Northern Fleet submarine units are also used for the Soviet squadron in the Mediterranean.

The Baltic Fleet consists primarily of older ships. Its missions are to defend the Baltic against penetration by hostile forces and to support amphibious operations against NATO or neutral countries adjacent to the Baltic in the event of war. It is generally believed that this Baltic Fleet is subordinated to the Ground Forces Command.

The Black Sea Fleet is approximately the size of the Baltic Fleet but has a somewhat larger component of newer and more heavily armed vessels. The Black Sea is also the site of substantial naval construction—new vessels for all of the Soviet fleets are often on trial or shakedown cruises in the Black Sea. The Mediterranean Squadron, known as the Fifth Squadron, is under the administrative control of the Black Sea Fleet.

The Pacific Fleet, although somewhat larger than the Black Sea and

Baltic fleets, generally tends to have older and more obsolescent vessels than the Northern Fleet, and they appear to be less well-equipped for antisubmarine warfare. It usually has about four guided missile cruisers, four gun cruisers, and a dozen destroyers. It does have a large number of nuclear submarines of all classes (although not as many as the Northern Fleet). The Soviet fleet detachment operating in the Indian Ocean is under the administrative command of the Pacific Fleet. It is often somewhere in the vicinity of the Indian subcontinent, but frequently it visits East African ports, and it was especially visible in Somalia (until the spring of 1977) and the People's Republic of Yemen (formerly the Aden Protectorate). It is usually smaller than the Mediterranean Squadron, but composed of similar ship types.

Soviet naval communications are based on a series of redundant and reliable systems to ensure secure links to all operational units. Several very low frequency (VLF) radio stations, in addition to landlines, satellite relays, and conventional high-frequency transmitters, provide a variety of channels from the commander-in-chief in Moscow to regional commanders and ships at sea. Strict control is exercised through this system over the SSBNs at sea, which are, of course, like all other strategic systems, under the direct centralized command of STAVKA, the headquarters of the High Command.

The Naval Budget

The Soviet naval budget amounts to one-fifth of the total funds allocated to the Soviet armed forces. This proportion has remained constant for the last five years, but the actual amounts involved have risen by about 20 percent over that period of time, around the average rate of growth for the Soviet military budget overall. Most of the increase has gone to the strategic submarine fleet and the procurement of the Backfire bomber.

The U.S. Navy currently receives one-third of the defense appropriations, which are less overall than those of the U.S.S.R. United States and Soviet comparisons of military costs are inevitably misleading, however, owing, among other reasons, to marked differences in the relative costs of manpower and equipment. Differences in missions complicate attempts at quantitative comparison even further. Bearing these qualifications in mind, it is likely that Soviet naval expenditures were comparable to or greater than those of the United States in 1976; it is certain that the trend toward level expenditures (in constant dollars) in the United States and expansion in the U.S.S.R. has been under way for six years.

Constraints on Soviet Naval Operations and Growth

Geographic Constraints

In 1839 the Marquis de Custine noted in his commentaries on his visit to

Russia, "My traveling companions [near St. Petersburg] proudly explained the recent progress of the Russian Navy. I expressed admiration for this marvel without appreciating it as they do. It is a creation, or more correctly, a recreation of the Emperor Nicholas, who enjoys realizing the dominant desire of Peter the First. . . . As long as Russia does not exceed her natural limits, the Russian Navy will be a plaything of emperors—nothing more."

The Soviet Navy is no longer a plaything, at least since Stalin's death. Nonetheless, Russia's "natural limits" still inhibit her as she seeks to become a truly great naval power. The hard fact is that Soviet naval forces have access to the high seas only through a limited number of relatively narrow passages.

These passages seem narrower all the time because of long-duration bottom-moored mines, high-speed coastal vessels with homing torpedoes and antiship missiles, shore-based antiship missiles with ranges in excess of 20–30 miles, and higher performance land-based aircraft.

The Northern Fleet can gain the Atlantic basin only through the Norwegian Sea and adjacent areas. Access from the Baltic is even more restricted by the channels winding among the islands of the Danish Straits between Sweden and Norway on the north and Denmark to the south and west.

Access from the Black Sea to the Mediterranean is controlled not only by the geography of the Turkish Straits—the narrowest passage of them all—but also by the provisions of the Montreux Convention. Although that convention does not prevent the passage of naval ships in peacetime, it does impose irksome restrictions for the Soviet Union on virtually all types of combat vessels. In time of war, the Soviets must assume that passage through the straits will be denied them unless they are able to occupy the Dardanelles, free the straits from mines, and control the airspace above. Even if the passage to the Mediterranean were assured, there remain the Suez Canal and the Strait of Gibraltar, one of them virtually impassable in time of war and the other highly vulnerable to interdiction.

The Pacific coast of the Soviet Union is not so encumbered as those to the west by choke points, but the proximity of the Aleutian Islands and Japan and China imposes serious hazards from possible hostile action. Furthermore, the Pacific ports of the Soviet Union are themselves connected to the rest of the nation only by the thin strands of the Trans-Siberian Railway and *Aeroflot*. The Pacific Coast is more like an island to be supplied from the sea than a home base for maritime operations. This analogy does not fully apply in the case of the Soviet submarine fleet, which can rely on prepositioned supplies over an extended period of time. It would, however, be a major factor for the Soviet Navy in considering the mounting of amphibious operations or sustained surface operations. It is most applicable to the problems of sea lines of communication (SLOCs).

FIGURE 3-1
SOVIET GEOGRAPHY

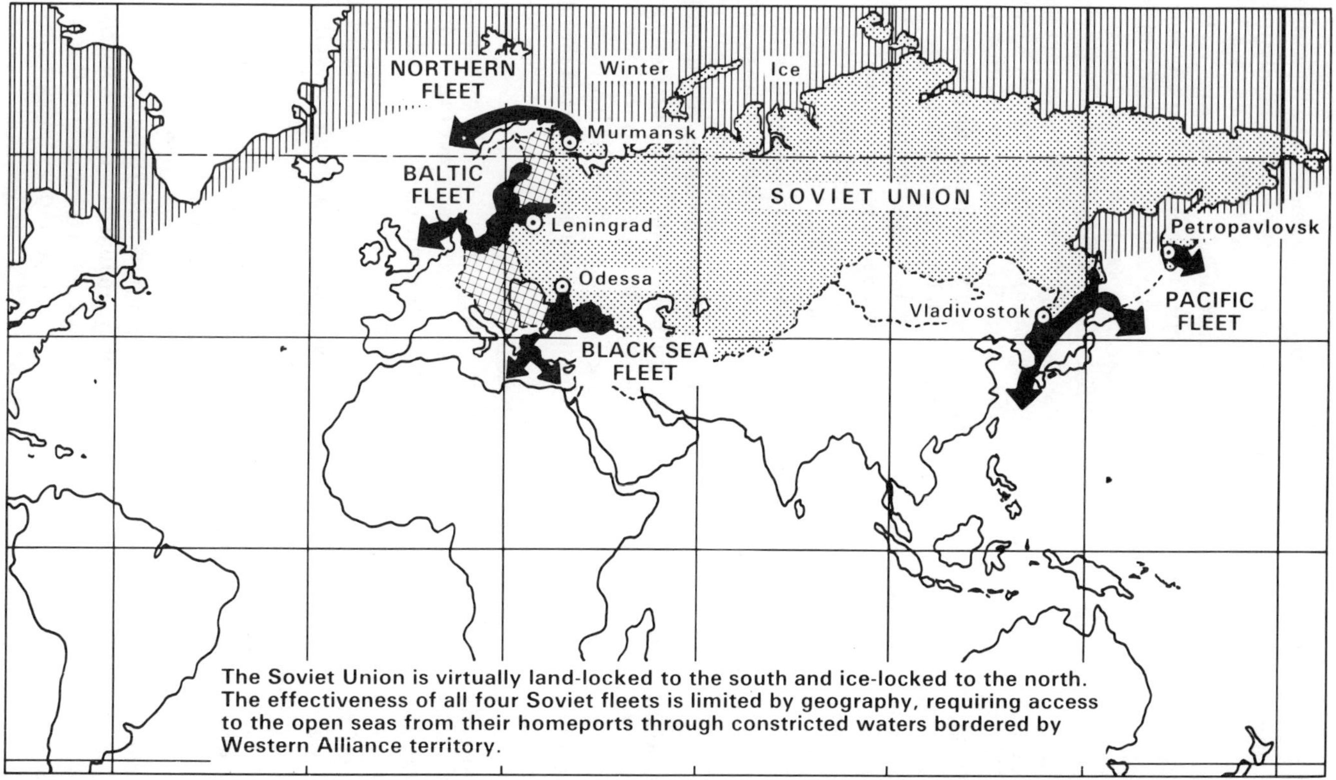

The Soviet Union is virtually land-locked to the south and ice-locked to the north. The effectiveness of all four Soviet fleets is limited by geography, requiring access to the open seas from their homeports through constricted waters bordered by Western Alliance territory.

The Soviet SLOC from west to east is the longest and most vulnerable in the world. The northern sea route across the Arctic Ocean is open to merchant shipping for about three months a year, permitting perhaps a hundred ships to make the passage. These constraints rule out the Arctic as an alternative SLOC from Soviet Europe to Soviet Asia. Soviet naval exploitation of Arctic ports west of Archangel and east to the Bering Sea has never been an attractive alternative because of the severity of the climate, the hazards of navigation, and the difficulties of maintaining effective bases in the area. Even the Sea of Okhotsk is subject to heavy winter icing.

One of the Russian dreams—with origins well before the Revolution—has been a warm water port in the south. Russian preoccupation with the Middle East and the Turkish Straits (which Stalin demanded as a part of the settlement after World War II ended), with Iran (the northwestern province of which Stalin tried to seize in 1946), with Iraq (where the Soviet Union is by far the most influential foreign power), and with Afghanistan (where Soviet influence is dominant) is evidence of this concern.

East of the Mediterranean, the two most logical areas for the establishment of a warm water port are the coasts of Iran and Pakistan. As noted above, the Soviet Union tried to take over northwestern Iran, including the city of Tabriz, after World War II, claiming it was a southern extension of Azerbaijan. The major barrier to obtaining a route to the sea through Iran is that country's strong alliance with the United States. Given a continuation of direct U.S. concern for the security of Iran, a Soviet move is most likely to occur at a time of great political instability there, such as might be occasioned by the death, abdication, or removal from power of the Shah.

Beyond these considerations there lies the question of access to the ocean through the Strait of Hormuz, where the main channel for large vessels—only three miles wide—is within the territorial waters of the Sultanate of Oman. Iran's only port on the Indian Ocean itself is at Chabahar, which has a capacious natural harbor. Communication overland to Chabahar, however, is almost nonexistent. The Shah is planning to build a major naval base there and hopes to develop the countryside as well, but the establishment of overland communication is well into the future.

Some analysts of Middle Eastern affairs have suggested that Soviet encouragement given to Afghanistan in its irredentist disputes with Pakistan has as an ultimate goal the establishment of a Soviet port on the Indian Ocean in what is now Baluchistan, the westernmost province of Pakistan. The physical problems involved in establishing a port in Baluchistan are greater than those of Chabahar, owing to both the terrain ashore and the very shallow water off the coast. However, the Russians have always loved grand projects and there may be political opportunities here that would be more difficult for the United States to counter than those involving Iran and Oman.

"In 1973, Admiral Sergeyev, chief of the Naval Staff, was asked by a Western naval attache what his greatest problem was as a result of the shift to forward deployment. He replied without hesitation, 'Bases.' "[1]

The implications of the U.S.S.R.'s landlocked geography for its navy are that it must keep its ships close to home, support them with auxiliaries over long distances, rely on foreign bases, or consider them expendable in time of conflict. It follows from this that the Soviet Navy should be reluctant to commit major elements of its fleet to remote areas during a crisis. The only alternative is to accept the loss of these units early in a general war, whether nuclear or conventional. At the same time (if one is thinking dialectically), the frustrations that geography imposes on Soviet naval planners may also contribute to the urge to expand the sphere of operations of the fleet into the broad oceans and away from the narrow passages that lead to home. Considering the geographic constraints on its navy, if the Soviet Union is to continue to expand and to assert its peacetime presence in more parts of the globe—particularly beyond its own Eurasian landmass—it must find much better means to maintain its combat units abroad. In wartime it would appear basic that the Soviets would attempt operations aimed at alleviating those geographic constraints.

The Soviet Navy until recently used a base and an airfield at Berbera in Somalia and received some support from various ports in India. It still uses ports in West Africa, Cuba, and South Yemen. It is looking for additional bases and port rights in various parts of the world. Although Soviet naval fleet support is weak, the Soviet Merchant Marine, whose ships ply all the seas, also furnishes supplies, including fuel, to the navy. These factors add significantly to the ability of Soviet naval detachments to remain on remote stations for long periods. In the event that hostilities seemed probable, Soviet naval units could also be sent out from the confines of coastal waters to escape through choke points before war began. In that circumstance, the units already abroad might be supported by the merchant fleet at least for a time, depending on the nature of the conflict. Such a mass exodus of the Soviet Navy from its home ports, however, would reduce the likelihood that the Soviets could surprise the West militarily. A recent Soviet naval exercise involved the mass movement of submarines plus surface vessels, including the *Kiev* and naval aircraft, out of the Northern Fleet base area and through the Norwegian Sea out into the Atlantic. (*New York Times*, July 29, 1977.)

Political Constraints

The Strategic Arms Limitation Agreements impose a limit of 950 missile launchers on the Soviet SSBN fleet. Beyond this modest restriction, there are no appreciable international obligations as to the size of the Soviet Navy.

The tempo and size of naval building programs in other countries, particularly the United States, have been frequently cited as an influence on the Soviet program. (The Soviet preoccupation with U.S. carrier and strategic submarine forces that threaten the Soviet Union directly and the construction of fleet units to counter these threats are well documented. Beyond that, it would be difficult to demonstrate that the Soviets are caught in any spiral to match U.S. naval progress.) It is equally unlikely that deceleration on the U.S. side would influence the Soviets to follow suit. In fact, the U.S. Navy appropriations have remained about the same for the past five years, while the budget of the Soviet Navy has increased by around 20 percent, with most of the increase going to the SSBN force.[2]

The expanse of the Soviet Union across Europe and Asia and its ability to employ aircraft and land-based missiles against hostile fleets call into question the idea that the deployment of Soviet naval forces beyond the littoral seas and into the Atlantic, the Mediterranean Sea, and the Indian Ocean is purely defensive in nature or simply responsive to U.S. initiative.

Perhaps the most immediate political constraints on bases are imposed by nations that are unwilling to receive or to fuel and supply Soviet naval units and to whom the presence of those units nearby would be considered provocative. This consideration applies to certain nations in the Middle East and South Asia.

Soviet concern with the militantly anticolonial Chinese influence in the Third World is also a factor, albeit of a different sort. There is something inevitably imperial about a high seas fleet. Moreover, a fleet remote from home bases is in part a projection of a nation's force and in part a hostage for a nation's good behavior. Given the lack of expenditures in maritime efforts of the Soviet political leaders, and given, furthermore, their preference for the traditional style of expanding one step at a time and only advancing when the rear is secured, naval ventures into the Indian Ocean must be upsetting to at least some members of the Politburo.

There is one political constraint imposed by communist ideology that might tend to inhibit the yen to acquire foreign bases. The reputation of the Soviet Union in the Third World and even the public opinion of its own population have made the Soviet leadership very cautious about foreign entanglements and commitments of a military nature beyond the "Socialist camp." Soviet preoccupation with preserving the antiimperialist image is real. The current political battle with China and other dissident leftist groups, including some of the European communist parties, has undoubtedly exacerbated sensitivity on this point.

Domestic Constraints

Fundamentally, the political constraints—international or domestic—imposed on the Soviet Navy are those of the Politburo of the Central Committee of the Communist party. The military hierarchy is still primarily oriented toward the ground forces. There are no independent advocates or critics of naval policies in the Soviet Union—no investigative reporters, no Navy Leaguers, no defense contractors, no unilateral disarmers, not even an appropriations subcommittee. Institutional interests exist, of course, and some individuals are influential. Sometimes there is no coherent policy on a subject. (The Law of the Sea conferences have demonstrated that.) But those used to the American style of countervailing influences, veto power, and consensus decision should not attempt to interpret Soviet policies through criteria valid for Washington.

That said, there would be clear penalties for the Soviet Union in either expanding the navy at a greater rate or broadening the scope of its activities. In addition to higher construction costs, at least minor economic problems could be involved in having to pay for offshore procurement of fuel and supplies in hard currency. Furthermore, the Soviets are preoccupied with the political contamination of crews and work forces by exposure to foreign ports and bases and related issues, such as security of classified equipment, ease and efficiency of repair, and efficient, reliable communications. All these factors work to inhibit a Soviet commitment to stationing units abroad and the development of many bases in other countries. As Gorshkov has said:

> One must say that our fleet, moving out onto the expanse of the world ocean, on the question of rear support finds itself in an unequal situation compared with the fleets of other countries. The naval forces of the United States, for example, have at their disposal more than 500 bases from which American ships and naval aviation are supported.... The Soviet Union does not have overseas military bases and does not intend to have any because the desire to seize the territory of another is alien to it.... Our ships, when on the high seas, only in rare circumstances visit the ports of friendly countries for short-term stays of rest for the crew or taking aboard fuel supplies, water, and food.[3]

This is not to say that the Soviet Union will not establish naval bases abroad. In fact, the general tenor of the article quoted above can be interpreted as a plea for more bases (and in the process it may considerably overstate the U.S. Navy's dependence on overseas bases). It does mean, however, that such a step will not be taken without careful consideration and awareness of the costs and complications involved.

The Soviet decision to predicate forward deployment on the availability and use of overseas bases and facilities provides some indication of the economic constraints within which the U.S.S.R. naval policy is forced to operate. The alternative to reliance on foreign bases would be construction of large numbers of warships and provision of specialized support capabilities afloat.

Economic Constraints

There are some suspicions that the Soviet economy will not be able to continue indefinitely to pour so many of its resources into military forces and hardware. Soviet productivity appears to be relatively stagnant at present, possibly suffering from insufficient investment in plant modernization. Soviet agricultural production still lacks the necessary growth, owing to inadequate mechanization in food growing and processing. The rate of development of the U.S.S.R.'s own natural resources appears inadequate to meet demand—as indicated by the fact that the Russians must now import oil and gas despite the existence of substantial untapped domestic reserves. Soviet demographic trends indicate that it may soon be impractical to maintain military forces at current levels. Relative to their own satellite states, the Soviets' domestic economy appears to be falling behind. These trends and others suggest that eventually Moscow may be forced to reallocate resources from defense to the civil sector. It is hard to imagine that the Soviet Navy would take less than a proportionate cut relative to the ground and air forces—both of which are more directly involved in the defense of the Russian homeland. None of the aforementioned trends, however, is serious enough to suggest a near-term curtailment in current Soviet military expenditures.

Peacetime Influence of the Soviet Navy

Nuclear Intimidation

The major threat the Soviet Navy poses for its potential enemies comes from its submarine forces carrying nuclear missiles. The striking power of the Delta-class submarine and its successors presents a substantial and relatively invulnerable threat worldwide. The Soviets also maintain a large force of submarines with shorter-range missiles, many of which now appear to be targeted against "theater" objectives in Western Europe. When this seaward threat is augmented by the newly deployed land-based systems, it is conceivable that an increasing number of European countries might decide that neither a nuclear war nor a conventional one with Soviet forces is winnable in Europe. From there, the conclusion is not far away that the only sane course for Europeans is to accommodate to the Great Power in the East. Equivalent submarine forces in the northwest Pacific might make it equally difficult for the Japanese to continue to see the advantages of their ties to the Western Alliance. Soviet naval strength could thus contribute to the Russians' apparent objective of achieving such a preponderance of force on and around their own continents that the Western-oriented nations may eventually undergo "Finlandization" of their own accord.

Influence in the Third World

The Soviet Union's overseas allies and friends, such as Angola, Cuba, Vietnam, and now Ethiopia, need what Soviet merchant ships and transport ships can bring them, including the protection provided by a Soviet high seas fleet. As indicated in numerous examples, the Soviet Fleet has been effectively used as a political instrument in the tradition of navies since the seventeenth century, but that has little to do with defense of the homeland.

In view of the power of the surface forces of the U.S. Navy, efforts at political influence or intervention through the instrument of the Soviet Navy are likely to be aimed at areas where both the difficulty of responding and the relatively low level of distress evoked would make it unlikely that either the United States or NATO would react militarily.

Expansion of the Soviet naval presence, particularly in Third World areas where it would serve Soviet purposes best, would depend on: an increase in the auxiliaries available to support warships abroad; an addition to the number of ships such as the *Kiev* with military capabilities for force projection on beachheads; and changes in Soviet diplomatic relations with other nations.

Soviet influence in the Middle East waxes and wanes as the receptivity of the major nations of the Indian Ocean basin vacillates with local political developments. The nations at the mouth of the Red Sea—both in Africa and the Arabian Peninsula—still attract the Soviets and their allies. North Yemen is now strongly dependent on Saudia Arabia and receives substantial support from the United States and other Western powers. South Yemen (the "People's Republic of Yemen") is largely dependent on Soviet and East German economic and military support. Across the strait in Africa are Somalia, Djibouti (formerly the Territory of the Afars and Issas), which won its independence from France in 1977, and Ethiopia. Soviet fortunes in Somalia have ebbed since 1975, but they are now high in neighboring Ethiopia, and Soviet interest in the area remains strong. The choke point of the Bab El Mandeb Straits is likely to increase in strategic and economic significance as the Suez Canal expands its capacity.

Going on east, the Soviets have long backed the People's Front for the Liberation of Oman from across the border in South Yemen. Although the movement is now dormant, it could perhaps be revived at some time. The tanker fleets that go forth from the Persian Gulf to supply the world with oil pass through the straits in the territorial waters of the Sultanate of Oman.

Influence in the Mediterranean

The Soviet presence in the Mediterranean was initiated in 1958 with the basing of eight Whiskey-class submarines with a tender at Vlone, Albania. In 1960, Soviet intelligence ships and submarines conducted an exercise in the Aegean Sea that appeared to be directed toward sinking a carrier task force. However, as a consequence of the loss of the Albanian base in 1961, there was little further Soviet naval activity in the Mediterranean until 1964.

In June 1964, fifteen vessels from the Black Sea Fleet under the fleet's commander made a grand Mediterranean cruise. Since that time, the Soviet Fleet has been regularly represented there. Buildup of forces continued until 1972, when approximately the current levels were attained. It should be noted as a possible prelude to the '64 cruise that the U.S. Navy introduced Polaris submarines into the Mediterranean on a regular basis in 1963. The Soviet Mediterranean Squadron is primarily designed for antisubmarine and anticarrier operations. As mentioned previously, however, it also includes some landing forces.

The Mediterranean Squadron spends most of its time at anchor. Maneuvers and steaming from one port or anchorage to another occupy something less than a quarter of its time. The Squadron also visits various Mediterranean countries including Algeria, Egypt, France, Yugoslavia, Morocco, Syria, Tunisia, and Italy. Those near the major choke points of the Mediterranean and around the Island of Crete are particularly favored.

The Mediterranean Squadron was notably employed in an exercise of Soviet diplomatic support (or so it appeared) in 1969 during the time of the Libyan coup against King Idris. Soviet, Syrian, and Egyptian military units were engaged in maneuvers involving a practice landing on the Egyptian coast close to the Libyan border. The Mediterranean Squadron was strung out between the Egyptian coast—very close to the Libyan border—and the Island of Crete in a disposition apparently aimed at preventing the penetration from the Western Mediterranean of a hypothetical U.S. carrier task force. The precise relation of the timing of this exercise to the coup is impossible to identify, but it seems highly likely that some sort of coordination took place. The most significant force in Libya to protect the King's government in the event of an Egyptian attack was a British tank detachment stationed near the Egyptian border. The crews of these tanks, however, were in Cyprus. To fly them to Libya would have required that the transport aircraft overfly a substantial part of the Soviet squadron, which was bristling with surface-to-air missiles.

On September 26, 1969, Radio Cairo commented on the Libyan coup as follows: "The presence of the Soviet fleet at this strength is a guarantee for neutralizing the effectiveness of the Sixth Fleet and deterring it from carrying out new imperialist adventures."

Only a year before, in November 1968, the present first deputy commander-in-chief of the Soviet Navy, Admiral Smirnov, wrote in *Red Star* that: "No one can be allowed to turn the Mediterranean into a breeding ground of a war that could plunge mankind into an abyss of a worldwide nuclear-missile catastrophe. The presence of Soviet vessels in the Mediterranean serves this lofty, noble aim." One can think of other explanations as to why the British did not fly the tank crews in, but the Soviet squadron must have given pause to those who made the decision.

Although not as dramatic as later events, perhaps the most significant use of the Soviet fleet during the Arab-Israeli conflicts was the stationing in the early 1970s of Soviet surface-to-air missile (SAM) -equipped destroyers in Egyptian ports to inhibit Israeli air attacks. In 1973, prior to the October attack by the Arab states on Israel, a detachment of 1,800 Moroccan soldiers was transported by truck from Morocco to Algeria, where they boarded Soviet ships that took them to Syria prior to the attack. This Moroccan force participated with the Syrians in the attack on Israel. Furthermore, the Soviet squadron was augmented to ninety-six ships, more than double its normal size, and stationed close to the war zone. The squadron's ships were in position to shadow the U.S. carrier task force with three surface-to-surface missile (SSM) and SAM-equipped ships near each U.S. carrier. In addition, four guided missile submarines were within range of the carriers. United States forces, including carrier aircraft and submarines, were on alert for a possible initiation of hostilities by the Soviets.

The Mediterranean Squadron was again used for political purposes with the visit in 1974, between December 11 and 17, of the squadron commander and two guided missile ships to Alexandria, Egypt. The following week Admiral Gorshkov himself went to Cairo. These visits seem to have been a last-ditch attempt to protect Soviet access to naval bases in Egypt.

More recently, ships of the Mediterranean Squadron reportedly jammed the radio circuits used by Egyptian attack and fighter planes in the border conflict with Libya in 1977. Because the Egyptian planes were Soviet-made, it was particularly easy for the Soviets to intrude on their transmission frequencies.

Influence in the Indian Ocean

The first Soviet involvement in the area was in the Yemeni civil war in the early 1960s. Soviet TU-16 bombers manned by Soviet crews but bearing Egyptian markings flew bombing missions against the Royal Yemeni forces from Cairo.

Soviet fleet units began to appear regularly in the Indian Ocean in 1968. Overall, including both warships and auxiliaries, the Soviet Navy had 1,800 ship-days (the number of ships multiplied by the number of days present in the area) in 1968, 2,800 ship-days in 1969, 3,400 ship-days in

1971, and 8,800 in 1972. The anomalous increase in 1972 was related to the Indo-Pakistani War and the establishment of independence for Bangladesh, with the consequent involvement of the Soviet Navy in minesweeping and repairs to the harbor of Chittagong. Since then, the number of ship-days has remained near the 1972 level. Soviet ship-days in 1974 equalled 9,060; 2,460 of these were for combatant vessels. Only one-third to one-half of the Soviet Indian Ocean units are warships, including, usually, one landing ship for vehicles. The rest are auxiliaries and hydrographic survey vessels. Judging from the amount of hydrographic surveying that the Soviets have done in the Indian Ocean basin, they must have the best data on bottom profiles, acoustic properties, and other bathymetric and oceanographic measurements.

The combatant ships of the Soviet fleet deployed in the Indian Ocean have consistently improved in quality and striking power. The first submarine and first guided missile submarine deployment took place in 1969; the first nuclear-powered submarine deployment in 1970. In 1974, the first advanced nuclear-powered submarines (Victor and Charlie classes), as well as the first modern guided missile cruisers, entered the Indian Ocean. As in the Mediterranean, the Soviet fleet is often at anchor in shallow areas on the high seas. Most of the Indian Ocean anchorages are off the African coast or in the Bay of Bengal. The Soviets have paid goodwill visits to twenty-two countries; since 1969 they have made frequent use of the ports of Berbera in Somalia, Hodeida in the Yemen Arab Republic, and Aden in the People's Republic of Yemen.

Significant uses of Soviet naval forces for diplomatic and political purposes include, most notably, the Soviet naval buildup during the Indo-Pakistani war of late 1971. Before the crisis, the Soviet Navy had four combatant ships in the Indian Ocean. An additional missile-equipped destroyer and several submarines arrived on December 1 as part of the normal rotation pattern. The ships already on station remained. On December 8, the day before the formation of the U.S. Naval Task Force 74, four additional Soviet naval vessels were dispatched from Vladivostok, including a guided missile cruiser and a nuclear-powered submarine with cruise missiles. The following day, two conventional attack submarines were dispatched from Petropavlovsk. On December 12, three days after U.S. Task Force 74 was formed, another guided missile cruiser and a destroyer left Vladivostok. In addition, other Soviet ships in the area in December and January included a collection ship, a conventional attack submarine, and a tanker. Most of these vessels were dispatched prior to the formation of Task Force 74—that is, they were assembled and dispatched not to counter U.S. intervention but to show a Soviet presence for its own sake. During the crisis, the Soviet ambassador in New Delhi was reported to have remarked that the Soviet fleet in the area would not allow Task Force 74 to intervene.

SOVIET NAVAL PRESENCE

Modern Soviet surface combatants like this Kynda-class guided-missile armed light cruiser now make possible a substantial Soviet naval presence virtually anywhere in the world. (Courtesy U.S. Navy)

In March 1973, Iraq occupied an outpost manned by Kuwait in a disputed section of the border between the two countries. The outpost was close to the Iraqi harbor and naval base at Umm Qasr, which is used as a harbor for Soviet imports including military supplies. During the period of this dispute, Admiral Gorshkov and several Soviet naval vessels paid Iraq an unprecedented visit of friendship.

In late April 1970, the Government of Somalia, which received substantial military support from the Soviet Union, announced it had evidence of an attempt at overthrowing the government. A few days prior to this announcement, ships of the Soviet Indian Ocean Squadron arrived in Somalian ports. There were nine Soviet vessels present at that time, including an oiler, a submarine tender, three destroyers, one amphibious ship with a marine complement, one cruise missile nuclear submarine, and two conventional submarines. These ships were in the Indian Ocean as part of the Soviet worldwide exercise Okean-70, but the stay in Somalia was extended from April 17 through the second week in May.

Influence in Other Areas

Soviet fleet units have visited most areas of the Pacific Ocean beginning in 1963 and 1964. (This is in addition to intelligence collection and surveillance operations aimed primarily at the U.S. Pacific Fleet.) Regular visits to Caribbean ports began in 1969. Apparent attempts to establish a submarine base at Cienfuegos called forth a strong U.S. protest. In 1970, West African ports in the South Atlantic also became regular places of call.

During the final months of the civil strife in Angola, Soviet naval forces lent moral and military support to their clients and were in a position to protect the ships and aircraft (also Soviet) delivering supplies, weapons, Cuban volunteers, and other useful items. A Kotlin guided missile destroyer, a large landing craft (LST) with Soviet naval personnel embarked, and the largest Soviet replenishment ship were in the Gulf of Guinea. Farther north, a Kresta II cruiser and an oiler were in the vicinity of the Guinea coast. There were TU-95 aircraft at Conakry. Farther north still, near the Strait of Gibralter, a Sverdlov cruiser and two guided missile destroyers were apparently standing by in the event that their support might be needed in Angola.

In March 1969, Soviet combatant ships were sent to Ghana when the Government of Ghana seized two Soviet fishing trawlers for violation of Ghanaian fishing regulations. Coincidentally, the trawlers were released. In May 1971, Soviet combatants called at Sierra Leone—apparently to support the then shaky pro-Soviet regime. The schedule indicates that Guinea and Sierra Leone have become regular ports of call.

Soviet naval units have been used in various parts of the world for security patrols and coercion of small vessels belonging to other nations. A

Danish fishing trawler recently had its tow cut off deliberately about a week after another Danish trawler tried to succor a Soviet citizen who was trying to flee his homeland in a rowboat. More emphatically, since 1945, 1,536 Japanese vessels have been seized by Soviet naval ships in the waters north of Japan. Only 941 have been returned; 25 were sunk. Over 1,200 Japanese sailors have been arrested, and 37 have died in Soviet custody.

Future Prospects

All contemporary great powers are maritime states. (Admiral Gorshkov)

Naval Nuclear Strategy

Soviet atomic submarines are first class modern warships of universal importance. They resolve a wide circle of tasks on the high seas... not only bearers of tactical weapons, but they make up an indispensable part of the strategic nuclear shield of the motherland. (Gorshkov, in *Sea Power of the State* [Moscow: Military Publishing House, 1976], p. 317.)

As mentioned in Chapter 2, Soviet strategy called for the use of submarine-launched ballistic missiles (SLBMs) from Yankee-class submarines against shoreline targets, apparently chiefly naval and military installations. Now the naval ballistic missile is considered virtually on a par with the strategic rocket as a major element of the Soviet nuclear strike capability.

The claims for equivalence and even superiority to other strategic weapons that Gorshkov and others had first raised seven years ago became more emphatic as the Delta-class submarine with its much longer-ranged and probably more accurate missile became operational in 1973 and 1974. On patrol since 1974, this submarine has largely remained in far-northern waters, well beyond the capability of normal U.S. Navy ASW operations and relatively close to its bases on the Kola Peninsula. Gorshkov's writings in recent years appear to advocate—or to announce in Delphic passages—that the Delta class will be withheld from a first strike in a nuclear war and used as a reserve, as a second strike weapon, or perhaps as a source of pressure during negotiations to terminate a nuclear war after the first exchange.

As part of overall Soviet strategy, the Yankee and Delta classes of submarines must be considered in the context of other Soviet developments relating to nuclear war. Soviet organization and construction in civil defense, the setting aside of major reserve food supplies, the apparent preoccupation with high accuracy on their newer nuclear-tipped missiles, and their continuing program to construct more and larger nuclear ballistic missile submarines—these are all parts of a whole. It would appear that, while not planning to begin a war, the Soviet Union takes seriously the possibility of fighting and winning a nuclear war if one should develop. Its leaders apparently foresee the possibility of a nuclear exchange stopping short of the total destruction of the U.S.S.R. and hope to protect their country in such a way that the result would be the surrender of the United States and its allies to a still viable Soviet Union. In those circumstances, their naval forces would be expected to diminish the effectiveness of Western strategic submarines and aircraft carriers while protecting their own SSBNs against Western ASW efforts and preserving the threat of a survivable second strike capability from the sea. This objective is likely to continue to rank foremost in Soviet naval planning.

In contrast to the practice of the U.S. Navy (which has two crews to provide almost continuous manning of each SSBN), the Soviet Navy has only one crew for a boat and limits the number on patrol such that more than half of the operating boats are in port most of the time. This procedure economizes on maintenance and operating expenses, but it does mean that an alert involving the deployment of the SSBN force would be promptly noted as the SSBNs left home port. It is also an indication that the Soviets consider a surprise attack by NATO unlikely.

Conventional War at Sea

The dominant characteristics of many Soviet surface combatant ships—high speed; great striking power; and relatively limited cruising ranges and reload and resupply capabilities—all suggest that their employment in a long drawn-out conventional war was not foreseen as a major mission when they were built. Soviet writings concerning the possible naval engagements of a major war confirm that assumption. Soviet ships appear to be configured for independent operation rather than for Western-style task forces. Under current doctrine, the Soviet Navy would most likely be dedicated to the destruction of enemy platforms capable of launching sea-based nuclear weapons, primarily U.S. and NATO SSBNs and aircraft carriers or other naval combatants.

Soviet statements on strategic planning for a war with the NATO countries mainly foresee a short, intense conflict involving a nuclear exchange. The alternative of a prolonged worldwide war between the two groups of allies, in which nuclear weapons are not employed (or used only in limited and isolated instances), does not appear to be discussed unambiguously in Soviet strategic writings. Admiral Gorshkov, for example, seems at times to be writing about naval warfare among first-class navies in a nonnuclear context, but only by implication. Nonetheless, the Soviets do maintain ample stockpiles and mobilization capabilities for their land forces for a relatively long conventional war (certainly in excess of one year).

In discussing sea control in his most recent book, *The Sea Power of the State*, Gorshkov covers the influence of nuclear weapons in concise terms:

> With the appearance of nuclear, and later also missile, weaponry, many theoreticians asserted that the question of gaining control of the sea had supposedly been thrust into the background owing to the fact that the new combat and technical means of warfare at sea had fundamentally altered the conditions for conducting operations and combat actions and, consequently, also the methods of supporting them.
>
> One of the arguments denying the need to gain control of the sea was that since combat operations have been developing so rapidly, so effectively, the forces conducting the battle at sea did not need to establish favorable conditions. The question is even raised in this manner: What will a fleet do in a nuclear war—destroy the enemy or gain control, subjecting itself to the risk of being destroyed by the enemy before it is able to achieve its own goal? ... The time frame within which one can maintain control of the sea has been considerably reduced as the speed of ships and other naval forces has increased and as communications and intelligence have improved.

Gorshkov goes on to cite historical examples from the prenuclear age and mentions submarines as the "main arm of the forces of modern navies." He adds that "establishing the conditions for gaining sea control has always required prolonged periods of time in the execution of a series of measures while still at peace."

Following these observations, he proceeds from the historical accounts of the nonnuclear age to the present: "We may draw the conclusion that the gaining of sea control depends ... on the prosecution of the primary missions assigned to the navy in the course of the armed conflict as a whole. ... The gaining of sea control continues to retain its validity and, therefore, the development of it in all the aspects applicable to the present day is one of the important tasks of naval science." Unfortunately, he does not deal more precisely with the question of sea control under conditions where nuclear warfare is possible. He appears to imply that denial of the seas is more important than control in his references to submarines. His treatment of the importance of preparation before a war begins seems to emphasize the ability to exploit one's naval assets as rapidly as possible during the war.

There is little evidence from recent writings of the Soviets—or from observation of their recent maneuvers for that matter—to support the thesis that they plan to conduct an extensive campaign against Western sea lines of communication (SLOCs) during a major war with the United States. The Soviets are still clearly aware that their navy is not large enough to carry out all conceivable missions. While the anti-SLOC mission is often mentioned and in some articles has been singled out for special attention, it appears to be of relatively low priority. The Soviets must recognize that the assignment of only a few submarines to that mission would be enough to cause the Western Alliance to devote a large part of its ASW assets to countering them, thereby possibly removing some of the threat to its other primarily strategic submarines. The Soviets frequently mention that each German World War II submarine diverted 25 ships and 100 priority aircraft. Moreover, the destruction of the receiving ports in Europe is often described as a higher priority mission—one more directly in support of the land force battle the Soviets are institutionally committed to support with high priority. Additionally, there are coastal SLOCs within NATO Europe which, in that context, would be perceived as more immediately threatening to the success of the land battle. Finally, since the Soviets tend to plan for a short, decisive land battle—with the potential for rapid escalation (by the West, initially) to use of nuclear weapons—it is not surprising to conclude that they do not regularly accord the anti-SLOC mission great importance. At the outset, they would probably expect to accomplish this mission by the assignment of a portion of their diesel submarines, some SSNs perhaps, and a fraction of their long-range naval air arm. Nonetheless, the West is extremely dependent on those SLOCs if the war is *not* decided quickly (in favor of the Soviets) and does *not* escalate or if the conventional aspects of the war continue after a nuclear exchange. It is fully appropriate for the United States and her allies to accord the SLOC protection mission higher priority than current Soviet planning might indicate. Also, the Soviets have more than enough submarines and aircraft to mount a very serious anti-SLOC campaign should they elect to do so at the expense of other mission priorities.

Possible Roles in Small Wars

The Soviet Navy has not played a direct part in small wars, insurrections, and other disturbances, although their merchant marine clearly has. There have been instances, however, when elements of the Soviet fleet were positioned off the coasts of countries at war, where insurrections or *coups d'etat* were taking place, with the apparent intent of strengthening one faction or country in the conflict. In addition, Soviet aircraft manned by Soviet crews have participated in military action in the Middle East. It should only be noted here that the continuing expansion of the Soviet surface fleet and the acquisition of aircraft carriers, amphibious craft, and related fleet units increase the capability of the Soviet fleet to engage in such activities. Statements of various Soviet officials indicate a distinct possibility that the Soviet Navy may intervene directly in such situations in the future. To quote Admiral Gorshkov in *The Sea Power of the State*: "In the policy of our Party and State, the Soviet Navy is emerging as a factor for stabilizing the strengthening of peace and friendship between peoples and acting as a deterrent to the aggressive aspirations of the imperialist states." Such intervention without surface fleet elements would be very difficult. Nonetheless, interventions of the kind exercised by the United States in Korea, Lebanon, and Vietnam are considered to be the "local wars of the imperialists" and not in keeping with Soviet doctrine. It appears more likely that the Soviets may eventually attempt to use their conventional naval assets to deter U.S. intervention than that they will conduct their own interventions using Soviet forces. But they will certainly continue to use their air and naval assets to support the movement of supplies and proxy forces required to assist their clients.

The odds would be heavily against the provision of such Soviet support if an engagement between the Soviet and U.S. fleets seemed likely to result. Yet situations are imaginable where the Soviet Union might presume that military interposition would not be countered directly by the United States.

The Soviet Navy is not equipped to handle shore bombardment or an assault operation against a hostile beachhead if confronted with the tactical air power and coastal naval strength of some of the better-armed Third World nations, particularly in the Mediterranean. The large majority of Third World nations, however, would be vulnerable to such moves from the Soviet Union. The Soviets, in addition, know how to conjure up the spectre of their "strategic" power when necessary. They have not hesitated to apply military force to deal with political problems—e.g., Czechoslovakia in 1968, the Bay of Bengal in 1971, and Angola in 1976.

Soviet attitudes and propaganda are typified in an excerpt from leading Soviet journalist Oleg Orestov. He wrote in the *Soviet Military Review* for November 1976 about the Fifth Non-Aligned Conference at Colombo, Sri Lanka. In his article, "Cohesion of the Forces of Peace and Progress," he says: "In their speeches the delegates to the Colombo conference made it clear that to extend détente to Asia, Africa, and Latin America, the developing countries were sure that it was necessary to step up the fight against imperialist intrigue, to abolish the hotbeds of colonialism and racism, and to extinguish the existing military conflicts."

Domestic Economic and Political Influences

It may be that future developments will refute the assumption that the Soviet regime acts patiently and deliberately and pursues policies designed to minimize the risk of a major war. As long as their country's influence has been expanding somewhat, Soviet leaders have traditionally avoided military threats or actions that ran real risks of war with the West. In considering how future economic and political developments might influence their naval policies and missions, we should first look at the negative side from a Soviet point of view. What would happen if Russian domestic economic and political problems became so acute that the leaders in desperation sought solutions in foreign adventure? (The reverse of this scenario—that the United States might attack the Soviet Union under such circumstances—is a fundamental assumption in Soviet writings concerning the most probable origin of the next world war.) Political temptations appear, in part, to have prompted Khrushchev to move in the Cuban Missile Crisis in 1962 and in the earlier Berlin crises from 1958 to 1961.

Economic and political pressures might push the leadership toward rash and risky acts (what the current leaders criticized in Khrushchev as *prozhektorstvo* or "harebrained scheming"). These pressures might include continuing failures to meet agricultural goals, major unrest in Eastern Europe, and military engagements with China. Other pressures are also possible, but these three appear to be among those least susceptible to amelioration by purely political actions on the part of the Soviet leadership. The first, serious and chronic agricultural shortfalls, could be the inevitable result of adverse climatic conditions over the next two decades, as predicted by some meteorologists. The first and third eventualities could produce an increased rate of expansion of the Soviet Navy—for the purpose of increasing Soviet influence in seeking additional food supplies on the one hand, or providing assured resupply of Soviet forces engaged with the Chinese on the other. The second eventuality, prolonged unrest in Eastern Europe, could cause a slowing of naval expansion if the Soviets turned their resources to an increased land threat on their immediate western frontier.

On the other side of the coin, the Soviet commercial and naval fleets may be expected to contribute significantly to the further economic and political development of the Soviet Union and thereby earn a more influential role in Soviet affairs.

Fishing should continue to provide a large fraction of the protein required in the national diet, particularly if weather trends hold back the growth of feed grain for beef cattle and pigs. There is no indication that the Soviet Merchant Marine has yet saturated the sectors of the shipping market for which it is well adapted. Such trade, as well as continued sales of Soviet ships abroad, can produce much-needed foreign exchange. Moreover, as the economy of the Soviets continues to expand, it is reasonable to expect increases in both their imports and exports, which will probably be carried predominantly in Soviet bottoms. As the merchant marine expands, and as other countries come to depend more on it, there might be pressures within the U.S.S.R. to increase naval presence on the high seas in order to assure the safety and right of passage of their merchant ships.

On the political side, the Soviet Union remains only a "continental superpower," in contrast to the United States, whose intercontinental alliances and commitments make it the sole "world superpower."

SOVIET MARITIME PRESENCE

Fish provide a large portion of the protein in the national Soviet diet. Here a Soviet factory ship prepares to receive the catch of a smaller Soviet fishing vessel. Such operations are routine worldwide. (Courtesy National Oceanic and Atmospheric Administration)

The Soviets maintain the world's largest oceanographic research fleet. This intelligence collector (AGI) was photographed off the coast of Florida awaiting the test firing of a Poseidon missile. (Courtesy U.S. Navy)

Although Europe will remain the focus of Soviet concern, as the Russian leaders become more confident of their newfound position of military "parity" and as they find their ability to influence the Third World growing, they may well strive to become the other world superpower. This means the formation at the right time of credible alliances beyond their own continent on all three planes: economic, political, and military. To form such alliances will require proof of their willingness and capability to support allies across the oceans. This in turn requires the development of an oceangoing conventional navy roughly equal to that of the United States and its allies, which implies reliable access to warm water ports and bases on the coasts of the open oceans. The best way to cultivate the possessors of these ports and bases is probably through nautical intercourse by the fishing fleet, the merchant marine, and the navy. In short, the key to Soviet attainment of world superpower status depends crucially on maritime prowess. It is safe to predict that the Soviet maritime expansion, both commercially and militarily, will facilitate the growth of influence beyond the Eurasian continent. To the extent, then, that the Soviets have surplus energies and resources during the remainder of this century, some fraction of this surplus will no doubt be applied to the expansion of their naval capabilities.

Advances in Naval Technology

Contemporary Soviet naval developments reveal a high degree of innovation and competitive technology. Given the substantial resources devoted by the Soviets to these areas in recent years, the Western Alliance must be prepared for continued advances in the effectiveness of Soviet naval elements, even if their force levels stabilize or, as in the case of submarines, drop off somewhat with the retirement of their diesel boats. The following advances could have serious implications for the projected balance of naval power within the next decade or so:

Antisubmarine Warfare. The Soviet Navy has devoted great effort in recent years to its ASW forces. Yet the Russians still write openly about the need for an effective submarine detection system. If a breakthrough in locating enemy submarines were achieved, it could be rapidly exploited by forces now available, which are numerous and well-equipped to close in for the kill. The Soviets are known to be working on several nonacoustic methods of detecting submarines. As Gorshkov has noted: "Submarines disturb many fields." Success could be doubly beneficial if such detection systems were not "blanked out" by the use of tactical nuclear weapons at sea—a serious problem for all acoustic systems.

Anti-SSBN Warfare. The Soviets place exceptional importance on the neutralization of our SSBN force and the SLBMs they carry. They might reasonably be expected to deploy a system capable of disrupting or destroying U.S. SLBMs during their launch phase using ships stationed in U.S. SSBN patrol areas. They appear to have considered a system that could backtrack from early SLBM launches through some launch detection system to allow the destruction of an SSBN before all its missiles had been fired. They might also attack U.S. SSBN command and control or navigation systems and they might well be willing to deploy such systems even if they were only expected to be successful one-third of the time or against only one-third of the opposing missiles or submarines.

Increased SLBM Accuracy. If Soviet SLBMs were to become accurate enough to threaten U.S. missile silos and other precise targets, such as strategic command, control, and communications centers, they would significantly add to Soviet counterforce capabilities. Continuous efforts to upgrade missile accuracy have been a hallmark of Soviet strategic developments, as they have been for the United States.

Improved Antiship Missiles. The introduction of a several-hundred mile-range ballistic missile with terminal homing against major surface ship targets could substantially increase the current vulnerability of major surface combatants, particularly if accompanied by some large-area surveillance system capable of tracking discrete targets. As noted previously, there is much evidence that some of the Yankee-class SSBN missiles are designed for short-range (500-nautical-mile) use against marine targets.

Sub-Launched Antiaircraft Missiles. The Soviet submarine force almost matches in numbers the long-range patrol aircraft operated by the Western Alliance to detect them. Under these conditions, it would not be unreasonable for the Soviets to consider attacking our low-performance patrol aircraft rather than trying only to evade them. Such a mission is believed to be currently assigned to a portion of the Soviet surface fleet in coastal waters that Soviet submarines must traverse in order to reach their operational areas. A sub-launched antiaircraft capability would add a new dimension to the threat against NATO patrol and transport aircraft, while releasing some Soviet surface ships for other missions. Although some observers believe that antiaircraft capabilities would only increase submarine vulnerability, others feel that such air defense emphasis would be consistent with Soviet military philosophy.

The aforementioned items are not intended as predictions of imminent Soviet advances. Rather, they suggest that Soviet naval progress has not yet reached its zenith and that its momentum is still increasing. This trend is doubly worrisome because the momentum of naval development is matched by that of the Soviet naval "industrial base" for ship, aircraft, and missile production. Unlike U.S. and allied naval shipbuilding and aircraft industries, which have been allowed, and, in fact, encouraged, to shrink, Soviet production rates and capacity appear to have been steadily maintained or increased (see Chapter 2).

4
Allocation of Soviet Naval Forces

Earlier chapters have attempted to outline the strategic goals and motivations of the U.S.S.R. and trace the history, progress, and future potential of its naval forces. Next we venture to suggest the most likely allocation of the various classes of those forces by mission and by region, in accordance with their known operational concepts. This review should provide a basis for assessing the threats presented by Soviet seapower in various parts of the world.

The judgments in this chapter are speculative at best. Although the regional deployments of Soviet aircraft and naval vessels are reasonably well known and relatively stable, one of the great attributes of naval units is mobility. Should the situation so dictate, the Russians are quite capable of changing the composition and relative strengths of their four major fleets. Even more speculative, of course, are the primary mission assignments of the various fleet elements. After all, the second most valuable characteristic of naval assets is versatility. Nonetheless, amphibious units are not well-suited to sinking aircraft carriers, and Delta-class SSBNs are not likely to menace merchant shipping in transit. Consequently, we can make some educated guesses in these areas and attempt to bound the limits of danger to Alliance sealanes during a superpower confrontation.

Furthermore, we make no pretense that the specific order of battle numbers used on the tables throughout this chapter is precisely correct. The figures have been gathered and compiled from open sources available prior to the spring of 1978. High accuracy would not change the trends noted, however, and those who require precise numbers should consult other more authoritative sources.

Wartime Mission Structure

The types of forces employed in the various missions need to be outlined first. On the basis of Soviet pronouncements and operations, there is general agreement among Western naval analysts on current Soviet wartime missions. These include:

1. Strategic nuclear strike;
2. Destruction of enemy naval forces;
3. Support for ground force operations;
4. Interdiction of enemy sealanes; and
5. Protection of own sea lines of communication.

Overlapping these specific missions are the more general requirements to secure control of the four fleet areas and to contest control of adjacent waters such as the Eastern Mediterranean and the South Norwegian and North seas.

Strategic Nuclear Strike

This mission involves both strike forces (the ballistic missile submarines with their nuclear-tipped missiles) and naval forces assigned to their protection and support. The Soviets place very high priority on the attainment of a capable, survivable SSBN fleet. As their missile and submarine technologies improve, they are continuously developing and deploying more lethal, more flexible, and longer-range systems that may be used during any phase of a nuclear war. As we have noted, there is a growing body of opinion that the Soviets may "withhold" their most capable long-range assets from the early nuclear exchanges for later use or postwar negotiations. There are frequent implications of such a role in the recent writings of Admiral Gorshkov, and he is well aware that other naval assets have served a similar purpose in earlier days. For instance, the blockade of Germany after World War I was not lifted until after negotiations had been completed at Versailles. Presumably, these assets would be deployed from their home bases early in a large-scale conflict to some protected or relatively invulnerable holding area, where they would be comparatively safe from U.S. ASW patrol aircraft and from our capable SSN force.

Soviet SSBN protection operations are of two distinct types. First, there is a need in adjacent waters to secure certain sea areas (or redoubts) against intrusion by enemy antisubmarine forces to allow the Soviet High Command maximum flexibility in the use of their SSBNs. Second, there is a need in more distant waters to secure the transit and deployment of the shorter-range Yankee SSBNs to within missile range of the United States; this entails breaching enemy antisubmarine barriers and denying the enemy target localizing information by disposing of his ASW aircraft.

This "pro-SSBN" mission, demanding that enemy ASW forces be

countered at sea, is a force-consuming task and an important function of Soviet submarine and surface forces. It is seen as one of the primary missions of the *Kiev* antisubmarine cruiser and the post-1966, large antisubmarine ships.

Destruction of Enemy Naval Forces

The two major elements involved in the mission to destroy enemy naval forces are (1) countering the enemy's sea-based strategic nuclear strike systems, and (2) denying the projection of tactical military force by aircraft carrier and by amphibious assault groups.

The defense of the Soviet Union against strategic attack is probably almost as important as the Soviet Navy's own strategic mission. Apparently the Soviets feel that they have developed an effective counter to the aircraft carrier—placing primary reliance on synchronized missile attacks by submarine and aircraft, with the missile-armed surface ships playing a lesser role. The problem of countering the U.S. SSBNs and SSNs is surely of a different order, and the Soviets appear to be allocating considerable resources to its solution.

Defense against the projection of tactical force is a traditional Soviet naval mission and remains important. Such operations can range from "defense of the homeland" against enemy landing forces supported by carrier tactical aircraft to the interdiction of enemy, sea-based reinforcement of such places as the Turkish Straits or parts of Norway. The long-range submarine, air, and surface capability that has been developed against the aircraft carrier can also be used against amphibious assault groups. These distant water forces are backed by submarine, air, and surface forces operating within range of shore-based systems and by weapons emplaced ashore.

Support for Ground Force Operations

Support for ground force operations is a traditional, important mission whose scope ranges from providing direct support (tactical and logistic) to the army's advance along maritime axes to executing combined assaults on more distant objectives such as the Baltic and Black Sea exits, parts of the Norwegian coast, and perhaps key offshore islands. Besides the amphibious forces and the naval air force's ground attack aircraft, distant-water surface units (including ships armed with surface-to-surface missiles) are reassigned to this role as they near obsolescence.

Support of ground force operations would also include the ability to deliver nuclear weapons within the combat theater. Many of the older Soviet ballistic and cruise missile submarines, initially designed for a strategic role (that of countering U.S. aircraft carriers), are believed to have been reassigned to this role. These older forces appear well suited to support land force operations because of their relatively limited range. However, if they are to remain on patrol for any extended period of time, the Soviets might well decide that they need to be escorted in order to lessen their vulnerability to Alliance ASW assets, which would most likely be active in the same areas. In fact, the Soviets might attempt to "sanitize" some relatively small operating areas for these submarines.

Command of Contiguous Waters

The general requirement to ensure control of contiguous waters (the home fleet areas) in turn facilitates the direct support of army operations and the free passage of friendly shipping while preventing enemy intrusions against the shore. This is the primary mission of the coastal defense forces, comprising missile-, torpedo-, and gun-armed patrol vessels of various sizes, subchasers, and larger escort ships. Medium-type submarines form part of the team, and these forces operate within range of shore-based air cover. They are supported by coastal missiles and artillery, shore-based ASW and strike aircraft, and an extensive surveillance and command and control system.

Distant-water surface ships are relegated to this contiguous waters role as they become older. In the Baltic and Black seas, the concept of operations appears to involve seizing the exits in order to help retain control and ensure egress. In the north and in the Pacific off Kamchatka, there are no geographic features that facilitate this mission, and the relevant force requirements will tend to merge into the exclusion of enemy forces from the SSBN redoubts.

Interdiction of Enemy Sea Lines of Communication (SLOCs)

Although the interdiction of enemy sea lines of communication (SLOCs) is a traditional mission, its importance has fluctuated with changing perceptions of the nature and duration of a possible East-West war. More recently, the possibility of protracted nuclear conflict or of conventional war has increased the relative importance of this mission. This is viewed in its broadest sense, including the destruction of terminal facilities and assembly areas by air or missile strike and extensive mining to deny the use of surviving port facilities. In terms of quick results, the denial of the West's receiving ports in Europe would seem far more effective than a campaign against the SLOCs themselves. However, although such attacks on SLOCs would appear to be less urgent than some other missions, they would have the great advantage of tying down Western ASW forces and diverting them from posing a threat to the Soviet SSBN strategic reserve. Therefore, although the anti-SLOC mission might not initially be primary, sufficient forces would doubtless be allocated to ensure the diversion of Western ASW forces from areas of primary Soviet concern. The mission would include

SOVIET AMPHIBIOUS AND COASTAL CRAFT

The 4,000-ton Alligator-class tank landing ship (LST) shown above is typical of the modern amphibious fleet being constructed by the Soviet Navy for support of ground force operations and the control of neighboring coastlines. (Courtesy U.S. Navy)

The 800-ton Nanuchka-class missile-armed patrol craft is one of the newest additions to the Soviet fleet of coastal defense boats. Over 600 earlier-design coastal patrol craft have been provided to nineteen different countries and present a substantial potential threat to free use of the seas within 250 miles of shore. (Courtesy U.S. Navy)

minelaying as well as direct attacks on shipping. Every Soviet submarine can carry torpedoes and mines. All major surface vessels and practically all long-range naval aircraft can carry mines.

Protection of Soviet Sea Lines of Communication

Soviet sea lines of communication are primarily envisaged as traversing contiguous waters, and their protection is enhanced by securing command of these waters. Longer-range seaborne assault would raise additional escort requirements, and in the event of war with China, the Soviet Union would also be concerned with protecting her SLOCs with the Far Eastern front.

Wartime Operational Concepts

The assessment of force allocations can benefit from a review of the key concepts that underlie Soviet naval operations.

Area Defense

Fundamental to Soviet naval strategy is the concept of area defense based on two main zones: an inner one, where superiority of force would allow local command of the sea to be secured, and an outer zone, where command would be actively contested. Beyond this outer defense perimeter, naval forces would operate on an encounter basis. The greater part of Soviet naval policy and procurement since the 1920s can be explained in terms of attempts to extend this maritime defense perimeter and, within it, the zone of effective command.

If the four, widely separated fleets of the Soviet Navy are to be ensured the superiority of force necessary to establish command in their respective areas, they must be able to deny the enemy the opportunity to concentrate his force against one fleet; this is most economically achieved by preventing his physical access to the fleet areas. In this defensive respect, Russia is favored by her geography. Three of her main fleet areas comprise semienclosed seas, and access to the Northern Fleet is canalized by ice during much of the year. Only the Pacific Fleet base at Petropavlovsk lacks any geographic advantage of this kind for defensive purposes. Of course, this very "advantage" is a severe liability in the use of the fleet *beyond* the protected waters.

Until 1961, the Soviet Navy's primary concern was to extend the inner zone of effective command to these natural defensive barriers, none of which are under Soviet sovereignty. These would presumably be subject to seizure by Soviet forces in the event of war. The outer zones did not extend very far beyond these geographic constrictions and were primarily seen as areas for interdicting the reinforcement of enemy forces defending these natural barriers.

After 1961, the outer zone was extended to take account of the qualitatively new danger to the Soviet Union posed by the Polaris submarine and the continuing threat from carrier strike aircraft. In the Far East, the maritime defense perimeter was pushed out to the East China Sea and the Pacific. In the West, the outer zones were extended to include the Norwegian and North seas and the Eastern Mediterranean, and the Soviet Navy progressively contested the West's maritime domination of these seas.

When the Delta-class SSBN entered service in 1974, the requirement for effective command of the inner zones in the Northern Fleet area and in the Pacific off Petropavlovsk is likely to have increased, both spatially and qualitatively.

Combined Arms

The principle of an "all arms" approach to maritime defense evolved as much from historical necessity as from proletarian revolutionary doctrine, but this makes it all the more persistent. In the early 1930s, area defense was only practicable within a relatively narrow coastal zone and depended more on coordinated operations by submarines, torpedo boats, and aircraft than on the capabilities of the pre-World War I surface ships. As more and larger ships joined the fleet, tactical concepts were adjusted to include them. The defense perimeter was progressively extended, but the principle of coordinated operations remained. Submarine, aircraft, and shore-based systems were seen as integral parts of the main fleet, the emphasis being on defense in depth and successive coordinated attacks. Moreover, the navy's priority mission to provide support to army operations on land served to accentuate the all-arms approach, which extended beyond the different naval components to include other services.

The same driving principle is very much in evidence today. Examples include: the use of long-range air force aircraft for maritime reconnaissance; the targeting of naval "groupings" by land-based aircraft; the use of merchant fleet for logistic support, and the navy's approach to antisubmarine and antisurface operations.

Warfighting

Soviet concepts of warfighting need to be stressed here because of Western reluctance to think through the full implications of what happens if deterrence fails. The Soviets do not appear to attach a high probability to war with the West in the near future (they certainly do not seek such a war), but they take the long-term possibility seriously enough to plan thoroughly for such a contingency. This, in turn, largely determines their force requirements. Their doctrine defines world war as a fight to the finish between the two social systems. While there continue to be internal arguments about the nature of nuclear war and its possible duration, the

Soviet military fully consider not only the initial and follow-on nuclear exchanges of such a war but also the subsequent phases to the final resolution of the conflict. At the same time, they take full account of other potential threats that might survive, such as the People's Republic of China.

This emphasis on warfighting, which must allow for disruption of supply systems and base facilities, has major implications for the employment or withholding of forces in the initial stage of a war. It also heightens the awareness that war is in large measure a matter of attrition and that victory goes to the side that gives up—or runs out—last. This leads to the Soviet practice of never allowing an enemy force a "free ride" and the continuing use of suboptimal and obsolescent weapons in order to complicate the enemy's problems. It may also explain various aspects of the maritime infrastructure the Soviets are seeking to establish overseas.

Equipment Adaptation

In the practical application of the basic concepts discussed below, the Soviets have to make do with existing assets. A substantial proportion of these were originally intended to operate in scenarios very different from the present ones. Some were designed for different tasks than those they now discharge. Many derive from building programs that were cancelled because of technological obsolescence before the first units entered service. Even when the design concept remains valid, competing priorities mean shortages in certain key categories. In reviewing the operational evidence, therefore, one must remember that it reflects considerable adaptation and getting along with less than optimal assets.

Antiship Warfare

The basic Soviet concept of operations against surface ships relies on coordinated attacks (synchronized, if possible) by as many different types of systems as allowed by the geographic scenario. The primary Soviet task is to counter Western aircraft carriers in waters beyond the inner defense zone. The two requirements of target location and strike are handled somewhat differently in each of the three main types of scenarios: continuous company, encounter, and distant targeting.

Continuous company describes the situation in the Eastern Mediterranean, which is an outer defense zone. When carriers operate in this area, primary responsibility for providing target location data lies with the "tattletale" surface units that remain in close company. The main strike arm is now the cruise missile–armed submarines. While some contribution of aircraft is hoped for, it is recognized that they lack the rapid response time essential to this scenario. After flying out of Russian bases, they must skirt or overfly portions of the NATO air defense system. The continuous scenario allows the use of the nonnuclear Juliett as well as the nuclear-propelled Charlie (and the occasional Echo) submarines. This provides a mix of missile range and flight profiles. Large missile ships may also contribute to this mix, and the "tattletale" surface units are now being fitted with their own horizon-range SSM system. The surface ships can also provide a secure communications link with headquarters ashore and local command and control.

The encounter scenario can be illustrated by a case where carriers deploy from U.S. East Coast ports to launch strikes against the U.S.S.R. from, say, the Iceland-Faeroes Gap. In such a circumstance, target location data would be provided primarily by forward pickets (intelligence ships) and by aircraft and satellite surveillance. The force would be harassed by air and submarine attacks en route, possibly including the use of medium-range SLBMs in the tactical mode, but the main engagement would take place in the encounter zone. Here the force would be subjected to successive, heavy, and synchronized attacks by air- and submarine-launched missiles at the same time as it was transiting a torpedo-attack submarine barrier.

If the carriers were known to be configured for nuclear strike against Russia, the encounter zone would be located to the west of the probable launch area. If they were known to be configured for operations in the Norwegian Sea (e.g., in support of counter-SSBN operations or flank reinforcement), the main encounter would more likely be north of the Gap in order to enhance the role of shore-based systems. Surface ships armed with surface-to-surface missiles would probably be used in the latter case if available but would be held back in the former. The large antisubmarine ships would probably be deployed forward to hinder attempts by Western ASW forces to prevent the missile-armed submarines from launching their weapons. Variations of this operational concept would apply in the Pacific and in the Western Mediterranean.

The distant targeting scenario covers those carriers that do not immediately threaten the Soviet Union in the event of war but that could contribute to the U.S. strategic reserve and thus affect the subsequent course of events. In this less well-defined scenario, target location information would be provided by air and satellite reconnaissance. It appears that the strike component would be carried out by the same systems intended to bring down fire on U.S. SSBNs once they had been located. Two methods are believed to be envisaged, both of which rely on terminally-guided ballistic missiles: land-based systems using IRBMs and possibly ICBMs; and sea-based systems using 500-mile missiles carried by submarines that would maintain station within range of their targets. The present status of this concept is not clear. The land-based capability against surface forces was explicitly claimed in 1972. At that time, the Soviets were actively developing a new tactical SLBM, the SS-N-13. The program appears to have been shelved in 1974. We do not know if the equivalent capability exists in some other missile such as the SS-N-6.

The first two scenarios depend heavily on the concept of a defense perimeter and area defense. All three are applicable to high-value surface targets other than carriers.

Antisubmarine Warfare

Part of the difference between U.S. and Soviet concepts of antisubmarine warfare derives from the early lead established by the West in submarine silencing and passive-acoustic methods of detection. But a more fundamental distinction is that Soviet concepts stress area defense of a static offshore zone, whereas Western concepts were initially developed for defending moving formations such as convoys and task groups.

The evolution of Soviet ASW capability largely matches the seaward extension of the antisubmarine defense zone, although it continues to reflect the ideas developed when the zone was comparatively narrow. At that initial stage, shore-based systems played the major role, with the various sensors operated by the Observation and Communications Service providing detection data for shore-based helicopters carrying sonobuoys. It was still an all-arms solution: offshore defense units were vectored to join the hunt and prosecute enemy contacts; and a portion of the torpedo-armed diesel submarines (originally intended to provide defense in depth against surface groups) was switched to the antisubmarine role. All these operations were controlled by naval headquarters ashore, and procedures were developed for coordinating the different types of units.

When it became necessary to extend the seaward limit of these defense zones beyond the effective radius of shore-based helicopters, it was natural to think of a seagoing platform—hence, the helicopter-carrying antisubmarine cruiser. Meanwhile, the elimination of large surface ships from the counter-carrier mission released destroyers for antisubmarine area defense, and methods of coordinating the various airborne, surface, subsurface, and land-based systems continued to evolve. In due course, submarines were teamed directly with one or more large antisubmarine ships operating in company.

While the concept of an antisubmarine defense zone is most effective in waters that are directly contiguous to one's coastline, similar procedures have been adopted in the outer zones, including the Eastern Mediterranean. However, area defense as such is not possible in such areas; there, greater emphasis is placed on various types of detection barriers and on a Soviet variant of hunter-killer groups involving surface ships and submarines working together.

This concept has little relevance to the problem of detecting Western SSBNs outside these areas, since the Soviets lack any real open ocean ASW capability—although they seek to develop one. Meanwhile, there have been numerous reports over the last ten years that the Soviets are attempting to trail Western SSBNs with their nuclear submarines.

Long-Range Interdiction

The Russian Navy has a tradition of long-range interdiction, as exemplified by the innovative torpedo-boat attack that largely destroyed the Turkish Fleet in port in 1887 and by the development of the self-propelled mine for penetrating harbor defenses. The Soviet concept of operations in the 1930s envisioned air strikes at enemy naval bases and minelaying off their ports. In the late 1940s, the submarine torpedo was designated as a delivery vehicle for nuclear weapons directed at the U.S. mainland. Foxtrot submarines, for instance, were deployed to U.S. waters at the outbreak of the Cuban crisis. It is likely that some Soviet naval forces will continue to be assigned to long-range interdiction in support of naval missions.

Soviet Naval Force Levels, Composition, and Fleet Allocations

Submarine Forces

While the present status of the nuclear submarine force is reasonably clear, the future is obscure. By the beginning of 1978, the Soviet Navy had taken delivery of more than 155 nuclear submarines, over 100 of which are still less than ten years old. Assuming that the Soviets will continue to allocate reactors to submarine propulsion at the present rate and that the submarines have a twenty-year maximum useful life, their submarine force should stabilize at about 200 nuclear submarines by 1990 (250, if the submarines last twenty-five years).[1]

During the last ten years almost two-thirds of new nuclear construction has been configured as SSBN, but eventually this rate should decline considerably in accordance with SALT limitations. There have been recent references to the construction of an even larger SSBN (Typhoon) comparable to Trident, and it might well be built at a lower rate. In any case, it is the projected size of the SSBN force—rather than what programs continue—that remains crucial. Once that size has been achieved, the general-purpose SSBN force can begin to build up.

There are considerable uncertainties about the future composition and characteristics of the SSN force. A family of third-generation submarines should have begun delivery in 1978, but it now appears that this schedule will not be achieved, possibly reflecting development problems. Two prototypes, the Alpha SSN and the Papa SSGN, have been under test for five to seven years. The new generation is expected to incorporate a radical new type of propulsion as well as advances in weapons and sensor systems, with particular emphasis on antisubmarine warfare. These third-generation units may begin delivery in 1980 or soon thereafter. This surmise is supported by reports of a greater than 50 percent increase in Soviet submarine-building ways since 1967.

Ballistic Missile Submarines. There are about sixty-two modern SSBNs in the Soviet fleet, plus eight first generation units. The twenty-eight Delta boats can strike at North America from home waters if desired, while the thirty-four older Yankee boats would need to leave home waters and transit unfriendly waters to launch missiles at the United States.[2] About five Yankees are permanently deployed forward and may be tasked to strike at time-critical targets within the United States. However, there seems to be a good possibility that these Yankees may be given a theater nuclear role once the desired number of strategic submarines has been achieved and the older submarines have been retired.

The older Hotel submarine was the world's first SSBN. Its first generation nuclear hull-propulsion unit was not a successful design. Since this class is nearing obsolescence, it is probably not worth configuring the Hotel as an SSN, as was done with the equally old Echo I. This class has already been reassigned to theater targets within the European area—in support of land force operations. There are also twenty-two diesel-powered Golf SSBs, which are now fifteen to nineteen years old and are also assigned targets within the European area. Six Golf II's were redeployed to the Baltic in 1977 and may also have such a theater nuclear role.

Cruise Missile Submarines. Nuclear propulsion was initially reserved for the strategic delivery mission, and the anticarrier SS-N-3 cruise missiles were intended to go to sea aboard two classes of diesel submarines—the Longbin (a conversion of the Whiskey-class submarine) and the Juliett (a new construction program). The qualitative change in the carrier threat, however, resulted in the cancellation of the diesel programs and the reallocation of nuclear hull-propulsion units to the counter-carrier mission. The SS-N-3 systems procured for the diesel Juliett were therefore used by the nuclear Echo I and II programs. The SS-N-3 had many drawbacks, including the missile's long time of flight, the need to launch from the surface, the dependence on external target location data, and midcourse guidance. The Charlie SSGN was intended to overcome these deficiencies with the shorter-range launched while submerged SS-N-7 (target data were provided by the submarine's own sensors).

Sixteen Juliett submarines were constructed and are used in the continuous company scenario of the Mediterranean, where their slow submerged transit speed is less of a handicap. The twenty-nine Echo II's are mainly deployed in the North Atlantic and Pacific, where transit speed to

MODERN SOVIET SUBMARINES

The modern Yankee-class nuclear-powered ballistic missile submarines form roughly half of the Soviet's current SSBN fleet. Production of the thirty-four units of this type did not begin until after the U.S. Polaris fleet of forty-one SSBNs had all become operational. (Courtesy U.S. Navy)

This Charlie-class nuclear-powered cruise missile submarine (SSGN) was photographed in the South China Sea in April 1974. Its primary mission may be in the anticarrier role. About fifteen of these SSGNs were operational with the Soviet Fleet in 1978. (Courtesy U.S. Navy)

the encounter zone can be critical. The SS-N-3 is now being superseded by the supersonic SS-N-12, which will improve the capability of both these classes. Meanwhile, the seven Longbin submarines are confined to trials and training, and the Echo I class has been converted to SSN.

At least eight Charlie I's and six Charlie II's have been built in the past 10 years. It seems likely that they were originally programmed to be built at a higher rate, but the shift in mission priorities back to strategic strike preempted the nuclear propulsion systems. In addition to the SS-N-7 SSN systems, the Charlie II's now carry the SS-N-15 missile-flight ASW torpedo systems, which could substantially improve their antisubmarine capability.

Attack Submarines. The thirteen November-class and five Echo-class nuclear-powered SSNs are essentially the same type. These first-generation submarines are now fifteen to nineteen years old, and two have already been placed in reserve. They remain effective in the antishipping role and certain aspects of area defense, but their noisiness and relatively low speed restrict their usefulness in the ASW role and against heavily defended surface forces. The second-generation Victor SSN is a greatly improved submarine whose role is primarily antisubmarine warfare, although its high speed and relative silence make it an effective antisurface system. About ten Victor I's and ten Victor II's have been built during the past ten years. Still in production, the Victor II carries the SS-N-15 missile-flight ASW torpedo and the SS-N-16 missile-flight depth charge.

There are about 145 submarines in the nonnuclear attack force, of which some 65 are over twenty years old and only 12 are younger than 10. The Soviets do not appear to intend to keep a large force of nonnuclear submarines. It would require a significant near-term building rate of around ten to twelve units a year to maintain this force at about 120 boats, and there are no firm indications of such a program.

The first-generation diesel units are not only obsolescent but reflect early postwar design and material limitations. The seventeen larger-type Zulus continue to be used in the Mediterranean, but they are almost past this task. The forty medium-type Whiskeys are probably mainly employed in the general area defense and training role, although this class does have some capability to operate in the mid-Atlantic against convoys.

The second-generation units represent a substantial advance. The fifty-five large-type Foxtrots, which comprise the bulk of the operational force, have proved very successful and can be found in the Mediterranean, the Atlantic, the Indian Ocean, and even the Caribbean in the antisubmarine and torpedo-attack roles. The twelve smaller Romeos have comparable performance and some capability for mid-Atlantic operations. However, their primary role is probably antisubmarine area defense.

Allocation of Soviet Naval Forces 97

TABLE 4-1
SOVIET SUBMARINE FORCES

		Fleet Allocations Current/Obsolescent*				
Type & Designation		Northern	Baltic	Black	Pacific	Total
Ballistic Missile Submarines (TOT)		(42/14)	(0/6)	(0/0)	(20/8)	(62/28)
DELTA	SSBN	19/0	0/0	0/0	9/0	28/0+
YANKEE	SSBN	23/0	0/0	0/0	11/0	34/0
HOTEL	SSBN	0/6	0/0	0/0	0/2	0/8
GOLF	SSB	0/8	0/6	0/0	0/6	0/20
Cruise Missile Submarines (TOT)		(36/1)	(0/2)	(0/2)	(22/2)	(58/7)
CHARLIE	SSGN	10/0	0/0	0/0	4/0	14/0+
ECHO II	SSGN	14/0	0/0	0/0	14/0	28/0
JULIETT/LONGBIN	SSG	12/1	0/2	0/2	4/2	16/7
Attack Submarines (TOT)		(56/40)	(8/16)	2/21)	(21/23)	(87/100)
VICTOR	SSN	14/0	0/0	0/0	6/0	20/0+
NOVEMBER/ECHO I	SSN	0/7	0/0	0/0	0/9	0/16
TANGO	SS	5/0	2/0	1/0	0/0	8/0+
FOXTROT/ZULU	SS	36/12	5/1	0/0	14/4	55/17
B-Class/R,W,Q-Class	SS	1/21	1/15	1/21	1/10	4/67
Total Submarines		135/57	8/24	2/23	64/28	207/135
Submarine Support Ships (TOT)		(12)	(3)	(8)	(15)	(38)

*Obsolescent if average class age equals or exceeds 20 years by 1980
(Underlining indicates still being built)

Only about eight units of the third-generation Tango have been delivered in the past five years. This is so atypical of normal Soviet shipbuilding practice that some explanation is needed. Three hypotheses come to mind: this represents "trickle delivery" from a cancelled program (such as the Juliett); there has been some delay in the development of its intended weapon system; or there are problems with its design, possibly involving a new type of closed cycle propulsion. Whatever the reason, it seems likely that this submarine will be used primarily in the ASW role in waters that are either relatively constricted or close to home.

Submarine Fleet Allocations

Table 4-1 presents all the various classes of submarines currently in the Soviet inventory, showing their approximate distribution by home fleet and indicating which of these total forces are modern and which are approaching obsolescence. More information on their size (displacement), dates of construction, and major onboard weapon systems is provided in the Appendix.

Table 4-1 shows that most of the Soviets' contemporary submarines—

including virtually all of their strategic nuclear delivery submarines (SSBNs)—are assigned to the Northern and Pacific fleets, with roughly twice as many deployed to the Atlantic as to the Pacific. The Baltic and Black Sea fleets include relatively few submarines, and most of these are now reaching obsolescence. Over 130 of the total Soviet fleet of almost 350 submarines are approaching the age of mandatory retirement. As mentioned earlier, the current Soviet submarine construction program appears consistent with a long-range goal of retaining a fleet of from 200 to 250 submarines.

Table 4-1 also indicates that among the more modern submarines, the ballistic and cruise missile boats outnumber the attack submarines by a ratio of approximately three to two. Moreover, the Soviet Navy still operates only about thirty-three nuclear-powered attack submarines, of which thirteen are obsolescent. Almost two-thirds of those, including all the Victors, serve the Atlantic and Mediterranean from the Northern Fleet.

Major Surface Combatants

The Soviet Navy has about 260 surface combatants displacing 1,000 tons and capable of open ocean operations. About 120 of these are in the 1,000 to 1,200-ton range and were designed primarily for the inner defense zones. Since these smaller ships deploy regularly to the Mediterranean and the Indian Ocean, they have been included in this category. Assuming current building rates are maintained and allowing twenty-five to thirty years of useful life, there will be about 130 units of 3,000 tons or more in 1990 compared to about 133 today. This part of the force would stabilize at about 160 units by the year 2000, comprising 10 carrier-sized, 50 cruiser-sized, and 100 destroyer-sized units.

ASW Aviation Ships. Although probably designed to operate in the inner defense zone, the two Moskva-class helicopter ships appear at present to be tied to the ASW role in the outer defense zone of the Mediterranean. The new Kiev class clearly has a more ambitious design. Within the Soviet context, its characteristics suggest a ship intended to carry out ASW operations in the face of an air and surface threat and without dependence on shore-based support—possibly after a nuclear exchange, for instance. Called a large antisubmarine cruiser by the Soviets, its design role is generally assessed to be protection of Soviet SSBNs, although obviously it can evolve a more general-purpose capability as suitable aircraft become available. Its present building rate is about one unit every three years.

Large Antisubmarine Ships. At present, three different categories of ships carry the Soviet designation of large antisubmarine ships: new cruisers and new and converted destroyers, with two classes within each category. The capability of the cruiser-sized ships is far greater than that of the smaller ships. Kresta I was the earlier design, appearing first in 1967, followed by Kara in 1972. The Kresta II married the weapon systems from the cancelled Moskva program to the original Kresta hull-propulsion unit. Both classes carry the SS-N-14 antisubmarine missile system and the SA-N-3 system, which has some antisurface capability. It appears that the Soviets intend to continue construction of these cruisers at a rate of about one each per year.

The older of the two destroyer-sized new construction ships is the Kashin. It was originally designated as a destroyer and designed to operate against aircraft carriers in company with the older Kynda missile cruiser. The nineteen Kashins carry two SA-N-1 SAM systems and 1962-vintage ASW equipment, although some are being modified to carry variable-depth sonar and horizon-range SSMs. The second class, Krivak, supplanted the Kashin in 1970, and the delivery rate has recently risen to four per year. The Krivak carries the SS-N-14 ASW missile, but its air defense missile systems are limited to the short-range point defense SA-N-4's.

Of the two converted destroyer classes, the eight SAM Kotlins were fitted with ASW systems from the cancelled Kynda program, and their ASW capability is less than that of Kashin. The later conversion, Kanin, married systems from the cancelled Kresta I program to eight older Krupny hull-propulsion units and, in terms of antisubmarine warfare, is probably comparable to Kashin. Both classes lack the dual purpose, 76-millimeter guns and the second SAM carried by Kashin. These ships are eighteen to twenty-three years old, but they will have gained a new lease on life in the process of their two-year conversion.

The primary role of these six classes is antisubmarine warfare, although all have a general-purpose capability. In ASW work, they are expected to operate in small groups (possibly one cruiser and two destroyers, together with submarines) as hunter-killers in the antisubmarine defense zones. Although the destroyer-sized units have an autonomous ASW capability, the Krivak appears more effective when operating as part of a team in company with the cruiser-sized ships or the helicopter carriers. This ASW role includes the mission to protect the accompanying submarines—including the defense of cruise missile submarines when they surface to fire at their target. Some Kashins operating in the Mediterranean have been fitted with horizon-range SSNs to assist in this task and to enhance their combat capability when deployed in close company with carriers as "tattletales."

Surface Missile Ships. The major components of the surface missile type of ship are the eight Kynda and Kresta I cruisers that carry 250-mile SSMs and were originally designated as "missile cruisers" by the Soviets. Each of the four Kyndas carries two SS-N-3 tubes and was designed to operate within range of shore-based air support. The four Kresta I's replaced the second SSM system with a second SAM and a shipboard helicopter, which provides them with autonomous target location and mid-course missile guidance. It is presumed that the supersonic SS-N-12 system will be fitted to these ships, which are only ten to fifteen years old.

The Soviets include these two classes within the general category of large antisubmarine ships, their ASW capabilities being comparable to those of the converted SAM Kotlin and Kanin destroyers, respectively. However, their primary role continues to be against the carrier. During the 1971 Indo-Pakistani war, one of each class (together with missile-armed submarines) was deployed to the Indian Ocean to counter the U.S. nuclear-powered carrier *Enterprise*. Their effectiveness as general-purpose units is limited by the relatively small number of missiles they carry. They do, however, have a continuing role as command ships, and they can be deployed effectively during peacetime for "presence" purposes.

The third component of this type, the destroyer-sized Kildin, is of quite a different order. This class, composed of four ships, is being converted to carry four horizon-range missiles and 76-millimeter guns, giving these twenty-year-old ships a new lease on life. They, too, are designated as large antisubmarine ships, and their primary role may be comparable to the SAM-fitted Kashin (i.e., carrier "tattletale" and support of cruise missile submarines).

A fourth class of antiship combatants is the Nanuchka missile patrol vessel, which, although it is considerably smaller, must be included because it has been deployed to distant areas and seems to have been designed to operate beyond the limits of the inner defense zone. This 800-ton vessel carries six 90-mile missiles as well as point defense antiaircraft missiles. Although it needs external target location data to exploit the missiles' full range, the Nanuchka provides a potent system for interdicting enemy operations in constricted waters such as transit through straits or the passage of reinforcements.

Old Gun Ships. The Soviet Fleet still includes about sixty twenty- to twenty-six-year-old gun ships. Most of them are based largely on prewar design, and they reflect the contemporary material shortages and production limitations of the early postwar years. The largest of these are the eleven Sverdlov cruisers still in service. Two of these have been converted to command ships so far, sacrificing part of their 152-millimeter gun armament in the process. These will continue to have a distant-water role for several more years, while the remainder of the class appears to be assigned to defending the inner zone and providing gunfire support to operations on land.

In addition, there are about thirty-eight Skory- and Kotlin-class

Allocation of Soviet Naval Forces

destroyers still in service, both carrying 130-millimeter guns. The slightly younger Kotlin is the more effective ship, and its ASW capability was upgraded during the 1960s. Both classes appear to have been relegated to the inner defense zone, although the Kotlin retains the capability for distant-water operations in company with SAM-armed units. Finally, there are probably about ten of the smaller Rigas still in service. They carry 100-millimeter guns but have a very modest ASW capability and are of limited value, even within the inner defense zone.

Small Antisubmarine Ships. There are about 110 of these 1,000-ton ships comprising some 67 Mirka/Petyas, delivered between 1962 and 1969, and 30 Grishas, which began delivery in 1970 and continue to be built at about 5 per year. They have deployed regularly to the Mediterranean and, more recently, to the Indian Ocean. The older ships carry 76-millimeter guns, while the Grishas carry 57-millimeter guns. They have a general-purpose capability in the area defense role, although they are somewhat small for open ocean operations. Three units of a new class of "escort" have been delivered over the last three years, and another new class is expected within the next five years with improved open ocean capability.

Major Surface Combatant Fleet Allocations

Table 4-2 depicts the total inventory of major Soviet surface combatants and their allocation among the four Soviet fleets. As in Table 4-1, those classes of ships that are still under construction are underlined. From a numerical standpoint, the Black Sea Fleet is the largest—primarily because it contains the largest number of small ASW ships and the second largest number of old gun ships, which might prove useful in support of local ground force operations. It also contains a sizable number of large ASW ships for operations in the Mediterranean. The Northern and Pacific surface fleets are roughly the same size, with the Northern Fleet having a somewhat higher fraction of newer ships—including the *Kiev*.

It is of interest that the Baltic Fleet contains relatively few support ships and that the Northern Fleet has a somewhat larger number of support ships than the Pacific Fleet, probably making it substantially more capable of distant open ocean operations under wartime conditions. However, all four fleets contain major combatants that are capable of exercising a variety of naval roles under peacetime, crisis, or limited war situations. These surface combatants have been used extensively to "show the flag" in the seven seas.

Other Surface Combatants

Minor Surface Combatants. The Soviet Navy has nearly 1,050 minor surface combatants of less than 1,000 tons. About 300 of these are mine

TABLE 4-2
MAJOR SOVIET SURFACE COMBATANTS

Fleet Allocations
Current/Obsolescent*

Type & Designation		Northern	Baltic	Black	Pacific	Total
ASW Aviation Ships (TOT)		(1/0)	(0/0)	(2/0)	(0/0)	(3/0)
KIEV	CVG	1/0	0/0	0/0	0/0	1/0+
MOSKVA	CHG	0/0	0/0	2/0	0/0	2/0
Large ASW Ships (TOT)		(22/0)	(10/0)	(20/0)	(16/0)	(68/0)
KARA, KRESTA II	CLG	7/0	1/0	6/0	2/0	16/0+
KRIVAK	DDG	6/0	3/0	4/0	4/0	17/0
KASHIN, KANIN, KOTLIN	DDG	9/0	6/0	10/0	10/0	35/0
Surface Missile Ships (TOT)		(2/0)	(1/0)	(5/0)	(4/0)	(12/0)
KRESTA I, KYNDA	CLGM	2/0	1/0	2/0	3/0	8/0
KILDIN	DD	0/0	0/0	3/0	1/0	4/0
Old Gun Ships (TOT)		(0/9)	(0/14)	(0/17)	(0/19)	(0/59)
SVERDLOV	CLG	0/1	0/1	0/5	0/4	0/11
KOTLIN, SKORY	DD	0/8	0/9	0/9	0/12	0/38
RIGA	FF	0/0	0/4	0/3	0/3	0/10
Small ASW Ships (TOT)		(22/0)	(31/0)	(41/0)	(25/0)	(119/0)
New, GRISHA, MIRKA, PETYA	FF	20/0	25/0	34/0	19/0	98/0+
NANUCHKA	PM	2/0	6/0	7/0	6/0	21/0+
Total Major Surface Combatants		47/9	42/14	68/17	45/19	202/59
Fleet Support Ships (TOT)		(40)	(6)	(29)	(33)	(108)

*Obsolescent if average class age equals or exceeds 25 years by 1980
(Underlining indicates still being built)

warfare units, including about 200 oceangoing sweepers and 100 coastal minesweepers. There are about 140 missile-armed craft that carry four horizon-range missiles, about 65 small antisubmarine ships, and over 140 subchasers. There are also about 210 gun-equipped patrol craft, most of which are torpedo-armed, including some 90 hydrofoils that carry four torpedoes each.

These forces are designed to operate in coastal waters within range of shore support, defending the offshore zone and assisting in securing command of the home fleet areas. The missile- and torpedo-armed units would probably also work beyond the line of battle, attacking enemy ships in their own coastal waters. These units tend to be "counted" as part of the Soviet Navy by those analysts who wish to emphasize its numerical strength, despite the fact that their size severely restricts the method and location of their use. Moreover, a large fraction of these small craft are obsolete and are slowly being dropped from inventory.

Amphibious Assault Ships. There are about 85 oceangoing landing ships in the Soviet inventory, plus about 180 smaller landing craft. The bulk of this force comprises 60 Polnocnys, which can lift 350 tons, and about 14 Alligators, which can lift about 1,700 tons. Polnocny is no longer being built, but its follow-on class, Ropuchka, is almost as large as Alligator, and about 10 have been delivered to date. There are reports that a new class of Landing Ship Dock is now being built.

This amphibious lift is commensurate with the 12,000-man size of the naval infantry, which is trained as the seaborne assault component of a combined arms attack on heavily defended coasts such as are found on NATO's flanks and the exits to the semienclosed seas. Operations along the Northern coast of Norway, the Danish Straits, the Bosporus, or even along contested exits from the Sea of Japan would appear to be quite plausible. How much farther from home these amphibious forces might go is subject to considerable speculation. If they could acquire suitable land bases for friendly air cover, they have the potential to operate anywhere along the North Sea, the Eastern Mediterranean littorals, and possibly along the Yellow Sea. Whether they will take part in intervention operations in Third World countries cannot be judged with certainty. Nonetheless, they have already been used to transport "proxy forces" to assist the cause of friendly client-states. Their major vulnerability is to air actions if they stray far from friendly land-based fighter air cover.

Other Surface Combatant Fleet Allocations

Table 4-3 displays the numbers and fleet allocations for these smaller naval vessels used for coastal patrol, amphibious operations, and mine warfare. The Baltic Fleet has the largest numbers of mine warfare ships and motor torpedo boats. The Northern Fleet, on the other hand, has noticeably fewer than the other three—possibly because of its isolated location on the Kola Peninsula and its inhospitable weather and sea conditions for small boat operations.

Their extensive experience with all of these classes of smaller coastal craft has put the Soviets in good stead when it comes to sales to their allies and client-states. As discussed elsewhere, there are literally hundreds more of these effective small ships in the inventories of various littoral client-states. In several of the patrol craft categories, there are almost no equivalent designs in the Western world—and none in the U.S. force structure. A partial listing of recent Soviet small craft transfers is provided in Table 4-4.

Allocation of Naval Ship Construction

Soviet ship construction rates appear to have been quite stable over the past several years, with new classes being introduced to replace the older

TABLE 4-3
OTHER SOVIET SURFACE COMBATANTS

Fleet Allocations
Current/Obsolescent*

Type & Designation		Northern	Baltic	Black	Pacific	Total
Mine Warfare Ships (TOT)		(35/25)	(50/40)	(35/35)	(40/30)	(160/130)
NATYA, YURKA/T-58,						
T-43	MSF	15/25	20/40	15/25	20/30	70/120+
ZENYA/VANYA	MSC	20/0	30/0	20/10	20/10	90/10+
Small Missile Patrol Craft (TOT)		(25/0)	(36/0)	(36/0)	(25/0)	(122/0)
SARANCHA, OSA	PMH, PM					
Small Torpedo Patrol Craft (TOT)		(30/15)	(51/15)	(44/10)	(25/15)	(150/55)
New, POTI, STENKA,						
PCHELA/SO-1	PC, PCH					
Small Gun Patrol Craft (TOT)		(15/5)	(35/20)	(20/15)	(20/20)	(90/60)
TURYA, SHERSHEN/						
P-6,-8,-10	PT					
Total Small Patrol Craft		70/20	122/35	100/25	70/35	362/115
Amphibious Assault Ships (TOT)		(22/0)	(21/0)	(23/0)	(18/0)	(84/0)
ALLIGATOR, ROPUCHKA,						
POLNOCNY	LST, LSM					
Landing Craft (TOT)		(25/0)	(50/0)	(50/0)	(55/0)	(180/0)
VYDRA, MP-10/						
MP-2,-4,-6	LCT, LCM					
Total Amphibious Support Ships		47/0	71/0	73/0	73/0	264/0
Total Other Surface Combatants		152/45	243/75	208/60	183/65	786/245

*Obsolescent if average class age equals or exceeds 20 years by 1980
(Underlining indicates still being built)

ones at a reasonably steady pace, at least in comparison to Western shipbuilding rates. Table 4-5 summarizes current allocations of Soviet naval construction and indicates the "steady state" fleet size that would result from an indefinite continuation of these building rates—assuming useful ship life equivalent to that of Western counterparts.

There appears to be little pressure within the Soviet military system for the retirement of ships and submarines despite their advancing age. In part, this is probably due to the relatively low cost of Soviet military manpower. In comparison, the large recent reductions in U.S. fleet size were produced primarily by the rapidly rising operating (i.e. manpower) costs of obsolescent U.S. ships. Hence, Table 4-5 differentiates between the current modern Soviet fleet and those units which appear to be rapidly approaching obsolescence. The projected future size of the Soviet Navy is roughly equivalent to its current nonobsolete assets.

TABLE 4-4
SOVIET SMALL CRAFT TRANSFERS (Thru 1975)

Country	KRONSTADT	OSA	KOMAR	SHERSHEN	P-6,P-8,P-10	P-4	Tot.
Algeria		3	6		12	12	33
Bulgaria	2	3		4		8	17
China	24	17	10		80	70	201
Cuba	18	2	18		12	12	62
Cyprus						6	6
East Germany		12		15	18		45
Egypt		12	6	6	24		48
Guinea					4		4
India		8					8
Indonesia	14		12		14		40
Iraq		5			12		17
Nigeria					3		3
North Korea			6			40	46
Poland	8	12			20		40
Romania	3	5				13	21
Somalia					2	4	6
Syria		5	3			17	25
North Vietnam					6		6
Yugoslavia	—	10	—	13	—	—	23
TOTAL	69	94	61	38	207	182	651

This rudimentary analysis suggests that the Soviets intend to maintain something as large as a "775-ship navy" consisting of one-third submarines and two-thirds surface vessels over 1,000 tons. This is supported by a building program of over 30 ships per year. No attempt has been made to estimate the equivalent size of their coastal navy of smaller vessels because it has essentially no counterpart in the U.S. Navy.

Soviet Naval Aviation Forces

The Soviet Naval Air Force comprises some 1,200 aircraft. About 365 of these are configured for intermediate-range maritime strike, being supported by another 200 aircraft configured as tankers, reconnaissance, and electronic warfare aircraft. There are about 170 fixed-wing open ocean ASW units and 270 ASW helicopters. Long-range aviation assets are used to support the naval mission with reconnaissance and tanker aircraft, as are those of the air defense force (PVO Strany) in the form of surveillance satellites and the Moss air control intercept aircraft.

Bomber and Support Aircraft. About 50 Backfires have been delivered to the navy, which is currently taking one-half of total production. This supersonic variable-geometry aircraft, the strike version of which carries the AS-4 ASM system, is entering service at the rate of about 15 units a year.

TABLE 4-5

IMPLICATIONS OF CURRENT SOVIET NAVAL CONSTRUCTION

Component & Class	Present Fleet Current/Obsolete	Yearly Production	Estimated Life (yrs)	Class Size	Future Fleet Size
Submarines	207/135				250
DELTA/CHARLIE/VICTOR		10	20	200	
TANGO		2	25	50	
Aviation Ships	3/0				10
KIEV		1/3	30	10	
Large ASW Ships	80/59				155
KARA		1	30	30	
KRESTA II		1	25	25	
KRIVAK		4	25	100	
Small ASW Ships	119/0				120
GRISHA		3	20	60	
NANUCHKA (or new class)		3	20	60	
Amphibious Ships	84/0				90?
ALLIGATOR		1?	30	30?	
ROPUCHKA		2?	30	60?	
Support Ships	146/0				150?
MISCELLANEOUS		5?	30	150?	
TOTALS	630/194 (824)	32+?			775?

The Backfire doubles the range at which Western surface forces can be attacked and is expected to replace Badger as the backbone of the Soviet Naval Air Force (SNAF), appearing in several configurations. There are also about 275 ASM-armed Badgers, the majority carrying the 175-nautical-mile AS-5 (Kelt) system, and about 40 Blinder aircraft, which carry free-fall bombs. These latter aircraft forces are declining, the Blinder at a much higher rate.

About three-fourths of these strike and support forces are deployed against NATO forces in the three Western fleets, the remaining one-fourth being stationed in the Pacific. The primary task of the strike units is to attack carrier task forces; the initial deployment of Backfire to the Northern and Black Sea fleets underlines this priority. However, some units could be tasked to attack other surface forces and the sea lines of communication, the latter to include attacks on commercial port facilities and naval installations. The more modern ASM systems are capable of delivering nuclear or conventional ordnance with considerable accuracy from substantial standoff ranges.

Antisubmarine Aircraft and Helicopters. The land-based component of the open ocean ASW capability comprises about 15 Bear E's, 55 Mays

Allocation of Soviet Naval Forces

(whose patrol range is comparable to the American P-3 Orion) and about 100 Mails. Production of these aircraft has stopped, and new types are expected in due course. Besides these patrol aircraft, there are also some 60 Hormone A ASW helicopters carried aboard the ASW aviation ships and the cruiser-sized large antisubmarine ships. There are about another 200 ASW helicopters operating from facilities ashore in the area defense role, covering the offshore zone. Given the length of Russia's coastline, this number is not excessive.

Ship-Based Fighters. About thirty Forger jet VSTOL fighters are now in service, some ten of which are at sea aboard *Kiev*. The primary roles of this aircraft have yet to be clarified, but they represent a new capability that appears likely to become widely adopted. They should be capable of both air-to-air and air-to-ground combat.

Close Support Aircraft (Land-Based). The Baltic Fleet has recently been provided with a force of about forty Fitter C's, an aircraft used by frontal aviation in the close support role. It is not clear whether this allocation reflects the particular circumstances of the Central Front or whether it will be repeated in the other fleet areas. In any case, this naval subordination would enhance the capability of amphibious forces in the Baltic to seize the Danish Straits. It could possibly denote an interest in more distant targets such as the southern tip of Norway, where seizure would help in securing the exits and in the battle for command of the Norwegian Sea.

Naval Aviation Fleet Allocation

The allocation of naval aircraft among the four major Soviet fleets is shown in Table 4-6. In the case of their 200-odd, shore-based ASW helicopters, no estimate of allocations has been found. Of primary interest, of course, is the distribution of their long-range bombers, most of which carry antiship standoff missiles, and their ASW patrol aircraft.

In terms of both numbers and capabilities, the bomber fleet assigned to the Northern Fleet is both the largest and the most capable, especially since the recent introduction of the new Backfire. As yet, none of these aircraft has been deployed in the Pacific Fleet, although the Black Sea Fleet already has a substantial number for operations over NATO's Southern Flank. The Baltic Fleet, quite naturally, has the smallest number of long-range aircraft because of its primary orientation toward that enclosed sea. It has been provided the Fitter C instead.

The Northern Fleet also has a much larger complement of ASW patrol aircraft than does the Pacific Fleet. Although aircraft can be redeployed to different forward-operating bases, it appears that Soviet naval aviation is primarily directed toward the North Atlantic region rather than the vast expanses of the Pacific Ocean.

TABLE 4-6
SOVIET NAVAL AVIATION

<table>
<tr><th rowspan="3">Type & Designation</th><th colspan="5">Fleet Allocations
Current/Obsolescent*</th></tr>
<tr><th>Northern</th><th>Baltic</th><th>Black</th><th>Pacific</th><th>Total</th></tr>
<tr><td></td><td></td><td></td><td></td><td></td></tr>
<tr><td>Naval Bombers & Support A/C (TOT)
BACKFIRE/BADGER B,C,G,
  BLINDER
BEAR D, BADGER D,E,F</td><td>(60/110)

30/80
30/30</td><td>(20/80)

0/60
20/20</td><td>(40/100)

20/80
20/20</td><td>(25/125)

0/95
25/30</td><td>(145/415)

50/315+
95/100</td></tr>
<tr><td>ASW Patrol Aircraft (TOT)
MAY, MAIL/BEAR F</td><td>(70/15)</td><td>(10/0)</td><td>(50/0)</td><td>(25/0)</td><td>(155/16)</td></tr>
<tr><td>ASW Helicopters (TOT)
HOUND, HORMONE</td><td>(?)</td><td>(?)</td><td>(?)</td><td>(?)</td><td>(260/0)</td></tr>
<tr><td>Ship-Based Fighters (TOT)
FORGER</td><td>(10/0)</td><td>(0/0)</td><td>(20/0)</td><td>(0/0)</td><td>(30/0)+</td></tr>
<tr><td>Close Support Aircraft (TOT)
FITTER C</td><td>(0/0)</td><td>(40/0)</td><td>(0/0)</td><td>(0/0)</td><td>(40/0)</td></tr>
<tr><td>Miscellaneous Types (TOT)</td><td>(?)</td><td>(?)</td><td>(?)</td><td>(?)</td><td>(70/70)</td></tr>
<tr><td>Total Naval Aviation</td><td>?</td><td>?</td><td>?</td><td>?</td><td>700/500</td></tr>
</table>

*Obsolescent if average class age equals or exceeds 20 years by 1980
(Underlining indicates still being built)

Wartime Mission Allocations of Soviet Naval Forces

This section estimates the application of Soviet naval forces to the major missions discussed earlier on the basis of the fleet force allocations developed in prior sections. While any such allocations must be considered speculative at best, they are felt to be representative of the mission emphasis that would be applied at the outbreak of a major conventional war in the four main theaters: the North Atlantic, the Mediterranean, the Pacific, and the Indian Ocean. Possible concepts of operations for each region are outlined below.

The North Atlantic

This theater of operations would be the combined responsibility of the Northern and Baltic fleets. The total assets of these two fleets are listed in Table 4-7. These forces cover the spectrum of Soviet naval missions. The dominant requirement appears to be ensuring the security of the Northern Fleet Yankee and Delta SSBN forces as well as the older Hotel and Golf forces, which are expected to be reserved for theater nuclear strikes against major NATO targets. Additional Soviet naval forces would be assigned the

TABLE 4-7
THEATER ALLOCATION BY MISSION – ATLANTIC
Current/Obsolescent

Naval Forces	Designation	Soviet Navy — Class of Assets	Fleet Allocation — Northern	Fleet Allocation — Baltic	Fleet	Strategic — Strategic Strike	Strategic — Theater Strike	Strategic — SSBN Protection	Counter-Navy — Outer Area Attack	Counter-Navy — Counter-Carrier	Counter-Navy — Counter-SSBN	Support of Ground Forces	Command Contiguous Waters	Port & SLOC Interdiction	Allocated to Mediterranean
Submarines	SSBN	DELTA, YANKEE	42/0	—		42/0									12/0
	SSB/N	HOTEL, GOLF	0/14	0/6			0/20								2/0
	SSG/N	CHARLIE, JULIETT, LONGBIN	22/1	0/2					–10/3–						2/0
	SSGN	ECHO II	14/0						12/0						
	SSN	VICTOR	14/0					–8/0–							10/0
	SSN	NOVEMBER, ECHO	0/7					–0/4–		4/0					
	SS	TANGO, FOXTROT, ZULU	41/12	7/1				–20/0–							
	SS	B, R, W, Q-CLASS	1/21	1/15				–2/10–							
Air Craft		BACKFIRE	30/0				10/0			20/0					
		BADGER, BLINDER	0/80	0/60						0/80					
Major Surface Combatants	CVG	KIEV	1/0	1/0				–1/0–							2/0
	CLG/M	KARA, KRESTA II	7/0	9/0				–8/0–					2/0		1/0
	DDG	KRIVAK, KASHIN, KANIN, KOTLIN	15/0	1/0				–20/0–							
	CLGM	KRESTA I, KYNDA, KILDIN	2/0	0/1					–2/0–					0/1	
	CLG	SVERDLOV	0/1	0/13								0/1			
	DD/DE	KOTLIN, SKORY, RIGA	0/8	25/0					15/0			0/21			
	FF	New, GRISHA, MIRKA, PETYA	20/0	6/0				10/0				8/0	12/0	0/3	
	PM	NANUCHKA	2/0										8/0	17/13	
Other		Small Patrol Craft	70/20	122/35									192/55	0/60	
		Amphibious Support Ships	47/0	71/0								118/0			

task of assuring the appropriate deployment of these forces against opposition if necessary. Only slightly less important is the requirement to counter Western Alliance naval units operating in the North Atlantic and the Norwegian Sea, particularly submarines, carriers, and Alliance SSBNs capable of strikes against the Soviet Union. There is also a substantial requirement to support ground force operations on land. With the significant exception of logistic support, the Soviet Navy's direct contribution to an advance across the North German Plain is unlikely to be crucial: more important is the need to prevent seaborne interdiction and reinforcement by the West.

Most of these differing requirements would be met through the concept of an extended area defense, with the Soviets seeking to establish a defensive perimeter running from Greenland to the Netherlands through Iceland and the United Kingdom, encompassing the Norwegian and North seas. To this end, a substantial fraction of the major assets of the Northern and Baltic fleets would attempt to clear these areas of Alliance surface and subsurface combatants. This would include the use of some of the most capable Soviet conventionally and nuclear-powered submarines (SSs and SSNs), as well as diesel- and nuclear-powered guided missile submarines (SSGs/SSGNs), specifically against carrier task forces. The bulk of their ASW surface combatants would also be involved in these operations—as would the largest share of their long-range naval aviation assets.

Effective command of the Soviet naval inner defense zones would also be sought: in the Barents to enhance the security of the SSBN holding areas, and in the Baltic to facilitate support of the land battle. Operations to this end would probably include attempts to seize the Baltic Straits and to occupy key positions on the northern Norwegian coast. Such missions would entail the extensive use of the older Soviet gun ships and the bulk of their smaller naval and amphibious combatants. Moreover, the Soviets appear prepared both to employ mines extensively and to counteract their use by Western forces. In addition, submarine barriers would doubtless be established to interdict Western attempts to reinforce the northern flank by sea, backed by smaller missile-armed surface units.

The battle for the outer defense zone would most likely be engaged, from the outset, by air attacks on NATO surface forces at sea in the area, and by forward movement of Soviet naval forces and the establishment of submarine barriers across the Norwegian Sea. This might involve further landings along both the northern and southern Norwegian coasts. Additionally, attempts would probably be made to neutralize Iceland as an airbase and surveillance platform. The "Battle for the Norwegian Sea" could be one of the major naval engagements in any "World War III" between the Alliance and the U.S.S.R.-Pact nations.

While these operations would not be allowed to draw down the naval

Allocation of Soviet Naval Forces 111

forces directly involved in the defense of the SSBN "bastions" or those held back to engage the carrier task forces, they would serve the same general objective and contribute to the defense of the inner zone.

As a means of drawing NATO units away from the crucial battle for the Norwegian Sea, limited air and submarine forces would probably be deployed to attack military and merchant shipping and lightly defended warships in the North Atlantic. Table 4-7 indicates that on the order of thirty to forty submarines might be assigned to this task from the outset, but probably not many more than that. These submarine operations could be expected to move progressively further west and south. Such Soviet anti-SLOC operations would almost certainly include the bombing and mining of naval bases and resupply ports in NATO Europe and, in due course, the mining of selected ports and bases along the East Coast of North America and the mining of the SLOCs as well.

Certain submarine forces would already be operating in distant sea areas on their peacetime task of trying to keep track of Western SSBNs. Despite the recognized importance of countering Western SSBNs at the outbreak of such a major war, lack of Soviet capability means that relatively few forces are assigned to this mission at the present time—except insofar as the defense of the outer zone serves this purpose as well as others.

Obviously, this study cannot specify with any accuracy the wartime allocation of Soviet naval forces in the Atlantic. Nevertheless, Soviet priorities are not totally unknown. Some naval assets are certain to be devoted to the defense of their SSBN forces and to the attack of our carrier and SSBN forces. If the Soviets place higher than expected emphasis on the control of the Norwegian Sea—or the Mediterranean—then less than 40 submarines may be directed against the sealanes. Conversely, if the northern and southern flanks are accorded lower priority, then possibly as many as 100 submarines could be assigned to interdiction of the Atlantic SLOCs. It is the considered opinion of this working group, however, that the most likely figures range from 30 to 60 Soviet submarines working against the Atlantic SLOCs during the early phases of a major conventional war in Europe. The allocation of Soviet long-range naval aviation assets is equally uncertain. However, there are strong indications that the Soviets would give higher priority to the destruction of Western carrier task forces than to the sinking of merchant ships in transit. By the same reasoning, only 50 to 60 long-range antiship missile-equipped aircraft—primarily Badgers—might be assigned to attack the sealanes, although this number might be doubled if the Soviet emphasis on or opportunities against Western carriers were reduced.

The Mediterranean

Table 4-8 suggests the level of Northern Fleet and Baltic Fleet assets that could be applied to the various Soviet naval missions in the Mediterranean area. A sizable number of submarines from the Northern Fleet are assumed to be diverted to this area of operations. (This was indicated in Table 4-7 and repeated in Table 4-8.) In this region, the dominant Soviet requirements would be: to counter nuclear strikes against the Soviet Union; to seize the Black Sea exits in order to facilitate military operations against Greece and Turkey; and to prevent NATO reinforcement of the Southern Flank. Neutralizing of the Sixth Fleet and associated NATO naval forces would be essential to all three of these objectives and would permit the Soviet Navy to establish effective command of the Eastern Mediterranean. In this theater, the Soviets must be prepared for several operational contingencies: the encounter and continuous company scenarios and the gradual buildup versus the sudden crisis. Some ideas of the size of force required can be seen from the Soviet buildup of combatants and support ships during the 1973 renewal of the Middle East war, although at that time, other theaters were quiescent. Interdiction of NATO seaborne reinforcements for Greece and Turkey appears to be a prime Soviet naval mission. If the Black Sea exits could not be seized, then the Soviets could not rely on their major naval facilities at Sevastopol in the Black Sea, and all their Mediterranean naval forces would have to deploy from the Northern Fleet through the Strait of Gibralter.

As indicated in Table 4-8, Soviet naval forces allocated to Mediterranean operations would be intended to counter NATO carrier task forces and SSBNs and to conduct support of ground operations associated with controlling the Black Sea exits. There are no Soviet strategic assets operating from within the Mediterranean or the Black Sea. Moreover, the submarine forces assigned to the Black Sea Fleet are almost entirely obsolescent, diesel-powered units of rather limited performance. Higher-performance units would need to be drawn from the Northern Fleet. In fact, the battle for the Mediterranean would probably be heavily influenced by the relative availability of airpower to each side. A substantial force of land-based, long-range naval aircraft from Soviet bases would be pitted against the extensive carrier-based aircraft of the Sixth Fleet. The outcome could well hinge on the ability to supplement U.S. naval carrier-based aircraft from various land bases on the Mediterranean littoral. Given U.S. control of the air, it would then be reasonable to expect that control of the surface—and the subsurface—would follow.

In any event, the threat to NATO Mediterranean sealanes is expected to come primarily from Soviet submarines of relatively limited capabilities and from some attacks from Soviet aviation, if they are not primarily involved in attacking the carrier task forces. The submarine threat could vary from ten to thirty units, and the air threat could vary from ten to sixty bombers equipped with standoff antiship missiles.

113

TABLE 4-8
THEATER ALLOCATION BY MISSION – MEDITERRANEAN
Current/Obsolescent

Naval Forces	Designation	Soviet Navy Class of Assets	Fleet Allocation - Northern Fleet	Fleet Allocation - Baltic Fleet	Strategic Strike	Theater Strike	SSBN Protection	Outer Area Attack	Counter-Carrier	Counter-SSBN	Support of Ground Forces	Command Contiguous Waters	Port & SLOC Interdiction
Submarines	SSBN	DELTA, YANKEE	12/0										
	SSB/N	HOTEL, GOLF											
	SSG/N	CHARLIE, JULIETT, LONGBIN	2/0	0/2					12/0			0/2	
	SSGN	ECHO II	2/0						2/0	2/0			
	SSN	VICTOR	—										
	SSN	NOVEMBER, ECHO	10/0	1/0					5/0	6/0			
	SS	TANGO, FOXTROT, ZULU	—	1/21								0/2	1/19
	SS	B-,R-,W-,Q-CLASS											
Air Craft		BACKFIRE		20/0		10/0			10/0	2/0			
		BADGER, BLINDER		0/80					0/50	6/0			0/30
Major Surface Combatants	CHG	MOSKVA		2/0									
	CLG/M	KARA, KRESTA II		6/0					–16/0–				
	DDG	KRIVAK, KASHIN, KANIN, KOTLIN	2/0	14/0					6/0				
	CLGM	KRESTA I, KYNDA, KILDIN	1/0	5/0									
	CLG	SVERDLOV		0/5							–0/5–		
	DD/DE	KOTLIN, SKORY, RIGA		0/2							–0/2–		
	FF	New, GRISHA, MIRKA, PETYA		34/0								34/0	
	PM	NANUCHKA		7/0								7/0	
Other		Small Patrol Craft		100/25								100/25	
		Amphibious Support Ships		55/0							55/0		

The Pacific

As in the Atlantic, the dominant Soviet naval requirement in the Pacific Ocean is to assure the security of the Pacific Fleet SSBN force based at Petropavlovsk on the Kamchatka Peninsula and to secure its deployment if necessary. The strategic forces and the naval elements most likely to be devoted to their security are shown in Table 4-9. Again, a substantial fraction of the Soviet Pacific naval forces would be involved in protecting their own strategic forces and working against our carrier task forces and SSBNs. Beyond that, the larger number of smaller Soviet naval vessels assigned to the Pacific are clearly oriented toward command of their own contiguous waters such as the Seas of Japan and Okhotsk and support of ground force activities along the Soviet East Coast.

If a war were to begin between China and the Soviet Union and spill over into NATO Europe, many of the considerations that apply in the Atlantic would also apply in this theater. But if the war started with NATO, the Soviets might seek to limit the conflict in the Far East in the hope that neither Japan nor China would be drawn in. Alternatively, the Soviets might decide that preemptive strikes were the only way to handle China. In any case, the combined naval forces of China, Japan, and the Pacific component of the U.S. Navy present a formidable challenge, and the Soviet Pacific Fleet has to cover an extended coastline with relatively few forces. Moreover, most of the Soviet Pacific naval forces—other than their strategic submarines—are based at Vladivostok and could have considerable difficulty establishing effective control of the Sea of Japan and its few, crucial, exits to the open ocean.

With regard to Soviet air and submarine threats to Alliance trans-Pacific SLOCs, Table 4-9 indicates that the Soviets do not yet have enough assets to perform a major interdiction campaign against Western shipping. On the order of ten to thirty diesel submarines might be applied to this mission, and on the order of thirty to sixty long-range aircraft, some of which are not equipped with standoff antiship missiles. In short, the Soviet threat to the sealanes across the Pacific is probably no greater than it is in the Mediterranean and probably half as great as it might be in the North Atlantic. While such a threat is by no means negligible, neither is it a cause for serious speculation that the Pacific sealanes could be severed for any extended period by Soviet naval actions.

The Indian Ocean

Soviet Pacific forces are somewhat reduced by the requirements of the Indian Ocean Squadron. The combatants normally assigned to this mission are tabulated in Table 4-9. Moreover, there was some indication that the Russians may have intended originally to deploy a larger force to the Indian Ocean. The now defunct Soviet naval facilities at Berbera in

TABLE 4-9
THEATER ALLOCATION BY MISSION – PACIFIC & INDIAN OCEAN
Current/Obsolescent

Naval Forces	Designation	Soviet Navy Class of Assets	Fleet Allocation Pacific Fleet	Strategic Strike	Theater Strike	SSBN Protection	Outer Area Attack	Counter-Carrier	Counter-SSBN	Support of Ground Forces	Command Contiguous Waters	Port & SLOC Interdiction	Allocated to Indian Ocean
Submarines	SSBN	DELTA, YANKEE	20/0	20/0									
	SSB/N	HOTEL, GOLF	0/8		0/8								
	SSG/N	CHARLIE, JULIETT, LONGBIN	8/2				–8/2–						1/0
	SSGN	ECHO II	14/0					13/0					
	SSN	VICTOR	6/0				–3/0–						0/1
	SSN	NOVEMBER, ECHO	0/9				–0/6–					0/2	2/0
	SS	TANGO, FOXTROT, ZULU	14/4				–6/0–					6/4	
	SS	B-,R-,W-,Q-CLASS	1/10								1/10		
Air Craft		BACKFIRE											
		BADGER, BLINDER	0/95					0/60				0/35	
Major Surface Combatants	CLG/M	KARA, KRESTA II	2/0				–2/0–						2/0
	DDG	KRIVAK, KASHIN, KANIN, KOTLIN	14/0				–12/0–						1/0
	CLGM	KRESTA I, KYNDA, KILDIN	4/0					–3/0–					0/1
	CLG	SVERDLOV	0/4										
	DD/DE	KOTLIN, SKORY, RIGA	0/15							0/3	0/10		
	FF	New, GRISHA, MIRKA, PETYA	19/0				10/0			0/5	7/0		2/0
	PM	NANUCHKA	6/0								6/0		
Other		Small Patrol Craft	70/35								70/35		
		Amphibious Support Ships	73/0							73/0			

Somalia appear to have been designed to support a much larger naval force than the Russians normally deploy there. In the short term, there appear to be two potential requirements for a larger Soviet force in that area. First, in the event of a war with China, there would be a need to secure the sealanes of supply to the Far Eastern Front, either via Suez and the Red Sea or via the Persian Gulf. Second, in the event of a war with the West, there would be a strong desire to seize the Persian and Arabian oil fields and to interdict seaborne support and reinforcements to the area (i.e., the encounter version of the antisurface scenario). In the longer run, the Soviets may also feel that it is necessary to develop the capability to counter Trident SSBNs, which they may assume might be deployed to the Indian Ocean. In any event, the Soviet naval forces currently earmarked for use in the Indian Ocean would not present a serious threat to an American task force in the event of a major war. Nonetheless, these individually capable ships provide an important element of Soviet presence in that area and could be used to limit the freedom of action of Western forces during periods of crisis less than a major conventional war between the superpowers. (This subject is discussed in greater detail subsequently.)

Implications of Force Allocations

This review suggests several broad, tentative conclusions about the fleet-by-fleet allocation of Soviet naval forces and their most likely assignments, as summarized below.

- The offensive capabilities of the Soviet Pacific Fleet appear modest at best: the Soviets would be hard-pressed to assign more than twenty Pacific-based submarines to an anti-SLOC campaign, and it is unlikely that any of them would be nuclear-propelled for sustained operations at long distances from home ports. This makes the current threat to the Pacific and Indian Ocean SLOCs significant but manageable.
- The major missions of the Baltic and Black Sea-Mediterranean fleets would appear to be in support of ground force operations in the defense against Alliance offensive naval actions. They do provide extensive capabilities to harass and interdict Alliance naval and maritime operations in coastal areas close to their home ports. These fleets are clearly capable of mounting local offensive operations of their own in support of naval missions, including mining, countermining, and amphibious operations.
- The Northern Fleet is by far the most capable, but it is also burdened with the largest variety of both strategic and conventional naval warfare missions. It appears unlikely that the Soviet Navy would currently apply more than sixty submarines to an Atlantic-

Mediterranean anti-SLOC campaign; and most, if not all, of these would be diesel-powered. The Northern Fleet, like the Pacific Fleet, has a major strategic role and if, as suspected, these strategic assets are intended to be operated in a "withhold" role, then other major Soviet naval elements would most likely be assigned to their defense. If the Soviets did not perceive the threat of nuclear war to be high, then the sealanes could be far more seriously jeopardized.

- The major threat to Alliance surface ships, both merchant and naval, comes from the combined submarines and land-based bombers and the torpedoes, mines, bombs, and missiles they carry. Both forces would most likely be preoccupied with operations against Alliance carrier task forces—at least early in a major engagement. The Soviet surface fleet is probably not intended to take part in an anti-SLOC campaign.
- By the same token, Soviet submarine and bomber forces are less likely to form the initial, visible elements of crisis operations (interdiction and interposition). The role would more likely fall to surface combatants, whose capabilities are limited beyond the reach of friendly air cover. The Soviets would seem unlikely to risk these major surface combatants in a direct confrontation with the United States for some time to come, unless the stakes were very high or they were to misjudge U.S. reactions. If a shooting battle did develop, however, Soviet submarines and aircraft would soon become involved.
- In situations where a direct confrontation with the United States appears unlikely, the Soviet surface fleet, operating with merchant marine support, could have a substantial impact on the perceptions of many Third World countries and potential client-states around the world. However, the Soviets do not appear to have worked out any significant "forward-basing" concept; consequently, a substantial Soviet "presence"—from military vessels—in South Asia or the Western Hemisphere appears unlikely for many years to come.

The numerical preponderance of Soviet naval assets is evidently still allocated to the "support of ground forces" and "command of contiguous waters," as might be expected in a basically army-oriented military society. While Soviet naval strategic assets are impressive, the conventional warfare forces for open ocean operations still appear somewhat limited— particularly since the Soviets are pursuing our four-ocean navy. Probably for many years the Soviet Navy will have substantially more potential mission assignments than it could hope to carry out simultaneously. This situation is aggravated by the approaching obsolescence of some of their ships and submarines. Therefore, Alliance forces need not be able to counter all these potential assignments simultaneously either.

By the same token, the Soviet oceangoing navy is now large enough to afford considerable flexibility in its strategy, particularly in situations less than an all-out superpower confrontation. For purposes of intimidation the Soviet Navy could concentrate its assets along either the northern or southern flank of NATO and present a severe threat to the friendly nations of those limited regions. Similarly, a gathering of Soviet Pacific forces around the South Korean peninsula or the Islands of Japan could seriously menace those countries if they were not assured of U.S. and Alliance support. Likewise, if the Soviets were to devote all their available submarines to an anti-SLOC campaign—using torpedoes and mines—for a short duration, they might force at least a temporary cessation of essential shipping. In conclusion, although this chapter argues that the most likely allocation of Soviet naval forces would be for a full-scale superpower confrontation, the Soviets could employ a variety of strategies under different circumstances to produce severe local effects.

Attention will now be turned to the Western Alliance economic dependence on the seas, the extent to which that dependence represents a vulnerability or just a sensitivity, and the competition of Soviet maritime activities with Western interests.

5

Western Maritime Interests

The Meaning of Maritime Security

Soviet maritime developments significantly affect the seagoing activities of the United States and its allies. Soviet bottoms now carry cargoes that once would have been the business of West European shipowners. Russian trawlers compete with the Japanese on most of the world's fishing grounds. And, of course, the developing naval capabilities of the U.S.S.R. threaten the ability of the naval forces of the United States and its allies to carry out their missions in the event of war.

But it would be a mistake to view the new Soviet prowess at sea as a challenge to maritime activities alone. Interests in the oceans per se are relatively minor when compared with the enormous economic, political, and security considerations ashore. Soviet maritime operations are more properly viewed as part of a patient effort to expand Soviet power and whittle down Western economic strength and political influence.

The loss of seaborne imports is a real possibility. The Arab oil embargo of 1973 gave new prominence to this contingency. But overreaction could be costly. Concern about access to foreign supplies often leads to talk about "essential seaborne imports," "critical raw materials," "vital sealanes," and so on. Such statements are heavily weighted with political and economic judgments. Before investing in additional naval programs to enhance the security of raw material imports, we should think carefully about how dependent the economy is upon maritime activities.[1]

This chapter suggests some ways of thinking about maritime affairs, their importance to the security of the Western Alliance, and the uses to which the seas will be put in the future.

Sensitivity, Interdependence, and Vulnerability

Much of the concern of Western nations about security at sea focuses on potential interruptions of their extensive seaborne trade. Because of their understandable preoccupation with imports of raw materials, particularly oil, the Western industrial countries sometimes neglect other aspects of maritime activity. But trade is clearly a two-way matter. Imports must generally be paid for with exports. We should therefore be sensitive to the potential loss of access to export markets as well. Moreover, *sensitivity* to imports and exports—and to fishery problems, for that matter—does not necessarily imply *dependence*.[2] Because modern trade is complex, "interdependence" is a more descriptive term. Most nations both import and export raw materials and manufactured products. Some raw materials from abroad are later exported in finished products. No nation is wholly self-sufficient, and none is wholly dependent on seaborne commerce. Dependence is a matter of degree.

The importance of seaborne trade naturally varies widely according to the product or material. The importance of oil imports is widely recognized. But the Europeans also import all of their coffee, cocoa, tea, bananas, and pepper. The United States imports all of its natural rubber but only 30 percent of its wines, and its major exports include grain and manufactured items. Our focus in this chapter will be on measures of general economic welfare, for these—not the protection of specific markets or firms or jobs—are the proper national security concern.

International interdependence has grown enormously since World War II. World exports increased by 144 percent in total value between 1960 and 1970; by 1976 that figure had risen to 639 percent, by no means all of it attributable to inflation. Real growth has been substantial as well.

Table 5-1 shows average annual rates of increase in imports for the United States, Japan, and the European Economic Community in constant prices for the period 1960–1976. The table also includes yearly rates of expansion in Gross National Product (GNP), again expressed in constant prices. Trade has grown much faster than GNP.

The data in Table 5-1 also show that during periods of recession, when economic growth stagnates or declines, as in the years since 1972, trade contracts even more. In the recession year of 1975, for example, both exports and imports of most Western industrialized countries declined more sharply than GNP.

Other evidence of interdependence is at hand. About one-fifth of U.S. industrial production and one-third of agricultural production are exported. In addition, about a third of the profits of U.S. corporations come from foreign investments and other overseas activities.

Moreover, interdependence goes far beyond economics. The national security policies of the Western Alliance are rooted in common political and military interests; modern communications and trade have greatly stimulated cultural exchange among nations.

International interdependence and seaborne trade are certainly facts of

TABLE 5-1
RATES OF GROWTH OF GROSS NATIONAL PRODUCT AND IMPORTS

	1960-71	1972-76
Imports in constant prices		
United States	9.0 %	2.3 %
Canada	8.5	5.7
European Economic Community	9.7	4.5
Japan	13.3	4.9
GNP in constant prices		
United States	3.9 %	1.9 %
Canada	5.4	3.9
European Economic Community	4.5	2.2
Japan	10.3	4.1
Ratio: Import growth to GNP growth		
United States	2.31	1.21
Canada	1.57	1.46
European Economic Community	2.16	2.05
Japan	1.29	1.20

Source: Calculated from *International Economic Report of the President*, January 1977 (Washington: U.S. Government Printing Office, 1977), pp. 139,147.

modern life. To what extent does international interdependence create vulnerabilities that Soviet maritime activities can exploit in order to weaken the Western Alliance? When imports are high in relation to consumption there is a presumption of vulnerability—that loss of supplies would cause continuing and costly shortages.

There are important differences in the ratios of imports to consumption among the member nations of the Western Alliance. Table 5-2 shows the situation for fourteen important materials, including oil and coal. Our allies import a much larger proportion of their total consumption of these raw materials (including coal, copper, iron ore, lead, oil, and phosphate) than we do, and the situation is not likely to change. These differences in degree suggest that vulnerability to loss of seaborne trade is greatest for Japan and least for the United States. If supplies should ever be generally interrupted, our allies would come under the most pressure; they would undoubtedly urge U.S. leaders to act faster than purely domestic U.S. concerns would dictate.

The materials listed in Table 5-2 are important to industrialized economies; a similar table could be compiled for manufactured goods such as automobiles, clothing, electronics, and industrial equipment. But the ratio of imports to consumption is not a direct measure of dependence on seaborne trade or of vulnerability of the economy to embargo, blockade, or other interruption.

TABLE 5-2
IMPORTS AS A SHARE OF CONSUMPTION: MID-1970's

	European Community	Japan	United States
Bauxite	50%	100%	88%
Chromium	95	95	90
Coal	8	56	0
Cobalt	98	98	94
Copper	99	93	16
Iron Ore	85	99	35
Lead	85	78	12
Manganese	99	90	100
Nickel	90	95	61
Phosphate Rock	100	100	0
Petroleum	91	100	50
Tin	90	90	75
Tungsten	100	100	55
Zinc	74	63	60

Source: Central Intelligence Agency, *Handbook of Economic Statistics—1977*, p. 17, and various other documents.

The popular idea of vulnerability is captured by the words, "For want of a nail, a kingdom was lost." The idea is that one or a few "key" resources (goods, commodities, or processes) are so important to the strength of the economy that if they are destroyed or denied, economic performance suffers sharply, and military strength is cut accordingly.

The fallacy in this line of reasoning is that such rigid connections rarely exist in a large and resilient modern economy, particularly that of the United States, where tradeoffs or substitutions are usually possible, although at higher cost. Seaborne imports are valuable but not essential.

These points are widely recognized among economists. In an analysis of economics and national security, Charles Schultze put it this way:

> To what extent does our national security depend upon protecting access to overseas sources of raw materials and ensuring the safety of American investments abroad? In essence, the answer is simply "Hardly at all." One of the most pervasive myths about national security is that the United States is critically dependent on the steady supply of a number of vital materials, and that a slowdown or cessation in their supply would be disastrous for the economy and cirppling to our military capability. This is simply not true.
>
> In the first place, unlike many other nations, we import only a relatively small proportion of our needs. In 1971 merchandise imports were approximately four percent of GNP. In the second place, any modern

industrial economy, and particularly the United States, is incredibly quick to adapt to shortages of particular materials. Substitutes are rapidly discovered, synthetics developed, and ways found to minimize the use of short-supply items.

There is the problem of the initial shock should the United States be suddenly cut off from access to a particular material or fuel suply. But in the long run, the economy would adapt amazingly well. If imports to the United States were cut off and our overseas investments expropriated, the U.S. economy would not collapse. Our living standards would suffer, but not by a large amount. Nor would our military capabilities be substantially impaired.[3]

Determinants of Vulnerability

Still, where imports are large, there is often a presumption of vulnerability. Whether this presumption actually holds depends on these factors: (1) the uses to which imports are put, (2) the absolute levels of imports, (3) the availability of substitutes, (4) the availability of inventories and stockpiles, (5) the duration of the interruption, (6) the size of the economy, and (7) government policies. We shall illustrate these points with examples from the United States economy.

Uses of Imports. Imports include both raw materials for further processing and final products. The foreign trade of the United States is dominated by the shipments of manufactured goods, which represent 53 percent of imports and 66 percent of exports, by value. Over the past decade, trade in manufactured goods has grown fast; U.S. purchases of foreign manufactures—such as electronics and motor vehicles—have more than quadrupled since 1962.

But imports of manufactured goods do not present an important vulnerability because they are also a large sector of the domestic economy. In 1969, there were only eighteen products for which U.S. imports exceeded one-fifth of the total new supply. Moreover, these products—sewing machines, motorcycles, china, shoes, sporting goods, consumer electronics, and so on—do not seem vital. Many products that are not on this list—computing machinery, aircraft, machine tools, oilfield equipment, grains, etc.—are more important.

Another point about manufactured products: users have on hand far larger amounts of most finished products than this country imports (or produces) in a year. For instance, annual imports amount to only 2 to 3 percent of the more than 100 million passenger cars registered in the United States. If imports were stopped, the existing supply could be stretched to make up for the import losses.

As a net exporter of agricultural products the United States is not dependent on seaborne trade for food. The United States does, of course, import all of its supplies of some specific commodities—coffee, cocoa, tea, and bananas. But some commodities can hardly be said to raise important problems for the nation's security.

As for crude oil and oil products, the growth and level of U.S. imports have been widely publicized. In the early 1970s, U.S. imports of oil grew at an annual rate of more than 13 percent; by 1976, those imports amounted to half the total U.S. consumption. The United States has more domestic oil than its major allies (see Table 5-2), but the oil imports—increasingly from the Middle East—create a major vulnerability for the United States. We now face a problem that our allies have confronted for a long time.

With minerals, the picture for the United States is very different. For a number of metals and other minerals, imports exceed 50 percent as a share of total new supply, as shown in Table 5-2. These minerals are not all equally important to our national security, but dependence on imports (generally, seaborne imports) is great. The United States has long recognized that supplies might be cut off during major wars, seriously hampering our war effort. Since 1939, therefore, we have stockpiled some raw materials.

Magnitude of Imports. The effects of a loss of seaborne imports also depend on the tonnages involved. For some commodities, such as platinum and sheet mica, foreign sources account for 100 percent of U.S. consumption. Yet total needs are a few tens of tons at most, and the supplies needed can be airlifted.

Therefore, in an examination of the vulnerability of an economy to the loss of seaborne trade, it is necessary to look beyond the dependence criterion and consider the absolute level of transportation needed. For the foreseeable future, the United States will import large amounts of nine commodities by sea:[4]

*Oil	Barite
Iron ore and products	Copper
*Bauxite, alumina, and aluminum	Rutile
*Manganese	Zircon
*Chromium	

*The United States now plans to stockpile these commodities.

Availability of Substitutes. Some products are imported simply because they are currently cheaper than domestic supplies—iron ore, for example. And in modern industrialized nations, substitutions among materials is generally possible, although at a cost. For example, if imports of bauxite were halted, products that were made of aluminum might, instead, be made of steel or titanium or fiberglass. Such substitutes would not be cheap, and higher prices would induce conservation. An increase in recycling of discarded materials can be another substitute for imports. In either case, the products would cost more or the quality would be lower, and consumers might look elsewhere to satisfy the same wants. Moreover, the very process of substitution takes time, raising substantial problems of short-run adjustment. In the longer run, however, there are substitutes for everything.

Availability of Stockpiles and Inventories. The purpose of the U.S. stockpile of strategic and critical materials—now valued at $8.6 billion—is to protect the economy from the direct effects of an interruption of supply.[5] In August 1976 the president decided to plan stockpiles for a three-year (rather than one-year) emergency and to provide for civilian needs after allowing for belt-tightening. The United States is also building up a strategic oil reserve that will amount to 500 million barrels by 1980 and possibly a billion barrels two years later. Stockpiles reduce the vulnerability of the economy to interference with supply in wartime or in time of crisis.

Duration of Interruption. A modern market economy can adapt quite quickly to changes in supply if it is allowed to adapt freely. If the interruption is short, the adjustment is accomplished by inventory changes. If the interruption persists, however, firms seek substitute materials and consumers adjust their spending habits. Since such processes take time, there may be short and sharp local dislocations. After a while, however, the industry and the economy adapt, and the effects of the loss of supply are minimized.

Size of the Economy. The larger the economy, the more easily it can absorb the effects of a sharp and unexpected reduction in supply; in a large economy, there are more alternatives, and greater substitution is possible. If, for example, shipments to Hawaii and the continental United States were halted, the drop in income would be faster and proportionally greater in Hawaii.

Government Policies. Government policies can also affect the vulnerability of an economy to loss of supply. As we have seen, stockpiles help cushion the effects of such loss. In the event of major war, the government could also impose rationing or other belt-tightening measures. But government policies in peacetime can also reduce the use of imported

U.S. STRATEGIC STOCKPILES

Under the management of the Federal Preparedness Agency, the United States maintains strategic stockpiles of critical materials, both liquid (above) and solid (below), whose sources might be cut off during wartime. This report strongly urges all members of the Western Alliance to improve their strategic and economic stockpiles in order to offset the impact of temporary interruptions in the flow of seaborne commerce during the crisis of war. (Courtesy General Services Administration)

goods. Many examples of such policies have been promoted for energy conservation, including subsidies for insulation, research in solar power, and taxes on large automobiles.

The degree of vulnerability is a factual matter, susceptible to analysis. But, for the most part, the debate over the security of the sealanes has lacked careful commodity-by-commodity investigation. More important, there have been no estimates of the effects of interruptions of seaborne trade on aggregate economic activity—on GNP, employment, and production. Such an analysis is needed; it would play an important role in the debate about sealane defense forces.

Factors Affecting Use of the Ocean

What will happen to uses of the sea in the future? There are four main sources of change in ocean activities:

- World economic conditions
- Technological developments
- The international law of the sea
- Domestic policies

Economic Conditions

The economic uses of the sea grow when the world economy expands and decline when economic growth slows. This relationship can be shown most easily for seaborne trade. In the ten years beginning in mid-1965, the world's GNP grew at an annual rate of 4.3 percent, after the effects of price changes were accounted for. Measured by tons carried, seaborne trade grew at an annual rate of 6.2 percent in the same period; ton-miles of shipping grew at an annual rate of 10 percent. But the following data show the sensitivity of the volume of shipping to short-term changes in world economic activity:

	1972-1973	1973-1974	1974-1975
Change in world GNP	+ 6.5%	+1.5%	+0.2%
Change in seaborne trade			
Tons carried	+13.0%	+4.1%	-8.0%
Ton-miles transported	+17.6%	+6.4%	-7.1%

The volume of shipping rises and falls faster than total economic activity. Moreover, other ocean activities, such as fishing and offshore oil exploitation, respond to changes in economic activity ashore.

Although the pace of economic growth will continue to be uneven, the long-term prospects are for real economic growth at an annual rate of 2 to 4 percent. If past relationships hold, the importance of the seas—particularly for merchant shipping—will increase substantially more than that.

Technological Developments

Technological change is affected by market forces. Change can increase the uses of the seas by reducing costs and by opening up wholly new activities that were not technically or economically feasible before.

In ocean transport, the cost of shipping is reduced by the development of very large cargo-carrying ships—most notably, supertankers—and the ports to handle them. Pressure to capture these economies of scale in shipping has resulted in a growth of 50 percent in the average size of tankers since 1970. Similarly, the "unitization" of cargo by means of containers, barges, or pallets simplifies ship operations and reduces cargo-handling costs for general cargo shipments. The design and construction of specialized ships for carrying liquefied natural gas, an entirely new market for shipping services, has been created by technology. In general, new technology seems to be leading to increasingly specialized ships and ports.

Technological innovation is also increasing the yield and efficiency of fisheries.[6] With the development of shipboard processing and storage facilities has come the construction of factory ships that make it economical to fish in distant waters. Advanced methods for finding fish will employ infrared, photographic, and advanced acoustic technology— and not only aboard ships. The new fishing sensors will also be mounted on aircraft, satellites, and unmanned buoys or platforms. These sensors will make commercially important concentrations of fish easier to find; automation aboard the fishing vessels already makes catching them more efficient. Automation increases the proportion of detected fish that are actually landed and reduces the number of crew members needed. In all, new technology is increasing both the intensity and the extent of fishing operations.

As for exploitation of offshore energy resources, technical development has steadily increased the water depth at which oil can be economically extracted. In 1973, Esso drilled exploratory wells in water 2,600–3,500 feet deep, off the coast of Thailand.[7] One $60 million drill ship to be built will operate in water 4,500 feet deep, off the west coast of Africa.[8] New rigs are being designed and built to operate not only at greater depths but in more demanding environments, such as Arctic waters.

Although technology for mining the resources of the deep seabed has yet to be put into commercial operation, the *Glomar Explorer* proved the feasibility of operating heavy undersea equipment at great depths and lifting heavy, bulky weights from the bottom. Moreover, private groups have conducted pilot plant and testing operations, have surveyed potential mine sites, and have estimated the economic possibilities of exploiting the seabed for manganese nodules.[9] Although proponents of seabed mining declare that the technology for mining and refining seabed minerals is in hand, it has yet to prove itself commercially.

The state of technology, like the condition of the world economy, can lead to more use or less use of the ocean. Communications over long distances once handled by ships are now carried by electronics; long-range transportation of passengers is now done by aircraft. Advances in technology and new discoveries that reduce the costs of exploiting resources ashore tend to slow or even reverse the trend toward use of the seabeds. On the other hand, growing demand will tend to heighten interest in obtaining both oil and other minerals from the oceans.

It is hard to imagine any developments that would replace ships for long-distance movement of oil and such dry bulk commodities as grain and iron ore. Moreover, the technology for exploiting ocean resources seems to be moving more swiftly than any techniques for, say, squeezing more oil from long-used oil fields or working low-grade ore from land deposits.

In sum, technology is likely to increase the uses of the sea faster than it will increase comparable activities ashore.

Law of the Sea

The evolving law is a third factor that will have a major influence on the use of the seas. The Third United Nations Law of the Sea Conference has been negotiating a wide variety of issues since 1971, but failure to settle a few outstanding points may prevent agreement on a final treaty. Even if a pact does emerge, a number of uncertainties will remain. With or without a treaty, there will surely be change and adaptation as users of the sea learn to live with and exploit the new rules. Meanwhile, coastal states, including the United States, are unilaterally extending their territorial waters, economic zones, and fishing grounds seaward and imposing pollution controls and other restrictions on the use of offshore areas.

The main issues to be resolved include the width of territorial seas, rights of passage through straits, arrangements for exploiting seabed resources, rules to govern scientific research, and controls on marine pollution.

The regime that is agreed upon for each of these issues will affect maritime navigation. This is particularly true of the resolution of the width of the territorial seas and the related issue of transit through international straits. The new law of the sea, with or without a treaty, will extend the limit of the territorial seas from 3 miles to 12 miles. Such a change will apply to more than 100 straits that connect territorial seas, including the important straits of Gibraltar, Bab el Mandeb, Hormuz, Malacca, Lombok, Sunda, and Dover.[10] The manner in which the nations that border these straits choose to enforce their rights in the territorial waters could have important effects on the flow of seaborne trade and the nature of military deployments.

One possibility is that coastal or straits states will try to deny passage to shipping on the basis of environmental, scientific, or security considerations; if so, shipping costs will rise somewhat. According to one estimate, if Dover Strait were closed, transportation costs for U.S. shipping would rise by only $50 million a year.[11]

Strict exclusion seems unlikely, however, for the right to use these straits is valued by all nations. The straits states would be more likely to attempt to impose tolls. But such charges would not be set so high that alternative routes or methods of shipment would become economically attractive. The effect of the tolls would be some diversion of shipping and some reduction in the amount shipped, but the broad patterns of ocean shipping would not change significantly.

Military shipping might be affected differently. In periods of tension, a nation that could control passage through a strait might attempt to bar the naval ships of one side or of both sides if it were willing to bear the political risks. The ability of the superpowers' fleets to intervene in local wars could be seriously affected. In the event of general war, however, warships could be expected to ignore such efforts to restrict their movements.

As for fishing and mineral rights, more and more nations are claiming exclusive economic zones, generally 200 miles in width. Such claims may well be codified if an international agreement is reached on the law of the sea.

The effects on fishing will be felt mainly in those few nations—Japan and the Soviet Union, in particular—that operate fishing fleets in distant waters. Such nations will be forced to reach agreements with the littoral states or move their fishing efforts elsewhere—to the Antarctic, for example. In some cases, quotas will be imposed, and in others, compensation agreements will be worked out. In either case, the effect will be to increase costs and slow the development of fishing activities off distant shores.

Entrepreneurs complain that continuing uncertainty about the right to exploit seabed minerals is inhibiting development. This may well be true. Certainly there is a risk that potential investors may not be able to realize their profits even if they can overcome the huge technical and economic risks of undersea mining. But how a specific law of the sea might affect extraction of these minerals depends on details of agreements yet to be negotiated. The effects could operate in either direction.

In the long run, the uses of the seas will develop more in response to economic and political events than to the specifics of any international agreement on the law of the sea.

Whether or not a law of the sea gains international agreement, two broad outlines of a future legal regime can be discerned; namely, a 12-mile territorial sea and a 200-mile economic zone. Transit through international straits is less certain, as is the regime for mining the deep seabed beyond areas of national jurisdiction.

Domestic Policies

The extent to which nations use the seas depends as much on their domestic economic and political policies as on international law: tariffs and quotas inhibit seaborne trade, subsidies to shipbuilders and ship operators encourage trade, environmental policies inhibit offshore oil production, rights to exploit offshore oil fields are controlled by governments, government research activities subsidize some ocean uses, and so on. Most of the large industrialized countries maintain policies that favor domestic activities. They have the net effect of slowing the growth in uses of the sea for international trade. Nationalist and protectionist policies are likely to become more widespread, inhibiting somewhat the expansion of seaborne trade.

Maritime Activities Worldwide

How do the United States, Japan, and the nations of Western Europe exploit the seas? This section assesses their major maritime interests and analyzes the importance of those interests in the Atlantic, Pacific, and Indian oceans and the Mediterranean Sea.

The main peacetime activities on the oceans are economic. The oceans are used simply because using them is cheaper than the alternatives. This point is best illustrated by seaborne trade. Businessmen—and nations—engage in foreign trade because there are economic benefits to be gained. For the full benefits of trade to be derived, transportation costs must be minimized. Although great improvements have been made in aircraft speed and capacity, there have also been improvements in the capacity and productivity of ships. For the foreseeable future, the large merchant ship will be the cheapest way to move most goods across oceans.

There are no satisfactory estimates of the actual economic value of the oceans. In 1974, the National Ocean Policy Study prepared estimates of the "primary economic value" of the oceans to the United States.[12] "Primary economic value" measures the output of goods and services performed at sea but excludes closely related activities ashore. For example, the measure includes the direct costs of fishing but not the costs of processing the fish ashore.

Measured by this limited standard, the economic value of ocean activities to the United States is expected to grow about 10 percent a year, a rate that far exceeds the 3 to 4 percent growth rate expected for total U.S. economic activities. The growth in ocean uses is dominated by a large increase in the exploitation of offshore petroleum and natural gas as a result of the 1973 OPEC embargo and the price increases that followed. The "primary economic value" of the ocean (consisting of transport) is expected to grow at a rate of nearly 6 percent and to exceed $5 billion by 1985.

The primary economic value of the oceans to the United States is small relative to total economic output. The $8 billion of "primary economic value" in 1972 amounted to less than 1 percent of the $1.3 trillion Gross National Product (GNP) of the United States. If GNP grows at 3 percent a year while ocean activities grow at 10 percent, the ocean activities will amount to just over 1.3 percent of GNP in 1985.

The economic importance of ocean activities ranks differently in different nations. To Japan, for example, fishing and transport have great value; exploitation of offshore seabed resources has little. For the Persian Gulf states, on the other hand, it is of dominant importance to exploit offshore petroleum and ship it to market; fishing is of only token value. For the foreseeable future, the peaceful uses of greatest value to the United States, Western Europe, and Japan will be seaborne trade, fishing, and exploitation of offshore oil and gas. The next few pages are devoted to these ocean activities.

Seaborne Commerce

In 1976, the value of world exports totaled about $990 billion. Exports from the United States, Western Europe, Japan, and other developed countries amounted to nearly two-thirds of that total. A reasonable estimate of the proportion of total world trade carried by ship is two-thirds—nearly $700 billion. That is the total *value* of total trade, not an estimate of the *gains* from seaborne trade. The gains may be larger or smaller, depending on the costs of comparable supplies from other sources.

In analyzing seaborne trade, it is useful to divide the total cargo among three broad classes of commodities:

- *Petroleum and related products.* Shipments of crude oil, refined products, liquefied natural gas (LNG), and liquid chemicals.
- *Dry bulk cargo.* Shipments of bulk raw materials, such as coal, grain, fertilizer, mineral ores, semirefined mineral products, and semifinished iron and steel.
- *General cargo.* Shipments of finished manufactured products, such as automobiles, machine tools, television sets, toys, newsprint, and clothing.

One measure of the importance of seaborne trade to a nation's economic well-being is the *amount* of goods it imports. The United States, Europe, Japan, and the Soviet Union vary strikingly in this respect. In 1975, the amounts of goods unloaded, measured in millions of metric tons (MMT), were as shown in Table 5-3.

The United States, Japan, and our allies in Europe received nearly three-quarters of all the cargo shipped in international trade in 1975. The reason, of course, lies in the West's huge imports of petroleum and other raw materials. (The data in Table 5-3 lump together dry bulk cargo and general cargo as "dry cargo." Some 40 to 45 percent of dry cargo tonnage consists of bulk raw materials.)

When we look at the volume of shipping loaded in international trade—that is, exports—a somewhat different picture emerges (Table 5-4). The United States and its international allies ship far less than they receive. About 85 percent of Western Alliance exports consist of dry cargo.

The nations of Western Europe, taken together, continue to dominate the world shipping market. Three out of every eight merchant ships in the world fly the flags of Western European nations. The following data, in millions of tons of registered ships, summarize cargo-carrying capabilities.[13]

	Tonnage	Share of World Total
United States	13.4	4.2%
Western Europe	132.4	41.7
Japan	34.2	10.7
U.S.S.R.	11.7	3.7
Rest of the world	126.2	39.7
World total	318.2	100.0%

These data, however, understate the share of world shipping controlled by the West. Nearly 90 million tons were registered to "flags of convenience" in 1975, and most of this was surely controlled by shipowners in the developed Western world.[14]

To assess the effects of disruption of Western seaborne trade in war, it is necessary to forecast the amounts of trade and shipping.[15] Shipping in the interregional trade of 1985 is estimated here in two steps: the volume of goods to be moved is projected, and the shipping required to carry that volume is estimated.

For the most part, the projections of seaborne trade in 1985 assume that the trade patterns of the 1960s and 1970s will continue. This is generally a reasonable assumption, for these patterns depend on the location of large-scale manufacturing industry and the distribution of natural resources. For instance, emergence of a major new manufacturing center within the short space of a decade seems unlikely. But patterns of trade can, of course, be altered by discovery or exploitation of new sources of raw materials or exhaustion of old sources. The projections described here have been adjusted for the expected development of petroleum and gas in the North Sea and in Alaska.

Projections of the amounts of petroleum, dry bulk cargo, and general cargo to be transported must be translated into estimates of the number of transits. Estimates of transits are stated in terms of standard ship-types chosen to reflect recent developments in design:

Tanker:
Speed: 15 knots
Port time: 4 days per round trip
Capacity: 215,000 metric tons

Dry bulk carrier:
Speed: 14 knots
Port time: 4 days per round trip
Capacity: 35,000 metric tons

General cargo ship:
Speed: 22 knots
Port time: 6 days per round trip
Capacity: 8,700 metric tons

On this basis, the numbers of transits required each month to carry the projected totals of interregional trade in 1985 are as shown in Table 5-5. These estimates imply that the amount of goods shipped in seaborne trade will grow at an annual rate of 5.9 percent between 1974 and 1985. Considering the uncertainties about political and economic conditions, it seems reasonable to conclude that between 25,000 and 30,000 transits a month will be required for interregional trade in the free world in 1985.

Traffic in manufactured goods and other general cargo will be increasing faster than shipments of primary commodities. As a result, general cargo will account for nearly half of total transits by 1985 (at least, in terms of the standard ships used here). Shipments of petroleum will increase slowly, because high prices for OPEC oil will limit consumption and encourage development of domestic supplies.

Actually, there will be far more ships at sea than Table 5-5 suggests. The table does not include the seaborne trade of Communist nations; moreover, it excludes intraregional seaborne trade, and this can be substantial. In the Mediterranean, for example, at any given time there are 1,500 to 2,000 ships at sea carrying cargoes among the littoral nations.

Fishing

Fishery products are an important part of the diet for much of the world's population, although their importance varies from place to place. Fish is far more important in Asia, for instance, than in the United States.

About 92 percent of the total catch is taken by local fishermen, and more than 98 percent of the catch is taken within 200 miles of the shore. Only a few fleets—prominently, those of the Soviet Union and Japan—range the world's oceans. In 1975, the world's fishing fleet, measured in millions of registered tons, was:[16]

	Tonnage	Share of World Total
United States	0.4	3.6%
Western Europe	1.9	16.8
Japan	1.2	10.6
Soviet Union	5.9	52.2
Rest of the world	1.9	16.8
World total	11.3	100.0%

Most fish are caught from ships that are generally too small to be registered. Therefore, despite the Soviet's preponderance of registered tonnage (in ships of 100 tons or more), their share of the world's fish catch is only 15 percent. By contrast, Japan, with 10.6 percent of the fishing fleet tonnage, lands more than 17 percent of the total. In 1975, the world's open-ocean fish catch, measured in millions of metric tons, was:[17]

	Tonnage	Share of World Total
United States	2.7	4.6%
Western Europe	10.8	18.2
Japan	10.3	17.4
Soviet Union	8.9	15.0
Rest of the world	26.6	44.8
World total	59.3	100.0%

In the past ten years, the world's fish catch increased at an annual rate of 2.8 percent. But all of the growth took place in 1965–1970; the total annual yield of ocean fisheries stayed essentially constant at 60 million metric tons from 1970 through 1975. This does not mean, however, that 60 million tons is the "maximum sustainable yield."

During the 1970s there was a drop of 9 million tons (75 percent) in the yield of the Peruvian anchoveta fishery. As a result, Peru's share of the total ocean catch fell from 20 percent in 1970 to just under 6 percent in 1975. The decline in the Peruvian catch was made up by the continuing increase in the fish catch in other oceans.

Even if the Peruvian catch does not recover fully, the world's catch can be expected to grow to 85 million metric tons by 1985 (Table 5-6). If the

TABLE 5-3
SHIPS UNLOADED IN SEABORNE TRADE: 1975
(Millions of metric tons)

	Total	Tanker	Dry Cargo
Europe	1,236	715	521
Japan	549	247	302
United States	391	245	146
Canada	46	23	23
U.S.S.R.	36	6	29
Rest of the world	787	404	384
World Total	3,045	1,640	1,405
Europe + Japan + N.A.	2,222	1,230	992
Share of world total	73%	75%	71%

Source: OECD, *Maritime Transport 1976* (Paris: Organization for Economic Co-operation and Development, 1977), p. 25. Great Lakes traffic has been excluded.

TABLE 5-4
SHIPS LOADED IN SEABORNE TRADE: 1975
(Millions of metric tons)

	Total	Tanker	Dry Cargo
Europe	394	114	280
Japan	70	2	68
United States	228	0	228
Canada	84	6	78
Middle East	969	961	8
U.S.S.R.	120	72	48
Rest of the world	1,274	587	687
World Total	3,139	1,742	1,397
Europe + Japan + N.A.	776	122	654
Share of world total	25%	7%	47%

Source: OECD, *Maritime Transport 1976* (Paris: Organization for Economic Co-operation and Development, 1977), p. 25. Great Lakes traffic has been excluded.

TABLE 5-5
MONTHLY TRANSITS BY STANDARD SHIPS:
1974 and 1985

World Totals	1974	1985
Petroleum tankers	2,725	3,625
Dry bulk carriers	5,775	11,075
General cargo ships	6,700	13,775
Total	15,200	28,475

TABLE 5-6
WORLD FISH CATCH: 1975 and 1985
(Millions of metric tons)

	1975	1985
Atlantic Ocean	24.5	32.6
Mediterranean Sea	1.3	1.8
Pacific Ocean	30.4	47.5
Indian Ocean	3.1	4.8
Total	59.3	86.7

anchoveta share does return to former levels, a total catch of 90 million metric tons is possible.

These trends do not indicate sharply increasing dependence on the seas for food. During 1965-1975, in fact, world meat production and the total fish catch grew at about the same rate, less than the increase in production of grain.

Seabed Resources

For at least the past ten years, there has been a great deal of interest in the economic potential of the resources of the seabed. Along the continental margins, petroleum and gas are the main resources. In the seabed, metals have attracted the most attention.

For the United States, extraction of offshore petroleum and gas has greater primary value than other uses of the seas. Extraction of metals from the seabed, on the other hand, will not have significant economic value for the United States (as far ahead as can be seen).

As long as the oil-producing countries continue to act as a cartel and the metal-producing countries do not, the world will be far more interested in offshore oil and gas than in seabed deposits of metals. The development of North Sea sources, in fact, has already relieved the United Kingdom of dependence on petroleum imports. Norwegian production of North Sea oil doubled in 1975; in the United States expanded exploitation of the oil and gas of the continental shelf is part of emerging energy policies.[18]

In 1975, offshore wells yielded more than 8 million barrels of oil a day, about 15 percent of the world's total production:

	Thousands of Barrels a Day	*Share of World Total*
United States	910	11.0%
Western Europe	319	3.9
Japan	1	—
Soviet Union	230	2.8
Rest of the world	6,804	82.3
World total	8,264	100.0%

Petroleum production offshore is generally associated with production ashore. The Persian Gulf states and Venezuela—all included here with "rest of the world"—account for 55 percent of the world's offshore oil production. Like oil, natural gas is produced from wells, offshore and on land, but the geographic distributions of the two products are not the same. The United States and Western Europe, for example, accounted for nearly 80 percent of the production of natural gas for sale, but only 15 percent of the petroleum.

RESOURCE EXTRACTION FROM THE SEA

The world extracts over 60 million metric tons of fish from the sea each year. The 7,500-ton Japanese crab factory ship *Koyo Maru* carries a crew of 321 men. It is but one of the world's 13,000 oceangoing fishing vessels. (Courtesy National Oceanic and Atmospheric Administration)

Offshore wells, typified by this semisubmersible drilling rig in the Hutton Field of the North Sea, yielded more than 8 million barrels of oil per day in 1975—about 15 percent of the world's total production. (Courtesy Continental Oil Company)

On the deep seabed, manganese nodules are the resources of prime importance. Nodules have been found in all the oceans; those with the highest commercially attractive content lie in the deepest portions of the Pacific.

The United States, Western Europe, and Japan are interested in the development of seabed resources. Exploitation of nodules, in fact, could reduce these countries' reliance on imports of the minerals they comprise: nickel, copper, cobalt, and manganese.

Moreover, production and reserves of these minerals ashore are generally limited to a few developing nations. Zaire alone, for example, accounted for more than half the world's production of cobalt in 1976 and held about a third of the world's reserves. Production of cobalt in developed economies—Australia, Canada, and Finland—amounted to only one-sixth of total production, and these countries had only 5 percent of the world's reserves.[19] Although cobalt is the extreme case, production of other minerals is concentrated in ten nations. The possibility that mineral cartels may limit production and raise prices cannot be ignored.

There is, therefore, substantial incentive for some industrialized nations and some individual industries to exploit seabed deposits. They need the minerals and are developing the technology to recover them. But uncertainty about the law of the seas and about future markets for the minerals is retarding commercial development.

In addition, large amounts of minerals can be economically extracted from mines on land for many years to come. At current rates of use, reserves of manganese will last for more than 200 years; of nickel, for 70 years; of copper, for 60 years; of cobalt, for 40 years.[20] World resources include, in addition, far larger quantities of minerals that cannot be extracted economically at today's prices by today's techniques.

For all these reasons, it is unlikely that seabed minerals will be produced in commercial quantities from manganese nodules in the near future. By 1985, a small number of firms from an even smaller number of nations may be so engaged, but the economic importance of this activity will be small.

Western Uses of the Seas—By Region

The maritime activities of the United States, Western Europe, and Japan reach into all the world's oceans for varying purposes and to differing degrees. The purpose of this section is to examine the four major regions of maritime competition—the Atlantic, the Mediterranean, the Pacific, and the Indian Ocean—in order to show the amounts and varieties of maritime activities of the Western Alliance.

Atlantic Ocean

From almost any point of view, the Atlantic Ocean will represent the most important security-at-sea concern until at least the year 2000.

The United States has close cultural, political, and military ties with Europe. The North Atlantic lends its name to the most important of our military alliances. This commitment by the United States to support Europe is now about thirty years old. During these years, Europe has recovered from the devastation of World War II and has built up modern industrial economies. In 1976, the total Gross Domestic Product of the European Economic Community amounted to $1,390 billion, about 81 percent as large as the United States' output of goods and services.[21]

The need to defend NATO has guided U.S. plans for general-purpose forces. Although airlift capabilities are being expanded, deployment of large-scale reinforcements to Europe would require sealift. Seaborne resupply for our own forces and those of our allies would also be necessary.[22]

Some naval forces will therefore be needed to keep open the sea lines of communication in the Atlantic. Other naval forces may be able to play a role in a European conflict by projecting power ashore. Carrier-based tactical aviation and amphibious forces can add to NATO's capability, particularly on the flanks.

The United States has other security agreements on and near the Atlantic. An agreement with Spain provides for air and naval bases. The Rio Treaty (formally, the Inter-American Treaty of Reciprocal Assistance), which was signed in 1947, commits the United States to a share in the defense of thirteen Latin American nations that border the Atlantic.

These military commitments also reflect the great economic importance of seaborne trade in the Atlantic. Eighty percent of U.S. seaborne imports of manufactured products move through Atlantic ports. And, of course, all of Western Europe's seaborne trade moves on the Atlantic. Trade in engineering products, mainly machinery, flows in volume in both directions between Europe and North America.

The distribution of foreign direct investment provides another kind of evidence of economic interests. The citizens of the United States have close to $76 billion invested in countries that border the Atlantic Ocean, more than 70 percent of all direct U.S. investment overseas.[23] Most of the investment in Atlantic nations—half of the total U.S. overseas direct investment—is concentrated in Europe. In turn, the Europeans have invested more than $12 billion in the United States.

Trade and investment imply shipping. Table 5-7 gives a projection of monthly transits across the Atlantic in 1985—by the standard ship-types defined earlier. More than half the world's shipping will travel these routes.

The main trade across the North Atlantic is in manufactured goods. The Europeans import some phosphate rock, coal, aluminum, nickel, and other materials from the United States and Canada, though they get most of their raw material imports elsewhere. But trade in manufactured products is important to both Western Europe and North America. More than half of all the manufactured products imported by North America is shipped across the Atlantic, and about 43 percent of European imports of finished or manufactured products comes from North America.

On the South Atlantic, the most important maritime interest is, beyond question, the movement of Persian Gulf oil to the United States and Europe. About 90 percent of that oil is shipped through the South Atlantic. Although the Suez Canal will be widened and deepened to accommodate larger ships, the volume of imports from the Persian Gulf will continue to grow.[24] As Table 5-7 shows, the growth will be at a modest 2 percent annual rate, slowed by high OPEC prices and exploitation of North Sea oil and gas resources. Nonetheless, the route around the Cape and up the sealanes of the South Atlantic will predominate in importance.

The South Atlantic region is also a source of raw materials. Imports of iron ore and semifinished products account for most of the trade. The United States also imports other metals from sources on the South Atlantic: beryllium, chromite, cobalt, columbium, manganese, platinum, tantalum, and vanadium. But the United States does not depend heavily on these imports; they are, in fact, of small economic importance, at least to nations in the Northern Hemisphere. Not much shipping is required for these raw materials or for the manufactured products that are transported through the South Atlantic.

In sum, the importance of the Atlantic Ocean to shipping derives from the exchange of manufactured goods between the industrialized nations of North America and Western Europe and from the movement of Middle East oil to North America and Europe.

The Atlantic is heavily fished. Table 5-8 shows that about 40 percent of the world's open ocean fish catch comes from the Atlantic, and two-thirds of this share from the North Atlantic. When Communist states are included, the proportion of fish caught in the Atlantic by coastal states rises to 97 percent. Japan, Korea, and a few others catch the remaining 3 percent.

Among the littoral states, Western European nations took 10.4 million metric tons in 1975, 42 percent of the total. The Soviets took 5.2 million tons; the United States and Canada, 2.8. The remainder was taken by smaller states.

About 12 percent of the world's catch comes from the South Atlantic. Half is taken by South Atlantic nations; the South Atlantic is not an important fishing ground for the U.S. and European fishing fleets.

The Atlantic contains a wide variety of seabed resources, but in quantities far smaller than are available elsewhere. In the North Atlantic, offshore oil and gas production is concentrated in the North Sea and the Caribbean. Production in these areas accounts for something less than 20 percent of all offshore oil and about 3 percent of total oil production. These percentages will grow as the North Sea wells are developed. Exploration off the east coast of the United States is just beginning. West Africa accounts for only 3 percent of the estimated world reserves of offshore oil.

Manganese nodules have been located in the west-central Atlantic, off Florida, and along the Mid-Atlantic Ridge. In the South Atlantic, they have been concentrated along the Rio Grande Rise, about 800 miles off the coast of Brazil, and on the Agulhas Plateau, about 300 miles off the coast of South Africa. Large-scale exploitation of these resources is many years away.

Mediterranean

Compared with the vast shipping and fishing enterprises in the Atlantic, maritime activity around the Mediterranean is minor. But three members of NATO—Italy, Greece, and Turkey—are best reached by sea. To some strategists, the Mediterranean flank of NATO represents one of the main weaknesses of the Alliance. The largest regular deployments of the Soviet Fleet take place in the Mediterranean.

Moreover, there are many sources of conflict in the Mediterranean, particularly at the eastern end. Arab-Isaeli hostility continues, as does U.S. commitment to Israel. Greek-Turkish differences over Cyprus and the Aegean could erupt. Splits in the Arab world could continue, and the course of Libya under Qaddafi is not predictable.

The United States has deployed naval forces in the Mediterranean since 1947: a carrier and assault force from 1947 through 1951, two carrier task forces ever since.[25] Naval forces are also maintained in the Mediterranean by Britain and, of course, by France and other Mediterranean states.

Most of the shipping in the Mediterranean is intraregional. North African oil and gas and Moroccan phosphates are shipped to Europe. Food and manufactured goods are transported to the European nations of the Mediterranean and, to a lesser degree, to North African states.[26] West Germany and other NATO nations dominate the trade of the Mediterranean nations. The United States' trade with the Mediterranean area amounts to about 5 percent of our imports and a slightly larger share of our exports. As Table 5-9 shows, shipping through the Mediterranean amounts to only 5 percent of the world's interregional trade.

When the Suez Canal is widened and deepened, the importance of the Mediterranean to the world's oil trade will increase. Some of the larger ships will be redirected through the Mediterranean (unless Suez tolls are excessive). Very large tankers will, of course, continue to round the Cape.

The other maritime activities in the Mediterranean are of mainly local importance. In 1975, the fish taken in the Mediterranean and the Black Sea amounted to 1.3 million metric tons, or 2.2 percent of the world's ocean catch. Modest continuing growth—3 percent a year—will raise this catch to 1.8 million tons in 1985. As for seabed resources, Italy and Spain pump small amounts of oil from offshore wells, but heavy development from those sources is unlikely.

Pacific Ocean

The huge Pacific Ocean basin contains a rich variety of resources: Chilean copper, Alaskan fish, Australian alumina, Malaysian tin, Indonesian oil, and the Japanese force of skilled labor, to name a few. It also encompasses a variety of political and security interests. The United States has a territory in Guam, bases in the Philippines and Japan, forces in Okinawa and Korea and at sea, and defense treaties or security arrangements with the Philippines, Australia, New Zealand, Japan, South Korea, and Taiwan. There have been striking changes in international relations in the Pacific during the 1960s and 1970s: the Sino-Soviet split, the U.S. diplomatic initiatives to China, the Nixon "shocks" to Japan's economy, and the Communist takeovers in South Vietnam and Cambodia.

Although some find in all this a reduction of U.S. interests in Asia, the fact remains that we continue to have major interests and political commitments there. Several of these changes increase the importance of a U.S. maritime presence to support the credibility of our remaining commitments.

Our relations with Japan, involving major military and economic interests, are at the core of U.S. involvement in the Pacific. Japan's spending for its self-defense forces is small in relation to its economy— about 0.9 percent of GNP. But the United States has a large military presence in Japan, including airfields and naval facilities. Some ships from the Seventh Fleet operate in the Western Pacific from Japanese home ports.

The Japanese economy depends on seaborne commerce.[27] Japan's main economic resource is a skilled and productive labor force. With almost no domestic sources of industrial raw materials, the Japanese must import them from all over the world. They also import a substantial portion of their foodstuffs—wheat, soybeans, and sugar, for example. Moreover, their economic prosperity depends on access to markets for selling the goods they manufacture from imported materials.

Shipping is important to the other nations of the Pacific as well. For most, it is their only means of trade. As a result, ocean shipping in the Pacific amounts to one-third of the world total, when measured in standard ships (Table 5-10). The figures in Table 5-10 reflect the heavy flows of primary products to Japan and the shipments of finished products from Japan to the rest of the world.

To limit their dependence on other nations for food, the Japanese have developed a large, modern fishing fleet. Throughout Asia, in fact, fish is an important part of the diet; more than half of the world's catch is taken from the Pacific Ocean (Table 5-11).

The seabed resources of the Pacific are virtually unexploited. Some oil is produced off the coasts of Indonesia and California, and much interest—some of it resulting in conflicting claims—is being shown in the East and South China seas for their petroleum potential. No production has yet begun there, however. There are also major sources of manganese nodules in the Central and Eastern Pacific.

Indian Ocean

Although formal Western defense and security commitments in the Indian Ocean have declined steadily, important new economic and security interests have developed during the 1970s. The SEATO and CENTO arrangements are no longer important. The U.S. commitments to Australia and New Zealand—represented in the ANZUS treaty—remain strong. By all measures but one, the United States, Europe, and Japan have shown only small interest in the resources and markets of the Indian Ocean.

The single exception—and the key to renewed Western interest—lies in the vast oil resources of the Middle East. These are truly essential to the economies of both Japanese and Western Europeans. For the United States, they represent the one important case of dependence on foreign suppliers. This dependence, moreover, is likely to continue for at least ten to fifteen years for the United States and indefinitely for Japan. The only way Middle East oil can reach the markets of the industrialized nations is by shipment through the Indian Ocean.

The amount of interregional activity in the Indian Ocean is shown in Table 5-12. In contrast to other ocean areas, where dry cargo shipments dominate, oil generates half the standard ship transits in the Indian Ocean.

Because the local economies are not developed and because there are alternative sources closer to the developed economies, ores and other mineral resources of the Indian Ocean area are largely unexploited. This fact is reflected by the small numbers of dry bulk cargo shipments (largely iron ore) on the Indian Ocean. On the other hand, shipments of general cargo represent a significant number of the interregional transits in the area.

The Indian Ocean fish catch in 1975 was 3.1 million metric tons, 5.2 percent of the world total. The Indian Ocean states—mainly India, Pakistan, Yemen, Indonesia, and Thailand—took 96 percent of the catch.

TABLE 5-7
MONTHLY SHIP TRANSITS IN THE ATLANTIC: 1974 and 1985

	1974	1985	Growth Rate
Petroleum tankers	1,575	2,000	2.2%
Dry bulk carriers	3,150	5,875	5.8
General cargo ships	3,850	8,000	6.9
Total	8,575	15,875	5.8%
Share of world total	56.4%	55.8%	

TABLE 5-8
ATLANTIC OCEAN FISH CATCH: 1975 and 1985
(Millions of metric tons)

	1975	1985	Annual Growth Rate
North Atlantic	16.0	19.0	1.8%
Central Atlantic	5.1	9.2	6.1
South Atlantic	3.4	4.4	2.4
Total	24.5	32.6	2.9%
Share of world total	41.3%	37.6%	

TABLE 5-9
MONTHLY SHIP TRANSITS IN THE MEDITERRANEAN SEA: 1974 and 1985

	1974	1985	Growth Rate
Petroleum tankers	125	200	4.8%
Dry bulk carriers	300	600	7.2
General cargo ships	350	650	6.4
Total	775	1,450	6.5%
Share of world total	5.1%	5.1%	

TABLE 5-10
MONTHLY SHIP TRANSITS IN THE PACIFIC OCEAN: 1974 and 1985

	1974	1985	Annual Growth
Petroleum tankers	400	550	2.9%
Dry bulk carriers	2,300	4,550	6.4
General cargo ships	2,050	4,300	7.0
Total	4,750	9,400	6.4%
Share of world total	31.3%	33.0%	

TABLE 5-11
PACIFIC OCEAN FISH CATCH: 1975 and 1985
(Millions of metric tons)

	1975	1985	Annual Growth
North Pacific	19.3	27.8	3.8%
Central Pacific	6.2	12.6	7.2
South Pacific	4.9	7.1	3.8
Total	30.4	47.5	4.6
Share of world total	51.3%	54.8%	

TABLE 5-12
MONTHLY SHIP TRANSITS IN THE INDIAN OCEAN: 1974 and 1985

	1974	1985	Annual Growth
Petroleum tankers	625	875	3.1%
Dry bulk carriers	25	50	6.5%
General cargo ships	450	825	5.7%
Total	1,100	1,750	4.3%
Share of world total	7.2%	6.1%	

Although outsiders (the Soviet Union, Japan, Taiwan, and Korea) took 4 percent, their total catch has been declining. The Indian Ocean yield has been growing at a 4 to 5 percent annual rate; it should approach 5 million metric tons by 1985, well below the estimated potential harvest of 15 million tons.[28]

Except for offshore oil in the Persian Gulf, the development of seabed resources in the Indian Ocean can be expected to lag behind that in the rest of the world. The same factors that limit the development of mineral resources on land will slow the development of offshore deposits.

Summary

The seas are important to Western nations. In the past decade, Soviet maritime capabilities have grown significantly (see Chapter 9). To the extent that these emerging capabilities could be used to jeopardize important Western interests, new strategies and programs are needed.

Security of the sealanes will become more important as the years go by. Seaborne trade has been growing faster than overall economic activity. Imports of raw materials, particularly oil, represent the major potential vulnerability for the Western Alliance. The effects of interruption in the supply of these materials depend on extent and duration. Some government policies—especially stockpiling or raw materials—can help protect against loss of supply from any source, including hostile naval action.

The use of the seas is likely to continue to grow as world economic activity expands. Developments of technology will give further impetus to this growth. But future developments in the law of the sea and in protectionist domestic policies are likely to raise the cost of sea activities and thereby slow the rate of growth.

By almost any measure, all the nations of the Western Alliance are heavy users of the oceans. Commerce in primary commodities is likely to remain the most important of the various ocean activities for the foreseeable future. The sealanes in the Atlantic will certainly be the most intensively used.

Seaborne commerce is more important to Japan than to Europe and more important to Europe than to the United States. The allies of the United States must therefore be concerned about maintaining the security of their sea lines of communication. By its strong commitments, the United States demonstrates that it shares the responsibility.

6

Implications of Soviet Maritime Capabilities

In a recent book called *The Seapower of the State*, Admiral Sergei Gorshkov, commander of the Soviet Fleet, set forth a comprehensive analysis of the Soviet view of maritime activities. As defined by Gorshkov, "seapower" includes merchant shipping, fishing, oceanographic research, and, of course, the navy. In each of these particulars, Soviet capabilities are strong and growing. Gorshkov says:

> we regard sea power as an intricate complex of various components linked to the area of the economy of the country and to the policy of the Communist Party, to the area of the country's defense capability, science and the training of cadres, and to the area of the practical realization of all those possibilities which the exploitation of the seas and oceans will open up for the building of Communism.[1]

He adds that seapower supports foreign policy, strengthens trade and cultural ties, and carries economic aid to developing nations.

This chapter analyzes the effects that Soviet maritime activities in peacetime, crisis, or war might have on the nations of the Western Alliance. It concludes by examining the implications of these developments for our naval forces and those of our allies.

Soviet Maritime Activities

Extensive maritime activity by the Soviets does not mean that they themselves are dependent on the seas. Actually, they depend very little on imports of raw materials. Although the Soviet Union imports perhaps 40 percent of the bauxite it consumes (and almost all of its natural rubber), it has vast natural resources and a tradition of economic self-sufficiency. Trade with the West for food and advanced technology has been increasing, to be sure, but the basic independence of the Soviet economy has not been sacrificed. The Soviets' foreign trade is small in relation to their economy, and nearly half of this commerce is with their Eastern European neighbors.

The GNP of the Soviets is estimated at a little more than half that of the United States. Yet they import only 18 percent as much as the United States in dry cargo and only 3 to 4 percent as much as the United States in tanker cargo. (In 1975, the Soviet Union imported 29 million metric tons of dry cargo by sea; the United States, 164 million.) The Soviets depend far less than the Western Alliance on seaborne trade.

Seaborne trade is more important to the other members of the Warsaw Pact, who already import nearly three times as much by sea as the Soviet Union; these imports have been growing about 10 percent a year since 1970.

Shipping

In maritime transport—tankers, freighters, bulk carriers, container ships, and passenger ships—the Soviets now rank fourth in numbers of ships and ninth in total tonnage.[2] Since the 1950s, the Soviets have become a real competitor in the international shipping market. Buying and building ships, the Soviets have increased their cargo capacity by 750 percent. By far the most impressive period of expansion was from 1960 through 1965, when their merchant fleet, seaborne foreign trade tonnage, and total international trade rose at an average annual rate of 15-17 percent.

Since 1965, that growth has slowed to a rate no higher than the world rate of expansion. In fact, since 1970, the slackened rate has caused a drop in position for the Soviets, whose fleet now comprises 2.7 percent of the world's trading vessels; in 1970, the figure was 3.5 percent.

One result of the growth is that Soviet merchant ships are newer, on the average, than their Western counterparts. But they are generally of smaller capacity. Shallow harbors in the Soviet Union have limited the average size of Soviet merchant ships to less than half the average of the world fleet. The Soviets are just beginning to acquire large ships with modern cargo-handling technology (see Chapter 3).

One motive for the expansion of their merchant fleet seems to be self-reliance. Soviet flagships carry 60 percent of their overseas trade. This merchant fleet affords significant advantages: Soviet cargoes are not subject to foreign scrutiny and the Soviets do not have to lose foreign exchange for transporting what they import, with the rare exception of grain. Approximately 80 percent of the Soviets' trade cargoes carried by their own fleet consists of exports; the main one is petroleum, which accounts for nearly half of all their seaborne trade. Exports accounted for 77 percent of their total seaborne trade in 1975.

Since imports are generally limited to industrial goods from developed countries, a great deal of cargo space is available on the Soviet ships once they have delivered their exports. The Soviet Merchant Marine has found that by offering low shipping rates to carry cargoes between foreign ports ("cross-trading") it can earn substantial reserves of hard currency. In mid-1975, of the fifty-eight Soviet international lines, twenty were engaged largely or entirely in cross-trading. Cross-trades contribute about 20 percent of all cargoes carried by the Soviet Fleet.

Although the Soviets preferred to operate outside the rate-setting conference system in the past, two Soviet lines joined conferences in 1975. Together with plans for greater fleet capacity, this move may reflect a willingness by the Soviets to accept commercial rate structures (adding their voice to rate-level discussions) and to place some economic priorities ahead of political ones.

Tapping the market between the United States and Western Europe and earning hard currency in the process, the Soviets carry about 13 percent of the volume to and from West Germany and 22 percent of the volume of seaborne trade between the United States and the rest of Europe. Following a 1972 agreement that opened forty U.S. ports to Soviet ships and forty Soviet ports to U.S. ships, trade between the two nations increased sixfold. Combined with the U.S.-Europe cross-trading the Soviet Merchant Marine engages in, it now transports 8 percent of all U.S. seaborne trade. Most Soviet cross-trading shipments, however, go to Communist or less-developed trading partners, where payment is often in soft currency.

The Soviet Fleet brings Canadian flour to Cuba and Middle East petroleum to Eastern Europe. Soviet trade with less-developed countries accounted for 9 percent of the Soviets' total trade in 1965. It increased to 12 percent in 1970 and has remained fairly constant since then.

In size and type, the general-cargo vessels that make up much of the Soviet Fleet are well suited to commerce with less-developed nations and ports and are even suited to military supply for some types of conflict. The large number of roll-on/roll-off ships scheduled for construction would be particularly useful for delivering military equipment through poorly developed ports.

Shipping to North Vietnam, Cuba, Egypt, India, Iraq, Angola, and Ethiopia provides clear examples of use of the merchant fleet to support Soviet allies. This merchant shipping also promotes diplomatic contact with the Third World and yields intelligence about commercial and naval activities. Merchant ships sometimes serve under naval command, providing logistic support or taking part in naval exercises.

Beyond these direct benefits, the Soviet Merchant Marine enhances the Soviet image among the nations of the Third World. Its newer ships demonstrate that the Soviets have mastered the latest techniques of cargo handling and shipbuilding. The size of the fleet and its frequent

SOVIET CARGO SHIPS

Modern Soviet cargo ships like the *Pridneprovsk* shown above cruising the Western Pacific are limited in average size to less than half the average size for the world merchant fleet and are well-suited to shallow, undeveloped harbors. (Courtesy U.S. Navy)

Relatively small ro-ro (roll-on/roll-off) ships of the Soviet merchant fleet like the Inzhener Machulskiy class shown above are involved in "cross-trading" between foreign ports to earn hard currency. (Courtesy U.S. Navy)

appearance in foreign ports show the size and strength of the Soviet economy. Moreover, Soviet ships deliver technical and economic assistance as well as military aid. The Soviets acquire both the good will and the knowledge of local ports and operating conditions that is a prerequisite for development of naval facilities. Such was the sequence of events for the Soviets in Somalia in 1965-1975.[3]

If war broke out, the Soviets could lose a substantial part of their merchant fleet. Although that prospect may inhibit Soviet actions under some circumstances, it is hardly likely to be a major factor in Soviet thinking during a major crisis. After all, earnings of hard currency are important only if the Soviets expect to continue trading with the West.

Fishing

As outlined in the preceding chapter, the Soviet Union's wide-ranging fishing fleet is second to none in registered vessels.[4]

Fishing provides 13 to 15 percent of the animal protein and about 6.5 percent of all protein in the Soviet diet. Like maritime transport, the fishing industry is a source of foreign exchange and naval intelligence to the U.S.S.R.

Nonetheless, the Soviet leaders probably do not regard the fishing industry as vital. They can certainly feed their people and sustain their economy without any fish from the deep oceans. In a war with the Western Alliance, they would probably be willing to sacrifice much of their investment in oceangoing fishing vessels.

Offshore Resources

The Soviets are conducting research efforts to find and develop offshore resources. They are particularly interested in oil and gas.[5] The main reason seems to be a strong desire to maintain energy independence. They have a long coastline and a large continental shelf, and three-quarters of this area is thought to have good potential for oil and gas. But much of this is in the Arctic, where climate, geography, and economics suggest that development will be slow.

The technology for exploiting offshore energy resources is available to the Soviets. They have more than 2,000 offshore rigs in the Caspian Sea, producing oil and gas, and they have explored for both in the Black and Baltic seas, off the Kola Peninsula, and in the Sea of Okhotsk. Much of the needed technology has been acquired from the West. For use in the Caspian Sea, for example, they are building offshore rigs that are essentially copies of a Dutch-built rig they bought in 1967. The Soviets have also been acquiring foreign technology for submersible vehicles to be used for seismic exploration of the seabed and for pipelaying, drilling, and testing.

The Soviets are also interested in extracting other minerals from the sea and the seabed.[6] Since the Soviet Union is self-sufficient in most minerals and an exporter of many, the purpose of this activity would probably be to earn hard currency in order to finance imports of foreign technology. In comparison with the West, the Soviets' capabilities for deep seabed mining are small. They have dredged up manganese nodule samples but have made little progress toward commercial exploitation.

Contests at Sea

The United States, Japan, and the nations of Western Europe use the seas more intensively than the Soviets. And the Soviet Union has no important vulnerabilities arising from its ocean activities. Because of this basic asymmetry in the extent and importance of the use of the seas, the Soviets may think that competition at sea is a relatively attractive way to achieve their political, economic, and strategic objectives.

The commander of the Soviet Navy seems to employ this logic in *Seapower of the State*. There is no doubt that Gorshkov recognizes the significance of the sealanes to the United States and its allies in Europe and Asia. He says that "some 90 percent of the total volume of foreign commercial shipping consists of raw materials and food" and points out that petroleum shipping has been growing by about 10 percent a year.

By emphasizing seaborne trade in raw materials, petroleum, and food, Gorshkov implies that not all shipping has the same strategic significance. Although trade in manufactured products is great in volume and value, it is of less immediate economic consequence to the West than trade in the commodities he mentions.

Gorshkov's assessment of the relative importance of the various oceans, at least for shipping, takes account of their different degrees of significance and is consistent with the analysis in the preceding chapter.

In assessing the implications of Soviet maritime capabilities, therefore, one must consider which Western activity is threatened and where. The most important consideration is whether the Soviet capabilities are employed in peacetime, during a time of crisis, or in a shooting war.

Peacetime Competition

Since World War II, the Soviets have become active competitors with other merchant and fishing fleets on the world's oceans. New competitors are, of course, seldom welcomed by existing interests.

Still, the total economic effect of these Soviet maritime activities has been small, especially in comparison with other factors that influence world markets. The closing and reopening of the Suez Canal, the OPEC embargo and price rise, the development of supertankers and container ships, and the subsidy programs in various countries—all have had greater influence on shipping markets than the advent and growth of the Soviet Merchant Marine.

Three types of Soviet effort have attracted special attention: cargo preference, cross-trading, and price-cutting.

The Soviets prefer to carry their own trade in their own ships and are not alone in this preference. But they can not always manage it; some 40 percent of their cargoes move under foreign flags.

Soviet cross-trading is sometimes viewed as harmful to Western ship operators. By engaging in this kind of activity, Soviet ships do indeed carry cargoes that would otherwise sail under other flags. But the motivation for cross-trading is to utilize capacity that would otherwise be wasted. The revenues thus raised would be forgone if the ship returned to the Soviet Union in ballast. Sometimes, the Soviets' ships are chartered out during the months when most of their ports are icebound. Recently, they have used some newer and larger ships in cross-trading full time, mainly for carrying bulk cargoes for Communist and less-developed countries.

Because the Russians have generally remained outside the organized shipping conferences or cartels, their pricing policies have, on occasion, upset established shipping interests. Because their ships are smaller and slower, some discount is required in order to attract cargo; but, as with cargo preference, rate-cutting is not a monopoly of the Soviets.

Penetration into the major shipping markets of the free world, however, has been slight. Soviet cross-trading among the industrialized nations of the West may be an economic threat, but it does not affect their security. In any case, a halt in Soviet shipping to and from the United States and its major allies would not do significant economic damage. At worst, rates would rise a little; at best, underemployed Western ships would get the cargoes.

Because shipping is a state activity of the U.S.S.R., the operations of the Soviet Merchant Marine may have more political meaning than the purely commercial activities of its Western counterpart. A visit by a Soviet ship to pick up or deliver cargo can represent a state decision. Such a visit may, therefore, have a somewhat greater effect than the comings and goings of the private merchant fleets of Western countries.

The Soviets' maritime successes have not always lasted. For instance, they made heavy use of their merchant fleet for a period of time for deliveries to Indonesia, Egypt, Somalia, and India. Yet their influence in these nations has since waned.

Seen from a longer perspective, the Soviets seem to be adopting new attitudes with respect to the use of the seas. As they become more and more involved in exploitation of the ocean for economic gain, they are coming to share many of the views of the other seagoing nations. This tendency is already evident in the Law of the Sea conferences. Whether the underlying motives are military or economic, the U.S.S.R. has a growing stake in stability and order at sea.

But it would be a mistake to think of the Soviets' peacetime maritime activities as wholly benign. Although their immediate motive is generally economic, their ultimate purpose is projection of power and influence.

Crisis

In the past thirty-two years, political crises have occurred in many places over many issues, and usually they have not been expected. More than 200 times since World War II, the United States has used its military forces for political objectives.[7] These actions have taken place throughout the Northern Hemisphere: in the Caribbean, Europe, Asia, and the Middle East. Incidents in the Southern Hemisphere are likely in the future.

The hottest issues have included Soviet missiles in Cuba, access to Berlin, the capture of the Pueblo, the conflict in Cyprus, the Arab-Israeli fighting, fishing rights near Iceland, and the seizure of the Mayaguez. The military forces of the Western Alliance must be flexible enough to cope with unexpected situations of these kinds.

Our naval units were called upon in more than 80 percent of past crises. Typically, naval forces were sent to the scene ready for action, but they rarely had to act. Maritime interests were seldom involved.

Twice since World War II, the United States has taken action to stop selected shipping activities—by quarantining Cuba in 1962 and by mining the territorial waters of North Vietnam in 1972. The Soviets have never taken similar steps against Western shipping.

In the future, there are almost certain to be situations of competitive intervention, when superpower support for opposing states or factions leads to a confrontation between naval elements of East and West. This possibility may well become a major factor in the design and operation of both the U.S. and Soviet fleets.

The Soviets now have enough naval forces—if unopposed—to halt traffic through any of the world's major straits or to blockade or quarantine almost any of the world's nations, at least temporarily. Whether they would try and whether they would succeed, if opposed, is another matter.

Until the mid-1960s, Soviet naval forces seldom deployed away from home waters. Direct naval encounters between the United States and the Soviets were therefore very rare. But the large and steady deployments of the Soviet Fleet into the Mediterranean, the Indian Ocean, and elsewhere have since made such situations more likely. United States and Soviet forces faced each other in the Mediterranean during the events associated with the Middle East crises of 1967, 1970, and 1973; both nations deployed forces to

CRISES INVOLVING NAVAL FORCES

Eighty percent of the more than 200 crises in the past thirty-two years have involved the deployment of U.S. naval forces, although they have rarely had to act. The Soviet cargo ship *Anosov* is shown above carrying eight canvas-covered missiles from Cuba in November 1962. (Courtesy U.S. Navy)

United States task forces, like TF-60 shown above in the Mediterranean in 1976, are forward deployed in peacetime and are ready if needed to respond to crisis situations. This formation included the new nuclear carrier U.S.S. *Nimitz* (CVN-68) and two nuclear-powered cruisers (CGN-36 and CGN-37). (Courtesy U.S. Navy)

the Indian Ocean during the Indo-Pakistani war of December 1971 (see Chapter 3).

The Soviets are generally cautious; were they to make a naval move against the Western Allies, it would have to be for an important goal or stake. They might well undertake confrontation or blockade in hopes of forestalling the need for more direct use of military power. Nevertheless, any such military action, though localized and for limited goals, could result in conflict with the United States. Just how far the two sides would be willing to go would, of course, depend on their capabilities, on the area, and on the stakes involved.

If the issue were not fundamental, the United States and its allies might choose not to respond to a Soviet blockade with force, but rather (initially, at least), to take roundabout routes or drop out of the specific areas involved. Diversion of traffic can impose some costs, however, especially if shipping is already fully employed. If the Suez Canal were capable of handling 250,000-deadweight-ton tankers and if, at the same time, the Bab el Mandeb were closed by blockade, the cost of shipping oil from the Persian Gulf to the east coast of the United States would rise by 20 percent.[8] Access to the Malaccan Strait is worth perhaps $75 million a year to the United States and more to Japan. The United States' trillion-dollar economy could afford to pay such costs, and even the $500 billion Japanese economy could absorb substantial costs without seriously affecting the standard of living of its people.

Some local crises could have wide effects. A successful blockade of the Strait of Hormuz would impose great costs on the economies of Japan, Western Europe, and the United States.[9] Military or political closure of the Strait of Gibraltar would be devastating to the nations of the Mediterranean but much less harmful to the economies of the rest of Europe and the United States. The military consequences, however, would be dramatic. A blockade of Japan could hardly be called a local crisis, for it would be a major challenge to the United States that could easily lead to war.

The Soviet Navy—and some Third World navies—can harass or temporarily cut the flow of shipping in local areas.[10] But, with rare exceptions, *local* seaborne trade is not essential to the general functioning of industrialized Western economies.

The political consequences of a maritime crisis might be harder to bear than the economic effects. Nations not directly involved would observe the course of events and draw their own conclusions. If one side gained a major strategic advantage because the other was unwilling to intervene or counter a blockade, alliance partners might begin to doubt the strength of commitments. In many cases, therefore, it would be desirable to have the ability to keep seaborne trade flowing, if only for broader, political reasons.

If, on the other hand, the Western Alliance harassed or seized Soviet merchant or fishing ships, the Soviets could not protect them easily. The Soviet Union has invested a substantial amount in the development of its merchant marine and fishing fleet. In a maritime crisis, Soviet leaders, too, might find the political consequences of a failure harder to bear than the economic effects.

The Soviets are less likely to take direct naval action against Western shipping than to try to stem the flow of materials at the source through political action. To forestall these possibilities, Western Alliance policies—such as diversifying sources of supply and stockpiling—are directed against political as well as military threats to foreign suppliers.

Wartime

Competitive intervention or other conflicts of basic interest could lead to serious hostilities between the United States and the Soviet Union. Chapter 13 analyzes such a war fought with conventional weapons and suggests that the Western Alliance might lose several hundred ships in the first three months, while the Soviets might lose most of the submarines they had committed to the battle. This, in itself, would be a serious disruption of the flow of seaborne trade. But other, less direct causes would probably have a greater effect on the amounts of material moved by sea.

Convoying has usually been resorted to when shipping is under attack by a hostile power. But organizing and operating a convoy system takes time and reduces the flow of shipping. Loaded ships must be held in port until enough are assembled to make up a convoy and sometimes they must wait for escort ships. The convoy, once under way, is restricted to the speed of the slowest vessel. On arrival there is another delay because ports may be saturated and ships must wait to be unloaded. The cumulative effect of the various delays could reduce shipping capacity by perhaps 25 percent, so that 200 ships might be needed to carry cargoes that 150 could handle in peacetime.

Another effect is harder to assess. The prospect of losses tends to cause shippers to ship less and to make ship operators limit their sailings. Even apart from any unwillingness of neutral crews to sail in war zones, war insurance rates are high, reducing the demand for shipping.

Some factors act in the reverse direction. Shipping volume is not an end in itself; importing nations are concerned with receiving goods, not merely ships. Experience has shown that ships can be used more intensively than is normal in peacetime—by carrying refined metals rather than ores, for example. When these factors are taken into account, the estimated drop of 25 percent in shipping capacity seems high. More intensive use of ships could reduce that figure by perhaps 5 to 10 percent.

It is hard to estimate the economic effects of interruptions in shipping in wartime. There is no recent experience, and there are major uncertainties about the fighting itself. Finally, there are difficulties in predicting the policies of all the governments involved.

What little evidence there is about the effects of blockades and antishipping campaigns is drawn from World Wars I and II. In the short run, stockpiles and business inventories of imported materials can offset import reductions. Over the long run, the experience of the world wars suggests that reductions of seaborne imports cannot, *by themselves,* bring about surrender. Germany showed little sensitivity to the blockade in World War II, and there is good reason to doubt that the blockade was important in World War I. In World War II, Great Britain and Japan, both extensive trading countries, managed to survive extreme reductions in shipping. Investments were made in import-replacing industries. Major shifts occurred in the size, employment, and character of the labor force, and temporary use was made of domestic resources that would not have been available over the long run.

Although levels of consumption may be related to imports in specific cases, the relationship is often complex, depending on the role of the country in the war, the availability of capital, labor, and raw materials, and the alternative demands for shipping. Moreover, the relation between consumption and political stability is obscure. The effect of imports on political stability is certainly complex and probably beyond analysis.

Is there cause for worry if the Japanese GNP falls by 25 percent in a conventional war? How much should the United States spend to hold the reduction in Japan's GNP to 20 percent, or 5 percent? The United States should consider the political effects of low levels of shipping traffic, and, alternatively, of levels of imports that maintain GNP at peacetime levels. Concern with imports should not be allowed to obscure an alternative such as maintenance of food and fuel stockpiles if continuation of high levels of shipping proves costly.

Prudence dictates the stockpiling of many materials—minerals, foods, and fuels. But stockpiling against the possibility of a long war is probably impractical; a flow of needed materials (especially food and oil) must be reestablished and maintained if war should come.

Nevertheless, strong confidence in the dependability of help from the United States is fundamental to Western solidarity. Any perception that the United States could not or would not support its allies during a war with Soviet forces would undermine the Western Alliance.

The Japanese, of course, are highly dependent on continuing use of the seas for their economic well-being. Yet they cannot defend the full length of their sealanes and they are vulnerable to blockades or antishipping campaigns. They know it, we know it, and, we must assume, the Soviets know it. The growing capabilities of the Soviet Pacific Fleet lend substance to Japan's concern about security of the sealanes.

ALLIANCE NAVAL FORCE IN THE PACIFIC

Modern units of the Japanese navy like the Tachikaze-class (DD-168) destroyer shown above and the Haruna-class (DD-141) shown below could provide valuable naval assistance in retaining control of the seas in the Western Pacific during time of war. Whether or not Japan would side with the West in a war with the Soviet Union might well depend on its perceptions of the strength of U.S. naval forces in the Pacific. (Courtesy Government of Japan)

Since World War II, the Japanese have had close political, military, and economic ties with the West. This is important because Japan is in a strategic location relative to the Soviet Union. Forces operating from Japan could pose a real threat to the Soviet Pacific Fleet and could exact substantial attrition if Soviet forces were caught at their bases. The task would be very difficult if the Western forces could not operate from Japan. If, in the event of war, Japan were to opt for neutrality, the ability of the United States to contend for control of the Western Pacific would be sharply reduced.

If a worldwide war should erupt between the United States and the Soviet Union, the Japanese would face a difficult choice. If they elected to stand by the Western Alliance, they would expose their vulnerable sealanes to considerable risk. If they chose neutrality, they would face long-term political, military, and economic readjustments that could also have major domestic effects. The choice would not be a happy one.

In any event, the choice would most likely result from perceptions built up in peacetime. The assessment of the naval balance in the Western Pacific is particularly important. If the Japanese (with the current levels of their maritime self-defense force) believed that the U.S. Fleet could not prevail against the Soviet Pacific Fleet, they would have no real choice. They would simply not be able to join the West in its collective defense effort.

The actions and pronouncements of the United States and the U.S.S.R. all contribute to Japan's perception of the naval balance in the Pacific. In recent years, the United States has drawn down its naval forces in the Western Pacific, and U.S. leaders have declared frequently that the United States would "have difficulty" in keeping open the sealanes to Japan and the rest of the Western Pacific. At the same time, the increasing strength of the Soviet Pacific Fleet has been evident.

These actions and statements—coupled with the primacy of the Atlantic theater in U.S. force planning—must give the Japanese pause. Actions to reassure the Japanese and other Asians that the United States will honor its commitments are called for. These actions must go beyond routine force improvements if they are to have any real effect. What is true of the Japanese applies to our other Alliance partners.

The implications that growing Soviet maritime capabilities have for Western Alliance naval forces are discussed in the next section.

Implications for U.S. and Allied Naval Forces

The flow of seaborne commerce is heavy in peacetime. And the Soviets can interfere with it, to the detriment of the Western Alliance. What are the implications for naval forces?

The key forms of interference with the flow of shipping are:

1. Political or labor actions to close ports;
2. Closing of straits or narrows by threat of local military action;
3. Ship seizures to intimidate shipping through an area;
4. Attacks against merchantmen in specific sealanes by submarines, surface craft, or aircraft;
5. Blockades or quarantines of selected ports or coastal areas;
6. General destruction of port facilities; and
7. General attack on major sealanes of the Alliance around the world.

The adversary's choice of action depends on the level of conflict and tension at the time, as well as the risk of escalation that is considered acceptable.

The Soviets are not likely to use their own forces to accomplish any of the first four of these categories of interference. The risk of escalation is high, and their own maritime activities would be endangered without the promise of large returns. The serious concern, however, is that they might stimulate such actions by others.

The ships of many nations sail the sealanes, often flying flags of convenience and carrying the cargoes of other countries. Identifying individual vessels is difficult for an attacker and determining their cargoes without inspection is virtually impossible. A ship under fire may also find it hard to recognize its assailant. These factors reduce the chances of limited attacks on the sealanes, except for acts of terrorism.

In any event, such limited measures cannot result in serious economic loss if the members of the Alliance are willing to adopt significant stockpiling practices, whether they be governmental, private, or both. Alternative sources and outlets will be available in most cases, and the diversified and resilient economies of the Western Alliance should be able to absorb the modest incremental costs of rerouting shipping.[11] Military response may, therefore, be neither appropriate nor necessary.

If a military response is in order, it is probably best to aim at punishing the aggressor rather than to mount a defense of the sealane or area involved. If local coercion and intimidation occur while superpower tensions are low, U.S. naval battle groups can be available to threaten retaliation or provide local protection. If they occur while tensions are high, on the other hand, naval forces may not be available. In any event, coercive measures against Western commerce are not likely to persist.

Nations other than the Soviet Union are not likely to engage in any of the last three forms of maritime interference. The Soviets have a full understanding of the escalation that might follow if they engaged in blockades, destruction of ports, or worldwide war at sea.

To date, the Soviets have not attempted blockades. But, given their increasing naval capabilities, their announced role of protecting the Third World from Western intervention, and their growing aggressiveness, such a confrontation sometime in the next twenty years would not be surprising. It could result from a conflict between Soviet and U.S. clients or from a U.S. attempt to intervene on behalf of friendly powers.

The outcome of such a confrontation would depend on the relative posture of the opposing forces—and, of course, on the broader political interests at stake. Nevertheless, the possibility of blockades imposes no direct requirement on the Western Alliance to build special forces for defense of the sealanes; current forces could be brought to bear on the blockading force.

Nor does the possibility of a Soviet tactic of destroying port and dock facilities during a major conflict create a requirement for sealane defense forces. The possibility does suggest, however, that Allied merchant ships should not be dependent on sophisticated dockside equipment for loading and unloading essential material. Direct action against the ports—bombing and mining—may be the Soviets' preferred antisealane approach, at least in the early stages of a war. If this is true, it will be far more important for the Alliance to increase its emphasis on forces for port defense.

The main need for sealane defense forces would arise during a major and protracted conventional war with the Soviet Union, either including or excluding NATO.

The *minimum* requirement for such sealane defense is to protect military cargoes for reinforcement and continued support of combat forces. The volume of military shipping, in turn, depends on the level of stockpiling and prepositioning in the theater and on the vulnerability of these supplies. These subjects are discussed in more detail in Chapter 13.

With 200–300 nominal shiploads of dry cargo per month, the United States can deploy active and reserve military forces and keep them supplied for six months. The fuel to keep these and local forces operating will require about 50 nominal 70,000-ton tanker loads a month. The United States' naval forces can defend this much shipping, unless they are engaged elsewhere in projection operations.

The *maximum* requirement for sealane defense depends on the levels of economic shipping that must be maintained. It would be neither necessary nor possible to defend all peacetime ship traffic (3,600 tanker, 11,000 dry bulk, and 14,000 dry cargo transits per month are projected by the middle 1980s). The United States' military requirements would, by then, represent less than 1.5 percent of normal peacetime traffic. In fact, a requirement to protect the peacetime tanker flow alone would lead to sealane defense requirements over ten times as heavy as might be expected for all U.S. military shipping.

Only a small part of the shipping devoted to dry cargo and finished goods would be essential to the Western Alliance in wartime. It may be more

Implications of Soviet Maritime Capabilities

practical to stockpile dry bulk materials in advance than to protect them in transit during a war.

The major unanswered question concerns the need for continued petroleum shipments during a possible large-scale protracted war with the Soviets. If that war is centered on NATO, how much oil is required to keep Europe and Japan from yielding for lack of energy? If the war should take place in the Northwest Pacific, how much oil must be shipped both there and to Western Europe to avoid intimidation? If the war should be centered on the Middle East, and the area's oil production capacity is destroyed, how much oil must be delivered to both Japan and Europe, and from where?

There are no simple answers to these questions. The many imponderables include the issues at stake, the levels of prewar stockpiling, the extent to which these stockpiles escape destruction, and the ability to ration. Protection is probably warranted for a substantial fraction of peacetime oil shipments—say, between one-half and two-thirds, beginning soon after the war breaks out.

Table 6-1 compares shipping requirements for peacetime and a protracted war in 1985 on four oceans. Peacetime shipping levels are those developed in Chapter 5. Military shipping levels for the Atlantic are taken from available Department of Defense estimates and extrapolated to the other three areas. The economic shipping flows for a protracted war are derived as simple percentages of those estimated for peacetime; that is, 5 per-

TABLE 6-1
ILLUSTRATIVE MONTHLY SHIP TRANSITS IN 1985

	Atlantic	Mediterranean	Pacific	Indian Ocean	Total
Peacetime					
Economic:					
Tankers	2,000	200	550	875	3,625
Dry bulk	5,875	600	4,550	50	11,075
General cargo	8,000	650	4,300	825	13,775
Total	15,875	1,450	9,400	1,750	28,475
Protracted War					
Military:					
Tankers	50	10	20	20	100
General cargo	300	100	200	50	650
Subtotal	350	110	220	70	750
Economic:					
Tankers	1,200	120	330	525	2,175
Dry bulk	295	30	230	5	560
General cargo	800	65	430	85	1,380
Subtotal	2,295	215	990	615	4,115
Total	2,645	325	1,210	685	4,865
Of which:					
Tankers	1,250	130	350	545	2,275
Dry bulk	295	30	230	5	560
General cargo	1,100	165	630	135	2,030

cent for dry-bulk shipments, 10 percent for general-cargo shipments, and 60 percent for oil. Underlying these figures is the assumption that most raw materials either have been stockpiled in advance or are not needed during the war and that only a few commodities—probably bulk foodstuffs—continue to move. The general-cargo shipments are assumed to consist mainly of finished products needed to support the war effort; many of them may be replacing machinery and other items destroyed early in the war. The need for a continuing oil flow assumes that only small stockpiles have been built up (enough for sixty to ninety days) and that rationing is strict.

The table shows that military shipping amounts to a small fraction of the low level of economic shipping already postulated and that tankers account for a large share of the latter. The military shipments would probably be needed before the economic shipments, unless substantial military prepositioning had been effected.

Summary

The main purpose of the Soviets' merchant shipping and fishing activities is promotion of economic self-sufficiency and acquisition of foreign exchange for needed imports. Their penetration into major shipping markets has been relatively slight.

Their maritime activities generally make a good public impression in other countries. For better or worse, they expose developing nations to Soviet doctrine and symbolize Soviet economic strength and technical development.

The civil shipping of the U.S.S.R. can be harassed in crises and destroyed in wartime. This vulnerability would seem to limit risk-taking for minor goals on their part. But the Soviets would probably be willing to risk such losses in a major conflict with NATO or the United States.

In a local crisis, seaborne trade with a specific area may be cut off, but the economies of the Western Alliance are generally strong enough to absorb the loss. A complete stop to oil shipments from the Middle East would be an exception.

Sealane defense forces would be needed most in a protracted war with the Soviet Union. The economic effects of maritime shipping losses depend on the vulnerability of the economy and on such governmental actions as contingency stockpiling. The most important ocean routes to keep open in wartime would be: across the Atlantic from the United States to Europe (for military development and resupply); from the Persian Gulf to the North Atlantic (for the oil supplies of Europe and the United States); and from the Persian Gulf to the Western Pacific (for Japan's imports of primary products).

7
Evolution of the U.S. Navy

Early History

Until the last decade of the nineteenth century, the United States was concerned primarily with coastal defense, and most of its ships were constructed for that specific purpose. Although the U.S. Navy had a significant mission of maintaining a presence overseas and took action against Caribbean and Barbary pirates, its major concern was the protection of coastal cities and shipping. Throughout most of that century, U.S. naval objectives remained limited. The combination of remoteness of location, the protection afforded by British naval supremacy, and limited international objectives hardly demanded a massive navy that could stand up to European fleets on the open seas.

From about 1890 to 1910, U.S. naval objectives were entirely revised. Crises with England, Germany, Chile, and finally with Spain brought U.S. foreign relations impressively to the fore. The need to supply protection for U.S. citizens in South America and China, the threat of European penetrations in Central and South America, and the growing interest in the Pacific and in the acquisition of overseas possessions all forced a reevaluation of U.S. naval objectives. Under the influence of Alfred Mahan and the leadership of Theodore Roosevelt, the purely defensive navy gave way to the concept of the fighting fleet.

The Battleship Navy

The nineteenth century had seen a revolution in naval ship construction. The advent of steam propulsion, screw propellers, shell ammunition, rifled ordnance, and armor plate all contributed to a great change in naval warfare. Many of these innovations were of American origin.

The Russo-Japanese War established the supremacy of the battleship.

The early 1900s witnessed major debates over the optimum displacement of that vessel (similar to present-day arguments over aircraft carrier size). The United States emphasized big guns and heavy broadsides rather than speed. Its aim was to acquire an oceangoing battleship navy of second rank, with the heaviest and most powerful units in the world. At this time, aircraft were in their infancy, and their military potential had not been foreseen.

Although submarines had become an accepted part of naval forces, their enormous possibilities went unrecognized before World War I. Germany entered the war with only forty U-boats but managed to sink over 12 million tons of shipping during the conflict, nearly half of it in a single year (1917). Submarines threatened to end the war that year, and they forced the United States to suspend battleship construction in order to provide a huge force of antisubmarine destroyers. By the end of the war, however, a "solution" to the submarine threat had been found in underwater listening devices, "Q-ships," and destroyers. The success of the submarine was considered to be transitory. The bottling up of the German Fleet and the Battle of Jutland were believed to have been the deciding naval actions in World War I.

During the period between world wars, attention returned to the battleship. It grew enormously in size (as the carrier has done since the last war). Not everyone was oblivious to the increasing potential of the aircraft and the submarine; many naval officers, some of high rank, believed that the battleship was becoming obsolete. However, the controlling interest continued to reside in the battleship groups within the Congress and the navy. From four broadside 12-inch guns, armament increased to nine broadside 16-inch guns, and displacements grew to nearly 50,000 tons. Design studies were even made on an 80,000-ton ship mounting fifteen 18-inch guns. By the end of the 1920s, the U.S. Navy also had launched its first two rudimentary aircraft carriers. By 1940, the United States had built five more aircraft carriers, but ship construction continued to feature heavy cruisers, destroyers, submarines, and battleships.

Meanwhile, neither Germany nor the Allies had learned the submarine lesson of World War I, and neither side was prepared for undersea warfare in World War II. In fact, the Soviet Union had by far the world's largest submarine force at that time. Germany entered the second conflict with a very small force of fifty-seven submarines—that were larger and more heavily armed than their World War I counterparts. Although the Germans had not foreseen U.S. entry into that war, the initial impact of German forces on Allied shipping was devastating. Similarly, the United States entered World War II with fewer but more capable submarines than it had in the first. Again in World War II, the Axis submarine threat was only contained through the development of new technology, this time in radar and patrol aircraft—and cryptanalysis (see Chapter 13).

The Navy after World War II

The Japanese attack on Pearl Harbor all but sealed the fate of the battleship. Executed from six oceangoing aircraft carriers, the attack eliminated the heart of the U.S. battleship fleet. Further action by Japanese carrier aircraft against major British combatants—and eventually by U.S. aircraft against Japanese capital ships—established the aircraft carrier as the principal combatant of the navy. During World War II, the carrier became the leading tool for the projection of naval power through the Pacific Island chain into Japan itself. The United States built (or converted) over 100 large and small carriers during that time. It also built 11 battleships, 37 cruisers, 700-odd destroyers and escorts, over 140 submarines, and an enormous fleet of amphibious ships. Having energized its enormous latent production capabilities and being out of reach of enemy action, the United States truly became the Arsenal of Democracy.

The United States emerged from World War II as the foremost naval power in the world, essentially unopposed by any likely foe. It had built the strongest fleets of naval and merchant vessels ever assembled by any combination of nations. There were no naval opponents in sight. The German and Japanese navies had been smashed, the French and Italian navies were virtually eliminated, and the British fleet was allied with us and second in rank to our own mighty armada. The Russian fleet consisted of a small number of obsolescent surface ships and some 200 relatively ineffective submarines that were not considered a serious threat to U.S. sea-control capabilities.

The major issues confronting the U.S. Navy in the immediate postwar period were how to shrink to an affordable peacetime level and how to accommodate to the new technologies of nuclear weapons, jet aircraft, and intercontinental bombers. Naval proponents urged the construction of very large aircraft carriers to serve as platforms for jet aircraft delivering nuclear weapons. Although such proposals were eventually turned down in favor of long-range strategic aircraft, the Korean War again demonstrated the utility of carrier-based aircraft in projecting force across the Pacific Ocean. Recently "mothballed" ships were returned to active service, and a new, large aircraft carrier construction program was authorized by the Congress. The navy's role in strategic nuclear warfare was later settled with the successful testing of a nuclear-propelled submarine, sea-launched ballistic missiles, and precise inertial navigation.

By the late 1950s, the present course of the U.S. Navy had been largely established, with major offensive missions for its conventional air and amphibious forces, its tactical nuclear weapon delivery forces, and its submarine-launched strategic missiles. At that time, Khruschev was cutting back and reorientating the Soviet Navy toward land-based aviation

THE U.S. BATTLESHIP NAVY

The Japanese attack on Pearl Harbor, executed from six aircraft carriers, all but sealed the fate of the battleship in the U.S. Navy. The U.S.S. *West Virginia* (BB-48) and the U.S.S. *Tennessee* (BB-43) are shown afire above. (Courtesy U.S. Navy)

One of three U.S. Navy mothballed battleships, the U.S.S. *New Jersey* (BB-62), returned briefly to active service in 1968 for shore bombardment missions against North Vietnam. She is shown above performing similar missions near the 38th Parallel off Korea in 1949. (Courtesy U.S. Navy)

and long-range missiles. Only the Soviet interest in submarines remained constant. A readily perceptible threat from this Khruschev-Gorshkov navy only became evident in the early 1960s.

Given chronologically, then, overall U.S. Navy objectives since the conclusion of World War II have been: to perpetuate the air and amphibious force projection capabilities used so successfully in World War II and several times since; to accept and exploit the new and rapidly improving capabilities for sea-based nuclear warfare; and to counter the gradual but steady growth of Soviet naval prowess, primarily in submarine and land-based air forces. In conformity with these general objectives, we have endeavored to:

- Create a relatively invulnerable sea-based strategic deterrent;
- Maintain land- and sea-based ASW forces and sea-based antiaircraft forces capable of defeating conventional or nuclear operations of increasingly sophisticated Soviet attack submarine and aircraft fleets;
- Continue a substantial capability to project air power at sea or ashore in the face of increasing Soviet or Soviet-supplied defenses; and
- Preserve the capability to project amphibious forces ashore against substantial opposition.

Our pursuit of these goals has, by and large, been successful thus far. The Polaris-Poseidon fleet of SSBNs, soon to be improved by the deployment of Trident missiles and submarines, constitutes the backbone of our survivable nuclear deterrent forces. United States and Allied ASW capabilities are still considered superior to those of the Soviets. The projection capabilities of U.S. air and amphibious forces far exceed the comparable potential of the Soviet Union. The attack aircraft carrier is still the principal component—and primary symbol—of U.S. conventional naval strength. Like the battleship before it, the carrier has grown in size and effectiveness (as well as complexity and cost) far beyond the most liberal original projections. A number of observers attribute most of this growth in carrier size and cost to the increasing needs for self-defense, claiming that the attack aircraft have grown far less in capability than the AAW (antiaircraft warfare) and ASW complements normally kept aboard. Nonetheless, U.S. naval forces have played a substantial role in supporting U.S. policies in a variety of political situations around the world—from the Eastern Mediterranean to the Northwest Pacific and from Southeast Asia to the Caribbean.

Unfortunately, continued ability to support these ambitious objectives is now threatened by a combination of basic factors. While the "side-by-side" comparisons still appear encouraging, the "face-to-face" views of opposing naval forces are not. Soviet submarines have sufficient power to present a serious threat to Alliance naval vessels and merchant shipping. Soviet land-based aviation could pose an equally serious threat to our projection forces anywhere within its expanding reach. Even against non-Soviet opposition, U.S. and Allied naval units are more likely to be challenged by defending forces using longer-range and more sophisticated surface-to-surface cruise missiles from relatively small ships. If the Soviets continue to provide these and other more capable weapons to various Third World clients—as a means of expanding their own influence in Africa, the Middle East, and South Asia—the threats to Alliance naval forces will continue to rise.

Declining U.S. Navy Force Levels

The naval balance is not only altered by the increasing naval assets of the Soviet Union and her client-states but by the declining size of our own naval forces. The difficulties and costs associated with rapidly progressing technology have combined with the inevitable obsolescence of our residual World War II naval assets to bring about a U.S. Navy that is only one-third its size on V-J Day. In recent years, the navy's share of the defense budget has grown more than that of the other American military services. Nevertheless, the increases have not been nearly enough to compensate for rapidly rising manpower expenses and the escalation in shipbuilding and operating costs. The navy has attempted to offset the impact of these quantitative reductions through strenuous efforts to enhance the quality of each remaining ship.

The variation in U.S. naval force levels since before World War I is shown in Table 7-1. While advocates of increase often compare our present force levels to the peaks that followed both world wars, it is possibly more valid to compare them to the period immediately prior to each of those conflicts. In fact, peacetime force levels can only be discerned after the wartime peaks have gradually subsided. It appears, however, that during peacetime naval construction has favored the larger and more capable individual ships—originally battleships and cruisers, and now cruisers and carriers—while wartime production has pushed the smaller (and easier to build) amphibious forces, destroyers, escorts, and submarines. These trends also appear to indicate a preference for a smaller fleet of higher quality ships as a deterrent during peacetime, coupled with the rapid generation of a larger quantity of less capable ships for fighting during wartime. Such trends are also consistent with minimal peacetime military manning requirements and the latent capacity of the U.S. industrial mobilization base during wartime.

Evolution of the U.S. Navy

TABLE 7-1
UNITED STATES NAVAL FORCE LEVELS

Class / Date	Battleships	Cruisers	Fleet Carriers	Amphib. War Carriers	Dest. & Escorts	Submarines
1919	19	16			392	90
1921	20	16			489	90
1929	18	18	2		295	81
1932	15	19	2		260	81
1941	14	37	7		180	84
1945	25	74	27	88	892	223
1955	3	50	28	73	559	178
1960		25	33	21	545	156
1964		12	33	6	555	152
1970		10	19	7	264	145
1977		26*	13	9	156	115

*This increase over 1970 results from a redesignation of 16 destroyers as cruisers

One major uncertainty, however, is whether there will be sufficient time preceding or during any large-scale conflict to mobilize the U.S. industrial economy and civilian manpower pool to build and man a larger fleet. If there is not time for such a crash program, then the existing U.S. fleet will be far more vulnerable to attrition from a large Soviet force.

Table 7-1 shows that, although there have been decreases in all categories of ships within the U.S. Navy, the largest reductions have been in amphibious ships, destroyers, and escorts—the types that might be useful in either limited intervention operations or the defense of the sealanes against submarine attack.

Quality versus Quantity in Naval Forces

Assorted pressures have brought about the creation of the smaller "quality" fleet as opposed to a larger and less individually capable "quantity" fleet. These pressures include: tight defense budgets; the rapidly increasing cost of manpower; the American urge for technological sophistication; and the belief that each combatant should be capable of surviving a "worst case" threat. Nonetheless, the current situation suggests that a larger number of somewhat less-sophisticated ships might be a more realistic alternative for warfighting as well as for our far-ranging peacetime commitments.

The solution of smaller and cheaper ships would be a difficult option for the U.S. Navy to accept—particularly if versatility were lost. The size and cost of the modern attack carrier are determined largely by the requirements for nuclear propulsion and for the accommodation of the latest types of aircraft, features considered essential in certain high-intensity conflicts. The size and cost of our major surface escorts are also determined largely by the demands of defending those carriers against a "worst threat" from Soviet land- and sea-based forces.

Not all naval ships need to be designed for high-intensity conflict. Perhaps lower-level conflicts with a less-developed enemy could be handled by a more modest, nonnuclear-powered force mounting simpler aircraft and defended by more expendable ships. In precisely these lesser situations, a show of force is often required with units in exposed vulnerable positions. And it would be desirable in such cases not to use the most costly force or be embarrassed by damage to it. In many situations, however, surface combatants will remain vulnerable to cruise missile attack by even the smallest enemy, and unless the unit cost of U.S. ships can be reduced drastically, the increase in the number of available ships will not significantly alter the vulnerability of the fleet as a whole.

Opponents of the shift from quality to quantity point out that if individual ship prowess decreases too far a larger number of inferior ships would be essentially useless. There is a limit to how much excellence can be sacrificed. In many instances rigorous analysis will be required to determine whether some aspects of "quality" are really simply oversophistication, with attendant sacrifices in maintainability and standardization. Moreover, the quality-quantity options are not necessarily limited to ships of the same class. For instance, the elimination of nuclear propulsion (quality or oversophistication?) from a few very large ships would permit the construction of quite a few smaller, frigate-sized ships, with no reduction at all in their quality.

Even if a decision were made to increase the U.S. Navy from a 500- to a 600-ship fleet, a shipbuilding program of substantial size and duration would be needed, and the subsequent sustaining costs might well strain anticipated defense budgets. This suggests that it may be more reasonable to look for alternative means of rapidly mobilizing additional maritime assets to satisfy the need for warfighting quantities (see Chapter 12).

U.S. Naval Roles, Missions, and Versatility

There is certainly room for increasing concern that naval force levels are no longer adequate to meet currently accepted roles and missions. Following is a review of the future applicability of the navy's missions. The U.S. Navy is assigned two principal missions—sea control and power projection. Sea control is defined in DOD Directive 5100.1 as the primary mission:

To organize, train, and equip navy and marine corps forces for the conduct of prompt and sustained combat operations at sea, including operations of sea-based aircraft and land-based naval air components—specifically, forces to seek out and destroy enemy naval forces and to suppress enemy sea commerce, to gain and maintain general naval suppremacy, to control vital sea areas, and to protect vital sea lines of communication, to establish and maintain local superiority (including air) in an area of naval operations, to seize and defend advanced naval bases, and to conduct such land and air operations as may be essential to the prosecution of a naval campaign.

The Navy's officially assigned "collateral mission" of power projection includes the ability to:

- Interdict enemy land and air power and communications through operations at sea;
- Conduct close air and naval support for land operations;
- Furnish aerial photography for cartographic purposes; and
- Participate in the overall air effort as directed.

The U.S. Air Force, whose primary mission is to engage in offensive and defensive air operations over land and in support of the U.S. Army, also has a "collateral mission" to assist the Navy in its ocean surveillance and antishipping roles when needed and when possible. In short, the Navy's primary mission is sea control (with the assistance of the Air Force) plus the projection of ground power ashore through the Marines. The primary Air Force role, on the other hand, is air power projection, with the assistance of the Navy where and when needed.

Critics of postwar U.S. naval policy believe that the carrier task force has been developed for the projection of air power beyond the needs of the Navy's primary mission. Advocates of the carrier task force as the mainstay of U.S. naval operations claim that sea-based aircraft will make it possible to achieve sea control over enemy fleets—as they did in World War II—and permit the prosecution of an offensive naval and amphibious campaign. This debate has been waged sporadically since the end of World War II, and it will probably continue. In effect, it is a tribute to the versatility of naval task forces and their highly sophisticated aircraft.

Carriers may operate singly in lower threat areas or in groups of two to four where the threat is very high. They may be lightly or heavily defended by antiair warfare escorts or antisubmarine escorts, or both. Those same escort ships can also be used to operate singly or in smaller task forces in other sea control missions such as convoy defense, amphibious operations support, force presence, or force projection. An attack aircraft that can sink an enemy ship 500 miles from the carrier can also support amphibious operations with a different bomb load—and it can strike distant enemy land targets with a smaller bomb load in an interdiction role.

Similarly, a carrier-based fighter that can defend a task force from air attack can also defend a beachhead for the Marines—or it can escort attack aircraft into a deep penetration of high-value land targets. Carrier-based ASW helicopters and patrol aircraft can help defend the carrier from submarine attack or they can go somewhat farther afield and "sanitize" an amphibious force objective area or the approaches to a port. Carrier-based radar surveillance and electronic countermeasures aircraft can help defend the task force or the beachhead or they can escort attacking aircraft into a heavily defended land target.

In many instances carriers provide the only protected means to bring aircraft to bear far from friendly bases; they can be deployed without "permission" from any other nation; and they can be held offshore in readiness for action for extended periods. In short, it is the very versatility of these naval and marine assets that fuels the debate.

The fundamental issues in the carrier controversy revolve around the vastly increasing cost of self-defense, quality, and versatility and the reduction in quantities (force levels) produced by tight budgets. Arguments based on "cost-effectiveness" and "economy of scale" have led to the concentration of military capabilities in a small number of assets, while the growing threat from Soviet anticarrier forces has forced the conversion of an increasing share of those capabilities to defensive functions. Many analysts feel that the only way to break this spiral is to return to a navy comprised of larger quantities of less individually capable systems—both as a means of retaining the necessary worldwide deployment of friendly naval forces and as a way to reduce individual combat losses. Such forces, depending more on numbers and newer technology weapons, may well be more effective for sea control missions, particularly in the absence of any major Soviet fleets with which to duel.

Such an increase in primary sea control capabilities worldwide might well be accompanied by a reduction in the Navy's ability to perform its collateral mission of air power projection ashore. Pertinent questions are whether or not such a reallocation of naval priorities is worthwhile and whether or not other forces can now perform more of that mission. By some methods of calculation, more than half of the Navy's budget is devoted to the modernization and maintenance of carrier forces. United States naval power is customarily measured in terms of quantity and quality of carriers and carrier task forces. Carrier effectiveness, in turn, is popularly expressed in tons of bombs that can be delivered ashore per dollar. In view of the diversity of the Soviet threat, it may be appropriate to reallocate U.S. naval funding and revise the measures of naval capability.

To those who favor a greater U.S. concentration on sealane defense, for instance, the "normal" allocation of convoy escorts appears inappropriate. Of the U.S. ships suitable for this assignment, more than three-quarters are regularly assigned to the defense of carrier or amphibious task forces and

U.S. AIRCRAFT CARRIER GROWTH

The U.S. Navy had over thirty aircraft carriers at the end of World War II, typified by the U.S.S. *Langley* (CVL-27) and the U.S.S. *Ticonderoga* (CV-14), shown here leading a formation of battleships and cruisers into Ulithi in December 1944. (Courtesy U.S. Navy)

By the end of 1977 the U.S. Navy had only thirteen aircraft carriers of very large size, as typified by the 90,000-ton nuclear-powered U.S.S. *Nimitz* (CVN-68). The future of ships of this size is now being questioned. (Courtesy U.S. Navy)

the under way replenishment groups that resupply them. Some proponents of sealane defense would prefer to see the ports defended better, the carriers retired to sanctuary, and their escorts released for convoy protection. In future procurement, they would prefer to see more of the smaller escorts and fewer of the larger ships built—at a ratio of ten or fifteen to one.

On the other hand, to most naval strategists the best defense still remains a strong offense. Not surprisingly, they advocate the formation of more—and increasingly capable—carrier task forces that could go after the bases and facilities on which Soviet naval forces depend. This, they claim, will be a more effective long-range solution to the sealane defense problem. Everything finally depends on different perceptions of the priority tasks to be accomplished based on the types and phases of naval combat anticipated. The current U.S. Navy is not capable of carrying out all of its possible missions simultaneously, and not all of those missions are best accomplished by carrier task forces. Mining, for instance, may be more effectively accomplished from submarines or land-based aircraft, and the attack of Soviet naval bases may be more effectively carried out in the near future by tactical cruise missiles launched from any number of different naval or air force platforms.

Soviet postwar naval development contrasts sharply with U.S. efforts as befits a nation attempting to build up a navy in the face of the successful naval capabilities of the Western Alliance. Given their perceptions of the strategic and conventional naval forces arrayed against them and their political imperatives for the support of national liberation movements, the Soviets appear to have done a remarkable (and appropriate) job of naval development within three decades. They have managed this relatively unencumbered by past experience and predilections. Nonetheless, their progress has been accompanied by internal debate, and there is evidence of shifting priorities between defense and offense, strategic and conventional capabilities, submarines and aircraft versus surface ships, first echelon versus second echelon use, etc. The Soviets also appear to be caught in the dilemma of quality versus quantity, but the versatility of their individual naval assets seems to be increasing. As with Alliance forces, the Soviet Navy could not now or in the foreseeable future carry out simultaneously all of the missions that could be assigned to it. Again, the issues come down to priorities, timing, and the type of naval engagement involved.

The Soviet Submarine and Air Threats

Any large-scale naval conflict between the Soviets and the Western Alliance would be significantly different from past engagements. In the first place, the Soviets have not set out to "match" Western capabilities but rather to "counter" them. Moreover, their priorities and imperatives are quite different from those of the Germans and Japanese in World War II. As discussed earlier, there are also much stronger interrelationships between strategic and conventional forces that may dictate force allocations and "withhold" policies. Major fleet-on-fleet battles such as characterized some stages of the U.S.-Japanese war appear less likely. The Soviets' initial application of their submarines may not be primarily against merchant shipping, since they appear to seek a much shorter and more decisive war. Their emphasis on land-based attack aviation has no counterpart in the West. Encounters between dissimilar systems appear far more likely than battles between similar systems (such as ship-on-ship or aircraft-on-aircraft). Moreover, improvements in surveillance, guidance, and propulsion technologies now make antiship weapons lethal at far greater ranges than heretofore. Thus, Alliance surface fleets may be fully engaged at standoff ranges of scores, if not hundreds, of miles—by aircraft and submarines that are exceedingly difficult to locate and counterattack in the short time available.

For the foreseeable future, Soviet aircraft and submarines—and the standoff weapons they carry—present the greatest threat to Alliance naval operations. Fortunately from the standpoint of defending the sealanes, these weapon systems are not the best for coping with large numbers of merchant ships in convoy, owing to limitations in the numbers of standoff weapons that can be carried by each launch platform. Consequently, the threat to naval surface forces has increased in severity far more than the threat to the more numerous merchant ships, which are still more likely to be attacked at close range by bomb-carrying aircraft or torpedo-carrying submarines.

Over half of the total naval combatant displacement of the U.S.S.R. is currently contained in its submarine force, and roughly half of its current construction displacement is still in submarines. In fact, much of the Soviet surface ship construction in recent years also appears to have been at least partially directed toward defending and improving the operation of this submarine force. The Russians seem to consider their underwater fleet to be their first line of offense, if not their first line of defense as well. As discussed in Chapter 3, these submarines have at least four offensive missions, including strategic and theater nuclear attack with ballistic missiles, shore-target and surface combatant attack with cruise missiles, and merchant ship attack with torpedoes. In addition, they are capable of mining allied ports and choke points and of carrying out defensive barrier operations against Alliance naval intrusions.

Soviet naval aviation expenditures have been heavily concentrated in recent years on the production of the new Backfire bomber, which appears to be entering service with both Soviet naval aviation (SNA) and Soviet long-range aviation (LRA) in equal numbers. This emphasis is expected to continue for several more years until the SNA is equipped with roughly 200 of these capable, standoff missile-carrying, supersonic aircraft. These aircraft are destined to have high-priority assignments against Alliance naval task forces and other surface combatants and against ports, naval facilities, and other shore installations related to naval warfare.

The importance of the submarine in modern naval warfare is emphasized by the long-standing U.S. antisubmarine warfare research program and the expanding Soviet effort in this field. Since World War II, antisubmarine warfare has received continuing attention by the NATO nations. Developments in aircraft-carried sonobuoys, in hull-mounted towed and dipped sonars, in bottom-mounted hydrophone arrays, and most recently in surface- and submarine-towed arrays have to some extent counteracted the growth of the Soviet submarine threat. But if the sophistication of Soviet submarines increases, especially in the reduction of their radiated noise level, the prospects for effective acoustic detection of those boats will become more clouded. Although nonacoustic means of submarine detection have received attention, none as yet offers the high search rates that are possible with acoustic means.

Antisubmarine weapon developments have kept pace with detection developments. The acoustic homing torpedo, perfected after World War II, may be launched from aircraft, surface ships, or submarines to ranges compatible with reliable detection limits.

United States naval emphasis on antiair warfare has also been continuous since World War II, and some of the world's most capable fighter aircraft and surface-to-air missile systems have been developed by the U.S. Navy. In recent years, a very large fraction of the navy's aviation budget has been devoted to the procurement of the highly capable F-14, with its Phoenix multiple shot long-range missile capability, and its companion, the E-2C airborne early warning aircraft, which is capable of tracking hundreds of incoming airborne targets simultaneously. At the same time, families of increasingly effective air defense missile systems for shipboard use have been developed. These are now culminating in the multiple-target, electronic phased-array Aegis fire control system coupled with the latest version of the Standard surface-to-air missile system. New ship construction to support this sophisticated new air defense system is just getting under way.

At the same time, the Navy has recently begun to place greater emphasis on the development of both weapons and electronic countermeasures systems by which to defeat the cruise missiles themselves. Several promising systems are in engineering development or beginning to be fitted onto existing ships, but many years will probably elapse before an adequate anticruise missile weapon is deployed in quantity.

Although the United States has made considerable strides in antisubmarine and antiaircraft warfare since World War II, technology has strongly favored the submarine and homing standoff missiles. The ability to detect, localize, and classify large and noisy surface targets by means of airborne or spaceborne sensors or by sensitive underwater listening devices has enjoyed spectacular improvement—for both sides. While aircraft remain readily detectable, their standoff missiles present difficult, multiple targets to destroy.

On the other hand, the elimination of the snorkel, the systematic reduction in radiated noise, and the achievement of unlimited underwater endurance through the use of nuclear propulsion have greatly reduced the detectability of submarines. While nuclear propulsion for surface ships is considered by many to be of dubious value relative to its cost, virtually all experts agree that the underwater endurance and tactical flexibility it provides for the submarine have revolutionized many of the most demanding new submarine warfare missions—including strategic operations, barrier operations, and countersubmarine operations. In fact, almost the only submarine mission that does not benefit so markedly from the use of nuclear propulsion is the convoy attack assignment, where stealth and endurance are relatively less important than speed and rate of weapon delivery.

Vulnerability of the Carriers

Carriers, like other warships, have never been completely invulnerable. Four U.S. fleet carriers were sunk in 1942 and another in 1944. The Japanese lost eight modern carriers at the Battles of Midway and Leyte. Altogether, some thirteen major carriers and many smaller ones were sunk in World War II actions at sea. Interestingly, only three small carriers were among the vessels sunk by the 2,314 kamikaze planes launched at U.S. naval targets. However, on nine separate occasions, U.S. carriers were very badly damaged by such attacks, and a carrier need not be sunk in order to neutralize its primary onboard weapons, its aircraft. It is the high-density "parking" of these aircraft on the flight and hangar decks that increases the carrier's vulnerability—as was demonstrated by two disastrous incidents in the Western Pacific during the Vietnam War. In that war, Army and Marine units, Air Force tactical units, and naval air wings were heavily engaged in direct and protracted firefights with enemies using Soviet-supplied equipment. However, neither our surface fleet nor our submarine forces have been seriously attacked at sea since World War II. Hence, the U.S. Navy's operational experience against opposition is quite dated in these areas and excludes vast changes in the technological environment as well as in potential enemy tactics.

Despite the persistence of the Soviet air- and submarine-launched standoff missile threat, and despite continuing heavy U.S. investment in surface forces, high-confidence defenses against such attacks have not yet appeared in the fleet. There may be some hope that in open ocean combat, after a conflict has begun, long-range carrier aircraft, submarine pickets, and various protective air defense and ASW barriers may be able to keep Soviet aircraft and submarines beyond the effective range of their standoff missiles. At present, however, the advantage appears to lie strongly with the submarine and, to a somewhat lesser extent, with long-range, land-based aviation.

Before a conflict is initiated, little can be done to prevent Soviet submarine station-keeping on major U.S. surface forces, particularly in restricted waters such as the Eastern Mediterranean. Even if such submarines could be pinpointed and maintained under surveillance prior to a conflict, it would be difficult to deny an initial attack by high-speed, low-altitude missiles with large conventional warheads. A salvo of six to eight cruise missiles launched in rapid succession at close range from a single underwater platform would be difficult to defeat, even by our most elaborate fleet defenses in fully alerted condition. Simultaneous attacks from several underwater platforms, perhaps coordinated with surface and air strikes (if the Soviets could really pull it off) would make the defense of the carrier forces even more difficult. Some "leakage" of missiles through the defenses appears inevitable.

Although the United States has invested in long-term programs that promise some improvements in defense against the *current threat*, it is unreasonable to expect no further increase in the quality of that threat. There have already been hints of a tactical ballistic missile threat against the carrier forces—a threat for which no effective counter is in sight.

The aircraft carrier task force also remains vulnerable to standoff air attack. While the U.S. Navy has devoted substantial assets to the development of sophisticated air defense systems for its task forces, there is a limit to the number of these defensive weapons and surveillance systems that can be placed aboard ship, and their costs are enormous: a single radar early warning aircraft costs more than $33 million, while the F-14 fighter, with its highly advanced six-simultaneous-shot Phoenix missile system, costs over $26 million. The new Aegis surface-to-air missile system for installation aboard large 10,000-ton destroyers will cost well over $100 million per ship. Close-in, point defense missile systems will cost around $5 million for each installation.

Despite these costly systems and the highly complex central command and control arrangements for their integrated operation, it will always remain possible to "saturate" the defenses with a coordinated bomber attack.

Something on the order of a 50-bomber raid is likely to produce some attack weapon "leakage" through the defensive systems to the major task force ships, even if all the intricate systems are working properly at once. Such leakage is likely to be considerably higher under real-world operational conditions. The anticipated Soviet inventory of perhaps 200 naval Backfire bombers presents a major threat to carrier task forces—particularly in conjunction with a near-simultaneous attack from cruise missile submarines. Again, the sinking of the carriers is not necessary—only the disabling of their unprotected aircraft, roughly half of which are aboard ship at almost any time during combat conditions.

Naval Alternatives for the Future

The official view is that the U.S. Navy is marginally able to discharge its sea control responsibilities, at least in most areas of vital interest. There is strong dissension, however, from some congressional elements and from several naval authorities. The latter believe that, although the United States has sufficiently capable forces for power projection, it lacks survivable forces for sea control in some areas of vital interest. Admiral E.R. Zumwalt has stated that in a showdown with Soviet naval forces in the Mediterranean during the Yom Kippur War, we probably would have lost the naval engagement if action had been initiated by the Soviets. Others have suggested that we cannot protect Atlantic and Indian Ocean sea lines of communication (SLOCs) simultaneously. Another frequent cause for concern is the dwindling of U.S. capabilities to defend the Western Pacific SLOCs to Japan during a NATO war.

The United States might thwart the Soviet plan for sea denial merely by not offering its vulnerable surface force in combat until the Soviet submarine and air threats had been reduced to an acceptable level—through the actions of ASW barriers and ocean-clearing missions using U.S. submarines and land-based aircraft. This strategy, however, would require the prehostilities withdrawal of U.S. presence forces, such as the Mediterranean Sixth Fleet, as well as a standdown of naval task force support during the crucial early stages of a war in Europe. This could hardly be seen as a demonstration of firm sea control, effective power projection, or national will, although it may become a practical necessity.

Ideas for improving the overall effectiveness of the U.S. Navy or for shifting emphasis from power projection to sea control are as numerous as complaints about the Navy's lack of capability and its imbalance. Most of these schemes address the number, size, and propulsion of aircraft carriers or the size and composition of the remaining surface fleet, or both. However, some ideas do involve more radical shifts away from heavy dependence on surface forces.

Candidate carriers for future consideration are the current 90,000-ton Nimitz-class carrier, a proposed midicarrier at 60,000 tons, and a mini-VSTOL carrier at 20,000 tons. Candidates could be nuclear- or conventionally propelled, but much of the cost advantage of the smaller carriers would be lost in the nuclear version. It is estimated that two conventional midicarriers mounting a larger total air complement than the nuclear Nimitz might be built for little additional cost. Their primary mission would be in lower-threat environments. Although more vulnerable individually and less effective in power projection, midicarriers could also operate in high-threat areas by pooling resources—or they could dilute the enemy air denial forces by operating individually.

The turbine-powered minicarrier could be even more effective in diluting the sea denial threat than the midicarrier. It has been estimated that five minicarriers could be constructed for roughly the same cost as one Nimitz, but with possibly higher total operating costs. Although current limitations in VSTOL technology would not allow the minicarriers to project normal air power in many high-threat situations, together they might provide a significant improvement in sea control capability. They might even carry a substantial number of tactical cruise missiles to retain some highly selective long-range power projection capability. They could also double as amphibious carriers—in fact, they might well be versions of the 10,000-ton LHA (amphibious carrier) now under construction.

Although a fivefold increase in carrier assets would greatly complicate enemy targeting problems in sea denial, the surface naval forces would remain individually vulnerable to enemy direct attacks. Even with the inclusion of all NATO forces, the Alliance would remain short of effective surface escort forces for all its naval task forces and all its maritime shipping. The present U.S. construction policy will maintain at most a 500-ship navy with an annual shipbuilding and aircraft procurement budget of approximately $10 billion (see Chapter 12). Proposals for reducing the numbers of ships and the commitments they support outnumber the recommendations for adding ships to maintain or strengthen our current commitments. The principal reason for this contraction is the enormous cost of construction and maintenance of current ship types. The cost of increasing the U.S. Navy to 600 ships in five years is variously estimated at between $40 and $80 billion.

Ideas for improvements in the design or increases in the quantity of conventional surface forces vary from the nuclear strike cruiser to austere destroyer designs. The former extreme offers, at huge cost, substantial improvement to carrier air defenses but suffers from lack of ASW self-defense when operating independently. At the other extreme, ideas for

NEW SMALL U.S. AIRCRAFT CARRIERS

One new concept for small aircraft carriers of the future involves the 20,000-ton VSS class, which would be capable of handling only VSTOL aircraft but could be built in larger numbers. (Courtesy U.S. Navy)

The U.S.S. *Belleau Wood* (LHA-3), shown above during builder's trials, is the third of a new class of amphibious ships specifically designed to support amphibious landings with helicopters and landing craft. Not considered a "carrier" by the U.S. Navy, it could still handle VSTOL aircraft for various fleet operations. (Courtesy Ingalls Shipbuilding)

inexpensive, austere destroyer designs such as the FFG-7 are readily available. However, the low-cost alternatives have a habit of increasing gradually in complexity—and radically in cost—during the development cycle.

A number of other proposals for future naval construction programs have been presented by both Navy and civilian experts. One ex-submariner and former commander of the Seventh Fleet maintains that the best way to counter the Soviet naval threat is by the construction of more attack submarines. He argues that deploying them in large numbers would put the United States in an offensive, and the U.S.S.R. in a defensive, position. Another recently retired admiral suggests that U.S. attack submarine construction should be halted completely. Others note that the Captor mine, now entering the U.S. Fleet, poses a severe threat to enemy submarines, even in deep water, and may provide a substantially less costly alternative ($100,000 versus $200 million) to keeping Soviet submarines on the defensive.

Norman Polmar suggests that large carriers should not be escorted by vulnerable cruisers and destroyers but rather by other carriers that would provide more air and ASW defense than conventional escorts and, of course, more air strike capability. He also favors attack submarines because of their lower vulnerability. There have also been suggestions to use SSNs as carrier and convoy escorts by adding towed array sensors and more versatile weapons. According to a recent congressional Budget Office analysis, however, this appears to be a very expensive alternative.

Other plans call for increased cooperation between the Air Force and the Navy during major confrontations. During the period when the U.S. Navy had overwhelming superiority at sea, such cooperation was neither needed nor wanted. The Air Force was not interested in diversifying from its primary functions; neither was it convinced that Air Force weapon systems could contribute significantly to sea control. However, technological innovations now make it possible for the Air Force to contribute significantly to sea control with precision-guided munitions, extended aircraft ranges, and improved air surveillance capability. Operating from existing bases, the Air Force could intercept Soviet aircraft and shipping in the North Atlantic, Mediterranean, Northwest Pacific, South China Sea, and Bay of Bengal. Air refueling can further increase the range of aircraft and allow broadened operating areas. Questions here naturally center about the uncertain availability of the Air Force assets during a major confrontation with the Soviets. But it is clear that effective Air Force contributions would require special weapons, equipment, and training. Without real efforts in these areas, the Air Force role would be marginal at best, and, at worst, counterproductive.

With respect to sea surveillance, the U.S. Air Force could help keep track of Soviet surface ships as well as aircraft that might threaten friendly fleets, although some modifications in aircraft equipment would be required, and personnel would have to be trained for such missions. By combining these surveillance capabilities with the new precision-guided missiles and long-range, land-based interceptors, the U.S. Air Force could significantly enhance U.S. ability to control the seas. Air Force bombers are currently capable of helping the Navy in aerial minelaying and might be able to accept a larger role in this important mission.

Admiral Zumwalt wanted to go further and provide for some, if not all, of the Air Force's tactical air wings to be carrier-capable so the United States would be able to deploy optional airpower in any type of crisis. This proposal, however, would require a revised design of air force aircraft and significant organizational changes, to say nothing of the continuous training required to keep pilots proficient in carrier operations. Moreover, carrier-capable aircraft are noticeably more expensive than their land-based equivalents.

The foregoing proposals illustrate the dilemma of the U.S. Navy. The Soviet Navy has become a serious threat to U.S. sea control and power projection in areas of vital importance to the Western Alliance. The U.S. Navy must respond to this threat and still remain within politically acceptable budget limits. The proposals of various experts are sometimes diametrically opposed. Adding to the dilemma is the rapidly advancing technology in every conceivable area, while ship construction leadtimes continue to grow longer because of the sophistication of modern combatants. Hence, ships authorized today may not meet the requirements of the 1980s and 1990s, when they are to be deployed. Picking the optimum path for future naval forces is probably the most difficult problem currently facing U.S. defense leaders.

8
Allocation of U.S. and Allied Naval Forces

Organization and Missions of NATO Naval Forces
NATO Naval Organization

NATO naval forces are integrated within the complex organizational structure subordinate to the North Atlantic Council, as shown diagrammatically on Figure 8-1. It is virtually impossible to discuss the various echelons of command without becoming immersed in the "alphabet soup" that identifies the various elements of the command.

Three distinct Allied commands are involved: Allied Command, Atlantic (ACLANT); Allied Command, Channel (ACCHAN); and Allied Command, Europe (ACE). The Supreme Headquarters, Allied Powers in Europe (SHAPE), is commanded by the supreme allied commander, Europe (SACEUR), a U.S. general officer who also serves as commander-in-chief, U.S. Forces, Europe.

ACLANT, headquartered in Norfolk, is responsible for Atlantic littoral security, for NATO sea-based strategic forces, and for Atlantic SLOC protection. Its commander (SACLANT) is a U.S. flag officer who also serves as commander-in-chief, U.S. Forces, Atlantic (CINCLANT). During peacetime, SACLANT commands only a token fleet of seven ships heavily involved in multinational training—the Standing Naval Force, Atlantic (STANAVFORLANT). During periods of high tension or actual hostilities, however, SACLANT would assume command of all NATO naval forces operating in the Atlantic, and cooperative arrangements provide for integrating NATO and French naval forces. Five lesser commands are subordinate to ACLANT: Western Atlantic, Eastern Atlantic, Iberian Atlantic, Striking Fleet, Atlantic, as well as United Kingdom striking forces, and the Submarine Command. Nuclear deterrent and strike forces (U.S. and U.K. SSBNs and U.S. carrier-based aircraft) are subordinated to both SACLANT and SACEUR.

FIGURE 8-1
NATO NAVAL ORGANIZATION

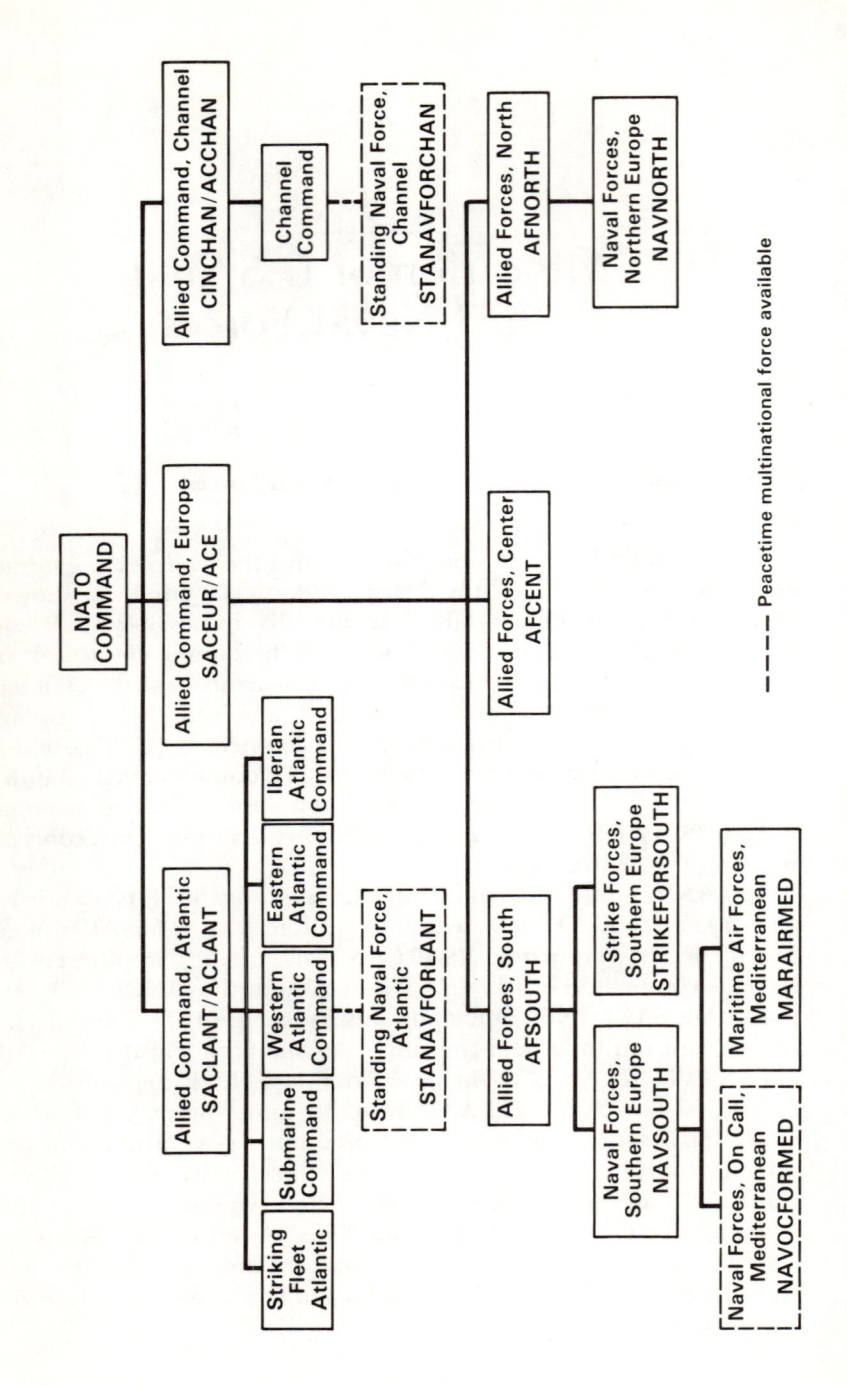

- - - - Peacetime multinational force available

NATO COMMAND

- **Allied Command, Atlantic SACLANT/ACLANT**
  - Striking Fleet Atlantic
  - Submarine Command
  - Western Atlantic Command
    - Standing Naval Force, Atlantic STANAVFORLANT
  - Eastern Atlantic Command
  - Iberian Atlantic Command

- **Allied Command, Europe SACEUR/ACE**
  - Allied Forces, South AFSOUTH
    - Naval Forces, Southern Europe NAVSOUTH
      - Naval Forces, On Call, Mediterranean NAVOCFORMED
    - Strike Forces, Southern Europe STRIKEFORSOUTH
      - Maritime Air Forces, Mediterranean MARAIRMED
  - Allied Forces, Center AFCENT
  - Allied Forces, North AFNORTH
    - Naval Forces, Northern Europe NAVNORTH

- **Allied Command, Channel CINCHAN/ACCHAN**
  - Channel Command
    - Standing Naval Force, Channel STANAVFORCHAN

ACCHAN, headquartered in London, is responsible for protecting the English Channel and the southern North Sea. British, Dutch, and Belgian ships are earmarked for use in this command, and agreements exist for French cooperation. There is also a token peacetime Standing Naval Force, Channel (STANAVFORCHAN), which is primarily an open-water mine countermeasure force.

Allied Command, Europe (ACE), headquartered in Casteau, Belgium, is broken into three subordinate comands: Allied Forces, North (AFNORTH); Allied Forces, Center (AFCENT); and Allied Forces, South (AFSOUTH). The Danish and Norwegian navies and the German Baltic naval forces are designated for AFNORTH. (Some experts believe ACCHAN forces should be combined with AFNORTH.) The Greek, Italian, and Turkish navies and the U.S. Sixth Fleet report to AFSOUTH through two separate commands: Naval Forces, Southern Europe (NAVSOUTH); and Strike Force, Southern Europe (STRIKEFORSOUTH). Maritime Air Forces, Mediterranean (MARAIRMED) and the five-ship Naval Forces On-Call, Mediterranean (NAVOCFORMED), report to NAVSOUTH.

One can only wonder at the complexities of the command structure for the naval forces involved in the defense of NATO. In fact, most of these arrangements were established when Allied navies were stronger and the Soviet Navy was substantially weaker. Consequently, command lines could be drawn that satisfied local political interests without major concern for their impact on effectiveness. It would appear, at least on the surface, that serious inefficiencies are implicit in the current command relationships—these inefficiencies may seriously reduce the total effectiveness of Alliance naval forces: certainly their flexibility and deployability would be inhibited by command boundaries. Given the increasingly precarious naval balance in the NATO theater, it may well be time to streamline these command relationships for greater overall naval impact. It may also be desirable to provide more direct linkage with air force elements that can contribute to the success of any possible naval battle.

NATO Naval Strategy and Missions

The eleven NATO nations possessing oceangoing combatant resources (not including Iceland and Luxembourg) are vested with the following missions, discussed individually hereafter:

- Offensive operations
  Strategic deterrence and nuclear warfighting
- Blockade of key straits and "gaps"
- SLOC defense

There are still basic questions about whether these missions have been sufficiently blended into a coherent Alliance strategy to counter the growing Soviet naval threat.

Under certain circumstances it is expected that the French and possibly the Spanish navies would cooperate in the mutual defense of NATO maritime interests, particularly in convoy escort and mine and countermine missions. Port defense and port mine countermeasures are considered to be primarily individual national tasks not under NATO jurisdiction. These missions are discussed in later sections.

Offensive Operations. A major war between the NATO nations and the Warsaw Pact would most likely arise as the result of Western resistance to Soviet aggression in Western Europe—either directly in the "Central Region" or against either or both of the flanks. In any event, it would be primarily a contest for the control of the Western European landmass and its population. To the Soviets, such a war must be considered primarily a battle between ground forces, and their navy would be expected to contribute to the support of their ground elements. They would undoubtedly seek to make the war as short and decisive as possible. They would not "need" a navy to prosecute that ground war themselves. But they would need a navy to prevent the United States from providing reinforcements, from diverting Pact forces to defensive missions, from prolonging the war and wresting the initiative, and from threatening escalation to nuclear warfare. To accomplish these aims as fast as possible, they would seek to gain full control of the Norwegian Sea, to seal the European ports against reinforcements, and to blunt or destroy the offensive capabilities of NATO naval forces. These consist primarily of U.S. carrier task forces that can counterattack and, secondarily, of NATO ASW assets and SSNs. The need to concentrate on interdicting Western SLOCs would only arise if their initial objectives were not achieved.

The initial stages of a NATO naval war, therefore, are most likely to be a contest for the neutralization or disruption of the NATO receiving ports and a contest for the destruction of NATO carrier task forces. If the West could surmount these initial attacks, then the character of the war could change and a more protracted engagement might result, with surviving NATO naval units on the offensive and Soviet submarines focusing on the open ocean SLOCs.

The major offensive elements of AFSOUTH in the Mediterranean consist of Sixth Fleet aircraft carriers accompanied by their fifteen to twenty major surface combatants and possibly augmented by the two French aircraft carriers. These units would be certain to become almost immediately engaged in a sharp battle with the Soviet Mediterranean Squadron. NATO forces would be expected to prevail—but with substantial losses. Any subsequent naval battles in the Mediterranean

NATO NAVAL FORCES ON THE NORTHERN FLANK

The navy of the Federal Republic of Germany contains many fast attack craft like the *Kondor* (P-6070) and *Kabicht* (P-6075) pictured above. As yet these craft are not equipped with antiship missiles. (Courtesy U.S. Navy)

Destroyers of the Federal Republic of Germany like the *Schleswig-Holstein* (D-182) shown above would play an important role in gaining control of the North Sea in any major war involving NATO naval forces. (Courtesy U.S. Navy)

would probably center around the operations of surviving Soviet submarines and aircraft, interfering with NATO operations on the Southern Flank.

The major offensive naval elements available to AFNORTH are mining units and the carriers of the British Navy and the U.S. Second Fleet. Soviet attacks against these carrier task forces would probably be somewhat more difficult in the North Atlantic, but the Soviet Northern Fleet operating from the Kola Peninsula in the Barents Sea comprises the most capable naval units of the U.S.S.R. The outcome of this contest would help determine the ability of NATO forces to defend and to reinforce the Northern Flank and the Baltic Straits.

It is generally assumed that NATO offensive naval forces would be augmented by carrier task groups sent around from the U.S. Pacific Third Fleet. The assignment of these additional forces would obviously depend on the progress of battle by the time they arrived. If required, carrier-based aircraft from any of these units could also provide some support to NATO land forces, in the event that Pact forces advanced to within practical range of carrier-based aircraft.

NATO ASW patrol aircraft (VP) provide a substantial offensive capability against Soviet submarines operating in the North Sea, the North Atlantic, or the Mediterranean. So do Western aircraft carriers if not otherwise engaged. The United States operates by far the largest number of VP aircraft, with significant contributions from the British navy and the French navy. German, Dutch, and Norwegian VP aircraft could contribute to antisubmarine operations in AFNORTH, while Italian VPs could considerably extend MARAIRMED ASW coverage. Spanish VP units could also provide support in the Western Mediterranean. These VP aircraft would have little ability to distinguish among various classes of Soviet submarines. Consequently, Soviet submarines assigned strategic or theater nuclear roles would be susceptible to attack from these aircraft within VP surveillance areas.

There would be, of course, a substantial competition for resources among the various possible missions for NATO naval forces. The carriers, their escorts, and the patrol aircraft could contribute significantly to the SLOC defense missions as an alternative to their offensive roles. Trade-offs between these two missions would have to be made continually as the overall war progressed and as SACEUR set the relative priorities in response to Soviet tactics and strategy.

Mine warfare represents yet another form of NATO offensive operations that could seriously impede enemy naval operations, although it is by nature a double-edged sword. The United States possesses no task-specific minelaying ships, and other NATO nations maintain only a handful suited primarily for coastal operations. However, most U.S. naval and air

NATO NAVAL FORCES IN THE NORTH ATLANTIC

Units of the British Royal Navy like the guided missile destroyer *Glamorgan* (D-19) pictured above provide significant contributions to overall NATO naval force levels required to defend North Atlantic sealanes. (Courtesy U.S. Navy)

Escorts from five NATO nations including Canada (DDE-207), the Netherlands (F-815), West Germany (F-225), the United Kingdom (F-10), and the United States (DDG-2), exercise together as part of the Standing Naval Force, Atlantic (STANAVFORLANT). (Courtesy U.S. Navy)

force aircraft are, or can be made, capable of, laying mines, as are most NATO aircraft. Virtually all NATO submarines can also lay mines. Submarines offer the most covert method of installing mine fields, although aircraft offer the advantage of being able to cover larger areas in a shorter period of time. Some knowledgeable observers believe that NATO has devoted too little attention to improving mining capabilities. If so, the lack is likely to be in the area of modern mine technology and stockpiling of suitable weapons. The delivery means appear to exist in substantial quantities.

Strategic Deterrence and Nuclear Warfighting. The strategic missions are to be carried out by the combined U.S. and U.K. SSBN forces based at Rota, Spain, Holy Loch and Faslane, Scotland, and Charleston, South Carolina. United States aircraft with tactical nuclear weapons may be flown from the four carriers of the Second Fleet and the two carriers of the Sixth Fleet if necessary. SACLANT commands the majority of these SSBN and carrier resources, but all four British SSBNs and several U.S. SSBNs are subordinate to SACEUR. The SSBN missions are primarily oriented toward deterring Warsaw Pact aggression. If that deterrence failed and escalation to nuclear warfare followed, these highly capable submarines would be prepared to engage selected enemy target sets with their SLBMs.

Blockade of Key Straits and Gaps. Geography confronts Warsaw Pact naval forces—air, surface, and submarine—with serious problems in gaining access to the seas vital to NATO. Effective NATO air and sea barriers and blockades could seriously hinder enemy mobility and reduce the threat of flanking thrusts. NATO navies have a clear primary mission to interdict the Soviet Baltic Fleet entering the North Sea through the Kattegat, the Northern Fleet—with its many submarines—entering the North Atlantic through the Greenland-Iceland-United Kingdom Gap (G.-I.-U.K. Gap), the Black Sea Fleet entering the Mediterranean through the Dardanelles and the Bosporus, or any enemy units infiltrating the Strait of Gibraltar from either direction. Land-based interceptors could provide attrition of Soviet long-range aircraft overflying the G.-I.-U.K. Gap, the North Sea, or the Mediterranean.

AFNORTH would utilize Norwegian, Danish, and German fleet units to control Soviet naval movements to and from the Baltic. These would include surface combatants as well as NATO aircraft and some forty-five NATO coastal submarines, almost one-third the NATO total. Control of the G.-I.-U.K. Gap and any other more northerly submarine barriers would fall to the forces assigned to SACLANT. Whether sufficient air force assets are assigned to support naval operations in either of these areas is currently subject to question.

AFSOUTH Naval forces include many NATO ships as well as additional NATO aircraft and submarines, which would have one mission of trying to seal off egress from the Black Sea. French and Spanish forces would be useful in securing access to the Western Mediterranean and providing shore bases for aircraft and ships.

SLOC Defense. The Atlantic SLOC defense mission is the responsibility of SACLANT, while the Mediterranean SLOC defense mission falls to SACEUR's CINCSOUTH. The U.S., U.K., Dutch, Norwegian, and German navies together could theoretically contribute up to 195 surface combatants (over 1,000 tons) to the defense of the Atlantic SLOC, while Italy, Greece, Turkey, and the United States can contribute some 76 more combatants to the defense of the Mediterranean SLOC. These assets could be augmented by up to 49 French and 29 Spanish surface combatants—adding 40 percent to the combined NATO total.

As many as 100 NATO oceangoing submarines are potentially capable of supporting the SLOC defense mission directly or indirectly. These include some 40 U.S. and U.K. SSNs. Three-quarters of these submarines would probably support the Atlantic SLOC defense task; the remainder, that of the Mediterranean. Again, France and Spain could contribute 29 more oceangoing submarines. Direct submarine SLOC defense contributions, however, are still a nascent development requiring a degree of command, control, and communication integration with surface and air escorts that probably exceeds current NATO capabilities. Nonetheless, there appear to be more NATO submarines available than would be required for other missions such as mining and attack of what little Warsaw Pact shipping there might be. Operations against enemy submarines in one form or another, then, appear to be a primary mission for them.

Aviation support of NATO SLOC defense comprises land-based and carrier-based aircraft. The Soviet threat to both Atlantic and Mediterranean sealanes consists primarily of submarines and long-range aviation. Against the Soviet submarine threat, NATO forces operate long-range, land-based ASW VP from bases in North America, Bermuda, Iceland, the Azores, and the United Kingdom out to a radius of about 1,000 miles. Supplementing these VP squadrons are carrier-based ASW patrol aircraft (VS) operating from U.S. carriers out to a radius of about 300 miles.

The open ocean threat posed by Soviet land-based aviation includes bombers armed with conventional bombs and rockets as well as standoff weapons of 150 to 300 miles range. The latter require defensive operations far beyond the range of the antiaircraft weapons of the surface escorts. The standoff threat would have to be met by carrier- or land-based interceptors. To avoid overflying NATO ground defenses, Soviet aircraft would have to adopt circuitous routes over the Norwegian Sea or North Africa, rendering them vulnerable to detection and attack during their long flights.

NATO ASW helicopters, operating from many classes of surface combatants, are primarily useful in extending the range of shipboard ASW sensors and weapons. They have neither the payload nor the endurance features of the land-based or carrier-based fixed-wing aircraft specifically designed for surveillance of large ocean areas. Both helicopters and VS aircraft, however, might be useful at shorter ranges—near the receiving ports, for instance.

The southern extent of the SACLANT ocean areas of responsibility is bounded by the Tropic of Cancer—essentially the longitude of Havana, Cuba. When this boundary was established it must have seemed more than adequate. There could have been no inkling at that time of the growing importance of the SLOCs around Africa from the Indian Ocean to the South Atlantic and thence north to Europe and North America. Consequently, there is currently no NATO jurisdiction over these vital routes. This is a purely political situation that could be changed at any time: it has no "legal" implications. Nonetheless, it appears that those southern SLOCs will remain, at least for the present, a unilateral responsibility for CINCLANT and U.S. forces. The Soviet air and naval facility at Conakry in Guinea, for instance, is almost exactly 1,000 miles south of the Tropic of Cancer. United States use of roughly equivalent naval facilities at Recife in Brazil was recently terminated as a result of U.S.-Brazilian political disagreements.

The importance of "officially" extending the southern boundaries of SACLANT further to the south is difficult to assess. On the one hand, it would imply a thinning out of NATO naval assets to the north. On the other, there is nothing to stop joint naval operations south of that imaginary line in time of war if they are deemed important by the participating nations. The NATO ministers have authorized the planning for such contingencies.

The NATO Flanks

NATO's northern and southern flanks are rather thinly protected, and they are the areas where naval and marine forces could provide the greatest marginal improvements in Alliance capabilities—particularly if they were accompanied by suitable land- or sea-based air cover. That the military balance on the flanks has been given so little attention is due, in large part, to the historically popular view that the major NATO objective is to deter military aggression straight across the east-west borders of the Central Region into Western Europe. That priority was certainly more appropriate when the naval forces of the Russians were less formidable, when their overall military capabilities were substantially lower, and when it was anticipated that they might attempt to expand their sphere of influence by the swift application of direct military force.

NATO NAVAL FORCES IN THE MEDITERRANEAN

Participation of French naval units like the destroyer *La Galissonniere* (D-638) would have a substantial impact on the strength of naval forces on NATO's Southern Flank, thus helping to keep Mediterranean SLOCs secure. (Courtesy U.S. Navy)

Logistic "interoperability" of NATO naval forces is demonstrated in the Mediterranean as the U.S.S. *Severn* (AO-61) refuels the British aircraft carrier *Ark Royal* and the U.S. destroyer *Wallace L. Lind* (DD-703). The latter has since been transferred to the South Korean Navy. (Courtesy U.S. Navy)

However, a different view of Moscow's intentions has recently emerged in some quarters—that is that the real purpose of Soviet military buildups is to engender the peaceful collapse of the Western Alliance through the simple display of preponderant force at all possible combat levels (see Chapter 1).

The political "surrender" of either Northeast Asia or Western Europe could then seriously jeopardize the independent course of the People's Republic of China—and ultimately the ability of the United States itself to remain a viable economic and political entity. Such a process of intimidation could well involve the "Finlandization" of the European flanks (or the Northeast Asia "flank" of South Korea and Japan, for that matter) in the hope that the rich and vital Central Region would then see the light and join the Communist fold without intervention from the United States. In this scenario, preservation of the confidence of the Alliance nations on the flanks deserves substantially higher priority relative to the Central Front.

This scenario also suggests the need for a more capable naval counterforce posture on the Atlantic, Mediterranean, and Pacific flanks. In this respect, one's views of the Soviets' intentions, including the real rationale for their massive military buildups, has a direct impact on Alliance naval priorities. In short, the more emphasis is placed on Soviet intentions to accomplish their aims of world domination without resort to military force, the more important become the naval capabilities of the Western Alliance to preserve the confidence of the maritime nations of the flanks, and the more important become the naval contributions of such countries as France, Spain, and Greece.

National Missions of Naval Significance

The NATO military organization does not encompass all of the supporting missions that would be required to prosecute successfully a large-scale defense of Europe against Pact aggression. Possibly the best known instance of national—rather than NATO—responsibilities is the logistic support for NATO fighting forces. This remains a task for each member nation and is not directly subject to NATO guidance or supervision. The consequence, of course, is a considerable degree of inefficiency and duplication in the support of engaged forces, which must depend on their own national logistic chains to provide for their maintenance and resupply. This, however, is not of unique importance to the NATO naval campaign, although it has produced a depressing lack of standardization among logistic resupply components, including many items of consumable naval ordnance. Nevertheless, there is a high degree of "interoperability" among NATO naval units insofar as tactical doctrine and communications are concerned. In fact, naval units of different countries frequently exercise and operate together, using NATO operational and communications procedures.

More significant to this analysis, however, is the retention of the mine countermeasures and the port defense missions as individual national responsibilities. Given the almost certain emphasis that the Soviets would place on mining operations and the attack of NATO ports, these shortcomings appear to be very significant indeed. They are discussed in the following two sections.

Mine Countermeasures. The Soviets are known to stress the use of mines for impeding Western naval operations if war should arise. They maintain vast stockpiles of mines, some of which are apparently sophisticated in their operation and resistance to sweeping. Since mines have a tendency to delay naval activities immediately, their use is consistent with a plan for a short and decisive campaign.

West European countries contribute substantially more resources to mine countermeasures than do the U.S. and Canadian navies. Most of them, including France and Spain, have invested heavily in minesweeping ships and, more recently, in mine-hunting craft. Mine hunters are designed to seek out unidentified mine fields and individual mines. Minesweepers, on the other hand, are designed to sweep areas of suspected or known mine concentration. Mine hunters may be substantially more effective than minesweepers in actions against the sophisticated Soviet mines likely to be encountered in any future conflict.

Despite the relatively even distribution of mine countermeasures craft between various NATO nations, there is no guarantee that the Soviets would distribute their mines in proportion to the ability of member nations to sweep them. To take an extreme case, Iceland has no minesweepers, yet its ports and adjacent waters are certainly excellent candidates for a Soviet mining effort. Many other areas of potential Soviet mining lie beyond the coastal waters of the member nations. Which nations will take on the responsibility for sweeping them, and how will they determine priorities between national needs and overall NATO requirements? These problems strongly suggest a need to combine these assets within the NATO naval command structure in order to achieve the best level of response to a known Soviet area of concentration.

Port Defense. The defense of ports against Soviet offensive actions from the air or the sea is also an individual responsibility of NATO nations, and one that is generally split between each country's air force and navy. There is, for instance, virtually no cognizance of the NATO member countries' port defense plans within the SACLANT headquarters. Until a few years ago, the air threat to NATO ports was not very high because most of the

Soviet aircraft lacked the range to perform effective strikes against these vital facilities. For the most part, NATO air defenses still face the East and are intended to defend the battlefield from attack. The situation has changed markedly, however, with the introduction of such capable Soviet aircraft as the Backfire and the Fencer. Both of these planes have more than adequate range and payload to make substantial strikes against the port areas with conventional ordnance—without approaching over NATO held territory.

The major NATO receiving ports in the Netherlands and Belgium are thus defended only by national assets. These two countries certainly contribute their share to the NATO defense. Nonetheless, they rank sixth and seventh in terms of GNP and defense expenditures among the NATO countries, and their combined national air defense assets consist of about seventy-two older F-104G aircraft and some twenty-four Nike Hercules air defense missile launchers—now virtually obsolete and phased out of U.S. inventory. Together, these obsolescent air defense assets do not offer their two countries as much air defense capability as a single U.S. carrier task force provides for itself. Moreover, one could easily expect the Soviets to attack the various installations (including SHAPE) in much greater total force than would be applied against the carriers. The importance of keeping these ports open far transcends the capabilities of these individual nations to defend them against air attack. Unless something is done to improve the defense of these receiving ports, one might reasonably question any greater emphasis on SLOC defense at sea.

The proper air defense of European ports requires a combination of "point defense" missile systems and "area defense" fighter aircraft systems. The former would allow a higher rate of defensive fire against aircraft attacking close-in with bombs or mines. The latter would permit the attrition of longer-range aircraft carrying standoff weapons. NATO air defense fighters and airborne early warning radars would probably be sufficiently versatile and long-ranged to permit reorientation as the threat developed without base relocation. The necessary surface-to-air missile (SAM) systems, however, might have to be relocated from the eastern "SAM belt." Or, more likely, additional units would have to be procured and properly situated in hardened sites near the ports.

In mine countermeasures, the Netherlands and Belgium appear to be in considerably better shape, with a total of sixty-seven craft divided almost evenly between the two. One would have to conclude that they are probably more capable in the area of mine defense than in air defense.

NATO Order of Battle (1978)

Table 8-1 presents a tabular summary of the combined naval strength available to NATO in time of war—not including additional U.S. naval

TABLE 8-1
NATO ORDER OF BATTLE (1978)

Region & Country	Submarines SSBN	SSN	Torpedo Attack Ocn/Cstl SS	(TOT)	Aviation Capable Ships CV	CH	Surface Combatants Cruisers	Destroyers	Frigates	(TOT)	Small Combatant Ships Msl & Torp	Mine CM	Amphib Ships	Naval Aviation Carrier Based	Land Based
Northern Flank															
Norway	—	—	6/45	(51)	—	—	—	21	23	(44)	144	152	—	—	48
Denmark	—	—	-/15	(15)	—	—	—	—	5	(5)	48	15	—	—	5
W. Germany	—	—	-/6	(6)	—	—	—	—	2	(2)	40	14	—	—	20
Netherlands	—	—	-/24	(24)	—	—	—	11	6	(17)	45	57	—	—	23
Belgium	—	—	6/-	(6)	—	—	—	10	8	(18)	11	37	—	—	—
									2	(2)		29			
Atlantic	35	30	30/-	(60)	5	3	10	37	109	(156)	29	38	27	420	231
U.K.	4	9	19/-	(28)	1	1	2	10	60	(72)	11	34	7	60	43
Canada	—	—	3/-	(3)	—	—	—	2	10	(12)	—	—	—	—	20
Portugal	—	—	3/-	(3)	—	—	—	—	17	(17)	18	4	—	—	8
U.S. 2nd Flt	31	21	5/-	(26)	4	2	8	25	22	(55)	—	—	20	360	160
Mediterranean	—	12	27/4	(43)	2	1	8	41	27	(76)	103	94	28	180	78
Italy	—	—	5/4*	(9)*	—	—	3	8	10	(21)	14	44	2	—	18
Greece	—	—	8/-·	(8)	—	—	—	9	4	(13)	24	26	9*	—	—
Turkey	—	—	14/-·*	(14)*	—	—	—	12*	2*	(14)*	65	34	2*	—	—
U.S. 6th Flt	—	12	—	(12)	2	1	5	12	11	(28)	—	—	15	180	60
France & Spain	5	—	25/4	(29)	2	1	2	32	44	(78)	57	60	10	170	38
France	5(1)	—	17/4	(21)	2	—	2	19	28	(49)	32	38	2	120	35
Spain	—	—	8/-·*	(8)*	—	1	—	13	16	(29)	25	22	8*	50	3
NATO Subtotal	35	42	63/49	(154)	7	4	18	99	159	(276)	276	284	55	600	357
NATO + FR. & SP.	40	42	88/53	(183)	9	5	20	131	203	(354)	333	344	65	770	395
U.S. Only	31	33	5/-	(38)	6	3	13	37	33	(83)	—	—	35	540	220

Notes: *Ships obsolescent
(1)includes one French SSB

assets that might be transferred from the U.S. Third Fleet in the Pacific. The table divides these resources by type (submarines, surface combatants, and naval aviation), and by region (Northern Flank, Atlantic, and Mediterranean). It indicates the naval forces of France and Spain that might be considered additive to the total, and it sums up U.S. assets of the Second and Sixth fleets for comparison to the contributions of our allies. NATO assets include the following:

Submarines. A total of some 154 attack submarines are available to NATO, including 42 U.S. and U.K. SSNs Thirty-five SSBNs must be added to these numbers. France and Spain could contribute another 29 conventional attack submarines and 4 SSBNs. Some 49 of the diesel submarines are considered adequate for coastal work only, and these are concentrated in the shallow waters of the Northern Flank.

Aviation-Capable Ships. The predominant naval aviation force is provided by the six U.S. supercarriers. To this total, however, can be added one British, two French, and one Spanish carrier, plus at least three U.S. helicopter ships. A total of some 770 carrier based aircraft are assigned to these ships, of which the vast majority—and most capable—are the U.S. combat aircraft.

Surface Combatants. NATO can count on 276 major surface combatants, plus another 78 from France and Spain if they join forces. These are the classes of ships most likely to be involved in the SLOC defense missions, and it is of some interest to note that the U.S. contribution is less than one-quarter of the grand total. However, elements of the Greek, Turkish, and Spanish surface fleets are obsolete and need replacement.

Small Combatants (Mine Countermeasures). NATO contains a total of over 280 mine countermeasures ships, while France and Spain could add 60 more. The U.S. contribution in this category is only a dozen MCM craft. NATO countries have almost as many small missile and torpedo boats (333) as do the Soviets in their Northern, Baltic, and Black Sea fleets (372).

Amphibious Ships. NATO can count on fifty-five amphibious ships, plus perhaps ten more from France and Spain: the United States contributes roughly half of these.

Land-Based Patrol Aircraft. Counting the 38 VP aircraft of France and Spain, the NATO grand total is just under 400 patrol aircraft, of which the United States contributes 220.

Regional Comparison. The three regional fleets are somewhat

Allocation of U.S. and Allied Naval Forces

analogous to the Soviet Baltic, Northern, and Black Sea fleets. On the NATO side, the Atlantic Fleet is by far the strongest, as is the Soviet Northern Fleet. NATO naval forces on the Northern Flank are by far the weakest, as is the Baltic Fleet of the U.S.S.R.: both are primarily intended for coastal operations within the immediate vicinity. The NATO Mediterranean Fleet is about halfway between the Atlantic and Northern Flank fleets in strength and appears more than adequate to balance the Soviet Black Sea Fleet, given Soviet geographic difficulties. If the French and Spanish fleets are added to the normal NATO Mediterranean Fleet, then it is almost exactly the same size as the Atlantic Fleet in numbers of ships. In this latter case, the U.S. contribution is only about one-quarter of the total, although it contains the most powerful aircraft carriers and submarines.

U.S. Atlantic Posture without NATO

The superficial naval balance in the Western Mediterranean changes markedly when the naval assets of our Atlantic allies are excluded from consideration, for the European contribution to NATO's naval strength is substantial. By comparison, the Polish, East German, Bulgarian, and Romanian naval forces contribute virtually nothing to Warsaw Pact strength. Hence, there is a very significant difference between the Warsaw Pact versus NATO and the U.S.S.R. versus U.S. comparisons. If, as is likely, the Soviets have set out unilaterally to provide a naval balance to the Western Alliance, then it will be essentially impossible to establish a naval balance between the United States alone and the Soviets. This prospect presents a dilemma that could have serious implications in a U.S.-Soviet confrontation that did not involve vital NATO interests.

For instance, in a confrontation over some Third World nation on the North Atlantic or Mediterranean coast of Africa, it is possible to conceive of the Soviet Northern and Black Sea fleets opposing the U.S. Atlantic Fleet without NATO support. Likewise, a confrontation in the eastern end of the Mediterranean over Lebanon, Israel, Egypt, or Libya could occur between the Soviet and American fleets without NATO involvement. Similarly, a dispute on the Western Indian Ocean littoral, involving, say, Iran, Saudi Arabia, or Somalia, could find U.S. and Soviet naval forces in opposition—each with a long line of naval communication exposed to harassment by the other. Without NATO participation, the naval balance is clearly less favorable to the United States. Although the opposing forces might be smaller and the desire to avoid escalation much higher, imbalances in available forces could be pronounced. This is exemplified in Table 8-1 by the U.S. contribution to the NATO Atlantic Fleet totals in, say, escorts suitable for convoy protection. While the overall NATO total appears to be substantial (156 surface combatants), only one-third of this total is comprised of U.S. ships, and a good fraction of these are U.S. "escorts" required to defend the U.S. carriers. Without NATO (or at the very least, British) assistance, we might be hard-pressed to provide escorts for any sizable number of noncombatant ships.

These facts reinforce the view that the "standard" NATO-first scenario may not, in fact, be the most demanding one for U.S. naval forces. Some lesser contingency, excluding NATO support, may actually be more challenging to U.S. naval asssets.

Organization and Missions of Allied Pacific Forces

Pacific Naval Organization

Treaties. The Southeast Asia Treaty Organization, SEATO, was the partial Pacific counterpart to NATO in the Atlantic. Seven of the eight original members, including the United States, the United Kingdom, France, Australia, and New Zealand, jointly agreed to terminate SEATO on 30 June 1977. However, they agreed to retain the Southeast Asia Collective Defense Treaty, SEACDT. Pakistan formally left SEATO—and denounced the treaty—in 1973, the only nation to do so.

SEATO was originally envisioned as an instrument by which member nations agreed to jointly defend each other's national security interests against outside aggression. Primarily a naval force, SEATO depended on U.S. and U.K. (as well as Australian and New Zealand) naval elements for its backbone. There are many reasons for the demise of SEATO. These include the minimal Soviet naval threat in Asia; the collapse of Soviet influence in Indonesia; the withdrawal of U.K. forces "East of Suez"; and the political neutralization of Thailand following the collapse of the Republic of Vietnam in 1975. Conspicuously Japan, South Korea, Taiwan, Malaysia, and Singapore did not (or could not) sign the treaty or join the organization.

Other agreements exist which serve the interests of former SEATO nations as well as others. The 1951 ANZUS Treaty—involving Australia, New Zealand, and the United States—remains a joint defense pact. The 1971 "Five Power" agreement, whereby the United Kingdom, Australia, and New Zealand agree to support the defense of Singapore and Malaysia, essentially ensures Western Alliance presence along the important oil SLOC between Japan and the Middle East and is intended to secure Alliance control of the critical Malacca Strait.

U.S. Pacific Forces. By far the predominant naval force in the Pacific area is that of the United States. Our Pacific naval assets are organized into two primary fleets: the Seventh Fleet is primarily deployed forward in the

Western Pacific, while the Third Fleet is primarily an administrative command for ships in service, training, or repair along the west coast of the United States. The bulk of our Pacific assets are assigned to the Third Fleet during peacetime.

Pacific Naval Strategy and Missions

The Alliance naval presence in the Pacific is considerably enlarged by the not-insignificant navies of Japan, Taiwan, and Australia, which add a total of 110 to 120 oceangoing combatants to U.S. forces in the area. Together, they pose a serious challenge to the success of any potential Soviet or People's Republic of China naval offensives, although they are dispersed across the vast span of the Western and Southwestern Pacific and serve primarily national interests during peacetime. With these allies, the U.S. Pacific fleets present a major obstacle to any attempted establishment of Communist maritime supremacy throughout the Pacific Ocean. Western Alliance naval strategy appears to encompass five distinct missions:

- Strategic Deterrence
- Neutralization of Soviet SLBM Forces
- Offensive Operations in Support of Allied Security Interests
- Atlantic Reinforcement in a "NATO-First" Scenario
- Defense of Pacific and Indian Ocean SLOCs

Strategic Deterrence. The U.S. Navy operates a single squadron of about ten Polaris (A-3) SSBN submarines from a forward base in Apra Harbor, Guam. These submarines patrol North Pacific waters as part of the overall U.S. strategic nuclear deterrent. The SSBNs do not, as far as is known, patrol Indian Ocean waters, although, of course, they could. United States SSBNs are not integrated within Western Alliance general-purpose naval forces; they are, for obvious reasons, in a separate command. Nonetheless, these SSBNs contribute in a real, if inconspicuous, manner to Western presence and deterrence of Soviet attempts to expand regional influence. In view of the relatively small Soviet naval presence in the Pacific, it is generally assumed that these SSBNs remain rather invulnerable to Soviet detection techniques. The introduction of the newer Trident submarine and missile system, with its greatly expanded range, promises to keep U.S. SSBNs quite invulnerable in the Pacific for the foreseeable future.

Neutralization of Soviet SLBM Forces. Soviet naval missions in the Pacific include deployment of SSBNs and SSGNs supported by general-purpose naval and air assets. These Soviet SSBNs have patrolled Pacific waters since the early 1960s. The 1,600-mile range of the SS-N-6 missiles aboard the Yankee-class submarines requires operations relatively close to their intended U.S. or Asian targets, well beyond the normal range of their supporting forces. The introduction of the Delta-class submarines, with their 4,000-mile missiles, on the other hand, permits these newer SSBNs to operate within Soviet regional waters and within protective coverage of general-purpose defensive forces. The Soviets are expected to maintain screens around their deployed SSBNs made up of attack submarines, ASW surface ships, or ASW and bomber aircraft. These forces could be drawn from a total of about 44 attack submarines (a mix of nuclear- and diesel-powered), about 64 surface combatants, and about 100 medium- and long-range naval aircraft. Soviet long-range aviation could augment Pacific based naval aviation from bases in the western regions of Russia if priorities so dictated.

United States, Japanese, and Canadian forces normally operate in Soviet SSBN patrol areas. However, given the superior performance of U.S. naval elements, any mission to neutralize Soviet SSBNs would be likely to fall to U.S. forces, probably some of the thirty to thirty-five U.S. SSNs normally assigned to the Pacific fleets. Japanese and Canadian forces are better suited to SLOC-defense missions and the protection of coastal waters. Other U.S. SSNs would normally be expected to be assigned to antisubmarine barrier operations—to attack Soviet underwater assets as they depart and return to their home ports in the Northern Pacific. This country's SSNs in the Pacific appear more than adequate for that task.

Surveillance of the Pacific Ocean is carried out by an extensive network of ASW patrol aircraft bases stretching from Hawaii and Okinawa to Taiwan, the Philippines, and Guam. These P-3 aircraft, in addition to other, more strategic surveillance systems, are virtually assured of providing the Alliance with better information on the location of Soviet naval units than will be available to the other side concerning Alliance submarine positions. To the extent that the Russians chose to "withhold" their SSBNs and other naval strength, however, the Alliance would have increasing difficulties in rooting them out of their defended sanctuary areas.

Offensive Operations in Support of Allied Security Interests. The U.S. Navy retains a major conventional capability for offensive operations throughout the Pacific in the form of forward-deployed aircraft carriers and amphibious forces for power projection ashore. Two large aircraft carriers are normally deployed forward with the Seventh Fleet as well as one Marine Battalion Landing Team during peacetime. Additional carriers are stationed on the west coast of the United States, and marine units are available from Okinawa or California. The Soviet Pacific naval forces

ALLIANCE NAVAL FORCES IN THE PACIFIC

Units from four nations operated together in the Pacific exercise "Valiant Heritage" in 1976. Pictured here are a New Zealand frigate, four Canadian warships, a British light cruiser, the nuclear-powered U.S.S. *Enterprise* (CVN-65) and two U.S. cruisers (CG-11 and CGN-35). (Courtesy U.S. Navy)

Extended U.S. naval operations in the Western Pacific are made possible by the important U.S. Naval Ship Repair Facility at Subic Bay in the Philippines. Without such facilities U.S. naval operations would be seriously curtailed. (Courtesy U.S. Navy)

currently have no equivalent capabilities, although their relatively modest Pacific marine units are presumably capable of some operation along their adjacent coastline to the south or toward the offshore Kurile Islands. Operations against Japan or the Aleutian Islands appear beyond their capabilities for the foreseeable future.

On the other hand, Soviet naval forces are well equipped to defend against attacks from U.S. carrier-based aircraft. The Soviet ocean surveillance network, consisting of land, sea, undersea, air, and space elements should have little difficulty tracking any carriers headed toward the Soviet Pacific coast. Moreover, the Soviets now maintain an active fleet of cruise missile submarines (SSGs), some of which are nuclear-powered (SSGNs). Their primary purpose would be to counter the U.S. carrier threat. Within roughly 2,000 miles of the Soviet coast, U.S. carriers could be attacked by a variety of submarine and surface vessels and land-based aircraft carrying cruise missiles—in the Soviets' customary "all-arms" approach to such a tactical engagement.

Although the carriers' main mission, then, is to "carry the war to the enemy," their first objective would be to diminish the capabilities of Soviet general-purpose naval assets set against them. This would include elimination of the "tattletale" ships that follow the carriers and a concerted search for any Soviet submarines within carrier striking distance. A direct engagement between U.S. surface combatants and Soviet Pacific surface combatants does not appear likely, unless the Soviets could not escape it. The success of Soviet long-range aviation against the carriers would depend in large measure on whether or not sufficient resources could be marshalled in a coordinated attack to saturate carrier in-depth air defenses. This seems less likely in the Pacific than in the Atlantic or Mediterranean. Yet it also seems unlikely that the United States would emerge from Soviet anticarrier efforts unscathed.

On balance, U.S. carriers should be able to carry out their missions in the Pacific, and our Air Force long-range bombers in the Pacific should be available to assist. Whether the United States would send its carriers on the offensive at the outset of a major confrontation or withhold them for action at a possibly more crucial phase of the war is not clear. Until they are committed, however, the Soviets would be forced to hold back some of their own assets also. But in general, as the assets of both sides decreased, the carrier would emerge as a relatively more powerful residual force.

In situations less than an all-out confrontation with the Soviets, the U.S. Navy in the Pacific at present appears adequate to handle most contingencies, even though it might have to operate without help from Alliance naval assets. In prior contingency operations in the Pacific, our naval forces have gone essentially unchallenged. This may not be the case in the future as Third World countries improve their own naval capabilities. Nonetheless, although they may become capable of damaging some elements of U.S. naval forces (and embarrassing us thereby), there seems to be little question that U.S. strength would prevail. By comparison, the Soviets do not retain "power projection" forces in the Pacific other than for a nuclear war.

Augmentation of NATO Forces in the Atlantic. Judging from normal peacetime deployment patterns, friendly naval forces appear to be more than a match for their Soviet counterparts in the Pacific. However, as mentioned earlier, a substantial fraction of U.S. Pacific naval forces would probably be redeployed to the Atlantic to support a "NATO-First" scenario. Those redeployments would require thirty to forty-five days, and the ships would be away from combat roles for most of that time. Although the specific number of ships to be transferred is not available—and is not necessarily fixed—major elements of the U.S. Third Fleet are thought to be earmarked to reinforce the Second and Sixth fleets. Such a redeployment would have a large impact on the force balance in the Pacific, particularly since the carrier task forces seem prime candidates for transfer. If so, their greatest utility would be to contribute to Atlantic offensive "power projection" missions rather than to the defense of the sealanes. Since distances are greater across the Pacific and friendly bases farther apart, carrier task forces are probably more useful to Pacific SLOC-defense than they are to Atlantic SLOC-defense. Hence, the justification for the redeployments appears to center on the need for additional offensive airpower in support of Europe or its flanks. Since the carriers are also less vulnerable in the Pacific than in the Atlantic, their redeployment must be based on high priority and high risk assignments.

United States Department of Defense planning for many years assumed that a "NATO war" would be something less than a world conflict and that the engagement would be primarily confined to the European theater. In that case, it would have been normal to plan to concentrate one's naval forces in the Atlantic, regardless of the specific missions planned. More recently, it has been recognized that wars with the Soviet Union might also involve conflict in the Pacific or the Indian Ocean—and include the need to assist in the defense of our Pacific and Middle Eastern allies. It is no longer so clear that the higher-priority naval missions are all in the Atlantic, particularly in view of the larger naval contributions available from our NATO partners. The increased significance of the Indian Ocean may also suggest the need to augment the U.S. Seventh Fleet rather than the Second.

There are additional powerful reasons for maintaining strong U.S. naval forces in the Pacific during a large-scale confrontation with the Soviet Union. These deal with the perceptions of the People's Republic of China (P.R.C.). The ability of the P.R.C. to remain outside Soviet hegemony

U.S. NAVAL FORCES IN THE PACIFIC

Carrier-based strike aircraft like the heavy attack A-6A and the light attack A-7E pictured above on the U.S.S. *Enterprise* (CVN-65) provide the U.S. Navy's "power projection" capabilities across the Pacific. CVN-65 is being escorted here by the British light cruiser *Glamorgan*. (Courtesy U.S. Navy)

Naval elements of the U.S. Third Fleet in the Pacific include ships like the frigate U.S.S. *Quellet* (FF-1077) and the guided missile destroyer U.S.S. *Joseph Strauss* (DDG-16) shown here off Hawaii. This report questions the value of "swinging" these forces to the Atlantic during a major war. (Courtesy U.S. Navy)

depends crucially on the retention of an appropriate balance of power between the Western Alliance and the Soviet Union both in NATO and in the Pacific. It is no surprise that the P.R.C. is one of the greatest proponents of a strong and dynamic NATO. By the same token, it is to the Alliance's advantage for the P.R.C. to continue to present a threat to Soviet Asian forces. The ability of the P.R.C. to do so depends on the retention of a balance of power in the Northwest Pacific. Clearly, this balance would be lost if the Soviets could "neutralize" Japan and if the North Koreans, at Soviet urging, could take over South Korea. Keeping Japan aligned to the West and maintaining the freedom of South Korea both depend on a strong Western naval presence in the Northwest Pacific, by which the sea and air lanes are held open and the conventional and nuclear threats presented by Soviet Pacific naval forces are diminished.

Because of all the foregoing considerations, planning to divert a large measure of our Pacific naval forces to the Atlantic during a large-scale war with the Soviet Union appears increasingly unwise.

Defense of Pacific and Indian Ocean SLOCs. As previously mentioned, the Soviets maintain roughly ten older-vintage SSNs (1957–1962), six newer Victor SSNs, and about thirty diesel-powered SSs, of which roughly half are approaching obsolescence. Relative to estimates of the levels of merchant shipping plying the waters of the Pacific and Indian oceans, the number of anti-SLOC Soviet submarines is considerably lower than it might be in the Atlantic or Mediterranean. Allied merchant loss rates, then, would probably be lower. Moreover, the extent of Soviet naval aviation assigned to the Pacific theater is also rather modest. To undertake an anti-SLOC campaign, the Soviets would be faced with a choice between concentrating their attacks at various marshalling points near the SLOC terminals—where they would be more vulnerable to ASW forces of the Alliance—and randomly attacking the long and open SLOCs, where their effectiveness would be lower.

Employed in a surge, Soviet attack submarines could disrupt Allied shipping, particularly in Japanese and Korean waters, but only for a limited period of time before Allied ASW forces—and their own operational limitations—would reduce the Soviet level of effort. If, instead, they withheld their submarine attacks until logistic concentrations had developed in SLOC marshalling areas, then their effectiveness might be higher, but so would their attrition through Allied mine and submarine barriers. Soviet long-range aviation might also be used to strike congested port areas, but, at least until now, none of the more capable Backfire bombers has been assigned to the Pacific forces.

Employed in a protracted war of attrition against the open ocean SLOCs,

Soviet submarines would probably be less effective in sinking ships but might succeed in diverting Allied naval assets from more threatening offensive uses. In all likelihood, Allied naval forces would be required to conduct both offensive and defensive missions, and there would, of course, be some inevitable losses to Allied shipping in the process.

Allied SLOC defenses in the Northern Pacific would include U.S., Japanese, and Korean naval forces. The major responsibility, however, might well have to fall on the Japanese Maritime Self-Defense Force (MSDF) since the U.S. Seventh Fleet would likely be preoccupied with other open ocean missions. The MSDF currently possesses some ninety long-range patrol aircraft and over sixty modern ASW surface combatants and submarines. Japan has additional submarines under construction and will gain forty to fifty more P-3 patrol aircraft during the 1980s. The MSDF is designed to deter or defeat a Soviet offensive against its uniquely vital SLOCs, without which the Japanese economy could not survive. It is designed to operate close to home waters, but there is no inherent reason why its forces could not eventually extend to Taiwan and possibly even as far as Guam in the Marianas—a favorite vacation spot of the Japanese, where their presence stimulates no alarm.

Japan controls the key La Perouse Strait connecting the Sea of Japan with the Pacific basin, and, together with the Republic of Korea, commands the Tsushima Strait—the western exit from the Sea of Japan. Soviet forces based at Vladivostok and its satellite installations must expect to fight their way through these straits or to transit north along Sakhalin Island and out through the Sea of Okhotsk, where they could expect to obtain some security from their forces at Petropavlovsk on the Kamchatka Peninsula. Thus, in addition to its SLOC-defense role, the MSDF has an important sea-denial mission proximate to its home waters. Without active Japanese naval participation in a major confrontation between the Alliance and the Soviet Union, the Pacific-based Soviet Navy would appear to be a somewhat more formidable opponent, and the chances of maintaining a low-attrition SLOC to Japan or Korea would be reduced significantly.

In the Southwest Pacific, the potential threat from Soviet submarines, particularly the older diesel boats, is greatly diminished. So are the naval forces that could be marshalled to oppose them. Less than two dozen escorts would be provided from the Philippines, Australia, and New Zealand acting together. Some U.S. units would have to be dispatched to this area if an anti-SLOC campaign materialized, but their major function might have to be the securing of the Malacca Straits. In some instances, it might be necessary to risk the losses associated with individual sailings and accept whatever small level of submarine attrition could be exacted by merchantmen defending themselves.

Indian Ocean Strategy and Missions

Western Alliance naval strategy in the Indian Ocean appears limited to a relatively minor continuous American and French presence, with occasional deployments by additional U.S. warships and one or two Dutch or French vessels. The French naval presence actually exceeded that of the United States in 1976. Our Pacific allies do not deploy into the region. The U.S. land-based presence is confined mainly to communications facilities in western Australia, plus the new air and naval facilities being built at Diego Garcia. These are primarily designed to enable a quick-response buildup of forces to the region should the necessity arise and to help counter the presence of the Soviet Indian Ocean Squadron (IOS).

The Soviet Pacific Fleet provides the primary support for the IOS, which has a nominal strength of eight to ten combatants and ten replenishment and support ships. Soviet research and fishing vessels routinely operate throughout the Indian Ocean. The peacetime IOS mission is essentially political—"in support of state interests"—and appears designed to offset any perceptions of unilateral Western influence in the area. Having been expelled from their rather elaborate naval facility at Berbera, the Soviets are now more limited in their combat capabilities to what can be maintained at sea. The IOS naval potential is mainly a threat to Alliance oil SLOCs from the Middle East and to U.S. carriers, which are shadowed throughout the ocean by alert Soviet forces. The IOS and its fleet marine force and cruise missile platforms could presumably interfere with U.S. use of Diego Garcia, at least temporarily, but these forces would be subject to considerable risk operating virtually without air cover.

In a war at sea, the Soviet IOS could engage in operations against the Western SLOCs and any hostile forces operating in the area. This force would soon be depleted of stores, munitions, etc., owing to its attenuated lifelines. However, it could draw down considerable U.S. forces that could otherwise be used more effectively elsewhere. In a more localized contingency, the Soviets might attempt to interpose their IOS in the path of some intended U.S. intervention in the Indian Ocean region. Which side would ultimately gain the upper hand would depend on what specific U.S. vessels were there at the time and how much each side might be willing to "up the ante" in such a local showdown.

There is a broad range of opinion concerning the need for U.S. military and naval forces in the Indian Ocean area. Were it not for the unique dependence of the Western Alliance on Middle East oil, it is doubtful that the political and societal instabilities of that area would draw so much attention. Nonetheless, the Indian Ocean littoral remains important to the Soviet Union for several prime reasons. Potentially, it offers the Soviets a source of excellent naval access to the Indian Ocean, the South Atlantic,

U.S. NAVAL CAPABILITIES IN THE INDIAN OCEAN

A U.S. naval task group (77.6) is shown in the Straits of Malacca, returning from the Indian Ocean to Subic Bay in the Philippines. The aircraft carrier U.S.S. *Constellation* (CV-64) is flanked by two destroyers (DDG-12 and DDG-15), led by an escort (DE-1065), and trailed by a fast combat support ship (AOE-2). (Courtesy U.S. Navy)

U.S. naval construction on the island of Diego Garcia in the Indian Ocean will provide a badly needed logistics way-station for U.S. naval units operating westward beyond the Pacific Ocean. (Courtesy U.S. Navy)

and the Pacific. The political affinities of several eastern littoral states are germane to Soviet attempts to "contain" an unsympathetic People's Republic of China. Indian Ocean ports could also provide the Soviets with ready access to Southeast Asian markets and raw materials. On the western littoral, the ability to influence the Arab states will probably grow in importance as the Soviets become net importers of natural gas and oil as a result of their apparent inability to exploit their own native resources rapidly enough. Moreover, the political orientations of the countries of the northeast quadrant of Africa, from Libya to Somalia, are of more than passing interest to the U.S.S.R.—and to the overall stability of the Middle East.

In some respects U.S. interests in the area are driven by the negative imperatives of counterbalancing these Soviet objectives. We are not receptive to the notion of intimidating the P.R.C.; neither do we share the Soviet view of a suitable resolution of Middle East instabilities. While we would presumably not object to the Soviets having increased access to Southeast Asian markets or to their importing Mideast oil, our primary interest will obviously remain the continued availability of essential petroleum products for ourselves and the rest of the Western Alliance. Possibly the situation would appear more stable if the Soviets *did* share our dependence on oil imports. Nonetheless, the Middle East oil fields are much closer, militarily speaking, to Moscow than they are to Washington, London, Bonn, or Tokyo.

The Soviet cause appears to have little appeal for the Arabs, Iranians, Indians, or North Africans, who have tended historically to be attracted more by Western lifestyles and technology while enjoying a political framework of their own choosing. Economically, the oil-producing states enjoy the benefits of sales to the West and would normally be reluctant to impose more than a temporary embargo.

On the other hand, there are many relatively simple ways to interrupt the oil flow, which depends, in fact, on a very small number of wells. Saudi wells, for instance, pump an average 12,000 barrels each per day compared to the U.S. domestic average of only 18 barrels each per day. The energy sources that power these pumps and the gas-oil separators are even less numerous, and the collection points where the oil is piped to awaiting tankers are few in number as well. Finally, the Strait of Hormuz presents a natural geographic choke point only a few miles wide. As a consequence, there seem to be many system vulnerabilities other than the one-by-one sinking of tankers along the Indian Ocean SLOCs. Hence, although it may appear desirable to protect the oil SLOCs from attack, doing so would by no means assure the continued flow of Middle East oil.

Oil does not represent the only SLOC of potential interest in the Indian Ocean. The need might arise to establish a sea line of communication in support of a large task force or other military operation along the Indian Ocean littoral or within the Arabian or Red Sea, the Persian Gulf, or the Sea of Aden. Such a SLOC, whether it flowed from the South Atlantic or the Pacific, would be long, exposed, and lacking in receptive way-stations. As a matter of interest, the Iranian port of Bandar Abbas is roughly 13,400 miles from San Diego and 13,600 miles from Norfolk: more than three times the distance from Norfolk to Rotterdam and about twice as far as it is from San Diego to Pusan, South Korea.

Support of a military operation in the Indian Ocean littoral would be further complicated by uncertainties concerning the moral or material support of other Alliance nations. There are some who believe that any intervention primarily justified by the need to keep the oil flowing would be supported by most of the Alliance. Others believe that if there were any reasonable doubt concerning the outcome—or fear of making a bad situation worse—the reaction of our allies would be studious neutrality, as in the Arab-Israeli war of 1973 (even though the cause might be quite different). Certainly, for U.S. naval forces neutral allies would constitute a "worst case."

Finally, resort to the use of military force—or even a firm display of force—at the end of such a long lifeline would demand exhaustive consideration of the potential consequences downstream. To what extent could we afford to persevere in the face of serious resistance from the Soviets or their surrogates? What would we be willing to risk, and how close to the nuclear threshold would we be willing to approach? To what extent would we be willing to lower the conventional deterrent to aggression either in Europe or Northwest Asia by redeploying forces toward the Middle East? Would we unwittingly force a choice between nuclear warfare and the more permanent interruption of the flow of Middle East oil?

The answers to such questions exceed the scope of this study. Nevertheless, U.S. intervention in the Middle East at some future date cannot be excluded on either emotional or political grounds, although it might be ruled out for realistic military considerations. But contingency planning for such an event would probably reveal that current U.S. naval and maritime force levels are inadequate. Our current force options appear so limited that a hasty commitment could seriously lower the current deterrent values of our forces in other parts of the world. In this case, the military resources required for such a contingency should be considered additive to, rather than subsumed within, the minimum conventional force requirements to deter aggression in Europe or Northeast Asia. A more thorough analysis of the demands of this additional scenario is warranted.

Pacific-Indian Ocean Orders of Battle (1978)

Western Alliance forces operating in the Pacific and Indian oceans include some 300 naval combatants and some 370 land-based ASW and maritime surveillance aircraft. United States and Australian carriers operate more than 500 ship-based aircraft. United States and Australian carriers operate more than 500 ship-based aircraft. Against these forces are about 130 Soviet naval combatants and about 100 land-based naval aircraft. Both sides, of course, can augment their naval aviation assets with long-range bombers from their air forces. In only one category do the Soviets hold a slight numerical advantage—submarines. They have about 90 submarines, compared to some 62 for the West.

Numerical comparisons are a rather poor measure of relative effectiveness, but the qualitative advantages tend to be on the side of the West too. Both the Japanese and the Australian navies are considerably more potent in antisubmarine warfare and antiaircraft warfare, as well as in conventionally powered submarines. United States naval forces are superior to their Soviet counterparts in all respects, save possibly cruise missiles—a a situation that will be equalized in the near future with the introduction of the Harpoon.

The primary strength of the Western Naval Alliance in the Pacific lies in the U.S. Third and Seventh fleets. The Third Fleet, in the Eastern Pacific, holds 4 carriers, almost 500 land- and sea-based aircraft, 70 surface combatants, and 30 attack submarines. Many of these assets are in normal overhaul. The forward-deployed Seventh Fleet in the Western Pacific contains 2 carriers, 200 to 250 aircraft, 20 surface combatants, several amphibious units, and 10 to 15 submarines, all of which can be augmented from Third Fleet assets on short notice.

Canadian, Japanese, Australian, New Zealand, and Malaysian naval forces add about another 100 surface combatants and submarines and about 200 naval aircraft. The Republic of Korea, the Philippines, and Taiwan possess considerable but increasingly obsolescent assets, including another 55 surface combatants, 2 submarines, and 50 land-based naval patrol aircraft. While those forces are generally obsolescent for offensive ASW operations, their ability to initiate an attack on a submarine based on a "flaming datum" (i.e., a ship-sinking indicating general submarine location) and to deter attacks on convoys by conventionally powered submarines provides a valuable asset. This is particularly true in view of the somewhat limited Soviet anti-SLOC capabilities in the Pacific.

Pakistani, Iranian, and South African naval forces are both weak and widely dispersed around the shores of the Indian Ocean. Together, they could add about twenty-five combatants and submarines and only about fifteen land-based aircraft to the West's resources. Nevertheless, these assets could be valuable in combined operations to defend oil SLOCs against a modest level of submarine attack. The Soviets would not neglect these units in their own computations of the naval balance in the region.

Table 8-2 lists all of the naval strength potentially available to the West by region and by major unit types. While the U.S. Pacific fleets contribute the largest number of assets of any country, they form no more than half of the aggregate in any areas except for carriers and their aircraft, and nuclear submarines.

Alliance Naval Posture without the United States

Conceivably, the United States could find itself in a confrontation at sea against the Soviets without allied participation, perhaps in some remote place. By the same token, our allies ought to assess their own capabilities for limited naval encounters in the absence of immediate U.S. support. Clear understandings are needed of where the threshold for U.S. entry begins and where the independent or combined capabilities of our allies end. A gap between these two thresholds would undermine the capability of the Alliance to deter an opportunistic adversary and could even lead to the piecemeal defeats of the navies of its member nations, leaving the United States ultimately to face the Soviet Navy alone.

Our allies, then, need to retain the confidence, will, and balanced naval capability to respond to lesser contingencies and exact some noticeable naval counterforce penalty from the aggressor. No Alliance navy should be devoid of the capability to defend against and, in some form, retaliate against intimidation by elements of the naval forces of the Soviet Union or her client-states. The aggressor should be unable to achieve a limited naval objective without raising the confrontation to a level that assures U.S. intervention. The independent Alliance reaction, modest though it may be, should force the aggressor to desist or "raise the ante" to the point of assured U.S. attention. Such individual capabilities, added together, could contribute significantly to the total Alliance naval counterforce capabilities in a major confrontation.

Minor naval confrontations appear increasingly likely in the waters adjacent to Soviet naval bases and possibly off the shores of nations where Moscow is supporting local wars directly with proxy forces. The North Sea, the Eastern Mediterranean, the Sea of Japan, possibly the Gulf of Aden, and even the Gulf of Mexico represent such areas. The United States, within its present resources, cannot hope to be the naval policeman for every remote confrontation. The Russians could exploit a variety of situations to demonstrate expanding naval prowess and sea control capabilities. Acts of intimidation might include seizure of fishing vessels, quarantine of offshore oil rigs, interference with merchant vessels, and even the seeding of mines to prevent shipping through key areas. Those acts might be carried out by Soviet naval forces or, more likely, through surrogates.

TABLE 8-2
PACIFIC ORDER OF BATTLE (1978)

Region & Country	Submarines SSBN	SSN	Torpedo Attack Ocn/Cstl SS	(TOT)	Aviation Capable Ships CV	CH	Cruisers	Surface Combatants Destroyers	Frigates	(TOT)	Small Combatant Ships Msl & Torp	Mine CM	Amphib Ships	Naval Aviation Carrier Based	Land Based
Eastern Pacific															
U.S. 3rd Flt.	—	26	5/-	(31)	4	2	11	28	31	(70)	—	3	22	360	128
Canada	—	26	5/-	(31)	4	2	11	26	22	(59)	—	3	22	360	110
	—	—	—	—	—	—	—	2	9	(11)	—	—	—	—	18
Western Pacific															
U.S. 7th Flt.	10	5	17/-	(32)	2	2	4	63	52	(121)	51	81	73	180	187
Japan	10	5	—	(15)	2	2	4	10	8	(22)	—	—	8	180	40
South Korea	—	—	15/-	(15)	—	—	—	30	15	(45)	20	37	5	—	117
Taiwan	—	—	—	—	—	—	—	7	9	(16)	14	12	18	—	20
Philippines	—	—	2/-	(2)	—	—	—	18	10	(28)	9	22	28	—	10
Malaysia	—	—	—	—	—	—	—	—	10	(10)	—	4	11	—	—
	—	—	—	—	—	—	—	—	1	(1)	8	6	3	—	—
Oceania															
Australia	—	—	6/-	(6)	—	1	—	5	10	(15)	16	4	—	20	27
New Zealand	—	—	6/-	(6)	—	1	—	5	6	(11)	12	3	—	20	22
	—	—	—	—	—	—	—	—	4	(4)	2	—	—	—	5
Indian Ocean															
Iran	—	—	-/6	(6)	—	—	—	8	12	(20)	30	18	2	—	16
South Africa	—	—	-/3	(3)	—	—	—	3	8	(11)	11	5	2	—	6
Pakistan	—	—	-/3	(3)	—	—	—	1	3	(4)	—	6	—	—	7
	—	—	—	—	—	—	—	4	1	(5)	19	7	—	—	3
Pacific/IO Totals	10	31	28/6	(75)	6	5	15	106	105	(226)	97	106	97	560	358
U.S. Alone	10	31	5/-	(36)	6	4	15	36	30	(81)	—	3	30	540	150

219

While a detailed assessment of the many possible naval confrontations at the lower end of the spectrum is beyond this study, these illustrative questions may be helpful: Can Turkey, alone, assure its ships free passage through the Dardanelles? Can Norway, by itself, protect its drilling rigs in the North Sea? Can Israel, unaided, guarantee its egress to the Indian Ocean through the Red Sea? Can Japan protect its own fishing rights in the Sea of Japan? Could Indonesia enforce the security of maritime passage through its archipelago? Can the Australians be sure of getting their raw materials to market? Can Iran unilaterally guarantee Western access to the Persian Gulf?

Finally, is the United States Navy, on its own, expected to handle all of these problems if they arise? That answer must be no; but increasingly the preceding questions must bring affirmative replies, assuming that reasonably substantial threats materialize and that the cooperation of friendly states in the immediate area will be forthcoming. Regional cooperation to guarantee the security of vital local sealanes and commercial zones appears both essential and somewhat overdue.

Alliance Naval Exercises

There are a number of signs that the combined naval exercises currently conducted in both the NATO and Pacific arenas are inadequate to assure effective international operations. Some Alliance observers consider NATO maneuvers as "ritualistic" rather than real attempts to improve efffectiveness. United States commanders, on the other hand, often believe that these activities are designed to "avoid the embarrassment of failures" amongst other Alliance naval forces. Some Alliance units are even said to be hesitant to move out into open water operations far from their home bases. In some cases, lack of standardization and interoperability appear to limit seriously the effectiveness of joint operations. There are also suggestions that the lack of an agreed Atlantic or Pacific naval strategy hinders the development of realistic exercises. In any event, the combined resources of all the navies of the West would be required to promptly neutralize the Soviet fleet. The less effectively Alliance navies work together, the longer this task would take and the greater would be the dependence on the dwindling seapower of the United States.

9
Comparative Force Levels, Merchant Marines, and Overseas Bases

Soviet and Alliance maritime comparisons are derived primarily from naval force levels, the sizes of the merchant marines, and the extent of the overseas bases and facilities. These factors are discussed in the aggregate in this chapter.

Soviet-Alliance Force Level Comparisons

When comparing total Western and Warsaw Pact naval strength, one should recognize that the missions, objectives, and deployments of the two groupings differ greatly and that, in general, like forces do not oppose each other. The Soviets obviously have no counterpart to our attack aircraft carriers, and perhaps they do not need one. Their nonstrategic submarines are built specifically for antisubmarine warfare or for attacks on surface warships (using cruise missiles) or on civilian shipping (using their larger numbers of conventional torpedoes), whereas U.S. nonstrategic submarines have been generally configured for a range of antisubmarine missions. Moreover, amphibious forces, coastal defense units, minelaying or minesweeping vessels, and strategic submarines would not be expected to oppose one another directly in battle.

Because quantitative comparisons do little to reflect the factor of quality, they can be misleading. For instance, U.S. ships are generally larger, have more endurance, and are less vulnerable than those of the Soviets. On the other hand, many Soviet ships, submarines, and aircraft carry longer-range standoff missiles. The U.S. Harpoon antiship missile is only now being introduced. It is somewhat ironic that the initial cruise missile developments were carried on in the United States in the 1960s and subsequently dropped as unnecessary. A higher-powered submarine is bound to be faster than a comparable medium-powered version—but it is also likely to be far noisier. In engagements with ships, the value of speed may outweigh the disadvantage of the associated noise, but in a submarine duel, the opposite conclusion is likely. In addition, numbers per se certainly do not reflect combat superiority. History is replete with examples of the defeat of larger forces by qualitatively superior but smaller ones, especially if the latter could avoid being "saturated" or surprised by the enemy.

Finally, a static "snapshot" of opposing forces is not truly indicative of future trends unless age and current building rates are taken into account. As discussed in Chapter 4, there are several rather large classes of Soviet vessels for which there are no apparent replacement modernization programs. Consequently, in certain categories both the Soviets and the Alliance are "coasting" on prior expenditures that may not be duplicated. In fact, several elements of the Soviet naval postwar building program now face the same "bloc obsolescence" problem that befell the U.S. Navy in the last decade after our World War II building program.

Nonetheless, current force level comparisons are widely used—and misused—by various advocates for change in the current Alliance naval posture. Therefore, Soviet and Alliance overall force levels as of January 1978 are depicted on the somewhat complex Table 9-1, divided into the six major categories described below. The first two columns indicate force levels for the Soviet Union and the United States, followed by separate columns for non-U.S. NATO, France and Spain, and our Pacific and Indian Ocean allies. The last column gives a conservative Alliance total.

Submarines

In the most important category of submarines, the number of currently operational Soviet submarines (about 340) is significantly larger than the U.S. total (116) and somewhat larger than the Alliance count of 299. This comparison appears even less favorable in view of the relatively large number of Western submarines (59) that are less than 200 feet long and, hence, primarily coastal-oriented. The Soviets also lead in nuclear submarines (150 versus 123), although all of this advantage is in ballistic missile submarines, which would not normally be accorded sea control missions. In torpedo attack submarines, the Soviets actually lag the West by a factor of two (36 versus 74)—although the large number of their cruise missile submarines with nuclear propulsion is a testimonial to their concerted effort to counter our aircraft carriers. Moreover, their large remaining inventory of ocean-going diesel submarines (151) are still useful, although they are gradually aging and unlikely to be replaced one-for-one with nuclear units. As noted in Chapter 4, it is expected that the Soviets would assign some nuclear submarines to the disruption of our intended antisubmarine barriers and some cruise missile submarines to theater nuclear targets, further reducing the number that would be

223

TABLE 9-1
COMPARISON OF MAJOR SOVIET AND ALLIANCE NAVAL ELEMENTS
AS OF 1/1/78

Categories	Soviet Union	United States (active/reserve)	Non-US NATO	France & Spain	Pacific & IO Allies	Alliance Totals
Submarines (Tot)	(342)	(116)	(120)	(34)	(29)	(299)
SSBN (12-16/3 tube)	64/8	41	4	4	0	49
SSB	20	0	0	1	0	1
SSGN/SSG	42/23	0	0	0	0	0
SSN	36	65	9	0	0	74
SS	151	10	107	29	29	175
Aviation Ships (Tot)	(3)	(21)[1]	(2)	(3)	(1)	(27)
CTOL a/c Carriers	0	13	1	2	0	16
VTOL/Helo Carriers	3	8	1	1	1	11
Major Combatants (Tot)	(237)	(200)[1]	(191)	(78)	(145)	(614)
Cruisers	35	28	5	2	0	35
Destroyers	94	78/30	62	32	70	272
Frigates/Escorts	108	64	124	44	75	307
Small Combatants (Tot)	(788)	(31)	(560)	(117)	(200)	(908)
Missile Craft	143	1	81	6	0	88
Patrol Craft	355	5	195	51	97	348
Mine Warfare Craft	290	3/22	284	60	103	450
Amphibious Ships (Tot)	(84)	(55/3)	(20)	(10)	(67)	(155)
Naval Aviation:						
Carrier-Capable (Tot)	(290)	(2850)[2]	(210)	(120)	(80)	(3260)
Combat Aircraft	30	2000/300	90	60	50	2500
ASW/AEW Patrol	0	250/50	20	30	20	370
ASW Helicopters	260	250	100	30	10	390
Land-Based (Tot)	(865)[3]	(400)[3]	(250)	(40)	(200)	(890)
Antiship Aircraft	365	0[4]	0	0	0	0
Patrol/Recce/ASW (incl Helos)	500	400	250	40	200	890

Notes:
1. Does not include 5 carriers, 10 cruisers, & 4 battleships in "mothballs."
2. Includes all Navy/Marine fighter, attack, recce, tanker, & ECM aircraft.
3. Does not include possible contributions from Soviet LRA or U.S. B-52s & F-111s.
4. All 400 U.S. P-3s will be fitted with HARPOON antiship missiles.

available to attack Allied sealanes unless the Soviets were certain there was little chance of escalation to general nuclear war.

Aviation Ships

The table shows that the Western Alliance retains a commanding lead in aviation-capable ships, although the Soviets apparently intend to close that gap somewhat. They have no counterpart to U.S. attack carriers and their aircraft complements. Moreover, it is doubtful that their first three aviation-capable ships are better aircraft platforms than the fourteen smaller Alliance carriers.

Major Surface Combatants

In numbers of large surface combatants, the Soviets lead the United States in virtually all categories by a small margin but have less than one-third the total of destroyers and frigates available to the Western Alliance as a whole. The Soviets' current shipbuilding program is adequate to sustain their current number of surface combatants over the long haul, while it is by no means clear that Western shipbuilding plans in the aggregate will sustain current force levels.

Small Combatants

In numbers of small combatants for coastal operations, the Soviets dwarf the United States, which recognizes no equivalent mission. However, when the capabilities of our allies—who do have such missions—are included, then the Alliance total is somewhat larger (908 versus 788).

Amphibious Ships

The increasing number of Soviet amphibious ships would suggest more than a purely defensive intent, although this dispersed fleet has relatively little overall capability. The Russian total is roughly half that available to the Western Alliance, and the displacement of the U.S. ships alone is substantially greater than that of the Soviets at this time.

Naval Aviation

Naval aviation is, of course, the other category in which the vast asymmetry clearly favors the West and the United States in particular. While numbers of land-based patrol aircraft are roughly equal, the Alliance has an enormous lead in carrier-capable combat and patrol aircraft and helicopters. On the other hand, the West has no naval equivalent of the Backfire bomber, although the P-3 equipped with Harpoon missiles will soon be able to exact heavy surface ship losses if required to do so.

Alliance Contributions

Table 9-1 shows that, collectively, the other members of the Alliance maintain larger naval forces than the United States does, emphasizing conventional submarines, destroyers and frigates, and small surface combatants.

According to the criteria that popularly rate the U.S. fleet as a "500-ship navy," our Allies command another "600-ship navy." Unfortunately, much of this additional force is approaching obsolescence as our partners share our own uncertainty about what units are needed and affordable for the future. This indecisiveness is hard to understand in the face of the increased dependence of the Alliance countries on the seas and the growing ability of the Soviets to interfere with free passage.

Other Comparisons

Figures 9-1 and 9-2 are more frequently used than the preceding comparisons. They indicate the trends in numbers and tonnage of U.S. and Soviet warships over the past ten years. These statistics, presented repeatedly by the Defense Department, reveal that Soviet naval capabilities relative to those of the United States *alone* have been improving in both numbers and displacement. This could be particularly important in a U.S.-Soviet confrontation outside the NATO arena.

These trends are further demonstrated by the bar charts in Figure 9-3. While the United States has maintained a lead of roughly 50 percent in total tonnage—primarily in major combatants over 10,000 tons—the Soviets have built 40 percent more major combatants in the size range from 1,000 to 10,000 tons, and almost three times as many submarines.

The Defense Department view of the current U.S.-Soviet maritime balance is summarized in Figure 9-4, and the relative trends in force levels and total tonnage are portrayed in Figures 9-1 and 9-2.

Another measure of maritime capability is the number of combatant "ship-days" spent on distant deployments. This is shown in Figure 9-5, although this graph does not account for the high fraction of time spent by deployed Soviet ships at anchor. Soviet progress toward the attainment of a competitive deep-sea navy is shown more clearly by the two graphs in Figures 9-5 and 9-6. Although these graphs compare only the United States and the U.S.S.R.—not including the Western Alliance—it is clear that the trends are converging, although the United States alone still maintains a substantial advantage in both the Atlantic and the Pacific. That advantage has been lost, however, in the Mediterranean and in the Indian Ocean.

There do not appear to be any equivalent statistics on the relative number of port visits to the Third World by U.S.-Alliance and Soviet merchantmen. Such tabulations, however, would almost certainly indicate

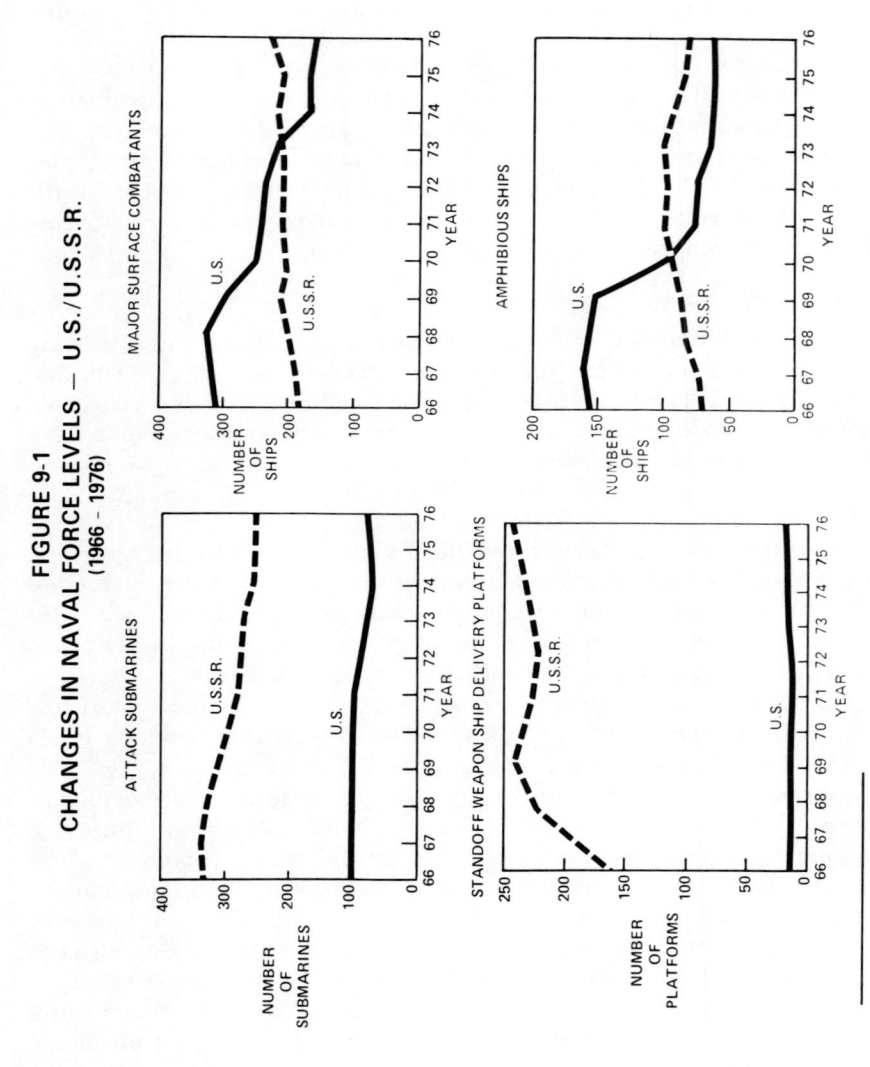

FIGURE 9-1
CHANGES IN NAVAL FORCE LEVELS – U.S./U.S.S.R.
(1966 – 1976)

Ref: U.S. Defense Perspectives, FY 1978, DoD, January 1977

FIGURE 9-2
CHARACTERISTICS AND CHANGES IN GENERAL PURPOSE* NAVAL FORCES — U.S./U.S.S.R.

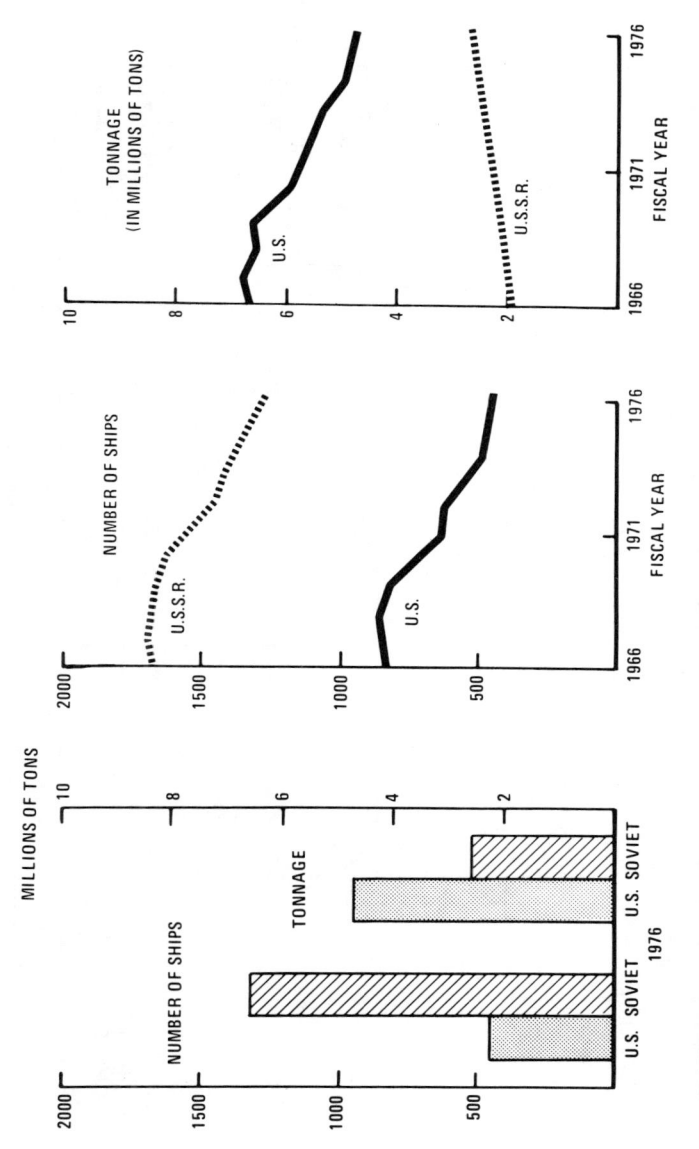

*DOES NOT INCLUDE BALLISTIC MISSILE CARRYING SUBMARINES

Ref: U.S. Defense Perspectives, FY 1978, DoD, January 1977

228

FIGURE 9-3
U.S./U.S.S.R. COMBATANT SHIP DELIVERIES*
(1966 - 1976)

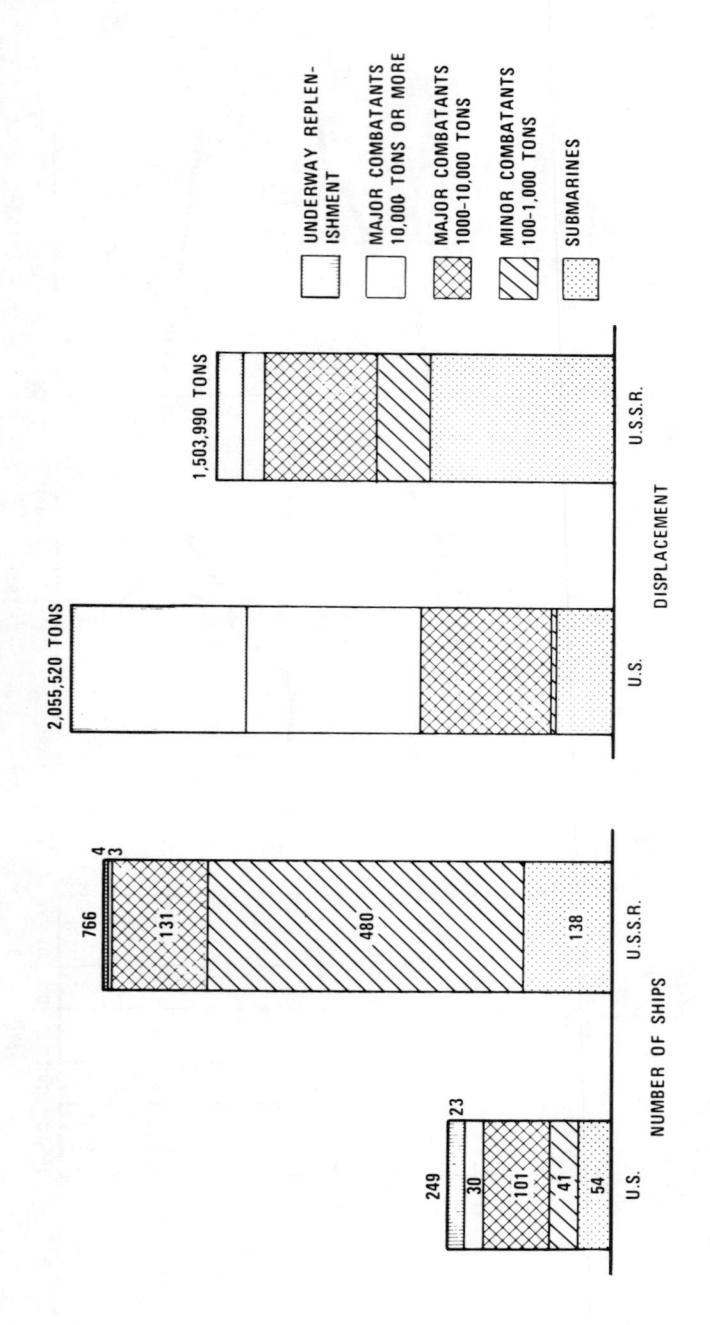

Legend:
- ☐ UNDERWAY REPLENISHMENT
- ☐ MAJOR COMBATANTS 10,000 TONS OR MORE
- ▨ MAJOR COMBATANTS 1000-10,000 TONS
- ▧ MINOR COMBATANTS 100-1,000 TONS
- ░ SUBMARINES

NUMBER OF SHIPS:
- U.S.: 249, 23, 30, 101, 41, 54
- U.S.S.R.: 766, 4, 3, 131, 480, 138

DISPLACEMENT:
- U.S.: 2,055,520 TONS
- U.S.S.R.: 1,503,990 TONS

*SUPPORT SHIPS OTHER THAN THOSE CAPABLE OF UNDERWAY REPLENISHMENT ARE NOT INCLUDED.

Ref: U.S. Defense Perspectives, FY 1978, DoD, January 1977

FIGURE 9-4
CURRENT U.S./U.S.S.R. MARITIME BALANCE

U.S.	FACTOR	SOVIET UNION
• OPEN ACCESS TO OCEANS • LONG DISTANCES TO ALLIES	GEOGRAPHY	• CONSTRAINED ACCESS TO OCEANS • SHORT DISTANCES TO ALLIES
• SEA CONTROL/POWER PROJECTION	MISSIONS	• SEA DENIAL/PERIPHERAL SEA CONTROL • LAND BASED NAVAL AIR FORCE
• FEW LARGE SHIPS • SEA BASED AVIATION • ATTACK SUBMARINES • AMPHIBIOUS FORCES • MARGINAL ANTI-AIR WARFARE CAPABILITY	OFFENSIVE CAPABILITY	• MANY SMALLER SHIPS • ANTI-SHIP MISSILE SYSTEM • ATTACK SUBMARINES
• ANTI-SUBMARINE WARFARE • AIR COVER	DEFENSIVE CAPABILITY	• MARGINAL ANTI-AIR WARFARE CAPABILITY • INADEQUATE ANTI-SUBMARINE WARFARE • INADEQUATE SEA-BASED AIR
• EXCELLENT UNDERWAY REPLENISHMENT • WORLD WIDE BASE STRUCTURE	SUSTAINED OPERATIONS	• LIMITED UNDERWAY REPLENISHMENT • LIMITED OVERSEAS BASE SYSTEM
• MAJOR ADVANTAGE--OFFENSIVE AND DEFENSIVE TECHNOLOGY	TECHNOLOGY	• ANTI-SHIP MISSILES AND SURFACE OCEAN SURVEILLANCE
• EXTENSIVE EXERCISES • VOLUNTEER FORCE • WARTIME EXPERIENCE	EXPERIENCE	• LIMITED AT-SEA TIME • MANNING BY CONSCRIPTS

Ref: U.S. Defense Perspectives, FY 1978, DoD, January 1977

FIGURE 9-5
U.S./U.S.S.R. COMBATANT SHIP-DAYS ON DISTANT DEPLOYMENT

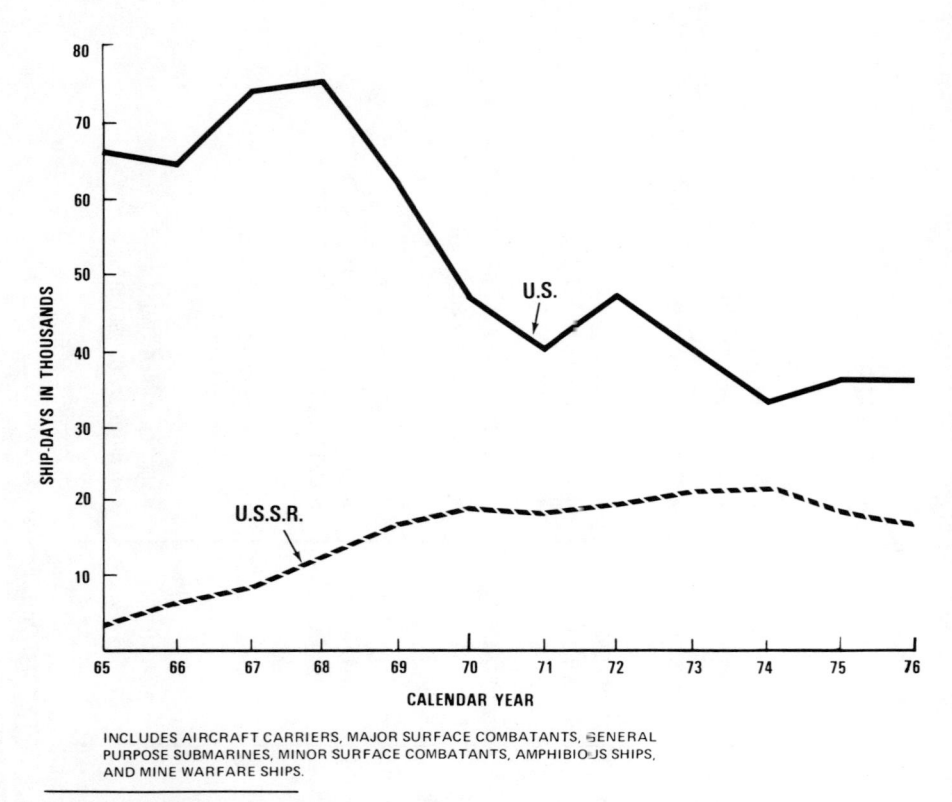

INCLUDES AIRCRAFT CARRIERS, MAJOR SURFACE COMBATANTS, GENERAL PURPOSE SUBMARINES, MINOR SURFACE COMBATANTS, AMPHIBIOUS SHIPS, AND MINE WARFARE SHIPS.

Ref: U.S. Defense Perspectives, FY 1978, DoD, January 1977

a growing predominance of Soviet visits to most countries that are not large exporters of raw materials.

Regional Comparisons of Major Naval Elements for Conventional War

In assessing the East-West naval balance, American numerologists tend to overlook the extensive fleets of our Alliance partners. Their results can thus be made to look excessively gloomy. On the other hand, the Russians tend to give special attention to Alliance forces operating close to the Eurasian continent. The Soviets can also darken their view of their own sea strength: if they eliminate their strategic forces from their calculations; if they leave out the conventional elements they may dedicate to defending their SSBNs or attacking ours; if they do not count the conventional forces assigned to the assault of our aircraft carriers; and, finally, if they credit our side with the seapower of France, Spain, Taiwan, Japan, Australia, and so on. This approach is illustrated in Table 9-2 for the major ocean battlegrounds: the Atlantic, including the Northern Flank, the Mediterranean, and the Pacific. The Soviet naval allocations employed are from Tables 4-7, 4-8, and 4-9; the Alliance distributions are those of Tables 8-2 and 8-3.

For simplicity only two categories are shown: "submarines" and "surface combatants" (including aviation-capable ships). In virtually every case except Pacific submarines, the Soviets are outnumbered by non-U.S. Alliance naval assets alone. On the other hand, in all categories except Pacific surface combatants, the Soviets outnumber the United States alone. If they also made realistic estimates of the number of their combatants that might not gain egress from the Black Sea, the Baltic, or the Sea of Japan, the "balance" would look even less favorable for them. A case could be made from the aggregate numbers that the Russian navy would have difficulty contending with non-U.S. navies in any region, while the involvement of U.S. units could only make matters worse for them. Only if the Soviets were to confront the U.S. elements alone would the advantage appear to go to them, and then only if the effectiveness of U.S. ASW and naval aviation capabilities were disregarded. This subject will be discussed in Chapter 10.

Soviet-Alliance Merchant Marine Comparisons

Static Balance

The distribution of ships and tonnage among the eleven largest merchant fleets is shown in Table 9-3 as of the end of calendar years 1965 and 1975. Between those times, the Soviet merchant fleet had risen from fifth to fourth in numerical size but dropped from seventh to ninth (just ahead of the United States) in total tonnage. However, the showings of Liberia and Panama on this listing indicate the bias produced by the extensive use of foreign registry or "flags of convenience." In fact, all ten of these countries other than the Soviet Union are really part of the Western Alliance as far as their merchant shipping fleets are concerned. Thus, the overall comparison would indicate that of the over 14,000 merchant ships, the Alliance controls 89 percent of them by number and an even more impressive 96 percent of the aggregate tonnage. From a gross standpoint, then, the Alliance nations still operate and control the vast preponderance of the world's merchant fleets—as is appropriate for the huge maritime trade they conduct.

Advocates of a larger U.S. Merchant Marine are more concerned, however, about the individual balance between the United States and the Soviet Union. The table clearly implies that the United States carries a far smaller percentage of its trade in its own ships than does the U.S.S.R. As a

**FIGURE 9-6
U.S./U.S.S.R. COMBATANT DEPLOYMENTS***
(AVERAGE CY 66 AND 76)

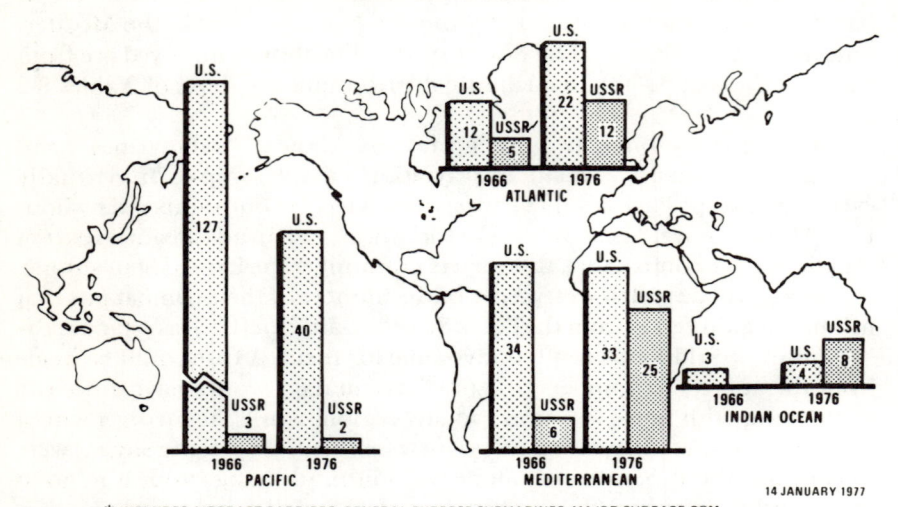

Atlantic: 1966 – U.S. 12, USSR 5; 1976 – U.S. 22, USSR 12
Pacific: 1966 – U.S. 127, USSR 3; 1976 – U.S. 40, USSR 2
Mediterranean: 1966 – U.S. 34, USSR 6; 1976 – U.S. 33, USSR 25
Indian Ocean: 1966 – U.S. 3; 1976 – U.S. 4, USSR 8

* INCLUDES AIRCRAFT CARRIERS, GENERAL PURPOSE SUBMARINES, MAJOR SURFACE COMBATANTS, MINOR SURFACE COMBATANTS, AMPHIBIOUS SHIPS, AND MINE WARFARE SHIPS.

14 JANUARY 1977

Ref: U.S. Defense Perspectives, FY 1978, DoD, January 1977

**TABLE 9-2
REGIONAL COMPARISONS OF MAJOR NAVAL ELEMENTS FOR CONVENTIONAL WAR[1]**

	No U.S. Involvement[2]		U.S. Involvement		
	Soviet	Non U.S. Alliance	Soviet	Alliance With U.S.	U.S. Alone
Atlantic					
Submarines	62	100	91	126[4]	26
Surface Combatants	83	186[3]	85	247[4]	61
Mediterranean					
Submarines	24	45	51	57[5]	12
Surface Combatants	48	87[3]	78	118[5]	31
Pacific (incl. I.O.)					
Submarines	34	23	60	69[6]	46
Surface Combatants	54	114	57	216[6]	102

[1] Rules out SSB/SSBN's and those conventional Soviet assets earmarked to defend theirs or attack ours.
[2] Rules out U.S. Naval elements and Soviet submarines and ships dedicated to anticarrier functions.
[3] Includes one-half of French and Spanish navies.
[4] Includes U.S. 2nd Fleet.
[5] Includes U.S. 6th Fleet.
[6] Includes U.S. 7th and 3rd Fleets and Canadian Pacific Fleet.

TABLE 9-3
ELEVEN LARGEST WORLD MERCHANT FLEETS
(Source: Maritime Admin.)

AS OF END 1965

Rank	By Number of Ships		By Deadweight Tonnage (Mil.)		Average Tonnage
1	U.K.	2052	Liberia	30.9	23,600
2	Norway	1365	U.K.	26.4	12,800
3	Japan	1333	Norway	23.5	17,200
4	Liberia	1313	Japan	16.4	12,300
5	U.S.S.R.	990	U.S.	14.7	15,500
6	U.S.	948	Greece	10.4	11,400
7	Greece	916	U.S.S.R.	8.0	8,100
8	F.R.G.	843	Panama	7.2	12,800
9	Italy	588	F.R.G.	7.2	8,500
10	Panama	564	Italy	6.9	11,800
11	France	542	France	6.4	11,800
Subtotals:	Alliance	10,464 (91%)	Alliance	150.0 (95%)	12,300
	U.S.S.R.	990 (9%)	U.S.S.R.	8.0 (5%)	8,100
Totals		11,454		158.0	

AS OF END 1975

1	Liberia	2546	Liberia	132.7	52,000
2	Japan	2051	Japan	63.2	30,700
3	Greece	1804	U.K.	54.9	34,700
4	U.S.S.R.	1655	Norway	47.8	48,100
5	U.K.	1576	Greece	37.6	20,800
6	Panama	1556	Panama	22.1	14,200
7	Norway	991	France	17.7	39,900
8	Italy	633	Italy	16.1	25,300
9	F.R.G.	611	U.S.S.R.	15.4	9,300
10	U.S.	580	U.S.	15.0	25,900
11	France	444	F.R.G.	13.4	22,000
Subtotals:	Alliance	12,792 (89%)	Alliance	420.6 (96%)	26,300
	U.S.S.R.	1,655 (11%)	U.S.S.R.	15.4 (4%)	9,300
Totals		14,447		435.9	

matter of fact, the United States carried only about 5 percent of the volume of its trade (but 20 percent by value), while the Soviets carried roughly 60 percent of their volume in their own ships and under their own flag in 1975. However, the United States owns another 460 ships aggregating 30.9 million deadweight-tons (DWT) and operates them under foreign flags (see Chapter 5). Using ownership rather than registry presents a very different picture of the comparative standings of the superpowers. By this measure, the United States has half the number of merchant ships but three times as much tonnage as the Soviet Union. The average U.S.-owned ship is almost 45,000 DWT, while the Soviet average is roughly 9,300 DWT. As discussed earlier, this is indicative of the U.S. preference for "economy of scale" in large specialized ships. The Soviets have in the past concentrated primarily on smaller, general-purpose ships—which have the additional advantage in many areas of the world of being able to load and unload without extensive dockside facilities.

Despite these advantages in size and performance of both Western and U.S. merchant fleets relative to the Soviet Union, there are adverse trends both in modernization rates and in fleet composition that are of serious concern for the future—at least with respect to the possible military contribution of the opposing merchant fleets. These are discussed in the subsequent sections.

Trends

At the end of World War II, the Soviets had lost almost half of their merchant fleet and could count only about 400 ships with a total of 2 million DWT. One-quarter of those ships were the newest and best provided by the United States under the Lend-Lease Act. At that time, the United States could boast a wartime residual of 4,900 merchant vessels totalling almost 51 million DWT. As in the case of the navies themselves, the United States was able to "coast" on its wartime investments, while the U.S.S.R. was forced to undertake the significant shipbuilding program discussed in Chapter 1. In the past three decades, then, we have allowed the U.S.-owned merchant fleet to decrease numerically by a factor of five while retaining almost the same total tonnage. Meanwhile, the Soviets have increased their fleet size by a factor of four and their tonnage by a factor of eight. At the same time, U.S. employment in the merchant marine has dropped to 55,000—well under half the Soviet total, and we are graduating less than 800 licensed merchant marine officers per year, while the Soviets are apparently training roughly 9,000 full- and part-time officers. As a result, our officer corps and crews are approaching fifty years of age on the average, while the Soviet force remains more nearly the equivalent of their active naval forces, with whom they are very closely allied.

Perhaps indicative of future trends is the fact that U.S. shipyards average only twelve new merchantmen each year, which is not sufficient to maintain our current fleet size, whereas the Soviets have an ambitious plan to increase fleet tonnage by over 20 percent within the next five years. In the last ten years the tonnage of the U.S. fleet has remained constant, while that of the rest of the Alliance has grown threefold.

Composition

The majority of the U.S.-owned merchant fleet is composed of specialized tanker, container, and dry bulk cargo carriers of large size, almost all of which require extensive dockside cargo handling equipment. By comparison, as noted in Chapter 6, the Soviet fleet is currently composed almost entirely of smaller, self-loading, general-cargo vessels. New Soviet shipbuilding plans call for more tankers and dry bulk carriers, but also for an increasing number of roll-on/roll-off (ro/ro) and sea barge (Seabee) vessels, which are more capable of self-loading and unloading and which were technological innovations of the United States, abandoned because of their relative "inefficiency." Often, however, machines, techniques, and policies that appear economically inefficient in the competitive commercial sector turn out to be more useful under the "off-optimum" conditions of crisis and war. Consequently, new Soviet merchant ships are more applicable to conversion for military missions than their U.S. counterparts.

There is, in fact, a serious and growing shortage of U.S.-owned ships that can contribute to currently envisioned military roles in the transport of military cargoes to potentially damaged European ports. As is well known, the United States does maintain a National Defense Reserve Fleet that can be used in time of national emergency to transport military cargoes. Of the 450 U.S. flag vessels listed as available for this mission, however, 130 are obsolete "Victory" ships over thirty years old. Among the 320 remaining ships of that earmarked fleet, only 35 are general-cargo vessels with self-contained cargo handling capabilities. Despite the 1970 Merchant Marine Act, which approves subsidies for the construction of a "well-balanced merchant marine" in this country, general-cargo vessels are no longer being built. The Maritime Administration claims that a large percentage of the 58 ships contracted for under subsidy allowances since that time are suitable for direct support of military forces, but the Defense Department is not so optimistic.

Government Responsibilities

The dilemma of the U.S. Maritime Administration has been to

U.S. MILITARY SEALIFT CARGO CAPABILITY

The *Alaskan Mail*, owned by the American President Lines, is typical of the newer cargo ships with container capability that might be used to transport military cargoes in time of war. Very few of these ships are owned by the United States. (Courtesy U.S. Maritime Administration)

Ships of the U.S. "Mothball Fleet" are shown in the James River Reserve Fleet Area. Most of these ships, left over from World War II, are obsolete "Victory" ships over thirty years old. Only thirty-five are general-cargo vessels with self-contained cargo-handling capabilities. (Courtesy U.S. Navy)

subsidize—with the limited funds available—a merchant marine capable of meeting direct defense needs and other national security interests along with more demanding commercial requirements. Defense interests have been taken into account in the construction subsidy program, but in the effort to balance the various requirements under the law, the less efficient general dry cargo ships have lost out in the competition for funds to the more efficient specialized cargo vessels. Soviet naval and maritime planners are not faced with the level of conflict in this area that besets our free competitive society. As noted in other connections, they have been able to develop a merchant fleet with varied roles, including influence-building in the developing world, where the presence of American ships has all but disappeared.

National security considerations in government subsidy programs have never been very controversial. It is generally accepted that the United States needs a balanced merchant marine to serve as an auxiliary force to the navy in times of emergency and to haul a "substantial portion" of overseas trade in times of peace. The Maritime Administration of the Department of Commerce is responsible under the law to administer the maritime program in such a way as to provide for a strong U.S. Merchant Marine to meet the needs of national defense and security. Section 101 of the Merchant Marine Act of 1936, which has never changed in subsequent revisions of the Act, reads:

> It is necessary for the national defense and development of its foreign and domestic commerce that the United States shall have a merchant marine (a) sufficient to carry its domestic water-borne commerce and a substantial portion of the water-borne export and import foreign commerce of the United States and to provide shipping service essential for maintaining the flow of such domestic and foreign water-borne commerce at all times, (b) capable of serving as a naval and military auxiliary in time of war or national emergency, (c) owned and operated under the United States flag by citizens of the United States insofar as may be practicable, (d) composed of the best-equipped, safest, and most suitable types of vessels, constructed in the United States and manned with a trained and efficient citizen personnel, and (e) supplemented by efficient facilities for shipbuilding and ship repair. It is hereby declared to be the policy of the United States to foster the development and encourage the maintenance of such a merchant marine.

Experts disagree as to whether the Act has been properly implemented. Only in recent years has the government paid substantial subsidies for the construction and remodeling of merchant vessels under the Merchant Marine Act of 1970. But has the size and composition of the subsidized fleet sufficiently taken into account defense needs?

The number of government-owned ships operated by the Military Sealift Command has never been enough to move more than a fraction of a major support requirement. The Department of Defense has always depended heavily on the U.S. Merchant Marine to support major military contingencies. The degree of dependence on the merchant marine and the National Defense Reserve Fleet is likely to grow even further in the future because most of the remaining government-owned ships will have to be retired on account of age and material conditions. In the event of a NATO war, commitments have been made for early availability of ships belonging to NATO partners to help support U.S. deployments. Those NATO ships would surely be needed because the U.S. Merchant Marine and National Defense Reserve Fleet can supply substantially less than projected U.S. shipping requirements in a major war.

Recent studies show that, given the movement requirements anticipated in a NATO-Warsaw Pact war, the U.S. and NATO merchant fleets together would only be marginally adequate to meet the deployment and resupply objectives. This concern becomes significantly more serious in view of the possibility of a major involvement in a distant region where the United States would most likely be unable to count on the support of her NATO partners. In a major contingency in the Middle East, for instance, it is quite possible that U.S. military operations would be constrained by a shortage of available sealift capacity.

The U.S. intervention in Vietnam provides a warning for similar military operations in the future. The United States could minimize its negative experiences with foreign shipping during the Vietnam War because we had a larger general-cargo merchant marine than we have today. Consequently, the Military Sealift Command could be very selective in choosing the foreign ships to be used. But even then, the situation was not considered satisfactory; foreign ships were employed, and eventually we took the time, cost, and trouble to build unloading facilities for container ships. Although North Vietnamese resupply requirements were admittedly much smaller, the Soviets apparently had no trouble in providing their own general-cargo ships—which, incidentally, were able to continue to unload needed military supplies along the North Vietnamese coast after we mined Haiphong.

There are other reasons for avoiding dependence on foreign vessels. If the United States were totally dependent on foreign shipping, groups of maritime nations unsympathetic to U.S. objectives or desirous of gaining political advantage would be capable of exercising undue leverage during periods of tension or crisis. For example, OAPEC oil exporters have stated their intent to increase control of the shipping of their commodity to the industrial nations. At some point during the 1980s when the United States is projected to be importing roughly 5 million barrels per day from OAPEC countries, those countries might conceivably be in a position to control a significant fraction of the available tanker fleet. Control of tanker tonnage by the oil producers, along with wellhead control, could assure the success of an embargo by denying access to alternative sources. Such economic pressure and intimidation could be used for political advantage, to help determine the outcome of a war between rival superpower client-states, or to deter U.S. intervention against some Third World state.

Another question that has received virtually no attention among U.S. national security planners is the requirement for merchant shipping in the aftermath of a major nuclear exchange with the Soviet Union. Such a strategic war would by no means necessarily produce a clear "winner," and the struggle to determine its real outcome might involve the ability to recover—or to prevent occupation by a hostile force. The need for some level of sea control might be imperative under such conditions, and industrial recovery could depend on the ability to continue to import or export certain crucial materials. An extensive and far-flung merchant fleet could conceivably avoid total destruction in such a war, and the surviving ships could play a vital role thereafter. In such a scenario, unlikely as it may seem, the ownership and control of some residual merchant fleet could be influential; at such a time, dependence on a foreign fleet could be extremely unwise.

Other Potential Applications for Merchant Ships

Defense needs are also supposed to be taken into consideration by the Maritime Administration in the so-called National Defense Features (NDF) program—by adding certain defense standards such as hull compartmentalization (to minimize the effects of torpedo hits), improved shock resistance, additional electrical power and evaporating capacity, and increased speed. Admiral Zumwalt wanted to go considerably beyond the current, seldom-used NDF program. He had merchant ships successfully tested for refueling at sea and examined the feasibility of using commercial container ships for replenishment of ammunition and other logistics in conjunction with heavy lift helicopters. A few commercially operated ships are now used for refueling the U.S. Navy.

When Zumwalt was chief of naval operations, the Navy also examined the feasibility of giving container ships the capability to handle VSTOL aircraft and antisubmarine helicopters during wartime together with the necessary shipboard equipment so they could provide their own fighter, antimissile, and antisubmarine capability. Although each of those programs would have initially been costly to implement, they might have proved cost-effective in the end. Admiral Zumwalt maintains that each of these plans was technically feasible, but it was politically impossible to resolve jurisdictional disputes between the Defense Department and the Maritime Administration.

The feasibility of some of those Zumwalt proposals was confirmed in a recent study by the Transportation Institute. The study suggested several self-defense modifications to merchant ships to facilitate their use in military sealift. Installation of passive electronic (decoys, jammers) and active (gun and missile) defenses, plus convertible helicopter facilities, were listed for consideration. If planned prior to construction, such defense features can generally be added at relatively low cost. Providing for these features during normal construction scheduling would significantly reduce the shipyard workload during critical periods or actual hostilities.

There are a number of other specific recommendations in the Institute study, suggesting modification of roll-on/roll-off, container, Lash, and Seabee ships to make them adaptable to various uses as amphibious assault ships, helicopter VSTOL carriers, maintenance and communications ships, etc. The study observes, however, that since the 1947 Defense Reorganization there has been no senior individual in the executive branch to ensure the coordination of the navy and the merchant marine as provided for in the Merchant Marine Act of 1936.

Despite such potentially resolvable bureaucratic problems and the fact that some of the Zumwalt proposals might be ahead of their time, it seems that a modern, dynamic merchant marine could serve a variety of fundamentally useful services to national security. As time goes on and the merchant fleets of the world continue to grow as naval fleets diminish, it would appear eminently sensible to look again at whether or not our overall national security objectives can be enhanced through greater use of the Western Alliance's civil assets. This would require real changes in current trends, incentives, subsidies, and special interests. However, it may offer the only realistic alternative.

Economy of Scale Considerations

The vulnerability of merchant shipping is increased by the use of smaller numbers of larger ships—since a single torpedo will almost certainly sink any one of them. It is important, then, to examine the economic merits of "economy of scale." Tanker shipping has probably benefited the most by such economies as a result of the large oil transport requirements. Projected U.S. imports alone are shown in Table 9-4. Operating cost differentials between large and small tankers increase not only with the tanker size but also with voyage length, as shown in Table 9-5. The Persian Gulf has accounted for an increasing share of U.S. petroleum imports in recent years and will almost certainly continue to do so for many years to come. There are also very large cost differences between tankers built in the United States and operated with American crews and foreign flag tankers (also shown in Table 9-5). More than 95 percent of U.S. petroleum imports have been carried in foreign flag tankers in recent years for the obvious reasons of economy shown.

ECONOMY OF SCALE IN TANKER DESIGN

The 270,000 deadweight-ton *Conoco Europe* carries crude oil from the Middle East to northwest Europe. This very large crude carrier (VLCC) holds over 2 million barrels of oil, travels at 16 knots, and is manned by a crew of thirty-six. (Courtesy Continental Oil Company)

The *Globtik Tokyo*, at 476,025 deadweight tons, is the largest ship at sea and is manned by a crew of thirty-five to forty men. It is over five times the weight of the U.S.S. *Nimitz* aircraft carrier. In wartime the virtues of "economy of scale" may become the folly of "too many eggs in one basket." (Courtesy American Petroleum Institute)

TABLE 9-4

ESTIMATED U.S. WATERBORNE PETROLEUM IMPORTS
(Millions of Barrels per day)

	1980 Estimates Low	1980 Estimates High	1985 Estimates Low	1985 Estimates High
Western Hemisphere[a]	2.50	2.50	2.70	2.70
West Africa—Med	1.23	1.23	1.33	1.33
Persian Gulf[b]	3.68	7.68	7.50	11.50
TOTAL	7.41	11.41	11.53	15.53

[a] Includes imports from Caribbean and South America.

[b] Includes small import from Indonesia. Low estimates based on successful federal energy policies to reduce consumption and imports.

TABLE 9-5

SHIPPING COST OF U.S. PETROLEUM IMPORTS BY SOURCE AND TANKER SIZE
(Dollars per Barrel)

Tanker Size & Flag	Western Hemisphere[a]	West Africa—Mediterranean	Persian Gulf
225,000 DWT[b]			
U.S. Flag[c]	0.41	0.75	1.62
Foreign Flag[d]	0.31	0.56	1.21
60,000 DWT[e]			
U.S. Flag	0.82	1.53	3.45
Foreign Flag	0.45	0.84	1.90
30,000 DWT[f]			
U.S. Flag	1.19	2.18	4.97
Foreign Flag	0.61	1.15	2.62

[a] Simple average of South American and Caribbean rates.

[b] Nominal size Very Large Crude Carrier (VLCC).

[c] Freight rate required to cover all costs including 10% return on capital as of 1977.

[d] Market rate as of early 1977.

[e] Approximate size limit of Suez Canal at current depth.

[f] Normal size refined product carrier and/or military POL carrier.

The cost of shifting all or part of these imports from larger tankers to smaller ones would depend on the volume shifted, the trade routes involved, and whether the smaller tankers were of U.S. or foreign registry. Here it is significant that federal subsidy programs (to date) have been limited to ships built in the United States and operated by U.S. crews.

If all imports were shifted from tankers of 225,000 DWT to those of 60,000 DWT, the ships involved in U.S. imports would approximately quadruple. The outside cost limits of such a shift are estimated for 1980 and 1985 in Table 9-6.

TABLE 9-6

ESTIMATED ANNUAL COSTS[a] OF LIMITING U.S. PETROLEUM IMPORTS TO SMALL TANKERS IN:
(Millions of Dollars)

Tanker Size	Western Hemisphere	West Africa-Mediterranean	Persian Gulf Low	Persian Gulf High	Increment in Shipping Cost
60,000 DWT		1980			
U.S. Flag[b]	465.4	435.5	3008.8	6279.2	3909.7- 7180.1
Foreign Flag[c]	127.7	125.7	926.8	1934.1	1180.1- 2187.5
30,000 DWT					
U.S. Flag[b]	803.0	727.3	5050.4	10540.0	6580.2-12060.3
Foreign Flag[c]	273.7	264.9	1893.4	3952.5	2432.5- 4491.2
60,000 DWT		1985			
U.S. Flag[b]	502.6	470.8	6132.0	9402.4	7105.4-10375.8
Foreign Flag[c]	138.0	135.9	1888.9	2896.3	2162.8- 3170.2
30,000 DWT					
U.S. Flag[b]	867.2	786.4	10293.0	15782.6	11946.6-17436.2
Foreign Flag[c]	295.7	286.4	3859.9	5918.5	4442.0-10360.5

[a] Differential between rates for 225,000 DWT tankers and smaller tankers (Table 9-4) multiplied by volume of imports (daily rate in Table 9-3 times 365). This exaggerates the cost increment in shifting to smaller tankers because part of U.S. petroleum imports are already carried by such tankers—primarily refined products and crude oil from Western Hemisphere sources.

[b] These estimates reflect the cost differences between small U.S. tankers and large foreign tankers.

[c] These estimates reflect the cost differences between small foreign tankers and large foreign tankers.

Assuming that our imports from the Persian Gulf remain high through 1980 and that we continue to use primarily foreign tankers, then the annual cost of retreating toward 60,000 DWT tankers for all our imports could run as high as $2 billion. By 1985, even if we have adopted stringent energy conservation and reduced import measures, these costs could still rise to $4 billion annually if we are still using foreign flag tankers. Were we to switch to U.S. flag ships in that later period, the incremental costs could exceed $10 billion annually.

While these costs seem high, a sunk supertanker is also very expensive. A 225,000 DWT tanker could easily cost $55 million and carry $45 million worth of oil. Loss of a single supertanker, then, represents $100 million. Only ten such supertankers have to be "saved" to prevent a billion dollar loss. Moreover, not all tankers would need to be reduced in size—only those that would continue to be used during wartime. On this basis, the penalty for the use of 60,000 DWT foreign flag ships might only reach $1 billion annually by 1985. The question, of course, is whether it would then be worth spending $1 billion annually during peacetime to save $5 to $50 billion (50-500 supertankers) during a war. Such a decision would be difficult to make but probably deserves serious consideration.

Comparisons of Soviet and Alliance Naval Bases and Facilities
Importance of Shore-Based Support

All navies are inescapably dependent on shore-based support. The farther from home a navy is projected, the more its effectiveness is diminished without access to shore-based installations on foreign soil. In some respects technological innovation is reducing such dependence: underway replenishment, worldwide communications and navigation systems, afloat servicing and maintenance, and nuclear propulsion all make it possible for combatant ships to spend more time away from friendly ports. Nonetheless, the crews are land species, and all of their sustenance except air and water comes from the land. If the combatants themselves can be resupplied at sea, then their resupply elements, in turn, must have access to sheltered and secure harbors.

Such afloat support can provide means for refueling, restoring, and rearming as well as furnishing the personnel and equipment needed to service propulsion, electronic, and machinery systems. However, refits, overhauls, major engineering repairs, and most battle damage normally require shore-based installations. So does the crew itself. During wartime, crews cannot maintain peak efficiency without port calls every few months. During peacetime, extended family separations and the cramped life aboard ship become alien to the Western lifestyle unless interspersed with opportunities for normal life ashore.

In short, whether or not a distant-deployed naval force can achieve its politico-military objectives depends in large measure on access to regional, land-based installations. The effectiveness of naval ships can be greatly expanded by shore access in the vicinity of their forward deployment stations. Even our strategic nuclear submarines—the most self-sufficient of our combat elements—benefit from forward bases on Guam and in Scotland and Spain in minimizing their "turnaround time" and maximizing their time on station. The United States has repeatedly sought "home ports" for its other major combatants at the far sides of both the Atlantic and the Pacific as a means of increasing the effectiveness of the Sixth and Seventh fleets—of which the most valuable asset is their crews.

Shore-based installations are an essential part of naval operations besides the direct servicing of ships and submarines. These facilities also provide needed surveillance and communications capabilities as well as airbases for ocean surveillance and counterforce operations by land-based aircraft. They also permit aerial resupply of critical items to surface units at sea.

Comparisons of the worldwide potential of Soviet and Alliance naval forces, then, are not complete without some assessment of the relative availability of overseas bases and facilities. There is a non-trivial difference between a "facility" and a "base" that cannot be overlooked. A facility generally refers to a port or other location where access has been granted to another country's naval forces, including ships, aircraft, or submarines. A base, on the other hand, generally refers to ports or installations on foreign soil exclusively built, maintained, and operated by the visiting country for a specific duration under some sort of treaty or agreement with the host country. In many cases, the host's forces may be restricted from operations at that base, as in the Soviet airbase near Aswan in Egypt and the U.S. base at Guantanamo in Cuba.

While base-rights treaties may be broken or renegotiated at the insistence of the host country, it is far easier to deny access to a facility—where that access is by invitation rather than by "lease"—for the duration of some particular crisis. Both superpowers have found their access to facilities abroad interrupted by sudden changes in circumstances. The Soviets lost their use of facilities in Albania in 1961, in Egypt in 1976, and in Somalia in 1977. Similarly, we have found our forces unwelcome in Turkey as a result of the Cyprus situation and unwelcome temporarily in Spain and some NATO countries during the Middle East war of 1973.

Relative Trends in Shore-Base Access

The relative status and trends in the availability of bases and facilities, then, are a significant measure of the worldwide naval potential of the superpowers. There is general concern that the Soviets' overseas access is increasing, while that of the United States is declining. Certainly the number of overseas bases and facilities available to the United States has declined since the end of World War II. At that time, we had access to ports, airfields, and installations in virtually every corner of the globe. Some were established for the purpose of fighting World War II, particularly in the Pacific. Others were captured from our opponents and occupied for the duration of the war. Still others were part of worldwide "empires" of our allies that have since been lost. Others were built for our strategic bombers in the era prior to the intercontinental B-52 and have subsequently been relinquished. Still others have been voluntarily closed as redundant or uneconomical to operate during peacetime. While detailed statistics on our "losses" have not been gathered, there has been a definite reduction in available shore-based installations since the late 1940s, and this trend appears to be continuing.

Soviet Overseas Facilities

By comparison, the Soviet Union has made some progress in acquiring its first overseas bases and facilities. Often, however, these arrangements have been somewhat transient, as the loss of the Soviet base in Somalia in 1977 exemplifies. In fact, the relatively secure overseas bases and facilities that the Soviets could rely on in time of war can probably be counted on one's fingers. They are maintained in Conakry in Guinea and, to a less active extent, in Cienfuegos in Cuba. The Soviet Navy also operates four permanent anchorages in the Indian Ocean: near Socotra Island off the African Horn; near the Comoro islands between Tanzania and the Malagasy Republic; along the Cargados Carajos Shoals near Mauritius; and in the Chagos Archipelago, near the developing U.S. facility on Diego Garcia. The Soviets also maintain "bunkering rights" for naval auxiliaries (not combatants) with Mauritius and Singapore.

All of these locations are far from the U.S.S.R. and in or near nations that could not help the Soviets defend them in time of war. Hence, the primary threat posed by these installations is not the real level of damage they could exact against Alliance shipping (primarily petroleum) but rather the level of Allied forces that might have to be diverted to neutralize them in an otherwise relatively unimportant theater of operations.

The Soviets currently also have access to shore-based facilities of three countries on the Mediterranean: Yugoslavia, Syria, and Libya. The Yugoslav government tightly controls access to its ship repair facilities and makes them available on an equally controlled basis to other nations. The Syrian government grants access to the small, crowded ports of Latakia and Tartus, but there has been some indication of dwindling interest in a large Soviet presence. The Soviets also maintain four rather permanent anchorages in the Mediterranean: in the western part near the Spanish island of Alboran and in the eastern part near the Greek island of Kithira; in the Gulf of Sollum, north of Egypt; and in the Gulf of Hamamet, between Tunisia and Sicily. There are no Soviet overseas bases bordering the North Atlantic or the Pacific, the normal operating areas of their two primary open ocean fleets.

U.S. Overseas Bases and Facilities

Admiral Gorshkov's claim that the United States has access to "over 500" ports and bases overseas would appear to be somewhat exaggerated. Nonetheless, the U.S. Navy is in substantially better position than the Soviet Navy in the North Atlantic, Mediterranean, and Pacific. In the South Atlantic and Indian oceans, the situation is somewhat more analogous for the two superpowers.

The United States and Canada, of course, are Atlantic powers, sharing well over 5,000 miles of Atlantic coastline, while eight more members of the NATO Alliance have substantial naval facilities bordering the North Atlantic and the North Sea. During periods of major confrontation

OVERSEAS NAVAL BASES

The Soviet Navy uses anchorages at sea like this one at Kithira in the Mediterranean to compensate for its lack of overseas bases. Shown are a Kashin- and a Kotlin-class destroyer at anchor, each with a Nanuchka-class missile-armed corvette astern, and another Kashin moving past a Baskunchak-class missile range ship. (Courtesy U.S. Navy)

By contrast, this aerial photo shows the U.S. Naval Station at Rota, Spain. In addition to the Spanish helicopter carrier *Dedalo* (PH-1) in left center are six U.S. amphibious ships (AFS-2, LPA-249, LSD-21, LKA-03, LST-117, and LPD-1) and a guided missile frigate, the U.S.S. *Dahlgren* (DLG-12). (Courtesy U.S. Navy)

between NATO and Warsaw Pact nations, all of these naval installations would be available for the use of member nations, as would those in the Mediterranean. In all probability, so would those of France and Spain. They would also, of course, be vulnerable to Soviet attack.

The United States operates regularly from eight major facilities in the Mediterranean: Rota in Spain; Naples, LaMaddalena, and Catania in Italy, Sardinia, and Sicily; Suda Bay and Iraklion Airfield in Crete off Greece; and Iskenderun and Yormatakin in Turkey. Additional bases in Israel, Egypt, and Tunisia might possibly become available in a major confrontation with the Soviets in Europe, depending on the political situation at the time.

The United States is also a major Pacific power, with extensive naval facilities on our West Coast, in Hawaii, and on Guam. In addition, the United States operates a vast naval complex at Subic Bay in the Philippines and has extensive facilities in Yokosuka, Japan, and on Okinawa. In the South Pacific, the United States has access to Singapore on the Strait of Malacca and can gain virtually unlimited access to Australia and New Zealand through the ANZUS Treaty, should the need arise.

The United States is currently building a substantial facility at Diego Garcia in the Chagos Archipelago in the Mid-Indian Ocean. This British territory will provide an essential way-station for U.S. operations in the Indian Ocean. Although the United States retains limited access to Bahrain and Iran on the Persian Gulf, neither can be counted as a secure base of operations—in fact, either or both could become the focus of some future military contingency. Access to other shore-based facilities along the Indian Ocean littoral would be highly dependent on the crisis at hand and the politics of the moment in such countries as Thailand, India, Pakistan, Yemen, and Saudia Arabia.

In the South Atlantic, the situation for the United States is even less certain. Current political relations with Brazil and South Africa make port access uncertain, at least for the present. The United States currently has no bases or facilities anywhere on the South American coastline—on either the Atlantic or the Pacific—and none along the African coastline, for that matter. It is in these areas that decreasing U.S. naval access and increasing dependence on the oil SLOCs is a matter of some concern.

Scenario-Dependence of Overseas Facilities

The relative advantages accruing to the United States in naval balance as a result of our more extensive overseas naval facilities and access are highly "scenario-dependent." In what is generally considered our most demanding military contingency—a NATO-Warsaw pact confrontation—there can be little question that the Alliance, collectively, is far superior to the Soviet-Pact naval forces as far as base access is concerned. This would certainly be reflected in the relative effectiveness of opposing forces. The availability of NATO bases for U.S. naval elements would greatly enhance their contribution to the total Alliance effort.

On the other hand, the U.S. Navy may be faced with politico-military contingencies in which free access to Alliance facilities may be denied for the duration of some crisis. The United States maintains no "bases" within the Alliance—only "facilities." Outside the Alliance, our only real overseas bases are in Cuba and the Philippines, and the future of Guantanamo is uncertain at best. It is not difficult to imagine a scenario, as discussed in Chapter 1, involving a direct U.S.-Soviet confrontation outside the NATO area, quite possibly related to the continued availability of oil. In such a case, the relative balance of available overseas port and airfield facilities may no longer favor the United States. The effective utilization of U.S. naval forces under these conditions may be intimately associated with the level of foreign political acceptance of our proposed actions. Given the ambivalence of many normally friendly states over relations with the oil-rich and other nations of the Third World, such support might not be readily forthcoming.

The overseas base and facility structure of the West provides an important positive element in the retention of a favorable naval balance. However, in any confrontations between the United States and the Soviets that are not seen as vital to the interests of our allies or that strongly favor their neutrality, there appears to be little inherent base-related advantage for the United States in the Mediterranean, the South Atlantic, or the Indian Ocean. In the Pacific and the Caribbean, we are blessed with favorable geography that may exceed our political assets.

The critical scenario by which to test the adequacy of U.S. naval forces may well be other than the currently accepted standard of a "NATO war." An American military expeditionary force to the Middle East, for instance, would be smaller than that planned for NATO support, and its resupply tonnage less. However, distances are much longer, the essential economic shipping is much greater, the confrontation might be more prolonged, and the availability of cooperative shore-based facilities and friendly shipping would probably be much less.

10
Comparative Alliance Naval Capabilities

Introduction

This chapter is devoted to a detailed description of the various components of Western naval capabilities and a comparison of them with their Soviet counterparts where possible. Current characteristics of ocean surveillance systems are addressed first, followed by a comprehensive description of Alliance warships, submarines, and aircraft.

As previously explained, the primary missions of the two opposing navies have been significantly different since the end of World War II. The West continued its emphasis on sea control and power projection, while the Soviets concentrated on sea denial. Both sides devoted considerable energy to the introduction of sea-based nuclear ballistic missiles. The evolving Soviet Fleet has emphasized submarines and land-based aircraft. The West has placed greater reliance on surface ships and carrier-based aircraft. Soviet antisubmarine warfare has concentrated on neutralizing the West's strategic submarines. The West, more dependent on sea lines of communication (SLOCs), has focused on counteracting Soviet general-purpose submarines. The Soviets have developed and maintained an extensive naval coastal defense force that is becoming capable of offensive missions along the Eurasian littoral, which they share with many of their potential adversaries on the Atlantic, Pacific, and Mediterranean. The United States, on the other hand, has virtually no coastal defense forces for its own politically united continent, but it has the capacity to project power ashore on other continents.

Despite these fundamental differences in mission objectives and emphasis, the navies of East and West would most certainly collide in high-intensity combat should a major conflict arise. The equipments and weapon systems that would interact under such conditions are addressed in this chapter.

Comparative Surveillance Capabilities

Even in times of war, surface ships have, in general, been able to traverse the seas without undue attrition because of the difficulty of locating isolated ships or even convoys. Submarines have been even more difficult to locate. Once they became nuclear-powered so they could remain submerged quietly for extended periods, they were considered to be virtually invulnerable—particularly U.S. submarines, which have historically been quieter than their Russian counterparts.

The United States has become accustomed to depending on the seas for safe haven and passage of surface ships and submarines. The seas have been considered so safe, in fact, that submarine-launched ballistic missiles are considered to be the backbone of the U.S. strategic deterrent. However, the relative invulnerability of naval vessels is susceptible to technical change. It will inevitably erode as sensor technology evolves. We will then become more dependent on equivalent advances in countermeasures technology and more capable defensive systems. A question of concern is how much naval survivability may have eroded already, and how much it is likely to diminish over the next decade.

Present defense systems cannot ensure the survivability of U.S. ships once they are located by enemy forces. United States surface ships appear to be vulnerable to the standoff cruise missiles that the Soviets have deployed in large numbers. These high-speed, low-altitude, homing missiles can be very difficult to detect. Defense can be further complicated by the use of standoff jammers and coordinated attacks from several azimuths, both of which are known Soviet capabilities. United States submarines may also have survival problems if they are located. In particular, they may be susceptible to high-speed homing torpedoes and nuclear depth charges.

Because we cannot have high confidence in the survival of U.S. naval ships if their positions are known, we must assess how well the Soviets can locate U.S. surface ships and submarines now and in the future. Since the situation for surface ships is fundamentally different from that for submarines, separate discussions are presented.

In each case the problem breaks down into *wide-area detection* and *localization*. Once the approximate location of a unit is known, an intensive search can usually locate it well enough for weapons to be aimed at it. The wide-area problem is generally the more difficult because it requires continuous analysis of data from the entire ocean. The vast number of "non-targets" at sea guarantees that most targets will be concealed in noise—unless some signature unique to the desired targets is used to cue the intensive search systems. In this sense, decoying and deception are useful because they can merge the target back into the noise through which a wide-area search system must operate. Only if they fail at this task do they need to confound localizing search systems.

In principle, localizing systems could be used for wide-area search; but the costs, both in search units and in data processing, would be prohibitive. More commonly, separate systems are used. For example, the U.S. passive sound system, SOSUS, provides wide-area detection of Soviet submarines in the Western Atlantic (albeit without pinpoint accuracy). Once a submarine has been established in a given region, aircraft can fly out to seed the area with small passive hydrophones (sonobuoys) that more narrowly define the submarine's position. The aircraft may sometimes use an even shorter-range system, a magnetic anomaly detector (MAD), to increase the effectiveness of attack.

Surface Ship Surveillance

The fundamental ways in which a surface ship can be located include the means enumerated below.

Receiving Radio Communications. Ships utilize radio communications. The frequencies usually employed can easily be heard for many thousands of miles by ground-based receiving antennas capable of sensing the direction of the incoming signal. When widely spaced, shore-based receiving stations pick up these signals and their directions are compared, a shipborne transmitter's position can be localized, although the identity of the ship is not necessarily known. This process has been in use for many years.

Visual Observation. Visual observations over the open ocean can be maintained by long-range aircraft—which can check out a search area defined by the aforementioned communication receivers. Small trailing ships such as trawlers can pick up a high-value target as it leaves port and stay with it. Both the aircraft and the "tattletale" are, of course, vulnerable to a warship's weapons.

Acoustic Detection. Submarine or surface ship hydrophone arrays for acoustic detection can be used to detect high-value surface ships or to trail them at a safe distance.

Long-Range Radar. Most large ships reflect back so much radar energy that they can be detected for a thousand miles or more by a fairly low-powered radar with a clear line of sight. Such a radar can readily be carried on a satellite and can detect ships at sea if they are as large, say, as a freighter. The radar does require a long-lived power source of appreciable strength, but this is available from small, spaceborne nuclear power sources or from large solar panels. Only current levels of sophistication of technology are involved. A nuclear-powered Soviet radar satellite recently crashed in Canada. In the United States, NASA launched in June 1978 a synthetic aperture radar having a resolution of about 25 meters, as part of the SEASAT program. This should be discriminating enough to detect and characterize most ships of importance. Such systems obviously have continuous and all-weather capability. However, the radar data processing requirements stretch current capabilities. Simpler radar systems with poorer resolution can still easily track a ship's movement from relatively low, nonsynchronous orbital height.

Shore-based, over-the-horizon (OTH) radar presents another alternative. It, too, faces serious data processing problems but has the advantage that it can track ships continuously for a considerable time, whereas nonsynchronous satellites must track intermittently since they obtain data only on each pass over the ship every ninety minutes or so. Isolated ships present little problem in this respect because they do not move far in ninety minutes and will not be confused with neighbors.

Receiving Radar Signals. Most ships have radars that operate almost continuously and transmit appreciable powers at high frequencies. A receiver located on a satellite has a clear line of sight and can pick up these signals with a properly designed antenna. By comparing the directions of origin as the satellite moves, the location of the transmitter can, in principle, be determined. The small power required is readily supplied by solar panels, and the technology is largely available. Since certain types of radars are usually associated with particular classes of warships, naval ships using their radars can probably be distinguished from merchantmen.

Visible and Infrared Satellite Pictures. Infrared and visible wavelength telescopes on satellites can be used to detect ships at sea or their wakes, although rather large optical equipment may be needed to obtain adequate resolution. Also, clouds and precipitation will often obscure the signal. As an example of such a system, NASA's Landsat D infrared sensor is reportedly able to resolve an area as small as 200 square feet. Thus, it should be able to detect most ships.

There are open literature references attributing operational capabilities to the Soviets for a number of the aforementioned functions, particularly radar satellites. Even if they do not now have all the above-named capabilities, they undoubtedly will within the next decade. The United States has no military radar or optical satellite sensors dedicated to sea surveillance and none are planned for the near future—although both will probably be available within the foreseeable future. The United States probably already has most or all of the other surveillance capabilities mentioned. The implication is simple: Present technology makes it prudent to assume that within the next decade both superpowers will be able to determine the precise position of any surface ship of value whenever they wish, unless extensive counter-sensor operations are undertaken. It is likely that the U.S.S.R. already possesses both these capabilities.

In many cases, however, these radar systems will not be able to recognize particular ships. For example, a satellite radar might be designed to be "cued" by ship length in order to reduce the number of sightings relayed and thereby cut the signal-processing load. Assuming that it could compensate for the different radar images presented by ships at different bearings relative to the satellite track, the radar might still be fooled by large merchant vessels and tankers. The more these ships approach carriers in size and speed, the harder the job of the data processor. This is inadvertent decoying and is applicable to some other surveillance systems as well. Combining the data from radar satellites and other satellite sensors tends to obviate this problem.

The major limitation on the widespread use of most of the new large-area surveillance systems remains inability to make *positive identification* of a specific ship. In an all-out conventional or nuclear war, such positive identification might not be essential for the Soviets—particularly if very few of their own ships were at sea. However, under less than full-scale war conditions, both sides would presumably want to avoid the inadvertent sinking of a friendly or non-belligerent vessel. In periods of crisis or tension, over-the-horizon surveillance or guidance systems would probably not be employed unless prior "eyeball contact" had verified the identification of the target in question. Systems to provide positive identification from greater range are still needed from the research and development community.

Submarine Surveillance

The technological alternatives for surveillance of submarines are, on the whole, poorly understood compared to those for surface ships. However, the United States has been trying for years to develop passive acoustic detection of submarines and is probably well ahead of the U.S.S.R. in this technology. It is open knowledge that the United States has operational acoustic arrays that would be useful against Soviet submarines; the Russians write articles about them. These arrays, both stationary and towed, are coupled through various secure communications links to extremely elaborate shore-based processing centers that utilize the data from multiple arrays to localize an enemy submarine's position. The accuracy is presumably sufficient (at present Soviet submarine noise levels) to allow our P-3 or S-3 aircraft with their sensors to fly out,

SATELLITE OCEAN SURVEILLANCE

The National Atmospheric and Space Administration's SEASAT-A ocean surveillance satellite illustrated above was launched in May 1978 into a near-polar orbit 500 miles high. It is designed to cover 95 percent of the ocean's surface every thirty-six hours and can resolve surface objects as short as 80 feet. Earlier naval satellites have been used to track ships suspected of transporting illegal drugs to the United States. Such satellites, used by both superpowers, promise to make surface ships far more vulnerable to attack than ever before. (Courtesy National Atmospheric and Space Administration)

search the area of uncertainty, find the submarine and attack it.

Since we understand acoustical technology very well and continue to rely on the survivability of our own submarines, it can be inferred that our submarines are quieter than Soviet submarines, Soviet detection equipment is inferior to ours, or probably both. However, it would be no surprise if the Russians produce a generation of quieter submarines within the next decade.

One might conclude that our submarines are safe because we have a strong acoustical technology base and probably cannot reliably detect our own submarines with our best present-day equipment. But this conclusion is questionable for several reasons. One is Admiral Gorshkov's statement with respect to the submarine threat: "On the basis of the latest advances of science, technology, and production, the mission to repulse and disarm that threat was successfully accomplished."[1]

Perhaps Gorshkov is bluffing, but he may be basing his statement on some output of his country's extensive nonacoustic ASW program. The Soviets seem to have been keenly interested in this area since about 1962, possibly due to the impetus of some chance experimental observation. Since that time, they appear to have explored nonacoustic ASW technology far more vigorously than the United States has. It would not be surprising to learn that they have devoted far more effort and resources to this area than the United States and that perhaps they have a five to ten year lead.

The Soviet open literature discusses a number of nonacoustic techniques, including the following:

- Extremely low frequency electromagnetic waves arising from galvanic currents around the submarine's hull.[2]
- Thermal detectors (e.g., infrared sensors) to measure temperature differences in the ocean and on its surface caused by the hydrodynamic disturbances associated with the movement of a submarine.[3]
- Internal (subsurface) hydrodynamic waves that are generated when the submarine moves through regions with water layers of differing temperature. The Soviet literature suggests that internal waves might be detected either by direct subsurface measurements with conductivity gauges, etc., or by radar measurements of the accompanying distortion of the ocean's surface.[4,5]
- Detection of the trail of radioisotopes created in the water by the passage of the submarine's nuclear reactor.

In addition, for many years the Soviets have carried on an extensive study of basic ocean phenomenology over large regions of the world. The U.S.

understanding of nonacoustic technologies appears to be not nearly as far advanced. We cannot rule out the possibility that the U.S.S.R. has made a breakthrough in the area of reliable nonacoustic submarine detection or will make such a discovery before we do.

Implications of Surveillance Capabilities

The capabilities of Soviet surveillance systems imply that the survivability of U.S. surface ships is poor and that fear of the unknown concerning the detection of U.S. submarines is justified.

What should be done?

The United States certainly cannot hide surface ships if the Soviets wish to spend the rubles to find them. Sinking them may be another matter. It does not seem appropriate to spend large amounts of money on building additional ships if their survivability in a major U.S.-Soviet war is in serious question. It can be argued that a larger number of lower-cost ships may be more survivable than a smaller number of high-value targets. But there is the accompanying question about the value of the missions that such a fleet could perform. The U.S. Navy's "high-low mix" philosophy is, of course, the current approach to this long-standing dilemma (see Chapter 12).

There seem to be several areas where additional U.S. effort could be fruitfully spent on the surface ship problem. In the surveillance area, the United States should not let an asymmetry develop—or should move rapidly to eliminate any asymmetry that has come about because of Soviet progress. If the Soviets have the capability to locate and attack surface ships quickly and we do not, then the United States is clearly at a disadvantage. Moreover, the United States' greater dependence on the sea justifies the development of countermeasures to mask ship signatures.

A long overdue and even more urgent need in the fleet is the deployment of defenses against cruise missiles. Among candidate systems that have been under development for years are the very large and expensive Aegis radar-missile combination and the less costly, more compact, Vulcan/Phalanx radar-gun system. Survival of U.S. surface ships in the opening stages of a war with the Soviet Union would be much more certain if both these systems were deployed in appropriate numbers at the earliest possible time. Development of more capable antiship missile defenses should also be pursued.

The United States should also place much greater emphasis on its nonacoustic ASW programs. This country may well be spending only a fraction of what is appropriate in this area, even though the potential payoff from increased nonacoustic ASW research is twofold. First, it can improve understanding of the associated vulnerabilities and countermeasures needed for the U.S. submarine fleet. Second, the research may provide a viable alternate detection mechanism if and when the Soviets produce a new generation of quiet submarines. The United States should also evaluate defensive tactics such as spreading out ocean operations in order to make submarine surveillance as difficult as possible. We must also recognize the growing vulnerability of all of our own shore-based facilities that contribute to surface and underwater ocean surveillance.

As a final note, the size of the Trident submarine tends to be a disadvantage as far as nonacoustic detection is concerned, since most nonacoustic signatures are aggravated by increased body size. There is a serious question as to the wisdom of continuing to place heavy reliance on small numbers of this large submarine in the face of the poorly understood nonacoustic threat. Prudence calls for the establishment of alternative submarine programs that will hedge against the possibility that Admiral Gorshkov's statement concerning the submarine threat is well-founded.

Comparative Ship Characteristics

Aircraft Carriers

The current U.S. carrier force is the end product of over fifty years of specialized development, based on the key theme that the carrier force as a whole gains in effectiveness as nonaviation features of the carrier are sacrificed for improved aircraft performance. Thus, on current carriers, nonaviation weapons are limited to last-ditch self-defenses such as the Basic Point Defense Missile System, which requires little sacrifice in weight or space. The airplane-oriented features of flight deck dimensions and area, catapults, arresting gear, hangar volume, aircraft size and maintenance provisions, and space for aviation fuel and ordnance largely determine carrier dimensional characteristics. Moreover, even if a carrier were an unpowered barge designed to operate the current carrier air group, it would not be substantially *smaller*, although it would certainly be less expensive.

Current carriers have a unique value to the Alliance because of their highly capable aircraft and strategic mobility; i.e., both high sustained speed and long range—nuclear range in some cases. These very large "supercarriers" provide weight and volume margins which permit considerable hardening; it is realistic to imagine a carrier surviving those Soviet weapons that might get through the defenses provided by its aircraft, escorts, and, finally, its last-ditch weapons. Their great size also allows carriers to be spotted more easily by ocean surveillance systems. Moreover, because of their size and cost, they are few in number. Should one be sunk or disabled, it would be very difficult to replace. Additionally, the aircraft on deck are far more vulnerable to damage than the ship itself.

Critics of large carriers find these last points extremely persuasive. For the past several years, the Navy has been under intense pressure to give up supercarrier construction in favor of something substantially smaller. It is not clear whether "substantially smaller" implies the abandonment of nuclear power, which contributes greatly to carrier acquisition costs. In any case, the critics would like to replace the present generation of very large (circa 90,000-ton) carriers with a smaller (60,000-ton) class. The first of these new carriers would operate conventional aircraft, but most of them would be designed to fly only vertical/short-takeoff and landing (VSTOL) aircraft.

The VSTOL aircraft would require no catapults or arresting gear and, quite possibly, no angled decks—all of which are substantial contributors to carrier weight and cost. VSTOL aircraft can also contribute to a carrier's survivability against damage short of sinking, since they might be able to operate effectively from a partially destroyed flight deck. On the other hand, the carrier's value is in the capabilities of its aircraft, and VSTOL aircraft certainly cannot match the payload capabilities of conventional-takeoff types. Considering that much recent carrier employment has been in the nonnuclear strike role (e.g., in Korea and Vietnam, where the tonnage of ordnance carried per sortie has been of great consequence), adoption of the smaller VSTOL carriers might imply some curtailment of this conventional bombing role, unless precision guided munitions can continue to reduce the desired munitions load or unless such capabilities are additive to those of existing carriers and their conventional aircraft. Such smaller carriers might be better suited to ASW, antisurface ship, or amphibious projection roles. Whether any change in total capability is warranted depends on how the United States perceives the mission of its future navy. As noted at the outset, this study does not specifically address the future need for naval power projection forces.

The Soviets have completed their first warship comparable to a carrier, the *Kiev*, which has an angled deck and a complement of subsonic VSTOL fighter-strike aircraft. Unlike a Western carrier, *Kiev* is provided with a substantial nonaviation battery: eight tubes forward for a powerful surface-to-surface missile, SS-N-12 (with reloads below), a heavy launcher for ASW standoff missiles, and a powerful surface-to-air battery—all of which fills the forward third of the ship and quite definitely restricts the space available for aircraft. Moreover, the Soviets do not designate their new warship a carrier; they call it an "ASW cruiser." They mount large sonars on it, both a variable depth sonar aft and, probably (from the shape of the bow), a big bow sonar. Certainly, *Kiev* cannot be characterized as a specialized airbase intended only to take high-performance strike and fighter aircraft to sea. Such reliance on aircraft for antiship strike, for instance, would have precluded locating the massive SS-N-12 battery forward.

Kiev appears to be designed to operate with fewer escort ships than U.S.

carriers since it is not optimized for aviation in such a way as to require other ships to supply other defensive or offensive needs. In view of past Soviet practice, it also seems unlikely that it would be considered essentially an SS-N-12 platform, with its air group designed merely to provide targeting data. One possible role for *Kiev* would be to break a NATO ASW barrier in the G.-I.-U.K. Gap, a mission that would be vital for successful Soviet submarine operations in the North Atlantic. In such a mission, *Kiev*'s air group could shoot down the relatively low-performance NATO ASW patrol aircraft, and its SS-N-12 battery would destroy NATO ASW surface ships. *Kiev*'s ASW battery would provide both self-defense and a means of destroying those NATO submarines trying to form an active barrier. In this situation, the *Kiev* could also be supported by Soviet landbased aviation. Note also that Soviet doctrine calls for the establishment of sanctuary areas in which Soviet SSBNs can operate. *Kiev* might well be intended as the basis for a Soviet/G.-I.-U.K. barrier designed to keep Western submarines and other ASW forces out of the sanctuary zone. Such a mission would correlate well with the Soviet doctrine that considers the SSBN role to be paramount. In either case more than one such ship would be required, and more Kievs are under construction.

The missions postulated are very limited ones, but it is clear that a ship like *Kiev* can do far more. It can, for example, support Soviet clients in small conflicts like the civil war in Angola and raise the the ante for Western intervention. The ship's YAK-36 VSTOL aircraft have been observed practicing strafing attacks against surface targets. Should the Soviets learn to use their new air-capable ship in this way, it seems likely that they may ultimately decide to build true carriers and the task groups to go with them. It is unlikely that such a momentous decision would be made until some experience with *Kiev* and its sister-ships has been acquired.

Kiev (about 37,000 tons) is the largest warship ever built in the U.S.S.R., although not a very large one by U.S. standards. Its immediate predecessor was *Moskva*, a "helicopter cruiser" completed in 1967 that has no precise U.S. counterpart. Basically, *Moskva* presaged the *Kiev* configuration but without provision for either SS-N-12 or VSTOL aircraft; it operated only ASW helicopters. Only two ships of this type were built, a fact which has led some observers to suggest that the design was unsuccessful or that changing circumstances demanded the construction of the larger Kiev instead.

The only Western near-equivalents to *Moskva* are the Italian helicopter cruiser the *Vittorio Veneto* and the French *Jeanne d'Arc*, both substantially smaller. The French ship appears optimized for commando operations and is, therefore, analogous to the U.S. helicopter carriers. The Italian helicopter cruisers are fleet escorts similar to enlarged guided-missile (AA) destroyers and would be useful in convoy operations.

SOVIET AVIATION-CAPABLE SHIPS

The Soviet aircraft carrier *Kiev*, shown above, is the first of several such ships under construction. It will be capable of handling both helicopters and VSTOL aircraft. It displaces roughly 40,000 tons and carries SS-N-12 standoff antiship missiles on its foredeck. (Courtesy U.S. Navy)

The Soviet helicopter cruiser *Moskva*, shown above, and her sister-ship, the *Leningrad*, were the first truly aviation-capable ships in the Soviet Navy. Their primary mission appears to be antisubmarine warfare, possibly against Alliance Poseidon SSBNs. (Courtesy U.S. Navy)

Unless the Soviets visualized a need to convoy their shipping in the future, it seems more likely that *Moskva* and her sister-ship were intended to sweep anticipated Alliance SSBN approach routes. This idea is not entirely impractical, since early U.S. and U.K. Polaris submarines and French SSBNs would have to approach the Soviet coast in the north or the Eastern Mediterranean to strike Moscow. But by the time *Moskva* entered service, the range of U.S. missiles had been so improved that other alternatives were possible.

Surface Combatants and Escorts

Most of the West's major surface combatants are classed as escorts: missile cruisers (formerly "frigates" in U.S. parlance); destroyers (both ASW and AAW); destroyer escorts, which are now called frigates in the West; and lesser ASW craft. The reason for this lies in the heavier Alliance use of integrated task force operations in the exercise of sea control.

Soviet ships of similar size appear designed for operations associated with Soviet submarines and for offensive missions associated with sea denial. Many of these ships are probably intended to operate alone, despite the submarine threat, because any concentration of ships lacking serious air support is extremely vulnerable to NATO aircraft.

In Western task forces, air support is assured by the organic carrier aircraft. A serious, often unperceived problem in Western navies (both U.S. and foreign) is the decline of naval air arms as hulls built in World War II are retired. This reduction in carriers leaves the ships that were designed to operate with them more vulnerable to attack with standoff weapons.

The U.S. escort force consists of a series of guided-missile cruisers optimized for the antiair warfare (AAW) defense of fast carrier forces; guided-missile destroyers of lesser capability intended to supplement the cruisers or to replace them in areas of lesser risk; ASW-oriented destroyers and frigates; and missile-armed frigates of lesser capabilities—particularly less speed—than their destroyer and cruiser counterparts. All of these ships are armed with some ASW weapons, but they differ according to the sophistication of the sonars installed, the degree of silencing demanded, and the level of ASW weaponry provided.

ASW Systems. The basic ASW weapons are an acoustic torpedo (launched either from shipboard or from a helicopter) and a standoff rocket that can carry either a homing torpedo or a nuclear depth charge about five miles. In the newest escorts, the Perry (FFG-7)-class frigates, the standoff rocket has been discarded in favor of helicopter delivery, which provides a greater range at the cost of some bad-weather capability.

The weapons are only the visible part of the ASW system. Much depends on the sensors which, in the U.S. Navy, are predominantly very powerful

SOVIET AND U.S. CRUISERS

The Soviet Kara and Kresta II classes of surface combatants are roughly equivalent to U.S. cruisers and generally similar to the Kresta I shown above. These ships are designated as "ASW cruisers" by the Soviet Navy. (Courtesy U.S. Navy)

The nuclear-powered guided missile cruiser U.S.S. *Virginia* (CGN-38) is shown above. Its primary mission is antiair defense for aircraft carriers. It displaces roughly 10,000 tons as compared to 6,000 to 9,000 tons of the Kara and Kresta cruisers of the Soviet Navy. (Courtesy U.S. Navy)

active sonars. All of the fleet ASW units are equipped with large, low-frequency active sonars, either SQS-23 or SQS-26 (or their transistorized counterparts, respectively SQS-56 and SQS-53). The SQS-26 is credited with "convergence zone" capability, meaning that under favorable circumstances submarines can be detected as far away as 30 miles. Recently, the U.S. Navy has begun to experiment with large, towed, passive arrays, which may perform more efficiently—especially against relatively noisy Soviet submarines.

A particularly appealing feature of the passive array is that it deters a submarine from accelerating to engage a moving force. The submarine becomes increasingly detectable as it accelerates. As technical developments increase the array's effectiveness, the area from which a submarine can approach a task force or convoy with impunity shrinks but does not vanish entirely. Additionally, the helicopters flown from many ASW ships can sow fields of sonobuoys that can greatly extend the effective range of shipboard ASW sonars. Similarly, aircraft and helicopters give the carriers effective ASW sensing systems.

An essential element of surface ship ASW design is *silencing*. The detection range of a warship employing either passive or active sonar is limited by extraneous noises (static) that interfere with significant signals. This limiting factor includes both unavoidable ambient noise and self-generated noise, although the latter is (at least in theory) avoidable. Moreover, much of modern underwater warfare is conducted passively—i.e., with each opponent attempting to listen for the sounds generated by the other without being heard itself.

Silencing can be extremely expensive in terms of other ship characteristics. For example, engines must be acoustically isolated from the surrounding hull structure so that most of their operating noise is not transmitted into the water. Such isolation necessitates greater machinery box volume for a given horsepower. Simply put, it means less power and less speed in a ship of a given size. Although U.S. submarine silencing programs have received appreciably more publicity, silencing efforts were also an important contribution to the character of U.S. surface ships.

One other ASW point well worth mentioning has to do with weapon reloads. Most U.S. ASW units have substantial weapon capacities. For example, the new Spruance-class destroyers are supplied with three launcher loads (twenty-four rounds) of antisubmarine rocket-propelled torpedoes (ASROC), fourteen Mk-46 torpedoes for firing from onboard torpedo tubes, and another six such torpedoes to be dropped by helicopter. A normal salvo might involve firing two Mk-46 torpedoes; in that case, the Spruance weapon load would permit the equivalent of as many as twenty-two engagements. Other U.S. ASW escorts have lesser but still comparable weapon loads.

Electronic design could also have significant impact on the future U.S.-Soviet naval balance. The efficiency of a lightweight ASW torpedo such as an Mk-46 depends critically on its builder's ability to produce very compact electronic circuitry—a field in which the Soviet Union lags significantly. For example, the smallest Soviet torpedoes are significantly larger than Mk-46 (16 versus 12.75 inches in diameter).

AAW Systems. Antiaircraft weaponry is a matter of great complexity. U.S. naval AA missile development began late in World War II and has since produced three major series: a large, long-range ramjet, Talos; a long-range, two-stage rocket, Terrier; and a short-to-medium-range, single-stage rocket, Tartar. Initially it appeared that Talos and probably Terrier would be limited to installation aboard cruisers, while the smaller Tartar might well fit aboard destroyers and even destroyer escorts.

As a result of rocket fuel development, Tartar has moved well beyond the capabilities of early Terriers. In addition, the two programs have since been merged under the designation Standard, in which Terrier is replaced by a Standard plus booster, and Tartar is replaced by the single stage alone. Most Standard/Terrier/Tartar installations have capacity for about forty missiles, which can be fired off in rapid sequence. Talos is far more cumbersome and, indeed, is rapidly leaving fleet service as the cruisers that were converted for its operation wear out. Future AA missile ship construction is likely to be based on Standard, which is the missile component of the new Aegis system (discussed in later text).

In recognition of Soviet emphasis on standoff antiship cruise missiles, much U.S. effort is now going into "point defense" or "last-ditch" defensive measures. These include the Phalanx, a very rapid-firing 20-millimeter cannon, and the already operational Basic Point Defense Missile System (BPDMS), essentially a modified Sparrow air-to-air missile launched from shipboard. The BPDMS is to be mounted aboard nearly all U.S. warships, so even non-AAW types like the ASW frigates will have some, at least limited, organic air defense. Phalanx will see similar applications in the near future.

U.S. post–World War II missile ships fall into four basic categories: large cruisers converted to missile ships, of which four remain (plus a nuclear cruiser built for the role); the "superdestroyers" (formerly called *frigates*, now, for the most part, redesignated cruisers) built as Terrier launchers but without the sensors and command facilities of the converted cruisers; the Tartar-launching destroyers and destroyer escorts (the latter now redesignated frigates); and the two new series of nuclear-powered cruisers, the California and Virginia classes, equipped with the improved Tartar.

The simplest way to characterize the sensor capabilities of the various categories is to note the type of air search radar used. The big cruisers generally have the SPS-43A, the largest U.S. two-dimensional radar, which is used on most aircraft carriers. Missile cruisers often have the SPS-43, a radar that has similar electronics but a much smaller antenna and a shorter range; however, it does provide the minimum essential radar coverage. Destroyers have the next most capable radar, the SPS-40, in many cases.

Larger and more complex ships generally have greater "target-handling" capability. The largest of the cruisers, the Albany class, are "double-enders," which have Talos fore and aft and radars capable of controlling four missiles at once—as well as controls for Tartar amidships. Many of the ex-frigates can also control four missiles at once, but they have only one or two missile directors. These considerations are of great consequence in view of known Soviet saturation tactics designed to be used against task forces.

The Naval Tactical Data System (NTDS) enables ships in a task force to exchange information automatically—almost instantaneously. This computer-based system permits a task force to operate in an extremely integrated fashion against incoming threats. It also makes possible the layered defense on which U.S. task forces depend: carrier-based fighters with their long-range Sparrow or Phoenix positioned where the Soviet bombers must operate, then Talos, then the Standard in both long- and short-range forms, and, finally, the point defenses. All defenses must be coordinated if incoming threats are to be handled properly. Unfortunately, much of this equipment may be too costly and sophisticated to permit standardization with some of the less affluent members of the Western Alliance.

The overall weapon systems of Western ships have very impressive capabilities. However, these ships do not *look* particularly impressive compared to Russian combatants of similar size. The Soviets seem to have Phalanx-like weapons already in place; we have ours only in advanced development. The Soviets have more different missile systems; they seem to have a greater variety of weapons types; and to the casual observer, their ships appear individually more capable and threatening than their Western counterparts. While such perceptions may favor Soviet attempts to influence the less sophisticated members of the Third World, they do not necessarily connote greater combat capabilities.

Antiship Systems. The question of our surface fleet's vulnerability is not merely a matter of the real or apparent lack of defensive weapons, but also a matter of the apparent inability to strike at the enemy. Considering the visible number of offensive weapons carried by the latest Soviet surface combatants, such a dearth of offensive power on Western ships seems puzzling, at least at first. But most of the supposed Soviet antiship missiles are actually ASW weapons. Moreover, the U.S. Navy has now moved to provide its escorts with a very capable antiship missile, Harpoon.

Harpoon will replace many of the ASW or AA weapons aboard existing ships (e.g., it can be fired from the ASROC antisubmarine rocket "pepperbox" launcher). In effect it dilutes the escort character of the U.S. surface combatant force, and one might ask whether this dilution makes sense in view of the predominance of air and submarine forces in Soviet anticarrier formations. On the other hand, it will vastly increase our antiship capabilities in formations that do not include scarce aircraft carriers.

Most of our offensive power still lies in our carriers (to which there is still no real Soviet equivalent), but the Soviets' surface fleet is not their key means of naval attack on surface ships.

A great deal must depend on the relative reliability of Soviet and U.S. guided weapons, about which little is really known. In many cases, the Soviets seem to have serious problems with the "invisible" parts of their weapon systems, such as fire control and search radar. On the other hand, the United States has withheld deployment of its Phalanx system largely because the radar, which was to fire automatically upon the approach of a missile, sometimes picked up erroneous signals from other targets. By comparison, photographs of Soviet combatants armed with analogous weapons do not appear to show much in the way of automatic fire controls. Such a lack could prove costly in the defense against a missile such as Harpoon. Yet the guns themselves provide some manual capability, and their presence is both impressive to observers and reassuring to the crews.

Soviet Surface Combatants. The Soviet surface fleet on the high seas today contains elements of at least three distinct design periods. The first, built under Stalin, consisted of cruisers and destroyers of conventional pre–World War II design: Sverdlovs, Skorys, and Kotlins. These were elements of a much larger program which Stalin ordered to provide the Soviet state with the trappings of a world power, i.e., a large oceangoing navy. His successors in the Soviet leadership did not support his approach, and Stalin's program was curtailed after his death in 1953. Two of the big Sverdlov cruisers were converted to command ships and provided with limited SAM defense capability, but other than peacetime presence, the remainder seem to play little role in current Soviet strategy (see Chapter 4).

The main survivors of Stalin's surface ship program were destroyers, which developed along two main lines: cruise missile-armed Kildins and Krupnys in which the SSN-1 missile provided (in effect) a longer-range antiship torpedo, and conventional torpedo-armed destroyers equipped with AA missiles in place of AA artillery, the Kashins. Neither series appears to have been part of any larger strategic design.

The next design period produced the anticarrier fleet, to which Western tacticians have devoted considerable attention. The major surface components were the Kynda- and Kresta I-class missile cruisers, armed with the long-range, air-breathing SS-N-3 missile. It appears that Soviet tactics called for coordinated strikes by surface ships, submarines (Echo II and Juliett classes), and missile-dropping Badger bombers against carrier formations. Such coordination was intended to saturate the formidable carrier task force defenses.

The fairly small ships Kynda and Kresta I were intended to derive their effect from the large missiles they carried—albeit in very small numbers. Kynda has quadruple surface-to-surface missile launchers fore and aft, with a reload for each tube, but the reloads would be difficult to manhandle in any kind of sea. Moreover, it has only a single AA missile launcher, which would be inadequate in the event of a serious air attack. Kresta I, which is roughly the same size, is more heavily equipped. It has a second antiaircraft missile launcher aft, but no reloads (which would probably constitute a fire hazard rather than a serious capability). In both ships, the radar fire control for the AA missile is so designed that it can handle only a single target at a time.

A major problem for the kind of anticarrier missile strike postulated is that the missiles coming into the carrier formation may home on the wrong ships; none of the launching ships can actually tell visibly which ship in the formation is the carrier. Hence, the Soviet practice of "tattletaling" (a destroyer or AGI tags along with the formation, so it can relay back the vital data). At the time of attack, the "tattletale" must leave the formation or it, too, will attract missiles intended to strike the carrier. Recently, the Soviets have begun to fit destroyers assigned to "tattletale" duty with short-range (20-mile) missiles (SS-N-2) firing aft—the proper direction for launch by the "tattletale" as it exits the carrier formation.

These tactics make sense only in the event of a preemptive attack at the moment war begins; otherwise the carrier's aircraft, which far outrange SS-N-3, will merely seek out and sink the prospective anticarrier forces. Also, "tattletaling" does not seem a viable operation once war has begun. Hence, the Western name usually given Soviet anticarrier (surface ship) tactics—"the D-Day shootout."

For quite some time it was assumed that anticarrier warfare was the main function of all modern Soviet surface ships, but that was not the case. Submarines and aircraft were generally far more efficient. Only four Kyndas and four Kresta I's were ever built. Their successors formed the third Soviet design period—the strategic ASW fleet.

Soviet ASW Ships. In 1964, the Soviets redesignated most of their major combatants "large ASW ships." This redesignation included the Kresta I's, clearly *not* ASW ships, which were then under construction. However, *Moskva* soon appeared, then came a new series of surface ships (Kresta II and Kara-class cruisers and Krivak-class destroyers), all of them armed with a new missile. At first this missile was assumed to be a shorter-range anticarrier weapon, but it is now known to be a short-ranged cruise missile carrying an ASW torpedo, a rather long-ranged Soviet equivalent of ASROC. Therefore, the new generation of Soviet major surface combatants is not so very different from the series to be found in Western navies—ASW ships, often with effective AA missile defenses.

However, there are some important differences. Because their primary ASW weapon is quite large, the Soviets cannot afford reloads—thus Kara and Kresta II carry only eight missiles each, and Krivak only four. Aside from the missiles, there are torpedo tubes, which may carry antiship weapons for self-defense. The Soviets also provide their newer ships with AA missiles to which they ascribe important antiship capabilities—but at relatively short range. Consequently, although Soviet ships have more launchers on deck, their total missile load generally falls short of their Western counterparts.

Another major difference between Soviet and Western ASW ships is speed. It is generally assumed in the West that speeds above 30 knots will be required so rarely and will be so expensive that they are not particularly worthwhile, thus the 30 knots of Spruance. The Soviets, on the other hand, had the problem of maneuvering into attack positions relative to 30-knot carrier groups—hence, the somewhat higher speeds of Kynda and Kresta I, which are about 34 knots. The ASW ships show the legacy of this requirement, even though their sensors cannot be worth much above 20 to 25 knots. However, the new destroyers of the Krivak class are substantially slower than their production predecessors, the Kashins, which were classical (SAM-armed) destroyers of very high speed.

Soviet Ship Deficiencies. Perhaps the most striking self-defense deficiency of the new Soviet surface ships is their very limited target-handling capability compared to Western destroyers. A Kara, comparable in size to U.S. missile frigates, mounts two double SA-3 launchers, which on paper represent a battery more than comparable to the two single-armed launchers of a U.S. cruiser of the California class. But each Soviet launcher is served by a *single* fire control device that can direct missiles onto only one target at a time. The equivalent U.S. ship has two fire control directors per launcher and can engage twice as many targets at once. In addition, the new Aegis system is being developed to enlarge raid-handling capacity a great deal by controlling several missiles with each director.

Other basic differences between Soviet and Western design practices

SOVIET AND U.S. DESTROYERS

One of the latest classes of Soviet "ASW destroyers" is the Kashin class pictured above. It displaces roughly 4,300 tons and carries missiles, guns, and antisubmarine torpedoes. (Courtesy U.S. Navy)

The U.S.S. *Arthur W. Radford* (DD-968), shown above, is one of the new 7,800-ton Spruance (DD-963)-class destroyers currently being built for the U.S. Navy. Its primary mission is ASW defense for carrier or amphibious task forces. Its capabilities probably exceed the minimum required for escorting convoys. (Courtesy U.S. Navy)

suggest that the Soviets are not yet prepared for protracted forward deployment during either peace or war. In general, the habitability of Soviet ships is poor, with cramped quarters, low overheads, and little, if any, air conditioning. As for battle damage, it appears that the Soviets have devoted less effort to assuring the survival of their ships if hit. While some attention is paid to protecting vital equipments, little consideration appears to be directed toward minimizing crew casualties.

Soviet Coastal Fleet. Just as Moskva does not quite correspond to any Western category of warships, neither do the various classes of coastal "escorts," which the Soviets often term "coast guard craft." These include the numerous postwar Rigas, which in the West are often dubiously categorized as destroyer escorts, and their successors of the Grisha, Petya, and Mirka classes. The Rigas were armed against the major coastal threat of their day, surface ships. They had twin or triple torpedo tubes. Their successors are light ASW units, roughly comparable to the old U.S. destroyer escorts and PCEs. However, they do not have particularly sophisticated ASW batteries—only unguided rockets and small ASW torpedoes. They are far faster than their Western counterparts, which may be a feature intended to permit ASW craft to concentrate more quickly on a "flaming datum." Some analysts think that recent Soviet work on wing-in-ground machines, which are hybrid aircraft-surface effect ships, may have a similar rationale.

Corresponding to the ASW coastal fleet is an antiship coastal fleet, the best-known units of which are the Styx-armed fast patrol craft, Komars (now nearly extinct) and Osas. These PT-like craft are heirs to vast numbers of true PT boats, which once formed an essential element of Soviet coastal defenses. Their successors appear to be the Nanuchka-class missile corvettes, with a longer-range weapon (roughly 90 versus 20 miles). Many Western European navies also operate fast missile boats, but there is a considerable difference in rationale. To the Soviets, a primary naval task is to prevent intruders from approaching the extraordinarily long and sparsely populated Soviet coast: in effect, to seal the Soviet Union off against seaborne aliens. Related to this task is the requirement that the sea frontiers be sealed against Soviet citizens who may wish to leave the Soviet Union. The task of securing the very long coasts of the country against intruders, who may be far from any point of strategic significance, is a very large one (even in peacetime) and one without serious counterpart in the West. Hence, the Soviets maintain an enormous flotilla of coastal craft, including coastal patrol craft manned by the KGB.

Relative Ship Capabilities. Capabilities of the Western and Soviet surface fleets are very difficult to compare. Except in a very few instances,

Soviet and Western surface ships are *not* designed to fight each other. They are intended to strike at or defend against other threats. For the Western fleets, the main threats against naval ships are air- and submarine-launched missiles, and against merchant ships, torpedoes; hence, the AAW/ASW orientation of Western escorts. Similarly, our attacks against the Soviet surface fleet would most likely be delivered by air or submarine. From a Soviet point of view, it is most important for surface ships to have either the ability to "tattletale" carrier formations in a pre-D-Day mode or else ASW capability against Western SSBNs. Nonetheless, the most likely confrontation between opposing surface ships might arise from some lesser scenario in which Soviet ships attempt to deny passage to U.S. or Allied ships involved in some Third World crisis. In this event, the outcome would depend on the individual ships involved. At present, Allied success could not be assured without the introduction of aircraft carrier assets.

Just how effective either force would be in a major confrontation is also a matter of speculation because official estimates of weapon reliability and sensor performance are classified and relatively uncertain. The Western navies are likely to be far more advanced in antisubmarine warfare than the Soviets; Soviet submarines are known to be fairly noisy (as noted elsewhere), which clearly does not improve their chances in wartime; considerable effort has gone into Western AA missile systems designed to defeat Soviet saturation tactics; and the Soviet surface fleet would not long survive if committed. It is also well known that for many years the primary U.S. Navy missile systems have suffered low reliability rates. No one can really say how well fleet units do under attack. For example, considerable effort is just now going into means of improving reaction times as a counter to Soviet short-range antiship missile fire (e.g., defense against Charlie-class submarines).

High Speed Ships. In the West there seems to be some feeling that current surface combatant displacement hull technology has reached its limits and that something new is required. Whether or not this view is sound, it has led to attempts at new kinds of ships. The usual desideratum has been greater speed in a seaway. The two current means to this end are hydrofoils and air-cushion (surface effect) ships. In the near future, small-waterplane-area twin hull (SWATH) configurations may also be demonstrated. The first two types share a relatively low load-carrying capability, high cost, and high speed. It is perfectly feasible, for example, to produce 100-knot ocean escort surface effect craft, which is what the U.S. Navy is about to do. Hydrofoils can operate at speeds as great as 60 knots. SWATH is in a somewhat different category in that it is not higher speed but better ride quality in rough seas that gives it advantage over conventional monohulls.

The question is, just what is all this speed worth? The very fast platforms are inherently quite noisy, which means the enemy submarines can detect them passively at great range and, presumably, attack them with weapons far faster than the fastest ocean vehicle. On the other hand, it can be argued that high speed confers a strategic mobility that may compensate for lesser numbers—as long as the fast platform survives. Speed might also be valuable for exploiting distant flaming data, for scanning large surface areas at very low altitudes, or for "sprint-and-drift" tactics of submarine detection by convoy escorts, which may permit the transit speed of the convoy to be increased. The Soviets have also indicated interest in unusual high-speed configurations with their very large "wing-in-ground-effect" machine. To date, none of these novel high speed configurations has progressed into operational inventories, and none appears likely to do so for other than specialized missions because of their higher costs. If, as appears more likely, the value of surface ships for tasks such as ASW is to be found in their staying power, load-carrying ability, and command-and-control facilities, it seems probable that the cheaper, slower conventional hulls will continue to dominate, except possibly for special escort detection schemes.

Submarines

In all major classes of warships, Soviet and Western requirements differ sharply. Nonetheless, in submarine development both sides have pursued very similar technology—but to different ends. In 1945, both the United States and the Soviet Union operated large submarine fleets consisting of vessels designed for surface operation with occasional submergence as a means of protection. Rather suddenly these fleets became obsolete with the emergence of the German Type 21 and Walter submarines, which were intended to operate submerged essentially all of the time. After the war, the United States and the Soviet Union each acquired complete Type 21 submarines, and both appear to have realized their significance. In fact, the United States viewed the acquisition of Type 21's by the Soviets as a disaster, and we initiated crash ASW programs even in the postwar period of severe budgetary retrenchment.

Both countries put submarines loosely based on Type 21 into production: the Whiskey and Zulu classes in the Soviet Union; the Tang class and Guppy conversions in the United States. However, the conventional submarine objective of the United States had vanished with the defeat of Japan and Germany; there were no longer any prospective enemies with large merchant fleets whose loss would be economically catastrophic. For their part, the Soviets had a definite requirement for antishipping units; even so, in the decade after 1945 they concentrated on medium-range units (Whiskey), which were unsuitable for long-range operation off the U.S. coasts.

American submariners considered a number of new roles for their craft. One which proved most important was antisubmarine warfare, which required that the U.S. submarine be able to stalk its Soviet quarry, using passive sonar wherever possible. This tactic required careful attention to quieting, both to improve sonar performance and to avoid alerting the quarry.

Although the U.S. submarines continued to have an antisurface-ship role, little effort was expended on antiship weapons, at least until very recently. The major postwar torpedo programs (Mk-37, Mk-48), have been directed toward antisubmarine warfare, some with secondary antiship capability. The U.S. nuclear torpedo, Mk-45, was designed exclusively for antisubmarine warfare, as its acronym, ASTOR (A/S TORpedo), indicates. The major nontorpedo submarine weapon of the 1960s was SUBROC, a submarine-launched rocket carrying a nuclear depth charge.

Soviet priorities were quite different. The main Soviet target, at least until the Polaris reached operational status in 1960-1961, was the carrier task force, a fast moving group of ships whose nuclear capabilities could be deadly for the Soviet Union. Consequently, when the Soviets developed nuclear propulsion, they used it primarily to achieve high underwater speeds at the expense of very quiet operation. They attempted to produce standoff weapons that would improve their submarines' chances of destroying carriers and their escorts. The first of these was probably a nuclear torpedo, which is a standoff weapon by virtue of its large lethal radius. It can be fired from a great range, and the aircraft carrier probably could not outmaneuver the torpedo during its time to target. Great effort also went into developing a long-range cruise weapon, SS-N-3, which could be fired from submarines over a hundred miles from the carrier group. In the late 1960s, the Soviets began to build two classes of fast attack submarines: Charlie, which could fire eight short-range (30 miles) SS-N-7 missiles; and Victor, a strictly torpedo attack submarine. Both were extremely fast; neither was particularly quiet by U.S. standards. In theory, the SS-N-7 presented an almost impossible problem for U.S. carrier defenses because of its very short flight time and the correspondingly brief reaction time it imposed.

Actually, the anticarrier mission conflicts with recent Soviet interest in anti-SSBN (i.e., antisubmarine) operations. It takes a very long time to reorient production of nuclear power plants toward quieter types, for design and production practices to change, and for new passive sonar technology to evolve.

The Soviets have two major options: One is to have the already fairly quiet conventional submarines of the Foxtrot (older) and Tango (newer) classes wait in bottlenecks through which SSBNs might have to pass, such as the Strait of Sicily in the Mediterranean. The other would be to try to

SOVIET AND U.S. ATTACK SUBMARINES

The nuclear-powered Victor-class attack submarine is now being produced in the Soviet Union; the rate of production is expected to increase in future years. This is one important category in which the Soviet Navy still lags behind the U.S. Navy by a significant margin. (Courtesy U.S. Navy)

The nuclear-powered Los Angeles–class (SSN-688) attack submarine is now being built in the United States. The U.S. fleet now operates over sixty-five SSNs of this type and the earlier SSN-637 class. They are significantly more capable—and substantially quieter—than their Soviet counterparts. (Courtesy U.S. Navy)

produce an effective ASW standoff weapon, relying on diesel submarines or other platforms for targeting, so the self-noise of the launching submarine would be relatively unimportant. In the latter case, the development of a Soviet submarine rocket equivalent of SUBROC might transform Victor into a very effective ASW platform—if the targeting problem could be solved. Just such a weapon has been reported as SS-N-15.

As in the other warship categories, it is very difficult to compare U.S. and Soviet submarines directly because they have such different missions. Only in the case of SSBNs do the two navies appear to approach mission similarity. However, the notable lack of interest in quieting SSNs appears to have carried over to Soviet SSBNs and should make them more vulnerable. It appears that the United States has achieved noticeably better operationally useful sonar performance, both passive and active, than has the Soviet Union. On the other hand, the Soviets have long believed in coordinated strikes by underwater, surface, and air platforms against carrier task forces. In such strikes, sensors *external* to the submarine can improve the submarine's targeting capabilities, and such operations may offset noise problems to some extent when standoff weapons are used. A concomitant to such tactics is the need for strong emphasis on communications, including communications through the air-water boundary. In this area, it is possible that Soviet capabilities may well be ahead of those of the West, since U.S. submarines have traditionally operated as lone wolves.

In either direct duel or static side-by-side comparisons, Western submarines appear to be more capable on a one-for-one basis. Nevertheless, the Soviets maintain a larger inventory of submarines, are willing to devote more surface ships to their protection, and have many fewer targets vulnerable to submarine attack. Consequently, Western quality appears to be offset by Soviet quantity, and Western vulnerability to submarine attack appears higher than Soviet vulnerability. For these reasons, the undersea war would be a most difficult one for the Western Alliance.

Naval Weapons

As already suggested, the U.S. and Soviet naval arsenals differ fundamentally, in accordance with the orientation of their navies. The Soviets, faced with large U.S. surface forces, have invested heavily in antiship technology. Their recent shift to antisubmarine warfare utilizes similar (cruise missile) technology. The U.S. Navy, on the other hand, began the postwar period with only one serious reminder of World War II difficulties—enemy submarines; consequently, the United States invested heavily in antisubmarine warfare. Somewhat later, the United States perceived a bomber threat: hence, the "3T" series of AA missiles—Tartar, Terrier, and Talos. More recently, AA development has shifted over to antiship missile defense (ASMD); and the United States has begun to develop its own antiship weapons as the Soviet surface fleet has grown.

Both navies' missions appear to coincide only in the case of long-range ballistic missiles. In each navy, the trend has been toward greater range and accuracy. The U.S. Navy went from 1,380-mile Polaris (1959) to a range of 2,875 miles in later versions (A-3); in the newer Poseidon the A-3 range was retained, but multiple independently targeted reentry vehicles (MIRVs) were introduced. At that time, U.S. strategists must have believed that the 2,875-mile range allowed an SSBN enough sea room to evade Soviet ASW forces in the foreseeable future. Ten years later, however, the new Trident has emerged with a far greater range, 4,600 miles in its earliest version, and yet it will lag behind the introduction of the Soviet Delta SSBNs with equivalent performance. Both Trident and Delta submarines will be able to operate under the direct protection of shore-based forces. It is worth noting that Trident I SLBM deployment will overcome the effect of withdrawal of U.S. SSBNs from Rota, Spain.

The Soviets moved in a similar direction. They began more primitively with a naval version of the land-based Scud missile. The naval Scud was followed by the SS-N-4, a 350-mile-range SLBM, which has to be launched from surfaced Golf I and Hotel I-class submarines. These were followed by the 750-mile SS-N-5 on Golf II/Hotel II submarines, which could be launched submerged. The SS-N-5 could still provide a significant theater nuclear capability against short-range targets, most likely against NATO countries or Japan. In the early sixties, the Soviets began to develop a new series of SSBN weapons more nearly comparable to Polaris: SS-N-6 (1,500 and later 1,840 miles) for the Yankee class and then SS-N-8 (4,800 miles) for the newer Deltas. However, the Soviets took far longer to achieve effective MIRV technology, so the long-range SS-N-8 is not yet directly comparable with Trident. Newer Soviet SLBMs, the SS-NX-17 and -18, are reported to be under test with multiple warheads for greater effectiveness.

For a time in the early 1970s, the Soviets appeared to be testing a ballistic antiship missile, designated the SS-N-13. Owing to the absence of more recently observed testing, many analysts have concluded that the development was aborted. Others believe that the Soviets may retain an interest in the development of a tactical nuclear ballistic missile of modest range for use against various targets at sea—varying from other hostile SSBNs to carrier task forces or even high-value merchant ship convoys. Certainly such a development would be possible, and its emergence may depend on the Soviets' perception of its usefulness in some limited nuclear war at sea, during which they might wish to avoid using land-based systems. Such a missile would also make a logical replacement for the SS-N-5 in a theater nuclear role against shore targets.

From the early fifties on, the Soviets placed great emphasis on antiship cruise missiles, both air- and ship-launched. The first of the ship-launched series were an air-breathing weapon, SS-N-1, and a liquid rocket, SS-N-2, the notorious Styx. The former was mounted aboard missile destroyers; it had a radar homer and a range of about 30 miles in the absence of a forward observer. Apparently, SS-N-1 was not particularly successful, and it was succeeded by the better SS-N-2.

SS-N-2 is an autonomous missile: its launcher fires it in the general direction of the target, after which the missile itself begins to search with its internal radar. Such a weapon places very small demands on the launch platform. It is generally carried about by PT-like craft, such as the Soviet-built Komars with which the Egyptians sank an Israeli destroyer in 1967.

Since ships may move considerable distances during the time of flight of the missile, autonomous homing becomes inefficient at very great ranges. For example, a missile intended for the carrier in a task force may, instead, home on one of the escorts. Thus, the long-range Soviet cruise missile SS-N-3 is a far more elaborate system requiring a forward observer. This weapon is fired from both submarines and surface ships, as discussed earlier.

Of the remaining Soviet naval surface-to-surface missiles, the SS-N-7 is a submerged-launched, short-range weapon fired by Charlie-class submarines; it is functionally similar to SS-N-2. The SS-N-12 is an SS-N-3 replacement. An SS-N-9 is a medium- to long-range antiship cruise weapon carried by the Nanuchka-class missile corvettes. All of these weapons have substantial warheads, and in many cases there are nuclear options. Just what Soviet doctrine is governing the release and use of nuclear weapons at sea remains the subject of considerable debate.

There is another family of air-dropped antiship missiles. The earliest one, AS-1 (Kennel), was exported to Indonesia and Egypt and has apparently left Soviet service. It resembled a small jet fighter and had a range of about 60 miles. Two could be carried under the wings of a Badger (TU-16) bomber. Kennel was replaced by the far more sophisticated Kipper (AS-2), which could only be carried singly but has a range of about 130 miles. For some time the latter was the primary weapon of Soviet naval antiship aircraft. More recently, a one-for-one replacement of Kennel has been in service: Kelt (AS-5), with a range of about 200 miles. Kelts have been exported to Egypt, and several were used in the 1973 Middle East war. As in the case of naval ship-launched weapons, all of these missiles carry large warheads, many of which may be conventional or nuclear.

The Soviet Navy has many hundreds of long-range weapons available for anticarrier strike warfare. As explained earlier, the U.S. response has been improved air defenses ranging from fighters intended to destroy both missiles and missile carrying aircraft to longer- and shorter-range defense weapons to "point defense" or "last-ditch" missiles and guns.

A major fraction of the Soviet antiship threat is carried by Soviet naval bombers: Badgers at present; Backfires in the near future. The most efficient counter to such aircraft, once they are airborne, is probably long-range carrier-based interceptors with air-to-air missiles, backed up by very long-range radars. For the foreseeable future, the U.S. combination will probably be the F-14 armed with the Phoenix missile and controlled by E-2 aircraft, both of which are in production. One of the great virtues of the E-2 is its long detection range against low-flying aircraft.

It is difficult to say just how well the U.S. system of missile defense will perform in action or, for that matter, how well the Soviet cruise missiles will perform. One essential question for the defender is reaction time, the time it takes to shoot back *once the threat has been recognized.* Enormous differences will exist between the responses of alerted and unalerted forces. The question of how a force becomes alerted is very much one of timely intelligence—if the "D-Day shootout" scenario is realistic. In addition, there are questions of practical radar capability against low-flying aircraft, missile reliability and rate of fire, electronic countermeasures, and many other uncertainties. For a time in the mid-sixties, serious doubts about the efficiency of the "3T" missiles were entertained, even in public, and considerable funds went into a series of modifications.

As far as its own antiship capabilities are concerned, the U.S. Navy effort was relatively quiescent for many years because of a lack of a perceived threat, even though our NATO allies developed and deployed short-range missiles such as Exocet, Ottomat, and Penguin for their own ships. Even U.S. aircraft weapons received relatively little antiship standoff emphasis. This situation has now changed. United States forces are beginning to receive Harpoon, an autonomous antiship weapon launchable from ships, submarines, and aircraft, with a range of about 60 miles. Harpoon was designed for compatibility with existing launching systems (e.g., submarine torpedo tubes and the ASROC "pepperbox"); hence, its limited dimensions (13.5-inch diameter) and relatively small warhead (500-pound blast type). Relatively optimistic statements about the survivability of Western warships hit by one or two Soviet cruise missiles bring the lethality of Western antiship missiles into question. At 60 miles, Harpoon may also have problems finding the important target among a group of warships. Nonetheless, Alliance navies clearly need greater antiship capability as soon as possible. For the future, the navy is developing the much bigger and far longer-ranged Tomahawk (400-mile, 21-inch diameter, 1,000-pound warhead), which will be compatible with submarine torpedo tubes.

Tomahawk may also be built in a strategic version, with a thermonuclear warhead, a range of about 1,700 miles, and a high-precision, radar-mapping guidance system. Its advent may greatly complicate the problem of Soviet strategic antisubmarine warfare, since attack submarines could be equipped with Tomahawk. Even if it were carried only on U.S. submarines, the Soviets would then have to track all seventy-six U.S. attack submarines as well as the forty-one SSBNs. Therefore, the mere existence of Tomahawk may be an important factor in the survivability of the U.S. SSBN force in wartime. Mounted on surface ships, Tomahawk would also force the Soviets to conduct the equivalent of anticarrier operations against all U.S. surface ships—quite possibly even against all NATO surface ships. It could be a vital factor in restoring a favorable U.S. naval nuclear balance. However, it is not clear what the status of Tomahawk will be under a new SALT agreement.

Although ASW weapons have already been discussed in some detail, it should be noted that the Soviets appear to have applied their cruise missile technology in the SS-N-14 ASW missile, whereas the U.S. ASROC and SUBROC are ballistic weapons whose course cannot be updated during flight. As a result, extended-range ASROC is not very useful, since the longer the flight, the greater the chance that the submarine has left the lethal zone before impact. Thus, the Soviet technology is potentially more useful—if the Soviets can develop the sensors required. In the West, the Australian Ikara and the French Malafon use cruise missile technology to deliver a homing torpedo. Presumably Harpoon and possibly Tomahawk offer the United States similar possibilities should a command control link be developed for the basic antiship missiles.

Mine Warfare

The U.S. Navy retains only three ocean minesweepers (MSO) in active commission to support mine research and development activities at the Naval Coastal Systems Laboratory in Panama City, Florida. Another twenty-two MSOs are assigned to the naval reserve force and are manned by composite active-reserve crews. The Navy's principal mine countermeasures capability consists of one helicopter squadron (HM-12) flying RH-53D Sea Stallions. While these helicopters are effective in countering shallow-water mines, the Navy has only twenty-three of them, and their deployment aboard amphibious ships (LHA/LPH) displaces troop-carrying helicopters and marines.

The Navy has belatedly initiated development of a new class of oceangoing minesweepers, designated Mine Countermeasures Ships (MCM), to counter advanced Soviet deep-ocean mines. Several smaller, coastal minesweepers are also under construction for transfer to foreign navies. All U.S. coastal minesweepers (MSC) and minesweeping boats (MSB) have been discarded, while the surviving minesweeping launches (MSL) have been stripped of their specialized equipment and are employed as utility craft.

The U.S. Navy has shown only a limited interest in offensive as well as

U.S. TACTICAL STANDOFF ANTISHIP MISSILES

The U.S. Navy's new antiship missile, the Harpoon, is shown here being fired from the regular ASROC launcher of the U.S.S. *Knox* (DE-1052). This launcher is one of the most "standardized" items in Alliance navies, many of which will soon receive this important missile system. (Courtesy U.S. Navy)

The above sequence shows a Tomahawk missile leaving the water after a successful launch from the torpedo tubes of the U.S.S. *Barb* (SSN-596) during a February 1978 test. Designed for both land- and ship-attack missions, Tomahawk missiles have been successfully fired from aircraft, submarines, and land platforms. (Courtesy U.S. Navy)

defensive mine warfare. The principal navy minelaying platforms are carrier-based attack aircraft, land-based patrol aircraft, and submarines. No surface ships are currently fitted for minelaying.

Minelaying exercises are carried out by aircraft squadrons and submarines on a periodic basis. However, these can be considered severely limited in scope and interest. The stowage of mines aboard aircraft carriers reduces the number of conventional bombs and missiles that can be embarked in the ships. Submarines do not carry mines on normal patrols; to load mines they would have to return to port, steam to the target area to plant the mines covertly, return to base for torpedos (or more mines) after the field is planted, and then steam to an operational area. With the limited U.S. Navy interest in mine warfare, it seems unlikely that U.S. submarines will be diverted to minelaying operations.

The U.S. Air Force has a secondary sea control mission which includes minelaying. Approximately 80 air force B-52D's are configured for carrying mines as well as nuclear or conventional bombs. Another 250 B-52G/H strategic bombers would require modification to carry maximum mine loads; more significantly, those aircraft are committed to the U.S. strategic attack plan. Indeed, the availability of even the B-52D aircraft for minelaying during a conflict with the Soviet Union or a major crisis is questionable.

The recently developed CAPTOR mine is now entering service. This is a deep-moored mine which can detect passing submarines by their acoustic signature and launch an Mk-46 homing torpedo. Other mine programs were initiated in the early 1970s to replace the largely obsolescent U.S. mine stockpile and to compensate for the compromise of technology resulting from the extensive use of mines during the Vietnam War. The major development efforts are the propelled-rocket ascent mine (PRAM) and Project Quickstrike, the latter an extension of a concept of fitting general-purpose bombs with mine fuses.

The following table indicates the maximum mine-carrying capability of various U.S. aircraft currently in service. The mines are identified by "class," which indicates their approximate weight. Submarines carry mines in place of torpedoes. (The torpedo-carrying capacities of contemporary submarines are classified.)

There appears to be little current unclassified information on the Soviets' mine warfare capabilities. They maintain a large minesweeping force—which may be indicative of their own plans. They are known to have very large stockpiles of old mines as well as some newer models, including what appears to be a very capable deepwater mine.

Comparative Aircraft Characteristics

Naval aircraft fall into two categories: those that operate in the difficult

SOVIET AND U.S. LAND-BASED MINING AIRCRAFT

A Soviet-built TU-16 Badger (with Egyptian markings) is shown monitoring a NATO exercise over the North Atlantic, escorted by a carrier-based U.S. Navy F-8 fighter. Badgers have a long-range mining capability. (Courtesy U.S. Navy)

Long-range U.S. aerial mining capabilities are included in about eighty Air Force Stratofortress (B-52D) strategic bombers like the one shown above. These aging aircraft, extensively used over Vietnam, and other Air Force assets could contribute significantly to naval sea control operations. (Courtesy U.S. Air Force)

TABLE 10-1
MINES CARRIED BY VARIOUS AIRCRAFT TYPES

Aircraft	Wing Mounted Number	Wing Mounted Weight (lbs.)		Weapons Bay Number	Weapons Bay Weight (lbs.)
A-6	5	2,000		—	
A-7	6	2,000		—	
S-3	2	2,000	+	4	500
P-2	8	500	+	8	1,000
			or		
	8	500	+	4	2,000
P-3	10	500	+	6	500
			or		
	8	1,000	+	3	1,000
			or		
	6	2,000	+	1	2,000
B-52D[a]	8	2,000	+	56	500
			or		
	8	2,000	+	28	1,000

[a]Maximum B-52D CAPTOR Mk-60 mine capacity is 18.

environment aboard ship and those that operate from the more benign environment of land bases. The vast majority of the ship-based aircraft of the Western Alliance are of U.S. design and manufacture. As for land-based aircraft, the numbers maintained by the Western Alliance and by the Soviet Union are more comparable, but the capabilities are quite different. Both aircraft categories will be discussed in the ensuing paragraphs.

Ship-Based Aircraft Systems

Although the Soviets have improved their submarines and surface ships, there is still virtually no comparison between the capabilities of their few ship-based helicopters and aircraft and those of the West. In the U.S. inventory alone, there are roughly 2,500 ship-based aircraft and helicopters, with outstanding capabilities in the three functional areas of strike systems, air defense systems, and antisubmarine warfare systems. A good many of the U.S. strike and air defense aircraft are operated by the U.S. Marine Corps. All of the U.S. ASW-capable systems are operated by the U.S. Navy.

The backbone of U.S. naval strike capabilities resides in the 400-odd A-6 Intruder aircraft. The A-6 is capable of carrying as many as six or seven tons of sophisticated ordnance for ranges well in excess of 500 miles. This aircraft is equipped with all-weather navigation and weapon delivery systems and is capable of deep penetrations over land masses at very low altitude under bad weather conditions, using its own integral navigation and terrain-clearance systems.

These heavy attack aircraft are augmented by a larger fleet of lighter A-7 attack aircraft, which are also capable of poor weather operation, with ranges of more than 400 miles and carrying four or five tons of ordnance. In addition, the marines are currently replacing their older A-4 aircraft with the first group of truly operational VSTOL attack aircraft, the British-built AV-8A's, which are capable of carrying two tons of ordnance on missions of roughly 100-mile radius. These VSTOLs are primarily intended to perform ground support missions to the marine amphibious forces. However, they are capable of operating from a variety of large and small carriers and could, if required, perform limited operations from the helicopter pads aboard smaller naval ships.

All Navy and Marine strike aircraft are capable of carrying a broad variety of sophisticated ordnance from low-drag, free-fall bombs to high-accuracy, precision guided munitions, anti-radar missiles, electronic jamming pods, and many different families of "cluster munitions" for use against dispersed targets. They can also deliver a variety of land and sea mines, and the A-6 will soon be equipped with antiship Harpoon missiles. Altogether, these weapons and aircraft present the Western Alliance with a capability for "force projection" which is unmatched by anything currently foreseen for Soviet naval aircraft. It would not be amiss to observe that those aircraft can (or can be wired to) carry nuclear weapons, and that for some time the carriers figured in the primary Single Integrated Operational Plan (SIOP) strike. Presumably, that is why the Soviets invested so heavily in anticarrier warfare.

These strike aircraft are also augmented by highly capable electronic warfare aircraft, the EA-6B, which allow strike forces to penetrate very high enemy defenses with a good chance of suffering only modest attrition. Many authorities believe that U.S. naval aircraft electronic warfare capabilities have consistently exceeded those available to U.S. Air Force tactical aircraft. Moreover, each aircraft carrier includes a small complement (four to six) of tanker aircraft, which are capable of refueling all aircraft in the naval inventory. This permits strike forces to perform even longer-range missions than are possible with their own internal and external fuel provisions. Altogether, these strike forces represent the culmination of roughly forty years of concerted development in ship-based naval aviation, an extremely specialized field which the Soviets probably could not hope to duplicate within a generation.

The air defense capabilities of U.S. naval aviation also appear unique in the world. The F-14 air defense fighter and its Phoenix missile system provide the only manned aircraft in the world capable of shooting air-to-air missiles simultaneously against six different maneuvering enemy aircraft over 75 miles away from the launching aircraft. The Navy will shortly have a total of approximately 500 of these aircraft to use in conjunction with an

SOVIET AND U.S. NAVAL STRIKE AIRCRAFT

This is the only available photograph of the new Soviet swing-wing Backfire bomber now in full-scale production for Soviet naval aviation. It is a long-range, supersonic aircraft capable of launching standoff missiles or conventional weapons and mines. It operates from land bases. (Courtesy U.S. Navy)

The U.S. Navy's all-weather heavy attack capabilities reside in some 300 carrier-based Intruder (A-6A) aircraft (shown above) and their companion electronic countermeasures aircraft, the EA-6B. This aircraft became operational in the mid-1960s and its missions include power projection, mining, and naval counterforce. (Courtesy Grumman Corporation)

equal number of F-4 fighter aircraft. These older F-4's are also capable of all-weather air defense with their fully mature Sparrow missile systems. Derivatives of this basic naval aircraft design have been widely adopted by the air forces of the United States and many other Western Alliance countries. Current planning calls for the eventual replacement of these naval F-4 aircraft with a higher performance and more modern aircraft such as the F-18, which will also be used by the Marines in an attack version known as the A-18.

The fighter forces are supported by airborne early warning (AEW) aircraft that are capable of maintaining airborne orbits several hundred miles from the carriers for several hours. They can track literally hundreds of enemy planes simultaneously and compute automatic intercept information for as many aircraft as the carrier could launch. These E-2C's are as modern as any AEW aircraft in the world and have been sold in limited numbers to Israel.

These air defense systems, together with the variety of antiaircraft missile systems aboard ship, assure the Navy and Marines a very good air defense capability against moderate-sized air raids of any sort. Their weaknesses lie in a somewhat limited capability against certain Soviet air- and ship-launched, long-range antiship missiles. The Navy's and Marines' defenses can be "saturated" if the enemy mounts a large coordinated air raid—although such a raid would require substantial operational precision on the enemy's part.

Ship-based antisubmarine aircraft include both patrol planes and helicopters. The Navy has just finished procuring almost 200 S-3A ASW patrol aircraft capable of search, detection, localization, and attack operations against most known submarine types out to a radius of approximately 300 miles from the task force. The sophistication of their onboard sensor and weapon system is essentially a match for their longer-ranged land-based counterpart, the P-3C.

In addition to these aircraft, the Navy operates approximately 250 ASW helicopters, both from carriers and from smaller ships, including cruisers, frigates, and destroyers. Current models are beginning to age, and the Navy has just recently begun a modernization program to replace existing helicopters with the LAMPS III model, which will not only have extensive antisubmarine capabilities but will also be able to provide over-the-horizon guidance for the Harpoon antiship missiles.

Finally, the Marine Corps has several models of helicopters which are operated from its helicopter ships. These include large troop-carrying versions and smaller troop and command models as well as armed helicopters—all for support of Marine amphibious operations. These same assets, incidentally, can be used for a variety of other conflicts and crisis scenarios—including disaster relief, evacuation of endangered U.S. or

SOVIET AND U.S. CARRIER-BASED FIGHTER AIRCRAFT

The Soviet's first carrier-based jet fighter is shown here hovering over the deck of the *Kiev* during sea trials. This YAK-36 Forger VSTOL is no match for U.S. fighters, but it could give the Soviet Navy an air defense capability against Alliance ASW patrol aircraft. (Courtesy U.S. Navy)

Long-range U.S. naval carrier task force air defense is currently provided by the highly capable and sophisticated F-14A fighter aircraft, shown here in formation with the carrier-based Hawkeye (E-2C) radar warning and control aircraft. Procurement cost of the three aircraft shown was roughly $80 million in 1978. Their prime mission is to shoot down enemy bombers 200-300 miles from the carriers. (Courtesy Grumman Corporation)

Allied personnel, and various "presence" missions. Presumably they are also capable of such tasks as the recapture of hijacked merchant ships. These Marine assets, which are virtually unique in the world, together with their helicopter carriers, provide a substantial capability for the less-than-full-scale conventional war scenarios mentioned in Chapter 1 and are sure to find application in many peacetime-force "presence" roles.

By comparison, the Soviets have a limited ASW helicopter capability, some over-the-horizon missile guidance capability for ship-launched missiles, and some budding jet VSTOL capability in the form of the new YAK-36 mentioned in Chapter 3. The full mission capability of this jet aircraft is not yet known, although it appears to be designed primarily for some air-defense role, presumably against unarmed Alliance naval patrol craft. It will be some years before the Soviets have any number of Kiev-class carriers on which to base these VSTOLs—and many more years before they gain the necessary proficiency in sea-based aircraft operations. Within the next ten years, there is virtual certainty that the Soviets could not afford to risk a fleet-on-fleet battle involving naval aircraft. It is by no means clear at this time that the Soviets even aspire to the development of such a capability; neither could they hope to profit from a war at sea. Nonetheless, the disparity between naval aviation capabilities on the two sides presents a difficult situation should a confrontation at sea develop (perhaps in the pursuit of some lesser intervention objective by both superpowers). This class of scenarios was mentioned in Chapter 1 and will be treated again at the end of this section.

Land-Based Aircraft

The land-based aircraft inventories of the Western Alliance have concentrated almost exclusively on the development of long-range patrol aircraft for ocean surveillance and the conduct of ASW "search and destroy" operations. Most of these aircraft will be equipped with the Harpoon antiship missiles mentioned previously in order to give them a substantial capability against enemy surface ships. Even so, these are relatively low-performance aircraft, incapable of making offensive strikes against defended targets ashore. The 400 P-3, Atlantique, and other maritime patrol aircraft of the Alliance were specifically designed for ocean surveillance and ASW operations only. In these roles it is almost certain that Alliance aircraft, with their extensive surface search radars, sonobuoy data processing equipment, and underwater magnetic detection gear, are vastly superior to anything in the Soviet inventory and can perform their mission at greater distances than Soviet aircraft.

By comparison, over three-quarters of the 800 Soviet land-based naval aircraft, including the new Backfire, have had their genesis as long-range bomber aircraft designed for Soviet strategic long-range aviation. The

SOVIET AND U.S. LAND-BASED ASW PATROL AIRCRAFT

This Soviet IL-38 May ASW/maritime patrol aircraft was photographed over the Indian Ocean during the 1977 Ugandan crisis, escorted by an F-14A from the U.S.S. *Enterprise* (CVN-65). Its ASW capability appears limited. (Courtesy U.S. Navy)

The mainstay of U.S. land-based ASW patrol aircraft forces is the P-3C Orion, shown here launching the Harpoon antiship missile in a recent test. Addition of the Harpoon gives the P-3C, currently the finest ASW aircraft in the world, a substantial antiship capability for the first time. (Courtesy McDonnell Douglas)

designs were later modified and produced for Soviet naval aviation to perform several missions including bombing, inflight refueling, ocean (surface) surveillance, and electronic intelligence gathering. Only the 150-odd May and Mail aircraft appear to have been designed primarily for ASW patrol operations. They are not considered to have nearly the performance (range and endurance) or ASW capability (detection and destruction) of Alliance patrol aircraft.

As discussed in Chapter 4, most of the Soviet naval bomber aircraft are equipped with standoff missiles, and it is reasonably certain that they were initially designed as anticarrier forces. However, these aircraft may now have gained additional missions against shore targets such as harbors and port facilities—particularly the new supersonic Backfire. The equivalent capability in U.S. land-based forces still resides in our Air Force, and similar missions would require the use of the F/FB-111 and the B-52. (As mentioned elsewhere, striking or mining Soviet port facilities would have been an important collateral mission for the B-1.)

Soviet land-based naval aviation has been assigned some missions that are the domain of the U.S. Navy carrier forces and others that are the province of the U.S. Air Force. Of course, strict equivalence in operational capabilities from like force elements on both sides is by no means an end in itself. However, extreme dissimilarities may have some undesirable side effects in making it difficult to constrain a seemingly limited confrontation between naval elements of the superpowers.

For instance, the third class of conventional war scenarios discussed in Chapter 1 cites the possibility of Soviet naval force interposition to deny the United States a capability to resupply a friendly state that is involved in some conflict with a Soviet client-state. Assume that U.S. merchantmen, escorted by one or two older and less capable U.S. frigates, are challenged by a Soviet cruiser which seeks to blockade the receiving port of the U.S.-supported state. If U.S. frigates are not equipped with a ship-to-ship missile, they would probably have to back down or risk relatively certain defeat. United States response to this situation might be to dispatch an aircraft carrier to the scene which has unmistakable ability to sink the Soviet cruiser. The Soviets' response, lacking equivalent sea-based capability, might then be to alert and launch elements of their land-based long-range naval aviation—perhaps a squadron of Backfires. These Backfires might be expected to at least partially damage the U.S. carrier with one or two of their long-range antiship missiles. What is the next step? Would the United States then threaten to send strategic bombers to destroy the home airfield of those Backfires?

This hypothetical scenario only demonstrates how rapidly such a confrontation could escalate. Both the U.S. carrier and the Soviet land-based aviation are unnecessarily large jumps up the escalation ladder. The illustrative confrontation might have been more stable and less dangerous if the United States could have augmented these older frigates with a more capable surface combatant that would have been a match for the Soviet cruiser but not an "overkill." The danger of such rapid escalation may ultimately constrain the use of U.S. aircraft carriers in this type of confrontation and add urgency to developing a greater antiship capability for individual U.S. surface combatants. Better antiship capability may be particularly desirable for U.S. ship classes that may be involved in conflicts less than all-out conventional war.

11
Projected Alliance Technology and Force Requirements

Introduction

This chapter surveys the prospects for improving the naval effectiveness of the Western Alliance through new technology over the next decade and reviews the inherent difficulties in that process. A study of the forces required to perform sealane defense missions concludes the chapter.

New Naval Technology (RDT&E)

The U.S. Navy's expenditures for research, development, test, and evaluation (RDT&E) during 1978 will be in excess of $4 billion, and our NATO partners will probably spend an additional $2 billion. The annual rate of increase for these outlays has exceeded the growth of inflation for many years, and there is no reason to assume that we have reached any sort of plateau in the development of new naval technology. To the contrary, that science appears to have been accelerated by the increasingly visible threat of a worldwide Soviet naval capability.

Near-term improvements will probably benefit most from the West's burgeoning capabilities in electronics and computers—in which the Soviets still appear to lag significantly. Although details remain classified, some general projections can be made concerning technological developments during the next decade and their influence on the composition of naval inventories by the end of the century.

Ocean Surveillance

Satellite surveillance of the surface of the world's oceans—and the air above them—should continue to improve. Basically, the technology required to detect surface ships and aircraft has already been developed. This field will probably involve improvements in processing and the delivery of collected data to military users. Development of multiple sensors such as radar and infrared will probably also be continued as a significant aid in the positive identification of individual ship classes.

Because satellite navigation is already a reality, it appears that these navigation systems could guide "over-the-horizon" missile systems containing homing seekers against individual surface targets with little additional technology. As already projected by Admiral Gorshkov, surface units will only require "strategic placement," while their long-range weapons will provide the "tactical mobility."

The extent to which satellite systems can also be used to detect submarines remains problematical. Although the undersea boats create many detectable disturbances, it is not yet clear that they can be detected from space. It seems more likely that submarines may be detectable from closer to the ocean's surface, but the reliability of this type of detection has not yet been assured.

Major improvements are expected in acoustic detection and processing systems—another area in which the West maintains a substantial lead over Soviet research and development efforts. New varieties of very long linear arrays are known to be under development. Towed arrays have already been discussed, and there are other versions that may be moored or permitted to drift in areas of anticipated submarine traffic. The advent of new communications and relay equipment—again using satellites—may make it possible to perform remote data processing almost instantaneously. These deployable systems will markedly lower the West's current dependence on fixed arrays on the ocean floor, with their cable connections to somewhat vulnerable shore facilities. Of course, there is always a possibility that the satellites themselves may become more vulnerable to attack.

In any event, all naval systems will have to evolve under the assumption that they *can* be detected. Further efforts must therefore go into countering detection systems through such techniques as jamming, deception, decoying, and, of course, attack.

Antisubmarine Warfare

Detection remains the key to antisubmarine warfare. Improvements in both acoustic and nonacoustic surveillance and detection systems will remain fundamental to improvements in antisubmarine warfare. Second only to these will be advances in the "localization" systems that allow the attack to be made with homing weapons. As yet, the radius of action of homing weapons is not as large as the radius of uncertainty associated with the detection. Active sonar systems currently provide the bridge between the two. By using helicopters to deploy weapons to the target area, the delivery time is shortened, thereby improving the radius of detection. In other cases, uncertainties can be reduced by getting more accurate detections or simultaneous detections from separate directions. The towed arrays are helpful in this respect. Nonetheless, technology has not yet permitted the elimination of the "localization" phase as a separate function, with the possible exception of submarine-on-submarine engagements. Either torpedoes with significantly greater area search capability or a more capable helicopter localization system are still sought. Although minor improvements in both are foreseen, a significant breakthrough is not likely in the near future. Unlike antiaircraft warfare, antisubmarine warfare still lacks a highly effective defense against attacking submarines.

One solution to this problem may eventually lie in providing some kind of terminal defense against the submarine's attacking weapons. It might ultimately be possible to attack the torpedo itself, although such a defensive system would be very expensive and possibly impractical, at least in the near future. Another approach would be to deceive or jam the terminal homing and fusing system of the torpedo. An effective system of this type, however, is not expected to evolve in the foreseeable future.

By far the most practical method for defending against submarine attacks seems to be the various mine systems now being developed that can attack the submarine before it reaches its target area. Significant improvements in this field are now under way. Long-lived "intelligent" moored mines that will recognize submarines and launch homing torpedoes when they come within range are now completing development. Current technology also permits the remote guidance of mines to their optimum waiting position in shallow or otherwise constricting waters. Because these mines are virtually undetectable, they are a serious threat to passing submarines.

Antiaircraft Warfare

For many years great emphasis has been placed on the defense of surface ships from attacking aircraft, and the results have been eminently successful. As discussed earlier, the combination of E-2 early-warning aircraft, ship surveillance radars, F-14 aircraft and their Phoenix missile system, and now the new Aegis surface-to-air missile system all provide defense against incoming aircraft. In addition, both the F-14 and the Aegis will make it far more difficult for the enemy to "saturate" the defenses of a large task force.

To a certain extent, the air threat has forced the evolution of large task force operations in which the various ships and aircraft provide each other with protection. The high capability of these mutually supporting task force elements, on the other hand, has forced the Soviets to develop long-range standoff weapons which are vastly more difficult targets for fighter aircraft or surface-to-air missile systems. In recent years, the need for a last-ditch defense against these standoff weapons has been widely recognized in

NEW U.S. NAVAL SHIPBOARD AIR DEFENSE SYSTEMS

The U.S. Navy's new air defense missile control system, Aegis, is shown here in an artist's rendering aboard a nuclear-powered guided missile cruiser. This billion-dollar escort would provide substantial capability against both enemy aircraft and their standoff cruise missiles. (Courtesy U.S. Navy)

This very high speed photograph shows the U.S. Navy's new Phalanx ship defense system (far left) as it destroys an incoming antiship missile in a recent test. Sophisticated "last-ditch" defense systems such as this will be required to enhance the survival prospects of surface combatants. (Courtesy General Dynamics, Pomona Division)

the R&D community and has resulted in the development of weapon systems to cope with this problem. These systems include high-speed guns and missiles that are self-contained in relatively small packages (now being added to navy ships). They can be used aboard small combatant ships and may eventually provide for the self-defense of merchant vessels. These "modular" antiaircraft and antimissile systems will undoubtedly be installed aboard many classes of surface ships in the near future.

Antiship Warfare

For the first time in many years, the new Harpoon antiship missile will provide the United States with a highly capable system for attacking enemy surface ships, large or small, probably exceeding the performance of equivalent Allied systems. Variants to these basic designs will probably evolve for years to come. Far longer range than the current nominal 60 miles is technically feasible, and alternate seekers will almost certainly be developed to broaden the classes of targets that can be hit.

"Mid-course" guidance remains the major limitation on increased standoff performance. Standoff effectiveness will be improved by the new ship-based helicopters, and, as mentioned earlier, may benefit further from satellite navigation. At the same time, Alliance antiship torpedoes are being upgraded to provide additional versatility and performance. In general, the West should have little difficulty in providing a variety of weapons capable of keeping enemy ships at bay.

Electronics and Electronic Warfare

In view of the rapid developments in tiny electronic components, the revolution in electronics appears destined to continue. Simplification in systems design will be a major emphasis. Stationary phased-array radars appear certain to replace the heavier rotating models which now clutter the mast tops. In addition, microcomputers associated with specific functions and equipments will most likely replace the large central computers that are difficult to program and to modify. The increasing significance of the central combat control and information center will, however, require its relocation to more protected spaces below decks.

Shrinkage in electronic components is also producing another important change for ship's weapon systems—it is now possible to build a broad variety of weapons for different applications. Ships, planes, and submarines can be alternate targets for the same basic missile, fired from a common magazine and launcher. This development is producing a substantial increase in the versatility of weapon loading for a given ship. Moreover, the adoption of a standard vertical-launch technique will make possible a more compact and less vulnerable storage arrangement aboard ship. While this factor may detract from the appearance of "fierceness," it can add measurably to combat effectiveness—as well as to the ease of changing weapon loads. As discussed later, it is becoming realistic to visualize the construction of ships whose weapons and fire control systems can be changed from one mission emphasis to another within the space of a few weeks, thereby increasing fleet versatility.

At the same time, growing dependence on electronics brings increased vulnerabilities for both sides. Denying the proper operation of an opponent's electronic systems becomes a goal, and navies will be forced to expand their knowledge to the complexities and subtleties of electronic warfare. Technology must seek to permit operation in electronic silence, to intercept enemy electronic communications, and to create deceptive signals in order to confuse enemy radars and missile seekers. In addition, as the West becomes more dependent on fewer naval and merchant ships, the ability to blind—or at least blur the vision of—enemy detection and homing systems becomes more important. Moreover, these electronic countermeasures must be capable of rapid modification or replacement to keep up with changing technolgy. This represents yet another area where the ability to change a major ship's components on short notice—quite possibly during a war—is of growing importance. Consequently, even though electronic systems are becoming smaller and more versatile, the ship space and weight that must be devoted to countering enemy electronic capabilities is growing larger and more critical. Meanwhile, dependence on highly sophisticated equipment—and the men who can understand, operate, and repair it—is increasing sharply.

Laser Warfare

While most of the efforts in this area are classified, it is now possible to transmit destructive energy by laser beam. Whether or not lasers can be converted to a practical antiaircraft, antimissile, or antiship weapon system within this century remains problematical because of the high power requirements needed for operation within the atmosphere. Laser weapons may therefore have their first application in space.

Mine Warfare

Recent advances in electronics for guidance systems and many different classes of sensors appear applicable to mine warfare. Some, of course, have been applied to the new Mk-60 CAPTOR mine and to the minesweeping equipment of the RH-53D minesweeping helicopters. Nonetheless, the relatively low interest in mine warfare exhibited by the U.S. Navy virtually assures that some new technological opportunities have been neglected for higher priorities. This may represent a technological area where the U.S. Navy could benefit from research and development assistance by other members of the Alliance who are "closer to the problem." Both non-U.S.

U.S. MINE WARFARE ASSETS

The U.S. Navy's Sea Stallion (RH-53D) minesweeping helicopter is shown above towing a minesweeping sled. The U.S. Navy maintains only twenty-two of these aircraft, which were used for sweeping the approaches to Haiphong and the Suez Canal. (Courtesy Sikorsky Aircraft)

Roughly half of the U.S. Navy's current active fleet of ocean-going minesweepers (MSOs) are shown in this photo taken at Subic Bay in 1961. The U.S. Navy will have to depend heavily on Alliance minesweepers if it ever becomes necessary to counter the Soviet Navy's heavy emphasis on mines. (Courtesy U.S. Navy)

NATO countries and Japan might do well to accept this challenge.

Shore Target Attack

For many years, major naval interest has centered on the use of carrier-based aircraft for attacking shore targets with conventional ordnance. As a result, a variety of highly accurate, terminally guided munitions are available for launch from the Navy's attack aircraft. Technology, however, is bringing a rebirth of interest in the use of surface-to-surface missiles, such as the new Tomahawk cruise missile with a conventional warhead, for this attack role. Such tactical cruise missiles should not be confused with the more publicized nuclear cruise missiles included in strategic arms limitation agreements. In addition, there have been major technological advances in the development of guided, homing gun shells. Future ships with a shore attack role will almost certainly be equipped with rapid-fire 8-inch guns, firing laser or radar-guided shells. These guns may also be used against ships and possibly air targets as well.

Both the missiles and the guided shells open up new alternatives for the attack of shore-based targets. While it would be premature to suggest that these weapons could replace manned, carrier-based attack aircraft, there may well be some shore attack missions that could be accomplished by gun or missile fire from a few individual ships instead of committing an aircraft carrier and its escorts to the task. This in turn may start a trend back toward the battleship approach, or, as it is called today, the "strike cruiser." The major virtue of the strike cruiser concept is that it permits the use of more heavily armed—and armored—individual ships in a threatening offensive role, without the involvement of a complete task force. The use of separate attack elements within a numerically constrained navy may become a new trend in naval warfare, if their cost and vulnerability can be kept within bounds.

Ship Design

Many innovations in ship design are under evaluation and preliminary construction. These include hydrofoils, air cushion vehicles, surface effects ships, and twin submerged hulls. All of these concepts provide increased speed or sea-keeping capabilities, but they also entail some penalties in cost, power requirements, and configuration awkwardness. Although some of these specialized designs, such as the hydrofoil, are bound to find applications for critical mission requirements, none of them appears to offer sufficient promise to replace conventional displacement hulls in the majority of Alliance fleets in the foreseeable future.

Similarly, there appear to be no giant strides in the offing for ship propulsion. The use of nuclear propulsion in surface ships remains a

NEW U.S. SHIP DESIGNS

The 230-ton Pegasus is shown here during trials in Puget Sound carrying five of the planned eight Harpoon missiles astern and a 76-millimeter gun on the bow. This 40-kiloton patrol hydrofoil missileship (PHM) is the first of a new class that may find application in U.S. and Alliance navies. (Courtesy Boeing Aerospace Company)

Shown above is an artist's conceptualization of a 3,000-ton surface effects ship (SES) based on recently completed research and development. Ships of this type may find application as specialized high-speed ASW escorts, but are not expected to replace conventional hull ships in the foreseeable future. (Courtesy Rohr Marine, Inc.)

mixed blessing at best. Its installation and manpower costs, as well as its overhaul expenses, are so high that they make its broader application unlikely, despite the obvious advantages in unrefueled range. Gas and steam turbines, powered by fossil fuels of some sort, appear destined to remain our primary propulsion systems for the conceivable future. Composite propulsion systems, using one power source for sustained operations and another for maximum performance, may become more common for certain classes of ships. In addition, the naval application of cryogenics may extend to the use of "superconducting" electric machinery for power transmission. This application of very low temperature electrical systems could eliminate the need for large reduction gears, heavy propeller shafting, controllable (and reversible) pitch propellers, and the in-line mounting of these components within the hull. Significant weight and volume economies for the propulsion system could also result. The penalty, of course, would be the necessity for dependence on highly reliable, damage-resistant, cryogenic systems.

Except in a few areas aboard ship (such as the bridge), there appear to be no major opportunities for automation to reduce crew sizes. Moreover, demands are rising for greater crew space for comfort, and automated equipment almost inevitably seems to require more maintenance personnel—either aboard the ship or elsewhere.

The most important innovation in ship design could be the growing use of modular components. As described subsequently, the natural life spans of various items of equipment aboard ship differ markedly from one another and from the hull itself. The ability to change modules—either to facilitate maintenance or to stave off obsolescence—could be a vital factor in getting the most from a numerically and financially constrained naval force. It might be possible to make greater use of standard hulls and ship's machinery while specializing the sensor and weapon modules to perform different missions. This technique could also serve to economize on Alliance ship construction costs, while still permitting nations to specialize their preferred on-board equipments for nationalistic or operational reasons. Other applications for modules might be in the modernization of fighting ships in Alliance inventories or the preparation of merchantmen for military duties during a period of major hostilities. In any event, the ability to make selective removals and replacements of primary ship system components offers a new versatility in naval design.

Aircraft Design

Since the advent of the jet aircraft, research and development appear to have stressed speed and range, until additional speed is now physically impractical, and additional range appears largely unnecessary. Attention has now shifted to making naval aircraft less dependent on the ships from which they operate by efforts to improve the reliability of parts, increase the electronic "self-testing" of onboard equipments in flight, and eliminate catapults and arresting gear.

As aircraft sizes aboard ship have increased, so have the bulk and complexity of demands on catapult and arresting gear. In an effort to reverse the trend toward larger carriers and fewer aviation-capable ships, the Navy is investing heavily in aircraft technology for vertical and short-takeoff and landing (VSTOL) capabilities. The AV-8 Harrier aircraft provides the first operational VSTOL jet in Navy and Marine history and has clearly demonstrated its ability to work from smaller and less complex ships. Lighter and less fuel-consuming engines, more compact electronics, and higher accuracy ordnance combine to make VSTOL aircraft more practical than in the past, even though their cost and complexity have considerably increased.

How far the Navy will be able to move toward an all-VSTOL force depends on many factors, possibly the least of which is technology. The major development questions are more concerned with relative cost and complexity and the practicality of operating broadly dispersed, highly sophisticated equipment. Obviously, the rate of development of VSTOL-capable ships is also a major consideration. In view of the long remaining lives of the existing carriers and planes, one cannot realistically project a major conversion to an all-VSTOL force within the next two decades.

Even though many questions remain, powerful forces are at work to change carrier aviation: (1) The same technology that permits the extension of range and endurance for carrier-based planes is equally, if not more, applicable to land-based aircraft. Eventually, some tasks now performed by carrier aircraft may be performed equally well from land; (2) The advent of terminally guided gun munitions and long-range tactical cruise missiles may supplement tactical aircraft in some attack roles, just as the more capable surface-to-air missiles may take over more of the antiaircraft defense from manned fighters; (3) The helicopter is also improving in speed and payload; it, too, may supplant some of the roles currently accomplished by fixed-wing aircraft; and (4) The cost and vulnerability of large carriers may diminish the range of scenarios in which they are useful.

The current period may prove to be the zenith of carrier-based fixed-wing aviation. It may well be followed by the distribution of some of the traditional missions of these aircraft among other systems and the allocation of the remaining missions to VSTOL aircraft operating from smaller ships. The result might be a more nearly even apportioning of the functions of the Navy among its components, a reduction in dependence on a few key ships, and a more versatile fleet.

NEW ALLIANCE SHIP-BASED AIRCRAFT DESIGNS

The first British-designed-and-built (for the U S. Marine Corps) Harrier VSTOL attack aircraft is shown here in trials in Dunsfold, England. The U.S. Marine Corps now operates several squadrons of these aircraft both ashore and at sea. New VSTOL designs may provide the U.S. Navy with increased versatility. (Courtesy U.S. Navy)

A mock-up of the U.S. Navy's new Light Airborne Multi-Purpose System (LAMPS III) is shown above. This new helicopter will provide the fleet with greatly improved ASW and antiship surveillance and targeting capability. New electronics and helicopter technology such as this will provide more elements of the fleet with a significant aviation capability. (Courtesy Sikorsky Aircraft)

Submarine Design

Progress in attack submarine design will be primarily evolutionary, including the use of higher-strength materials for lighter hulls or lower operating depths and further advances in machinery quieting. Sonar performance is not likely to undergo major improvements in the near future. Radical design changes in SSBNs may be possible if their missiles are carried outside the pressure hull and if missile ranges permit a return to nonnuclear propulsion for more restricted deployments under shore-based defenses.

The major determinant of attack submarine size and performance is the propulsion system, and current power plants are not likely to change much over the next decade, since they work very efficiently now. Within the next decade or so, however, it should be possible to evolve a new generation of considerably smaller and more efficient nuclear power plants for submarines. In this event, we may be able to look forward to a new class of smaller attack submarines which, by virtue of lower cost, might enable the Alliance to increase its total acquisitions. Meanwhile, the continued development of improved nonnuclear submarines—by other members of the Alliance if not the United States—would appear worthwhile. They can still be usefully applied to such missions as minelaying, the attack of other nonnuclear submarines, barrier operation, harassment of surface shipping, and various clandestine operations. Under certain conditions they might even escort merchant convoys if the major threat were from Third World submarines.

In conclusion, no "breakthroughs" in technology are forecast that would rank with the advent of nuclear propulsion or solid state electronics. But a steady progress is predicted in the refinement of systems and technologies already in hand. In many ways, this evolution will increase the complexity of naval combat. In a few areas, however, the principal advantage of improved technology may be to increase the versatility of the West's limited navies and forestall the obsolescence of its capital ships.

Nothing on the technological horizon would tend to alter the current judgment that the major threat to friendly navies is the enemy submarine, while enemy aircraft with standoff missiles represent a significant danger, and enemy surface combatants constitute only a modest threat. That relative ranking is likely to persist throughout the remainder of this century.

Problems in Adopting New Naval Technology

Some critics see U.S. and Alliance naval developments as too little and too late. The implication is that naval society exhibits an institutional resistance to adopting new technology that may not be found in other military organizations. Those who proffer this thesis often cite the U.S. Navy's initial reluctance to accept nuclear propulsion (until Admiral Rickover and a forward-looking Congress forced it through), gas turbines, and even roll stabilizers for ships. These critics generally believe current Alliance naval difficulties can be alleviated by more rapidly adopting the latest technology.

Navies are also criticized for failing to recognize the need to change their mission priorities and for a propensity to "fight the last war." The fact that the battleship was perpetuated and early acceptance of the aircraft carrier forestalled is a prime example of the validity of this criticism.

Yet others believe that many of the Navy's difficulties arise from the acceptance of too much technology too soon, resulting in sophisticated weapon and support systems that do not work very well and are difficult to maintain. These critics note the early failures of the "3T" surface-to-air missile systems and the Navy's current intention to move toward all-VSTOL aircraft for use on ships.

All three criticisms are partially justified by experience. They illustrate the inevitable problems associated with modernizing naval forces in a period of rapid technological advances and changing military balances.

The real problems are fundamental, stemming from the fact that major warships take a long time to build, are acquired in small numbers, and last for many years. Modern submarines, for instance, have an expected life of twenty to thirty years in active duty, after requiring two or three years to design and another two to four years to build—at a rate of only one to six per year. Major surface combatants such as aircraft carriers or nuclear-powered cruisers may require even longer to design and up to six years to build, and their service lives may be extended to forty years. Their "production rates" tend to be, at best, one per year and are frequently only one every two to four years. Moreover, these ships and submarines undergo major overhaul and equipment modernization only once or twice during their useful lives.

In contrast, the useful life of the weapons and other equipment that a particular navy vessel carries may be only ten to fifteen years, after a development cycle of roughly five years. To make matters worse, a technological component—particularly in the case of electronics—may only operate five years before it is outdated by a more capable device. The merging of a new component into a new technology weapon system to use aboard a new or existing class of naval platforms thus becomes extraordinarily difficult. It virtually guarantees the evolution of a naval force equipped with dissimilar systems of varying obsolescence—none of them built in sufficient numbers to remove their inevitable development "bugs." This condition is symptomatic of all peacetime navies.

PROBLEMS IN ADOPTING NEW NAVAL TECHNOLOGY

Navies are criticized for failing to recognize the need to change their mission priorities and for a propensity to "fight the last war." The perpetuation of the battleship, like the U.S.S. *New Jersey* (BB-62) above, is used as an example of this tendency. Others believe that many of the Navy's difficulties arise from the acceptance of too much technology too soon, resulting in sophisticated weapons that are difficult to maintain. (Courtesy U.S. Navy)

These timing difficulties are aggravated by budget and funding problems as well as the limited availability of shipbuilding facilities. Budget processes strongly discourage sudden changes in a single appropriation account such as "shipbuilding." Even if Congress becomes convinced of the need for a sudden spurt in construction (as it did at the time of the original Polaris decision), it is unlikely that the required shipbuilding capacity would be available. This would be particularly true if the new demands came after several years without large-scale construction. Hence, "serial production" of a given ship class may continue over ten to fifteen years.

Finally, maintaining a year-by-year naval balance is virtually impossible if the opposition is able to conceal its intentions until the end-products begin to take shape on the ways or in the outfitting docks. For instance, the Soviets might be able to devote four or five years to a new naval project before we could "see" it for the first time. It might then take three or four years more to discover whether the project is developmental or ready for serial production. If we seek funding for a counteractive system development only after we can demonstrate to Congress that serial production is under way, then, in all probability, we can look forward to a ten- to twelve-year lag before we can redress the perceived imbalance.

It is therefore virtually impossible to just keep up with a secretive opponent in naval capabilities. The time required to gather intelligence is too long. One must set out to achieve the capabilities one selects or be doomed to lag behind. Even then, a counterpoise for the navy that eventually emerges for the adversary's efforts may not be created. For example, the Soviets undertook to develop the Moskva-Leningrad-class of ships, only to find that the Polaris no longer provided the threat it had to counter. On the other hand, we appear to have authorized the construction of supercarriers without recognizing the rate of development of Soviet anticarrier forces—at least, in part, because of their unexpected reallocation of long-range strategic aircraft, coupled with the development of capable antiship missiles and satellite ocean surveillance systems. In any event, the *Moskva* and *Leningrad,* and our own nuclear-powered supercarriers, will be in our respective inventories well into the twenty-first century.

In short, the extensive lead-times, long lives, small numbers, and very high investment costs of individual naval systems will continue to make it extremely difficult for either side to assure that it will always match the capabilities of the other.

The following proposals are partial solutions to all of these problems:

- Naval research and development should pursue a broad variety of paths allowing the Navy to hedge its bets against unexpected Soviet developments.

- Naval craft should be built to perform a variety of roles in order to prevent their obsolescence if their primary function is no longer needed.
- Naval craft should be designed with the anticipation that there will probably be major changes in their onboard systems during the lifetime of the hull. This is far easier said than done when the weapon and equipment systems are virtually an integral part of the ship's design and construction.
- Naval craft should be produced in sufficient quantity to provide a continuous stream of new capabilities with systems that have been exercised sufficiently to work out the inevitable "bugs."

Within realistic budget expectations it is not possible to satisfy all four of these desirable conditions. Funds for RDT&E must compete with production and operational dollars. Unit costs must compete with production quantity. Acceptance of the latest technology must compete with the high operating and maintenance costs implicit in few-of-a-kind systems. It is no wonder that there has been no simple solution to this dilemma—or one that would satisfy the diverse interests within the Defense Department or the Congress.

Every nation's navy must be a compromise among many conflicting demands and pressures. This is no reason to believe that naval developments in the United States are any more constrained by "inherent" or "institutional" problems than those in any other country—including the Soviet Union. The basic issue, then, is whether or not we have selected the most appropriate naval missions and whether we can maintain the mission objectives somewhat independently of the decisions of our opponents. This study focuses on the need to keep the sealanes open and the level of national and Alliance effort that should be devoted to this objective. As we have repeatedly pointed out, this would probably *not* be the immediate objective in a major war with the U.S.S.R.; the immediate objective would be command of the seas. We should seek solutions that are at least partially independent of Soviet mission emphasis and that will minimize the costs if the Soviets do not follow the path we expect for their naval objectives and capabilities.

Two other aspects of the introduction of new technology deserve mention. One is the increasing difficulty of getting young, largely unskilled volunteers who can operate the highly sophisticated new equipment. This problem affects the U.S. Navy as well as the rest of the Alliance. The other is the growing problem of retaining standardizatiion and interoperability between the U.S. Navy and the fleets of the less technologically advanced Allies. Both of these limitations deserve careful attention. There is some indication that the U.S. Navy has begun to field equipment that cannot be operated by its own personnel, to say nothing of its allies. It may well be time to redirect some of our technological planning toward the development of more basic equipment that is easier to operate and maintain and more "transferable" to our allies.

Characteristic Forces Required for Sealane Defense Missions

The neutralization or destruction of Soviet naval capabilities during a large-scale war would have several distinct aspects, requiring different types of sensor, weapon, and delivery systems. The most advantageous mode of warfare would be to seek out and destroy elements of Soviet naval power before they could be brought to bear against Allied forces. This would involve heavy strikes against the Soviet ship and submarine home ports and the airfields customarily used for naval long-range aviation. As discussed elsewhere, however, defenses around these major installations would be extraordinarily heavy. The Soviets have spent more than a generation perfecting their defenses against penetration of their home waters by U.S. aircraft carriers or their airspace by U.S. aircraft. The extent to which such strikes might actually be carried out would depend on many factors—including the availability of U.S. Air Force elements.

The second class of warfare against Soviet naval assets would involve attempts to exact heavy attrition as their units deploy from home bases or return for rearming and refurbishment. As previously discussed, Soviet home ports are relatively scarce and, with the exception of Petropavlovsk in the North Pacific, require the navigation of constricted and sometimes shallow water. Likewise, their long-range aircraft would, in general, be forced to fly near landmasses held by nations friendly to the United States in order to get within reach of our fleet elements and critical ports in any of the major contested ocean areas. This would permit the effective Alliance use of air, surface, and undersea barrier operations.

One obvious mission for U.S. nuclear attack submarines (SSNs) would be against submarines and surface vessels attempting to gain access to the Atlantic, the Mediterranean, or the Pacific from their home ports. In addition to these manned weapon system barriers, there would be extensive opportunities for floating and bottom mines to make passage extremely hazardous for both surface and undersea vessels. For example, the new U.S. CAPTOR mine will provide moored homing torpedoes capable of waiting for months, if necessary, before being released to attack their targets. Other systems are under development that will permit friendly submarines to sow their mines in relatively safe waters, after which they will propel themselves to more optimal locations (e.g., in harbor mouths) to await their prey.

As far as we can foresee, the continued improvement of antisubmarine barrier operations appears to offer the best means of assuring or regaining the security of the seas against Soviet naval forces. The numerous Soviet submarines are the most difficult offensive naval systems to detect, classify, and localize. Antisubmarine operations are made simpler when the search areas are limited, when the enemy subs must generate certain speeds and noise levels in transit to or from operational areas, and when the ASW detection systems can remain relatively stationary and free of self-generated noise. Convoy defense against submarines represents a far less effective operation for much the same reasons: the convoy and its escorts, with their sensors, must maintain a reasonable forward speed, while the attacking submarine can remain quiet. In other words, barrier operations place the ASW systems in their preferred posture and the enemy submarine in its least-advantageous situation, while convoy defense operations place the ASW detection systems at a disadvantage and permit the enemy submarine to operate in its least-detectable mode. The most important use for Alliance attack submarines, both nuclear and operational, then, appears to be for counterforce against Soviet submarines through barrier operations.

The third offensive aspect of the naval campaign would involve "search and destroy" missions where Soviet naval elements are expected to be active. These operations could be carried out by Alliance submarines, surface units, or long-range, land-based naval patrol aircraft (P3C), possibly augmented by suitable Air Force craft such as the B-52 and the FB-111. The availability of Air Force elements would depend on other considerations and mission priorities. Nonetheless, these aircraft are capable of operations well over a thousand miles from home and are equipped with sensors and weapons that give a reasonable probability of kill against any ships they detect. Their major limitation, of course, is their vulnerability to Soviet air defense systems. While the sea-based air defense systems do not yet present a very serious threat (as discussed earlier), it would be extremely hazardous for our patrol aircraft to penetrate within reach of Soviet land-based interceptor forces. Areas where Soviet ships and submarines can be protected by interceptors are relatively restricted, however, and the P-3 aircraft in both U.S. and Allied hands presents a significant threat to Soviet naval forces beyond the reach of Soviet air defenses.

In any event, it would be necessary to defend Allied task forces and convoys from attack by Soviet offensive forces that had not been destroyed nearer their home bases. This threat would consist primarily of submarines and, to some extent, long-range aircraft. The following sections discuss the forces required to defend Allied shipping both on the open ocean and approaching destinations near the Soviet homeland.

Convoy Defense System Characteristics

Since convoys are generally accepted to be of lower value as enemy targets than major Alliance task forces at sea, their defenses can be somewhat more Spartan. While task forces have the capability to detect, challenge, and "defend in depth" against any enemy aircraft, submarines, or surface ships within approximately 300 miles, the defense of shipping convoys will probably be considered adequate if it provides good protection against enemy units within about 30 miles of the convoy center. The latest American warship designed for this type of convoy protection is the Perry-class frigate, the FFG-7, an austere design which entered service in 1977. This design specifically sacrifices maximum speed, growth potential, and sonar capability to achieve lower costs and larger numbers of escort ships. They are not suitable for escorting aircraft carriers. For defense against penetrating aircraft, they are equipped with the Standard missle (SM-1), with launchers which can also fire the 60-mile Harpoon missile against attacking surface ships. The main defenses of the Perry, however, are in its antisubmarine capabilities. These include the new tactical towed-array (passive) sonar system (TACTAS) as well as a limited active-passive hull-mounted sonar as a backup system. The TACTAS system is expected to provide outstanding detection—and reasonable localization—capabilities while traveling at convoy speeds. Each Perry-class frigate will also carry two LAMPS III helicopters capable of converting the TACTAS detections into kills with their own sonobuoy systems and air-launched torpedoes. The LAMPS III helicopters are also capable of providing over-the-horizon guidance for the Harpoon antiship missiles, and they should provide a good capability against attacks from small surface patrol craft. The overall cost of these frigates is roughly $150 million exclusive of their helicopters. The current Navy shipbuilding plan calls for the construction of more than seventy of these craft "at a rate consistent with shipyard capacity," according to Secretary of Defense Rumsfeld's Fiscal Year 1978 Annual Report. If the Navy were to increase its emphasis on convoy defense forces, these ships would presumably be strong candidates for construction.

In areas of increased submarine threat, it is possible to augment the ASW capabilities of these escort ships by providing a moving ASW screen ahead of the convoy. This would entail P3C aircraft dropping patterns of sonobuoys and attacking with air-dropped homing torpedos. Such augmentation, however, is probably only worthwhile in heavily traveled sealanes where concerted opposition is expected—such as in the North Atlantic or the seaward approaches to Japan. Attack submarines offer another capable means of defending convoys from attack. Their use in this role appears unlikely, however, owing to their relatively high cost and their seemingly more appropriate use as offensive sub-killers far from the sealanes themselves.

As explained in Chapter 13, these convoy defenses will not by any means assure that there will be no losses in transit on the high seas. Reducing the

Alliance Technology and Force Requirements

enemy submarine threat is—and will remain—an exercise in cumulative attrition as the submarines pass through the various barriers, screens, and escort defenses. Major purposes of these convoy escorts, however, are to increase the price paid for attacking shipping and hasten the elimination of the submarine threat.

The number of escorts assigned to convoy will obviously depend on their availability, the size of the convoy, the value of the cargo being shipped, and the anticipated threat along the route. Up to eight escorts have been used in the past, with the World War II average being around seven. In general, the provision of adequate sonar detection capability has been the critical factor in determining the number and pattern of the escorts. To the extent that TACTAS increases submarine detection range, it might be possible to consider using fewer escorts—such as four or five. The inclusion of the capable LAMPS III helicopters, because of their speed and radius of action, would also appear to reduce the number of escorts required to assure that detected enemy ships can be destroyed. The problem, of course, is that the submarines are also becoming more capable. Hence, it is by no means clear that required escort levels would be significantly reduced.

Sealane "Sanitization" System Characteristics

There are areas of the seas where continuous freedom from enemy submarine and surface ship penetration is much more desirable than a simple moving defense for ships in transit. Such "sanitized" areas in the Atlantic might well include the western approaches to the English Channel and Mediterranean, where heavy warship and cargo vessel traffic may be expected. In this case, continuous, extensive surface and underwater surveillance would be required, and land-based aircraft or attack submarines could be used to prosecute detections.

The success of these operations would depend on the availability of adequate sensor systems to keep track of all ships and submarines transiting the area. Existing long-range passive sonar listening systems, such as the SOSUS, would be useful for this purpose. The major limitations of these systems are the time required to install them and the relative ease with which they can be rendered ineffective by dragging the bottom with cable cutters.

New developments are well under way in the United States that will provide alternative underwater surveillance systems, according to the FY 78 congressional statements of the director of Defense Research and Engineering. One is a slow-speed, towed-array system designated SURTASS, and the second is a relatively easily deployed semipermanent sonobuoy. Apparently one or both of these systems will be able to transmit acoustic data to shore stations for extensive processing and read-out, thereby minimizing the onboard complexity of the system equipment and easing the problems of replacing a lost or malfunctioning unit.

These "sanitized" sealanes or areas would generally be within reasonable distance of friendly territory. Consequently, the reactions to submarine or surface ship detection could be performed by a variety of shore-based aircraft or coastal patrol craft. At the longer ranges, such reaction forces might include P-3 or equivalent Alliance aircraft, while at shorter distances it would be possible to consider the normally carrier-based S3A aircraft or LAMPS III helicopters. If, as discussed elsewhere, the Soviet emphasis were on attacks against the ports as opposed to fleet-to-fleet combat, it might be fruitful to enhance our defenses of the European port approaches with any "surplus" carrier-based antisubmarine, antiship, and antiaircraft weapon systems deployed ashore. Such an alternate assignment of some of our carrier-suitable assets might more directly "support ground force operations"—to use the Soviet naval parlance. Whether such an approach is practical remains hotly disputed within the Working Group.

Sealane "sanitization" systems—and other naval counterforce operations—depend heavily on shore-based installations and facilities that are becoming increasingly vulnerable to long-range Soviet naval aviation. These include not only the P-3 bases themselves, but also the various smaller sites that collect, process, and transmit vital ocean surveillance information concerning both surface ships and submarines. The defense of these installations seems certain to become increasingly important.

Potential for Merchant Ship Self-Defense

As discussed in Chapter 2, the need for shipping during a protracted conflict with the Soviet Union—either before or after initial nuclear exchanges—might vastly exceed U.S. (and Alliance) naval convoy defense capabilities within either a "500-ship" or a "600-ship" navy. In a direct wartime confrontation between U.S. and Soviet forces outside the NATO arena, the requirements for U.S. naval forces might be even more crucial, owing to the absence of a meaningful NATO contribution. The question, then, is whether it would be practical in the foreseeable future to provide commercial ships with weapon systems during open hostilities. Four factors seem to combine affirmatively.

First, the number of cargo and tanker vessels available to the West has grown tremendously and will continue to expand in the foreseeable future. The wide availability of these ships provides a possible "hiding" place for essential cargoes. This approach might become acceptable if there were a reasonable chance that these ships could defend themselves to some extent—and have their crews rescued (by helicopter) in case they went down.

Second, the average size of commercial ships has grown until many of them dwarf their military counterparts in displacement. For example, the average of the current Liberian-registered merchant fleet of over 2,100 ships is approximately 39,000 tons, or ten times the average tonnage of Allied shipping losses during the first three months of World War II (see Chapter 13). There are now less than two dozen ships in the U.S. Navy of that size. Consequently, it should be much easier to install weapon systems aboard these merchant ships than it was during World War II, when the vessels were much smaller.

Third, technology is making contemporary weapon systems more compact and self-contained. For instance, the Harpoon antiship missile can be released from a self-contained deck launcher readily mountable on a 60- to 70-foot patrol craft displacing less than 100 tons. The SM-1 surface-to-air missile system, while considerably larger, still requires less volume than twenty standard shipboard containers and should be available for vertical launch from a relatively simple "drum" containing over fifteen "rounds" which can be installed as a single unit. The LAMPS helicopter can also be operated from shipboard, and a four to six helicopter unit can be contained (including crew living quarters) within forty-two containers of standard dimensions.

Last, and probably most important, underwater surveillance and submarine detection equipment is now becoming relatively independent of the vessel that tows it, instead of being an integral part of the hull. This circumstance has made it possible for the seventeen new-construction Coast Guard cutters (roughly 150 feet long) to have facilities for towing the new TACTAS mentioned earlier and for onboard signal processing equipment. Later versions of TACTAS might benefit from remote processing—as is planned for the SURTASS system previously discussed. Eventually, a single processor may be able to utilize the data collected by several towed arrays in a convoy.

These sensors and weapons systems are relatively independent of the ship's basic structure, and they can easily be adapted for many of the older U.S. and Alliance naval escort vessels. As a result, high "ship effectiveness" can be maintained in the naval reserves for only a fraction of what it costs for active forces. Of course, properly motivated and trained reservists are essential to this concept. This weapons adaptation process also helps to avoid the construction and peacetime operation costs of a larger active fleet. (The fifteen-year operating expenses of a navy ship are roughly equal to its construction costs.) Equipping merchantmen with advanced weapon systems should have substantial appeal for U.S. forces as well as for allies who operate large commercial fleets but find it difficult to maintain a large defense establishment. Whenever possible, the converted merchant ship escorts should operate with active naval combatants that would provide command, control, and communication functions not available to the converted vessels.

The adaptability of these new weapon systems provides an opportunity to pit another segment of Western economic strength against the Warsaw Pact's military prowess. Even if a large number of merchant ships cannot be armed for complete ASW operations, it may be possible to increase the chance of sinking any submarine that attacks an Allied ship. The advent of high-performance homing torpedoes enables the merchant ship to shoot back when hit by the attacker's torpedo. The attack itself provides the means of detecting the presence of an enemy submarine (see Chapter 13). Modern technology should make armed merchantmen visibly more formidable than their World War II counterparts.

The concept of mobilizing the civil sector during times of crisis or impending large-scale war is by no means a simple one. First, the civilian component of the nation involved would have to be agreeable. There are at least superficial indications that organized labor in some Alliance countries, unlike the situation in the United States, might resist such actions. Second, a great deal of advance planning, organization, and training would be essential. An effective mobilization plan would take substantial time, thought, and cooperation. Fortunately, most nations of the Western Alliance have enough skilled manpower with prior military experience to make such an effort practical. Third, special legislation might be required to permit the timely activation of reservists and conversion of civil assets. Fourth, considerable expenditure would be needed during peacetime to assure the availability of the necessary components (such as ASW helicopters or towed sonars). This requirement is bound to engender stiff competition between the active military budget and the financing of a mobilization potential. Most military commanders can be expected to favor the former. Nations accepting the concept of mobilization, then, may well need to establish a separate agency—within or outside their defense organization—with its own source of revenue that cannot migrate to the support of the active forces.

In summary, providing merchant ships with self-defense and mobilization capabilities in time of war may prove to be more practical than developing a considerably larger navy to protect convoys. But the program would require substantial planning, manpower, and money.

12
Anticipated Constraints on the U.S. Navy Budget

There are very few problems associated with the naval balance that could not be solved eventually by increasing the budget of the U.S. Department of the Navy. Therefore this chapter explores the possibilities of enlarging the defense budgets or the Navy's share of them over the next few years. Since the maximum long-range planning within the U.S. Government covers only the next five years, this discussion will be limited to that period.

There would appear to be five different ways to allocate more funds to the construction of a larger and more capable navy. These include:

- Increasing the Defense Department share of federal expenditures;
- Increasing the Navy's share of defense spending;
- Increasing the procurement share of the Navy's budget;
- Increasing the ship construction share of the Navy's procurement budget;
- Changing the "mix" within the Navy's procurement program.

These five options are discussed in the ensuing sections as well as the implications of significantly lowering the Navy's procurement budget in accordance with the proposal of the Carter Administration.

Increasing Defense's Share of Federal Spending

Over the past twenty years, Defense's share of federal expenditures as a percent of total outlays has dropped steadily—even during the height of the war in Southeast Asia. This is shown in Table 12-1. In 1957, national defense accounted for over 55 percent of federal spending, while in 1977, this category had dropped to 24 percent. Projections for the next five years are prepared annually by the Congressional Budget Office (CBO). While

TABLE 12-1

MAJOR COMPONENTS OF ACTUAL FEDERAL SPENDING AS A PERCENT OF TOTAL OUTLAYS
FY 1957 - FY 1977

	1957	1962	1967	1972	1977
National Defense	55.1	47.2	43.7	33.3	24.0
Benefit Payments to Individuals	20.3	25.4	25.3	36.7	44.4
Grants to State & Local Govts.	2.7	4.3	6.4	9.0	11.6
Net Interest	7.0	6.4	6.5	6.7	7.0
Other Federal Operations	14.9	16.7	18.1	14.2	13.0

TABLE 12-2

MAJOR COMPONENTS OF PROJECTED FEDERAL SPENDING
AS A PERCENT OF TOTAL OUTLAYS
FY 1976 - FY 1982

	1976	1977	1978	1979	1980	1981	1982
National Defense	24.6	24.0	24.2	24.8	25.0	25.0	24.8
Benefit Payments to Individuals	45.6	44.4	43.2	44.1	45.2	46.2	47.3
Grants to State & Local Govts.	11.0	11.6	11.9	11.0	10.3	9.9	9.6
Net Interest	7.3	7.0	7.6	7.6	7.4	6.9	6.6
Other Federal Operations	11.5	13.0	13.2	12.6	12.3	12.1	11.7

Ref: CBO Staff Working Paper, July 1977: Update to Five-Year Budget Projections FY1978-1982.

the forward planning arrests the precipitous decline of the past twenty years, it is not likely that the Defense share of federal expenditures will increase under any conditions short of a major war. The projections for the next five years are shown in Table 12-2.

The basis for these projections, however, may well be optimistic. There are many reasons to anticipate real pressure for further reductions in Defense spending. This is indicated indirectly in Table 12-3, which shows the projected spending trends in outlays within all the major federal budget categories. In order to limit federal outlays to the levels indicated and permit defense spending to rise at 3 or 4 percent a year in real terms as shown, it is assumed that there are virtually no other "new initiatives" for federal spending than those already on the books. For instance, annual spending for natural resources, environment, and energy shows virtually no growth other than for anticipated inflation. Community and regional development, as well as revenue sharing and general-purpose fiscal assistance actually show declines. Health, education, and social security benefits are increased only to the extent required by existing statute. In short, these projections are virtually the minimum conceivable expenditures for human resources, based on current legislation. If, in reality, spending in these areas is going to increase over the next several years, then

Anticipated Constraints on the U.S. Navy Budget

TABLE 12-3
OUTLAY PROJECTIONS BY FUNCTION: BY FISCAL YEARS, IN BILLIONS OF DOLLARS

Function	1976 (Actual)	1977 (Third Concurrent Resolution)	1978	1979	1980	1981	1982
National Defense (050)	90.0	100.0	111.2	121.6	130.6	139.5	148.3
International Affairs (150)	5.1	6.8	7.0	6.9	7.1	7.6	7.9
General Science, Space and Technology (250)	4.4	4.4	4.6	4.9	5.2	5.6	5.9
Natural Resources, Environment, and Energy (300)	11.3	17.2	19.3	20.1	20.1	21.4	22.0
Agriculture (350)	2.5	3.0	3.1	2.8	3.4	3.7	4.0
Commerce and Transportation (400)	17.2	16.0	19.5	19.8	20.6	21.2	22.2
Community and Regional Development (450)	5.4	8.4	10.7	9.6	8.0	8.1	8.7
Education, Training, Employment, and Social Services (500)	18.2	22.7	27.3	27.8	28.1	28.5	28.9
Health (550)	33.4	39.3	44.9	50.6	56.2	64.6	73.0
Income Security (600)	126.6	141.3	147.2	158.8	173.0	187.5	203.5
Veterans' Benefits and Services (700)	18.4	18.1	19.4	20.4	21.1	21.7	22.5
Law Enforcement and Justice (750)	3.3	3.6	3.8	3.9	4.1	4.4	4.6
General Government (800)	2.9	3.5	3.7	3.9	4.2	4.3	4.6
Revenue Sharing and General Purpose Fiscal Assistance (850)	7.1	9.9	9.7	9.1	8.5	8.6	9.2
Interest (900)	34.6	38.0	44.2	47.0	48.7	49.6	50.8
Allowances (920)	—	0.8	1.1	1.2	1.1	1.2	1.3
Undistributed Offsetting Receipts (950)	-14.7	-15.6	-16.0	-17.3	-17.7	-18.6	-20.1
Total	365.6	417.45	460.5	491.0	522.2	558.9	597.3

Ref: CBO Staff Working Paper, July 1977: Update to Five Year Budget Projections FY1978-1982

the difference will have to come out of currently projected defense spending, or total federal expenditures must rise accordingly.

The extent to which federal spending can exceed the levels projected is primarily a function of the level of deficit spending acceptable to the Congress and the public. Consequently, the CBO also makes projections of the size of the federal deficit under varying economic conditions. The major economic problems facing the current administration appear to be inflation and unemployment—the latter caused partly by the continuing influx of women into the labor market and, more basically, by the "baby boom" of the 1950s.

President Carter has established a goal of reducing unemployment to a

TABLE 12-4
ALTERNATE APPROACHES TO REACHING 4.5% UNEMPLOYMENT BY FY 1982

By Federal Tax Reductions
(Billions of Dollars)

	1977	1978	1979	1980	1981	1982
Current Policy Outlays	417	460	491	522	559	597
Current Policy Receipts	348	400	457	520	590	660
Required Tax Reductions, Assuming:						
Moderate Nonfederal Demand	—	—	-14	-58	-100	-134
Strong Nonfederal Demand	—	—	-14	-36	-49	-70
Deficits (-) or Surplus, Assuming:						
Moderate Nonfederal Demand	-70	-60	-48	-60	-69	-72
Strong Nonfederal Demand	-70	-60	-48	-39	-18	-8

By Increased Federal Spending
(Billions of Dollars)

Required Fed. Spending, Assuming:						
Moderate Nonfederal Demand	—	—	9	41	74	105
Strong Nonfederal Demand	—	—	9	26	37	55
Deficits (-) or Surplus, Assuming:						
Moderate Nonfederal Demand	-70	-60	-44	-44	-43	-42
Strong Nonfederal Demand	-70	-60	-44	-29	-7	7

Ref: CBO Staff Working Paper, July 1977: Update to Five-Year Budget Projections FY1978-1982

level of roughly 4.5 percent by 1982. Barring an extremely strong economic recovery and a previously unattained strength in nonfederal demand, there are two basic government approaches to stimulating the economy: one is to reduce taxes; and the other is to increase federal spending. Table 12-4 illustrates the CBO estimate of the federal deficit using each approach if the nonfederal demand trend stays "moderate" over the next five years. Taxes would have to be reduced by a total of $134 billion by 1982 to achieve the lower unemployment rate, or federal spending would have to be increased by $105 billion. In the former approach, the deficit would increase to $72 billion in that period. Even if a uniquely strong nonfederal demand should develop, either approach produces a barely balanced budget by 1982.

Unfortunately, raising employment through increased spending for defense is substantially less effective than other means because of the relatively high labor skills demanded in defense production. Consequently, either approach will result in mounting pressures for reduced defense spending. In short, increased defense spending over the next few years can readily be equated with increased unemployment and failure to reach the president's stated economic objectives. These assumptions concerning national priorities make it highly unlikely that the defense fraction of federal expenditures would grow very much in the near future, short of a highly visible increase in threat. This means that past Defense five-year spending projections have probably been somewhat optimistic—and they did not allow much growth in naval resources.

However, recent public opinion polls have shown increased concern by Americans over the possible inadequacies of their defense posture. Congressional response to public concern often lags by as much as four or five years. Yet congressional deliberations over the FY 79 defense budget during calendar year 1978 have indicated—for the first time in many sessions—that Congress may be willing to add funds to the president's request rather than to delete 2 to 4 percent as in the past. At the time of writing of this study, the majority of the congressionally proposed defense add-ons have been for the Navy's budget. If these recent congressional actions are a valid response to changing public concern, then there is some possibility that U.S. defense spending may in fact increase in future years, at some slight sacrifice in other national domestic objectives. In this case, additional funding for the Navy may exceed that granted to the other military departments. This Working Group would strongly support such increased naval spending.

Increasing the Navy's Share of Defense Spending

It is commonly believed that the Defense Department divides the pie evenly among the three military departments. Actually, this is not the case. Table 12-5 is a representative summary of spending by Defense (as proposed in its FY 78 budget, unamended). The Department of the Navy receives the largest fraction, and the Army the smallest. In part, of course, the Navy's share is the largest because it has significant strategic force expenditures as well as conventional force expenditures (like the Air Force). It also develops and maintains its own "army" and its own "air force." The Navy's "army," the Marines, is roughly one quarter the size of the Army, while its tactical "air force" is almost as large as that of the Air Force.

There is, of course, intense budget competition among the services; each believes its mission is the most vital to the nation's security, and each can demonstrate that it is inadequately financed to maintain properly modernized and ready forces. In recognition of this situation, the Defense Department has been regularly asking the Congress for increases in the procurement and operations and maintenance accounts, as well as in the research and development accounts—which have remained stable at roughly 10 percent of Defense spending for many years. By Defense calculations, it will require approximately 3 percent "real growth" (beyond inflation) to maintain active forces at their current strength and force levels. The new administration appears willing to accept some level

TABLE 12-5
DISTRIBUTION OF DEFENSE SPENDING—PROPOSED FY78 BUDGET

Total Obligation Authority—Millions $

Department of the:

Major Account	Total	Army	Navy	Air Force	Defense Agencies
Military Personnel	26,193[1]	10,129	8,419	7,644	
Retired Pay	9,036				9,036
Operations & Maintenance	34,169	9,525	11,764	9,805	3,075
Procurement	35,143	6,342	15,378	13,066	358
Research & Development	12,044	2,626	4,239	4,381	798
Military Construction	1,494	618	470	372	34
Family Housing, Mil. Asst. + Unassigned Contingencies	5,071	100	32	35	4,904
Total	123,150	29,339	40,303	35,302	18,206

Total Personnel

Military Personnel	2,090,000	790,000	728,000[2]	572,000	
Civilian Personnel	1,030,000	378,000	317,000	256,000	80,000
Total	3,120,000	1,168,000	1,045,000	828,000	80,000

Notes: 1: Of this, 24,142 is for active forces; 2,051 for Reserves.
2: Of this, 536,000 is Navy; 192,000 is Marine personnel.

of growth, as indicated by the FY 79 budget submittals. This is also consistent with the CBO budget projections shown in Figure 12-3.

If the Navy's budget were to be increased by, say, $2 to $5 billion annually—in order to build a larger navy, for instance—these funds would have to come from the Army or Air Force. Either of these transfers would almost certainly require a reduction in the numbers of active forces retained; a cut from the sixteen active army divisions or from the twenty-six active air force tactical fighter wings. This procedure would require a reversal of the recent national decisions to restore these forces to their 1964 (pre-Vietnam) level. Unfortunately, there has been no equivalent national decision on needed naval force levels, which have now been allowed to drop to roughly half of their 1964 levels (see Chapter 7) with no explicit rationale for why this smaller force is adequate to retain the security of the seas against an increasing naval threat.

It is beyond the scope of this paper to dissect the Defense budget in detail or to recommend specific force allocations. Estimates of cost savings associated with specific force reductions are complicated by two additional factors: (1) The Defense Department already benefits from the economies of shared support resources; i.e., the addition of the last army division or the last air force wing was not as costly in support requirements as the establishment of the first unit, and consequently the "savings" by eliminating the last unit are not as large; and (2) modernization programs are sufficiently far behind that the elimination of a division or a wing would not proportionately reduce the procurement requirements of the Defense Department for many years. Of course, many other temporary costs are associated with force reductions (such as relocation of remaining personnel, separation costs, etc.) which make the first year savings almost nonexistent. Nonetheless, in the considered judgment of the Working Group, it would not be unreasonable to estimate the following long-term annual savings asssociated with marginal force reductions—assuming that the units mentioned are transferred from an active to a reserve status:

- Transfer one army armored division to reserve status: Save $350 million/annually;
- Transfer one air force fighter wing to Reserves: Save $150 million/annually.

A "balanced" force reduction might reduce the Air Force by one wing for every army division eliminated. Hence, it might be possible to transfer approximately $500 million from the Army and Air Force to the Navy annually for each "division + wing" transferred from active to reserve status. As will be shown in this chapter, however, the elimination of several divisions and wings would be required to provide the funds for a substantially larger navy.

The real issue is whether it is in the nation's best interests at this time to shrink our conventional land forces—and their air support—in order to provide a larger conventional navy. The vast bulk of our conventional forces are earmarked for use in the NATO theater to preserve what most qualified observers consider a marginal balance of conventional ground forces with the Warsaw Pact forces, even when more U.S. light divisions are "heavied up" with armor. Given the high priorities assigned by the current administration to improving the European ground force balance, and the increased emphasis on "standardization" of our forces with those of our NATO allies, it would appear particularly inappropriate to suggest significant reductions in our NATO commitments ashore in an effort to increase our NATO commitment to securing the sea lines of communication. Certainly, it would appear desirable to achieve equivalent force reductions by the Warsaw Pact rather than making such force reductions unilaterally.

The only other alternative within a fixed level of defense spending would appear to eliminate completely those Army and Air Force units that are also available for contingencies elsewhere in the world. Such a step would appear to be in direct contradiction to the president's recently reported directive to Defense to improve the posture of American light forces available for global contingencies.

In short, all U.S. force levels are probably marginal, and a proposal to reduce our ground forces to build up our amphibious and naval capabilities would seem starkly inappropriate. However, if defense spending were authorized above current levels, it would appear desirable to halt or reverse the current decline in naval forces while holding constant the present Air Force and Army strengths and modernization rates.

Increasing the Procurement Share of the Navy's Budget

If it is inappropriate to seek increases in Navy funding through Army or Air Force cuts, then it may be wise to look within the Navy's own budget for possible reallocations.

Table 12-5 illustrates the major annual expenditures of each military department. Within each service there is intense competition among these various accounts for additional funding. Virtually all of the services' funds are spent in these four categories.

Military Personnel

Twenty-five percent of the service budgets are spent on military personnel pay and allowances. Personnel expenditures ultimately determine U.S. force levels.

Operations and Maintenance

Thirty percent of service funds are spent to operate and maintain forces and equipment. Expenditures in this account are primarily associated with current "readiness."

Procurement

Roughly 34 percent of service funds are spent for the procurement of major "end items" of military hardware. It is through this account that force modernization is accomplished and equipment is provided to our fighting forces to equal or better that available to our potential adversaries. Underfunding in this account produces gradual force obsolescence, as will be discussed in the following section.

Research, Development, Test, and Evaluation (RDT&E)

Approximately 10 percent of service funds are spent on the development of new technology and military capabilities for the future. There is considerable concern that the Soviets are applying substantially greater resources to their future military capabilities than the United States. This belief is beginning to generate pressure for increased U.S. RDT&E spending—and for the elimination of duplication of RDT&E efforts among the members of the Western Alliance in order to stretch our own RDT&E dollars.

Compared to the defense totals, the Navy spends proportionately more for procurement and less for military personnel than the average for all services, while spending roughly the same fractions on R&D and Operations and Maintenance (O&M). In fact, the Navy's procurement share is already larger than that of any other service, and its RDT&E spending appears to be marginal in view of the many diverse systems that must be created for operations across the spectrum of naval missions at sea, in the air, and across the shore. Increases in Navy spending for procurement would most likely have to be drawn from military personnel or O&M accounts. This does not appear practical for at least two reasons: (1) Additional naval forces would probably require more, rather than less, military personnel; and (2) among the services, the Navy has been singled out in recent years as possibly less "ready" for action than the others because of overdue ship overhaul and aircraft maintenance. Recent budget revisions imposed by the Carter Administration have forced a shift of naval funding away from procurement into the O&M account to improve naval readiness.

For these reasons, the Navy cannot be expected to derive any significantly increased procurement funding from within its own budget. There may even have to be some reductions in procurement spending, both to improve the condition of existing equipment and to develop new generations of equipment. Even with a larger defense budget and an increased naval budget, it is unlikely that a greater fraction of naval spending could properly be devoted to procurement.

Increasing the Ship Construction Share of the Navy's Procurement Budget

The Navy's procurement budget must be spent on a variety of hardware, from ships and submarines to aircraft, missiles, and torpedoes—as well as combat vehicles and other items for the Marines. The distribution of procurement funding in the typical fiscal year of 1978 is shown for each of the military departments in Table 12-6. In that year, the Navy proposed to spend almost half as much as the Air Force on aircraft, as much as the Air Force on missiles and ordnance, almost a third as much as the Army on combat vehicles and weapons, and as much as the Army on electronics and communications equipment. There were also plans to spend $6.5 billion on ship and submarine construction. These budget requests were subsequently amended (downward) by the incoming administration, but not enough to make a significant difference to this analysis. The predominant expenditures, between which some trades might be made, are tactical aircraft and ships. The missile expenditures are large but inescapable because of the Navy's need to procure Trident missiles to replace Poseidon missiles and for its new class of strategic submarines, as well as more capable air defense missiles for their combatants. (The air force missile procurement account is unusually low at this time because it is "between" procurements of the Minuteman III and the newer "MX" replacement.)

To explore whether the Navy's procurement funding for ships and aircraft is possibly out of balance, it is most convenient to generalize the problem and estimate how much must be spent each year to keep the proposed constant force levels suitably modernized for "steady state" conditions. This can be done by estimating how many of each type of ship or aircraft will make up the Navy's inventory objective, estimating each item's useful life and replacement cost (in FY 78 dollars), and determining how much should be budgeted annually in each category. This is done in Table 12-7 for a nominal "500-ship navy" and a 3,250-aircraft naval "air force." The results indicate that the average navy ship today costs $400 million and may be expected to last twenty-nine years. On this basis, the Navy should be spending roughly $7.2 billion for construction of 18 ships annually. Navy aircraft, on the other hand, cost roughly $17.5 million each and have an expected life of eighteen years. This requires that at least $3 billion be spent annually on 180 planes of various types. At the moment, however, the Navy is buying aircraft primarily at the high end of its cost spectrum and consequently spending more than "normal" for this

TABLE 12-6

PROPOSED MAJOR PROCUREMENTS FOR FY78 (UNAMENDED)
(Millions $)

| | | Department of the: | | |
Item	Army	Navy	Air Force	Total
Aircraft	665	3700	8652	13017
Missiles	657	1999	1909	4565
Ships	--	6493	--	6493
Combat Veh./Wpns./Torpedos	1799	508	--	2307
Ordnance/Trucks/Equip.	1450	526	507	2483
Electronics/Commo. Gear	834	955	573	1362
Other Procurement	937	1197	1425	3559
Total	6342	15378	13066	34785

TABLE 12-7
GENERALIZED ANNUAL NAVY PROCUREMENT REQUIREMENTS

System & Category	Force Level	Useful Life (yrs.)	Yearly Buy	Average Unit Cost ($M)	Yearly Procurement ($M)
Ships	(500)				
Submarines	(130)				
SSBNs	40	25	1.6	1000	1600
SSNs	90	25	3.6	400	1440
Aircraft Carriers	(20)				
Strike Carriers	12	40	0.3	2000	600
Amphibious Opns.	8	32	0.25	800	200
Surface Combatants	(180)				
Cruisers	30	30	1.0	750	750
Destroyers	75	25	3.0	500	1500
Frigates/Escorts	75	25	3.0	150	450
Other Ships	(170)				
Amphibious Ships	60	30	2.0	100	200
Small Combatants	10	20	0.5	40	20
Support Ships	100	36	2.75	160	440
Total/Average, Ships	500	29 yrs.	18.00/yr.	$400M	$7200M
Aircraft	(3250)				
Ship Based	(2850)				
Combat Aircraft	2300	17	130	15	1950
ASW/AEW Patrol	300	19	16	25	400
ASW Helos	250	15	17	10	170
Shore Based	(400)				
ASW/Recce/Patrol	400	25	16	30	480
Total/Average, Aircraft	3250	18 yrs.	179/yr.	$17.5M	$3000M

purpose, while it is spending a little less than "normal" on its ships. Over the long run, however, this process would be expected to average out. More serious is the fact that for many years the Navy has been buying neither 18 ships nor 180 aircraft per year. This situation has led to the current problem of dwindling forces. There is no simple way for the Navy to transfer, say, $2 billion from aircraft to ship procurement without substantially reducing the size—or capability—of its "air force." The addition of one "average" ship would require the elimination of about twenty-three "average" aircraft.

In short, the distribution of procurement funding between ships and aircraft appears approximately right, given the force levels projected for each and the level of sophistication demanded. The Navy's current attempts to arrest the spiraling cost of its aircraft are illustrated in the development of the F-18 as a companion to the F-14, which costs almost twice as much. Even so, there is little hope that future aircraft procurements can be reduced sufficiently to provide significant additional funding for ship construction.

Three sidelights to Table 12-7 may be of interest. First, the Navy, like the other services, procures equipment to last a long time. There is no allowance for the replacement of any capital equipment before it wears out. In short, there is virtually no "arms race" in which active equipment is discarded and replaced prematurely in order to "keep up with the threat." All military planning assumes this capital equipment will remain competitive with Soviet weapon systems until it wears out.

Second, the Navy's total investment in major weapon systems is staggering. At today's prices, the replacement value of the Navy's nonaviation equipment is roughly $200 billion and of its "air force," roughly $60 billion. Given all the other items procured and operated by the Department of the Navy, its total replacement cost must be considerably in excess of $300 billion. Without question, the navy is forced to stretch the life of its current equipments as much as possible.

Third, the same type of calculation can be used to develop the annual ship and aircraft procurement budgets required by all the other nations of the Western Alliance. Collectively, they could maintain another "600-ship navy" and a 1,000-aircraft naval air arm for roughly $5 billion in shipbuilding and $1 billion in aircraft procurement annually. This would provide 180 diesel submarines, 10 LPH-sized carriers, 250 destroyers and frigates, 60 amphibious ships, 100 support ships, 500 helicopters, and 500 land-based patrol aircraft on a continuing "steady-state" basis. Since the cumulative defense spending of all other Western Alliance nations is approximately 80 percent as large as that of the United States alone, it should not be unreasonable for them to devote 60 percent as much to their naval forces. In the short term, however, Alliance naval procurement would have to be somewhat higher to "catch-up" with advancing obsolescence.

The numbers of Table 12-7 only apply for "steady state" conditions on

NEW LOWER-COST U.S. NAVAL DESIGNS

Shown above is an artist's sketch of the U.S. Navy/Marine F-18 carrier-based fighter and attack aircraft. It is intended to provide the "low" component of the Navy's "high-low" mix of jet fighters, while the F-14A is to provide the more capable and more expensive "high" component. (Courtesy U.S. Navy)

The Perry-class frigate (FFG-7 shown above) has been designed to provide a lower-cost convoy escort that can be built in larger numbers than more sophisticated and expensive ships like the Spruance-class (DD-963) destroyers. (Courtesy Bath Iron Works)

an annualized basis—i.e., when current forces are suitably modern and of the desired size and when annual funding is adequate to maintain that size and modernity. But since the Navy has been procuring neither 18 ships nor 180 aircraft each year for the past several years, then some force aging is inevitable, and force levels must eventually decline unless there is a sudden infusion of additional funds. The Navy has already fallen below its prescribed complement of 500 ships, and its aircraft inventory is somewhat below the desired 3,250. Additional procurement funds will be needed in both areas to restore the specified force levels or unit costs will have to be reduced substantially.

A decision to create a "600-ship navy" over the next fifteen years would necessitate additional procurement funds for ten years. For instance, if the Navy should seek to increase its fleet size from 500 to 600 ships with the same ratio of ship types it now has (a 20 percent increase in each type), then $40 billion over the next ten years would be required (in FY 78 dollars), or $4 billion annually. This could not even be accommodated within the Navy's budget if its planners gave up *all* of their aircraft procurement for ten years. On the other hand, if the Navy were to increase its active fleet by 100 escorts only (with a proportionate increase in support ships), then about $18 billion would be required over ten years, or $1.8 billion annually. Even this could only be accommodated by reducing the naval "air force" by more than half.

Changing the Mix within the Navy's Procurement Program

As indicated in Table 12-7, the unit costs of the various ships that make up the "500-ship navy" cover a spectrum from $2,000 million to $40 million. Changing the mix of ships within the total, then, would make possible many different kinds of navies with varying sizes and capabilities. A navy centered around supercarriers and their antiaircraft and antisubmarine escorts will have the greatest ability to project airpower against distant land targets. It will also be the smallest navy within a given expenditure ceiling. Navies primarily optimized for ASW work or for amphibious operations will be less capable of projecting airpower against opposition but will be able to hunt and kill more submarines or simultaneously deliver more amphibious forces to a distant beachhead. They would be significantly larger navies in terms of total ships. In the extreme, the same level of funding could be applied to an all-coastal navy of small combatants. In this case, one might be able to devise a "3,000-ship navy" within the same budget constraints. Any nation's actual navy is the result of complex compromises among missions, budget limitations, and desired capabilities. Perhaps the least valid measure of overall capabilities is the number or tonnage of its ships.

Table 12-8 presents two illustrative fleet compositions that require annual procurement funds essentially identical to the "current mix" shown in Table 12-7. One fleet would move in the direction of costlier, higher-capability ships, such as carriers and cruisers, while the other would favor a numerically larger fleet of less costly ships, emphasizing frigates and attack submarines. The first is a "400-ship navy," the second a "600-ship navy." Because the most significant variation between the two is in the number of aircraft carriers, there are also important differences in the allocation of procurement funds for ship-based aircraft. Further, some tradeoff is assumed between shore-based and land-based aircraft, such that the fleet with the smaller number of strike carriers has the larger number of shore-based aircraft.

The purpose of Table 12-8 is not to present a preferred alternative to the one the navy is currently pursuing; it simply indicates that navies of broadly differing capabilities can be achieved by changing the mix within a relatively constant—and constrained—procurement budget. Other alternatives can be drawn from Table 12-7. For instance, halving the number of SSBNs—or preferably, halving their cost—would allow the *doubling* of the number of cruisers, or a 33 percent increase to sixteen large strike carriers plus their combat aircraft. On the other hand, a 50 percent increase in support ships (to compensate for a dwindling overseas base structure) could require a 50 percent reduction in frigates and escorts. Halving the number of large cruisers, on the other hand, could double the number of ships and carriers available for amphibious operations. In yet another variation, a 50 percent reduction in destroyers could be used to increase by 50 percent the number of nuclear attack submarines.

This simplified analysis demonstrates that there is broad room for variation in the composition of the future U.S. Navy within relatively limited procurement budgets and that it may not be necessary to press for increased funding for the Defense Department or for the Navy. The basic issue remains one of deciding what missions will be of highest priority in the future and then beginning to shape a navy in that direction. In any case, we will never be able to afford a navy that could perform all of its potentially desirable missions simultaneously. The primary justification for larger naval ship construction expenditures, and hence a larger defense budget, would probably be to allow the conduct of more missions simultaneously. For instance, if the objective is to perform more peripheral or contingency operations without reducing the NATO deterrent, more amphibious and escort ships are probably justified. But to perform more offensive operations while still defending the sealanes against Soviet attack during a NATO war, more aircraft carriers may be appropriate. If we wish to hedge against greater vulnerability of surface ships, then a larger SSN and patrol aircraft fleet may be warranted. Even a 50 percent increase in the

TABLE 12-8
ALTERNATIVE ANNUAL NAVY PROCUREMENT REQUIREMENTS

System & Category	Higher Mix	Current Mix	Lower Mix
Ships	(400)	(500)	(600)
Submarines	(120)	(130)	(140)
SSBN's	40	40	40
SSN's	80	90	100
Aircraft Carriers	(25)	(20)	(20)
Strike Carriers	16	12	8
Amphibious Opns.	9	8	12
Surface Combatants	(125)	(180)	(255)
Cruisers	40	30	20
Destroyers	60	75	60
Frigates/Escorts	25	75	175
Other Ships	(130)	(170)	(185)
Amphibious Ships	50	60	60
Small Combatants	0	10	25
Support Ships	80	100	100
Average Ship Cost	$500M	$400M	$300M
Annual Procurement Cost	$6755M	$7200M	$7340M
Aircraft	(3800)	(3250)	(3000)
Ship-Based	(3500)	(2850)	(2500)
Combat Aircraft	2800	2300	1800
ASW/AEW Patrol	375	300	200
ASW Helos	325	250	500
Shore-Based	(300)	(400)	(500)
ASW/Recce/Patrol	300	400	500
Average Aircraft Cost	$16.5M	$17.5M	$17.5M
Annual Procurement Cost	$3430M	$3000M	$2790M
Total Annual Ship & A/C Cost	$10185M	$10200M	$10130M

size of the U.S. Navy would probably not permit the execution of all possible missions simultaneously.

This analysis has omitted any consideration of the Reserve Fleet or possible wartime conversions of commercial ships to military tasks. In fact, such additional capabilities are virtually "free," from the standpoint of this analysis, of budget trends. The inherent issues for decisions in this area are related to conversion time, readiness, utility, and effectiveness—not to budgetary limits.

Reducing the Navy's Procurement Budget

The foregoing analysis assumed an average total naval aircraft and ship procurement budget of $10 billion annually in constant FY 78 dollars. If this figure is substantially reduced, then even a "low mix" procurement

TABLE 12-9
**"STEADY STATE" SIZE OF U.S. NAVY FLEET AND AIR ARM
AS A FUNCTION OF ANNUAL SHIP/AIRCRAFT PROCUREMENT**
(Ships/Aircraft)

Annual Ship/Aircraft Procurement (FY 78 Dollars)	Higher Mix	Current Mix	Lower Mix
$ 6B	240/2300	300/2000	360/1800
$ 8B	320/3000	400/2600	480/2400
$10B	400/3800	500/3250	600/3000
$12B	480/4600	600/3900	720/3600

program will produce a substantially smaller and much less capable U.S. naval force. While an almost infinite variety of programs could be postulated, it will suffice to demonstrate the point using the proportionalities given in Table 12-8.

Table 12-9 indicates the ultimate "steady state" size of the U.S. fleet and air arms for different total procurement levels for the current, higher, and lower mixes postulated previously. While this calculation is highly theoretical, it nonetheless demonstrates the need for a long-range commitment to a substantial shipbuilding and aircraft program in order to maintain a viable U.S. naval force, particularly if it is assumed that the U.S. Navy should be able to confront the Soviet Navy without extensive Alliance support. Our allies must establish equivalent programs to maintain their own contributions to the security of the West.

An $8 billion annual procurement for ships and aircraft will not support a "500-ship navy" even at the lower mix, while a $6 billion per annum procurement would support only a "300-ship navy" at the current mix. There is little question that a continuing naval procurement budget of approximately $10 billion (in FY 78 dollars) is essential for the maintenance of an adequate U.S. contribution to the naval strength of the West and that even more procurement funds could well be spent to increase U.S. unilateral naval capabilities (see Chapter 9).

Summary

The United States cannot realistically expect to achieve a larger or more capable naval force within current defense spending levels unless some quality is traded away for greater quantity. Annual aircraft and ship procurement expenditures of less than $10 billion (in FY 78 dollars) would continue the past decline in naval force levels at the currently accepted quality-quantity mix. Continued expansion of Soviet naval power and national recognition of the increasingly unfavorable superpower force balance may soon lead to higher U.S. defense budgets—as a result of figures proposed by the Executive Branch or increases voted by the Congress. A substantial fraction of any such increases could profitably be devoted to strengthening our naval forces.

13
Quantifying the Sealane Defense Problem

Introduction

Previous chapters have dealt with the systematic development of the Soviet Navy since World War II; the need of the Western Alliance to use the seas during periods of peacetime, crisis, and conflict; and the growth in naval capabilities of both sides. By virtue of geography, economics, and politico-military commitments, the West is more dependent on the seas than the Soviets. Each side assigns missions to its naval forces that reflect these differences. One major U.S. naval mission is to ensure continued access to the seas under a variety of international conditions, while a likely mission for elements of the Soviet Navy is to deny this access.

As chief of U.S. Naval Operations, Admiral James L. Holloway, 3rd, defined "sea control" as "the capability to use those portions of the high seas essential to our national interests. This includes the capability to deny their use for purposes hostile to ourselves or our allies."[1] Given the current balance of superpower strategic nuclear capabilities and the distribution of naval forces between the Soviets and the West, the achievement of sea control by the Alliance—or sea denial by Soviet forces—must become a relative matter. In the classic sense, total freedom of the seas may not be achievable either prior to or following a major conventional or nuclear war with the Soviets by either side.

Under circumstances less than major war between the superpowers, the retention of freedom of the seas by either side (given their present navies) must be achieved by the acquiescence of the other. A challenge to either side could result in a confrontation, and its outcome would depend primarily on the level of naval and other military assets that each side was willing or able to commit to the resolution of the issue at hand. During a major military confrontation, the choice of action and the outcome would depend largely on the mission assignments given the opposing forces, the duration and geographic focus of the conflict, and the availability of bases. For the foreseeable future, neither side appears to have sufficient forces, naval or otherwise, to thoroughly intimidate the other in all situations.

If the Soviets should elect to threaten Western Alliance sea lines of communication, they would have extensive naval resources for that mission. The Western Alliance—or the United States alone—would then be forced to apply substantial seapower to the defense of those SLOCs in order to keep them open. Regardless of the units deployed, however, substantial attrition among merchant ships and naval escorts should be expected. Like most interdiction battles, an anti-SLOC campaign would most probably be a war of attrition—for both sides.

The primary purpose of this chapter is to examine the plausible range of shipping casualties that might be expected during an anti-SLOC campaign and to explore various means for reducing friendly losses and for increasing damage to the enemy in such a campaign. Alternative means for limiting the destruction sustained during the crucial early stages of a major conflict are discussed. The possible impact of the use of nuclear weapons as part of the anti-SLOC campaign is also treated briefly.

The ensuing analysis is in the context of a major superpower conflict focused on NATO Europe. This has been the classic scenario used for the development of both U.S. and Allied forces, although it is certainly not the only plausible one or necessarily the most critical for U.S. force requirements. Several other conflict scenarios could place different demands on the United States depending on applications of Soviet forces, degree of Allied participation, and geographic dispersal of the SLOCs and their supporting naval bases.

At one end of the spectrum, an enemy might undertake a relatively low-level but long-term interdiction campaign directed at seaborne commerce. One example might be a submarine campaign to cut the SLOCs traveled by oil tankers—from the Persian Gulf to North America, Western Europe, or Japan. Another variation might be either a low-level or intense war at sea without simultaneous action on land, using either conventional or nuclear weapons. This scenario developed in the late 1960s out of recognition of the growing Russian naval power coupled with our increasing need to use the seas on the one hand, and on the other, of the greater danger of nuclear escalation of any land conflict between the United States and the Soviet Union. Nearer the other end of the spectrum is the possibility of a major Russo-American confrontation outside the NATO area—say, in the Middle East or the North Pacific—where the lesser forces involved might be more than offset by the greater distances and the absence of military support from our allies.

To assess the implications of any of these scenarios, it is important to understand the dynamics of the interaction of U.S. and Soviet naval forces.

Quantifying the Sealane Defense Problem

Studies done by and for the Navy explore the direction such campaigns might take. The vast majority of them contain classified information, but other sources are available, such as testimony before congressional committees by Department of Defense personnel, articles in military journals, and unclassified studies sponsored by such nongovernmental organizations as the Brookings Institution and the Center for Naval Analyses. The lessons of World War II can also be instructive. These and other unclassified sources can yield a pertinent picture of what an anti-SLOC campaign might involve. They form the basis for the analysis which follows.

Past Experience: The World War II Battle of the Atlantic

U-Boat Effectiveness

The German World War II U-Boat campaign against Allied shipping in the North Atlantic is often reviewed for its relevancy to current conditions.[2] Although the predictive value of lessons learned from World War II is a matter of opinion, the naval experiences of that period have had an effect on subsequent planning for protection of seaborne commerce and deployment of forces. A variety of analyses suggest that the dynamics of conflict during the first sixty to ninety days of any future war could be similar to early phases of World War II—if we dispatch our shipping and the Soviets deploy their submarines.

At the beginning of the war in 1939, Germany possessed 57 U-Boats, of which 49 were operational.[3] Of the operational boats, 31 were deployed—17 in the North Atlantic and 14 in the North Sea. The average building rate was 2 submarines per month. (An overview of German submarine strengths is presented in Table 13-1.) By contrast, the United Kingdom had 279 surface vessels, of which 271 were assigned to Atlantic or Mediterranean commands.

That German subs were the primary means for sinking Allied merchant ships is evident from Table 13-2. U-Boats accounted for nearly 70 percent of the tonnage sunk during the war. The German campaign against merchant ships was accompanied by attacks on combat vessels as well. But emphasis was obviously placed on merchantmen. In addition to sinking more than 2,800 commercial vessels, U-Boats also sunk 50 Allied warships.[4] U-Boat losses during the first three months of the war are particularly interesting. (Table 13-3).

Considering the small number of U-Boats in 1939, the results are consistent with present Defense studies which show that shipping losses early in a major war would be heavy. (More will be said about this later in this chapter.)

TABLE 13-1
GERMAN OPEN OCEAN SUBMARINES—WORLD WAR II

	1939	Jun. 1940	Mar. 1941	Dec. 1941	Jul. 1942	Jun. 1943	May 1944	Apr. 1945
Force Level	30	27	54	200	350	385	400	350
Built[a]		15	60	234	434	612	862	1042
Sunk[a]		18	36	64	114	256	455	689
Average Building Rate (Subs/mo.)		2	5	19	29	18	23	15
Average Number Subs @ Sea		6	10	30	57	104	61	39

[a]Cumulative.

Ref: George R. Lindsey and S. W. Roskill, *The War at Sea, 1939-1945*, vols. 1-4 (London: Her Majesty's Stationery Office, 1960).

TABLE 13-2
ALLIED MERCHANT SHIP LOSSES FROM ENEMY ACTION, BY CAUSES: TONNAGE (SHIPS)

Year	Submarine	Aircraft	Mine	Warship Raider	Merchant Raider	E-Boat	Unknown	Total
1939 (4 months)	421,156 (114)	2,949 (10)	262,542 (78)	61,337 (15)			7,253 (4)	755,237 (221)
1940	2,186,158 (471)	580,074 (192)	509,889 (201)	96,986 (17)	366,644 (54)	47,985 (23)	203,905 (101)	3,991,641 (1,059)
1941	2,171,754 (432)	1,017,422 (371)	230,842 (111)	201,823 (40)	226,527 (44)	58,854 (29)	421,336 (272)	4,328,558 (1,299)
1942	6,266,215 (1,160)	700,020 (146)	104,588 (51)	130,461 (31)	194,625 (30)	71,156 (23)	323,632 (223)	7,790,697 (1,664)
1943	2,586,905 (463)	424,411 (76)	108,658 (37)		41,848 (5)	15,138 (6)	43,177 (10)	3,220,137 (597)
1944	773,327 (132)	120,656 (19)	95,855 (28)	7,840 (1)		26,321 (13)	21,630 (13)	1,045,629 (205)
1945 (8 months)	281,716 (56)	44,351 (6)	93,663 (28)			10,222 (5)	8,869 (10)	438,821 (105)
TOTAL	14,687,231 (2,828)	2,889,883 (820)	1,406,037 (534)	498,447 (133)	829,644 (133)	229,676 (99)	1,029,802 (632)	21,570,720 (5,150)
Percent of Total Loss	68.1 (54.9)	13.4 (15.9)	6.5 (10.3)	2.3 (2.0)	3.8 (2.6)	1.1 (2.0)	4.8 (12.3)	100

Ref: George R. Lindsey and S. W. Roskill, *The War at Sea, 1939-1945*, vols. 1-4 (London: Her Majesty's Stationery Office, 1960).

Quantifying the Sealane Defense Problem 341

TABLE 13-3
ALLIED MERCHANT SHIP LOSSES
FROM GERMAN U-BOAT ACTION

	Tonnage	Ships
September 1939	153,870	41
October 1939	134,807	27
November 1939	51,589	21
	340,275	89

Ref: George R. Lindsey and S. W. Roskill, *The War at Sea, 1939–1945*, vols. 1-4 (London: Her Majesty's Stationery Office, 1960).

Countering the Submarine Threat

The value of convoying as one means of conducting antisubmarine warfare was a major "lesson learned" from World War II. From January to May 1942, the U-Boat campaign was directed primarily against ships sailing independently (Table 13-4)—i.e., without convoy protection. The overall exchange ratio of merchant ships sunk (by U-Boats) to U-Boats sunk was 12.8:1. The following year the emphasis shifted against convoys (Table 13-5: January to May 1943), and the exchange rate fell to 2.6:1. During the last twelve months of the war, the score averaged 0.6 merchants destroyed for each German submarine sunk. The rate of loss of ships sailing in ocean convoys for the entire war was 0.7 percent. The overall loss rate was at least twice as great for unescorted ships. The dramatic turnaround brought about by convoying (and other ASW techniques) was due primarily to the fact that after 1943 convoys sailed with adequate escort forces (Table 13-6). In December 1942, the U.S. had no destroyer escorts. However, by one year later, 224 were commissioned into the Atlantic Fleet.

Although most studies of German and Allied naval interactions focus on the effects of convoying and the buildup of Allied surface combatants, the important contribution of Allied intelligence activities should not be overlooked. The German naval historian Jurgen Rohwer believes that Allied success in breaking the German code was a major factor in reducing merchant vessel losses and in increasing submarine losses. This view is also reflected in Anthony Cave Brown's book *The Ultra-Secret*. Good intelligence would have enabled Allied forces to reroute convoys away from areas with deployed submarines while providing ASW forces with information as to their location. In recent years, considerable information has been made public on the positive contribution of code-breaking to the Battle of the Atlantic.

In summary, past experience provides valuable insights into the sea control operations. Although technical advances in antisubmarine warfare and improvements to the attack submarine have changed the operating environment, many studies suggest that the dynamics of opposing forces have not dramatically altered since World War II—at least for conventionally-powered torpedo attack submarines against slow-speed

TABLE 13-4
U-BOAT CAMPAIGN ON THE EAST COAST OF AMERICA
(January-May 1942)

Month	Allied Ships Sunk in Convoy By U-Boats	Allied Ships Sunk in Convoy Total	Allied Independently Sailed Ships Sunk By U-Boats	Allied Independently Sailed Ships Sunk Total	Total Ships Sunk	U-Boats Sunk By Convoy Forces	U-Boats Sunk By Other Forces	U-Boats Sunk Total
January	3	9	48	69	69	4	5	9
February	9	16	67	78	94	2	0	2
March	0	8	88	98	106	5	4	9
April	4	11	69	104	115	1	3	4
May	13	24	111	119	143	1	5	6
Total	29	68	383	459	527	13	17	30

Ref: George R. Lindsey and S. W. Roskill, *The War at Sea, 1939-1945*, vols. 1-4 (London: Her Majesty's Stationery Office, 1960).

TABLE 13-5
U-BOAT CAMPAIGN ON THE ATLANTIC CONVOY
(January-May 1943)

Month	Allied Ships Sunk in Convoy By U-Boats	Allied Ships Sunk in Convoy Total	Allied Independently Sailed Ships Sunk By U-Boats	Allied Independently Sailed Ships Sunk Total	Total Ships Sunk	U-Boats Sunk By Convoy Forces	U-Boats Sunk By Other Forces	U-Boats Sunk Total
January	15	18	14	19	37	5	6	11
February	34	38	16	18	56	17	6	23
March	72	77	23	25	102	6	10	16
April	25	29	22	24	53	9	8	17
May	26	31	19	19	50	28	19	47
Total	172	193	94	105	298	65	49	114

Ref: George R. Lindsey and S. W. Roskill, *The War at Sea, 1939-1945*, vols. 1-4 (London: Her Majesty's Stationery Office, 1960).

TABLE 13-6
LEVELS OF SELECTED U.S. NAVAL FORCES—WORLD WAR II[a]
AND EXCHANGE RATIO BETWEEN COMBATANT VESSELS AND SUBMARINES
(Forces Assigned to U.S. Atlantic Fleet Shown in Parentheses)

	Dec. 1941	Jul. 1942	Jun. 1943	Dec. 1944
Attack Carriers (CV)	7 (3)	4 (1)	10 (1)	17 (0)
Battleships	15 (5)	19 (6)	21 (6)	23 (4)
Cruisers	37 (17)	39 (12)	48 (10)	60 (10)
Light Carriers (CVL)	0	0	9 (0)	8 (0)
Escort Carriers (CVE)	0	10	33 (12)	63 (14)
Destroyers	145 (94)	194 (100)	291 (111)	343 (68)
Destroyer Escorts	0	0	224 (157)	365 (252)
Total	204 (119)	266 (123)	636 (297)	879 (348)
Exchange Ratio (ships sunk/subs sunk)	10:1	19:1	4.5:1	0.5:1

[a] Includes ships in overhaul, repair and training status and ships in both the Atlantic and Pacific.

merchant ships. These advances will next be addressed in the context of a present-day anti-SLOC campaign.

Sea Control Today

Progress in Submarines and Antisubmarine Warfare

The analogy between World War II and present-day anti-SLOC campaigns cannot be applied without limits. Current ASW and submarine weapons systems are far more advanced. For example, the U-Boat was more like a surface ship than today's models. It would submerge for only a few hours, since batteries had to be charged on the surface. This made the submarine especially vulnerable to air antisubmarine warfare. The first-line German submarine was 708 tons, carried fourteen torpedoes, had a maximum submerged speed of 7.6 knots, and remained on patrol an average of thirty five days. Advanced technology has produced far more versatile diesel submarines as well as nuclear-powered submarines capable of speeds faster than most surface ships and underwater patrols limited only by the endurance of the crew—and by the number of torpedoes carried. On the average, that number has changed little from World War II days, but torpedo accuracy has improved.

On the other hand, antisubmarine warfare has also made tremendous strides. There have been breakthroughs in acoustic detection, signal-processing, and prediction of oceanographic conditions as well as in torpedoes and homing mines. On balance, Alliance antisubmarine warfare has probably kept up with known Soviet submarine advances,[5] although it may not have matched U.S. submarine improvements. Today's nuclear submarines are probably less vulnerable than their World War II predecessors, while conventionally powered submarines are perhaps somewhat more vulnerable—at least when they are in motion. This is not a gloomy appraisal, since it must be remembered that the World War II submarine attacks on escorted merchant ship convoys were countered in time and since the majority of Soviet anti-SLOC submarines are likely to be diesel-powered for many years to come (as explained in Chapter 4). In short, there is no hard evidence indicating a dramatic change in the exchange ratios—either way—between ASW and submarine forces in an anti-SLOC campaign with conventional weapons. On the other hand, Alliance capabilities in barrier operations would substantially increase attrition rates against all classes of Soviet submarines.

To illustrate current sea control tactics, we will briefly examine a scenario emphasizing the material resupply of land forces in NATO. This situation, popular with Congress, defense planners, and our allies, recognizes the need for early resupply of forces fighting a conventional war against the Warsaw Pact.[6] It further assumes that there has been no useful "preparation time" prior to the outbreak of hostilities, which may or may not be realistic. In any event, it is consistent with a basic Defense Department objective: namely, to keep the SLOC open to Europe in the face of a growing Soviet naval threat. Although the example deals with NATO, many of the factors considered would apply to conflicts in other parts of the world as well, including the Pacific and Indian oceans.

In a NATO war, how would the Alliance ensure that essential military and economic supplies reach Europe in sufficient quantity and on time? The U.S. Navy is structured on the premise of protecting a minimum of fifteen convoys, including ten Underway Replenishment Groups (which support naval task forces) and five military resupply convoys.[7] Non-U.S. NATO destroyers and escorts number almost 200, while other allies such as France and Spain could add more than 70 more. Half of these Alliance assets could escort another fifteen or twenty convoys if available and properly trained.

These convoys would have to be escorted against Soviet submarine, surface, and air threats. Generally, the large number of Soviet submarines in the Northern Fleet is regarded as the most serious threat to North Atlantic shipping.[8] Soviet aircraft and surface combatants armed with antiship cruise missiles might also challenge the convoy and her escorts, making Allied ASW prosecution less effective. However, the Soviets might not use up their relatively scarce cruise missiles in this role. It should also be possible to deny aerial refueling through counterforce operations. Routing convoys south of a great circle route could also minimize the surface and air threats. Nonetheless, the overall hazard to shipping would still be substantial. Statements by the Department of Defense and published data suggest that losses during the first thirty days of a major war could, under some conditions, amount to half of all ships sailed. Thereafter, the rate of shipping losses would rapidly decline.[9]

The use of convoys is based on the premise that all but essential military and economic shipping would be curtailed during the conflict. With a substantial reduction in shipping density, unprotected high-value merchant ships would be extremely vulnerable, unless they could travel at very high speeds along random routes. Although some modern container ships have the requisite speed, most tankers and bulk carriers are not fast enough to evade an attacking submarine. Organizing ships into convoys enables the Navy to offer more escort protection than would be possible with independent shipping—and to exact attrition from those submarines that do attack the convoys. But convoys also solve two of the enemy's major problems—detection and identification.

Ocean shipping in peacetime is intensely active, with thousands of crossings taking place monthly in both the Atlantic and the Pacific. If a relatively high level of shipping were maintained during a conflict, ships carrying military supplies might be able to sail independently without increasing their vulnerability to submarine attack. The obvious reason is that submarines would be faced with the difficult problem of target identification.

An anti-SLOC campaign is basically a war of attrition. This means that the ASW campaign is characterized by many encounters, each having a low probability of kill. Figure 13-1, summarizing some 1975 Defense Department Atlantic Campaign study results, reflects this phenomenon. As shipping losses decline (after the first month), cumulative Soviet submarine losses would continue to climb. If about one-half of the ships sailing during the first month of the war were sunk, more than 200 ships would be lost. This represents about 50 percent of the shipping required to meet Defense Department early resupply objectives for NATO.

While detailed study results are not available, they are sensitive to: threat assumptions (e.g., number, type, torpedo load, and effectiveness of submarine deployed); performance estimates of friendly weapon systems (probability of kill); operating parameters; and tactics. It is interesting to note the similarity between the estimated losses in an anti-SLOC campaign, (given in the next section) and those of Figure 13-1.

The New Setting and Tactics

How might today's convoy and its defenses differ from those of World War II? The number of ships might be somewhat larger. Planners often think in terms of sixty-ship convoys rather than the forty five-ship average of World War II. These ships are likely to be roughly three times as large (15,000 tons versus less than 5,000 tons) and roughly 50 percent faster (15

**FIGURE 13-1
1975 DEFENSE DEPARTMENT
ATLANTIC CAMPAIGN STUDY RESULTS**

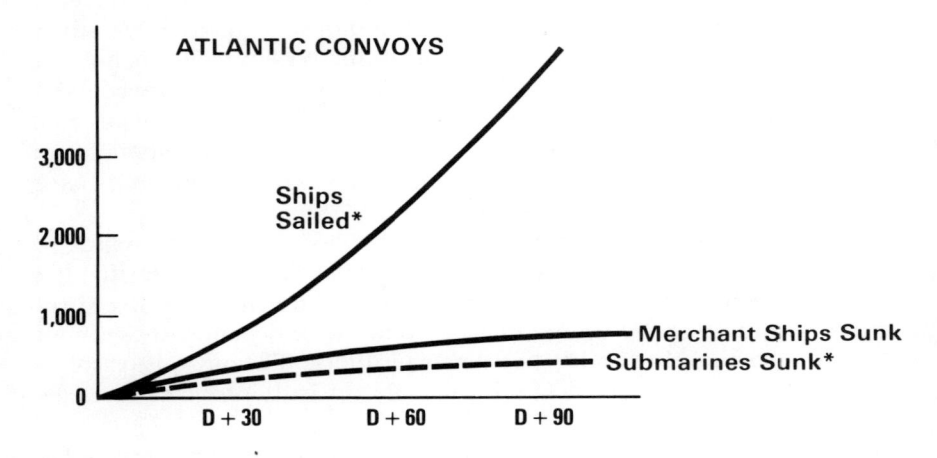

ATLANTIC CONVOYS

Ships Sailed*

Merchant Ships Sunk
Submarines Sunk*

*Cumulative Data

SOURCE: U.S. Congress, House Committee on Armed Services, Hearings, Military Posture, 94th Congress, 1st Session, 1975, H.R. 3689, H.R. 6674 (Washington, D.C.: U.S. Government Printing Office, 1975), Testimony of Leonard Sullivan, pp. 1817-1860.

knots versus 10 knots). Planners talk in terms of two convoy sailings per week instead of roughly one per day and estimate the unloading time in terms of two days instead of three. These factors mean that only six convoys would be "exposed" at sea on an average day (half traveling each way) rather than thirty, even though the material being delivered to Europe per day might be 20 percent greater than that during World War II.

The number of escorts required per convoy appears to have changed less than any other parameter. The World War II average was seven escorts, and planners currently talk about six to eight escorts—one of which, under special circumstances, might be a submarine. In addition, modern Atlantic convoys would probably be under virtually continuous coverage from land-based ASW patrol aircraft as long as bases are available in Bermuda and the Azores—effectively adding to the total number of escorts accompanying each convoy. With a "back-up factor" of eight (aircraft on the ground for each on station with the convoy), two P-3C's could be kept over each convoy, using roughly one-half of the Atlantic-assigned U.S. land-based patrol force.

Allocating 7 surface escorts to each of six merchant convoys would bring the total escort requirement to 42 destroyers and frigates. This is roughly the number available for these assignments from U.S. Atlantic fleet assets alone—with no allowance for losses. These same types of calculations would have indicated a need for roughly 210 escorts for convoy duty during World War II, and Table 13-6 indicates that the total number of U.S. ships in these categories ranged from 260 in June of 1943 to 320 in December 1944. (Some were clearly assigned to other missions such as the defense of the larger attack carriers, amphibious groups, and battleships.)

Our NATO allies could probably provide some additional transatlantic escort assets. As shown in Table 6-3, our NATO allies, plus France and Spain, could contribute over 260 additional escorts to sealane defense. From those destroyers and frigates less than ten years old, about 100 could be provided, leaving over 150 less capable ships to escort convoys through the Mediterranean and within other local NATO waters. The average escort, incidentally, would seem to be newer than the average Soviet submarine it might be defending against.

Our combined NATO forces currently appear to have adequate levels of surface escorts to handle the initial requirements for the escorting of military cargoes across the Atlantic. However, as Chapter 6 indicated, during a protracted war military shipments might equal only a small fraction of the total shipping requirements of essential economic commodities—possibly as little as one-sixth or one-seventh. If all of this additional shipping also required escorting, then the total requirements would substantially exceed any reasonably achievable level of Alliance naval escorts, particularly over the longer distances involved.

This recalls another significant factor mentioned earlier. If a requirement arose to escort U.S. military or economic convoys to or from a more distant battleground such as Korea or the Middle East and this had to be done without Alliance assistance, then the escort requirement could be substantially larger. As noted elsewhere, an Atlantic or a Pacific SLOC from the U.S. to Iran, for instance, exceeds 13,000 miles, and the ship unloading time would probably be greater than at NATO ports. The U.S. escort force would probably be, at best, marginally adequate to support a military shipping requirement only one-fifth as great as that presented by NATO—particularly since P-3 coverage for such convoys would not be

U.S. WORLD WAR II CONVOY EXPERIENCE

World War II convoy experience is still considered useful in projecting future sealane defense requirements, even though modern convoys might be 30 percent larger, 50 percent faster, and comprised of ships three times as large in capacity as their forerunners shown above. (Courtesy U.S. Navy)

World War II shipping losses to German U-Boats (from one of which the above photograph was taken) were substantially lowered in 1943 when roughly 225 new destroyer escorts were added to Allied naval force levels. Similar operations would probably be required to counter the larger Soviet submarine force. (Courtesy U.S. Navy)

possible over much of the routes.[10] United States escort force requirements could, then, conceivably be set by some military—or economic scenario outside of NATO.

In any event, escort force levels make an important difference, as the World War II experience taught us, even though they can by no means eliminate shipping losses at sea. The addition of nearly 225 destroyer escorts to Allied forces in 1943, however, made it possible to escort all of our convoys and substantially reduce our shipping losses. Submarine losses also rose very significantly, at least partially as a result.

Buying enough ships to stop an attack altogether or to win the war after only a very few engagements is difficult to conceive. As mentioned, an anti-SLOC campaign is basically a war of attrition. Of course, a point of diminishing returns is reached where the effectiveness of each additional escort ship is not worth the cost of merchant shipping saved. On the other hand, insufficient escort forces may not only decrease the rate of submarine attrition but could also add dramatically to the vulnerability of the merchant ships—by more than the proportional reduction in forces. In other words, a 25 percent decrease in escort forces may lead to more than a 25 percent increase in ship sinkings.

An Illustrative Atlantic SLOC Campaign

Figure 13-2 illustrates how opposing forces might operate in an anti-SLOC campaign in the Northeast Atlantic. To protect the convoys, one ASW phase of an anti-SLOC campaign consists of detecting those submarines already in open waters with a fixed underwater sound surveillance system (SOSUS). Submarines and aircraft are then sent out to localize and attack the target. Additional navy tactics feature submarine barriers, minefields, and ASW patrol aircraft at geographic choke points.[11] Soviet submarines deploying from Northern Fleet ports or returning for resupply must transit the choke point known as the Greenland-Iceland-United Kingdom passage, or "G.-I.-U.K. Gap." The requirement for Soviet submarines to move through defended choke points depends on their speed, endurance, weapon payloads, and location of homeports.

Another phase of ASW "defense in depth" consists of the convoy's screen of ASW surface escorts, patrol aircraft, and possibly even submarines. The surface escorts employ sonar systems capable of both active and passive detections. Unfortunately, active sonar detections are usually short in range even under the best ocean acoustic conditions.[12] Convergence zone sonars make longer-range detections. However, this occurs only a fraction of the time, when ocean conditions are favorable. The Navy is now developing and deploying new towed-array sonars (TACTAS) that improve the probability of submarine detection. Helicopters and fixed-wing, land-based (or carrier-based) ASW aircraft can carry out

FIGURE 13-2
SEA CONTROL IN THE NORTHEAST ATLANTIC – GREENLAND – ICELAND – UNITED KINGDOM (G-I-UK GAP) BARRIER CHOKEPOINT

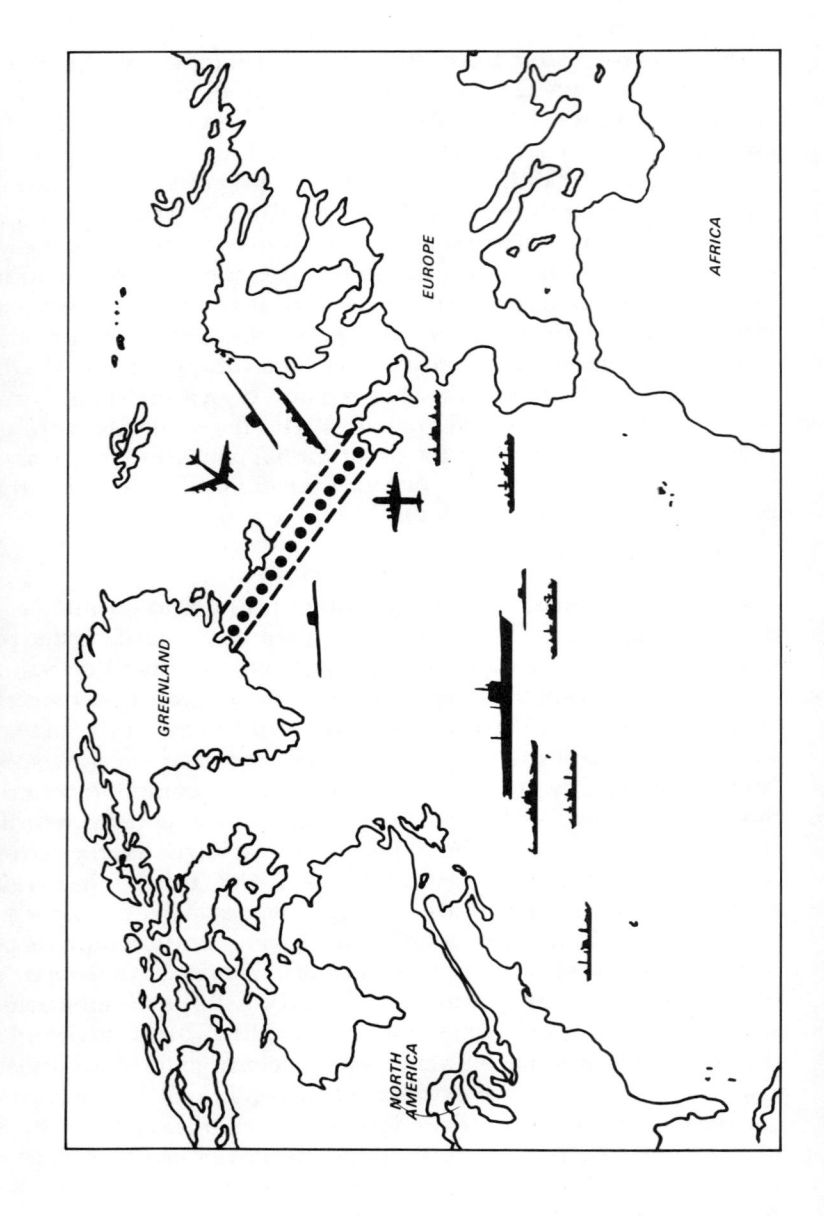

localization and torpedo attack once a sonar detection is made. Finally, nuclear submarine escorts could offer direct ASW support to the convoy if they could be spared from other mission assignments. The submarine is a better sonar platform than a surface ship, although identification, communications, and command and control problems would be of some significance.[13] Enemy submarines would have to contend with a wide array of ASW forces deployed in several barriers, which they would have to penetrate one by one to initiate an attack. Each barrier represents an opportunity to detect and destroy the hostile submarine, either prior to or subsequent to its attack on shipping.

Although an array of sophisticated systems is available for convoy protection, there is no evidence that convoy vulnerability has been substantially reduced since World War II. The number of surface combatants available for convoy protection remains a critical factor in the "last line" of SLOC defense.

Simplified Analysis of the Sealane Defense Mission

Given the many changes since World War II in the submarine, ASW forces, and the geographic setting, some structural analysis of interaction between opposing forces is needed. There are a number of sophisticated mathematical simulations of wars-at-sea in the classified literature that are not available outside the defense community. However, a simplified mathematical representation of the interaction among the submarine, its prey, and ASW forces can yield instructive results.

This section presents such an analysis. Although it examines a possible NATO conflict, the results are applicable to other situations as well. The exact outcomes of anti-SLOC campaigns are difficult—perhaps impossible—to predict, even for elaborate studies, because of the numerous estimates that must be made of technical, human, and environmental conditions. A gross approach can nonetheless suggest some useful points for thinking about the adequacy of our forces and the general course of anti-SLOC campaigns.

For our purposes a simple, flexible model has been used to analyze a high-intensity anti-SLOC campaign in the Atlantic. Accepting the allocations presented in Chapter 4, let us conservatively assume that the Soviets commit sixty submarines to attacking NATO SLOCs, one-half sailing on D-Day (or before that in the "pre-deployment" cases), and one-quarter sailing at fifteen-day intervals. A high activity rate of thirty-day submarine patrols is assumed. These submarines encounter NATO forces at a number of points, as described above. They pass through various fixed barriers, open-ocean search, and convoy protection forces. Different assumptions as to the performance of the ASW forces are used in different cases by altering the probability of kill.

Changes in the number of ocean barriers, area searches, and convoy screens are proxies for different assumptions as to force levels. Each submarine that survives the ASW forces on the way to the merchant ship convoy then sinks five ships before returning through the ASW gauntlet for a weapons reload in the Kola inlet.[14] This analysis is essentially independent of the number of ships sailed as long as that number exceeds the losses quoted. In other words, the analysis is basically a calculation of the number of torpedoes available to strike the convoys—factored by their individual effectiveness. For a conflict in the Pacific, it is assumed the Soviets would deploy no more than thirty submarines against convoys. In this simplified case, ship and submarine losses would be about one-half of those depicted in the following illustrations. In either case, this analysis assumes that the submarines can intercept the convoys with "perfect intelligence."

Figure 13-3 shows some results. Case A is considered the base example. The Soviet submarines do not predeploy (or we have strategic warning of those movements and contain them). They must pass through five lines of antisubmarine defenses:

- Two lines of forward barriers (submarines and mines);
- Open-area search (P-3 or carrier group supported by SOSUS); and
- Two convoy screens (P-3 or carrier outer screen and an inner surface escort screen).

Surviving submarines must pass through the same lines of defense in returning to port. The defense has an average probability of kill (PK, including initial detection) of 0.1 at each of these five lines of defense.

As shown on Figure 13-3, in the first thirty days we would stand to lose about 180 ships; by sixty days, about 60 more are lost. At the same time, 40 enemy submarines (out of 60 committed) are sunk; and more than 50 are sunk by ninety days. This accounts for the sharp drop in merchant vessel losses after sixty days of conflict.

Cases B and C halve and double the performance of the ASW forces as measured by their individual PKs. Improved individual performance in Case C brings a marked reduction in merchant losses; it halves them. The poorer performance represented by Case B increases ship losses by about one-half. It is interesting that nearly two-thirds of the enemy submarines are sunk in ninety days under even the pessimistic case. This reflects the fact that if many opportunities for engagement are possible because of force size, then, even though the job of detecting and killing a submarine is extremely difficult, the cumulative effect will be significant.

Even under the most optimistic case (Case C), we would lose 105 ships in ninety days, nearly all of them in the first thirty days.

**FIGURE 13-3
SIMPLIFIED ATTRITION ANALYSIS**

VARYING ASW CAPABILITY

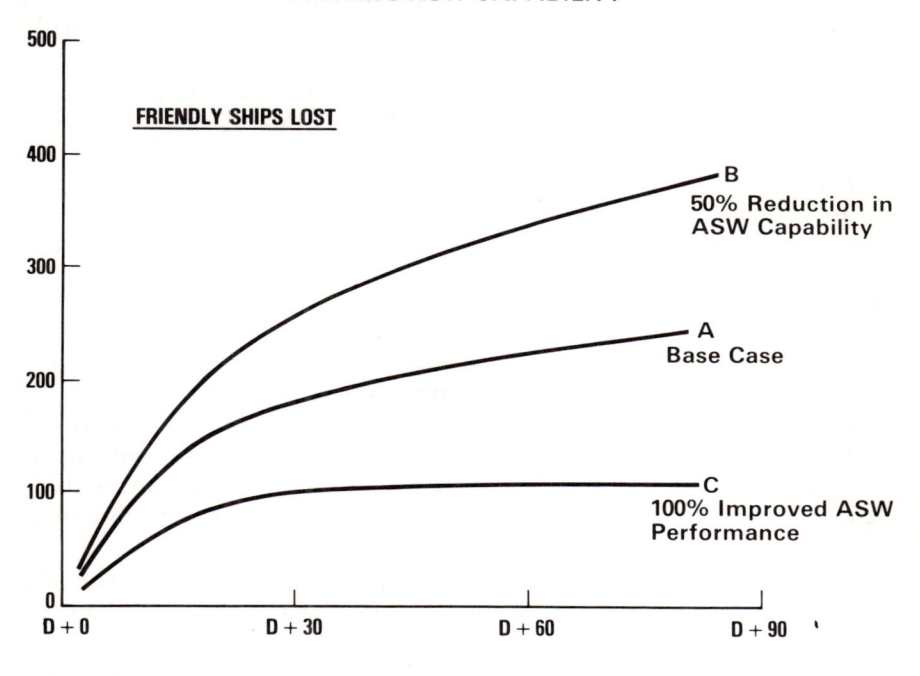

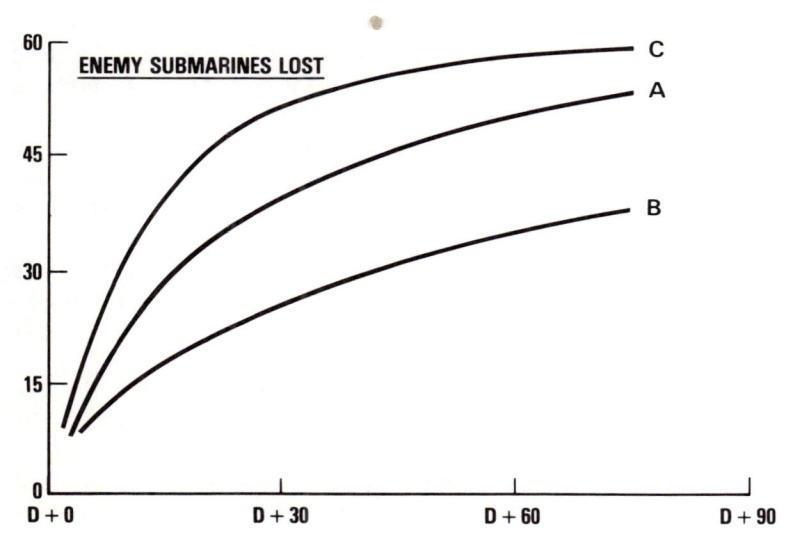

A major question concerns our ability to stop a predeployment of Soviet submarines before hostilities or to neutralize submarines once they are on station. Since U.S. policy rejects preemptive attacks by our forces, it is unlikely that much could be done to prevent predeployment or to neutralize submarines prior to the outbreak of hostilities. The graphs in Figure 13-4, however, suggest that our inability to do so would have startling consequences. Case A is shown for reference. Case AP has the same assumptions as Case A except that it allows thirty submarines to predeploy before the war, thereby exposing themselves to only the close convoy defenses before initial attack. There would be a sharp increase in the number of merchant ships lost in the first months—up almost 100 over the original 180 in Case A. A greater number of enemy submarines would be sunk at an early stage, but on balance it would be a better tactic for the enemy.

Case CP (Case C with predeployment) shows that even with highly effective ASW forces, the initial losses of merchant vessels are high—180 in thirty days. While the ASW forces rapidly destroy the enemy submarines (90 percent killed in sixty days), a high price in shipping losses is sustained.

Figure 13-5 carries this point a step further to show the obvious, that if the enemy predeploys effectively, even a large ASW force of units with an unlikely and extreme assumed PK of 0.33 could not prevent substantial merchant vessel losses.

Figure 13-6 shows the effect of reducing force levels. Case AW uses the same assumption as Case A, except that it gives a 40 percent reduction in ASW forces, thereby reducing ASW engagement opportunities by a like amount. A 40 percent increase in merchant ship losses over Case A results. Case BW, reflecting the lower ASW unit capability of Case B, plus smaller ASW forces, suggests a doubling of ship losses over Case A, or more than 450 in ninety days. More striking is the fact that the *rate* of loss of merchant vessels is hardly subsiding over ninety days of conflict.

Case AW can also be interpreted as indicative of the loss in Alliance ASW capabilities that would result from the elimination of two of the successive barrier stages. That might be the case if Soviet submarines were not constrained to deploy from and return to their present bases on the Barents Sea and the Sea of Japan through relatively restricted passages. Multiple Soviet bases on the northwest coast of Africa or along the Chinese mainland coast could considerably reduce the effectiveness of Alliance barrier operations.

Case BW can then be viewed as the consequence of inadequate Alliance ASW force levels (for both barriers and convoy defense) coupled with the availability of additional Soviet bases with unrestricted access to the open seas. In this event, use of the sealanes could be very seriously threatened indeed—even at the rather modest levels of submarine forces assumed to be

FIGURE 13-4
SIMPLIFIED ATTRITION ANALYSIS

VARYING SUBMARINE PRE-DEPLOYMENT

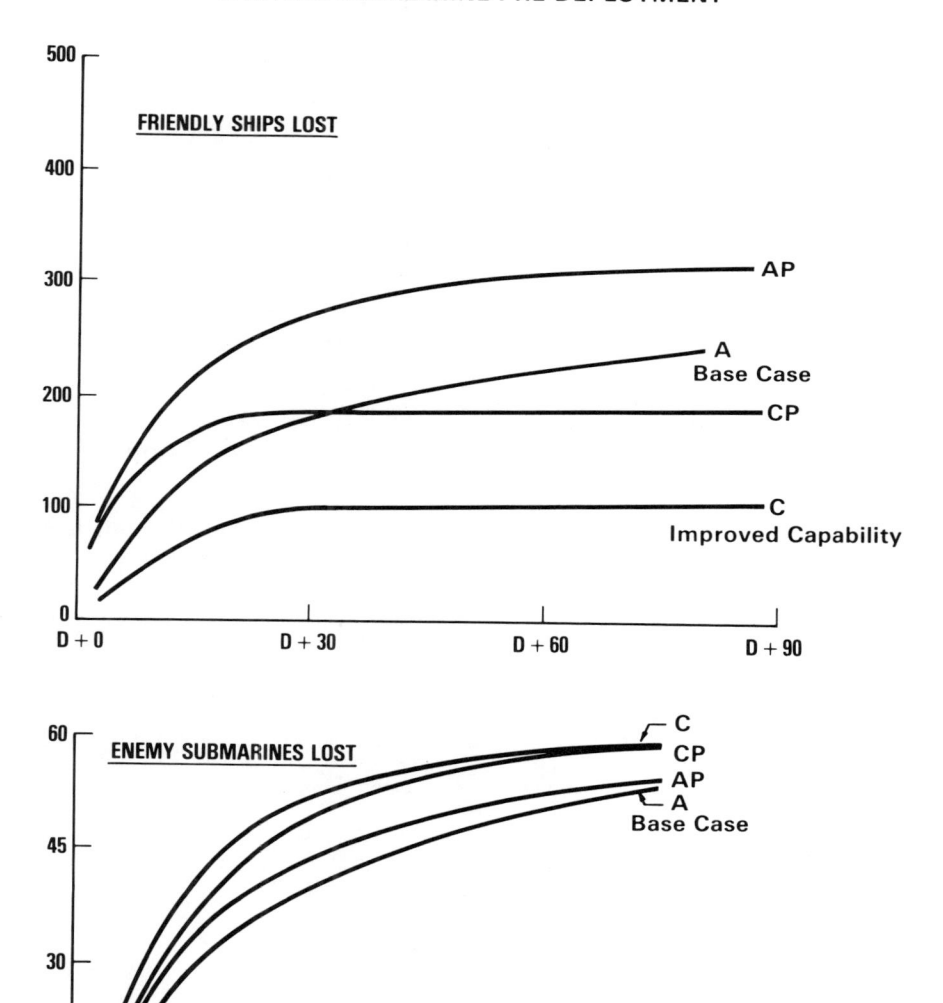

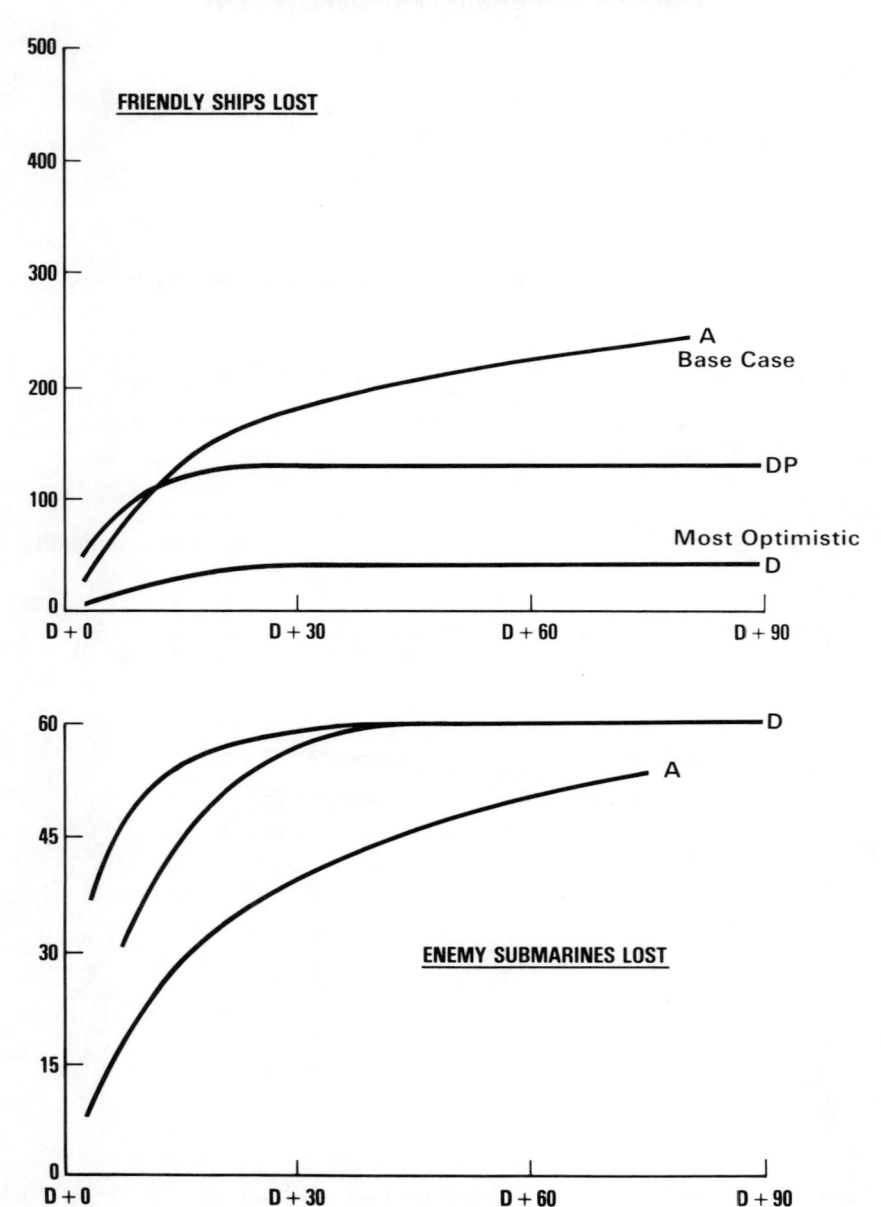

**FIGURE 13-5
SIMPLIFIED ATTRITION ANALYSIS**

MOST OPTIMISTIC ASW PERFORMANCE

357

**FIGURE 13-6
SIMPLIFIED ATTRITION ANALYSIS**

WORST CASE PERFORMANCE AND/OR FORCE LEVELS

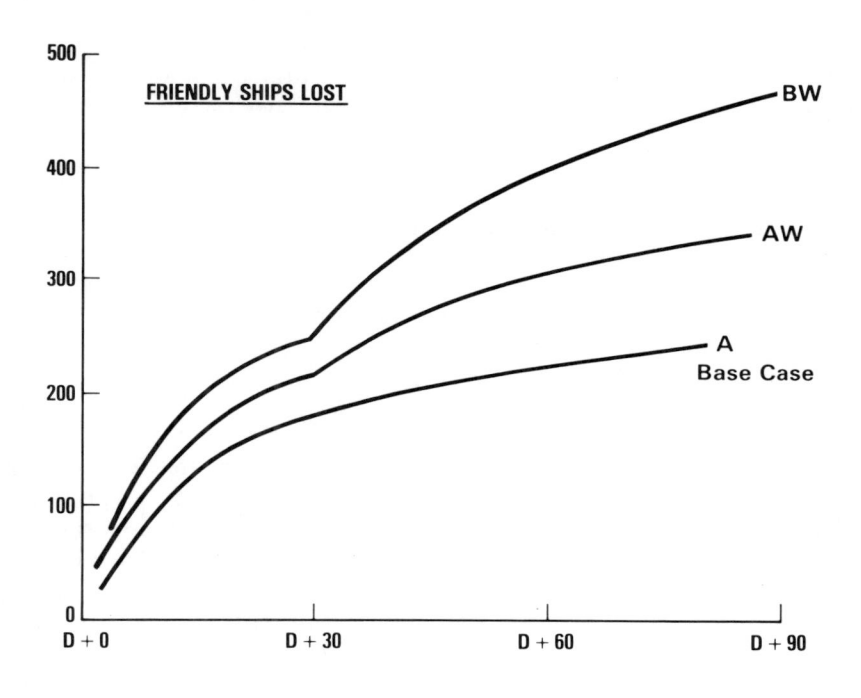

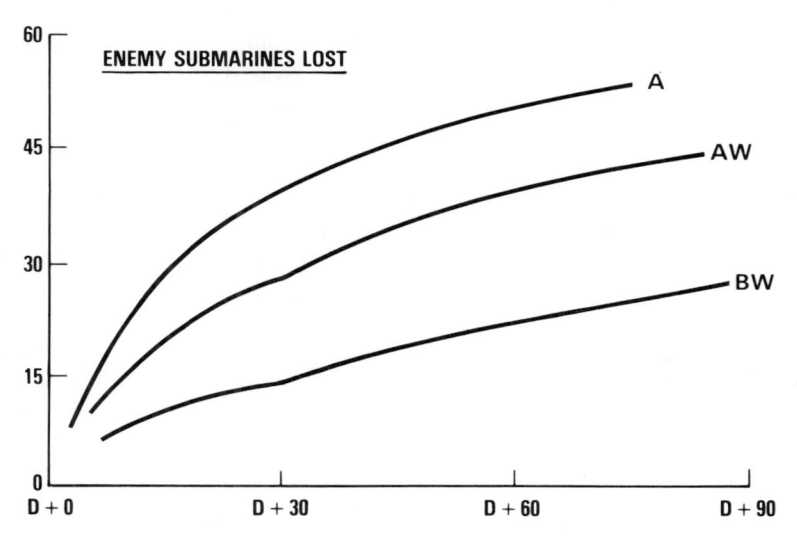

allocated by the Soviets to the anti-SLOC mission (see Chapter 4). This confirms the discussion in Chapter 9 of the limitations placed on Soviet naval forces by their current basing structure.

Case BW is the only case examined in which over half of the Soviet submarines survive for ninety days. Moreover, this case may be more representative of an anti-SLOC campaign against U.S. forces outside the NATO arena. In this case, there might be substantial constraints placed on the use of antisubmarine barriers for fear of excessive risk of escalation to nuclear weapons. Various forms of "Rules of Engagement" limitations equivalent to these seriously lowered the effectiveness of American fighting forces in Korea and Vietnam and cannot be dismissed in any confrontation involving less than total military commitment.

Moreover, under conditions short of a total superpower confrontation, the Soviets might reasonably have additional overseas bases available for the servicing and rearming of their general-purpose attack submarines. As discussed earlier, this could significantly reduce the effectiveness of any submarine barriers that were "allowed" by the rules of engagement.

Exchange Ratios

Possibly the most useful criterion for judging the effectiveness of a sealane defense campaign is the "exchange ratio" between friendly ships sunk and enemy submarines destroyed. For any set of assumptions concerning friendly and enemy force effectiveness, a characteristic "exchange ratio" results. For instance, in the preceding Case A, the characteristic exchange ratio turns out to be approximately 4.5:1. In other words, every enemy submarine committed to this mission succeeds in sinking 4.5 Allied merchant ships (or escorts) before being sunk itself. In the most optimistic case (Case D), this exchange ratio is about 0.7:1 (i.e., each enemy submarine kills less than a single merchantman before being sunk). At the other extreme, in Case BW—the most pessimistic case explored—each submarine accounted for eighteen friendly ships before being sunk by friendly ASW forces. It is pure coincidence that the exchange ratio of Case A is so similar to that experienced during World War II. From Tables 13-1 and 13-2, one can see that the overall World War II cumulative exchange ratio between merchant ships and submarines was 4.7:1 (when the ships lost to unknown causes are prorated to the various known causes).

This criterion is useful in estimating the impact of various possible Soviet allocations to the anti-SLOC mission. For instance, if an exchange ratio of 5:1 appears appropriate, and the Soviets dedicate 100 submarines to the anti-SLOC mission, then a total of 500 merchant ships and escorts would be lost before the submarine threat would be eliminated. It is, of course, tempting to ponder the relative availability of Alliance ships and

Soviet submarines. On this basis, one would readily conclude that we have more ships than they have submarines to lose. The fallacy in this argument, of course, arises from the fact that the essential cargoes those ships carry are the real losses. For instance, it has been estimated that all U.S. military material planned for the reinforcement of NATO could be carried in roughly 1,000 ships. Loss of one-half of those cargoes would be a very serious blow to the sustaining power of NATO forces.

While not specifically investigated in this simplified model, the Soviets might well adopt an anti-ASW tactic as the first step in an anti-SLOC campaign. In all cases studied here, NATO ASW forces are assumed to operate unimpaired throughout the war. If the size of our ASW forces is marginal, it might be worthwhile for the Soviets to lose some submarines, surface ships, and aircraft in attacks on the ASW forces themselves. This could well increase the effectiveness and survival of forces used in subsequent attacks. Larger ASW forces would preclude this tactic or reduce its value.

Conclusions from Simplified Analysis

While by no means conclusive, these results suggest the following generalizations concerning the submarine threat to the sealanes:

1. Under any reasonable set of assumptions about relative forces and their capabilities, we should expect to lose a substantial number of merchant ships and surface vessels in the first few weeks or months of an all-out submarine war. Predeployment or alternate basing of enemy submarines could make the situation markedly worse. This suggests some real utility for the stockpiling of strategic materials and the prepositioning of critical military equipments prior to the outbreak of hostilities—either permanently or during any available period of strategic warning. This high rate of attrition for early shipments has suggested the possibility of simply keeping ships in port until ASW forces can offset the temporary edge gained by Soviet submarine predeployment or of gaining the more permanent advantage offered by alternate basing. In a NATO context, supplies might arrive too late unless substantial prepositioning and stockpiling had taken place or unless there had been substantial and fully utilized strategic warning. In a war at sea campaign with no land conflict, the need to move supplies could be less urgent. Technological advances in wide-area surveillance, however, suggest that such a tactic might not be attractive. The Soviets could simply hold back their forces until merchant ships began to sail or perhaps increase the forces used to carry out attacks on naval combat forces. The potential contribution of prepositioning is discussed in a later section. In any event, the West must eventually regain the use of its sealanes and eliminate the submarines that threaten them.

2. The war is one of attrition for both sides. Once committed, the enemy

submarine force is destroyed at a reasonably fast rate, provided that our forces are large enough to ensure many engagement opportunities—and that our individual ASW forces are sufficiently effective.

3. In the representative scenario shown, 60 percent of the submarine attrition is exacted at the barriers and only 40 percent by convoy defense forces. This indicates the importance of attrition through antisubmarine barriers prior to attacks on the merchant convoys. The absence of such "filters" in more constrained scenarios could have a significant impact on continued high loss rates.

4. Improved individual systems capability—if possible in either the barriers or the convoy defenses—has a high payoff in both elimination of the enemy force and sharp reduction in merchant losses.

5. Unless considerably higher unit ASW capability can be achieved (which appears unlikely, given the recent advances already brought about by nuclear submarine performance but not yet fully exploited), then a large ASW force is essential to maintaining use of the seas without high and continuing merchant and naval losses. Given the uncertainty concerning relative performance to be expected from submarines and ASW systems (discussed later), conservatively large ASW forces represent a form of insurance.

6. This analysis is indifferent to the total number of ship sailings—as long as that figure exceeds the kill capability of the deployed submarines. Sailing additional ships means that more will get through since the submarines are "saturated" with available targets. This suggests several important options. One is to ship our essential and scarce military equipment in smaller ships, since this is one instance where the "economies of scale" are working to the detriment of the West. Second, one might consider sailing more ships with only a fraction of their cargo consisting of essential military goods. This is another way to reduce losses of essential cargoes, if not of ships. Finally, it may be either impossible or impractical for an enemy to differentiate between ships carrying military cargoes and those carrying lower-value economic goods. In this case, the attrition of essential military cargoes can be reduced in direct proportion to the increase in nonessential cargoes also being shipped by convoy. While the concept of using real ships to dilute the threat may not appear attractive, it may offer one of the most realistic means of reducing losses of vital military cargoes.

The Air Threat to Convoys

In addition to engagements between merchant ships and Soviet submarines, the role of Soviet naval aircraft must also be taken into consideration. These planes, some equipped with long-range air-to-surface missiles, would fly from bases in the Kola Peninsula and elsewhere.

Quantifying the Sealane Defense Problem

To attack U.S. carriers or convoys, they would have to survive land-based defenses and interceptors (operating from Norway, Greenland, Iceland, and Britain) as well as carrier-based interceptors. The air threat, which is formidable, has not been examined in detail because the most capable Soviet air assets and their expensive standoff missiles would probably be allocated against carriers and other elements engaged in force projection missions. If this assumption proved incorrect, the threat to convoys or their escorts would be substantially increased. Soviet aircraft armed with standoff missiles and refueled from aerial tankers could severely tax the antiair capabilities of normal convoy escorts. In fact, there is virtually no way that these escorts can be provided with a reliable means of shooting down the launch aircraft before they release their standoff missiles unless aircraft carriers are used as convoy escorts. Additionally, as discussed in Chapter 7, the Alliance has yet to deploy defensive systems capable of knocking down the standoff missiles themselves, although some encouraging developments are under way.

A more likely possibility for the foreseeable future, however, is that the Soviets would use less capable aircraft to attack shipping with shorter-range unguided weapons. Such attempts could probably be neutralized through the use of relatively available antiaircraft gun and missile systems. While troublesome, these assaults do not appear to present nearly as serious a threat as the submarine.

In any event, the best approach to countering the Soviet naval aviation threat—which would probably be directed at higher-priority targets than merchant ships—might be through attacks on their bases and a series of air defense barriers. Like the submarines, these aircraft—and their tankers—would probably have to attack Alliance targets from relatively limited distant bases. They could therefore be subject to en route attack by a variety of systems, including both carrier-based and land-based interceptors if they transit over water and land-based surface-to-air missile systems and interceptors if they overfly NATO territory. As in the submarine case, however, the availability of additional overseas Soviet bases for long-range naval aviation could significantly increase the air threat to the convoys.

ASW-Capable Merchant Vessels

Enemy submarines that survive or elude our ASW barriers could even exact a heavy toll on merchant ships escorted in convoys. If such barriers were not established, or if alternate Soviet bases were available that obviated the need to transit choke points, shipping losses could increase dramatically. Since a large increase in escort force levels or a major breakthrough in ASW technology does not appear likely in the near term, one alternative involves providing the merchant vessels themselves with some limited ASW capability.

A merchant ship is generally considered a defenseless prey for a stealthy submarine. As already discussed, convoying merchantmen is a necessary part of increasing the attrition rate of enemy submarines and reducing convoy losses. There may be other means as well. Current technology may now make it possible for the merchant ship itself to increase the attrition of attacking submarines. One such proposal was put forth in 1964 by Richard L. Garwin. He suggests that when a merchant ship is struck by a torpedo, it or a neighboring ship should have the on-deck capability to launch a homing torpedo—such as the Mk-46—in the general direction of the attacking submarine. The Mk-46 has a range roughly equivalent to any known Soviet torpedo and can be programmed to search a considerable area and home on an underwater submarine.

If past experience is any guide, the submarine skipper would try to position himself for a broadside attack on the ship. In World War II, about 80 percent of such attacks were made from within 20 to 30 degrees of directly abeam. An attentive crew may be able to spot the wake of an approaching torpedo. If it is contact- rather than influence-fuzed, the stricken merchant ship or a companion vessel could estimate from which side the attack was launched. Those odds can also be adjusted somewhat by ship-spacing within the convoy. Thus, if the Mk-46 can search the zone from which 50 percent of the torpedo attacks would come, and if the ship can tell which side the attack came from 50 percent of the time and launch an effective Mk-46 torpedo 50 percent of the time, then the merchant ship might have one chance in eight of sinking the attacking submarine with each torpedo launched. These are the same odds assumed for each of the separate barriers described earlier. Such odds might well make the attacking submarine alter its tactics and probably reduce its effectiveness. Moreover, unless a submarine launches all of its torpedoes in rapid succession (which is not customary practice), there is a reasonable chance of sinking that craft before it expends all its weapons, thereby possibly saving two or three other ships in the convoy.

An obvious question is whether an Mk-46 would home on friendly ships rather than the attacking submarine. Fortunately, a standard Mk-46 torpedo can differentiate between a surface vessel and a submerged platform, so surface ships are not at risk. Moreover, if the spacing of ships in a convoy is increased to make them less vulnerable to nuclear attack, then the chances of accidentally sinking another merchant vessel are further reduced.

This idea seems worth pursuing: an on-deck torpedo-launcher (ASROC, for instance) for each merchant ship may represent a very low-cost means of increasing submarine attrition. Figure 13-7 shows the marginal contribution of using the Mk-46 on merchant ships for cases A, B, and C. In assessing the effect of the Mk-46, a relatively optimistic probability of killing the submarine of 0.2 is assumed. (This might well require

ASW-CAPABLE MERCHANT SHIPS

This report suggests that it may be practical and desirable to be able to arm Alliance merchant ships like the S.S. *Arco Anchorage* shown above with ASW helicopters and other modularized ASW and AAW weapons in time of crisis or war. It would be virtually impossible to provide enough naval escorts to protect vital economic shipping along all the essential Alliance sealanes. By the end of 1975, the average Alliance merchant ship displaced more than 26,000 tons. (Courtesy U.S. Maritime Administration)

launching two weapons.) In additon, since submarines must launch their weapons from longer distances, the kill rate per submarine mission is assumed to drop from five to four ships. No credit was taken for avoiding unexpended torpedoes.

If these assumptions are valid, arming merchant ships with MK-46 torpedoes could have a substantial effect on ship losses. The effect would be both passive and active. Initially, ship losses would be reduced because of the reduced submarine weapon effectiveness associated with firing from longer distances. After the initial submarine attack, there would be the combined effect of both distances and increased submarine attrition. For Case A, ship losses would be reduced almost 25 percent. While this particular scheme may be neither practical nor optimal, it demonstrates the potential value of arming merchant ships to defend themselves.

There are, of course, more expensive—and probably more effective—means of protecting merchant vessels. Through the addition of towed arrays and ASW helicopters many of the larger commercial ships could become reasonable substitutes for—or adjuncts to—the average Alliance escort. Indeed, these merchantmen could accept some relatively simple, modularized air defense systems, if the air threat appeared to warrant them. These conversions should be considerably less costly than maintaining a larger active escort fleet during extended peacetime periods. A firmly funded and executed program for the mobilization of such capabilities might provide an alternative to constructing a larger escort fleet. Of course, some shipping would have to be curtailed until the conversions could be acomplished—probably not more than thirty days, which could well begin before hostilities break out.

Advanced Mine Barriers

Another concept that might produce effects similar to the use of armed merchant vessels involves the employment of CAPTOR mines, described in Chapter 10. CAPTOR has an effective blocking width of about 1 mile and a projected kill probability as high as 0.3. According to some estimates, a density of 300 mines per thousand miles of barrier might result in an attrition rate of 0.1 per barrier passage. Investment costs have been estimated at less than $60 million per 100 miles of barrier. Maintenance and delivery costs would be relatively slight, and delivery could be accomplished across the G.-I.-U.K. Gap with a dozen B-52D sorties (see Chapter 10). Even if these estimates prove highly optimistic, the concept of mine barriers appears sound for the future.

The Use of Nuclear Weapons at Sea

Nuclear weapons may be employed in a war at sea without being used in any simultaneous land combat. The oceans provide a natural boundary

**FIGURE 13-7
SIMPLIFIED ATTRITION ANALYSIS**

IMPACT OF ARMING MERCHANT SHIPS

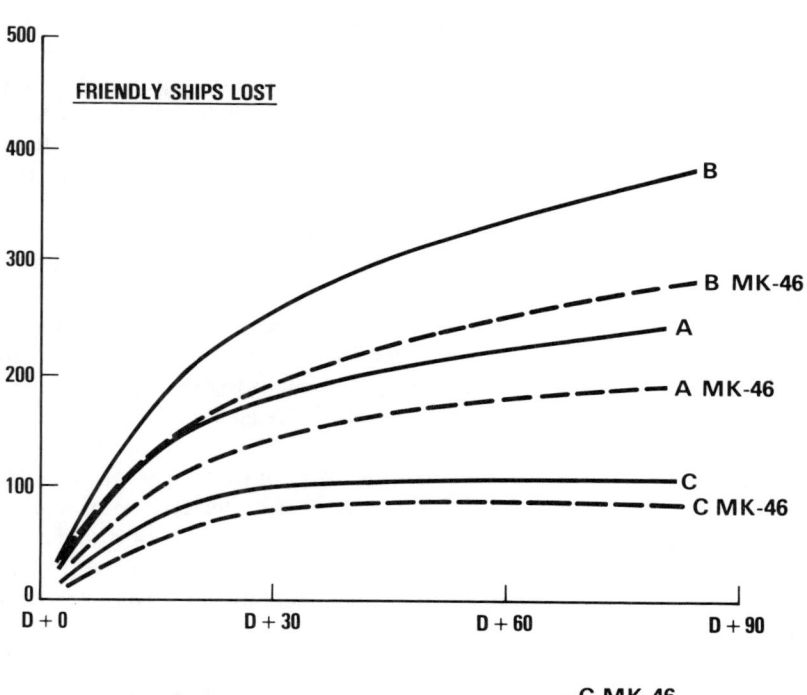

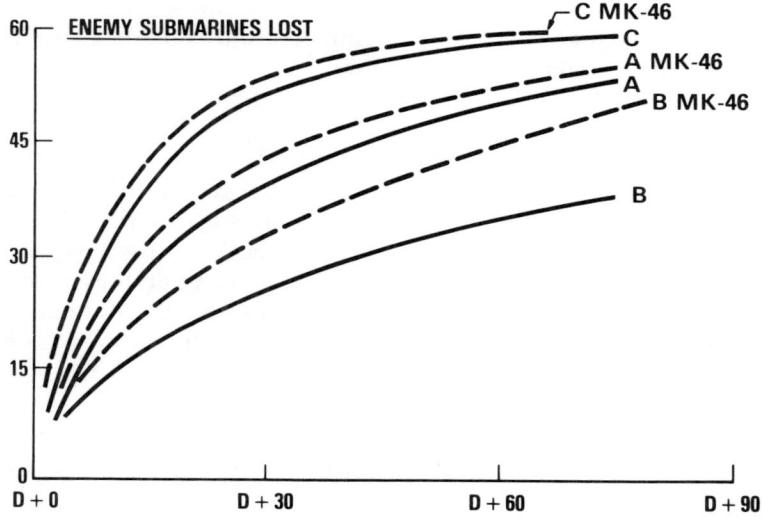

that both sides involved in hostilities might respect, and, of course, there are no large population centers at sea. The employment of nuclear weapons would sharply change the results described earlier.

The principal problem of antisubmarine warfare is to detect and localize the submarines initially. Nuclear weapons do not help with this task. While they do help solve the localization problem once a detection is made (by simply making accurate localization less necessary), the nuclear detonations may ruin the sonar environment for subsequent detections. Moreover, the use of nuclear weapons would require greater distances between convoyed ships, increasing the defended perimeter or reducing convoy size. On balance, antisubmarine warfare would probably be more difficult in the nuclear setting.

From the submarine point of view, nuclear weapons make the job easier. As shown in the calculations in the preceding section, the submarine is essentially carrying a weapons load through a series of dangerous barriers to a position where it can strike. Nuclear weapons enormously increase the killing potential of a single weapon load with little increase in exposure. Each nuclear weapon should have a higher probability of achieving at least one ship kill. Thus, merchant losses might increase by a factor of three or more during the early stages of a nuclear anti-SLOC campaign.

For naval surface forces or aircraft, the effect of nuclear weapons would probably not be so marked. For example, while the effectiveness of weapons launched from attacking aircraft would increase, the use of nuclear warheads on the defender's antiaircraft missiles could preclude the highly effective mass aircraft attack tactic. Thus, the effects might offset each other.

In summary, the use of nuclear weapons could significantly increase submarine attack capability. The results are likely to be so significant that they cannot be ignored. Even if the Soviets did not choose to go nuclear at the outset, they might elect to do so during the conflict if our ASW efforts were successful in a conventional conflict.

U.S. Sea Control and Merchant Ship Force Levels

The foregoing sections lay the groundwork for estimating the desired levels of Alliance sea control forces and merchant ships. Within U.S. and NATO circles, there is a wide divergence of views as to the adequacy of both. At one extreme are those who would base force level decisions on enemy potential. At the other are those who would decide on the basis of likely intentions and individual system capability. It is worthwhile to summarize the opposing positions.

The Opposing Views

Those who stress enemy potential as a guide for force sizing, like this

Working Group, tend to view the naval balance in terms of past and current trends, with particular respect for the lessons of World War II. They recognize that the Soviet threat has been increasing as Western naval forces have declined. They point out that the Soviets have a vast number of submarines, while we have allowed our destroyer and frigate force levels to decline to roughly one-third of what they were at the end of World War II (see Chapter 7). They note the great strides in both nuclear- and diesel-powered submarines over the past three decades. They observe that the number of merchant ships available to the United States has declined greatly. They see that the Soviets have many more submarines than the Germans did in World War II and realize that the code-breaking that provided the Allies with the information then probably could not be repeated. They also note that the average age of the remaining U.S. surface combatants is still greater than that of equivalent Soviet ships, and they are aware that the Soviet building program exceeds that of the United States.[15]

Despite their tendency to quote statistics, proponents of this approach depend basically on their "professional judgment" that Alliance—and particularly U.S.—force levels have dwindled too far. They feel that the current trends in naval force size are indicative of their role in representing a nation's military interests. More specifically, they feel that numbers of ships, submarines, and aircraft reflect a navy's ability to continue combat activities in spite of losses and to maintain a credible capability after the cessation of hostilities. To them, the lack of definite numerical superiority is a serious concern. They recognize that the sea control mission is more difficult than that of sea denial. Sea control forces must escort and defend high-value ships as well as locate and destroy enemy forces before those forces can approach their targets. Forces designed for the sea denial mission, they say, can emphasize fire power and first-strike capability, while sea control forces must stress endurance. The differences between the missions strongly suggest that the sea control job requires more assets than sea denial. They demonstrate that the experience of World War II supports this hypothesis: Allied forces were not able to contain the German submarine threat until they had achieved substantial numerical superiority—and successful code-breaking as well.[16] They believe there is an adequate analytical basis for concluding that the Soviets now have the capability to compete with the U.S. Navy on at least equal terms. Some naval experts have expressed the view (see Chapter 7) that the Soviets now have sufficient forces to deny the United States free access to the seas in some areas such as the Eastern Mediterranean or the Northwest Pacific.

Those of the opposite view place far less emphasis on number of assets. To them, what counts is each individual ship's effectiveness and manner of deployment. They note, as we do in Chapter 4, that the majority of Soviet submarines are unlikely or ill-equipped to attack the sealanes and that their individual quality is lower than our own (as discussed in Chapter 10). They note that the sea control battle will be fought by radically different types of forces on the two sides. They point out that our new submarines would be used to attack Soviet submarines and that our large fleet of ASW patrol aircraft did not exist in World War II. And they are apparently convinced that improvements in the West's ASW capabilities are more than a match for Soviet submarine improvements.

Moreover, they tend to accept the "NATO-first scenario" as the most critical one for the United States and point out that the United States would not be alone in conducting a campaign along the Atlantic SLOC. The naval forces of our allies would contribute to an anti-SLOC campaign also. The size and character of Allied general-purpose naval forces are described in Chapters 6, 7, and 8. Although the capabilities of most Allied navies do not match those of U.S. forces—only eight of the 134 NATO submarines are nuclear-powered, and over half of NATO's 260 destroyers and frigates are more than fifteen years old—NATO navies can make an important contribution to our total defensive effort. Many are capable of open ocean operations; others can clear enemy mines; conduct ASW operations in European sealanes, harbors, and shallow water areas; and provide some air defense near the SLOC termini. In addition, according to the argument, it may be feasible to develop modular packages that would enable older Alliance surface ships to serve as towed array or helicopter platforms for use in antisubmarine "search and destroy" missions.

The quality over quantity proponents also profess uncertainty as to the importance of code-breaking or the contribution of cryptology in the current sea control setting. Advances in technology have produced significant improvements both in cryptographic security and code-breaking techniques. How these advances would interact to affect anti-SLOC campaigns is unclear, they say. Improved and timely intelligence might result in improved detection and localization of enemy submarines. This could be important to ASW operations since these involve a process of attrition where individual encounters each have a low probability of success. The direct contribution of successful code-breaking to convoy operations may be less important in the modern setting, given the effectiveness of current surveillance systems and the speed and endurance characteristics of modern submarines.

Most of all, however, the holders of this more optimistic point of view place reliance on the validity of analytical calculations concerning the most likely "exchange ratios" to be achieved in a submarine-ASW campaign in the North Atlantic. Some believe that we should predicate our force levels on the achievement of an exchange ratio of 1:1 (i.e., a single merchant ship lost per submarine sunk). As will be demonstrated, such calculations are possible, but they might be more credible if they were not performed by analysts who want to reduce naval expenditures or those who want to redirect spending toward more offensive (force projection) systems. The major problem with such calculations is that they tend to produce "point solutions" that obscure the inherent uncertainties. This is the subject of the following section.

Uncertainties in Force Level Estimation

The preceding simple analysis demonstrates why studies suggest that it is impossible to provide enough ASW force to limit our initial merchant ship losses to very low levels (say 10 percent) in the early weeks of a war. The reasons are simply that the probability of destroying a submarine in an individual encounter is small and that submarines can, to a substantial degree, control the number of encounters. Encounters occur primarily when submarines attempt to move to the shipping lane and press the attack. Antisubmarine warfare is a time-consuming process. Nonetheless, a major fraction of ship sinkings—and submarine losses—is likely to occur during the first thirty to sixty days of conflict. Submarines are more likely to be destroyed in a series of barriers than in the sealanes themselves.

This is not an argument for smaller ASW forces. Increased convoy defenses and larger barrier forces would reduce the time needed to destroy enemy submarines. Also, the total ASW force must be sufficiently large at the outset to survive long enough to kill enemy submarines. Moreover, the size of the ASW force must prevent an enemy tactic of destroying the ASW force, then attacking the merchant ships. Unlike the situation in World War II, there probably would not be time for significant buildup of military forces during the conflict on either side—although there might be sufficient time for converting some merchant ships to help defend themselves.

Comparisons of opposing capabilities should consider a number of variables, such as weapon characteristics and performance, warning, tactics, logistics, command and control, dynamics of conflict, and force size. Unfortunately, information on many of these factors and the methodologies for analyzing them rigorously are not available outside the defense community. However, published data permit gross comparisons of the capabilities of opposing forces. Such comparisons include numbers of ships and aircraft, weapon systems available, force trends over time, and— most important—the range of performance characteristics that may be achievable. One of the major shortcomings of complex computer modeling is that it tends to assign a single performance value to each variable, even though there may be absolutely no test data to substantiate the point values chosen. In the ASW area, where virtually no combat experience has been gained for over thirty years, the range of uncertainty is so great that the value of complex modeling must be seriously questioned.

Two sample tables demonstrate the broad range of force level requirements that can be generated under different assumptions within the current band of uncertainty. Table 13-7 illustrates seven different computations of plausible convoy escort requirements for the defense of an Alliance SLOC across the Atlantic or the Pacific or to the Persian Gulf via either ocean. First of all, there is some uncertainty as to the number of convoys that would be dispatched per week. This would depend on many variables such as the amount of prepositioning, the duration of the war anticipated, the level of essential economic shipping that must be defended, and the extent of the submarine threat that materializes.

Next, there is at least some uncertainty as to the time required for any convoy to make a round trip to the war theater. While the speeds of ships are well known, their exact courses are not. Longer routes may be used to avoid an enemy air threat, for instance. The unloading time is not firm either, for it is related to the damage done to the receiving ports. Third, there is disagreement as to how many escorts should accompany each convoy; the number of escorts needed initially can vary very broadly. The examples show that the initial escort requirements across the Atlantic might vary from 18 to 124, while those in the Persian Gulf might range from 84 to 168 (depending primarily on whether attempts were made to escort tankers and other cargo vessels).

The next variable is the attrition of the escorts themselves. As mentioned, one reasonable Soviet tactic would be to concentrate on attacking the military escorts rather than the merchant ships in order to eliminate Alliance naval capabilities. Escort attrition could easily vary from none (0 percent) all the way up to the loss of half of our escorts on each round trip (50 percent). Another primary variable is the time it would take the ASW campaign to essentially eliminate the Soviet submarine threat. There is certainly no valid means of determining whether this can be done in four, twelve, or even twenty-four weeks. Those two parameters lead to an estimate of the number of replacement escorts needed. Replacements could range from 17 to 84 by varying escort attrition within reasonable limits. They may vary even more depending on the time it takes to neutralize the Soviet submarine force. If it takes twelve weeks to eliminate the submarine threat, as many as 149 replacement escorts could be needed to offset a 10 percent escort loss rate per week.

Therefore, it would be difficult at best to determine Atlantic escort level requirements more accurately than "somewhere between 18 and 273." By the same token, it is difficult to pin down escort requirements in the Persian Gulf other than somewhere between 53 and 370. A middle-of-the-road guess for Pacific convoys is about 175, with the same method of calculation.

Next, it is necessary to estimate what fraction of the total escort requirements must be provided by the U.S. Navy. Estimates of non-U.S.

TABLE 13-7
ESTIMATING ESCORT REQUIREMENTS

	Atlantic				Pacific		Persian Gulf	
Convoys Dispatched Per Week	1	2	2	4	2	1/2	3	
Weeks per Convoy Round-Trip	3	3	3	4	6	8	8	
Escorts Assigned Per Convoy	6	7	7	8	7	7	7	
Escorts Required Initially	18	42	42	124	84	28	168	
Escort Losses Per Week	0%	5%	25%	10%	10%	5%	5%	
Weeks to Neutralize Sub Threat	4	8	8	12	12	18	24	
Replacement Escorts Required	0	17	84	149	91	25	202	
Total Escorts Required	18	59	126	273	175	53	370	
Non-U.S. Escorts Available	100	75	75	50	100	0	0	
U.S. Escorts Required	0	0	51	223	75	53	370	
U.S. Escorts Available to Convoy	60	50	50	40	20	60	30	
U.S. Escort Surplus (+) / Shortage (-)	+60	+50	-1	-183	-55	+7	-340	

NATO escorts that could be used across the Atlantic vary between 50 and 100. There is little more certainty concerning the number of U.S. naval escorts that might be available for this mission. It would depend largely on the requirements to defend aircraft carriers and their underway replenishment groups or amphibious task forces that might be needed to support the NATO flanks. The best guess is between 40 and 60.

This rudimentary analysis demonstrates that it would be difficult to establish U.S. escort levels with any degree of confidence—even for the Atlantic: they could vary from 60 fewer than we now have all the way up to 183 more than we now have. Similarly, we might be "short" up to 55 escorts in the Pacific and somewhere between 7 too many and 340 too few for a Persian Gulf SLOC. According to this exploration of the uncertainty levels, those who focus on the enemy potential may be right when they say we have too few, and those who stress the effectiveness and deployment of individual ships may be right when they say we have too many. The decision will remain a matter of judgment rather than mathematics.

This Working Group is convinced that we have too few escorts—particularly if scenarios other than the "NATO-first" one are given serious consideration. Even if the United States developed a "600-ship" navy (see Chapter 12) composed of more lower-cost escort-type ships, it is doubtful that we could conservatively deploy an escort force to cover all contingencies. Escorts for our military cargoes may be adequate, but it appears virtually impossible to provide suitable escort for economic cargoes.

Table 13-8 illustrates the equal uncertainty concerning losses of merchant ships—and more important, cargoes—under a range of different assumptions. To begin with, as discussed in Chapter 4, there is considerable uncertainty about the number of submarines that the Soviets

TABLE 13-8
ESTIMATED MERCHANT SHIP 90-DAY LOSSES TO SUBMARINES

Soviet Submarines Allocated:			30			60			100		
Ship Kills per Soviet Submarine:		2	5	10	2	5	10	2	5	10
$P_{K_B}^*$	Number of Barriers	Pre-Deployed									
0.05	1	NO	155	385	775	310	770	1550	515	1285	2585
		YES	165	405	810	330	810	1620	550	1350	2700
	3	NO	120	295	590	240	590	1180	400	985	1965
		YES	125	310	620	250	620	1240	415	1035	2070
	5	NO	85	225	450	170	450	900	285	750	1500
		YES	105	265	530	210	530	1060	350	885	1770
0.10	1	NO	135	335	670	270	670	1340	450	1120	2240
		YES	150	370	740	300	740	1480	500	1235	2470
	3	NO	80	200	400	160	400	800	270	670	1340
		YES	90	220	440	180	440	880	300	735	1470
	5	NO	50	130	260	100	260	520	170	435	870
		YES	70	180	360	140	360	720	235	600	1200
0.20	1	NO	100	245	490	200	490	1180	335	815	1630
		YES	120	310	620	240	620	1240	400	1035	2070
	3	NO	40	100	200	80	200	400	135	335	670
		YES	50	130	260	100	260	520	170	435	870
	5	NO	20	55	110	40	110	220	70	185	370
		YES	40	110	220	80	220	440	135	370	740

*P_{K_B} = Submarines killed per barrier transit

Quantifying the Sealane Defense Problem 373

might dedicate to an anti-SLOC campaign in any part of the world. The table, therefore, shows 30, 60, and 100 (by no means the outer limits of total Soviet capabilities). Second, we do not know enough about Soviet submarines and torpedoes to predict with any certainty how many ships they should be able to kill with a single torpedo load. There is not even agreement as to the number of torpedoes carried in each of their many submarine classes. Hence, the table shows "ship-kills per Soviet submarine" varying from two to ten.

On our side, there is no sure way to tell what fraction of the Soviet submarines passing through a barrier will be killed. Thus, the table shows three values: one in twenty, one in ten, and one in five (i.e., PKB = 0.05, 0.10, and 0.20). Neither do we know how many successive barriers we will be able to establish. We currently count on five, but as discussed earlier, this estimate could vary broadly depending on the Soviet acquisition of overseas bases from which to operate in a major war or on the "rules of engagement" attendant to a lesser conflict. We thus vary the number of barriers from one to five. The combination of PKB and number of barriers tends to establish the number of "round trips" the Soviet submarines could make before they were all sunk. This could vary from twenty round trips to less than one. Moreover, we cannot know certainly how long a "round trip" will require: although four weeks is often used, this, too, depends on the Soviets' choice of submarine speed versus noise and on the location of their reloading bases. This uncertainty relates to the "weeks to neutralize sub threat" variable treated in Table 13-7.

Finally, there is no way to predict how many Soviet submarines would be "predeployed" to the sealanes before an outbreak of hostilities. As discussed earlier, this is important from the standpoint of how much attrition has been exacted at the barriers before those submarines could first strike our convoys. Hence, two extreme cases are shown: for no submarines predeployed (NO) and all submarines predeployed (YES). The truth would lie somewhere between and depend on political and military circumstances preceding any specific confrontation.

Table 13-8 shows the extraordinary range of uncertainty in the numbers of ships that might be lost during just the first ninety days of an anti-SLOC campaign. At one extreme, 100 Soviet submarines might sink 2,700 Alliance merchant ships if their torpedo effectiveness were high, if they predeployed, and if we established only one low-effectiveness barrier (for instance, only the escorts around the convoys themselves). This situation could arise in less than all-out confrontation in the event we were attempting to protect all shipping to and from the Persian Gulf and the Soviets had access to submarine facilities along the coast of Africa. The campaign could also persist longer than ninety days.

Near the other extreme is the case of a moderately effective 30-submarine attack on Western SLOCs with no predeployment and a series of five Alliance antisubmarine barriers of reasonable effectiveness (each killing 1 submarine in 10 that crosses). In this case, only 130 ships would be lost in ninety days and there would be little left to the threat. If technology could raise the PKB of each barrier to 0.20, if the submarines did not predeploy, and if each submarine could kill only 2 ships per cruise, then only 20 ships would be lost.

Again, the "correct" prediction cannot be selected by analysis—only by judgment. The judgment of this Working Group is that somewhere between 300 and 600 merchant ships (and escorts) would be lost within four to twelve weeks of the onset of a major war at sea. As mentioned previously, all of our war reserves could be carried in roughly 1,000 large modern merchant ships. Unless means were found to ameliorate those tolls—as previously and subsequently suggested—we would be faced with the destruction of one-third to one-half of our military equipment in transit across the seas, even if the Soviets dedicated a relatively small number of their submarines to anti-SLOC activities. These early losses cannot be substantially reduced by simply adding convoy escorts, submarines, or patrol aircraft. Other means to reduce these damages must be sought.

Resupply versus Prepositioning

The foregoing discussion has indicated that very substantial cargo and merchant ship destruction may result from even modest Soviet attacks on the sealanes. It is vital, then, to consider alternative means of meeting the resupply requirements for U.S. and Allied forces—either in NATO or in Northeast Asia. One alternative is "prepositioning." Such prepositioned material can be visualized as the military analog to a strategic or economic stockpile—but consisting of finished goods ready for combat application. Obviously, equipment that might be needed for contingencies elsewhere probably cannot be prepositioned.

Advocates of prepositioning urge that shipping losses would be avoided and that the material would be there even before it is needed. Those who do not believe in prepositioning point to storage cost considerations, warmup and linkup problems associated with getting stored equipment ready to use and into the hands of the user, vulnerability to air attack or seizure, and the costs of additional equipment for training in the United States or use in other parts of the world. This section looks at the costs of prepositioning versus convoying and some of the other considerations.

The costs of prepositioning combat stockpiles can be compared with estimated costs of transporting materials during war, based on shipping-loss assumptions. This analysis begins by illustrating the tradeoffs between combat stockpile and sealane defense costs.

U.S. PREPOSITIONED EQUIPMENT

The U.S. Army maintains heavy equipment (such as the M-60 tanks shown here at Germersheim Depot) in West Germany for several CONUS-based divisions. Additional prepositioning may be warranted as a hedge against highly uncertain, but probably serious, early shipping losses in a NATO war. (Courtesy U.S. Army)

The U.S. Army also maintains large stockpiles of artillery ammunition on Okinawa in the Pacific as a hedge against another war on the Korean peninsula. Such materials could be moved into South Korea several weeks before equivalent shipments from the CONUS could arrive. Prepositioning may be substantially cheaper than a larger wartime navy. (Courtesy U.S. Army)

The Defense Department estimates that 10 million tons of hardware and 15 million tons of petroleum, oil, and lubricants (POL) would have to be shipped to replace existing stockpiles within the first six months of a war in Europe. Some of these materials would be lost as the result of merchant shipping losses. As discussed previously, the loss rate would depend on many factors: when convoys sail, the number of available escorts, Allied success in antisubmarine barrier operations, and the number of ships used to transport the materials.

An analysis of the merits of shipping during wartime versus the merits of peacetime prepositioning involves anticipated shipping loss rates on the one hand and the cost of the material lost at sea on the other. The former has already been discussed. Next we need to estimate the replacement cost per ton for an average cargo. The items listed below are representative of the high priority material that would be needed to reinforce our combat units:

Guided missiles and munitions	$100,000 per ton
Radar and communications	$ 50,000 per ton
Tanks and personnel carriers	$ 20,000 per ton
Trucks and support vehicles	$ 5,000 per ton
Unguided munitions	$ 4,000 per ton
Food and personal equipment	$ 2,000 per ton
Fuel, oil, and lubricants	$ 200 per ton

Assuming from this cross-section that the replacement value of hardware averages $8,000 per ton and that POL is $200 per ton, the shipment values would be $80 billion and $30 billion, respectively, for a total of $83 billion. To compare the costs of increased combat stockpiles versus shipping during wartime, rates of loss must be estimated. At attrition rates of 25 percent, 50 percent, and 75 percent, material losses of $21 billion, $42 billion, and $62 billion would be incurred. This excludes the value of merchant ships and escorts.

The 25 percent example assumes losses of 250 merchant vessels and 25 escorts, losses that have already been shown to be optimistic. Replacement cost of the escorts is figured at $150 million apiece, which totals $3.7 billion for the 25 losses. The 250 merchant ships would be replaced with 62 larger vessels costing about $61 million apiece, for a total of $3.8 billion.

The analysis shows that charges of $90.5 billion for material and shipping ($83 billion + $3.7 billion + $3.8 bilion) must be incurred to deliver $62 billion worth of materials to combat areas, assuming a 25 percent attrition rate. Thus, the cost of delivery is $28.5 billion.

To compare this approach to the alternative of prepositioning larger stockpiles requires estimating the expenses of stockpiling $62 billion of materials. From various military documents, the major costs for hardware construction are estimated at $500 per ton, with maintenance requirements of $100 per ton per year. The total price would be $2,000 per ton over a fifteen-year period. Discounting the maintenance expenses at 10 percent yields a present value total of $1,260 per ton. Hence, the construction and maintenance cost for the 7.5 million tons of hardware would be $9.5 billion—roughly 16 percent of its procurement value.

For POL, according to data available from the American Petroleum Institute, construction costs would range between $10 and $30 per ton, depending on the type of storage facility required. The cost of underground storage in natural caverns such as salt domes tends toward the low end of the range, while aboveground storage in large steel tanks is at the high end. Maintenance costs for POL are generally low. To allow for maintenance and any special features associated with adequately protected prepositioned POL, a per ton value of $30 has been chosen for this comparison. At the extreme, the total cost to store and maintain 11.2 million tons of POL would thus be about $340 million—or 15 percent of its procurement value. Hence, the total costs of prepositioning would be approximately $9.9 billion.

Construction estimates of $500 per ton are sufficient to provide *underground* storage for military equipment like trucks and tanks at approximately the cost rate of the Washington, D.C., Metro subway station, which ran around $20 million per mile. Given a slightly different cross-section, it should be possible to store up to 40,000 tons per mile in such tunnels. Less than 200 miles of the tunnels would accommodate the entire 7.5 million tons. By comparison, the U.S. Mobile ICBM program is considering the construction of some 3,000 miles of tunnels to keep our strategic deterrent invulnerable. Underground storage would avoid usurping valuable surface land within the NATO area and would make the supplies essentially invulnerable to conventional air attack. Naturally, this Working Group would not advocate open, aboveground, high-density storage near the front lines for prepositioned material.

Some equipment would have to be purchased for forces in the United States to replace what is prepositioned. Certain duplication is bound to result, although by no means on a one-for-one basis. Much of the material to be prepositioned would be for reserve forces which are only intended for use in a NATO war. They would only need a fraction of their total equipment for a few weeks of U.S. training each year. Other material is war reserve consumables, such as munitions and spare equipments, which are not assigned to active operational units. In any event, if the total "savings" due to prepositioning were applied to additional procurement of material, it could replace 24 percent ($19.6 billion/$83 billion) of the equipment sent at the 25 percent attrition level. This would seem to be more than adequate.

Figure 13-8 shows the possible added costs of prepositioning versus the

**FIGURE 13-8
ADDED COSTS OF PREPOSITIONING
VERSUS
ADDED COSTS OF SHIPPING LOSSES**

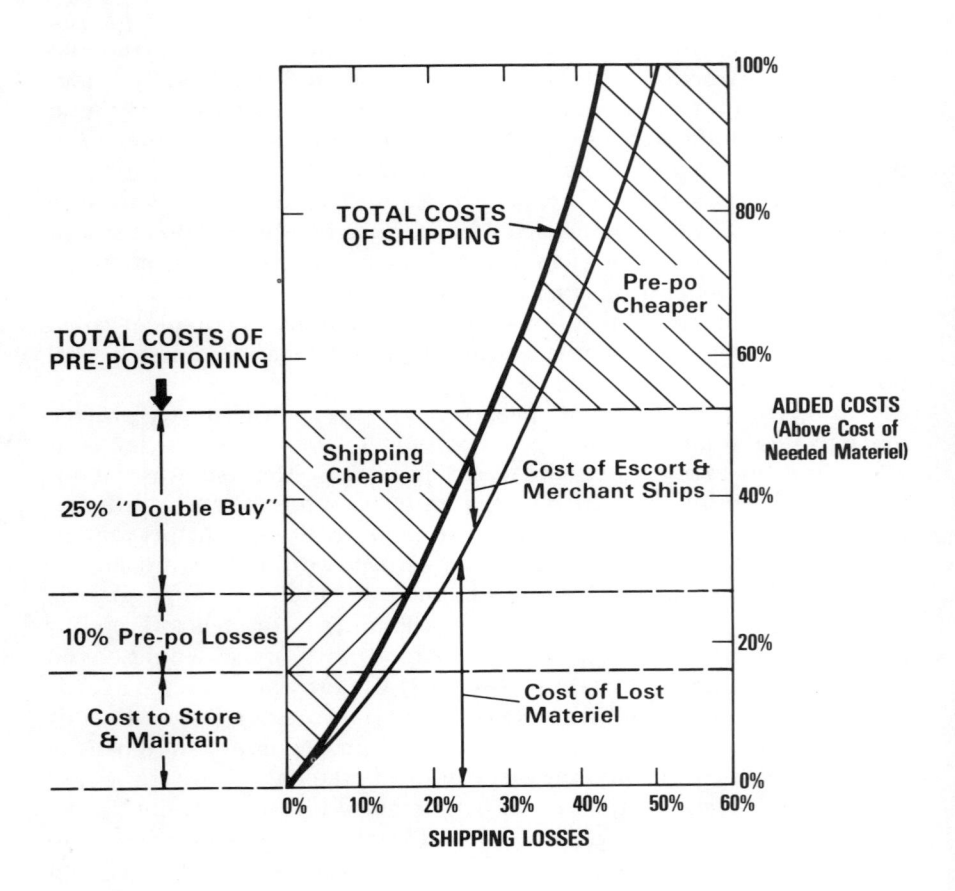

estimated shipping losses resulting from different levels of attrition. This illustrates how the tradeoff between the two might be made and where the "crossover" point falls—at which prepositioning is cheaper than accepting shipping losses. If only the cost of prepositioning is compared to the value of lost equipment and ships, then the crossover occurs at 10 percent shipping losses. If it is further assumed that 10 percent of the prepositioned equipment will be lost (to attack or poor maintenance, say), then the crossover comes at 16 percent shipping losses. Still another assumption that an additional 25 percent of the prepositioned material must be procured for peacetime training in the United States would move the crossover out to 27 percent shipping losses. These numbers will vary with the actual costs of equipment, ships, storage, and the like. This is a subject that deserves additional study, as does the feasibility and cost of providing reasonably secure storage for this material. Nonetheless, as the attrition rate of convoys increases above approximately 20 percent, so does the attractiveness of increased prepositioning as a substitute. This comparison considers only a limited number of variables. Many other factors have an impact on the costs and benefits of prepositioning versus shipping. These include:

- The implications of large shipping losses for the postwar period;
- The impact of large material losses on the ground campaign;
- Uncertainty as to the duration of combat and rate of consumption;
- Obsolescence of stored material, which is the same whether the material is in storage in the United States or in Europe;
- Sensitivity of results to changes in attrition rates and the time-horizon for calculating life-cycle costs;
- The location of material relative to the combat zone, and the problems of warming up the equipment and getting it to the arriving troops;
- The impact of prepositioning on base defense requirements;
- The effect of a shipping stand-down on ASW and other sea control operations; and
- The opportunity for game-playing on the part of the enemy.

When these and other factors are taken into consideration, the analysis becomes far more complex. Since the costs involved are substantial, a major analysis of the resupply alternatives seems justified. Nonetheless, unless the total costs of prepositioning are far higher than assumed in this example, prepositioning still appears preferable to convoying if losses on the order of 25 percent are anticipated.

One partial alternative to peacetime prepositioning is to be prepared to ship the equivalent equipment to the anticipated theater of operations during the period of increased tensions which is likely to precede the outbreak of hostilities. The use of strategic warning for preparation time could result in significant savings in losses at sea. On the other hand, there is always the danger that political authorities will refuse to ship (or receive) these equipments for fear of exacerbating an already difficult international situation. Such early shipments could also be used by the Soviets as a signal to predeploy their own submarines toward the sealanes. According to Table 13-8, this move could easily result in the loss of an additional 100 ships as soon as hostilities broke out. Whether this would present a net advantage or disadvantage is not clear. In any event, it would appear wiser to be postured in such a fashion that preparation time could be used as a "bonus" rather than as a prerequisite.

Summary

The preceding sections have described an anti-SLOC campaign, examined the wide range of uncertainities in the interactions between Soviet submarines and Alliance surface vessels, computed possible force requirements, and addressed one alternative to shipping. A number of observations can be made as a result of these considerations:

- A major anti-SLOC campaign could be similar to World War II in terms of the dynamics of combat. It would be a war of attrition, with ship losses almost certainly increasing faster than submarine losses during the early stages of conflict.
- In the event of a NATO-Warsaw Pact war, the United States currently plans to move approximately 10 million tons of American war supplies and 15 million tons of fuel to NATO ports within the first ninety days of hostilities to reinforce U.S. forces. This operation would require roughly 1,000 merchant vessels. In addition, NATO allies would require supplies by sea during the same period.
- In the absence of some technological improvement making Soviet submarines much more vulnerable to prompt detection and localization than they are today, there appears to be no way to avoid high shipping losses during the early days of a European conventional conflict if the Allies chose to maintain a major Atlantic resupply effort during this time. The uncertainties in predicting the outcome of the antisubmarine battle warrant the adoption of techniques and approaches that minimize the impact of poor estimating.
- Prudence may dictate that materials critical to the prosecution of a conventional war with the Soviets should be stockpiled during peacetime by all members of the Alliance in amounts that could assure an effective defense until resupply could be guaranteed. The costs of such stockpiles appear modest compared to foreseeable alternatives.
- Certain vital commodities such as food and energy supplies should also be stockpiled against the threat of shipping interruption during the early stages of a major conflict. However, it will probably be impracticable to stockpile adequately against a protracted war (over twelve months). Hence, a requirement does exist to reestablish

a flow of essential nonwar material under continuing periods of warfare. The most vital commodities within this category are probably food and oil.
- Compared to the costs of defending the sealanes within NATO against the potential Soviet submarine threat, there is an increasing premium on prepositioning essential supplies in or near the combat theater, where they would only have to be defended against the Soviet air threat rather than Soviet air and naval forces. Prepositioning would generally be favored if shipping losses exceeding 25 percent were anticipated.
- If the conventional NATO defense should be successful for more than a month or so, then the West should be able to regain the use of essential sealanes at acceptable attrition levels—unless Alliance naval elements had been destroyed in the initial stages of a Soviet attack.
- For the foreseeable future, the sealane defense mission in a major U.S.-Soviet conventional conflict would remain primarily an antisubmarine warfare operation. Moreover, there appears to be no justification for abandoning the use of escorted convoys as the best means of destroying enemy submarines, even if they do not markedly reduce convoy losses. Independent sailing of merchant ships is desirable only if a high density of commercial shipping can be maintained, and that appears unlikely.
- Alliance escort levels are probably marginal to defend military convoys alone. It would probably be impossible to build an escort force large enough to escort economic shipments too.
- Arming of merchant ships with homing weapons such as the Mk-46 torpedo appears to be a cost-effective means of reducing losses, although the overall losses would remain quite high. Other means to improve the self-defense of merchant ships appear to be in order. For instance, the conversion of large merchantmen to accept towed arrays and helicopters might make them as effective as many current escorts in the Alliance inventory.
- An anti-SLOC campaign sinks ships, not cargo per se. Compared to World War II, the total U.S. "arsenal" is considerably smaller and the cargo ships are much larger. There are several alternatives available to reduce military cargo losses: (1) Use more and smaller ships to carry essential cargos; (2) scatter essential cargoes among economic shipments to reduce the per-ship cargo losses; and (3) continue to sail commercially laden ships with military cargo vessels to dilute the effectiveness of the enemy operations. The loss of the ships during wartime is probably less significant than the loss of the scarce cargoes. If some form of cheaper unmanned "decoy"

can be developed, it might provide an even more attractive option.
- Although technology has resulted in substantial increases in convoy ASW capabilities since World War II, improvements in nuclear submarine performance appear to roughly offset them—within the limits of estimation uncertainties. Barrier ASW operations, however, offer significant opportunities to increase the rate of enemy submarine attrition, thus lowering the total exposure of friendly convoys to the submarine threat.

14
Overall Assessment of Naval/Maritime Balance

Introduction

This study assesses the capabilities of the Western Alliance members to maintain the security of the seas against increasing threats from the naval forces of the Soviet Union and its client-states over a range of possible confrontations. The threats perceived are evaluated within the contexts of differing naval backgrounds and objectives, dissimilar strategic doctrines, various conflict scenarios, and evolving naval technology. This chapter presents a short summary of these considerations, followed by general assessments of opposing capabilities across the gamut of naval missions. These broader assessments underlie the findings and recommendations of Chapter 15.

Historical Context

Soviet Naval Background

The Soviet Navy is part of a larger mechanism developed over the past sixty years to advance the interests of the regime. The navy's capabilities and intentions have been shaped by the Communist party leadership.

Owing to its limited resources, the Russian Navy was restricted to a minor defensive role in the early years after World War I, and it pursued no more ambitious goal. Although resources remained scarce through World War II and well into the postwar period, Soviet aspirations toward a broader use of sea power became manifest in the 1930s. Stalin wanted his country to take a place among the world's great naval powers. His aspirations led to a substantial building program that was subsequently delayed by World War II and finally abandoned after his death, under the pressure of economic problems and domestic political considerations. More important, changed strategic perceptions of Soviet naval imperatives as well as new options in military technology emerged in the post-Stalin era. This transition inspired Gorshkov to ask:

> Could the Soviet Union in the face of the imperialist threat agree to the eternal domination of the seas and oceans by the Western powers, particularly when broad regions of the ocean became the launch points of missiles with nuclear warheads? Of course not. In these circumstances, the only correct decision of the problem of the security of the country could be creation of those circumstances which would place before the militaristic circles of the West exactly the same problems with which they tried to encumber us.[1]
>
> Approximately in the middle of the 1950s in connection with the decision of the Central Committee of the Communist Party of the Soviet Union, major work was begun in our country for the creation of a powerful high seas rocket-nuclear fleet. This marks the beginning of the second stage in the development of the Soviet Navy. . . .[2]
>
> The fundamental directions by which the qualitative reform of the fleet was guided . . . were: change to the construction of an atomic submarine fleet; the introduction of rockets and nuclear weapons and the establishment of a submarine rocket-nuclear system of strategic significance; arming the fleet with long aircraft—high seas aviation; the introduction into the fleet of ships with aviation capabilities; qualitative change in the means of locating submerged objects and the forces and means for struggling with submarines; introduction of varied applications of radioelectronics, automation of control weapons and military technology and also mathematical methods of research using computers."[3]

Changes in foreign policy already under way when Stalin died also led logically to greater use of the merchant marine as a vehicle for influence as well as a potential earner of foreign exchange.

Current Soviet Naval Objectives

Over the past twenty years, Soviet naval forces have grown steadily and have become significantly more effective (after their post–World War II nadir), in conformity with the strategic context described subsequently. The responsible planners appear to have put high priority on:

1. The capability to counter U.S. sea-based strategic systems as they have evolved—initially with anticarrier systems, and later in the form of antisubmarine systems;
2. The creation and improvement of a naval strategic capability, primarily with ballistic missile submarines (both of longer and shorter range);
3. A submarine, land-based naval aircraft, and surface navy capable of inflicting immediate heavy damage on naval surface vessels and merchant ships with conventional or nuclear weapons, and of extensively mining the port facilities of the Western Alliance;

4. The maintenance of strong naval coastal defense and counter-mining capabilities as well as an expanding capacity to project naval infantry within areas of friendly land-based air cover;
5. Development of forward resupply capabilities consistent with sustained operations in distant waters—without extensive dependence on permanent shore bases abroad; and
6. Full civil maritime support of naval research, naval operations, and intelligence gathering.

The extent to which Soviet naval strength has grown over the past three decades to permit the accomplishment of these missions—for the first time in Russian history—will be assessed at the end of this chapter.

U.S. Naval Background

United States ambitions to become a major naval power began in the last decade of the nineteenth century—almost one hundred years ago. The U.S. Navy grew in the shadow of acknowledged British naval supremacy. It supplanted the British Navy as the world's unchallenged leader in naval forces in the wake of World War II. This was the result of the extraordinary American wartime ship and aircraft production effort. Naval opposition at sea had been virtually eliminated by the war, and the United States emerged as essentially the only nation with a vast and tested capability to project both air and ground force ashore from sea-based platforms. This unique capability has provided the focus for almost two generations of U.S. naval development, and it has been used—with varying degrees of success—in several political and military crises since World War II.

Current U.S. Naval Objectives

The imperative of U.S. naval evolution since World War II has been, in general, to develop a major sea-based nuclear war deterrent while maintaining the ability to control the seas and exploit that control in support of U.S. politico-military interests. This has led to four major naval objectives:

1. Maintenance of land- and sea-based ASW forces capable of defeating conventional or nuclear operations of an increasingly sophisticated Soviet attack submarine fleet;
2. Creation of a relatively invulnerable sea-based strategic deterrent;
3. Maintenance of a substantial capability to project air power at sea or ashore in the face of increasing Soviet or Soviet-supplied defenses; and
4. Maintenance of the capability to project amphibious forces ashore against substantial opposition.

A worldwide forward-base structure was "inherited" from World War II

SOVIET AND U.S. FORWARD DEPLOYMENT CAPABILITY

The Soviets have had to build up their distant deployment capabilities without benefit of readily available shore facilities. Here a Soviet Kazbek-class fleet oiler refuels a Kashin-class destroyer (bow visible) at sea, while a Kara-class guided missile cruiser steams alongside. (Courtesy U.S. Navy)

The U.S. Navy "inherited" a worldwide forward base structure from World War II. Shown here: an S-3A carrier-based ASW aircraft (far left) and three F-14A fighters aboard the U.S.S. *John F. Kennedy* (CV-67), which is departing from a routine visit—with shore leave—in Naples, Italy. (Courtesy U.S. Navy)

and expanded in some areas in the subsequent cold war era. Since then, there appears to have been no explicit policy for the retention of overseas bases beyond some minimum essential, economically practical, and politically acceptable level. Minimal demands have been placed on U.S. merchant fleet assets, consistent only with wartime requirements for resupply of NATO. In terms of both bases and merchant ships, the United States was able to coast along on the assets largely acquired during World War II. By comparison, the Soviets were forced to start from scratch in the postwar era.

The U.S. Navy's share of the defense budget has increased in recent years. Owing to rapidly rising manpower costs, the escalation in shipbuilding and operating expenses, and the perceived economies of scale in military vessels, however, it has been necessary to reduce the size of the navy substantially from its postwar zenith. Every effort has been made to improve the quality of this shrinking navy, with emphasis on smaller numbers of large, individually versatile ships. Much of the reduction has occurred in convoy escorts and amphibious warfare ships.

Comparative Force Level Trends

In the same period of time, the Soviet fleet has grown substantially. As many of the submarines and smaller craft built in the early postwar years reach obsolescence, it is expected to stabilize at about a "775-ship navy," while the United States appears headed for a "525-ship navy," according to the latest Executive Branch shipbuilding plan. Excluding the United States, other Western Alliance nations (including France and Spain) collectively maintain another "600-ship navy" at present, but their future plans are not available.

Strategic Context

No assessment of the Soviet threat to Alliance sealanes can be made without considering the fundamentals of Soviet military doctrine. Neither the Soviet armed forces nor those of the Western Alliance would be able to perform all their potential missions simultaneously. Consequently, the ability of the Soviets to deny Alliance use of the sealanes must be evaluated within the context of the most probable Soviet priorities in time-sensitive resource allocation.

Soviet Strategic Doctrine

The Russians emphasize the attainment and preservation of predominant capabilities at the higher levels of combat in order to broaden the opportunities for accomplishing their military objectives at the lower levels. They hope to achieve overwhelming military control as soon as possible during any conflict in order to hasten the achievement of the political aims for which the war is being fought. Consistent with this approach, and having endured a generation of strategic inferiority, the Soviets have placed high priority on achieving a prompt and radically favorable shift in the strategic nuclear balance. At the same time, they have built up conventional air and ground forces to defeat any opponents on the Eurasian landmass and exploit successes by "investing" and occupying enemy territory. Finally, they are developing naval forces to achieve Soviet "command of the seas" in certain areas for the support of other politico-military objectives.

In situations where the Soviets enjoy equal or superior military capability at the higher levels of potential combat, they believe in exploiting any advantage to support their stated objective of enlarging the Communist sphere of influence and control. They may employ socio-political or economic devices, or lower-level pressures or military action, seeking to minimize their risks by using client-states or sympathetic political movements whenever possible. They have resorted to these methods frequently in the past, and now naval forces are available for use directly or for the transport of client forces.

Soviet strategic military doctrine is clearly influenced by the military history of Russia, which has been invaded and ravaged on many occasions at tremendous costs in human life and physical resources. To the Soviets, no form of warfare is "unthinkable," regardless of the devastation it might cause. They appear to be driven by the concept that no form of warfare need be "losable" if sufficient resources are devoted to limiting their own damage and increasing the injury to their adversaries. Carrying this concept further, they can visualize a situation in which no major war need be fought because they will be able to accomplish their objectives by intimidation—or by proxy.

In conformity with the strategic principle of coordinating all available assets, the Soviets have given their trawler fleet extensive electronic monitoring capability; their fishing vessels contribute to hydrographic exploration and analysis; and their commercial ships support logistic and political tasks as well as providing a valuable source of foreign exchange.

This review seems to indicate that in a war involving the United States, the primary strategic objective of Soviet oceangoing naval elements would be to contribute to the support of the nuclear forces. The second aim would be to blunt the naval striking power of the Alliance, and the third would be to support their own ground forces. A fourth objective would be to impede Alliance reinforcements. In accordance with the Soviets' preference for a quick and decisive war, however, they are likely to concentrate initially on blocking NATO receiving ports through mines and bombing. Interdiction of Western sealanes is by no means the most important early Soviet naval mission.

In crisis situations where the threat of general war is not high, their navy is capable of carrying out lesser missions, from demonstrating presence and resolve to inhibiting the movement of Western naval and support forces. There is nothing in Soviet doctrine to hinder the use of seapower in this fashion unless the risks of failure or escalation appear to be unacceptable.

U.S. Strategic Doctrine

United States strategic concepts have evolved over a starkly different route from those of the Soviets. To begin with, our national political objectives are somewhat more limited: rather than pursuing the expansion of our own political ideology as a doctrinal imperative, we have sought only to retain the right to political freedom for ourselves and others with an avowed preference for it. Second, the United States has escaped major conflict on the American continent and tends to view nuclear, chemical, and biological war as morally and physically repulsive in terms of the losses that would be sustained. Third, having entered the atomic age from a position of technical supremacy, we have tended to view nuclear weapons as the ultimate deterrent to armed conflict as a means of achieving political objectives. At the very least, we believe that these nuclear weapons could restrain the conflict to lower and less destructive levels. For the United States, conventional conflict has only been justified for the purpose of resisting foreign aggression aimed at eliminating the political freedoms of an ally or a friend.

To the Soviets, the acceptance of nuclear inferiority appeared irrational, and the U.S. nuclear weapons provided an incentive rather than a deterrent for developing their own. Consequently, the era of American nuclear superiority was short-lived, and now the issue is whether or not the United States will accept a strategic nuclear balance that can be perceived by some as a "tolerable" level of nuclear inferiority. The weakening—or at least the partial folding—of the "nuclear umbrella" has forced renewed focus on the balance of conventional forces to deter aggression (keeping in mind the popular Western presumption that both sides would continue to view the escalation to the use of nuclear weapons as unprofitable). This has given rise to the Western concept of "stability," in which military developments that could be considered threatening to the adversary's nuclear retaliatory capability have been avoided. As a case in point, no American military assets have been developed or procured primarily to neutralize Soviet SSBNs—although available assets could be used in this role. On the other hand, there are no indications that the Soviets have resisted force developments specifically directed toward the neutralization of American SSBNs—or the active defense of their own. In fact, the opposite appears to be the case. There is considerable argument that "nuclear parity" and "nuclear stability" are Western conceptual goals that are not shared in Soviet doctrine.

In fact, the linkage between conventional and nuclear forces may be seen quite differently by the U.S.S.R. and the Western Alliance, and this in turn may create substantially different views of the most likely force allocations and mission priorities during a major confrontation. In some ways, it appears to this Working Group that it may be easier to estimate Soviet priorities in the assignment of naval forces than to predict the most likely strategy and precedence for the use of Alliance seapower.

The United States has a primary interest in preserving the political, economic, and military integrity of the Western Alliance and remains motivated to assist, where practical, in the preservation of political freedom for nations that desire it. Both objectives require use of the seas during the periods of peace, crisis, or war for a variety of national objectives, including the projection of military force and the reinforcement of allied defenses. The question at issue is how this can best be done.

Scenario Context

Naval elements, probably more than any armed forces, have application across an extremely broad spectrum of political, economic, and military situations. Capabilities must be assessed realistically with these various scenarios in mind. Moreover, naval force allocations and effectiveness are themselves scenario-dependent. The Working Group has thus concerned itself with sealane security under a variety of circumstances involving both nuclear and conventional conflict.

Nuclear Conflict Scenarios

The currently most dreaded form of warfare is a full-scale exchange of intercontinental nuclear weapons between the Soviet Union and the United States. At one extreme, such an exchange has been visualized as a essentially a "spasm" action and response, in which the vast majority of weapons on both sides are exchanged within a few hours or days. Primary aims for such exchanges could be industrial and population centers, military targets, or any combination of the two. At the other end, such exchanges can be visualized as controlled and limited, intended either to demonstrate resolve or force cessation of hostilities short of massive destruction. Such exchanges could involve only a few weapons and a small number of targets of special relevance, and they could be regionally limited. Between these extremes lies a variety of options in which each side would attempt to destroy the other's will or capability to persevere, while attempting to retain a reserve for a subsequent round if the initial objective were not achieved. Some analysts believe that such exchanges might not determine the final outcome of the struggle—and that both sides might elect or be forced to continue the battle at some lower level. There are even scenarios in which the battle for national reconstitution is the major element, with one side or the other still engaging in military activities to consolidate its own gains or to deny the other the ability to reconstruct until certain concessions have been exacted. In all these scenarios, naval forces both strategic and conventional would have a role.

There are also scenarios in which nuclear weapons are only used within the theater of military operations—such as Europe—while each superpower refrains from striking the other's homeland directly. Such operations might possibly characterize a war at sea in which land targets are kept immune from nuclear weapons. Conversely, either side might take advantage of an opponent's "Achilles' heel" ashore to cause a sudden change in the progress of the battle. One or two crucial resupply ports, for instance, might present such an attractive target to the Soviets, while the very few Soviet Fleet home ports might appear inviting to the West.

A scenario in which nuclear weapons are employed as the initial act of hostility does not appear likely to this Working Group under current force relationships, despite the extraordinary level of surprise that might be achieved. Some other observers feel that the Soviets might include selective nuclear attacks at the outset of a thrust into Western Europe. The risk of an unreasoned response would have to be carefully considered in such a case. One cannot help wondering, however, what the U.S. response would be if the Soviets, perceiving some extreme provocation or opportunity, attacked three or four forward-deployed carrier task forces with conventional or nuclear weapons, and then immediately sought a negotiated settlement of the grievance.

Conventional Warfare Scenarios

The primary role of general-purpose naval forces is to exploit—or to deny the other side the capability of exploiting—the lower portions of the conflict spectrum at a distance from the homeland, either before or after a nuclear exchange. Five principal classes of nonnuclear scenarios are pertinent now that the Soviets believe there has been a qualitative shift in the correlation of world forces in their favor. They have a significant capability to contest Western freedom of the seas in each class.

- One class includes a large-scale theater war involving the Soviet Union which has not reached the nuclear stage and which both sides are determined, if at all possible, to keep from escalating. The most obvious of these scenarios—but not necessarily the only or the most important one—is a NATO-Warsaw Pact conventional war.
- The second class includes potential conflicts at sea involving both Soviet and U.S. naval forces, with varying degrees of Allied participation, but no significant ground action on the perimeter of the Soviet Union.
- The third class envisages no direct Soviet military involvement, but

full Soviet support in the way of equipment, training, logistics, and other client-state military participation. The provocation has been such as to warrant direct U.S. military intervention. Direct or indirect Allied support to the United States would be a variable.
- In the fourth class of scenarios, the conflict would be between client-states supported by the Soviet Union and states resisting aggression—supported by the United States and various allies—but with no direct confrontation between U.S. and Soviet forces.
- The fifth class involves economic pressure and intimidation by the Soviets, their clients, or other Third World states who might wish to threaten the economic welfare of the Western Alliance by interrupting the flow of trade in raw materials or finished goods.

Some naval developments, particularly those relating to detection, classification, localization, and command and control, would appear not to be scenario-dependent, although the increasing dependence of both sides on space-based systems raises new questions. Similarly, strategic nuclear offensive and defensive capabilities appear less scenario-dependent, although the increasing Soviet potential for withholding some sea-based strategic systems as a determinant of the ultimate outcome of a major conflict introduces new considerations. In any event, these capabilities for higher levels of conflict can greatly influence scenarios at lesser levels.

Technology Context

Long-range nuclear weapons systems have never been tested in combat. Consequently, there must always remain some doubt as to how well they will work under realistic wartime conditions. Both sides may tend to misestimate their true effectiveness in war, as has happened with other new weapons. Among general-purpose forces, many elements of current naval systems have not been widely tested in combat since World War II. By comparison, our ground force and tactical aircraft systems have undergone extensive combat experience both in Southeast Asia and the Middle East. At the same time, significant technological developments are certain to change naval warfare to a substantial degree. The most important are singled out below.

Detection Systems

Modern electronics and satellites have produced significant improvements in the ability to detect naval units, largely depriving them of the stealth and surprise that have been so important in prior naval battles. The ability to detect, classify, and locate enemy surface, air, and submarine targets, to perform post-attack damage assessment, and to analyze, communicate, and use that information with speed has been increasingly valued by both sides. The competence of the Soviet Navy to utilize all source information, including satellite, electronic, over-the-horizon radar, and agent information, to pinpoint foreign naval surface vessels is now judged to be outstanding, possibly even better than our own. As yet, however, neither side can make positive identification of a specific ship without visual observation. The Soviet ability to detect, classify, and locate enemy aircraft is good in many areas and improving, although probably Alliance forces still maintain some advantages in "multiple target handling" capability. Soviet submarine detection does not appear good today, but it seems to be improving as a result of great effort. Alliance forces are believed to hold a substantial advantage in this field, but it may not persist indefinitely.

Submarine Propulsion

Important advances in aircraft and surface ship propulsion systems can profitably extend range and endurance. None of these developments, however, has anywhere near the advantage of nuclear propulsion for submarines, which gives them almost limitless range and endurance and allows them to remain submerged for weeks or months. These benefits apply to both Soviet and U.S. nuclear submarines, but U.S. submarines are significantly quieter, and that factor increases the advantages of U.S. acoustic detection systems. There is no inherent reason why the Soviets cannot achieve equally quiet running submarines. They have made considerable progress, but some time may be required before the improvement can be made fully operational. At that point, the task of destroying their submarine fleet would become much harder.

Homing Missiles

The advent of precision guided missiles that can "home" on surface ships against a sea clutter "background" represents a significant increase in antiship capabilities for both sides, although there remain some questions as to whether these missiles can adequately select the most important ship in a group. Coupled with modern missile propulsion systems that provide significant standoff capabilities, these weapons present an important threat to surface vessels—particularly when they are used with the newest ocean surveillance systems. Their effectiveness is amplified by the fact that the missiles can be launched from a variety of air, surface, and underwater platforms; and, in some situations, it would be extremely difficult to identify the launching platform ex post facto. They are also sufficiently modest in cost and bulk that they can be launched from a variety of relatively small patrol craft or coastal defenses operated by almost any nation.

U.S. ANTISHIP MISSILE CAPABILITIES

High speed photography "stops" a Harpoon missile (top) just before impact on a target ship. The damage done by this missile's relatively small warhead on the destroyer target sacrificed during development testing is shown below. Tomahawk will have a much larger warhead. (Courtesy U.S. Navy)

Implications

Such technological progress raises serious questions concerning whether surface ships can remain the backbone of future navies. Naval battles can apparently be waged increasingly from submarines or land-based aircraft. Although all technological advances are eventually matched by other developments that diminish their initial impact, the cost of defending surface ships will certainly continue to rise, and the wisdom of depending on a relatively small number of very expensive ships must be questioned. Meanwhile, although the Soviets place greater emphasis on land-based aircraft and submarines than does the U.S. Navy, they are also moving gradually toward larger and more capable ships. Their rationale is not yet clear.

Assessment of Mission Capabilities

The foregoing permits a general assessment of Soviet and Alliance naval capabilities across the spectrum of potential conflict for each of the seven categories of scenarios outlined.

General Nuclear Warfare

Both the United States and the Soviet Union have achieved highly capable sea-based nuclear strike systems. The Polaris-Poseidon fleet of SSBNs, soon to be improved by the deployment of Trident missiles and submarines, constitutes the backbone of American survivable nuclear deterrent forces. The current U.S. SSBNs, plus their British and French counterparts, are considered superior to the Soviet Yankee SSBNs in the range and accuracy of their missiles. In their newer Delta-class submarine and its various missiles, however, the Soviets now possess the most formidable SLBM weapons system in the world. Its production may be completed before the first U.S. Trident SSBN joins the fleet. No doubt this Delta system is largely responsible for the shift in Soviet strategic naval responsibilities from "fleet-against-fleet" to "fleet-against-the-shore." Deterrence, attack, and withholding as a reserve are all feasible SSBN missions—for both sides. The latest Delta missiles have a range sufficient to allow their operating stations to be under control of Soviet land-based aircraft and sea-based antiair and antisubmarine systems—thus remaining relatively invulnerable unless Alliance ASW efforts are substantially improved. Further improvements in the accuracy of Delta missiles may be expected.

The initial course of a general nuclear war would probably be dominated by the relative success of the first phase. Here, nonstrategic forces could play only a minor role, unless they had already neutralized a substantial portion of the other side's SSBN fleet with conventional weapons.

SOVIET AND U.S. STRATEGIC SUBMARINES

The Soviets have already deployed approximately thirty Delta-class nuclear-powered ballistic missile submarines (SSBNs). They are generally considered to be the most capable sea-based strategic weapon system in any naval inventory. (Courtesy U.S. Navy)

The U.S. Navy's Trident-class SSBN (artist's sketch shown above) will not begin to join the U.S. strategic arsenal until 1979-1980. By that time, production of the Soviet Delta class should have been completed. (Courtesy U.S. Navy)

Moreover, land-based ICBMs are likely to play a larger part in these initial intercontinental nuclear exchanges than the sea-based systems. In a full-scale nuclear exchange, or even in a limited one, U.S. SSBN submarines, major carrier task forces, and other concentrations of Alliance naval forces would be important targets. Probably each side would also target the major naval bases, port facilities, and airfields of the other. It is not so likely that low-value merchant ship convoys would be high-priority targets.

Both sides consider that major elements of their sea-based nuclear strike forces would survive the initial exchanges, owing to the difficulty of detecting and localizing at-sea submarines not otherwise obliged to give away their general location. It may be possible, however, given sufficient time, to locate individual submarines and destroy them or to attack SSBNs after their positions have been revealed by their initial launches. However, the final outcome of a general nuclear war may be crucially dependent on surviving naval forces—both nuclear and conventional.

Soviet doctrine now seems to call for the withholding of some SSBN forces in order to provide a predominant surviving reserve nuclear force that might be decisive in determining the ultimate negotiations or the outcome of the final phases of the war. In any event, a significant portion of the Soviet surface and submarine fleets will most likely be assigned to the defense of older SSBN forces, until they are retired. Such a mission assignment appears repeatedly in Soviet writings after 1971-1972. Acceptance of the "withhold" strategy would probably require the continued dedication of these assets to the defense of newer submarines against superior Western ASW capabilities, even after an initial nuclear exchange.

There is, as yet, no indication that the enormous and innovative Soviet effort to neutralize the U.S. SSBN-SLBM force has produced a capability to do so, although this is a stated objective. Soviet antisubmarine warfare does not appear to have advanced enough to overtake improvements in U.S. submarines and their missiles. Nonetheless, a significant portion of the Soviet Navy—as well as other military assets—would almost certainly be dedicated to this mission in any major confrontation with the United States. By comparison, there are no current Alliance plans to actively defend U.S. SSBNs with other naval units. Some Alliance naval assets are probably earmarked for the search and destruction of Soviet SSBNs, although it is doubtful we would distinguish the nuclear-armed Soviet submarines from the others during any antisubmarine offensive.

In short, both sides have growing sea-based nuclear arsenals capable of delivering substantial destruction during any stage of a nuclear war. On balance, Alliance ASW efforts would be likely to destroy more Soviet SSBNs than vice versa, even though the Soviets might dedicate more assets to the mission and allocate substantial naval resources to the defense of their own SSBNs. Nonetheless, both sides could withhold an impressive force of surviving SSBNS should they choose to do so. Soviet allocation of submarines to the defense of their own SSBNs—and the attack of ours— would remove some of their most capable units from anti-SLOC operations.

Theater Nuclear Warfare

Many of the older Russian missile-launching submarines (Golf and Hotel classes) have almost certainly been reoriented from anticarrier missions to serve as "frontal artillery" in support of land force operations— most likely during the anticipated theater nuclear stages. The new shorter-range missiles could provide a valuable adjunct to theater nuclear forces in support of land force objectives, when operating within local areas of Soviet sea control, if the more readily detectable Russian submarines could survive Alliance ASW efforts. On the Alliance side, some Polaris-firing submarines have been assigned a theater nuclear support role. Although no longer participants in the U.S. strategic operations plans, U.S. aircraft carrier task forces are also capable of delivering nuclear weapons against the Soviet Union or theater targets. The primary mission of major Soviet naval assets is against these carriers, regardless of their role. Soviet ability to counter U.S. carriers in a nuclear environment must be assessed as high and growing. To the extent that U.S. carrier task forces might be "withheld" for tactical nuclear purposes, the probability increases that the Soviets might husband their assets necessary to counter these "second echelon" forces. Such anticarrier forces would then not be available for interim use against the sealanes.

Given the current and projected nuclear balance, there could be the risk of nuclear escalation in a war solely at sea. Such limited escalation would not carry the full moral stigma associated with use of nuclear weapons on land and represents a relatively quick means of eliminating major elements of Alliance seapower. Consequently, Alliance maritime forces will have to be continuously deployed and maneuvered with this potential threat in mind. Soviet naval forces do not present nearly such an "attractive" target for tactical nuclear weapons because their capabilities are not so concentrated in a few large ships.

The naval forces of both sides are capable of contributing significantly to the application of tactical nuclear weapons against shore targets. A tactical nuclear war at sea remains a possibility, but appears to present a more inviting option for the Soviets than for the Alliance. The allocation of Soviet submarine assets to the theater nuclear role would withdraw some forces that would have marginal utility in attacks against Western sealanes.

Large-Scale Conventional War

Force Projection Ashore. The ability of the United States to project both air and amphibious power ashore from naval task forces remains the predominant advantage for the West in the relative naval balance. The Soviets have little, if any, means of projecting air power from the sea, and, despite their decision to build modest-sized carriers, there is yet no indication that they will be equipped with aircraft capable of presenting a sea-based air threat to more than the most meager array of targets. The Soviet Navy does include a limited capability to project amphibious forces along neighboring coastlines, but these units today have only limited landbased naval air support and very slim air or submarine defenses other than those that could be provided from shore. This situation could change if the Soviets gain access to more land bases beyond their own shores, thus permitting leapfrogging of their coastal forces. At present, however "side-by-side" comparisons strongly favor the almost unique Alliance capabilities.

In "face-to-face" engagements against Soviet forces, however, U.S. capabilities must be assessed as decreasing. Soviet ability to counter U.S. carriers in a conventional environment depends on the particular scenario envisioned (geography, surprise, level of synchronized defense, etc.), but it must be considered substantial if sufficient mass or tactical expertise is applied. The original Soviet goal of building a force capable of neutralizing Western aircraft carriers within range of the U.S.S.R. seems—in Soviet eyes at least—to have been largely accomplished. In fact, it would appear that the Russians now have more assets to do this job than are needed; some seem to have been released for other missions. The future balance will depend not only on the improvements they make to their systems but also on the West's ability to upgrade its defenses against them. The large Soviet naval air arm is designed primarily for offensive operations against Western surface ships and has essentially no counterpart among Western navies. The highly capable Backfire presents a serious new challenge to Western fleets and may well require an all-service approach to limiting its effectiveness.

Against non-Soviet military forces, U.S. carriers should continue to be able to do well, although longer-range and more sophisticated surface-to-surface cruise missiles constitute a growing threat in the hands of Soviet client- and Third World states. Conceivably, the network of treaties, mutual coooperation, and base arrangements which the Soviet Union is seeking to develop in Africa, the Middle East, and South Asia could also be strengthened by offers to provide willing countries with long-range aircraft, cruise missiles, air defense missiles, and mines. This would give

Soviet client-states a much more formidable defense than has been possible until now.

In short, the unique naval capabilities of the U.S. carrier task force appear destined to become a decreasing threat to the Soviet Union and possibly to many of its potential client-states. At best, an ever-increasing share of U.S. naval resources will have to be devoted to their survival as a conventional fighting force. Many Soviet submarines that could contribute to an anti-SLOC campaign appear to be allocated instead to anticarrier missions.

Navy-on-Navy Engagements. Each side recognizes that attacking the other's naval forces would be a primary objective from the outset of any large-scale conventional confrontation. Most of the Soviet surface units appear designed to inflict maximum damage during a short, intense initial period, in which they would have to get in the first blows, with little expectation of surviving long in the open ocean—unless U.S. and Alliance surface, air, and submarine forces had already been substantially reduced. Nonetheless, the striking power of the Soviet surface navy poses a major initial threat to Alliance surface forces, particularly in confined areas like the Eastern Mediterranean, the Norwegian Sea, the Baltic straits, or the Sea of Japan. In such areas, the West would need to establish air superiority to assure surface superiority and to establish surface superiority to assure eventual elimination of the submarine threat.

The large Soviet nuclear-propelled submarine fleet still has few modern attack submarines, although these forces are expected to increase as the Russians near the end of their accelerated SSBN construction program (in accordance with SALT limitations) and continue to expand their submarine construction yards. Their conventionally powered submarine fleet is still sizable, but becoming obsolete and increasingly vulnerable to Western antisubmarine warfare. In any event, the outcome of a series of encounters between surface forces (including attack submarines and aircraft) at the beginning of a war would most likely be the virtual elimination of the Soviet elements presented and considerable damage to the NATO unts. Surviving Soviet surface forces would probably thereafter be compelled to operate close to home under land-based defenses. Surviving Alliance forces would subsequently be threatened primarily by land-based aircraft or submarines. A good number of Soviet submarines and aircraft might be committed to, and lost during, such fleet-on-fleet engagements.

The underwater battles would almost certainly take longer to decide. In general, however, Western submarine forces appear capable of remaining on the offensive against Soviet submarines, both through barrier operations (made possible by restrictive Soviet port facility locations) and through submarine-on-submarine encounters, in which superior Western detection systems and quieter operation appear to provide a substantial advantage well into the future. The extensive land-based ASW capabilities of the Alliance have virtually no counterpart within the Soviet Navy, and they constitute another persistent advantage for the West, although their increasing vulnerability should not be overlooked.

Consequently, a war at sea involving only conventional weapons, with no ground war in progress, does not appear to be an attractive option for the Soviets for the foreseeable future.

In sum, the outcome of a major navy-on-navy nonnuclear campaign seems almost certain to favor the Alliance, although substantial damage would accrue to its surface combatants in the process. Surviving Alliance forces should, then, be able to establish effective sea control after the gradual elimination of remaining enemy submarines. The residual Backfire force could eventually be eliminated, probably with the help of Alliance air force assets. While the Soviet fleet is still not capable of carrying out long-term sea control missions with conventional weapons, it is becoming increasingly effective for short-term sea denial operations in specific areas (relatively close to land-based support), and it is constantly seeking to extend those areas.

Command of Contiguous Waters. The Soviet Navy's large fleet of relatively small coastal craft is effective for defensive operations within its own coastal regions. The United States includes no such forces in its own active fleets, but Alliance navies do maintain roughly equivalent capabilities. These counterpart forces are not likely to face each other in large-scale combat operations. There is little doubt, however, that Soviet coastal naval forces could defeat any small-scale incursions against their home shores. If a really major attacking force were assembled, it would certainly attract the assistance of extensive Soviet counter task force assets.

Support of Ground Forces. Ground forces are still the keystone of Soviet military operations on the Eurasian landmass. Support of ground operations remains a primary task of all military branches, including the Soviet coastal and amphibious navies. In addition to a sizable complement of increasingly efficient amphibious tank-carrying support vessels, these assigned naval forces include older gun-equipped ships and small diesel submarines. While the West holds relatively few gunfire support ships for an equivalent role, support of ground forces is an important mission for aircraft and amphibious task groups. Hence, the West's naval capabilities to support its ground forces with conventional weapons far exceed those of the Soviets at present. In "face-to-face" situations, with proper training and equipment, Alliance shore-based assets should find the task of eliminating Soviet naval and amphibious units supporting ground operations far easier than it would be for Soviet land-based elements to neutralize Western carrier and amphibious task forces, with their self-contained defensive systems. Nonetheless, it is doubtful that U.S. amphibious forces could be strong enough to project ground forces directly into Soviet Union territory, although they might well be stronger than required to secure more remote areas from Soviet client opposition.

Attacks of Sea Lines of Communications. The only large-scale Soviet military operations on the Eurasian continent that might depend to any degree on the sustained use of sea lines of communication would involve their forces and installations in Northeast Asia, and then only if their land lines of communication were severed—presumably by military actions of the People's Republic of China. Direct military intervention by a Soviet expeditionary force of any real magnitude in Africa would also require a secure SLOC and appears highly unlikely. On the other hand, the successful defense of Western Alliance territories in either the Western or the Eastern hemisphere depends crucially on military and energy shipments crossing the Atlantic, Pacific, or Indian oceans, or the Mediterranean Sea.

Alliance interdiction of Soviet SLOCs, should there be any, appears to be a relatively simple matter. The Soviets have very few naval assets that could be gainfully assigned to destroying Alliance submarines—particularly over the protracted distances envisioned to resupply Vladivostok or Petropavlovsk. In essence, all the Soviet maritime assets involved would be vulnerable to destruction by Alliance naval operations.

Naval interdiction of Alliance SLOCs is mentioned regularly in Soviet writings, although it does not appear to rate the same time priority as many more strategically oriented naval missions. Open ocean SLOC interdiction would not seem realistic for Soviet surface ships operating alone, and it does not appear to be a primary mission for naval aviation assets, unless their higher priority missions have been completed. Soviet attack submarines, however, would present a severe threat to NATO shipping (over the first few weeks or months, at least), even if only a fraction of those units were assigned to this mission (as projected in this study). At first, Allied shipping losses would probably be very high, and several weeks or a few months would be required before Soviet attack submarines could be reduced to manageable levels.

The effectiveness of Soviet submarine forces in this role could be substantially greater under four quite plausible conditions: if they were not constrained by a lack of reliable, forward, warm water ports; if U.S. forces were, for any reason, denied the capability to establish ASW barriers across the approaches to these ports; if non-U.S. Alliance ASW forces were not participating in the campaign; and if Soviet naval priorities changed to permit the allocation of more submarines to this role. This last factor applies essentially to all areas where Western SLOCs might be required, but seems more significant in the Atlantic, by virtue of the concentration of submarine assets in the Soviet Northern Fleet.

Anti-SLOC operations, however, tend to be rather indiscriminate. The Soviets would have to be willing to accept the consequences of sinking ships or cargoes of nonbelligerent nations still conducting international trade. In certain wartime scenarios short of a "world war," the risk of alienating neutral countries—or potential allies—could provide a significant deterrent to an anti-SLOC campaign.

The Soviets appear to view the anti-SLOC effort in its totality and to recognize the vulnerabilities in Alliance operations at the SLOC termini as well as across the open oceans. Attacks on the termini could afford a level of selectivity not readily attainable along the sealanes. The Soviets maintain extraordinarily high stockpiles of mines and are rapidly increasing their abilities to attack Alliance port, dock, and staging areas from the air with long-range aviation that need not traverse territory defended by the West.

In short, the Alliance retains the ability to attack Soviet SLOCs—if there need be any—and the Soviets could do little to defend them. The Soviets also have the resources to strongly attack Alliance SLOCs, both at sea and ashore. Therefore the West—and the United States, unilaterally—must be able to defend and reestablish those routes against substantial opposition. Recommendations concerning this task are contained in Chapter 15.

Intervention

Navies have substantial roles in military confrontations at many levels less than all-out conventional conflict between the superpowers. For instance, U.S. naval elements have been used several times since World War II in armed intervention scenarios supporting national objectives, and the United States may well be compelled to undertake such roles sometime again in the future. As Soviet military capabilities and political confidence continue to expand, however, there is no guarantee that the Soviets will retain their posture of reluctance to intervene themselves. Some qualified observers believe it would be totally out of character for the Soviets to risk any sort of military clash with the West, unless they were prepared to go "all the way." They feel that any such engagements will be limited to proxy forces. Others, however, believe that the Russians have now embarked on a more adventurous path and that the opportunities for miscalculation of the intentions or resolve of either superpower are increasing. Meanwhile, the willingness of the superpowers to intervene in the affairs of other states— the United States, defensively and the U.S.S.R., either aggressively or defensively—still seems to exist, and in some areas (Africa, for instance)

NAVAL ROLE IN INTERVENTION

Navies have substantial roles in military confrontations at many levels less than all-out conflict between the superpowers. The Soviet merchant ship *Volgoles* is shown here leaving Cuba with missiles on deck, with the U.S.S. *Vesole* (DDR-878) alongside and a U.S. Navy P2V overhead. (Courtesy U.S. Navy)

U.S. amphibious forces participated in Marine Corps "search and destroy" operations along the South Vietnamese coast near the DMZ. Here a landing craft is leaving the well deck of the U.S.S. *Monticello* (LSD-35) and is about to head for the beach with other landing craft in Operation "Beacon Hill I." (Courtesy U.S. Navy)

that kind of involvement appears to be increasing.

One stated purpose for the growing Soviet fleet is to protect Third World nations against such intrusions. In the face of increasing Soviet conventional naval capabilities and the relative decline of Western naval strength, superpower support for opposing factions within some state or region could lead to a collision—possibly unintentional—between naval elements of the East and West. This may well become a major factor in the continued evolution of both fleets. The Soviet Navy has already been used to inhibit somewhat possible Western responses to crises in the Third World, to strengthen Soviet client-regimes, and to protect Soviet maritime assets from the actions of another state. Actions of this type will almost certainly continue, and they may expand in scope, particularly if a marked disparity evolves between U.S. and Soviet forces available for these missions.

Against non-Soviet powers, the United States and the other Alliance nations should command superior naval capabilities as they did in Korea and Vietnam, although there may be some growing limitations depending on the availability of Soviet-supplied antinaval defenses. United States naval intervention, if required, would almost certainly continue to involve aircraft carriers or seaborne helicopters. Should the Soviets choose to challenge such a U.S. operation, the credibility of their position would depend on whether they could amass sufficient forces to threaten the carriers seriously and on the willingness of the United States to destroy Soviet lives and property in the conduct of some lesser operation. No prediction can be made of the outcome of such a confrontation. More important, perhaps, is the Working Group assessment that the Soviet Navy is now in a position to raise a very troublesome challenge to U.S. intervention operations.

Client-versus-Client Wars

Expansion of Soviet influence and control in other countries often occurs when an anti-Western, insurgent regime takes over. Combined with other elements of Soviet political, economic, and military power, naval and maritime support has played a crucial role in the achievements of many revolutionary movements. If one of the major long-range goals of Soviet foreign policy is the gradual extension of control over other states, then this method, now being demonstrated in West Africa, is likely to become more widely applied. The merchant marine will probably remain the principal vehicle for Soviet operations in such cases, with naval units standing by to deter intervention by others. The Russians have demonstrated that they intend to use their maritime assets, both civil and military, to supply their clients with both arms and "proxy forces" in support of "wars of national liberation." In their doctrine, there is no inconsistency between the avoidance of direct superpower confrontation through détente, or peaceful coexistence, and the continued support of armed conflict within the Third World.

Both superpowers now have the capabilities to use their navies and merchant marines to supply warring factions in client-states. Given the looser U.S. control of its merchant fleet, however, and the emphasis placed on its economic efficiency, one would have to judge that the United Sates has slipped markedly relative to the growing Soviet resupply capacity. The time may come when there are no longer U.S. merchant vessels capable of unloading in small undeveloped harbors—or when the marine unions might, under certain circumstances, refuse to man the ships, even if such operations were feasible. Furthermore, not only both superpower fleets but also many smaller navies would now be able to isolate or quarantine a neighboring foreign port against all forms of external resupply. These capabilities are certain to complicate the application of naval and maritime resources in support of national objectives by any outside nations.

Economic Pressure and Intimidation

Members of the Western Alliance would be unlikely to use their navies or merchant fleets for economic pressure or political intimidation on Third World countries, even though they have substantial means for doing so. In view of their doctrinal imperatives, however, the Soviets will not necessarily evince a similar reluctance as time goes on. For instance, several parts of the world are apparently becoming almost wholly dependent on Soviet shipping for the conduct of their trade, by choice if not by necessity. Moreover, the Soviet Navy has the capacity for at least limited worldwide operations to support, say, the blockade of a Third World port. In instances where important U.S. interests were not involved, and in view of the overall shift toward military equality between the superpowers, the Soviets would doubtless feel more confident of the success of such an operation than they did even a decade ago. Although somewhat unlikely, the future use of Soviet naval and maritime forces in this manner—without effective U.S. reaction—cannot be ruled out.

Military Presence

Ever since the formation of the NATO alliance, U.S. naval units have been forward deployed to the NATO area as a pledge of U.S. determination to support its treaty commitments. Forward deployments to the Western Pacific have accompanied similar U.S. guarantees. While there are many questions about the efficacy of such permanent "presence" roles, they have become institutionalized as proof of U.S. resolve. Until recently, the Soviet Navy was not capable of comparable demonstrations, and, in the main, it is still unable to support forward deployments over the long term.

Nonetheless, their growing naval strength makes it increasingly possible for the Soviets to undertake mutual support agreements with countries beyond their own continent and to demonstrate their commitment with fleet units in the area. In the long run, this could influence the alignment of presently uncommitted Third World nations. Certainly, the first appearance of an alien power in a region can give rise to new political tensions or uncertainties.

The presence of a more capable Soviet Navy can also be used to weaken the Western Alliance, an effect which is clearly a Soviet objective. The Alliance is accustomed to free use of the seas, and, to the extent that any of its member nations perceive the Soviets as capable of denying that freedom, the Soviet Navy could contribute substantially to the weakening of its resolve and cohesiveness. Although perceptions may vary in different circles, the Working Group believes that the West's short-term dependence on the seas can be greatly reduced. Moreover, the Soviet capability to deny free transit over the long haul remains relatively low. In any event, the continued demonstration of U.S. naval "presence" in some fashion can still contribute to the solidarity of the Western Alliance.

Prestige

The Soviet quest for a high seas fleet capable of representing Russian national strength has been successful. This fact has a symbolic significance beyond the specific applications of power noted above. For one thing, it is an indication of possible Soviet intentions toward Western Europe. Today's Soviet Union does not need the navy to defend itself from that quarter. Then too, it is an announcement to the world at large that the Soviet Union seeks to assert its influence globally and is acquiring, albeit gradually, the means to do so. Soviet merchant ships and their crews provide substantial opportunities to expose developing nations to communist visions of world social and political order. In many instances, these peaceful overtures intrude into areas historically identified with the West. This rising maritime presence can benefit the Soviet cause in several ways: by enhancing the image of Russian compatibility with Third World objectives; by symbolizing communist technological progress; and by suggesting to some of the nonaligned nations that the balance of power may be shifting inexorably toward Moscow. On the other hand, inept handling of their maritime presence could alienate the very nations the Russians seek to influence.

To the extent that there have been real shifts in the balance of world military power, economic capabilities, and technological skills, there is virtually nothing the Alliance could hope to do to prevent the Soviets from using their naval and maritime capabilities in demonstration of these developments. A more meaningful concern could arise from Alliance neglect of the importance of these trends and the significance of Soviet actions in demonstrating them. To the extent that the Alliance still represents the strongest and most appealing political, economic, and military coalition in the world, only our own neglect can keep the nonaligned nations from recognizing these realities.

Commerce

The Soviet Merchant Marine and fishing fleet make substantial contributions to the Soviet economy and provide significant opportunities to influence the economic growth and political affiliation of Third World countries. One option for the expansion of Soviet influence is accelerated construction and employment of these ships, especially in the Third World. As experience to date shows, the Soviets are strong competitors. If they can establish a virtual monopoly over the sea trade in some areas of the world, the West may find its commerce and its access to resources gradually reduced—or suddenly cut off. The West may also find that the Soviets have gained valuable overseas port and air base rights as a result of this commercial intercourse. The centralized Soviet government assures a high degree of cooperation between the uses of civil and military assets in pursuit of apparently well-coordinated objectives.

There is no reason for the United States to restructure its merchant fleet or its foreign trade to offset the benefits to the Soviet Union of its own commercial ventures. Nonetheless, it does appear sensible for the Western Alliance as a whole to compete with Soviet maritime interests on a purely economic basis. Comparisons of the U.S. and Soviet merchant fleets alone would suggest that the Soviets have certain advantages for dealing with Third World needs, but other Western nations still operate ships with the same general capabilities as those of the Soviet Union. They should continue to demonstrate that one of the strengths of the Alliance is the ability of its members to compete with the Soviets at various levels.

Summary

There can be no question that Soviet naval and maritime resources have gained worldwide stature and respect. In many cases, the Western Alliance need not be overly concerned. In other instances, there may be cause for apprehension, but little that can be done about it. In between, a number of Soviet naval developments do present a serious threat to the retention of Alliance solidarity, defense capabilities, and freedom of conventional military action. In these situations, an all-forces, all-nations approach is warranted, involving the coordinated use of all available resources, whether they be sea- or land-based, active or reserve, under the control of Navy, Air Force, or Army, whether they belong to one ally or another or are converted from civil assets. Such an approach seems to be needed in order to counter growing Soviet naval capabilities, particularly with respect to maintaining security of the seas.

15
Findings and Recommendations

Introduction

The following pages present the major conclusions and recommendations of this study concerning the future security of Western Alliance sealanes. They do not address the overall naval problem—or power projection, per se—except to the extent that various other naval objectives may preempt attention from this sea control mission. We believe that while many of these recommendations may appear to be broad, each could lead toward a change in thinking, construction, or deployment that could measurably help the Western Alliance maintain its ability to use the seas under a wide variety of conditions. Most of the recommendations involved are intended to minimize the expenditure of scarce resources. They are directed primarily toward a more effective use of both military and civil assets for sealane defense, but they are in no way substitutes for the retention of larger and more capable Alliance navies.

We recognize that Soviet naval capabilities—like many of our own—have not been tested in combat in more than a generation. How well they would work for either side remains unknown. We hope that they will never have to be tried in actual battle. We also claim no special wisdom that allows us to foretell the future intentions of the Soviets or even to grasp fully the motives implicit in some of their current activities.

Moreover, the importance of conventional naval forces, and of the sealanes themselves, depends crucially on the type of war that is envisioned and the circumstances leading to its initiation. Those who believe that a large-scale conflict between East and West would arise like a "bolt from the blue" and be settled within a few days or weeks see little contribution to the outcome from naval forces. They tend to believe that Europe would have been lost in that time or that the war would have been escalated to intercontinental nuclear exchanges. Others visualize a substantial period of warning and "preparation time," provided by gradually deteriorating superpower relations, possibly coupled with some lesser conflict elsewhere and followed by a protracted struggle, perhaps involving the limited use of nuclear weapons over an extended period. Still others foresee no general war and imagine that naval forces are basically an instrument of political persuasion. In any event, it behooves the Western Alliance to be prudent in its military, naval, and mobilization planning. The ability to fight a "long war" implies faith in NATO and confidence in the ultimate outcome and would place the burden on the Warsaw Pact nations to escalate to nuclear warfare if they should choose to do so. Surely, deterrence would not be enhanced by a generally accepted perception that the United States could not maintain its sea lines of communication to or from Europe, the Middle East, or the Far East, or that it would only be able to do so for a short time.

Hence, we have attempted to place some reasonable bounds on what the contingencies might be and then to propose solutions that would minimize the waste of resources if the more serious contingencies should not arise. At the same time, these proposed solutions would permit the development of additional Alliance capabilities at relatively low cost if our predictions understate the actual threat that materializes, possibly as a result of an unanticipated change in Soviet naval strategy.

There is no single magic solution in these recommendations concerning security of the seas. In fact, we are proposing that the Western Alliance needs to: broaden its sphere of concern; strengthen its resolve for cooperative action; reaffirm its commitment to retaining a favorable force balance; improve its planning for contingencies; expand the alternative missions for some of its existing military forces; and raise the level of cooperation between the civil and the military sectors. In this last category, an important, if seemingly novel, concept is worth noting. The strength of the West resides overwhelmingly in its civil sector and its economic prowess. The power of the communist world, which looms as our major potential adversary, depends primarily on its military capabilities—often pursued as a means of economic development and at the expense of its real growth. Mechanisms by which we can bring the unparalleled economic strength of the West to bear on the overall military equation are bound to be instrumental in assuring that the balance of real power does not shift away from us. This fact applies to the problems of retaining free use of the seas, and it doubtless has applications in many other military endeavors too.

Recommendations

Twenty-one sets of recommendations are presented on the following pages, each preceded by the pertinent findings of this study. Because of the very diverse nature of the recommendations, it is not possible to arrange them according to priority or to estimate their total cost impacts. However,

Findings and Recommendations

they do fall into groups related to different guiding principles, of which the first two are the most significant, as summarized below:

A. *Establish new Alliance long-range commitments to the retention of a favorable naval balance by:*
   A-1: Formulating definitive and cooperative Alliance naval policies and firm long-range construction programs that support them; and
   A-2: Establishing top priority for the development of Alliance naval counterforce capabilities against a potential enemy.

B. *Base future Alliance naval policies on a better understanding of the full range of possible requirements, including:*
   B-1: The increasing need for capable naval forces in the Pacific during a "NATO war";
   B-2: The growing capabilities of the Soviet Navy to interpose fleet elements to deny unilateral Alliance naval and maritime actions;
   B-3: The potential demands of a U.S. conflict which does not involve Alliance participation—and vice versa;
   B-4: The decreasing U.S. capability for continuous forward deployments for "presence" purposes;
   B-5: The continued importance of Alliance sealane security following the nuclear phases of a war; and
   B-6: Western merchant marine requirements in peace and war.

C. *Develop more threat-responsive Alliance capabilities by:*
   C-1: Creating numerically larger navies of less expensive ships;
   C-2: Adopting "modular" design of critical naval weapons and sensors to permit conversion of merchant ships in time of crisis, upgrading of Alliance escorts, greater Alliance standardization and interoperability of weapons and equipment and more frequent modernization of naval combatants; and
   C-3: Pursuing a variety of applicable technology programs on a priority basis to add strength and versatility to naval units.

D. *Make greater use of available assets to limit the effectiveness of a Soviet anti-SLOC campaign by:*
   D-1: Developing the capability to convert some merchant ships to auxiliary convoy escorts and to arm others for self-defense;
   D-2: Keeping the numbers of merchant ships up, mixing economic and military cargoes both within individual ships and within individual convoys, and assuring that those ships are not dependent on dockside unloading facilities;
   D-3: Assuring maximum effectiveness of Alliance contributions to the

SLOC defense mission through suitable standardization, interoperability, joint training, and streamlined command structures;
D-4: Giving NATO a collective responsibility for port defense;
D-5: Giving NATO a collective responsibility for mine warfare; and
D-6: Applying NATO air force assets to the naval counterforce mission.

E. *Reduce dependency on shipping during the early stages of a crisis or conflict by:*
E-1: Increasing prepositioning of military equipment in or near anticipated theaters of operations; and
E-2: Maintaining appropriate national economic stockpiling throughout the Alliance.

F. *Avoid increasing the projected Soviet anti-SLOC threat by:*
F-1: Resisting the extension of Soviet overseas bases; and
F-2: Maintaining or expanding U.S. overseas bases and facilities.

These recommendations and the findings that support them are elaborated on the following pages.

A. Alliance Long-range Commitment to Naval Superiority

A-1: Alliance Naval Policies and Construction Programs

Findings. As stated at the outset, this analysis is not directed toward total U.S. or Alliance naval and amphibious requirements. Rather, this study has concentrated on the problems associated with the defense of the sealanes. But we cannot come to that focus without considering the overall capabilities and mission requirements of Alliance and Soviet forces—both nuclear and conventional—well beyond sealane defense. Neither the United States nor the Alliance has sufficient naval forces to protect all the potentially essential shipping during a protracted war. The combined Alliance force levels are probably inadequate to protect essential military convoys—and they have virtually no capabilities to escort economic shipping. Yet this is only one aspect of our navies' broader missions.

The Soviet Navy has grown into a serious military threat at all potential levels of conflict. Moreover, the *trends* of the opposing superpower navies are not encouraging to the West. The circumstance is due not so much to Soviet expansion as to contraction on the Alliance side. During the twenty-four months of this study effort, the U.S. Navy alone has shrunk about 10 percent, presumably to its low point preceding the introduction of new construction ships already authorized.

It is easy to expound on the various options open to the Western navies for their future development and all too difficult to arrive at a nationally chosen course. For many years in the United States, there have been basic disagreements within the Navy, between the Navy and the Office of the

Findings and Recommendations

Secretary of Defense, between Defense and the Office of Management and Budget, between Defense and the Congressional Budget Office and the General Accounting Office, and between the Executive Branch and the Congress—which itself has displayed vastly differing views among its various Authorization, Appropriations, Finance, and Budget committees. It has become almost a national pastime to "help" design the future navy and to discredit all other designs. This lengthy debate has managed to delay any meaningful modernization program for many years—under three different presidents. By the summer of 1978, only minor progress had been made, and no firm multiyear shipbuilding programs had been established. One might remark that, apparently, members of the Soviet hierarchy have not been faced with an equivalent dilemma for the past twenty years, while most of the Alliance nations have neither a naval policy (or naval strategy) nor a long-range naval program. The Soviets seem to be on a steady course, with ample resources allocated to maintain at least a modern 775-ship navy, even though their mission priorities have changed several times. The contrast in consistency and resolve between the two efforts is stark. No area of the Western military establishment appears more in need than the navies of firm long-range decisions around which to rebuild a capable and competitive force.

No single naval shipbuilding program could be designed to the satisfaction of the assorted naval "experts"—nuclear and conventional, air, surface, and underwater—or all the analysts who seem willing to grind their proverbial axes right down to the handle. This Working Group, for instance, could never agree on a specific overall U.S. Navy configuration. Fortunately, naval vessels are designed to be versatile. Given enough of them, they can accommodate to a broad variety of scenarios during their useful lives—many of which we cannot presently foresee. What we need most for each Alliance country is a single nationally approved policy for the future roles and missions of its navy, a strategy for carrying it out, and a commensurate construction program for the next ten to twenty years. Those measures should be joined with a plan for augmentation of our naval forces from our merchant fleets. Nothing short of that will be adequate. Perhaps then the myriad specialists and critics can move to some other arena worthy of their attention.

Chapter 12 demonstrated that a U.S. shipbuilding and aircraft procurement of roughly $10 billion annually would be required to support a "600-ship navy" of a somewhat less expensive average unit cost than currently accepted. The study also showed that the other members of the Alliance should be able collectively to maintain another "600-ship navy" for approximately $6 billion annually, after a period of modernization. These levels appear consistent with total Alliance defense spending and should provide combined navies capable of defeating the "775-ship" threat of the Soviet Navy, if this should ever become necessary.

Recommendations. The Atlantic Council Working Group strongly recommends that the U.S. Congress take the lead in generating a long-term policy for the objectives of the U.S. Navy and Merchant Marine for the remainder of this century and that the Executive Branch initiate the development of a suitable naval strategy and construction program (for congresssional approval) that would be fully responsive to those policy objectives. Consultations within the Alliance could greatly assist in the evolution of an achievable naval strategy in which each country can share.

We further recommend that the findings and recommendations of this Study Group be taken into account in the deliberations of the Congress and the Executive Branch leading to the development of both the policy and the program. We urge the development of naval and maritime plans that will permit the Western Alliance collectively, or its members unilaterally, to retain the capability to use the seas for peaceful purposes, and we call for a construction program that will assure naval victory in any contest for the seas across the spectrum of plausible confrontations. Annual procurement requirements for the U.S. Navy should be at least $10 billion, and for the rest of the Alliance, roughly $6 billion. No Alliance navy should be sized or configured solely for the sealane defense mission.

A-2: The Importance of Naval Counterforce Capabilities

Findings. The early stages of Soviet naval development were dominated by the intent to defend the U.S.S.R. against naval attacks from the West. In more recent years, that country's growing naval capabilities, together with the emergence of a more confident and expansive Kremlin leadership, suggest that Soviet naval elements could now be used in more offensive roles. Meanwhile, the U.S. Navy has continued to evolve with substantial emphasis on the "projection of power ashore"—its principal role at the conclusion of World War II, when there was virtually no enemy naval threat. At the same time, Alliance navies have grown smaller, and, in some cases, they have become at least partially obsolete. Only the United States retains much capability for offensive operations against Soviet fleet units, while the navies of our allies have pursued primarily defensive roles in their own neighboring waters. More than ever before, however, the collective efforts of the Alliance will be required to maintain a favorable naval balance.

Our allies have become relatively less capable of individually undertaking any modest naval counterforce operations, while the U.S. Navy is no longer large enough to fight their minor battles for them. Moreover, the current superpower balance does not permit U.S. involvement in minor Allied confrontations at sea. At the same time, Soviet naval forces can now operate in some force across all the world's oceans, under a variety of strategies to threaten the West.

As in virtually all forms of warfare, the best Alliance defense against attacks on essential sealanes would be to take the offensive against the formidable Soviet submarine and land-based aircraft fleets, where they would be more vulnerable, and well before they reach within range of Alliance convoys. Such counterforce operations would be required to limit the effectiveness of emerging Soviet naval forces and to shorten confrontation. These operations cannot be performed by sealane defense forces only.

Recommendations. The primary naval requirement for Alliance forces must be to retain military forces large, strong, and versatile enough to neutralize or eliminate the diverse threats that Soviet naval assets—both ashore and at sea—could pose to Western security during periods of crisis, limited wars, or a major superpower confrontation. All members of the Alliance must retain some capabilities to perform naval counterforce missions. If this counterforce requirement is fulfilled, then the Soviet Navy can be kept on the defensive, the impact of alternate Soviet strategies can be minimized, and sealane security can be assured over the long run, even in a major conflict.

B. Future Alliance Naval Policies

B-1: Scope of a "NATO War"

Findings. Many analysts assume that the naval aspects of a "NATO war" could be confined to the North Atlantic and the Mediterranean. We often hear that it would not be in the best interests of the Soviets to expand such a war to the Pacific or the Indian Ocean. If that is true, then the Western Alliance might be served best by expanding the theaters of operations, to Soviet disadvantage. In any event, few things could be more damaging to that Alliance than the growth of a conviction among Middle East or Pacific nations—including the People's Republic of China—that the United States would be unable to provide its allies with essential reinforcements or economic shipping in either hemisphere during a major confrontation with Warsaw Pact forces.

Current defense planning appears to call for the transfer, in the event of a "NATO war," of most of the naval assets of the U.S. Third Fleet from the Pacific to the Atlantic, where the "action" is anticipated. In fact, these swing forces, consisting primarily of carrier task forces, would probably be more valuable to the protection of Pacific and Indian Ocean sealanes— where distances between friendly shore bases and facilities are greater and land-based aircraft cannot contribute as much to SLOC-defense operations. The transfer of these units would require thirty to forty days, during which they would be of little or no use in either theater of operations.

If Defense Department plans for depleting Pacific naval assets are predicated on the need to bolster Atlantic sealane defenses, it is not at all clear that such redeployments would be appropriate. Carrier task forces are almost certainly less vulnerable and more effective (relative to other available assets) in the Pacific and the Indian Ocean. U.S. naval presence—and bases—there may be more crucial to retention of the desired overall military balance and of the essential sealanes across those two-thirds of the world's oceans.

On the other hand, there may be some U.S. naval assets in the Pacific that could be more productive in naval counterforce operations in the North Atlantic against the Soviet Northern Fleet close to home. For instance, U.S. SSN attack submarines in the Pacific may exceed the minimum Pacific needs, while those in the Atlantic may be overcommitted. Such a selective redeployment may be warranted to reduce the Soviet threat in the Atlantic through naval counterforce operations.

Recommendations. We recommend that any plans the Navy might have for transferring naval forces from the Pacific during a "NATO war" be reconsidered with an eye toward keeping a more capable naval force in the Western Pacific and beyond, unless there are overriding requirements for these assets elsewhere.

B-2: Analysis of Soviet Interposition Capability

Findings. Because of the increasing strength of their conventional deep sea forces and the relative decline of Western naval strength, the Soviets may elect to resist U.S. involvement in some "local war." Moreover, even though the Soviets decry direct military intervention against lesser states by any major power, they have plainly demonstrated their intentions to use their maritime assets—military and civil—to supply clients with both arms and proxy forces in support of "wars of national liberation." In either case, future superpower support for opposing factions within some state or region—possibly exacerbated by some miscalculation of resolve on either side—could ultimately produce a confrontation between naval elements of East and West. This contingency could well become a major factor in the continued evolution of both fleets. There is considerable indication that the Soviets feel they have entered a new era in which they are less constrained from challenging the actions of the West. One stated purpose for the growing Soviet fleet is to protect Third World nations against "Western intervention."

Probably the U.S. naval forces assigned to such roles should either be small enough to be expendable or large enough to deter a challenge. In the latter case, however, the United States must be prepared to escalate even further if the Soviets decide to test our will—perhaps by attacking a supercarrier task force. Two plausible scenarios include: a Soviet blockade during another Arab-Israeli war; or Soviet resistance to U.S. attempts to reopen the Strait of Hormuz, blocked, let us say, by some smaller Middle East nation or an insurgent group supported by Soviet or Arab extremist interests.

Recommendations. We strongly recommend that the Western Alliance, and the United States in particular, devote special attention to the growing possibility of a limited naval confrontation stemming from Soviet interposition of forces to forestall U.S. or Allied intervention in some "local war" or revolutionary activity. The full range of possible actions and reactions needs to be thought through in substantial detail to avoid escalation to a major and possibly irreversible confrontation. Such considerations could lead to a change in the structure and character of Western naval forces and the bases required to support them.

B-3: Critical U.S. Scenarios Excluding the Alliance—and Vice Versa

Findings. Without NATO or Pacific Allied naval contributions, U.S. sea lines of communication required to support a major crisis-response in areas outside Europe, such as the Middle East or Northeast Asia, could become as vulnerable to Soviet naval interdiction as those that would be involved during a "NATO war," if not more so. This is particularly true if the Soviet perceptions of the likelihood of nuclear escalation were significantly lower and resulted in a reallocation of submarines to the anti-SLOC mission. In this case, a limited U.S.-Soviet confrontation at sea could heavily tax U.S. naval capabilities. Although the total shipping requirements might be significantly smaller than those required to support a major NATO conflict, the distances might be far greater and the Allied contributions much less or even nonexistent.

The "NATO planning scenario" may not even represent the realistic "worst case" for the application of U.S. conventional naval forces. For instance, NATO might supply well over two-thirds of the convoy escorts and merchant ships required for the North Atlantic reinforcement mission associated with that war. Likewise, the overseas base and facility structure available to the United States in a confrontation or conflict not involving vital Alliance interests might be very small and quite inadequate.

The naval and maritime support of, say, a four-to-six division operation on the Korean peninsula or on the Indian Ocean littoral could be more demanding in the face of Soviet resistance, particularly with the possibility of less than full-scale U.S. mobilization and little active Allied support. The most realistic scenario for U.S. force development probably differs for *each* military department, depending on individual mission requirements.

Efforts to force them all into the same mold, as is currently the case, may be very unwise and could result in limiting capabilities for independent response to contingencies of unique importance to this country.

The cooperation of allies and normally friendly client-states might be substantially reduced during crisis periods if they had reason to doubt that the United States could provide them with maritime support. The capability to provide such support against opposition is, therefore, of high importance. In any such scenario, the possibility of escalation of superpower involvement would always be present. In fact, judgments as to the relative capability and will of the superpowers to intervene could be dominant factors in the outcome.

From the standpoint of our allies, lesser naval confrontations might also develop with elements of the Soviet Navy wherein it is neither practical nor politically acceptable for the United States to intervene. It appears increasingly important for Alliance naval planners to assure that their own capabilities are great enough to cope with such contingencies without U.S. involvement or to raise the level of such limited conflict to the point where U.S. support is assured. In short, if the upper limit of Alliance capabilities were below the threshold of assured U.S. naval assistance, then a dangerous gap would exist, in which individual Alliance members could be intimidated by Soviet naval posturing. The development of such capabilities, albeit limited, would improve the naval counterforce potential of the entire Alliance.

Recommendations. We strongly recommend that U.S. naval force planning look to other contingencies than the customary "NATO-first" scenario to determine the desired size of U.S. naval and marine forces, base structure, and merchant fleet.

We also recommend that other members of the Western Alliance make sure that their own navies have the capability to undertake at least limited naval counterforce operations against isolated elements of Soviet or Soviet client naval forces without the assistance of the United States. Such capabilities will ensure that enemy navies cannot "nibble away" at individual Alliance nations below the threshold of U.S. participation.

B-4: Peacetime Naval Presence

Findings. The peacetime presence of naval forces in a given area can be an important signal of political will to use military force if necessary. The message could be ineffective if the military power backing the presence (there or elsewhere) is in doubt or if the will itself is not clear. If the will is real, some forward deployment may be necessary to assure the timely initiative—and prior training—essential to success.

Even in peacetime, the presence of Soviet naval forces has a clearly inhibitory impact on the free movement and deployment of Western naval forces. This is regularly demonstrated in the operations of U.S.-Alliance naval elements in the Eastern Mediterranean. This same phenomenon may soon be visible in other waters close to the Soviet homeland. Moreover, the anticipated new laws of the sea may somewhat reduce the classic freedom of peacetime naval actions by both superpower maritime forces.

Moreover, circumstances may change over time and thus warrant adjustment in the forward deployed forces. For instance, some observers would claim that the nature of the U.S. Sixth Fleet's primary mission in the Mediterranean has changed from force projection to sea control with the advent of the Soviet naval presence. If this is so, and if this dictates alteration in the Sixth Fleet composition, then such changes should be encouraged without regard to "presence" considerations.

Military presence, and particularly the naval form of it, however, may have unfavorable political effects if continued too long. Extended forward deployments can also cause excessive wear and tear on both the crews and the machinery of limited naval forces. This effect will become more pronounced as U.S. naval forces continue to decline in quantity—regardless of the quality built into individual ships.

We do not imply that U.S. presence should be eliminated from any current theater. However, the strain of continuous forward deployments of large and complex naval systems may be well beyond their value either for training purposes or for demonstrating the steadfastness of our political and military will. Too much peacetime presence in too few places may result in the neglect of other areas of growing importance—and a diminished capability to conduct sustained naval combat if the need should arise. A more selective policy of unit rotation to areas of interest might improve training, decrease stress, and send clearer signals of current intent. Naturally, care should be taken to avoid sending unintentional signals of political disinterest during such a realignment.

Recommendations. The United States, with Allied encouragement, should review the character, current missions, and extent of its more-or-less permanent forward deployments to Europe and the Western Pacific, with an eye to evolving alternative methods of achieving suitable "presence" in each area, such as in-and-out rotation of forces.

B-5: Post-Nuclear Naval Force Requirements

Findings. The United States tends to view strategic weapons primarily as a deterrent: a means of making nuclear war so unpalatable that no opponent would attempt it. Little planning is done by the West to cover the situation if the Soviets do make the attempt. For their part, the Soviets view nuclear war as very destructive but distinctly "thinkable." For instance, all major Soviet surface combatants appear to have extensive postnuclear "wash-down" capabilities. Typical Soviet war scenarios appear to envision a steady escalation toward all-out strategic exchange, with negotiation possible just before that point is reached—indeed, with the outcome of negotiation very much a function of the strategic status quo at that point.

Moreover, if nuclear war should take place, the Soviets envision a subsequent phase of war in which "the winner is decided." In other words, they recognize that an initial nuclear exchange might not, per se, determine the ultimate outcome in a contest between the superpowers. That final phase might include continued fighting, rearming, national redevelopment, and attempts to realign political allegiances of other nations.

Naval forces could quite conceivably have a very special role in this phase of the overall struggle, which is largely neglected in Western planning. Continued access to the seas for mutual help and reinforcement might be required. Further, any residual nuclear weapons at sea could provide a potent influence on the final outcome. Protecting our own surviving forces and neutralizing Soviet surviving forces could be sufficiently important missions to warrant realignment of present plans for the early utilization of some components of our naval forces.

Recommendations. We strongly recommend that the governments of the Western Alliance give careful thought to the possibly crucial roles to be played by surviving naval forces and installations in the residual conflict and struggle that could take place in the aftermath of serious, but indeterminate, nuclear exchanges.

B-6: Merchant Marine Requirements

Findings. The worldwide deployment of increasing numbers of Soviet maritime assets—and their crews—provides substantial opportunities to expose the developing nations of the world to Soviet doctrines of the "future world social and political order." In many instances, these peaceful overtures intrude into areas and regions heretofore believed to have been the exclusive interest of the West. Considerable concern has therefore been expressed in some circles about such Soviet "aggressiveness."

This increasing Soviet maritime presence can benefit the Soviet cause in several ways: by enhancing the image of Soviet compatibility with Third World objectives; by dramatizing Soviet technological progress and prowess; by contributing to perceptions in the nonaligned nations that the world balance of power is shifting inexorably towards the Soviet camp; and by allowing the Soviets to monopolize—or make sizable inroads in—the trading potential of some countries. On the other hand, the presence of Soviet crews does not always establish the desired Soviet image.

Findings and Recommendations

The Soviet Merchant Marine and fishing fleet make valuable contributions to the Soviet economy itself as well as providing significant opportunities to influence the economic growth and affiliation of Third World countries.

Soviet maritime assets have frequently demonstrated their usefulness in delivering military-related assistance to client-states. The centralized Soviet government assures the effective uses of civil and military resources in the pursuit of apparently well-coordinated objectives. This civil-military coordination extends to the collection of valuable local intelligence by virtually all elements of Soviet maritime forces. It also appears to assist handily in the acquisition of overseas basing and resupply points, on which Soviet naval forces would have to depend during wartime.

Despite some claims to the contrary, the penetration of the Soviet Merchant Marine into the major shipping markets of the Western Alliance to date has been relatively slight. Although the growth in U.S. shipping has been negligible over the past ten years in comparison to that of the Soviets, the increases in the vessels of our major Western Alliance powers—and the vast mechant fleets registered in Liberia and Panama—far exceed those of the Soviets.

To blame the relative decline of American merchant shipping on Soviet maritime performance would be neither accurate nor realistic. However, the benefits the Soviets derive from their large fleet of small vessels cannot be denied.

During peacetime, there appears to be no reason to compete with other members of our own Alliance for growth in merchant shipping. These ships should be available to the Alliance during any periods of crisis or tensions shared by our partners. Only in the event of U.S. crises or war situations which do not engage the interests of the rest of the Alliance (such as Korea or Vietnam) would the unilateral capabilities of the U.S. merchant fleet become critical. There is considerable concern as to whether our merchant fleet has now decreased to the danger point. This, in turn depends on whether we can rely on the use of U.S.-owned ships flying flags of convenience under such circumstances—and whether those ships are suitable for the missions demanded. As indicated in Chapter 5, the majority of them are not.

Recommendations. We recommend that the U.S. wartime requirements for merchant ship support be assessed for other cases besides a "NATO war," when we can rely on Alliance contributions. Other scenarios, such as a possible unilateral U.S. intervention or assistance to a warring client-state, might present the contingencies that can "size" the minimum U.S. maritime fleet for U.S. national security purposes.

We also recommend that the United States look to other members of the Alliance or to other means for retaining beneficial contacts with the Third World than to the creation of an economically unprofitable merchant fleet of very small ships.

C. Threat-Responsive Alliance Naval Capabilities

C-1: Numerically Larger Surface Navies

Findings. Technology has progressed to the point where detection and attack of surface vessels at sea are far easier than in the past. The cost of defending surface vessels against such attack—which is also technologically feasible—has risen enormously. Not only the Soviet Union but also some of its client-states and other nations of the Third World are continuing to increase their capabilities to attack major naval elements. The expansion of national sovereignty over extended coastal waters is likely to encourage this trend.

There is virtually no economically feasible way to prevent damage to shipping or to naval vessels themselves if any of these nations decides to take the risks associated with attacking Alliance shipping or navies—regardless of the level of naval defenses provided. The Western Alliance must accept the possibility of some losses at sea at the hands of various nations that might be using modern Soviet-supplied military and naval equipment—and be able to retaliate with appropriate military actions.

The West should avoid dependence on excessively large naval or commercial ships, whose loss or damage could cause acute embarrassment to us and thereby deter an appropriate response on our part or generate excessive escalation from what may have originated as a local incident.

What may appear to be an economy of scale during peacetime could turn out to be the folly of putting too many eggs in one basket during wartime—even during a local intervention operation. The development of navies with greater offensive capabilities—and less defensive orientation—might also result from some movement back toward a larger number of more expendable ships.

Recommendations. We recommend that Western nations avoid the tendency to base their navies (or merchant marines) primarily on a small number of expensive vessels subject to damage or loss, such as supercarriers and cruisers. Rather, emphasis should be placed on building a sufficient number of lower-cost systems such as destroyers, frigates, and smaller submarines which collectively can be made capable of delivering the appropriate military response in a timely fashion. All such small combatants should feature some counterforce capabilities against elements of enemy navies.

C-2: Modular Design in Naval Combatants

Findings. The nations of the Western Alliance, including the United States, appear to be experiencing difficulty in keeping their navies modernized—and standardized—at a time of continuing technological progress on both sides and in the face of changing priorities for Soviet naval missions. The rapidly increasing cost of surface combatants is making it difficult for some Alliance members to replace their aging fleets at all.

Naval forces require a long lead-time in decision-making, design, procurement, construction, deployment, use, and modification. Ships decided on today may not be initially deployed for ten years, and they may then have a service life extending for another thirty to fifty years. The original missions of combatant ships are generally made obsolete by their mission-related equipment rather than by the condition of their hulls, propulsion systems, and living spaces. The sensors, aircraft, missiles, torpedoes, mines, ECM equipment, and other hardware deployed on them are certain to have much shorter life cycles than the ships themselves.

Technology now makes possible the packaging of most weapons and other onboard equipments—including computers—in individual modules. Even power supplies, wiring, and cabling can now be made more versatile (through the use of multiplexing and optical fiber wiring) so they can be used to interconnect vastly different equipment components. While such design practices may somewhat increase the initial cost of the hull, in all likelihood this additional expense would be repaid severalfold in extended useful life and delayed obsolescence.

This modular design approach will also permit the gradual but continuous improvement of standardization and interoperability. Complete standardization and interoperability will probably never be achieved amongst large multinational fleets, unless a high level of modularity is incorporated to allow relatively easy equipment modification during the operational life of the ships. In some cases, the application of weapon and sensor modules to standard commercial hulls could present an economically attractive alternative to the construction of specialized naval combatants—particularly for less wealthy nations. These modules could also be added to older Alliance escorts as a means of extending their effective operational lives. In still other cases, common naval hulls and ship machinery could be used to carry different equipments and weapons for different missions or to satisfy individual nation requirements.

Recommendations. We strongly recommend that all the navies of the West adopt a modular approach to naval design to ease greatly the problems of modernizing, standardizing, adapting, and replacing onboard systems throughout the useful life of naval combatants and to facilitate the arming of merchant ships in time of war.

C-3: Important Technology Programs

Findings. The outcome of future naval battles will still depend on the ability to detect and localize enemy naval elements, be they submarines, surface ships, aircraft, or mines. Of these, the detection of submarines and mines probably remains the most difficult, plus the localization of submarines once they are detected. While Alliance capabilities in these areas are widely considered to be somewhat superior to those of the Soviets, the need to improve our effectiveness—and to maintain a substantial lead—is virtually certain to remain crucial to the outcome of the naval battle and the security of the seas over the long run.

The sealane defense mission in a major, protracted U.S.-Soviet conventional conflict is expected to remain primarily an antisubmarine operation and secondarily an antiaircraft task, for the foreseeable future. Moreover, there appears to be no justification for abandoning the practice of convoys for the most essential shipping—to the extent that escorts are available. Escorting provides one valuable means for raising the attrition of enemy submarines and thus progressively reducing merchant ship losses. Antisubmarine and antiaircraft barrier operations are additional devices for destroying enemy naval forces without waiting until they approach the sealanes. Moreover, the overall problem of protecting the sealanes must include the issues associated with defending the receiving ports against mining and air attack.

Attacking the Alliance sea lines of communication is almost certainly not the highest early Soviet mission priority in a large-scale war. Likewise, defending them may not be the highest priority naval mission for Alliance forces. To a large extent, the satisfactory execution of the sealane defense mission will thus depend on the outcome of direct counterforce operations between elements of the opposing navies. In considerable measure, then, the Alliance can bolster its sealane defense posture by enhancing its general offensive naval capabilities, particularly in ASW barrier operations, as well as improving its defensive potential against Soviet attack.

Moreover, if the Soviets do not already have the capability to perform very effective wide-area surveillance of the ocean surface, they must be expected to acquire it before long. Considering the extent of their research and discussion, we cannot afford to rule out the possibility that the Soviets will also develop a wide-area surveillance capability against submarines based on some nonacoustic principle with which the West may not now be familiar.

The foregoing suggests that the penalties associated with putting too many eggs in one basket will increase and apply equally to surface vessels, aircraft, *and* submarines. There is certainly no reason to believe that Soviet

Findings and Recommendations 427

naval progress has reached its peak. To the contrary, it is more likely to accelerate.

As discussed in Section D-3, the combined efforts of all the navies of the Western Alliance—and some help from their air forces as well (see Section D-6)—will be needed, in many cases, to counteract the growing Soviet naval threat. The United States must keep in mind the development needs and procurement limits of its Allies—and it behooves those nations to share the burden of development in areas where their special expertise (or their vulnerability) may exceed our own.

The long life and slow production rates for modern naval weapon systems virtually rule out the possibility of achieving a high level of standardization amongst Alliance naval ships. However, a much higher degree of interoperability, commonality in consumables, and overall system effectiveness could be achieved by the development of somewhat less sophisticated modular system components that could be incorporated in existing naval platforms during their overhaul periods.

Vast asymmetries in opposing naval systems can possibly lead to rapid escalation of a confrontation at sea (see Chapter 10). The use of a carrier to sink a destroyer could lead to the employment of land-based Backfires to sink the carrier. It seems important to be able to conduct a limited naval engagement successfully without risking unnecessary escalation. Primarily, this implies providing a substantial counteroffensive capability for smaller Alliance combatants.

All of these findings suggest the need for a dynamic and diverse research and development program for Western Alliance naval systems in sensors, weapons, and platforms.

Recommendations. We strongly recommend that the Western Alliance maintain an energetic and diverse naval research and development program, keeping in mind the following very important elements:

Sensors and ASW Operations

- All facets of sensor technology, detection, localization, and processing, active and passive, which have even remotely possible application to naval warfare should be pursued with vigor both for developing new systems and for upgrading present systems. Suitable data links and navigation systems will be needed to attain maximum performance from these new sensors. Many wartime situations would also require positive identification before engagement. Much more work in this area is warranted.
- The U.S. Navy should strive to complement its further development of acoustic sensors for the detection, localization, and attack of

enemy submarine forces by taking on an increased program in nonacoustic techniques.
- The prediction that Soviet ocean surveillance systems will be able to locate and track Alliance naval vessels and submarines points to the need for increased emphasis on countersurveillance systems. These may take a number of forms, from cover, deception, and decoys, to highly controlled communications, active jamming, and possibly direct attack. Gorshkov's vision of "antisensor warfare" must be developed in the R&D community.
- ASW barrier operations appear to offer inherent advantages by placing the ASW systems in their preferred posture and the submarine in its more valuable mode. Research and development to improve barrier effectiveness should be stressed.

Weapons
- Anticipation of reliable, longer-range submarine detection and localization systems suggests the need for longer-range conventional antisubmarine weapons. Torpedo-armed versions of Harpoon and SUBROC, for instance, may soon be justified.
- Weapons that can provide a greater offensive counterforce striking power from smaller naval platforms seem to be growing in importance—promising at least partially to reduce Western dependence on a handful of increasingly vulnerable supercarriers. Cruise missile technology should be exploited in many forms to give land-based aircraft, small surface combatants, and submarines a greater offensive capability when operating alone. Larger warheads than Harpoons are probably needed.
- "Close-in" weapon systems capable of countering Soviet standoff air-to-surface and surface-to-surface missiles appear to be of growing importance. We would do well to separate the problem of destroying the enemy's launch platform from that of destroying his weapons. These tasks may eventually fall to various friendly force elements, possibly even in different military services.

Platforms
- The U.S. Navy might do well to look at smaller submarines, which "disturb nonacoustic fields" less than larger ones and are more amenable to proliferation. An alternative to the huge Trident submarine may be in order.
- New platforms should be kept modest in overall unit cost with the aim of permitting larger numbers of ships, aircraft, and submarines. Technology could well be applied to lower cost and raise reliability in such new systems and enhance opportunities to achieve standardization and interoperability at the same time.

- U.S. Navy planners must learn to avoid the incorporation of marginally useful features in their surface ships which raise the cost more than is justified by their contribution to a broad variety of missions. Nuclear propulsion for all but the largest surface ships may well fall in this category.
- New systems should be made modular to the full extent possible for use on a variety of platforms: new and old; U.S. and Alliance; military and converted civil assets.

D. Making Greater Use of Existing Alliance Assets

D-1: Arming Merchant Ships for Escort Duty and Self-Defense

Findings. A relatively small fraction of essential shipping during a protracted war is made up of military cargoes. Collectively, the West maintains barely enough surface combatants to escort just those military cargoes, and then only if the Soviet Navy does not concentrate on attacking them. However, the importance of reestablishing transoceanic shipping increases as the war lengthens and economic stockpiles are drawn down. Such shipping might also be crucial in the aftermath of nuclear exchanges. To augment our limited escort force, it may be possible to rely on a short-term mobilization potential to increase Alliance capabilities to defend essential sealanes and continue the attrition of enemy submarines.

While the entire roster of active and reserve naval vessels is relatively small compared to the total of Soviet submarines, the number of commercial vessels available to the West exceeds the quantity of torpedoes and missiles the Soviets could reasonably put to sea in all their attack submarines. Moreover, it would appear virtually impossible to sustain navies large enough to defend all the non-military cargo shipments—or even the essential oil shipments—during a protracted war period.

During a very short war, of course, with proper prepositioning and stockpiling there might be little need to use the seas for shipping. Many observers believe a NATO-Warsaw Pact war might be short and are therefore reluctant to support construction and operation of a much larger escort fleet.

If the conflict were expected to last longer than a few weeks, a broad variety of large modern ships available within the civil sector could be mobilized and converted to assist in the accomplishment of the SLOC defense mission. Additionally, technology now makes possible the modular installation of suitable self-contained AAW and ASW weapons and sensors in these merchant ships. The peacetime costs of establishing such a mobilization potential appear far less than those for the creation of a vastly larger peacetime navy—for either the United States or our allies. There also appears to be an abundance of naval reservists with vague wartime assignments whose major purpose is also to provide a hedge against a protracted war and who could be retrained to operate these systems.

This concept presents a significant opportunity to bring the very superior civil economic strength of the West to bear against the seemingly burgeoning conventional military strength of the Warsaw Pact nations. It also offers an exceptional way to augment the wartime capabilities of those allies who must limit their peacetime defense spending, for internal political and economic reasons.

Examples of typical new systems that could be added to merchant ships include air and surface search radars, antiaircraft, antiship and antisubmarine weapon and control systems, helicopters, and towed sonar arrays. Moreover, if these highly effective equipments can be packaged and installed in a modular fashion, then there is a strong possibility that some of these same modules could be used to upgrade the capabilities of some of the older Alliance escort vessels. The Alliance still maintains several hundred escort vessels. Many of them, however, date from World War II and the period immediately following and suffer from obsolescence of their onboard equipments. The addition of Harpoon antiship missiles, a towed array, and limited helicopter facilities, as well as point defense missile systems against air attack, might well extend the useful life of these vessels for some years and lessen the immediate burden of modernization.

Recommendations. We recommend that all members of the Western Alliance explore the potential of converting a portion of their commercial tankers, container ships, and shipping fleets to provide auxiliary escorts and sealane self-defense. At worst, such converted ships could reduce enemy submarine effectiveness; at best, they could contribute substantially to submarine losses. The U.S. Navy's now defunct Arapaho project should be revived in some expanded form, in conjunction with interested allies, to demonstrate the practicality of incorporating helicopters and other ASW/AAW equipments on these converted commercial ships. The applicable technology should then be made available to all members of the Western Alliance. There are other techniques potentially applicable to the arming of merchant ships—both against air and submarine attack—which could be explored on a priority basis. One possibility is to place standoff ASW torpedoes aboard merchant ships to be used in a retaliatory mode.

We further recommend that new commercial ships built by the West should be designed to facilitate installation of military self-defense systems in case of war. These costs could well be borne by member nation governments as a cheaper alternative to creating large peacetime navies.

D-2: Reducing Convoy Losses through Merchant Ship Design and Use

Findings. Our analysis of the NATO sealane defense problem in a ninety-day war indicates that shipping losses would be substantial, at least initially, relative to the early demand for that shipping. If the conventional defense of NATO were successful for more than a month or so, then the West should be able to regain the use of essential sealanes at acceptable attrition levels—unless a major portion of Alliance naval elements had been destroyed in the initial stages of an enemy attack.

There appears to be no way to eliminate the anti-SLOC submarine threat other than by gradual attrition. In the meantime, our analysis indicates that much of our essential shipping at sea in the early weeks could be sunk. The loss of the ships themselves would be less significant than the destruction of the valuable and urgently needed cargoes they carry.

This problem is compounded by three Western peacetime economies that would prove to be very disadvantageous during mobilization or war. First, we have reduced our total war reserve stocks to what is probably well below acceptable minimums. In fact, until very recently, defense planning has not even made an allowance for shipping losses in war reserve calculations. Second, the average merchant marine ship has now grown to roughly ten times the size of the average convoy ship lost during the World War II Battle of the Atlantic. Consequently, we have less to send, and we send it in larger packages. Finally, despite the strong suggestion that the Soviets might tend to concentrate their initial antiresupply efforts on the receiving ports, significant vulnerabilities result from the fact that a constantly growing fraction of the Western merchant fleet requires dockside offloading facilities to unload cargoes promptly.

On the other hand, modern merchant ships such as container ships are considerably faster and may be able to outrun some Soviet submarines. This speed is not available, however, to other classes of bulk carriers and tankers that may fill the largest requirements for essential wartime shipping. Moreover, the concept of outrunning, with its connotation of a single ship-submarine encounter, may be misleading. A mixture of independent sailings of fast ships and convoys of slower ships appears inevitable.

Recommendations. We recommend that the West attempt to restrain its quest for economy of scale in certain areas and continue to construct some smaller cargo ships for wartime cargo movement—even though peacetime subsidies may be required for both construction and operation. These smaller ships should either offer, or be easily convertible to, a configuration for rapid self-loading and unloading.

Further, we recommend that consideration be given to mixing military and nonessential economic (or even ballast) cargo in each ship. In this fashion, the amount of critical material lost per ship sinking could be reduced to more tolerable levels.

Lastly, we recommend that consideration be given to mixing ships with nonessential economic cargoes in convoys with ships carrying essential military goods. It is unlikely that Soviet submariners would be able to distinguish among ship cargoes. The loss of one shipload of cement and one of ammunition would be far preferable to losing two shiploads of ammunition.

If it is technologically feasible to develop other means of providing the enemy with false targets to shoot at, these alternatives should be pursued with vigor. If not, then plans should be made to sail nonessential cargo ships with minimum crews. Shipboard helicopters could be integrated into each convoy specifically to enhance chances for crew rescue—if that is the price required to keep these additional ships moving.

D-3: Naval Partnership with Alliance

Findings. In any large-scale conventional war between Western and Warsaw Pact nations, the naval contributions of our Alliance partners would be instrumental in establishing the desired naval supremacy. Whereas the United States would provide the majority of carrier task forces and highly capable carrier-based aviation, the other Alliance nations could provide the bulk of the smaller escorts that would be used to protect the sealanes in the Atlantic, the Mediterranean, and, to a lesser extent, the Pacific and the Indian Ocean. The potential naval contributions of France, Spain, and Greece on Europe's Southern Flank are by no means insignificant.

The members of the Working Group are not satisfied that sufficient attention has been directed toward achieving the maximum effectiveness from this combined sealane defense force. Many nations have unique ships with specialized weapons and supporting systems aboard them. Some diversity in Allied weapons probably increases the difficulty of enemy countermeasures. Many standard operating practices have been worked out, but each ship is, for the most part, dependent on its own national logistic support system to keep it in action. Moreover, current exercises between the combatants of the different countries do not appear to be adequately realistic. In addition, the current NATO naval command structure appears excessively complex and a probable source of considerable inefficiency in force application. There also seems to be no clear command arrangement for the application of air force assets to the naval battle.

Standardization cannot be achieved around the most sophisticated and expensive equipment of the richest member of the Alliance. There appears to be considerable evidence that advanced-design U.S. equipments are hindering if not decreasing opportunities for standardization and interoperability of Allied naval systems. A trend toward larger quantities

Findings and Recommendations 433

of simple U.S. equipments could enhance overall Alliance capabilities even if U.S. unit effectiveness were somewhat reduced.

The rapid attrition of enemy submarines at the outset of any large-scale conventional war is crucial to assuring the reinforcements by which to sustain such a war without resort to the use of nuclear weapons. The conduct of successful ASW operations at sea is a highly specialized business, requiring extensive cooperation among all elements involved. This activity may involve not only commnd and control but also navigation precision and cooperative use of supporting elements such as helicopters. Many current combined exercises appear "ritualistic" rather than operationally educational.

Recommendations. We urge greater recognition of the importance of all Alliance navies in contributing to the future security of the seas. The restoration of full participation by France and Greece in NATO affairs and the acceptance of Spain into NATO would significantly enhance the naval security of Europe's Southern Flank.

We strongly recommend that all of the Alliance navies place more emphasis on the achievement of appropriate standardization of weapons, communications, and logistics elements and greater priority on the attainment of "interoperability" of naval elements. This may well require some reductions in the sophistication of U.S. contributions to Alliance naval warfare.

We further recommend that the frequency and depth of coordination and consultation be increased by those levels of command charged with the successful prosecution of the antisubmarine campaign. We believe these cooperative efforts should have as one of their early aims the conduct of more frequent and more extensive training exercises, with emphasis on counterforce operations and sealane defense—both in the Atlantic and in the Pacific.

Finally, we recommend that NATO give serious study to streamlining its naval command structure, which appears needlessly complex and could result in the effective application of limited force. At the same time, consideration should be given to improving training and the coordination between naval forces and land-based air forces capable of contributing to naval effectiveness.

D-4: NATO Role in Port Defense

Findings. Soviet naval doctrine addresses the problem of interdiction of the sea lines of communication in its entirety, including consideration of attacks on merchant ships and their escort forces at sea as well as the mining of ports and the disruption of terminal facilities and depots. Soviet naval forces are not designed for, or deployed in, Western-style task forces.

Moreover, most Soviet surface ships are not credited with the ability to survive their first encounter with Western naval forces—at least beyond the limits of Soviet land-based air cover. Soviet long-range aviation has some capabilities against shipping at sea with bombs and a limited number of standoff missiles most likely earmarked for use against Western task forces. The most capable new aircraft of the Russians, the Backfire, can only reach out into the North and Central Atlantic if there are no aerial barriers (see Section D-6) to prevent its high-altitude refueling over the G.-I.-U.K. Gap. Moreover, if they are planning on a short war with NATO, then destruction or denial of resupply material approaching shore or already landed at a few concentrated locations is a more time-urgent task than the piecemeal attack of voluminous shipping in transit dispersed over a large area. The protection of Alliance port approaches and dockside facilities should probably receive at least as high a priority as the defense of the sealanes themselves. This mission must be carried out by first-line military equipment against numerous and diverse attackers.

At present, the air defense and mine defense (see Section D-5) of NATO ports are the responsibility of individual countries and are severely limited by the fact that the two nations with a majority of the receiving ports (Belgium and the Netherlands) rank sixth and seventh in NATO GNP defense spending. France, the third country with extensive ports, is no longer a full member of NATO, and the use of her ports would not be assured. Our analysis indicates that a single U.S. carrier task force has greater air defense capabilities (both in point defense missiles and area defense aircraft) than the countries of Belgium and the Netherlands combined—for all their homeland targets, including SHAPE headquarters. There does not appear to be any practical way to meet this shortfall in available port defense other than making the mission a NATO responsibility, so the assets of all member nations may be distributed appropriately.

The NATO air defense system can probably allocate some air defense fighters to defending port areas if Soviet naval and air force aircraft are allocated to this mission. However, these ports and facilities are "point targets" that may be more efficiently defended by high-rate-of fire surface-to-air missile systems. Very few such systems, if any, are currently deployed in these areas. The latest U.S. systems, for instance, are all planned for deployment forward in West Germany. Moreover, the restrictive geography of the area would make the defense of port approaches against land-based Soviet aircraft, surface ships, or torpedo firing and mine-laying submarines a high-risk mission for a carrier task force, despite its extremely capable aircraft. On the other hand, there appears to be little reason to devote carrier task forces to the defense of the open-Atlantic sealanes. Hence, most of them should be available for other assignments—probably of a more offensive nature.

A substantial fraction of all carrier-capable aircraft (naval and marine) is in peacetime "pipeline" ashore in the United States. There is also some contest for deck space aboard ship among ASW, fighter, and attack aircraft and between naval and marine aircraft. Under wartime mobilization conditions, there should be more carrier-capable aircraft available for combat assignment than can be put aboard ship, although at present there is inadequate logistic support (or weapons) for them to use. Additionally, if some carriers are damaged, it would seem inefficient not to use their surviving assets to the utmost. Situations might even arise where the carriers themselves would be retired to relatively safe havens until the war had progressed to the point where their "second echelon" strike capabilities might be uniquely useful. This might possibly be after the initial nuclear exchanges, if any, had taken place, or at least after the threat from Soviet anticarrier forces had been reduced. In these circumstances, any available surplus naval aviation assets could contribute greatly to port defense. There is, of course, a long-standing issue as to whether aircraft are more valuable ashore in Europe than at sea in the Atlantic or the Mediterranean. This issue has not been resolved by the Working Group. The question here is whether any "surplus" naval or marine aircraft could be more effective in a port defense role in Europe than ashore in the United States.

Recommendations. We strongly recommend that NATO accept responsibility for the European port defense mission in view of increasing Soviet tactical and long-range aviation capabilities (such as the Fencer and Backfire). Any of several modern Alliance surface-to-air missile systems appears well-suited to this additional role as a replacement for the now-obsolete Nike Hercules systems operated by several of our NATO partners.

We also recommend that serious consideration be given to the suggestion that any potentially "surplus" carrier-suitable naval and marine aircraft be assigned to European port defense, at least during the early stages of a large-scale NATO war. If such assets exist, then Allied military planners should give serious thought to the advance preparation of suitable hardened and sheltered shore bases for the operation of appropriate aircraft, including surplus carrier-suitable aircraft (if available with deployable logistic and command support), in the port defense roles: antiair, antiship, antisubmarine, and antimine.

D-5: NATO Attention to Mine Warfare

Findings. The Soviet Union is known to place very high emphasis on the mining capabilities of its naval forces, which hold vast stockpiles of older mines and some relatively sophisticated newer ones for use against NATO naval activities. Actually, both the Alliance and the Pact nations are extremely vulnerable to enemy use of mines, owing to the European geography—which has been extensively exploited in this manner in previous wars.

NATO maintains rather extensive mining capabilities, but it is believed that the stocks of mines are relatively small and that the latest technology has not been applied as broadly as advisable to this form of warfare. The United States, for instance, has in the past placed relatively low emphasis on mine warfare developments. The offensive use of mines in selected areas still holds high promise in the conduct of counterforce operations.

On the defensive side, mine countermeasures (like port defense) are the responsibility of an individual nation rather than a NATO mission. This arrangement could result in inability to concentrate the not-insignificant mine countermeasures resources of the NATO nations in the areas where they may be most needed. The threat is serious enough, and NATO resources sufficiently poorly distributed, that a concerted Soviet mining campaign could be inordinately effective in the absence of suitable NATO resource management. Iceland, for instance, has no means at its disposal to protect its own vital ports.

Finally, a SLOC interdiction campaign is basically a war of attrition. The chances of finding and sinking a submarine in any one particular encounter remain very low. Only through repeated opportunities for contact can the submarine threat be reduced to acceptable levels. The least desirable "opportunity" for the defender in the long run is when the submarine has given notice of its presence by attacking a group of merchant ships. (Some such attacks appear inevitable, however, and Recommendation D-1 urges that the West be prepared to take advantage of the self-localization and identification provided by such actions.)

United States and NATO planning for an antisubmarine campaign against the Soviet underwater fleet involves the establishment of a series of barriers at choke points that the submarines must cross on the way to or from their patrols. These barriers may consist of areas of intensive ASW patrol, aircraft activity, a coordinated effort by our own SSN submarines, or the insertion of strings of homing mines that sense the passage of certain types of vessels and seek them out. The bottom-moored CAPTOR mines represent a relatively new and significant capability that has not yet gained wide acceptance. These mines are expected to have relatively long lives (several months) and to be capable of being controlled by friendly forces if necessary. The use of mines in barrier operations presents an important and relatively inexpensive means of increasing submarine attrition in areas the submarine must traverse before (or after) an attack on essential naval or merchant shipping.

Recommendations. We recommend that all the Alliance nations step up the development and stockpiling of modern mines and improve mine countermeasures against a possible Soviet naval threat.

We further recommend that NATO increase its planning for the use of the new types of mines, such as CAPTOR, as a means of exacting the substantial attrition of Soviet submarines that might threaten the Atlantic and European SLOCs. They could also be useful, of course, against Soviet surface ships.

We also recommend that NATO assume responsibility for the overall coordination and allocation of resources for the mine countermeasures missions.

Finally, we recommend that the United States share its mine and countermine technology—and production, if practical—with our Western Alliance partners in both the Atlantic and the Pacific. They may be closer to the potential minefields and can provide additional means for delivering the weapons. Moreover, they may be able to accord mine warfare a higher development priority than does the United States.

D-6: Air Force Contributions to Sealane Defense

Findings. The overall capabilities of the Soviet Navy to conduct either conventional or nuclear war have increased substantially. Many of the seemingly "conventional" Soviet naval vessels appear to have been given contributory responsibilities for enhancing Soviet nuclear warfighting resources. For this purpose, they may be accorded high levels of land-based defense to assure their survival until their nuclear roles have been played out. Furthermore, Soviet naval forces operating in contested waters close to home are certain to receive land-based air support.

The Western Alliance navies and naval aircraft, operating by themselves, should no longer count on overcoming these combined land and sea defenses and eliminating the Soviet naval threats when operating in Soviet offshore waters. Moreover, the Soviets have placed greater emphasis on land-based bombers and aerial tankers for refueling them. It is probably not practical for Western navies to attempt to neutralize this long-range aviation capability without air force assistance.

Far more than the Alliance, the Soviets must depend on a few home ports to maintain their naval capabilities. These vital installations are heavily defended by the Soviet Air Force and land-based SAM units. Nonetheless, these few facilities represent an inherent vulnerability for the U.S.S.R. that should be exploited by the West, even at the expense of high losses. Again, however, attacks on such installations may well exceed the capabilities of Western navies acting alone.

In addition to strike attack and air defense functions, Alliance air force units can also perform ocean surveillance and antiship missions: these could include bombers, aerial and electronic surveillance aircraft, or even military transports en route. For instance, there may well be more C-5's and

C-141's over the Atlantic at any one time than there are P-3's. If there is any question as to whether the Alliance has sufficient ocean surveillance assets, quite possibly both commercial airliners and the larger executive transports in the civil sector could also be modified during a mobilization period to contribute to this mission. There is already a precedent for this procedure in the adaptation of a commercial aircraft for Coast Guard offshore surveillance. This is another area in which the depth of the West's civil economy can be exploited to counteract the growing military strength of the East, if the proper preplanning is done.

Moreover, Soviet long-range aviation presents a greater threat to NATO SLOCs and shore-based facilities as its buildup and modernization programs proceed. Long-range bombers equipped with standoff weapons cannot be destroyed by organic convoy defenses. Many of them, however, require aerial refueling to achieve maximum range. Both these long-range bombers and their tankers would be subject to attrition as they transited aerial choke points to avoid overflying NATO territory and land defenses. The new U.S. and U.K. airborne radar warning and control aircraft, together with modern interceptors, would be useful in these situations by impeding, limiting the range of, and destroying aircraft that are threatening NATO navies, installations, and shipping.

In the recommendations for the NATO role in port defense (see Section D-4), we also suggested that both army and air force air defense units could make an important contribution to defending NATO ports against air and mine attacks.

It is becoming increasingly important to adopt an "all forces" approach to the neutralization and destruction of these elements of Soviet naval forces. Appropriate training, weapons, and equipment will be essential if air force elements are assigned naval targets. Moreover, some centralized command and control may be necessary to provide optimum targeting, control, and utilization of assets.

Recommendations. We recommend that Alliance air forces give more attention to the task of assisting in countering the threat to their sister naval forces. In the United States particularly, it is important that such assets as the B-52 and the FB-111 be assigned at least collateral missions—and proper weapons, equipments, and training—for the neutralization (bombing and mining) of Soviet home port facilities and their contiguous waters. This would have been an important collateral mission for the B-1.

We further recommend that the U.S. and NATO air force air defense units be assigned appropriate missions to protect naval and maritime shipping and vital shore-based installations from long-range, land-based Soviet air power transiting such areas as the G.-I.-U.K. Gap and the Black Sea-Eastern Mediterranean.

Findings and Recommendations 439

We also recommend that Alliance air force assets be considered for a greater contribution in the ocean surveillance role. In many cases, they might be able to contribute usefully to surface ship detection while carrying out their normal primary missions, if crews are properly trained and their communications are integrated with the ocean surveillance network.

E. Decreasing Dependence on Shipping at Crucial Times

E-1: *Prepositioning of Military Equipment*

Findings. Our analysis of the naval capabilities and priorities of the Soviets indicates that protection of their own strategic forces and destruction of our offensive forces would initially occupy most of their naval assets. Only a fraction of the very large Soviet submarine fleet is likely to be used to attack Allied convoys during the early stages of a large conventional war. Nevertheless, because of the capabilities of Soviet submarines, the initial attrition of Alliance merchant ships and their escorts is likely to be very substantial, almost regardless of the level of sealane defense assets that might practically be employed to defend that shipping. Moreover, the ports are likely to be heavily bombed and mined.

One way to reduce the impact of high early losses of essential war material at sea or in ports is to increase the prepositioning of equipment in or near the anticipated theater of operations. For instance, the entire inventory of U.S. tanks could be placed in shelters in Europe for the cost of ten modern naval escorts.

Prepositioning would almost certainly be cheaper than withstanding large shipping losses in crucial military equipment reinforcements. Even if losses that high were not realized, the added equipment made available to the Allies through prepositioning could be instrumental in stretching their conventional combat stamina, thereby raising the nuclear threshold for the West.

Recommendations. We recommend that all members of the Western Alliance, particularly the United States and Canada, give serious consideration to selectively increasing the levels of military equipment prepositioned in or near anticipated theaters of military operations in order to decrease the impact of inevitable early shipping losses once a war has begun. Such prepositioning should be established during peacetime or at the first indications of seriously rising tensions—if such preparation time is anticipated. The prepositioned material—either afloat or ashore—should be well dispersed or hardened against air attack and protected against sabotage.

E-2: Economic Stockpiling

Findings. The Western Alliance is becoming increasingly interdependent, and it will continue to require—and benefit from—increased levels of economic shipping worldwide. There is no practical alternative to the shipment of enormous quantities of raw and finished materials by conventional ships across the seas. The Soviet Union and many nations of the Third World are gaining both naval and political capabilities to interfere with, or even interrupt, that shipping flow for periods of at least a few weeks to several months. The economic impact of the interruption could be traumatic for Western nations if they remain unprepared. One practical alternative is for the West to maintain adequate economic stockpiles. Many nations of the West already operate various government and private-sector stockpiles, and some are currently increasing their oil storage. The adequacy of such efforts should be carefully reviewed.

Even if the Alliance were no longer dependent on the continuity of the seaborne trade flow, it might be highly desirable under certain circumstances to demonstrate determination to resist trade interruption at sea by the suitable application of naval force. However, there is no real expectation of providing enough naval forces to escort even a fraction of the West's economic shipping requirements against a concerted Soviet submarine campaign.

Soviet maritime units are no less susceptible to harassment, interruption, and internment than those of the Western Alliance. In fact, Soviet naval forces are probably even less able to "defend" their far-flung research, fishing, and merchant fleets than are those of the West. Direct Soviet harassment of Western trade during periods of economic crisis thus appears less likely than attempts to stem the flow at the source through strikes, embargoes, sanctions, and other means that do not place the Soviet commercial fleets in jeopardy. In this case, naval assets are no substitute for economic stockpiles.

Compared to the alternatives, stockpiling is relatively inexpensive, particularly if encouraged in the civil sector. Oil, of course, is the most important, but not the only material not adequately stockpiled at this time. The Working Group is in no position to specify adequate stockpile levels for all contingencies for all countries of the Alliance. The following levels appear to be reasonable, however, for all Alliance members: 120–180 days of normal oil consumption; 6–12 months of normal food imports; 18–24 months of "essential" economic commodities; and 24–36 months of essential war-related materials.

Recommendations. We recommend that all members of the Western Alliance seriously investigate their wartime import needs and review their current economic stockpile levels. Insofar as stockpiles are inadequate, they should be increased—either within their civil sectors, with appropriate government stimuli, or at the national level, if such inducements do not appear attractive to private enterprise. The practical supplements to stockpiling, such as substitution, recycling, and belt-tightening, should also be more thoroughly examined.

F. Limit Soviet Naval Effectiveness

F-1: *Soviet Acquisition of Overseas Bases*

Findings. For anything less than a full-scale protracted conventional war, the Soviet Navy does not appear to be seriously handicapped by lack of accessible, defensible, warm water ports. However, in a large conventional conflict, its current naval base infrastructure would not be adequate for sustained use. Geography would be a major constraint on the effectiveness of Soviet naval forces in such a war.

The acquisition of more warm water ports by the Russians on their own continent—on the Indian Ocean, for instance—could change the real naval balance significantly and should be viewed with considerable concern by the Western Alliance. Additional naval bases (particularly for submarines, aircraft, missiles, and sensors) beyond their own continent—in places such as Iceland, the Azores, Africa, or the Indonesian Archipelago—would also be dangerous and would require neutralization during a major conflict.

Recommendations. The Western Alliance should remain alert to political attempts by the Soviets to gain access to the warm water ports of their continental neighbors—particularly on the Indian Ocean. Such bases could significantly increase the Soviet naval threat and Soviet influence in world affairs.

It would be essential to neutralize naval bases and facilities controlled by the Russians beyond their own continent during any protracted large-scale superpower conflict. We recommend that Alliance planners take this need into account as they consider force requirements for successful prosecution of a major conventional war. Amphibious forces might find application in this mission, particularly if it appears practical to convert such bases to Allied use.

F-2: *U.S. Dependence on Overseas Bases*

Findings. With the exception of Guantanamo Bay in Cuba, Rota in Spain, and Subic Bay in the Philippines, the United States maintains no large, permanent naval bases overseas, although naval facilities such as Diego Garcia, Sigonella, Italy, and Yokosuka, Japan are available for our use in many parts of the world. Nevertheless, the number of overseas bases available to U.S. naval elements and aircraft has been declining significantly ever since the end of World War II. The vast majority of those remaining are essential NATO facilities that might well be unavailable for our use in some confrontation from which other NATO countries elected to remain aloof. Overseas bases remain an important element in stretching available naval assets—particularly for U.S. naval forces, which are more or less permanently deployed "forward." NATO facilities such as Keflavik in Iceland and Lajes in the Azores are a vital part of naval operations in the North Atlantic.

The United States will probably not be able to expand its overseas base structure to offset dwindling naval forces in the near future. In fact, the chances are that we will be unable to maintain our present overseas bases and facilities. Every effort should be made to retain these valuable assets, but we should also make plans for a naval force less dependent on permanent overseas bases.

The U.S. Navy's nominal 500-ship fleet currently consists of 80 percent combatants and 20 percent support ships. As overseas bases decline, this ratio may have to change in the direction of additional support ships. A larger noncombatant naval arm is one partial substitute for overseas bases and facilities. Another may be to rely more on commercial vessels that can be converted to naval service in the event of an emergency.

Such convertible civil assets might become necessary during wartime (after initial nuclear exchanges, for instance), and they would provide a hedge against the further loss of overseas bases and facilities. We might do well to observe how the Soviets use this approach to take advantage of their available merchant marine assets. Another alternative is to make sure we have the forces to secure needed bases and facilities during wartime or to place them under protective custody. It would still be difficult, if not impossible, to conduct sustained combat operations against significant opposition more than about 1,000 miles from the nearest air and sea base providing logistic and operational support.

Recommendations. The United States should endeavor to retain or possibly even expand bases and facilities in areas where the prospects justify the associated economic and political commitments. Furthermore, we should try to find comparable forward locations when political or economic circumstances force the abandonment of useful installations (such as Recife in Brazil). Without such assets, a larger noncombatant navy would be required, and many military operations might become impractical.

We also recommend that the U.S. Navy prepare for the eventual loss of more overseas bases and facilities and investigate the possibility of using more commercial ships for resupply and maintenance. A few commercial ships are already used in these roles, and the practice could undoubtedly be extended.

16
Additional Views

The members of the Working Group recognized from the outset that they would not be able to agree completely on every issue discussed in this report. They also realized that compromise for the sake of unanimity would diminish the integrity and usefulness of the study results. The group therefore agreed that members who differed strongly with any elements of the report, analysis, and recommendations would be encouraged to submit their views for inclusion separately and without change. In fact, every chapter of the report was reviewed at least three times in working committee sesssions, during which the areas of disagreement were discussed and clarified.

Six of the participants have elected to present their "additional views" on the following pages, where they sharpen the definition of the issues and testify to the vigor of the entire investigation. However, the fact that still other members did not prepare dissenting views does not connote their unquestioning approval of every element in the report. Their differences of opinion were simply not strong enough to require separate treatment.

Julien J. LeBourgeois

There are a number of assumptions, judgments, and ways of characterizing issues with which I do not agree or which I would have treated differently. My principal concerns are outlined in these additional views:

Long-Term Naval Policy Objectives—Recommendations A-1

I strongly disagree with the proposal that "the United States Congress take the lead in generating a long-term policy for the objectives of the U.S. Navy and Merchant Marine for the remainder of the century." The formulation of such a policy is the responsibility of the Executive Branch.

The fact that several administrations have not performed well in meeting this responsibility is not sufficient reason to shift yet another responsibility from the executive to the legislative branch of government. Rather, the Executive should get on with the job and deal with this most complex issue promptly and definitively.

Sea-based Air Power—Recommendations A-1, C-1, and C-3

The need is clear for sea-based air power into the twenty-first century—to defend the sealanes and to project power where land-based air power cannot reach or where bases are not available. The recommendations of the study do not deal specifically with this requirement. It seems equally clear to me that in the future there is a need (for reasons well treated in the body of the study) to emphasize the construction of large numbers of ships that may not be as individually capable as some already in service, being built, or authorized.

Specifically, the recommendations should have called for the construction of midicarriers, minicarriers, and other air-capable ships. Since progress in VTOL development is pivotal in determining the extent to which smaller ships may become air-capable, Recommendation C-3 should have included VTOL R&D as an essential element in "Western Alliance" R&D programs.

Making Greater Use of Existing Alliance Assets—
Overall Comments on Recommendations in Section D

The need for an "all forces" approach in dealing with maritime problems is agreed upon—as is the need to make the best use of all existing assets, military and civilian. Appropriate measures should be taken now so these additional capabilities will be in place, practiced, and properly supported *before* they are needed.

As a general comment, I believe the Working Group has done well to suggest areas for careful, open-minded analysis. The report overestimates the potential benefits and underestimates the cost and practical difficulties associated with some of these proposals.

For example, unless the B-52's and FB-111's (Recommendation D-6) could be dedicated to the mining mission and while they still have another primary task, it would be dangerous and self-deluding to base a mining plan on the assumed participation of these formidable aircraft.

Are the ideas about merchant construction and modularization of military capabilities for them (Recommendations D-1 and D-2) practical for accomplishment from the political and economic aspects? Has the situation changed so much that the previously intractable problems can be made to yield? My view is that the situation is more likely so in Allied countries than in the United States. Since such merchant ship measures would, at best, produce operational benefits at the margin, would they justify the high costs which the study acknowledges would be required by some of the proposals?

Regarding the proposal to consider diverting carrier aircraft to port defense tasks in Europe (Recommendation D-4), the study avoids reference to the policy and operational considerations that are disabling to such a proposal except in the most exceptional, obvious, and extreme situations—for example, there must be aircraft immediately available for them. On the operational side, it seems to be sheer folly to *plan* on scooping up "pipeline" aircraft and putting them down in Europe with the expectation that this would be a responsible way to employ assets. Unless the pilots and maintenance personnel have operated and worked together, unless they *know* the theater of operations, the terrain, the weather and operating conditions; unless they understand and have practiced the port defense plans along with the other U.S. and Allied forces involved in air defense—all this in the peculiarly crowded air space of Western Europe—it is unrealistic and dangerous to expect such forces to be effective. Rather, European assets should be created and earmarked for the specific task of port defense.

Prepositioning—Recommendation E-1

I believe the analysis in support of Recommendation E-1 is oversimplified and unconvincing. Of greater concern is the implicit assumption about the attrition of Soviet submarines that would supposedly occur during the early days of war while an Allied stand-down or reduced use of the seas was in effect. If we are to exact attrition, the Soviets must have a reason to commit their submarines. If we withhold, so do they—and we simply delay the problem for thirty to sixty days. While agreeing with the need for selective prepositioning (especially antiarmor capabilities), I believe that Allied strategic objectives are best served by causing the Soviet submarines to be active early in the war and thus more susceptible to the level of attrition essential to Allied sea control.

William Lind, Norman Polmar, Dominic A. Paolucci

We generally concur with the findings and recommendations of the study and believe that adoption of the recommendations would substantially improve the security of the free world. Although there are several details that we find troubling, particularly the refusal (p. 326) to trade off obsolete and largely useless army infantry units for more naval spending, these details do not detract from the potential utility of the study as a whole.

Naval Counterforce—Recommendation A-2

However, it is our collective view that three significant elements of the study require further comment. The first such element can be found in Recommendation A-2, concerning the importance of naval counterforce capabilities. We fully agree with the findings and recommendations presented here but feel that naval counterforce needs to be seen as an even more fundamental issue: the question of whether the sealanes are best defended with a strategy based on a "French-model" or a "Mahan-model" of naval warfare. In the traditional French-model strategy, the fleet is used primarily to support other operations, such as escorting convoys and landing troops in amphibious operations. In a "Mahanist" strategy, the fleet's main function is to destroy, or bottle up in port, the enemy's main naval force. Mahan argued that the destruction or immobilization of the hostile fleet was the best way to insure the safety of friendly maritime operations.

The U.S. and NATO navies have largely adopted the French strategy; both sea control and power projection are subsets of the overall French model concept of supporting other operations. In fact, the U.S. Navy is careful to distinguish sea control, which it defines as using one part of the sea for a specific purpose for a fixed time, from Mahan's concept of control of the sea.

Yet, it may well be that the Mahan approach could secure the sealanes more effectively than the French strategy. Certainly, history argues for Mahan. If the U.S. and Allied navies were configured largely for attacking the Soviet Fleet, even in its home waters, and if such a strategy were vigorously pursued in the event of hostilities, the Soviet Navy would have few forces available for attacking the sealanes. Indeed, such a strategy might well achieve its goal of sinking the Soviet Fleet—provided, once again, that Western navies were configured for that purpose.

Effective Configuration of Future Navy

This raises a second issue: the question not of *how large a force* is needed to defend the sealanes, but of *what kind of force* is most likely to be effective. If a Mahan-type strategy were adopted, more offensive systems would be required, with attack submarines and aircraft carriers (of various sizes) being the more capable systems.

However, even if the current French-model strategy is continued, the effectiveness of certain ship types is open to question. We disagree with the study's assertion that increased emphasis on convoy protection would logically lead to increased procurement of surface escorts such as the FFG-7 (Perry) class frigate (p. 314). In our view, traditional-design cruisers, destroyers, and frigates seem to be poor investments, even for defensive missions such as convoy escort. In antisubmarine warfare (ASW), the surface escort's only genuinely effective systems are its sonars and its onboard aircraft (although long-range, guidable shipboard ASW weapons, such as the Australian Ikara, may be useful). In antiair warfare (AAW), unless the escort has a highly sophisticated (and expensive) system, such as Aegis, it will have trouble even defending itself against sophisticated missile attacks, much less the ships being escorted. On balance, the traditional escort appears materially inferior to the threats it faces, especially modern (conventional as well as nuclear) submarines.

In our view, the Western nations would be well advised to cease most, if not all, construction of additional cruisers, destroyers, and frigates. Most of the missions for which new ships of these types would be procured could be performed more effectively by small VSTOL/helicopter carriers, such as the proposed Vosper Thorneycroft "Harrier Carrier" (at some 8,000 tons), the new Italian *Giuseppe Garibaldi* (12,000 tons), or the U.S. VSTOL Support Ship (VSS, at 25,000 tons). Such ships can incorporate the useful systems of traditional surface escorts, such as sonars, while offering the improved ASW and AAW standoff capability provided by sea-based aircraft. Diversion of funds from traditional surface escort building programs to submarines (nuclear and nonnuclear), land-based naval aircraft, offensive and defensive mining capabilities, lighter-than-air patrol/ASW vehicles, and new technology systems such as hydrofoils and surface effect ships would appear desirable to increase total force effectiveness.

Because this study fails to deal adequately with the qualitative issue of what kinds of systems are effective, it consistently underestimates the threat to the sealanes. If, as we believe, the conventional surface escort is not particularly effective, especially against the modern submarine, then Allied ASW forces have a substantially lower net effectiveness than this study, or U.S. Navy presentations, suggest. Both this study and the navy place heavy reliance on surface escorts to defend the sealanes. In its FY 1979 budget request, the navy asked $1.5 billion for surface escorts (eight FFG-7's), compared to only $433 million for attack submarines (one SSN-688) and $471 million for the air ASW systems (P-3's, S-3's, LAMPS). A review of unclassified navy operational plans shows a substantial role assigned to surface escorts. If they should prove unable to fulfill this role to the extent postulated, as we believe likely, overall allied ASW performance will suffer severely, and the task of defending the sealanes will be substantially more difficult than this study has assumed it will be.

Institutional Problems in the U.S. Navy

The final issue not adequately discussed in this report is the backdrop for and, to a substantial degree, one origin of the problem we have noted here as well as many of those mentioned in the main body of the report itself. The issue is institutional problems in the U.S. naval establishment; the study dismisses it in three sentences (p. 308). In our view, perhaps our *most* serious danger is the fact that the institutions responsible for structuring our naval stratgegy and forces—the U.S. and many Allied navies and defense ministries—have become sufficiently dominated by intra-institutional concerns that they are unable to perform their intended functions effectively.

In his book *On Watch,* the former U.S. chief of Naval Operations, Admiral Elmo Zumwalt, stated that:

> Internal forces in the Navy had contributed to unbalancing it in the 1960s. For the last quarter century or more, there have been three powerful "unions," as we call them, in the Navy—the aviators, the submariners, and the surface sailors—and their rivalry has played a large part in the way the Navy has been directed. . . . Whichever union a commander comes from, it is hard for him not to favor fellow members, the men he has worked with most closely, when he constructs a staff or passes out choice assignments. It is hard for him not to think first of the needs of his branch, the needs he feels most deeply, when he works up a budget. It is hard for him not to stress the capability of his arm, for he tested it himself, when he plans an action.[1]

In many cases the influence of intra-institutional factors causes the defense establishment to cling to dangerously outmoded systems and tactics and to reject new technologies and approaches. Ship types which have, by virtue of long existence, a substantial constituency behind them continue to appear in budgets, even when their continued utility is openly doubted both outside *and* within the service. New threats which promise to render cherished practices or systems unviable are ignored. Potentials or needs which lack a constituency—mine/countermine warfare is a prominent example in the U.S. Navy—are neglected. Ultimately, the defense establishment comes to live in a fantasy world of faith in obsolete ships and tactics which are likely to prove ineffective in war.

Unless the institutional problems can be effectively addressed, the recommendations in this "Additional Views" chapter in the study itself, or those in any other study, are not likely to be of much value. Conclusions based on objective analysis will be neither "right" nor "wrong" from the standpoint of a defense decision-making process dominated by intra-institutional concerns; they will simply be irrelevant. The service or defense department in question will always be able to produce a study rationalizing the course of action it wants to take in order to keep its internal interests satisfied. Logically, therefore, our first concern must be not the specific policies needed to kep the sealanes open, but the actions required to open our navies and defense departments to the need to secure the sealanes effectively even at the expense of internal interests within the defense establishment itself.

David B. Kassing

The issue I raise has to do with prepositioning of military supplies in the European theater. In Chapter 13, the report says: "Compared to the costs of defending the sealanes to NATO against the potential submarine threat, there is an increasing premium on prepositioning essential supplies in or near the combat theater. . . ." The chapter recommends "serious consideration" of more use of protected prepositioning of military supplies and equipment.

The report includes a careful assessment of the security of the sealanes of the Western Alliance. There is a detailed analysis of the Soviet Navy's missions and forces. There is a lengthy analysis of the importance of the sealanes and seaborne trade to the Western Alliance. Considerable attention is paid to U.S. and Allied naval organization, capabilities, technologies, and budgets. There is also an illustrative calculation of the results of a campaign by Soviet forces against Alliance sealanes.

But the report includes no similar assessment of prepositioning. At the very least, more thought should be given to the relative vulnerability of sealift and prepositioning, and the relative costs should be carefully estimated. I think the vulnerability of prepositioned military supplies is growing at the same time that the ability of the Western Alliance to protect its sealanes is improving.

Recent concern about NATO security arises from changes in the capability of Soviet forces in Eastern Europe. The possibility of an attack with little or no warning is taken more seriously now than a decade ago. So is the possibility of a swift Soviet move, deep into NATO. In fact, surprise and *blitzkrieg* tactics have long been stressed in Soviet military doctrine. But Western perceptions have undergone their recent change mainly in response to the obvious improvements in the capabilities of the Soviets' tactical air forces and the greater mobility of their ground forces:

- New Soviet tactical aircraft, deployed in Eastern Europe, are better equipped for deep-penetration attacks than their predecessors.
- The tank and motorized rifle divisions of Group of Soviet Forces Germany (GFSG) have been modernized with the latest tanks, self-propelled artillery, armored fighting vehicles, and attack helicopters.

These developments aggravate the vulnerability of material prepositioned on the Continent. The ability of the Soviets to destroy and overrun such material is clearly on the rise.

Meanwhile, the Alliance navies are becoming better able to protect the sealanes. The reason for this is, in part, that Soviet submarine force levels are declining and, in part, that the Soviets are finding missions of higher priority for their submarines.

But the improvement in the capability of the Alliance for sealane defense is also a result of intensive research and development as well as expensive procurement programs. New systems—towed arrays, computerized detection techniques, improved antisubmarine weapons—will soon be available in sizable numbers, reducing the losses to be expected from a Soviet campaign against the North Atlantic sealanes.

My judgment is that the report cites far too high an estimate of cumulative attrition of shipping in a lengthy campaign. Such a level—25 percent—might be reached briefly at the peak of an all-out sea fight, but over a six-month campaign, a figure no more than half that size is more likely. Losses of prepositioned materials to enemy action, on the other hand, could easily be as heavy.

The analysis in Chapter 13 suggests that prepositioning would save money. Would it? Could naval forces be reduced if more material were prepositioned? Not necessarily. A sound strategy for NATO is to be able to outlast the Soviets on the ground in Europe. This means that NATO must be able to sustain the fight. Ammunition, fuel, and other supplies would have to be replaced by sea. Naval forces to protect the sealift would be required in equal measure. The savings offered by prepositioning are exaggerated.

In the future, crises and contingencies outside Europe will become more important. The report recognizes this trend and discusses the role that naval forces might play in these situations. But army and air force units might also be needed, albeit less often, in such contingencies. The United States would have to be able to ship them to the combat zone and to protect the cargo ships that supported them as well. The savings that might result from prepositioning of material would be reduced accordingly.

If war material were concentrated in Europe, the ability of the United States to respond to crises elsewhere would surely be constrained. Moreover, military equipment stored in Europe would not be available for training. To keep the troops trained and ready for contingencies in NATO and elsewhere, additional equipment would have to be acquired. Any potential savings from prepositioning would therefore be reduced even further.

At the technical level, the analysis in Chapter 13 mixes wartime costs with peacetime costs, discounted costs with undiscounted costs. The usual practice in evaluating alternative defense programs, such as sealift and prepositioning, is to compare the peacetime costs of wartime capabilities. The costs of replacing wartime losses are incurred only if fighting occurs, but peacetime costs are incurred all the time, year in and year out. Yet the analysis in Chapter 13 treats the costs of material and ships lost in a possible war as though they were as sure as the peacetime costs of building and maintaining prepositioned sites. Clearly, they are not.

It is also customary to discount the cost streams associated with the options under evaluation. In Chapter 13, however, only the peacetime costs of prepositioned supplies are discounted. The peacetime costs of naval forces for sealane defense do not enter into the calculations; they should.

All this makes me doubtful that more prepositioning is desirable. The additional costs of prepositioning should not cost the nation a reduction in general-purpose naval forces. The need to pay more attention to naval capabilities, not less, is amply demonstrated throughout this report.

Richard L. Garwin

This participant agrees with nearly all of the text and recommendations and believes that the interests of the United States are best served in these "Additional Views" by reenforcing those findings and recommendations that seem to him especially pivotal.

The Navy shares with other large organizations—businesses, universities, and civilian government—the problems of maintaining vitality in a changing world of limited resources and ill-defined goals. As a bureaucracy it is further imbedded in the Department of Defense and the Executive Branch and interacts strongly with the Congress. It is not easy to adapt efficiently under these circumstances, and criticism is rampant, some of it warranted.

Quality versus Quantity

The long life of ships is invariably cited as a problem of adaptation, but the lesson is infrequently drawn that the shorter-lived, even expendable systems should be preferred at comparable costs for similar effectiveness. Finally, the emphasis on maximum capability per platform—nuclear attack submarine, aircraft carrier, guided-missile cruiser—is natural from the viewpoint of the individual skipper, but such an approach can seriously inhibit U.S. capability to fight and win against an opponent. Lanchester showed that the winning power of a force under often-applicable circumstances is proportional to the effectiveness of each element times the *square* of the number of elements. Thus, units of one-third effectivenesss need only be 1.73 times as numerous to match a nominal force, and if there are three times as many units of one-third.

effectiveness, the nominal force is wiped out without inflicting significant losses. For these reasons, I welcome the report's emphasis on *proliferation weapons*, such as the containerized weapons systems for addition of military capability to cargo ships, deck-launched torpedoes to threaten submarines which have attacked merchantmen, and CAPTOR mines for ASW barriers. Furthermore, such capabilities and their successful integration into U.S. doctrine and plans provide a better base for collaboration with our allies than the traditional approach of large ships of maximum capability.

Reducing Shipping Losses

We cannot eliminate losses to our shipping and our ports, but these losses need not be overwhelming if we act simultaneously to reduce the loss that can be inflicted by a given Soviet capability and prepare to exhaust that capability more rapidly than we would lose our own. Prepositioning, loading military cargoes on top of civilian cargoes, helicopter rescue plans for minimal crews, and self-defense torpedoes reduce the fractional loss rate to Soviet torpedoes and air-to-surface missiles. CAPTOR mine barriers, larger numbers of ships with lesser ASW capabilities, and planned attacks on Soviet submarine and aviation facilities can lessen the Soviet threat.

Bureaucracy and tradition severely inhibit progress toward an effective, affordable navy. I believe this report shows what to do if not how to get there.

Appendix: Soviet Ship Characteristics, Armament, and System Purpose

APPENDIX
SOVIET SHIP CHARACTERISTICS, ARMAMENT, AND SYSTEM PURPOSE

Ship	Type	Full Load Disp.	Approx. IOC	Hangar Capacity	Aircraft And Missile Launchers (# Missiles)	Guns	Torpedoes	RBU Rocket/DC	Mine Rails	Anti-shore	ASuW	ASW	AAW
KIEV	CVSG	37,000	1976-	35	Helicopter KA-25 VSTOL YAK-36 8 SS-N-12 ( ) 1 SUW-N-1 ( ) 2 SA-N-3 (~80) 2 SA-N-4 ( )	4 76mm 6 23mm	10 21"	? X		○ ? ● ○ ○	? ○ ●	? ? ● ○ ●	? ● ● ○ ○ ●
MOSKVA	CVHG	18,000	1968-69	18	Helicopter KA-25 1 SUW-N-1 ( ) 2 SA-N-3 (~80)	4 57mm	10 21"TT	 X		○ ○ ○ ○		● ● ● ● ●	
KARA	CG	9,500	1973-	1	Helicopter KA-25 8 SS-N-14 (8) 2 SA-N-3 (44) 2 SA-N-4 (36)	4 76mm 4 23mm	10 21"TT	 X		 ○? ● ○ ○		● ● ● ● ● ● ●	 ● ● ● ● ●
KRESTA II	CG	7,500	1970-	1	Helicopter KA-25 8 SS-N-14 (8) 2 SA-N-3 (44)	4 76mm 4 23mm	10 21"TT	 X		○? ○ ○ ○		● ● ● ● ● ●	 ● ● ●
KRESTA I	CG	6,500	1966-68	1	Helicopter KA-25 4 SS-N-3D (4) 2 SA-N-1 (44)	4 76mm	10 21"TT	 X		● ○ ○ ○		 ● ●	 ●
KYNDA	CG	5,700	1961-65		8 SS-N-3A (16) 1 SA-N-1 (22)	4 76mm	6 21"TT	 X		● ○ ○ ○		 ● ● ●	

○ = Primary Capability
● = Secondary Capability

APPENDIX (CONT)
SOVIET SHIP CHARACTERISTICS, ARMAMENT, AND SYSTEM PURPOSE

Ship	Type	Full Load Disp.	Approx. IOC	Missile Launchers (# Missiles)	Guns	Torpedo Tubes	RBU Rocket/DC	Mine Rails	Land Attack	ASuW	ASW	AAW
SVERDLOV CONV.	CC	19,200	1973	1 SA-N-4 (18)	6-9 152mm 12 100mm 32 37mm 8-16 30mm				● ○	○ ○		● ● ● ●
SVERDLOV (One ship is CLG/SA-N-2)	CL	19,200	1952-56		12 152mm 12 100mm 32 36mm			X	● ● 	○ ○ ○		
KRIVAK	DDG	3,900	1971-	4 SS-N-14 (4) 2 SA-N-4 (36)	2 100mm or 4 76mm	8 21"	X	X	○ ● ○ ● ●	● ○		● ● ● ●
KASHIN (MOD)	DDG	4,700	1973-	4 SS-N-11 (4) 2 SA-N-1 (44)	4 76mm	5 21"	X		● ○ ○ ○		● ●	● ● ●
KASHIN	DDG	4,600	1962-6	2 SA-N-1 (44)	4 76mm	5 21"	X	X	● ○ ●		● ○	● ●
KANIN	DDG	4,500	1967-	1 SA-N-1 (22)	8 57mm 8 30mm	10 21"	X		● ○ ●		●	● ● ●
KOTLIN SAM	DDG	3,885	1962-6	1 SA-N-1 (~20)	2 130mm 4 57mm	5 21"	X		○ ● 	○ ○		● ●
KILDIN	DDG	4,000	1973-	4 SS-N-11 (4)	16 57mm	4 21"	X		● ○	●	●	●

● = Primary Capability
○ = Secondary Capability

457

APPENDIX (CONT)
SOVIET SHIP CHARACTERISTICS, ARMAMENT, AND SYSTEM PURPOSE

Ship	Type	Full Load Disp.	Approx. IOC	Armament: Missile Launchers (# Missiles)	Armament: Guns	Armament: Torpedo Tubes	RBU Rockets	Mine Rails	Anti-shore	ASuW	ASW	AAW
KOTLIN	DD	3,885	1955-57		4 130mm 16 45mm 4 25mm	5-10 21" X	X		○	○ ● ●	● ● ●	● ● ●
SKORY	DD	3,500	1952-59		4 130mm 2 85mm 7-8 37mm	10 21" X	X		○ ● ●	○ ○ ● ○	● ● ●	● ● ●
NANUCHKA	PGG	930	1970-	6 SS-N-9 (6) 1 SA-N-4 (18)	2 57mm				●			● ●
NEW ESCORT	FFG											
MIRKA AND PETYA I, II, III	FF	1,000	1963-69		2-4 76mm	5-10 16" X	X		○ ● ●	● ● ○		
RIGA	FF	1,600	1955-59		3 100mm 4 37mm 4 25mm (some)	3 21" X	X		○ ● ●	○ ● ○		

● = Primary Capability
○ = Secondary Capability

APPENDIX (CONT)
SOVIET SUBMARINE CHARACTERISTICS, ARMAMENT, AND SYSTEM PURPOSE

Submarine	Type	Disp Surfaced	Approx IOC	Armament Missiles	Torpedo Tubes	Mines	Land Attack	ASuW	ASW
DELTA I, II	SSBN	8,300-9,500	1973-	12-16 SS-N-8/18 SLBM (I) (II)	6 21"		●	○	●
YANKEE	SSBN	8,300	1968-	16 SS-N-6/17 SLBM	6 21"		●	○	●
HOTEL II, III			~1961	3 SS-N-5 SLBM (II) 6 SS-N-8 SLBM (III)	6 21" 4 16"		● ●	○	● ●
GOLF I, II, III	SSBN	2,750	~1961	3 SS-N-4 SLBM (I) 3 SS-N-5 SLBM (II) 5 SS-N-5 SLBM (III)	6 21" 4 16"		● ● ●	○	● ●
PAPA	SSGN	6,700	1970	10 SS-N-7 SLCM	6 21"	?	●	○	●
CHARLIE II	SSGN	~5,000	1968-	10 SS-N-7 SLCM	8 21"	36	●	○	●
CHARLIE I	SSGN	4,700	1976-	8 SS-N-7 SLCM	8 21"	36	●	○	●
ECHO II	SSGN	5,100	1965-67	8 SS-N-3	6 21" 4 16"	36	●	○	● ●
JULIETT	SSG	2,800	1963-68	4 SS-N-3	6 21" 4 16"	36	●	○	● ●
ALPHA	SSN	2,800	1970		? 21" ? 16"	?		○	● ●
VICTOR II	SSN	4,700	1973-	~10 SS-N-15?	8 21"	?		○	●
VICTOR I	SSN	4,300	1968-	? SS-N-15?	8 21"	?		○	●
NOVEMBER	SSN	4,500	1961-65		6 21" 4 16"	64		○	● ●
ECHO I	SSN	4,600	1962-63		6 21" 4 16"	64		○	● ●
TANGO	SS	2,100	1973-		6 21"	?		○	●
BRAVO	SS	2,400	~1963		6 21"	?		○	●
ROMEO	SS	1,460	~1961		6 21"	36		○	●
FOXTROT	SS	2,600	1960-		6 21" 4 16"	44		○	● ○
ZULU	SS	2,000	1951-55		10 21"	44	●		
WHISKEY	SS	1,350	1951-57		6 21"	24	●		

○ = Primary Capability
● = Secondary Capability

Notes

Notes to Chapter 2

1. All the above quotations are to be found in Sergei G. Gorshkov, *Morskaya Moshch' Gosudarstva* [The sea power of the state] (Moscow: Military Publishing House, 1976).
2. Milovan Djilas, *Conversations with Stalin* (New York: Harcourt, Brace, Jovanovich, 1962), p. 182.
3. Except for the helicopter aircraft carriers, modern Soviet surface naval vessels are designated among NATO allies by class names beginning with "K." These names are assigned in the West and do not correspond to the names given the individual ships by the Soviet Navy. NATO designates Soviet submarines by using letters of the alphabet usually referred to in the international communications name system, such as "Alpha," "Bravo," "Charlie," etc.
4. *Jane's Fighting Ships, 1976-1977*, p. 702.
5. From David Fairhall, *Russian Seapower* (Boston: Gambit Publishers, 1971), p. 119, which contains an excellent treatment of the Soviet Merchant Marine.

Notes to Chapter 3

1. From Michael MccGwire, "Naval Power and Soviet Oceans Policy," in *Soviet Oceans Development* (Washington, D.C.: Congressional Research Service, 1976), p. 146.
2. Gorshkov does seem sensitive on the appropriations issue, however. In *The Sea Power of the State* (p. 118) he quotes from the diary of Kuropatkin, the Tsarist minister of war just before the Russo-Japanese war of 1904-1905: "Yesterday, Witte and I amicably persuaded the Tsar of the necessity to cut back on the funds for the fleet and the Far East." Gorshkov comments, "That testifies, if not to treachery, then to every manner of the crudest misunderstanding of the interests of the State." Lenin, who greeted Russia's defeat in 1905 as a victory for the workers and the peasants, must have quivered at those words, even in the fastness of his mausoleum.
3. Sergei G. Gorshkov, "A Most Important Factor of Military Preparations and Military Capabilities of the Fleet," *Rear and Supply of the Soviet Armed Forces*, no. 7 (1976), p. 4.

Notes to Chapter 4

1. Competing demands of the domestic economy for electric power generation reactors will increase as the oil squeeze gets tighter, with a concomitant effect on foreign exchange earnings. There is also the more direct competition with icebreaker propulsion systems.

2. On November 1, 1976 there were fourteen Delta I and one Delta II boats operational, plus another twelve units being built, being fitted out, or undergoing trials (U.S., Senate, Armed Services Committee, FY 1978 Appropriation Hearings, Part 1, p. 62).

Past experience suggests that if the program were to continue through 1978 there would have been seventeen to eighteen additional units rather than only twelve. Reports of the "63rd Ballistic Missile Submarine" (i.e., thirty-four Yankees and twenty-nine Deltas) lying in the Amur since summer 1977 tend to confirm this assessment (*Washington Post*, December 18, 1977, p. 46).

Notes to Chapter 5

1. Security of the sealanes is, of course, only part of the problem of assuring supplies. Embargoes and other interruptions at the source of supply may, in fact, be more likely. Trade negotiations can protect against some of these interruptions, and stockpiles can dampen the effects of all of them.

2. See Joseph S. Nye, "Independence and Interdependence," *Foreign Policy*, no. 22 (spring 1976), pp. 133-135 for further discussions of these issues.

3. Charles L. Schultze, "The Economic Content of National Security Policy," *Foreign Affairs* 51, no. 3 (April 1973): 525, 526. For similar analyses of vulnerabilities to interruption of raw material supplies, see: Richard Cooper, "National Resources and National Security," in *The Middle East and the International System*, Adelphi Paper no. 115 (spring 1975):11; and Raymond Vernon, "Rogue Elephant in the Forest," *Foreign Affairs* 51, no. 3 (April 1973): 578.

4. Arthur D. Little, Inc., *Dependence of the United States on Essential Imported Materials, Year 2000*, vol. 1, Table 1, (April 1974), pp. 13-14.

5. U.S., General Services Administration, Federal Preparedness Agency, "Stockpile Report to the Congress, October 1976–March 1977" (October 1977), p. vii.

6. In 1975 a conference at the University of Rhode Island on the law of the sea yielded three papers on future fishing technology: J. L. Jacobson, "Future Fishing Technology and Its Impact on the Law of the Sea"; S. Oda, "Impact of Fishing Technology on International Law"; J. Scharfe, "Interrelations between Fishing Technology and the Coming International Fishing Regime." The papers are printed in F. T. Christy, Jr. et al., eds., *Law of the Sea: Caracas and Beyond* (Cambridge, Mass.: Ballinger, 1975).

7. "Worldwide Listing of Deepwater Wells," *Offshore* 37, no. 6 (June 5, 1977): 43.

8. Leonard LeBlanc, "Ultradeep Age Now in Its Second Decade with 117 Wells," *Offshore* 36, no. 6 (June 5, 1976):58.

9. See two papers from the University of Rhode Island conference proceedings: J. E. Flipse, "Deep Ocean Mining Technology and Its Impact on the Law of the Sea"; and J. L. Miro, "The Great Nodule Controversy." These appear in Christy et al., *Law of the Sea*.

10. Robert E. Osgood, "U.S. Security Interests and the Law of the Sea," in R. Amacher and R. J. Sweeny, eds., *The Law of the Sea: U.S. Interests and Alternatives* (Washington, D.C.: American Enterprise Institute, 1976), p. 14.

11. See D. B. Johnson and D. Logue, "U.S. Economic Interests and the Law of the Sea," in Amacher and Sweeney, *Law of the Seas*, p. 65.

12. U.S., Congress, Senate Committee on Commerce, *The Economic Value of Ocean Resources to the United States*, 92d Cong., 2d sess. (Washington, D.C.: Government Printing Office, 1974). The work discussed in this report was done by Robert R. Nathan Associates, under contract to the Congressional Research Service.

13. Data taken from *Lloyd's Register of Shipping Statistical Tables, 1975*. These figures apply to cargo-carrying ships only. Tugs, ferries, supply ships, research vessels, and various other ship types that are often included in total fleets are omitted here.

14. At the end of 1975, U.S. companies owned vessels with a total of another 30.9 million gross tons. Of this total tonnage, tankers accounted for 87 percent, bulk and ore carriers for 12 percent, and freighters for the remainder. The eighty-six U.S.-owned foreign-flag freighters add only 8 percent to the 5 million-ton cargo-carrying capacity of the U.S. flag freighter fleet, providing no significant enhancement of the merchant marine's ability to support U.S. forces abroad in time of war. Data are drawn from U.S., Department of Commerce, Maritime Administration, "Foreign Flag Merchant Ships Owned by U.S. Parent Companies" (February 1977).

15. These projections were prepared by Professor Robert Athay of the Naval War College, with the help of the Maritime Administration.

16. Data from *Lloyd's Register of Shipping Statistical Tables, 1975*.

17. In order to focus on international competition in the world's ocean fisheries, these figures exclude the catch for inland fisheries (about 10 million metric tons). Data taken from Food and Agricultural Organization, *Yearbook of Fishery Statistics, 1975*.

18. The vulnerability of offshore structures for production and distribution of oil and gas raises serious problems. The structures are large, fixed, and easily damaged by conventional weapons. Consequently, planners will do well to assume the rigs would be attacked in any protracted conventional war. The British have concluded that the price of protecting their North Sea offshore facilities is worth paying; the Norwegians are moving in that direction. As the United States begins to pump increasing amounts of oil from offshore fields, investment to protect these structures must be considered.

19. See U.S., Department of the Interior, Bureau of Mines, *Commodity Data Summaries, 1977* (Washington, D.C.: Government Printing Office, 1977) for data on mineral reserves.

20. Calculated from Bureau of Mines, *Commodity Data Summaries, 1977.*
21. "Economic Report of the President," January 1978, Table B-107, p. 380.
22. In the event of conflict in Europe, the United States would need to move about 25 million tons of material to Europe. According to the secretary of Defense, "to reinforce and sustain our forces overseas—especially in Europe... we must turn to the sealanes for the movement of 95 percent of the tonnage...." Secretary Harold Brown, *Department of Defense Annual Report, Fiscal Year 1979* (February 7, 1978), p. 86.
23. At the end of 1976, U.S. direct investments abroad—excluding Canada—amounted to $103.3 billion. Investments in Europe were $55.9 billion; investments in other states bordering the Atlantic are estimated to be at least $20 billion. See Obie G. Whechard, "U.S. Direct Investment Abroad in 1976," *Survey of Current Business* 57, no. 8 (August 1977): 45.
24. In the 1980s the planned widening and deepening of the Suez Canal will increase the maximum size of loaded ships that can use the canal from 50,000 deadweight tons to 250,000 (U.S., Central Intelligence Agency, *Indian Ocean Atlas* [Washington, D.C.: Government Printing Office, 1976] p. 28).
25. H. Rivero, "Why a U.S. Fleet in the Mediterranean," *U.S. Naval Institute Proceedings* 103, no. 391 (May 1977): 66-89.
26. Ibid., p. 77.
27. The Japanese have long shaped their economic policies to limit the effects of their dependence. See L. B. Krause and S. Sekiguchi, "Japan in the World Economy," in H. Patrick and H. Rosovsky, eds., *Asia's New Giant—How the Japanese Economy Works* (Washington, D.C.: Brookings Institution, 1976), pp. 383-458.
28. The estimates of the potential fish catch are drawn from the Central Intelligence Agency's *Indian Ocean Atlas,* p. 15.

Notes to Chapter 6

1. Sergei G. Gorshkov, *Morskaya Moshch' Gosudarstva* [The sea power of the state] (Moscow: Military Publishing House, 1976), p. 19.
2. Calculated from Lloyd's *Register of Shipping Statistical Tables, 1975.*
3. Their efforts, however, were not enough to earn an enduring relationship with Somalia. The Soviets were asked to leave that country in 1977.
4. For a detailed analysis of Soviet fishing activities, see M. A. Kravansa, "The Soviet Fishing Industry: A Review," in J. Hardt and H. Franssen, eds., *Soviet Ocean Development* (Washington, D.C.: Government Printing Office, 1976), pp. 377-462.
5. See Joseph P. Riva, Jr., "Soviet Offshore Oil and Gas," in Hardt and Franssen, *Soviet Ocean Development,* pp. 479-500 for a detailed account of the Soviet offshore petroleum industry.
6. These activities are discussed in detail in James E. Mielke, "Soviet Exploitation of Ocean Mineral Resources," in Hardt and Franssen, *Soviet Ocean Development,* pp. 501-509.
7. A Brookings Institution study has identified 215 instances from 1946 to October 1975 in which the United States used armed forces to protect its interests. See Barry B. Blechman and Stephen S. Kaplan, *Force without War: U.S. Armed*

Forces as a Political Instrument (Washington, D.C.: Brookings Institution, forthcoming).

8. Estimated by D. B. Johnson and D. E. Logue, "U.S. Economic Interests in Law of the Sea Issues," in R. Amacher and R. S. Sweeney, eds., *The Law of the Sea: U.S. Interests and Alternatives* (Washington, D.C.: American Enterprise Institute, 1976), pp. 37-76.

9. The vulnerabilities of the West are not generated from its activities at sea per se. It follows that any attempt by the Russians to disrupt or interfere with seaborne trade in raw materials, oil, and food would have an adverse effect on their relations with *all* the countries affected—including, for example, Middle East oil suppliers.

10. A Soviet threat to oil shipping in the Indian Ocean is an oft-cited possibility. But the Soviet fleet would face real difficulty in an interdiction campaign against Indian Ocean oil routes. Soviet naval units would face logistic problems when operating in a hostile environment remote from their bases, without air cover and with inadequate support afloat.

11. The main exception is closure of the Strait of Hormuz, stopping the flow of Middle East oil.

Notes to Chapter 10

1. Sergei G. Gorshkov, "Historical Experience and the Present Day," *Voprosy Filosofi*, no. 5 (May 1975), pp. 26-38.

2. V. Nikyaylin, "Physics and ASW Defense," *Krasnaya Zvezda*, March 10, 1962, p. 6.

3. Sotnikov and Brusentsev, *Aviatsiya Protiv Podvodnikh Lodok* (1970), p. 101.

4. Ye. Brnzov, "Trends in the Development of Non-Acoustic Means of Detection," *Morskoy Sbornik* (September 1974), p. 85.

5. Demyanov, *Tekhnika i Vooruzheniye* (June 1966).

Notes to Chapter 13

1. U.S., Congress, House, Subcommittee of the Committee on Appropriations, Hearings, 94th Cong., 2d sess., H-181, 94-2 (Washington, D.C.: Government Printing Office, 1976), Testimony of Admiral James L. Holloway, 3d, passim.

2. George R. Lindsey, "Tactical Antisubmarine Warfare," *Power at Sea I—The New Environment*, Adelphi Paper no. 122 (London: International Institute for Strategic Studies, 1976), passim.

3. Historical information for this discussion was extracted from George R. Lindsey and S. W. Roskill, *The War at Sea, 1939-1945*, vols. 1-4 (London: Her Majesty's Stationery Office, 1960).

4. Lindsey and Roskill, *War at Sea*, passim.

5. For a discussion of ASW technology, see Hubert Feigl, "The Impact of New Maritime Technologies," in *Power at Sea I; The New Environment*, Adelphi Paper No. 122 (London: The International Institute for Strategic Studies, 1976), passim; and Robert Taft, Jr. and William S. Lind, *White Paper on Defense, A Modern Military Strategy for the United States* (Washington, D.C.: Government Printing Office, 1976), passim.

6. U.S., Office of the Secretary of Defense, *Annual Defense Department Report—FY 1977* (Washington, D.C.: Department of Defense, January 1976), passim.

7. Ibid., p. 127; and U.S., Office of the Secretary of Defense, *Annual Defense Department Report—FY 1976 and FY 1977* (Washington, D.C.: Department of Defense, February 1976), p. III-83.

8. Tonne Huitfeldt, "The Maritime Environment in the North Atlantic," *Power at Sea III—Competition and Conflict*, Adelphi Paper no. 124 (London: The International Institute for Strategic Studies, 1976), pp. 15-16; and Robert G. Weinland, *The State and Future of the Soviet Navy in the North Atlantic* (Washington, D.C.: Brookings Institution, 1975), passim.

9. *Annual Defense Department Report—FY 1977*, p. 17; and Christopher Cramer Wright, *Developing Maritime Force Structure Options for the U.S. Defense Program* (Washington, D.C.: Brookings Institution, 1975), pp. 49-73.

10. Peak annual shipping requirements to Vietnam and Korea ranged between 3.5 and 4.5 million tons, roughly 10 percent of those foreseen to support NATO, but perhaps considerably less than would be required for a high-intensity, armor-heavy war in the Middle East.

11. Taft and Lind, *White Paper on Defense*, p. 4c.

12. Ibid., p. 6c.

13. Ibid., p. 7c.

14. The results are very sensitive to this assumption, which depends on weapons load and effectiveness. The number might be as high as ten for some submarines carrying twenty torpedoes or more.

15. "An Analysis of the U.S. and Soviet Navies—Missions, Forces, and Capabilities" (Unpublished draft report, Center for Naval Analyses, Washington, D.C., 1975), passim.

16. Taft and Lind, *White Paper on Defense*, pp. 25-27.

Notes to Chapter 14

1. Sergei G. Gorshkov, *The Sea Power of the State* (Moscow: Military Publishing House, 1976), p. 290.

2. Ibid., p. 291.

3. Ibid., p. 296.

Note to Chapter 16

1. Elmo Zumwalt, Jr., *On Watch* (New York: Quadrangle, 1976), pp. 63-64.